Hellenic Studies 20

RITUAL AND PERFORMATIVITY

RITUAL AND PERFORMATIVITY

THE CHORUS IN OLD COMEDY

Anton Bierl

Translated by Alexander Hollmann

CENTER FOR HELLENIC STUDIES
Trustees for Harvard University
Washington, DC
Distributed by Harvard University Press
Cambridge, Massachusetts, and London, England
2009

Ritual and Performativity: The Chorus in Old Comedy
   by Anton Bierl; translated by Alexander Hollmann
New and Revised Edition
Copyright © 2009 Center for Hellenic Studies, Trustees for Harvard University
All Rights Reserved.
Published by Center for Hellenic Studies, Trustees for Harvard University, Washington, D.C.
http://chs.harvard.edu/Publications
Distributed by Harvard University Press, Cambridge, Massachusetts and London, England

LIBRARY OF CONGRESS CATALOGING-IN-PUBLICATION DATA
   Bierl, Anton, 1960–
      [Chor in der alten Komödie. English]
      Ritual and performativity : the chorus in old comedy / by Anton Bierl ; translated by
   Alexander Hollmann.
         p. cm. — (Hellenic studies ; 20)
   Originally presented as the author's thesis (Habilitationsschrift)—Universität Leipzig,
   1998.
   Includes bibliographical references and index.
   ISBN 978-0-674-02373-4
      1. Greek drama (Comedy)—History and criticism. 2. Drama—Chorus (Greek drama)
   3. Aristophanes. Thesmophoriazusae. 4. Dionysus (Greek deity) in literature.
   5. Phallicism in literature. I. Hollmann, Alexander. II. Title.

PA3166.B5413 2009
882'.010917—dc22   2009039179

Contents

Contents

Foreword to the First Edition

THIS BOOK IS A PARTLY REVISED AND UPDATED VERSION of my *Habilitations-schrift*, which I presented to the Philological Faculty of the University of Leipzig in the summer semester of 1998.

This wide-ranging and interdisciplinary work represents in many respects a new scholarly genre. The chapters on the chorus of the *Thesmophoriazusae* and on the phallus songs present a new and distinctive interpretation in the body of the text as well as an extensive commentary in the detailed footnotes, which take into consideration not only the general concept of the comic chorus, as does the Introduction, but also the entire context of the Greek choral culture, while treating even more extensive questions. The subject matter determines the complex and partly intertwined arrangement, which is designed to help the reader. The extensive introductory chapter can stand alone as a comprehensive study of the Greek chorus, but may also be read from the particular perspective of comedy. The chapter on the *Thesmophoriazusae* (chapter 1) begins with lines 947–1000, a choral dance song long considered to be irrelevant to the plot, but in which the twofold construction of the comic chorus with its opening onto the extradiscursive level can be shown in exemplary fashion. I use this as a point of departure from which to move both forward and backward in the play. The second chapter looks at the findings on a diachronic continuum: the comic chorus and phallus songs represent interim stages between literature and ritual.

I have been working on Aristophanic comedy since March 1992. Many experiences and positions in my academic life have converged in this work. My study of the history of scholarship with William M. Calder in 1990–1991 sharpened my awareness of my place within certain scholarly traditions. Bruno Gentili, with whom I studied in Urbino from 1982 to 1983 and whose ideas on orality in early Greek lyric would simply not let go of me, was a key figure. Likewise, the findings of my dissertation on Dionysus and the studies in my book on the performances of the *Oresteia* on the modern stage have also contributed to this interest. It was through my involvement with modern stag-

Foreword to the First Edition

ings that the performance character of ancient theater really became clear to me. Here I should like to thank my *Doktorvater*, Hellmut Flashar, for his scholarly company both during my time in Leipzig and during the course of this work. Claude Calame's dissertation, which was also begun under Gentili, gave me the impulse to extend the *Sitz im Leben* of choruses as a place of initiation to the comic chorus as well. One of my theses is that the comic chorus partly reworks rites of this type in symbolic fashion.

The present project was helped by a DFG *Habilitation* grant extending from February 1994 to January 1996, during which time I was at Harvard University. I am grateful to the Department of the Classics there for their hospitality. Harvard's *genius loci* has overseen among many other methodological inspirations John Austin's speech act theory, which he developed there in a lecture series some forty years before. A high point in my stimulating stay was Albert Henrichs' seminar on the Greek chorus, which I attended together with Greg Nagy, Paola Ceccarelli, and two graduate students, Fred Naiden and Tim Power. There and on other occasions I was given the opportunity to present various works in progress. I thank these συγχορευταί for stimulating discussions and the exchange of work not yet published at the time, and especially the χορηγός, Albert Henrichs. I owe a great debt, too, to Greg Nagy's interdisciplinary meetings at the Center for Cultural and Literary Studies and his brilliant contributions to discussions on various occasions. I owe equally much to my fruitful exchange with Charles Segal†, who at that time was the third member of the constellation of Hellenists at Harvard.

I count myself especially fortunate that Albert Henrichs and Claude Calame as experts in the material very kindly read parts of the book with close attention. Albert Henrichs discussed the second chapter with me and subsequently sent me further important comments. Claude Calame also read through the second chapter and the introduction critically, and I was able to incorporate some of his valuable suggestions.

For help with reading the proofs I thank Judith Habazettl, Sabine Vogt, Max Braun, and Christian Käßer.

I further thank the Deutsche Forschungsgemeinschaft for the *Habilitation* grant and the assistance given for printing and publication of the book.

I am also grateful to Ludwig Koenen, who accepted the work for the series *Beiträge zur Altertumskunde* quickly and with a minimum of red tape, and also gave me useful suggestions. I thank Frau Elisabeth Schuhmann of the Saur Verlag for the care and attention with which she saw the book through publication.

Leipzig, June 2000

Foreword to the English Edition

IT IS A SPECIAL PLEASURE FOR ME, almost ten years after finishing the manuscript of the first edition, to present this book in the English language and in lightly revised form. I have made a special attempt in my references to the scholarly literature both in the body of the text and in the footnotes to take into account the most important works in this area published before the end of 2006. In particular I have tried to include the editions of and commentaries to the *Thesmophoriazusae* that have appeared since 2000/1, together with any textual changes suggested therein. The fundamental argument of the main text remains unaltered.

The book seems as fresh and relevant to me now as it did in 2000/1. Interest in the chorus and the choral has increased substantially since then. There continue to be new conferences on this topic. In Urbino, at a conference organized by Franca Perusino and entitled *Dalla lirica corale alla poesia drammatica: Forme e funzioni del canto corale nella tragedia e nella commedia greca* (21–23 September 2005), I gave a presentation of my thesis as applied to the *Lysistrata* in which I connected the *exodos* with the *Partheneia* of Alcman.[1] More recently in Verona, at the symposium *". . . un enorme individuo, dotato di polmoni soprannaturali": Funzioni, interpretazioni e rinascite del coro drammatico greco* (14–16 June 2007) I gave a presentation on the same theme, this time with the focus on Pratinas' satyr play (cf. already Bierl 2006).

Even though the central theme of this book concerns the chorus of Aristophanes and Old Comedy and pays particular attention to the *Thesmophoriazusae* and certain phallus songs, it amounts to much more than that.[2] It introduces a new paradigm, that of performativity, to the study of the chorus

---

[1]   A. Bierl, "L'uso intertestuale di Alcmane nel finale della *Lisistrata* di Aristofane: Coro e rito nel contesto performativo," in F. Perusino and M. Colantonio, eds., *Dalla lirica corale alla poesia drammatica: Forme e funzioni del canto corale nella tragedia e nella commedia greca* (Pisa 2007), 259–290. I read an English version in Rethymno, Crete, at the International Conference on Archaic and Classical Choral Song (May 24–27 2007); it appears under the title "Alcman at the End of *Lysistrata*: Intertextuality, Chorality, and Ritual."

[2]   A critical evaluation is now to be found in M. Dorati, *QUCC* 81.3 (2005):143–149.

and of Old Comedy. Despite claims to the contrary, this approach antedates the work of Revermann (2006) by several years. Here the element of performance is importantly taken into account. This thesis is combined with a decidedly cultural-historical method and accompanied by a detailed analysis of the text, with the *Sitz im Leben* receiving proper consideration. The anchoring of the performance in ritual and festive occasion has an effect in turn on the performance and its concretization in the text. Through various newer perspectives meaning can thus be restored to the element of ritual, which traditional textual scholarship under the influence of the modern enlightenment had long studiously ignored.

At the core of drama lies the chorus. Its central activity, dance, is pure ritual. The chorus is in turn placed in an original, ritual context, namely, in the performances of adolescent youth on the threshold of adulthood. In these choral groups the performance of song and dance serves as the ritual demarcation of change of status, in particular as the foundation of an education in, and introduction to, the megatext of a traditional society, myth, and ritual practice. This megatext reflects social order, it affirms the social and theological cosmos, but it also undermines it and calls it into question. The chorus of drama is brought back to these functions diachronically in its development via choral lyric and the choruses of cultic practice. Because these ideas are so fundamental for the understanding of Greek *khoreia*, I have made the original subtitle of the German edition the main title here: *Ritual and Performativity*.

The present monograph is the first modern study to consider in an interdisciplinary and comprehensive fashion the phenomenon of the Greek chorus in the case of Attic Old Comedy, using more recent literary and cultural approaches (among others, speech act theory, performative self-referentiality, semiotic narratology, performance studies, gender studies, theater anthropology, the study of ritual, neurobiology, and the sociology of religion). In contrast to previous investigations, the relationship between ritual and Old Comedy is accordingly not understood here as a result of its historical evolution, but as a productive parallel relationship. The central thesis of my work is that the ritual and initiatory function of the chorus in Old Comedy is preserved in remnants and that the genre builds its plots upon this.

In the extensive introductory chapter the Greek choral culture of the archaic and classical periods as a whole is treated with a new set of hermeneutic tools. Here the attempt to grasp the chorus in its performativity as a cultural phenomenon using the concept of the performative turn is of course important. In addition, because of this historic and diachronic derivation the chorus becomes understandable in its diverse locations. The choral voice is contemporaneous with several locations and connected with various functions: it oscillates between the here and now of the citizens of the polis and the there of the dramatic role. Performative self-references have a hinge function and as shifters enable this oscillation. Among other things, the choral voice praises and worships, is fictional, ridicules, is political, comic, and purely performative. Using speech act theory, I show that self-referentiality, reference to the chorus' own singing and dancing in the orchestra, can also be connected with ritual. Further, I compare the comic chorus to the choruses of the other dramatic genres, tragedy and satyr play—an approach that has become prominent since my book was first published.

It can be shown how Aristophanes does not—as has been traditionally assumed—parody simple ritual songs that are based on a performative model and that strengthen the action in the orchestra in an illocutionary fashion by means of speech. Rather, as the representative of a living, performative choral culture, he reproduces them. Even embedded in a dramatic action that is diametrically opposed to an Aristotelian and naturalistic concept of illusion, the members of the chorus with their twofold nature continue to refer to the performance and the pragmatic connection with the real world, while symbolically reworking rites relating to transition in status on an intra- and extra-discursive level.

Rituality is explored in depth in a detailed commentary on micro- and macrostructure. The philological investigation in the central part of the book represents perhaps the most intensive treatment to date both of the *Thesmophoriazusae*, somewhat neglected both then and now by scholarship, and of Semos' songs of the Ithyphalloi and Phallophoroi, which have up until now been treated only incidentally in connection with the question of the origin of comedy.

Apart from this illustrative interpretation of the *Thesmophoriazusae* the book in general presents a comprehensive interpretation of the Greek chorus as well as of the genre of Old Comedy, using an anthropological and ritual foundation. Archaic and classical literature in its interdependent relationship with religion and with myth and ritual becomes thereby understandable in a completely new way. Scholarship in this area too is making definite advances. I myself organized a conference entitled "Literatur und Religion: Die Griechen, vorher, nachher und heute. Mythisch-rituelle Strukturen im Text" ["Literature and Religion: The Greeks before, after, and today. Mythic and ritual structures in the text"] in Basel with distinguished scholars in the field. The aim was to extend this approach to other genres. The conference papers in expanded form have recently been published in two volumes (Bierl, Lämmle, and Wesselmann 2007). In order to circulate these perspectives further I have founded a new series, *MythosEikonPoiesis*. In Basel two doctoral dissertations on this theme are under way: Rebecca Lämmle is writing on the satyr play from a ritual perspective, and Katharina Wesselmann is working on mythical structures in Herodotus. It also plays an important role in the newly formed graduate program there, Pro*Doc *Intermediale Ästhetik: Spiel-Ritual-Performanz* ["Intermedial Aesthetics: Play-Ritual-Performance"].

In this respect it is also no coincidence that Greg Nagy, friend and colleague at the Center for Hellenic Studies in Washington, D.C., made it possible for this book to be translated into English and for it to be published through the Center by Harvard University Press. The expression "ritual poetics" is a familiar term in the school of Greg Nagy[3]—and he has greatly influenced me. My most sincere thanks go to him: it was through him that everything here became possible in the first place.

It was also he who had the brilliant idea of entrusting the translation to Alex Hollmann, a graduate of the Harvard program in classical philology. As one brought up in this atmosphere of a new, anthropologically oriented approach to Greek studies with teachers such as Greg Nagy and Albert Henrichs, he was in an ideal position to translate the complex construction of arguments from German into elegant English prose. I thank him for his tireless work on the translation, which he completed in addition to his own work and faculty responsibilities in Seattle over the course of many late-night sessions. He will, I hope, receive due academic recognition for this work. Finally, I owe thanks to Leonard Muellner, who directed the publication process from behind the scenes in a remarkably calm fashion, as well as to the whole team at the Center for Hellenic Studies and those at Harvard University Press involved in its production.

May the book in its new form find many new readers!

Pro captu lectoris habent sua fata libelli!

Basel, September 2007

---

[3]   See, for example, Yatromanolakis/Roilos 2004.

Translator's Note

T HIS TRANSLATION IS LONG OVERDUE, both in the sense that it has taken me a long time to complete it and in the sense that it is a book that I feel deserves a wider audience than the original German version may ave found. It has been a privilege and a pleasure to have worked so closely ith it.

All translations of passages in ancient Greek are mine unless otherwise tated. I have of course followed the author's interpretation of these passages. ranslations from French and Italian are likewise mine unless otherwise cknowledged. In transliterating Greek words I have used â, ê, and ô to repre-ent ᾱ, η, and ω.

My thanks go to the author and to Greg Nagy, Lenny Muellner, and lbert Henrichs for their support and encouragement. I should also like to hank those who introduced me to German classical scholarship and encour-ged me to read in German: Eckart Schütrumpf, Christoph Konrad, and Albert lenrichs.

Seattle, September 2007

Abbreviations

A & A	*Antike und Abendland*
AION	*Annali dell'Istituto Universitario Orientale di Napoli*
AJP	*American Journal of Philology*
ARV	J. D. Beazley, *Attic Red-Figure Vase-Painters*, I–III, Oxford 1963²
Austin	C. Austin, ed., *Nova Fragmenta Euripidea in Papyris Reperta* (Kleine Texte für Vorlesungen und Übungen 187), Berlin 1968
B.	T. Bergk, ed., *Poetae Lyrici Graeci*, Leipzig 1882⁴ (= Bergk 1882⁴)
BCH	*Bulletin de Correspondance Hellénique*
BICS	*Bulletin of the Institute of Classical Studies*
BMCR	*Bryn Mawr Classical Review*
BzA	*Beiträge zur Altertumskunde*
CA	*Classical Antiquity*
CEG	P. A. Hansen, ed., *Carmina Epigraphica Graeca saeculorum VIII–V a. Chr. n.* (Texte und Kommentare 12), Berlin/New York 1983
CP	*Classical Philology*
CQ	*Classical Quarterly*
CR	*Classical Review*
D.	E. Diehl, ed., *Anthologia Lyrica Graeca*, I–II, Leipzig 1925 (I, 1–3, curavit R. Beutler, Leipzig 1949–1852³; I, 4–II, 5; 6, Leipzig 1935–1940²; *Suppl. Addenda et corrigenda fasc. 1–6*, Leipzig 1942²) (= Diehl 1925)
Davies	M. Davies, ed., *Poetarum Melicorum Graecorum Fragmenta*, I: *Alcman, Stesichorus, Ibycus*, post D. L. Page ed. M. Davies, Oxford 1991 (= *PMGF*)
FGrHist	F. Jacoby, ed., *Die Fragmente der griechischen Historiker*, Parts I–III, Berlin 1923–1930, Leiden 1940–1958; *Die*

	Fragmente der griechischen Historiker continued, Part IV, ed. G. Schepens, Leiden 1999ff. and *Indexes of Parts I, II, and III*, ed. P. Bonnechere, I–III, Leiden 1999 (= Jacoby)
Fraser/Matthews	P. M. Fraser/E. Matthews, *A Lexicon of Greek Personal Names*, I–III.A, Oxford 1987–1997
Frisk	H. Frisk, *Griechisches etymologisches Wörterbuch*, I–III, Heidelberg 1960–1972
GITA	Groupe interdisciplinaire du théâtre antique. Université Paul Valery–Montpellier
G.-P.	B. Gentili/C. Prato, eds., *Poetarum Elegiacorum Testimonia et Fragmenta*, I–II, Leipzig 1988²/85
GRBS	*Greek, Roman, and Byzantine Studies*
HSCP	*Harvard Studies in Classical Philology*
IG	*Inscriptiones Graecae*
JdI	*Jahrbuch des deutschen Archäologischen Instituts. Berlin*
JHS	*Journal of Hellenic Studies*
K.-A.	R. Kassel/C. Austin, eds., *Poetae Comici Graeci*, I, II, III.2, IV, V, VI.2, VII, and VIII, Berlin/NewYork 1983–2001 (= *PCG*)
KG	R. Kühner/F. Blass/B. Gerth, *Ausführliche Grammatik der griechischen Sprache*, I–II, Hannover/Leipzig 1890–1892³/1898–1904³ (Reprint of Vol. II, Darmstadt 1962)
Kl. Pauly	*Der Kleine Pauly. Lexikon der Antike*, I–V, ed. K. Ziegler and W. Sontheimer, Stuttgart 1964–1975 (Reprint Munich 1979)
Kock	T. Kock, ed., *Comicorum Atticorum Fragmenta*, I–III, Leipzig 1880–1888 (= CAF)
Lex. Bachm.	*Συναγωγὴ λέξεων χρησίμων ἐκ διαφόρων σοφῶν τε καὶ ῥητόρων πολλῶν*, ed. L. Bachmann, *Anecdota Graeca* I, Leipzig 1828, 1–422
LIMC	*Lexicon Iconographicum Mythologiae Classicae*, Zurich/Munich 1981ff.
L.-P.	E. Lobel/D. L. Page, eds., *Poetarum Lesbiorum Fragmenta*, Oxford 1955
LSAM	F. Sokolowski, *Lois sacrées de l'Asie Mineure*, Paris 1955 (= Sokolowski 1955)
LSCG	F. Sokolowsi, *Lois sacrées des cités grecques*, Paris 1969 (= Sokolowski 1969)
LSJ	H. G. Liddell/R. Scott/H. S. Jones, *A Greek-English Lexicon* (1940⁹). *With a Supplement*, Oxford 1968 (rev. Suppl. 1996)

M.-W.	R. Merkelbach/M. L. West, eds., *Fragmenta Hesiodea*, Oxford 1967
N	A. Nauck, rec., *Tragicorum Graecorum Fragmenta*, Leipzig 1889[2] (reprint with a "supplementum continens nova fragmenta Euripidea et adespota apud scriptores veteres reperta" by B. Snell, Hildesheim 1964)
n.F.	Neue Folge
NJbb	*Neue Jahrbücher für das Klassische Altertum, Geschichte und deutsche Literatur*, ed. J. Ilberg
n.s.	new series/nuova serie
Pape	W. Pape, *Griechisch-Deutsches Handwörterbuch*, I–II, Braunschweig 1902[3]
PCG	R. Kassel/C. Austin, eds., *Poetae Comici Graeci*, I, II, III.2, IV, V, VI.2, VII, and VIII, Berlin/New York 1983–2001 (= K.-A.)
PCPS	*Proceedings of the Cambridge Philological Society*
PMG	D. L. Page, ed., *Poetae Melici Graeci*, Oxford 1962 (= Page, Page 1962)
POxy	B. P. Grenfell/A. S. Hunt/E. Lobel, eds., *The Oxyrhynchus Papyri*, London 1898ff.
QUCC	*Quaderni Urbinati di Cultura Classica*
RE	*Real-Encyclopädie der classischen Altertumswissenschaft*, Stuttgart/Munich 1893–1978
REG	*Revue des Études Grecques*
RGVV	*Religionsgeschichtliche Versuche und Vorarbeiten*
RhM	*Rheinisches Museum*
Schwyzer	E. Schwyzer/A. Debrunner, *Griechische Grammatik* (Handbuch der Altertumswissenschaft II), I–III, Munich 1977[5]/1975[4] (1939–1953[1])
SEG	*Supplementum Epigraphicum Graecum*
SIG[3]	G. Dittenberger/F. Hiller von Gaertringen, eds., *Sylloge Inscriptionum Graecarum*, Leipzig 1915–1924[3]
S.-M.	*Pindari Carmina cum Fragmentis*, I: *Epinicia,* post B. Snell ed. H. Maehler, Leipzig 1987[8]; II: *Fragmenta. Indices,* post B. Snell ed. H. Maehler, Leipzig 1989; *Bacchylidis Carmina cum Fragmentis,* post B. Snell ed. H. Maehler, Stuttgart/Leipzig 1992[10]
Suppl. Hell.	H. Lloyd-Jones/P. Parsons, eds., *Supplementum Hellenisticum*, Berlin/New York 1983

Abbreviations

TAPA	*Transactions of the American Philological Association*
Tod	M. N. Tod, ed., *A Selection of Greek Historical Inscriptions*, I–II, Oxford 1933/48
TrGF	B. Snell/R. Kannicht/S. Radt, eds., *Tragicorum Graecorum Fragmenta*, I–V, Göttingen 1971–2004 (III and IV = Radt; V = Kannicht)
UaLG	*Untersuchungen zur antiken Literatur und Geschichte*
W.	M. L. West, ed., *Iambi et Elegi Graeci ante Alexandrum cantati*, I–II, Oxford 1989/92² (1971/72¹)
WüJbb	*Würzburger Jahrbücher*
ZPE	*Zeitschrift für Papyrologie und Epigraphik*

RITUAL AND PERFORMATIVITY

Introduction
The Choral Dance and Song as Ritual Action
A New Perspective

Introductory Thoughts, Performativity, and the Twofold Composition of the Chorus

To the extent that any kind of agreement can be attained in the irresolvable dispute about the origin of drama, this much is clear: tragedy as well as comedy developed out of choral and for the most part cultic festivities.[1] On these grounds alone the chorus forms the central element in the *Gesamtkunstwerk* of ancient drama. Among other things numerous technical expressions relating to production and performance prove this. For instance, when a poet applied to compete in the following year's dramatic contest (*agôn*), in the official language of the Athenian polis he did not present a proposal for a play named

---

[1] It is almost impossible to survey all the literature on the question of origin. Here we can only cover, using a few selected voices, the *communis opinio*, which sees the essence of drama as lying in the chorus. Aristotle's reflections in the *Poetics* (esp. 1449a9–24), which one should not however trust blindly, constitute the point of departure for nearly all studies. Cf. Lesky 1971³:260–278, esp. 273 ("In der Tat steht der Chor für die Komödie ebenso am Anfange wie für die Tragödie" [= Engl. trans. 1966:223–240, esp. 235 "In fact comedy begins with the chorus just as much as tragedy does"]). At the beginning of both genres were processions, ritual celebrations with dances and singing. For tragedy, cf. Latacz 1993:54: "Der Chor—so muß man schließen, wenn man diese Entwicklung über die ältesten Aischylosstücke hinaus rückwärts weiterverlängert—war offenbar ursprünglich der alleinige Träger jenes 'Gesangs,' den wir als Keimzelle der Tragödie aus dem Terminus 'trag-odia' herausschälten. Das heißt: die Urform der Tragödie war offenbar ein Chorgesang" ["The chorus—so one must conclude if this development is projected further back beyond the earliest plays of Aeschylus—was clearly at the beginning the only vehicle of the 'song' which we extract as the nucleus of tragedy from the term 'trag-odia.' That is: the original form of tragedy was clearly a choral song"]. Cf. among others Szemerényi 1975:325, Flashar 1991:23, Henrichs 1994/95:56, and Henrichs 1996:24–25. Cf. in particular Athenaeus 630c (perhaps quoted from Aristokles' *On Choruses* [cf. *ibid.*, 630b]); he thinks that the satyr play as well as tragedy originally consisted solely of choruses. Themistios (*Or.* 26.316d) credits Aristotle with the view that the chorus sang alone initially, and that Thespis came up with the prologue and speech. On the organic origin of comedy from *kômos* processions, cf. esp. Herter 1947 and Giangrande 1963. Against this view of a characteristic link between comedy and chorus cf. now the hyper-sociological approach of Stark 2004, esp. 97–99, 322–323. On the origin of comedies cf. also my observations in chap. 2.

X, but "requested a chorus" (χορὸν ᾔτησεν) for this play, which he would either "receive" (χορὸν ἔλαβεν) or not.[2] A wealthy private citizen in his capacity as *khorêgos* had to shoulder as a state "liturgy" the enormous costs of outfitting (masks, costumes), provisioning, and maintaining actors, extras, musicians, and chorus members, which included daily wages in compensation for income lost during the long rehearsal period. This type of "chorus management" in turn brought the individual, drawn mostly from the aristocracy, a considerable measure of prestige among his politically equal fellow-citizens in the democratic polis. The numerous choruses for dithyrambs, satyr plays, comedies, and tragedies constituted a traditional institution of training (παιδεία) for young men, retained from the archaic period. John J. Winkler goes so far as to say that he sees in these choruses remnants of initiation practices of a type common in tribal societies.[3] Choruses were so important for the continued existence of the city of Athens that a complex set of laws relating to them was enacted.[4]

Despite this fact, it must be admitted that the many choral songs of Attic drama remain peculiarly strange to today's recipients. For, as is well known, over the long road of written transmission only the text has remained intact, while all further semiotic performative levels of this multimedia spectacle— the melody, the musical accompaniment, the dance-steps associated with it, the entire complex of visual presentation—have all been irretrievably lost. For the modern reader, these songs represent at best enchanting lyric poetry. Yet

---

[2] Cf. Cratin. fr. 17, 1 K.-A. on the archon to whom the poet would apply: ὃς οὐκ ἔδωκ' αἰτοῦντι Σοφοκλέει χορόν; on χορὸν αἰτεῖν cf. Ar. *Equ.* 513; on χορὸν διδόναι cf. Plat. *Rep.* 383c2, *Leg.* 817d7, and Arist. *Poet.* 1449b1–2; on χορὸν λαμβάνειν cf. e.g. Ar. *Ran.* 94; χορὸν εἰσάγειν means "to begin the play" in Ar. *Ach.* 11; cf. *Thesm.* 390–391 ὅπουπερ ἔμβραχυ | εἰσὶν θεαταὶ καὶ τραγῳδοὶ καὶ χοροί (Mika complains: Euripides makes fun of us women, wherever there is an audience, actors, and choruses, i.e. in every tragedy). Here χοροί appears in a technical sense: tragedy consists of the three bodies audience, actors, and chorus; the expression χοροί often simply means "drama" or "dramatic performance" in a synecdotic sense; cf. Ar. *Ach.* 628, *Equ.* 521, *Eccl.* 1160, and Men. *Sam.* 737 (comedy), Ar. *Av.* 787, and *Ran.* 1419 (tragedy).

[3] Cf. Winkler 1990. He proceeds on the assumption that the tragic chorus represents a kind of military formation of ephebes. The members of the chorus symbolically transform themselves, in his opinion, into goats whose voices are breaking (τραγίζειν) (*ibid.*, esp. 58–62). On the initiation thesis, cf. already the negative attitude of Pickard-Cambridge 1927:159 and 172 (both passages were significantly left out of the second edition, Pickard-Cambridge 1962) and the suspicions of Thomson 1956:101–136. Winkler's theses have recently enjoyed the support of Graf (1998:25–27). On the concept of initiation in the study of religion, cf. the general overview in Grohs 1993. On initiation as a modern interpretative paradigm in the field of classics, cf. below, n61.

[4] Cf. MacDowell 1989 and Csapo/Slater 1995:139–157. On the prestige of the *khorêgia* cf. Wilson 1997, on the *khorêgia* in general see Wilson 2000.

a purely textual understanding is in no way sufficient to do full justice to the phenomenon of choruses. Beside the visual, rhythmic, and all other nonverbal elements, one must especially recognize the ritual foundation of the performance, which is radically different from the modern social context of a theatrical performance. All choruses of the archaic and classical periods consist of youths or girls—or, correspondingly, men and/or women—who honor particular deities—mostly gods associated particularly with choral dancing, especially Dionysus, Apollo, and Artemis—on specific cultic occasions. The dithyramb, the satyr play, and comedy as well as tragedy were all performed in honor of the god Dionysus, as is well known. In the case of Attic comedy, the Lenaia and the Great Dionysia were the festive occasions. In a system of communication still largely based on orality, "literature" thus had a particular pragmatic basis, that of its particular cultic *Sitz im Leben*.[5]

The performative and ritual aspect of the chorus was for a long time all but neglected by modern scholarship, which was oriented toward a form of communication that was largely written. Significantly, it was precisely the chorus that created the greatest difficulties for the movement to revive ancient drama on the modern stage, which was strongly influenced by naturalism.[6] Only in (post)modern staging practice is the performative potential of the ancient chorus being recognized. The interruption of the action of the play is here no longer felt as a disturbance, rather the emergence of ritual traces is now placed in the context of an overall ritualization of the theater.[7]

---

[5] In connection with the study in classical philology of extratextual frame, occasion, and performance, Bruno Gentili's research group on Greek lyric in Urbino, Wolfgang Rösler, and, in a narrower mythical-ritual connection, Claude Calame should be mentioned here as methodological examples of this work. Cf. among others Gentili 1984, Gentili 1990, Rösler 1980, and Calame 1977 (Engl. trans. vol. I, Calame 1997). Cf. also Kannicht 1989, Krummen 1990, esp. 1–9 (general), 10–30 (on Pindar), Käppel 1992, esp. 17–21 (on the paean), and Stehle 1997, esp. 3–25 (general introduction) and 26–169 ("public" poetry of male and female choruses).

[6] Cf. Flashar 1991:7, 22–24, 126–128, 148–152, 221, 234, 242, 248, 250–251, 261–262, 269–270, 298–302 and Henrichs 1996:61. The chorus does not fit in with most modern producers' plans; for this reason it is often drastically cut and split up into individual figures. For modern actors a role in the chorus is relatively thankless, because they are as a result unable to stand out and make their mark; for practical reasons resulting from specialized training actors also have problems with the presentation of song and dance. A corresponding realization of this on stage needs a lot of rehearsal time. Only in the best stagings of an ancient drama is the dimension of the chorus not neglected. In such productions the chorus sings and dances naturally; Ariane Mnouchkine's 1992 Atreid tetralogy was felt to be an outstanding event precisely because of the realization of the chorus; cf. Bierl 1996:54–77, esp. 62n122.

[7] On the re-ritualization of avantgarde theater, cf. Friedrich 1983:203–209; on corresponding tendencies in productions of ancient tragedy on the modern stage, see Flashar 1991:228–260. On postmodern theater in general, see A. de Toro 1995.

The interpretation that turns Aristotle's pronouncement about the unity of action into a psychological and naturalistic principle of the absolute unity of the plot no longer stands in the foreground. The chorus' predramatic (from a modern point of view) nature, rooted in the tradition of archaic choral lyric, now suddenly stands as the focal point of interest.[8] These points in turn also have an effect on the scholarly problems of classical philology. The chorus in its specific ritual aspects and its rootedness in a performative frame has thus recently been brought into the center of attention.

Modern trends in performance studies, which are connected mainly with contemporary stage practice, similarly emphasize the structural connection between theater and ritual. Here the field of theater-anthropology in particular should be mentioned.[9] Richard Schechner and Victor Turner, important proponents of this movement, have called into question the evolutionary hypothesis that has held sway since antiquity. According to this theory, the genesis of Attic drama lies in ritual origins, from which it freed itself during the course of the fifth century BCE, finally becoming fully aesthetic theater.[10] This theory of a diachronic movement from ritual to theater, vehemently advocated as a result of the work of the Cambridge ritualists at the beginning of the twentieth century, is removed by Schechner's demand for a relationship of interdependency. According to Schechner, ritual and theater ought not be understood as a "not yet" or "no longer," but as being simultaneously present beside each other. Ritual, too, has elements of entertainment and spectacle,

---

[8] Cf. Lehmann 1991:2, 47–50 and Baur 1997:26–28. On the choral in contemporary theater, cf. the contribution of Baur (1999), who presents a summary of his 1998 dissertation (= Baur 1999a) on this topic written with G. Erken (Munich). Cf. also Erken 1997:381–382 and Bierl 2004:157–183, esp. 164–167. On the continuities between melic choral lyric and dramatic choral songs, cf. among others Webster 1970:110–132, Herington 1985:103–124, Stoessl 1987:116–141, Nagy 1990:382–413, and the references to the latest literature below, n62.

[9] Cf. Helbo/Johansen/Pavis/Ubersfeld 1991, and esp. Helbo 1991 and Ruffini 1991. On theater anthropology, cf. also Barba/Savarese 1991.

[10] Cf. among others Schechner 1977, Schechner 1985 (for theater), and Turner 1982 (for ritual). On Jane Harrison's evolutionism and cult of origin, cf. Schlesier 1991:196–199 (in William M. Calder's excellent volume on the Cambridge ritualists [Calder 1991]). While the *communis opinio* continues to stick to a development from ritual to theater, theater anthropology emphasizes the structural commonalities. Both approaches have some truth to them; it is largely a matter of perspective. The connection between both categories is already acknowledged in the traditional approach; I am here mainly concerned with describing the ritual nature of the (comic) chorus from the most differing points of view. On the relation between drama and ritual, see now also Graf 1998:19–25 and Köpping 2003. On the relation between drama, myth, and ritual in a performative perspective see now also Wiles 2000:5–47, Bierl 2002, and Bierl 2007.

just as it cannot be denied that theater may have a serious effect in the sense of a transformation of those taking part in it, something that is particularly typical of ritual.[11]

The structural similarity lies ultimately in the element of performance and the complex of the performative, which has recently enjoyed a growing popularity, even if the concept remains somewhat vague and eludes precise definition.[12] According to the criteria of immediacy and the ephemeral imposed by theater-anthropology, everything that is presented by the performer in an appropriate context becomes a performance. Nevertheless, what appears to be critical is concentration on a definite action and the union of spectator and player in the process of performative transformation. Just as in the case of ritual, in every performance there is a lack of distinction between actors and audience. Rather, the spectators are fellow players and participants in the spectacle. The production of the artistic act coincides with the reaction to it, so that the performance is thereby completed through its execution. Bert O. States aptly formulates this connection as follows:

> Here is what we might call the kernel or gene of performativity from which all divided forms of artistic performance spring: the collapse of means and ends into each other, the simultaneity of producing something and responding to it in the same behavioral act.[13]

---

[11] Cf. Schechner 1977:63–98 ("From Ritual to Theatre and Back: The Structure/Process of Efficacy-Entertainment Dyad"), 108–139 ("Towards a Poetics of Performance"), Schechner 1985.

[12] Cf. States 1996; for a critique of Schechner, *ibid.*, 13–20. For a detailed criticism of the theses of Turner and Schechner, as well as of the performance approach in ethnology, which masks the fundamental differences between theater and social, ritual action, see Köpping 1998, esp. 65–71. This useful contribution correctly points out the problematic points of the fashionable equation of ritual and theater. To a large part one can agree with him; yet like Turner and Schechner, he relies heavily on an Aristotelian concept of theater. He sums up (67): "Die klare Unterscheidung zwischen Theater und sozialem wie rituellem Handeln muß aufrecht erhalten werden, sonst bleibt uns nichts 'Apartes' mehr für das Theater übrig" ["The clear distinction between theater and social as well as ritual activity must be maintained, otherwise we are left with nothing that is 'separate' for the theater"]. With regard to the picture of the chorus that results from traditional ideas of a theater of illusion (one-sidedly understood as "mimetic") with meta-reference, the present study shows that this kind of separation of categories impairs understanding of the phenomenon. Furthermore, both ritual and theater may here usefully be connected with the linguistic category of the performative, connections that Köpping does not pursue. But cf. now Köpping 2003.

[13] States 1996:25. Cf. also Schechner 1985:14–16, 117–150 and Gadamer 1992:415 (ritual), 425 (art). In connection with ritual, cf. also Friedrich 1983:186 and Morgan/Brask 1988:191, in connec-

In developed theater, this familiar constellation crystalizes out in a long cultural process: others, namely the performers, enact something from which bystanders, now called the theater audience, derive enjoyment. But countless opportunities arise in ancient performances, particularly in comedy, to nullify this communicative differentiation and to reduce the play to the pure aspect of performance. It is precisely the chorus, whose performance is always simultaneously embedded in the here and now of festive and cultic occasionality, that achieves this transparency of rituality when the fictional character, the "represented," fades out of the picture, yielding place to his simultaneously present ritual function as performer. This happens particularly in passages where everything of a narrative and descriptive nature disappears and the present of the performative experience is brought to the fore or both categories in the act of a ritual activity are simply brought into line together.

Before being integrated into an extensive dramatic event, the chorus has a primarily ritual, performative character, rooted in tradition. Even while being embedded in a defined course of action in which the chorus partly comes forward as player, the chorus nevertheless always possesses at the same time a good measure of performative presence. Above all, the chorus dances and sings, activities that also constitute completely autonomous patterns of behavior in the theater. The group acts for itself, completes an action that is an end in itself and in which it establishes contact with certain gods by means of rhythmic movements and the sung word. The transition to more complex plays of a developed comedy or tragedy is fluid. Aristotle significantly calls the

tion with avantgarde theater Friedrich 1983:208. I cite Gadamer 1992:415 for purposes of clarification: "Die Kultgemeinde darf sich durchaus nicht als Zuschauer fühlen. Sie gehört zu der Handlung. Sie kann mithandeln, etwa im Gesang, in den alle einstimmen, auch wenn es vielleicht nur geheimnisvolle, liedähnliche Texte sind, die am Ende gar einer fremden Sprache angehören, von der man kein Wort versteht. Oder man denke an die Tänze, die die heilige Handlung umkränzen. Selbst wenn es am Ende mimische Darbietungen sind, werden sie nicht eigentlich einer Zuschauerschaft angeboten, sondern der Gottheit selber" ["The cultic community never regards itself as spectator. It belongs to the action. It can also take part in the singing, for example, in which all join, even if these are only mysterious, song-like texts that are ultimately like some foreign language of which one understands not a single word. Or consider the dances that surround the sacred activity. Even though these are ultimately mimetic performances, they are not in fact performed for an audience, but for the deity himself"]. These remarks fit the performative and ritual passages of Old Comedy extremely well; cf. in particular chap. 1 below. Even Köpping (1998:66) has to concede that theater "becomes ritual" if the performance is carried out "for the gods." Of course this is usually the case for the Greek chorus even within the drama.

[14] Cf. the definition in Arist. *Poet.* 1450a4-5.: λέγω γὰρ μῦθον τοῦτον τὴν σύνθεσιν τῶν πραγμάτων. Cf. inter alia 1450a32-33 and 1451a16-19.

[15] On the distinction between μῦθος as fable and as plot, and between *histoire* and *discours* (using the terminology and interpretation of Benveniste 1966:237-250) cf. Kraus 1994:292-296. Kraus

story or tale underlying the action μῦθος,[14] from which the author then forms his specific plot, the *sujet*.[15]

It is precisely here that the use of *mythos* seems of decisive importance. Yet even ritual performances are not always purely ends in themselves and do not exhaust themselves in their own execution, but are frequently connected with a myth that frames their current action, raising it and establishing it in another realm belonging to the past or the divine. This mythical narration may be acted out in the ritual, in which case the rite becomes a staging of the myth and its transformation into action (enactment).[16] It is in this kind of arrangement that the first mimetic elements of the performing chorus emerged. These in turn probably eventually developed into plot. The leader of the chorus likely confronted the group as ὑποκριτής, as answerer and/or commentator. From this formation the first actor might have developed, and in his wake further actors emerged.[17]

Because of its historical development the dramatic chorus possesses a special status: it stands in the charged area between an inner, fictional and an outer, actual communications system, where the chorus, in contrast to the actors, ultimately remains itself, namely the theatrical entity of "the chorus," and role-specific characterization is applied only secondarily.[18] The ambiguous position of the chorus members, between representer and represented,

---

rightly refers to the action of the play, which is central for drama and which is found on two levels in Aristotle (289–290): "Tragödie ist für Aristoteles wesentlich Nachahmung *von* Handlung (μίμησις πράξεως) und *durch* Handelnde (δρώντων). Handlung ist Gegenstand *und* Mittel der Mimesis; Handelnde (πράττοντες, δρῶντες) sind sowohl die Schauspieler auf der Bühne als auch die dargestellten Figuren im Rahmen ihrer Geschichte" ["For Aristotle, tragedy is essentially the imitation *of* action (μίμησις πράξεως) and by means of those acting/doing (δρώντων). Action is the object *and* the means of mimesis; both the actors on the stage and the figures presented in the context of their story are agents (πράττοντες, δρῶντες)"]. Among other real-life actions, speech actions and speech acts occur frequently in drama: the locutionary act is actually completed on stage, while the illocutionary act is simulated. On the multidimensional nature of speech signs in theater, cf. Fischer-Lichte 1983:31–36. Flashar 1976:356 (= *Eidola* 175) and Flashar 1977:123–124 (= *Eidola* 60–61) already refer to speech actions, or speech acts in the sense of Austin 1994 in the *Oedipus Tyrannus* (threats, curses, apologies, laments, condemnations). For speech act theory in connection with the concept of the chorus see pp. 36–47 below. Both types of action mentioned here will be of particular importance in this study.

16 Cf. Leach 1982:5–6. Cf. Gregory Nagy's concise expression in the introduction to Martin 1989:xi: "The *mûthos* is not just any speech-act reported by poetry: it is also the speech-act of poetry itself. Viewed in this light, myth implies ritual in the very performance of myth. And that performance is the essence of poetics."

17 This account reflects current reconstructions of the genesis of tragedy. Cf. among others Lesky 1971[3]:265–266 [= Engl. trans. 1966:223–232].

18 Cf. Baur 1997, esp. 44–47 and now Baur 1999a:15–29, esp. 26–28. Baur and Käppel (1999:61–69) come to quite similar conclusions with regard to tragedy.

between their function as singing and dancing citizens of the polis and their dramatic role, is made apparent in exemplary fashion by the mask. In contrast to the traditional view, heavily influenced by veristic and naturalistic theater, the mask does not help the actor to embody a fictitious figure completely, but in ancient drama, as in many other ritual performances, it is there to prevent a complete absorption of the identity of the performer in the figure being represented in the action. Rather, the mask constructs a characteristic distance between these two dimensions, as Claude Calame has also recently demonstrated.[19]

Thus the here and now of the ritual performance always remains present behind the figure of myth. Consequently, by constantly fading in and out of the inner frame of the plot and the exterior reality, the chorus may glide back and forth between both levels of discourse. The emphasis on its own action of dancing and singing and so-called shifters—that is to say, words in which language as a code combines with the message—play a great role in this, as we shall see.[20]

In its assessment of the chorus scholarship on tragedy has so far fluctuated between two extreme positions: either the chorus is conceived of as purely a player alongside other players (a fourth actor)[21] or as a lyric "mouthpiece of the poet," in which case it is also ascribed the function of being a means of directing and controlling reception.[22] The flexible concept of divided function developed by Walther Kranz comes closer to the truth: this regards the

---

[19] Cf. Lohr 1986:78–79, Schechner 1985:4–10 and Calame 1995:97–115 (on the tragic mask), Calame 1989 (on the comic mask). On the convergence of drama and ritual in the mask (in its function as shifter), whose divinity Dionysus represents, cf. Henrichs 1994/95:70.

[20] Cf. Jakobson 1984. On the chorus in the interchange between intra- and extradiscursive function, cf. in the more recent scholarship Gould 1996 and the reply of Goldhill 1996.

[21] This opinion is based on Arist. *Poet.* 1456a25–27. Cf. with regard to tragedy Müller 1967, esp. 230, Rösler 1983, esp. 107–110 (Sophocles' *Antigone*), 123 (Sophocles), Gardiner 1987, esp. 1–9 (Sophocles), Paulsen 1989 (Sophocles' late tragedies), and in extreme form Thiel 1993, esp. 1–9, 441–456 (Aeschylus' *Agamemnon*). Hose II (1990/91:413) agrees with this conclusion with respect to Aeschylus and Sophocles. Paulsen (1998:77–81) has recently confirmed his results for all of Sophocles.

[22] Cf. Schlegel 1846:76–77, Wilamowitz 1921:517, and Kranz 1933:170–171 and 222, on directing reception, *ibid.* 207–215, esp. 213; on deflection into the general *ibid.*, 215–220.

[23] Kranz 1933:170–171 and 220–225. He talks of the "triple nature" (171) of the chorus; in his opinion "contradictions" may arise from the variety of aspects. Kranz 1933:171 and Rode 1971:85 make a fundamental distinction between the chorus' function in dialogue and in actual songs. Rode 1971:99–103 also sees its inclusion in the action of the play as secondary. Hose 1990/91 similarly treats Euripides' extremely heterogeneous chorus more along the lines of a broken model; cf. esp. the summarizing remarks of Hose I 1990/91:308–312 and Hose II 1990/91:404–413. Cf. also recently Paulsen 1998 (Aeschylus: fellow player, mouthpiece, and instrument [esp. 77]; Sophocles: fellow player [esp. 81]; Euripides: differentiated fellow player [esp. 82], not mouthpiece [85–86], not filler between acts [81–82]).

chorus alternately as wholly *dramatis persona*, voice of the author, and "ideal audience."[23] In contrast to this *communis opinio* I present a dynamic, open, and transversal model: the dramatic chorus can spread from the inner plot to external communication levels without entirely relinquishing the dimension of the fictional.[24] Conversely, it is never completely anchored in the plot as a fellow player because, as a result of the origins of theater, it always carries with it the ritual, real-life dimension. The dramatic chorus is thus a bearer of several juxtaposed voices or aspects, among which it is able to oscillate freely. These may be accentuated and activated to a greater or lesser degree, as needed, without the relation to the plot ever becoming lost. The development of drama from the ritual chorus with the resulting integration of the choral element, which is actually a hindrance to linear action, leads, in comparison to the naturalistic and closed concept of action, to the particularly rich possibility of expression of ancient drama. It is precisely through this that the poet obtains a highly flexible instrument with which he is able to have an effect on the play, the public, and the real world. The chorus functions both as transmitter and receiver of messages; both in the dimension of space and of time it can transcend the boundaries of the fictional into the here and now, without really breaking the so-called illusion. In this encroachment, which takes place mostly via the ritual and performative, the synaesthetic spectacle is not diminished in its impression, nor broken off in the sense of Brecht's epic theater for the purposes of reflection; rather, the emotional effect of the performance as *Gesamtkunstwerk* is intensified.[25] The members of the chorus act both as fellow players within the plot as well as ritual actors in the external frame of reference. The performative constitutes the hinge between the systems of communication, combining the fictional action on stage, decked out with all its theatrical signs,[26] with the action of speech and ritual into an emotionally effective spectacle.[27] Roman Jakobson's linguistic model of shifters, a category of doubly structured words that as conventional symbols simultaneously carry with them an indexical and deictic component and thus actually refer

[24] Cf. also Käppel 1999:61–69, esp. 66–69. Cf. already Bierl 1991, inter alia 83–84, 106–107, 114, 117–118, and 45–49 (on the tension between inner and outer). Cf. now similarly Calame 1999, esp. 148–153.
[25] Cf. Bierl 1991:114–118.
[26] Cf. Fischer-Lichte 1983, esp. 25–179; she views theater as a semiotic system that consists of various signs; she speaks of verbal, linguistic, paralinguistic, kinesic, mimetic, gestural, and proxemic signs, the appearance of the actor as sign, the sign of space, and nonverbal acoustic signs. These separate levels of signification are particularly important for the choral analysis in chap. 2. On theater semiotics cf. inter alia also F. de Toro 1995, esp. 63–96 (with further literature), who treats signs using the categories of Peirce 1983, esp. 64–67 (icon, index, symbol).
[27] In my dissertation I looked at Dionysus as doubly located shifter in his specific connection with performance and theater; see Bierl 1991.

to the object to be represented, i.e. the external communications situation, and to the actual expression or *énonciation*, is thereby transferred to the realm of the performative. For here too, reference is made both to the narrated or fictional event (*procès de l'énoncé*) and to the process of expression (*procès de l'énonciation*).[28]

Because of this ambivalent construction it is also incorrect to apply the veristic concept of theatrical illusion anachronistically to ancient theater. It is much more accurate to consider separately and in accordance with genre the sphere of action, whether it be fable/story (*histoire*) or theme (*sujet*) set in process (*discours*), against the sphere of pure performance. As has been seen, tragedy is based rather on a complex series of events, *mythos* in the Aristotelian sense condensed into plot, and accordingly thrusts the here and now more into the background, while comedy, with its preference for the episodic and paradigmatic as opposed to the syntagmatic plane of action, is lacking in the area of *mythos* as purposeful action: ritual performance thus comes to the fore precisely in the chorus.[29]

These characteristics lead me to my thesis, which may initially seem surprising: the chorus in ancient drama *is* to a large extent ritual. The choral lyrics of both comedy and satyr play are much closer to ritual than are those of tragedy. Apart from its quite simple plots, which for their part are based on mythic and ritual complexes,[30] comedy is thus to a large extent determined by ritual points of view with regard to the chorus. I return therefore to a theory which has for a long time been completely forced into the background after

---

[28] These connections with the performative in the speech act theory of Austin 1994 were already perceived by Johnson (1980:56): "The performative, then, acts like a 'shifter' in that it takes on meaning only by referring to the instance of its utterance." On the connection with the discourse of theater in general cf. F. de Toro 1995:5–33, esp. 24–28. Moreover, Johnson (1980:56–57) also refers to the self-referential nature of the performative utterance, to which I will also refer in what follows.

[29] According to Warning (1976:283–287) the purposeful plot or *sujet* is, using terminology borrowed from a distinction made by E. v. Hartmann, an ulterior plot (*anderweitige Handlung*) on which paradigmatic comic elements or actions (*komische Handlungen*, Hartmann 1887:334) operate, so to speak, in a "parasitic" fashion (Warning 1976:287).

[30] Cf. Bowie 1993. Riu 1999 has similarly suggested a ritual interpretation of Old Comedy that confines itself largely to Dionysus and the Dionysian; the monographis a slightly revised version in English of his 1989 Barcelona dissertation. See my critical review in *Gnomon* 74 (2002):196–203. On the connection of the plot structure of the *Plutus* to the Anthesteria see Bierl 1994. Generally, in scholarship on Greek drama one can see a recent boom in the discovery of ritual subtexts. For a performative-ritual interpretation of the *Ecclesiazusae* see Zeitlin 1999. On the interaction between religion and literature and on the mytho-ritual poetics of Greek texts, cf. Bierl 2002 and Bierl 2007 (with special emphasis on drama), Yatromanolakis/Roilos 2004, and Bierl/Lämmle/Wesselmann 2007. On the use of the interpretative paradigm of the *ephêbeia*, initiation, and *rite de passage* as definitive for structure in the construction of plot in tragedy and Old Comedy, see below, chap. 1, n481.

the excesses of the Cambridge ritualists and their successors, namely that the origin of drama lies in ritual. For more than two scholarly generations who prided themselves on their modern approach this belief was regarded as hopelessly old-fashioned. Richard Seaford and Walter Burkert must be credited with having rehabilitated these ideas at their true core.[31] Together with the theoretical movements and interpreters about which we shall soon speak, a new reworking of the connections between ritual and drama has recently met with great interest.

To understand the comic chorus better, one must also keep in mind the situation in its tragic counterpart, particularly since the phenomenon of the chorus has been far more thoroughly investigated in the area of tragedy. The dramatic chorus represents both a common, not particularly serious, and hypothetical preliminary stage (cf. Arist. *Poet.* 1449a19–21), out of which the separate genres crystalized and the common intersection of genres related to each other. This study will therefore examine the comic chorus in the diachronic dimension, i.e. with respect to its origin in choral poetry and lyric, and synchronically, in relation to the two other theatrical genres and in the context of a living choral culture that played a decisive role in the real world.

Performativity and Ritual: Theoretical Premises

To what extent, then, is the dramatic chorus ritual? Before a reply can be given to this question, we must first cast a brief glance at the overall theoretical background to this work and at the problem of ritual.

The frame of reference of this study is that of performance, currently the subject of much interest in cultural and social studies, where for some time now the field of performance studies has been flourishing. This trend in scholarship has also drawn attention in classical philology to a series of new formulations of questions. In this connection Eric Havelock and Bruno Gentili together with his lyric group in Urbino are regarded as the founders of an approach that concerns itself with pragmatic performative context, the relation of the customer or patron and audience, the communicative process, and in particular the problem of orality. In the field of early poetry, in particular Homeric epic, Albert Lord revealed the complementarity of performance and composition, which corresponds to that of *parole* and *langue*. Among societies that rely on oral communication structures, poetic compositions are therefore

---

[31] Cf. Seaford 1984:14. On the Cambridge ritualists see the extremely informative volume edited by Calder (1991).

[32] As further development of the theories of Lord 1960 see among others Havelock 1963, esp. 145–164, Havelock 1986, esp. 93, Gentili 1984, and Aloni 1998. The concept of performance has

generated in the act of performance with reference to the prevailing *mythos* and ritual.[32]

John L. Austin and Émile Benveniste's linguistic category of the performative has been transferred in the last two decades generally to the most diverse cultural and anthropological processes, such as ritual, everyday life, the theater, and poetry. Here one should mention the studies on performance by Victor Turner (ritual as social drama), Mikhail Bakhtin (the medieval carnival), Erving Goffman (everyday life), Judith Butler (function in the representation and consolidation of gender roles), Richard Schechner (connection of ritual and theater), and, recently, Erika Fischer-Lichte (theater-studies and "performative turn").[33] Finally, performativity has also entered into the study of literature and literary theory.[34] The concept has now become almost a paradigm in Thomas S. Kuhn's sense of the word, i.e. performativity represents an important theoretical frame of reference according to which social praxis is generally analyzed today.[35]

---

recently enjoyed a great vogue in countless publications in our field, especially in the English-speaking world. In the U.S. this has been particularly employed by Gregory Nagy as a framework for interpretation, chiefly in the areas of epic and lyric. See Nagy 1990, Nagy 1996, Stehle 1997, and Edmunds/Wallace 1997. On performance criticism as a trend in work on ancient drama, see Slater 1993 for a good overview. See now Wiles 1997 and Wiles 2000. On Aristophanes and performance in a political sense, see now Slater 2002 (with my critical review in *Gnomon* 78 [2006]:385–390); in general on comedy in a performative perspective, see now Revermann 2006 (who ignores the original German publication of this book).

[33] Cf. Austin 1994 and the restrictions of Benveniste 1966:267–276. Cf. among others Turner 1974, Bakhtin 1984, Bakhtin 1984a, Goffman 1959, Butler 1988, and Schechner 1985. Quite independently from me, while I was writing this book, Erika Fische-Lichte brought this paradigm to the fore, particularly in theater studies. This "performative turn" in humanities has a great impact on the interpretation of drama. See Fischer-Lichte 1998, Fischer-Lichte 1998a, Fischer-Lichte 1999. In this new approach *Geisteswissenschaft* focuses less on the reference and fixed significance of texts and other artifacts than on the process of synaesthetic performance. Body movements, dance, lighting, costumes, and all other semiotic signs yield to an effect of intense transformation. In such a highly stimulating event meaning is not prestabilized and fixed, but *emergent* in the actualization. On the performative see now Fischer-Lichte/Wulf 2001, Wirth 2002, Fischer-Lichte 2004.

[34] Johnson 1980:52–66 ("Poetry and Performative Language: Mallarmé and Austin") successfully applies Austin's theory of the performative and the speech act to lyric and dramatic poetry and to the problem of self-referentiality. On its use in classical philology cf. among others Martin 1989 (in the *Iliad*), Nagy 1990, and Nagy 1996.

[35] Cf. Kuhn 1968. Cf. the remarks of Versnel 1993:11–12 on this; in the field of anthropology different paradigms are not mutually exclusive. In particular, a broadly applied concept like performance and ritual combines various approaches. The attempt of Bell (1992, esp. 69–168), to understand ritual as social praxis in Pierre Bourdieu's sense (Bourdieu 1977, esp. 72–158) seems promising. On the concept of performance and its application to fifth-century BCE Athens see now also the excellent observations of Goldhill 1999 (esp. his overview of modern performance studies, 10–20), which introduce the collected volume Goldhill/Osborne 1999.

This model proves to be of the utmost use for our topic, especially since its different aspects come together in the phenomenon of the Greek chorus. Generally, and on countless occasions, choruses, in relation to which the theatrical chorus represents a secondary and further development, were performed in society. It is precisely religious activity and the initiation of the youth into the world of adults that furnish a central *Sitz im Leben* for the type of ritual dances that were spectacularly performed as social drama in a still living choral culture. Elements of this type of initiation are also reflected in dramatic choruses. My analysis of Aristophanes' *Thesmophoriazusae* (chapter 1) is strongly determined by these ritual and performative moments in the plot. Furthermore, textual references to these choruses can also be analyzed and interpreted from a performative point of view, using speech act theory and ethnological studies of ritual. Time and time again reference is made to the chorus' own action of singing and dancing. Thus we will see that choral self-reference must ultimately be traced back to rituality. But above all, precisely in the realm of Attic drama, which is anchored so strongly in the pragmatic and ritual reality of the polis and which symbolically reworks the everyday world, the performative not only represents a central metaphor that one may use to approach the phenomenon, but the members of the chorus also act directly in their own right and performatively (in the narrower sense of the term) even in the theatrical performance. In sum, the concept represents an intersection of stage, orchestra, and cultural, real-life practice. It is in the chorus in particular that the most diverse theatrical signs of different media are brought together in a comprehensive synaesthetic and spectacular presentation.

Given these connections, my thesis, that the chorus' dance-song is also ritual, will in no way emerge as merely a circular argument based on superficial connections and dependent on tropic connections, even if the concepts *performance* and *ritual* are admittedly extremely hard to define.[36] The extension of the concept of ritual to the performative dimension is of central importance in this connection. In what follows, therefore, ritual will be understood not merely as a particular series of events at a festival, a ceremony within the surrounding polis-cult of Dionysus, but will also be reflected in the micro-

[36] For criticism of the metaphor of performance and the difficulties of the concept, see States 1996. On the impossibility of a definition of performance see 1996:3; States maintains that the concept of ritual has lately expanded from religious actions to all manner of social everyday actions, which he believes makes it simultaneously increasingly more imprecise. The literature on ritual is practically impossible to survey; for a good general, theoretical view, see Bell 1992 and Bell 1997. For the field of classical antiquity see Versnel 1993:15–88 (esp. on the relation between myth and ritual) and Morris 1993.

structure of the text. Above all, the ritual nature of the comic chorus will be examined also in its cultural implications.

According to Stanley Tambiah's extremely useful definition, ritual is equally performative in three senses:

> Ritual is a culturally constructed system of symbolic communication. It is constituted of patterned and ordered sequences of words and acts, often expressed in multiple media, whose content and arrangement are characterised in varying degree by formality (conventionality), stereotypy (rigidity), condensation (fusion), and redundancy (repetition). Ritual action in its constitutive features is performative in these three senses: in the Austinian sense of performative, wherein saying something is also doing something as a conventional act; in the quite different sense of a staged performance that uses multiple media by which the participants experience the event intensively; and in the sense of indexical values—I derive this concept from Peirce—being attached to and inferred by actors during the performance.[37]

Here we should rely less on Julian Huxley's biological and ethological definition of ritual, which Walter Burkert takes as his starting point, since it is not quite extensive enough for cultural and aesthetic achievements. For human ritual forms are never simply conventionalized, stereotyped, and standardized behavior patterns. The aesthetic components, the expressive representation of ritual forms of expression, the symbolic, the element of play, the context of the festival, and the fact that it is an end in itself should be emphasized in particular here. The elements of the performative and theatrical, which are simultaneously conveyed through different media, are essential for ritual. Over the course of human history, simple, ritualized patterns of behavior were

---

[37] Tambiah 1985:128 and generally 123–166 ("A Performative Approach to Ritual," originally in *Proceedings of the British Academy* 65 [1979]:113–169). Tambiah relies here on Charles Sanders Peirce's well-known division of signs into icon, index, and symbol; see Peirce 1983, esp. 64–67.

[38] See Burkert 1979:37: "In other words, ritual is action redirected for demonstration. Characteristic features of ritual in this perspective are: the stereotyped pattern of action, independent of the actual situation and emotion; repetition and exaggeration to make up a kind of theatrical effect; and the function of communication." On Burkert's socio-biological concept of ritual see Versnel 1993:74–88. See also Burkert 1996. Bell (1992:73 [with 146n31]) rightly sees, along with Meyer Fortes, the danger of expanding the concept of ritual too far if one confines ritual, as Richard Schechner does for example, only to formalized communicative functions. As she pointedly remarks: "It is a short step from the proposition that everything is ritual to the practical reality that nothing is ritual." I meet this methodological objection by limiting the subject of my investigation to the chorus, which according to previous and current theories is undeniably connected with ritual and is strongly performative.

clearly further developed into artistic, expressive forms. Burkert has also of course wholly incorporated these communicative aspects into his theories.[38]

The transition to poetry and artistic drama is at the same time fluid. In the field of German studies Wolfgang Braungart has recently come to quite similar conclusions, independently of my studies.[39] These connections are even more compelling for the ancient dramatic chorus, since its practical frame of reference, in contrast to modern lyric, indicates a far greater state of ritual integration. We can speak in only a limited way about a process of secularization of drama in classical Athens. Rather, life in the polis, even in the fifth and fourth centuries BCE, was extensively defined by festivals, rituals, ceremonies, and customs. Contrary to modern practice, religion and society, politics and ritual do not here stand in diametrical opposition to one another, but are closely woven together. In particular, we have to rid ourselves of the assumption that ritual is primarily conservative. Quite the contrary: the polis produces, manipulates, and changes rituals in accordance with historical circumstances.[40]

Ritual is above all a program of actions that is set into action by speech, among other things. The performative approach enjoys a certain popularity in ethnological research into ritual, especially in the field of magic, since here word and action stand in a particularly close relationship to each other. The idea of performativity was introduced into the field of ethnology and anthropology by Ludwig Wittgenstein's criticism of James Frazer's *The Golden Bough*. Bronislaw Malinowski, who viewed speech utterances in magic as equiva-

---

[39] See Braungart 1996, esp. 139–253, specifically on theater 159–161. On theater from a cultural-anthropological perspective, see also Bachmann-Medick 1988.

[40] See among others Connor 1987, Morris 1993 (on the social function of ritual, with a good overview of various theories), and Osborne 1994. On ritual as an instrument of power, see Bell 1992:169–238.

[41] See Wittgenstein 1975 and Malinowski 1935:1–74, esp. 8–10, 45–60 (on the pragmatic context and potential of words), 211–250, esp. 231–240 (on 234–235 he lists alongside magic and sacral utterances typically Austinian speech acts: legal formulae, promises, agreements, oaths). I cite here a few passages straight from Malinowski because they will be of relevance in the course of this work for the connection between the ritual chorus and the speech act; see Malinowski 1935:8 (on the utterance of sacred words in a ritual): "Words, . . . the proper names of a field, path or garden plot, are used as significant actions side by side with bodily movements. Speech is here equivalent to gesture and to motion. It does not function as an expression of thought or communication of ideas but as a part of concerted activity." Equally 1935:9: "Words which cross from one actor to another do not serve primarily to communicate thought: they connect work and correlate manual and bodily movements. Words are part of action and they are equivalents to actions." See finally his concluding remark 1935:52: "All our considerations have led us to the conclusion that words in their primary and essential sense *do, act, produce* and *achieve*." On Malinowski see also Firth 1957 (on Malinowski's linguistic background), Tambiah

15

lent to actions in a practical context, opened the way to this approach at the time through several observations.[41] Obviously the complex problem of ritual cannot be completely explained simply by using the performative as explanatory metaphor. Yet it is precisely in the realm of the chorus, the performative *par excellence*, which in the theater becomes part of the drama, that this approach finds more than simply superficial analogies. The singing and dancing members of the chorus are theatrical sign-bearers and consequently are connected particularly to the speech act, to action in words. To be sure, Austin's linguistic theory, which was purely directed at the pragmatics of everyday communication, has now been built up into a more adaptable instrument, since in the theater we are clearly dealing with two systems of communication. Myth, the existing cosmology, and the system of belief are equally considered as context in choral ritual, especially since in their action the members of the chorus confirm precisely these values and norms.[42]

Ritual and performativity cannot however be investigated solely in terms of linguistic microstructure. From a cultural anthropological point of view new perspectives in social context arise. Not only are meaning and sense translated into ritual action through symbolic processes, but ideologically desired power relations are also internalized through corporeal experiences. As a result, following Catherine Bell and drawing on Pierre Bourdieu's *habitus* theory, we may understand the ritual nature of choral dance as a social practice.[43] Thus chapter 1 has as its theme the social practice of initiation, which is experienced directly on a physical level. Transition to adult status is primarily expe-

---

1985:30–34, and Adam 1990 (on the ritual effect of speech). The impetus for this theory came ultimately from James Frazer. On performativity and magic see Graf 1996:185–186. Austin was then received by Finnegan (1969) and Bloch (1974) into the field of ethnological reseach on ritual. In the study of everyday ritual Knuf/Schmitz 1980:7–11 ("Ritual als Handlung") are favorably inclined to performativity and the application of Austin.

[42] The stimulating criticism in Gardner 1983, which includes the actors' frame of belief as a central factor in more complex rituals, thus making the perlocutionary act not automatically, causally, and constitutively connected to locution, is not quite fair to Tambiah's complex idea, which does in fact address the interplay of belief and ritual (Tambiah 1985:130). Austin's model, which is directed purely at the pragmatic communication situation in a rather mechanistic and formal way, does not of course work in every ritual context. For an evaluation and critique of performative ritual theory, see Bell 1992:37–43. On the generally too restrictive and institutional concept of ritual and on the as-yet unclear assumptions behind the performative approach in the study of everyday ritual, see Rauch 1992:31–32.

[43] Bell 1992, esp. 69–168. Cf. her definition (81): "Practice is (1) situational; (2) strategic; (3) embedded in a misrecognition of what it is in fact doing; and (4) able to reproduce or reconfigure a vision of the order of power in the world, or what I will call 'redemptive hegemony.'" Cf. Bourdieu 1977, esp. 72–158; on Bourdieu's theory of *habitus* and the relationship to ritual see Braungart 1996:48–57, esp. 49–51.

rienced in the chorus as performative practice and social drama: by means of the combination of signs the strategic goal, the restoration of a clear differentiation of gender roles, is achieved in contrastive fashion. In comedy this ritual process is played out symbolically and humorously.

To what extent can we now connect these results from the study of ritual with dramatic choral dance? Let us first give by way of summary a cursory list of possible parallels:

1. In a manner characteristic of ritual, a beautifully arrayed group presents itself demonstratively to an audience using dance steps performed to the accompaniment of the *aulos* and song.[44] Of decisive importance are the extent of its elaborate arrangement, the self-consciousness of its staged stylization, the festive context, separated from everyday experience, and the development of actions that are completed using simple, stereotypical, and repetitive patterns. For Walter Burkert the combination of choral dance and ritual is fixed in an exemplary fashion: "Rhythmically repeated movement, directed to no end and performed together as a group, is, as it were, ritual crystalized in its purest form."[45] At the same time the songs that are sung involve myths, that is to say traditional narratives that are relevant for the unity of the community. As authoritative speech acts they thematize shared norms and values in marked form. At the same time myth generally has a close connection to the ritual framework, so that in traditional societies myth is often re-actualized in ritual and translated into action.

2. Apart from myths the members of the chorus also refer in their speech to their own activity in the orchestra. As a result of this, an arrangement typical of ritual arises: in its purest form ritual is completed through its own implementation.

3. The chorus represents a selected group of the entire community and itself portrays this as microcosm of the polis. Despite the separation into audience and performers, the differentiation in this complex formation is at the same time removed. The transition between ritual and theater consequently becomes fluid.

I shall explain my thesis of the extensively ritual character of the comic chorus on quite different levels, ranging from the macrostructure of the prag-

---

[44] On demonstration as constitutive element of ritual, see Burkert 1979:37 and Braungart 1996:45.
[45] Burkert 1985:102. On music and dance as ritual, see also Braungart 1996:246–248.

matic context to the microstructure of the transmitted text, and drawing on current research, particularly on the tragic chorus. It is important to realize here that comedy as a genre does not strive for a specific development of a myth or literary rendering, that is, the development of a closed narrative of a unified act, but that the syntagmatic element takes second place to the ritual sense.

As a result of this new perspective, typical characteristics of the comic chorus, in particular its frequent self-referentiality, become understandable. They do not appear as innovations of the comic playwrights but can be explained on the basis of the tradition of choral lyric and from the religious choruses and hymns of a living choral culture with its definite *Sitz im Leben*.

The specifically ritual nature of the comic chorus can be illuminated only partly from its historical development. One can of course make the following supposition: as is well known, it was only at a relatively late stage (487/6 BCE) that comedy was integrated into the Dionysiac *agôn* of the polis, in which theater was gradually transformed into art.[46] Because of this, comedy was isolated from poetic developments for a comparatively long time and completely rooted in folk traditions. These comic performance forms were thus limited to their immediate pragmatic use. Up to that time genre thus coincided with cultic occasion, so that the performance probably crystalized out of Dionysiac processions (κῶμοι). Because of the destabilization of its *Sitz im Leben* after 486 BCE, these ritual characteristics became fixed, preserved, or even partly created anew, evidently to differentiate it from tragedy. Typical of the comic genre is the total transparency between both communicative levels, namely between the only partly developed fictional plot and the pragmatic performative frame, which coincides largely with Dionysiac ritual.

The Current State of Scholarship Contrasted with the Thesis Advanced Here

Only with the broad interest in social and cultural anthropological questions that has recently arisen has the performative context of ancient dramatic performances moved more to the center.[47] Many peoples possessed and continue to possess choral dance songs. The members of the chorus represent a segment of the whole community and, while dancing, sing episodes of myth-

[46] On the agonistic principle, which appears also in the texts of the tragedies as a literary competition see Seidensticker 1996. On choral dance in agonistic context see also Henrichs 1996:28–34.

[47] See in particular des Bouvrie 1990 and des Bouvrie 1993.

ical cosmology. In intercultural comparative studies the following functions of ritual choral dancing have emerged as anthropological constants that may all be applied also to ancient drama and the Greek choral tradition:

1. As a stereotyped behavior for the sake of demonstration that permanently repeats itself, the choral dance is in an exemplary fashion ritual *par excellence*. The intensive rhythm, the movement of feet together, and the expression of the religious and ideological foundation of the human group simultaneously communicated in song contribute to its cohesion. In their staged theatricality choral performances come closest of all to a ritual game. As an essential part of education, *khoreia* is a means of social control and furthers the handing down of the society's values and norms. One could summarize this view in terms of a homoeostatic social theory as the social stabilization function of dance.

2. Following Victor Turner's theory of *communitas* and anti-structure, choral performances resemble a ritual drama that temporarily reverses the world.[48]

3. Collective dance rises autogenetically to an emotional highpoint that can be applied in a social fashion.

4. Choral dance is mostly performed in an agonistic context. In the competition, members of the chorus demonstrate the limits of their skill and ability.

5. The movements of the chorus are part of a performative, multimedia presentation in which song, visual charm, and movement are combined. Song and nonverbal communication by gesture are part of a metaphoric communication that in a marked and ritual fashion instills a behavior pattern both in the body and beyond it and perpetuates this in a public setting.[49]

It can be shown through a short overview of current scholarly theories how what has been said up till now builds on this and where the new directions of this study lie.

The most important contributions to the study of dance made by the early anthropological work come from A. R. Radcliffe-Brown and E. E. Evans-Pritchard. In *The Andaman Islanders*, a work first written in 1908 as a disserta-

---

[48] On *communitas* and "anti-structure" cf. Turner 1974:44–57, 201–202, esp. 272–274 and Turner/ Turner 1982:205–206.

[49] In compiling the above-mentioned five characteristics I rely among others on the conclusions of Lonsdale 1993, esp. 19; cf. also Tambiah 1985:123–166, 382–389, esp. 124, 149–150, 154–155, 164, and Ceccarelli 1998:10–12.

tion, then reworked in 1913 and only first published in 1922, Radcliffe-Brown brought together in passing extremely important findings about dance.[50] He stressed above all the effect of group cohesion. In contrast to this, in a study from 1928 Evans-Pritchard also brought to the fore the disruptive elements in tribal dancing.[51] Stanley J. Tambiah's pioneering contribution "A Performative Approach to Ritual," originally published in 1979, builds on these discoveries and has proved extremely useful for the connection of ritual, choral dance, speech, and music.[52] This study is among the best with respect to performative aspects in ritual in general, and is extremely applicable to phenomena in the Greek world.

In his book *Dance and Ritual Play in Greek Religion*, Steven H. Lonsdale gives a good overview of Greek dance from an anthropological perspective.[53] He unfortunately excludes dramatic choruses from his comprehensive treatment (6–7) because he makes a strong distinction between "ritual" and "dramatic" choruses, as if dramatic performances were not part of ritual festivals. In what follows I shall try to show just the opposite, namely that dramatic choruses, however embedded they may be in a plot, represent to a large extent ritual choruses.

The Greek chorus has been studied extensively from all angles, and here tragedy has been accorded a distinctly privileged position vis-à-vis other theatrical genres.[54] Up until the 1970s the chorus was seen primarily as a dramatic, artistic, and general cultural phenomenon belonging to Greece. It is only later work that has considered Greek *khoreia* in its broader social, anthropological, and performative context. In so doing, attention has been focused on the *Sitz im Leben*, on the interplay of dance and music, and on the specific

---

[50] Radcliffe-Brown 1964:246–254 and 334–335. On the social-anthropological functions of dance cf. Hanna 1979, Spencer 1985, and Cowan 1990 (on modern Greece). Naerebout (1997:293–409) erects a comprehensive theoretical framework, which takes into account findings from the field of dance and communication study as well as from anthropology and the sociology of religion.

[51] Evans-Pritchard 1928, esp. 460. Because of the Marxist perspective of Bloch 1974, which attempts to show ritual as the opium of the people, the latter views dance as a restricted code. This does not, however, fit in with the conclusions I have presented.

[52] Originally published in *Proceedings of the British Academy* 65 (1979):113–169 (= Tambiah 1985:123–166 and 382–389).

[53] Lonsdale 1993. Cf. the overly negative criticism of D. Sansone (*BMCR* 5.3 [1994]:230–233). Cf. also the review by F. G. Naerebout, *Mnemosyne* 49 (1996):366–369.

[54] Kinzl 1980:180, relying on Szemerényi 1975:319–330, esp. 326–330, in fact proposes an etymological connection between τραγικός and the Hittite root *tarkw-/tarw-*, "dance," "rave," which implies that the tragic chorus originally represented only dance. According to Kinzl's reconstruction (180–184) based on Hdt. 5.67 and 6.129, Dionysiac and orgiastic choral dance came to the area of the Isthmos from western Asia Minor and was there hellenized and domesticated (i.e. it took on a solemn character) by Kleisthenes of Sikyon.

production requirements in an orally-based song culture in a historical process that reached from the archaic period to the developed theater of Athens.[55]

The connection between choral lyric and polis drama is also of importance for understanding the comic chorus. For the purposes of our work, those studies that consider the chorus and choral poetry in connection with festival and ritual are particularly relevant. For an understanding of what follows, the findings produced by a pragmatic and functionally oriented interpretation of archaic lyric—especially that initiated and directed by the research group associated with Bruno Gentili—are fundamental. This "school" emphasizes in particular the oral nature of communication and the resulting anchoring of poetry in social and political life in which the cultic festival as occasion for the performance fully participates.[56]

In this connection Claude Calame's groundbreaking book, *Les chœurs de jeunes filles en Grèce archaïque*, must be mentioned. In the first volume of this work Calame gives a general morphology of the Greek chorus and emphasizes its social and ritual *Sitz im Leben*. In the second volume he illuminates the close connection between Spartan initiation rituals and the two *Partheneia* of Alcman (fr. 1 and 3 Davies = 3 and 1 Calame).[57]

---

[55] On "song culture" cf. Herington 1985. On Greek song culture in general from a dramatic, artistic, and cultural perspective see among others Warnecke 1932, Pickard-Cambridge 1968:246–257 (on the chorus 232–262), Koller 1963, Dale 1969, Webster 1970, Fitton 1973, and Kachler 1974. On individual dances and dance formations (choreographic studies of images and texts) cf. inter alia Weege 1926, Lawler 1964, Prudhommeau 1965, Stoessl 1987:23–47, and Brommer 1989. Mullen 1982, Henrichs 1996, and Ceccarelli 1998 are examples of more recent studies. See the detailed overview of the field by Naerebout 1997:1–113, esp. on trends since 1925 (72–101). For a supplement to the titles cited above see the detailed bibliography therein (114–145).

[56] Cf. inter alia Gentili 1984, Gentili 1984/85, Gentili 1990, Gentili 1990a, Rösler 1980, and Rösler 1983a; they emphasize the concrete nature of the discourse, myth as connecting link in oral culture, *deixis ad oculos* (in the sense of Bühler 1934, esp. 79–80, 105, 108, 125), and its direct reception and influence in early Greek lyric; Latacz 1985 rejects the narrow focus on concrete and pragmatic context and postulates the presence of imagination and fictionality even in lyric; Latacz 1985:69 correctly includes comedy among the genres influenced by actual everyday communication. On the discussion between Latacz and Rösler and an attempt to reconcile the two approaches, see Gentili 1990a:15–16; according to him, the cause of the difference lies in a misunderstanding of the term "fictionality," which should not be understood in the modern sense of the word.

[57] Calame 1977. On the connection between festival and choral poetry cf. also Kannicht 1989. In general studies of Greek dance there has also been something of a paradigm shift toward anthropological, ritual, and performative questions, which Calame's groundbreaking study introduced. After twenty years the first volume has now received an English translation, which the author has provided with updated references (Calame 1997). Cf. e.g. Lonsdale 1993 and Ceccarelli 1998 (esp. on the *pyrrhikhê*; cf. E. Stehle's review in *BMCR* 00.03.17), which emphasize inter alia the anthropological connection to initiation. On the chorus in Greek life cf. also Bacon 1994/95.

In his controversial but very stimulating piece, "The Ephebes' Song," John J. Winkler brings the ritual point of view in the Athenian tragic chorus to the fore by making a connection between participation in the chorus and the education and military training of ephebes. Even though the connection of members of the tragic chorus to the *ephêbeia*, which is only securely attested as an institution much later,[58] remains questionable, nevertheless the connection to initiation practices, as demonstrated by Calame in the case of the archaic choral tradition, cannot simply be dismissed. At the center of the *khoreia*, as has been said, is *paideia*, the process of teaching and learning in an age-group. Here young people are instructed in the highly important myths and rites that reflect and instill the values and norms of society.

In his monograph *Poetry into Drama* John Herington draws on the important concept of song culture and in so doing brings the performative aspect of choral lyric to the fore. Moreover, he draws attention to the fact that the performance of a traditional choral composition in archaic society was normally reserved for re-performance at important, periodically repeated festivals during the course of the year.

Gregory Nagy has recently summarized and synthesized important trends in scholarship relating to the development from choral lyric forms into the chorus of polis drama.[59] In *Pindar's Homer*, following Koller, Gentili, and others, he develops the concept of mimesis as reactualization or reenactment in an originally tribal society shaped by myth and ritual that hands on its ideology to the next generation by means of performances.[60] According to Nagy's theory, the key to the understanding of the tragic chorus lies in the ritual function of choruses in traditional societies like the *poleis* of the archaic period.

---

[58] Winkler 1990. The institution of the Attic *ephêbeia* is first attested only in the fourth century BCE (Arist. *Ath. Pol.* 42) and even the term *ephêbos* is a comparatively late usage; the earliest inscription concerning the ephebic class comes from 334/33 (Lycurgan military reforms). It remains controversial whether the fourth-century institution was something completely new or went back to very similar fifth-century antecedents. The detailed study by Pélékidis (1962:7–79, esp. 51–79 [on its history]) argues for the latter; in particular see 33 and 78–79. The question is also handled by Winkler (1990:26–27).

[59] Herington 1985 and Nagy 1994/95. My summary of current theories largely follows their presentation of the most important milestones, which range from Calame 1977 through Herington 1985, Burkert 1987a, and Winkler 1990 to Nagy 1990.

[60] Nagy 1990, esp. 42–45, 339–413, in particular 346, 349, 373–375; the reactualization of myth in ritual is thus fundamental; on this idea cf. Leach 1982:5–6; on mimesis in this sense cf. Koller 1954 (his thesis, that mimesis has its origin in dance, was for a long time not generally accepted), Gentili 1984:67–68 (2006⁴:87–88), De Angeli 1988, and Gentili 1990a:12–13. On the understanding of the term during the Second Sophistic, cf. Flashar 1979, which, relying on a different evaluation, defines mimesis in the fifth century BCE as "presentation on another level" (79–81, esp. 80 [= *Eidola* 201–203, esp. 202]).

Traces of this extensively ritual occasion can be found in the Athenian state theater. It is precisely in the nonprofessional status of members of the chorus that one may still recognize the old function of initiatory rites of passage.[61] As youths on the threshold of adulthood, in Nagy's opinion they play out in stylized ritual presentations the roles of marginal figures, thus completing, using the remnants of a tribal initiation preserved in the classical polis, the change in status from youth to full citizen in front of a collective of adult spectators.

This hypothesis of a survival of puberty initiation is of substantial heuristic value in considering dramatic choruses. In our consideration of individual rites in the action of Aristophanic comedies, initiation as important paradigm for the study of ritual will need to be subjected to a critical examination. But there remains the possibility that this point of view had a function in daily life in the archaic period, before the evolution of drama, and that it may help explain the existence of choruses of youths and maidens. In addition, the round dance forms part of the repertoire of cultic action in the polis during new year and fertility festivals. The ritual character of dramatic choruses is thus not exhausted by initiation alone. For ritual character can be seen not only in reflexes of cultic forms, but also in the structure of choral dance lyric. It is also in this sense that the tradition of choral lyric and customary hymns may be invoked.

[61] In a piece on choral performance traditions in Stesichorus, who is generally placed in the field of lyric monody by modern scholarship, Burkert 1987a, relying on a passage from the "Old Oligarch," Ps. Xenophon *Ath. Pol.* 1.13, in which the loss of the rich song culture in Athens of the archaic period is lamented, emphasizes the separation in choral culture of an aristocratic phase from a democratic one. It is of course significant that, contrary to Burkert's assumption of the professionalization in Stesichorus' time of the members of the chorus as well, the amateur status of choral participants continued in the classical period, even as the choral poet-producer now concentrated on this as his main activity. That professionalization did not take place should be regarded as evidence for a former initiation of the youth. It was not professional dancers, who might also be foreigners or slaves, but representative groups or age groups that on a cyclical basis formed the chorus, in which the polis as a whole clearly had a fundamental interest. On the religious concept of initiation see the general overview in Grohs 1993. As *rite de passage* it always requires symbolic dramatization; on this see van Gennep 1909 and Turner 1967:93–111. For discussion of initiation as puberty ritual see among others the following important works: Harrison 1927[2], Jeanmaire 1939, Burkert 1966, Vidal-Naquet 1968, Brelich 1969, Calame I 1977 (Engl. trans. Calame 1997); see also inter alia Bremmer 1978, Bremmer 1980, Vidal-Naquet 1986, Winkler 1990, Moreau 1992, Graf 1998:25–27, Baudy 1998:57–64, Calame 1999b, Bierl 2002:674–675. In particular on the Greek chorus as initiatory training institution see Calame I 1977 (Engl. trans. Calame 1997), Winkler 1990, and Calame 1999b:299–307. On the history of scholarship in this regard and for a critical survey of this paradigm (with extensive bibliography) see Versnel 1993:48–74, Bierl 2002:674–675, Dodd/Faraone 2003, and Bierl 2007:18–21, 23–25. On the application of the interpretative categories of *ephêbeia*, initiation, and *rite de passage* as structural determinant in the construction of plot in tragedy and Old Comedy cf. below, chap. 1, n481.

While the tragic chorus has in recent times been thoroughly investigated using new approaches, no such study has been undertaken in the field of comedy.[62] This seems all the more surprising given the fact that ritual and performative phenomena appear far more often in the comic chorus than in tragedy. This gap in scholarship will be addressed in the current work.

Self-Referentiality and Speech Act in Performative Context

In what follows I intend to construct a methodological instrument with which the ritual nature of the comic chorus can be understood more completely, using as background theoretical discussions of choral lyric and tragedy.

From a diachronic perspective and using modern narratology and semiotics as a foundation, Claude Calame shows how in the case of tragic choruses a second level of story or dramatic plot (*énoncé*) is layered over the purely ritual anchoring in the festive occasion, that is, over the frame of the actual communications situation (*énonciation*).[63] The members of the dramatic chorus

---

[62] There is now an impressive synthesis on the chorus in Attic tragedy in the form of a collective volume. The contributions stem from a conference on the chorus in Greek culture, held in the spring of 1992 as a cooperative effort between Harvard and Boston Universities. The first part focuses on the transition from choral lyric to tragic chorus; here the contributors reflect in exemplary fashion contemporary interest in choral performativity, self-referentiality, and ritual behavior. The second part, consisting mainly of contributions on the choruses of individual tragedians, is also published in the journal *Arion*; see *Arion* 3rd ser., 3.1 (fall 1994/ winter 1995) and 4.1 (spring 1996):1–114. Finally, on the tragic chorus see inter alia Segal 1995, esp. 180–181, Henrichs 1996, Henrichs 1996a, Baur 1997, Wiles 1997, esp. 63–113, Paulsen 1998, Käppel 1999, esp. 61–69, and Calame 1999, who for the most part consider archaic choral lyric as well. See now also Foley 2003 and Calame 2005. Baur 1999a:15–29 in his general characterization of the ancient chorus represents a notable exception, in that he includes the comic chorus in order to illustrate the phenomenon on the twentieth-century stage. Cf. also his "Überblick über die Forschungslage," *ibid.*, 10–12. At a conference held in Potsdam ("Der Chor im antiken und modernen Drama," 15–17 Oct. 1997) (= Riemer/Zimmermann 1999) comedy received its due alongside tragedy; see Zimmermann 1999 and Bierl 1999. See now also Perusino/ Colantonio 2007, the acta of the conference "Dalla lirica corale alla poesia drammatica. Forme e funzioni del canto corale nella tragedia e nella commedia greca" (Urbino, 21–23 Sept. 2005). On the Aristophanic chorus, particularly on the *exodoi* of *Lys.*, *Pax*, *Av.*, *Eccl.*, *Vesp.*, and *Ran.*, see now Calame 2004.

[63] Calame 1995, esp. 3–26, 98–100, and 106–111. On shifters see Jakobson 1984. On *énonciation* see Ducrot/Todorov 1972:405–410, Greimas/Courtés I 1979/86:125–128, and Greimas/Courtés II 1979/86:75–77; on the *énoncé* (i.e. the result of the act of utterance) cf. Greimas/Courtés I 1979/86:123–125 and Greimas/Courtés II 1979/86:74–75. A text as *énoncé* normally blends out references to its *énonciation*. Bühler's *deixis ad oculos* (on *deixis* see Bühler 1934:79–148, on *deixis ad oculos* 79–120, esp. 79–80, 105, 108, 125) is to some extent comparable to indexical reference to the *énonciation*, while anaphoric *deixis*, focused on the speech context, and *deixis* of the imaginary (*am Phantasma*) (Bühler 1934:121–140) are distinct from this; cf. Ducrot/

thus have a double identity: they dance as a ritual group in the here and now, specifically in Athens at the time of the performance in honor of the theater-god, Dionysus; on the other hand, they also undertake a dramatic role within the structure of the plot. All in all the chorus is given the role of inter-mediary between the heroes of the then and there and the audience of the here and now. It truly possesses, in the sense of August Wilhelm Schlegel, the features of an "idealized spectator," or rather an inner, double spectator.[64] On the one hand the dancers in the orchestra react as if they were themselves the audience in the theater of Dionysus; on the other, in their rather marginal roles—in tragedy they generally represent old men or young girls and slave women— they react to the actions of the heroes as a kind of external spectator and commentator, as if they were their contemporaries from the heroic age and were also "taking part" in the action on the stage.[65] Calame shows how the chorus, by means of fading in and fading out of the utterance situation and the frame of the plot—that is, by the accentuation of elements that refer respectively either clearly to the here and now or to the action on stage—is able to float freely between both worlds. In particular, deictic words and use of tense, mood, and person play a critical role in this regard. "Here," "now," the present tense and the "I"/"we" of the speaker and the second person of the addressee emphasize the performative present, for example; "there," "then," the past tense and the "he"/"she" of the third person tend to bring the plot of the action of the play to the foreground. Yet the text, or utterance, through the linguistic category of shifters (*embrayeurs*) ("now," "here," "I"/"we"), can also change the focus from the uttered/narrated dimension of mimesis

---

Todorov 1972:405–406. On these connections cf. also F. de Toro 1995:11–28, specifically on *deixis* 13–22. Even in a concrete, oral communication situation, as was also the case in Old Comedy, not every direct reference has to relate to the act of utterance, but may in accordance with its pivotal function also relate to the level of mimesis. Cf. the reply of Latacz 1985 to Rösler 1983a. On shifting in/out or *embrayage/débrayage* cf. Greimas/Courtés I 1979/86, 119–121 and 79–82, Greimas/Courtés II 1979/86, 73–74 and 61; on the nature of personal pronouns as shifters between *énonciation* and *énoncé* cf. Benveniste 1966:251–257. On the "I" in *énonciation* see Benveniste 1966:260: "Est «ego» qui *dit* «ego»" ["Whoever says *ego* is *ego*"]. On the status of "I" as shifter see Jakobson 1984:43–44 (= *Selected Writings* II, 132–133). The problem of the fluc-tuation between "I" and "we" is of central interest particularly in the chorus; the "I" as shifter here may also assume different voices: the speaker in the *énonciation*, the actor or narrator in the mimesis, and the collective voice of the "we," which also includes the audience and the author.

[64] Cf. Schlegel 1846:76–77. Arnott 1989:3–43 emphasizes from a spatial perspective that the orchestra, where the chorus performs, is closer to the audience than the stage on which the actors perform. On the ideal spectator cf. also Hose I 1990/91:32–37, on the question of space, 33.

[65] On συναγωνίζεσθαι (Arist. *Poet.* 1456a25–27) see inter alia Rode 1971:115n100 and Gentili 1984/85:33–35.

(*énoncé*) to the event of utterance (*énonciation*). References to one's own performance can be taken as instances in which the speakers are able to "switch" freely between levels of communication as if between gears. In the case of the chorus, one may especially point to expressions of its own activity in song and dance, particularly in the first person, and talk of ritual occasion as indicative of "gear changing" (*embrayage*). For the ritual chorus, which sings and dances at different festive occasions, the essential element is its limited role identity and its quality of being a hinge between mimesis and the actual communications situation. Regardless of whether one sees the chorus' dressing up as ghosts, spirits, and animals in terms of the three great religious and social paradigms of fertility, the new year, or initiation, these actors always function as shifters and a bridge to the audience. In the multimedia performance spectators are thereby drawn into a vortex of interconnected means of perception. In so doing they become participants in the action, and as a result a closeness between actor and spectator, characteristic of ritual, comes into being.[66]

Aristotle's requirement that the chorus "play/act/compete alongside" (συναγωνίζεσθαι, Arist. *Poet.* 1456a25–27) may clearly be explained from its historical evolution. In the case of tragedy, aspects of plot, descriptive narrative, and explanatory interpretation increasingly overshadowed the occasion of the ritual. This had developed to such an extent by the fourth century BCE that a poetological commandment arose to the effect that a stage production should not be interrupted by excessively obvious references to its own performance.

The process of extensive fictionalization in the golden age of tragedy between 450 and 400 BCE did not, however, develop as far as Calame suggests. In his essay "From Choral Poetry to Tragic Stasimon: The Enactment of Women's Song" he seems to absolutize the undeniable tendency for the frame of the here and now increasingly to fade out.[67] This follows the existing trend in scholarship to represent too schematically the gap between tragedy and comedy in the area of self-referentiality and possible encroachments of the dramatic action into the actual performance situation.[68] Nevertheless, he does recognize in this case the ritual function of the chorus, even in Euripides. The audience, gathered in the theater of Dionysus to honor the god of tragedy,

---

[66] Turner 1982:112 states: "Ritual, unlike theatre, does not distinguish between audience and performers." Cf. also the sound observations in Segal 1989:340–349 and Henrichs 1994/95:90 (on the cult of Dionysus in the orchestra and the connection with the audience).

[67] Calame 1994/95, esp. 142–146. Similarly, Segal 1995:180 stresses in the case of tragedy the extent of embedding in the plot and the distance from actual ritual. Cf. however the much more complicated model in Calame 1999, esp. 148–153 (with sketch, 152).

[68] Cf. Taplin 1986 and Möllendorff 1995:103–104.

identifies itself with the speaker of the unspecified "I"/"We," and in so doing chorus and audience, just as in choral lyric, are joined in a ritual act. In a piece on the comic mask Calame focuses his investigation on the actors and consequently does not go into the special properties of the comic chorus.[69]

In expansion of the precise narratalogical analysis of expressions of time, place, and person relationships, there are further indications that the chorus manages to refer to the actual here and now of the performance. These phenomena may best be described using the concept of self-referentiality. When members of the chorus refer to their own current action, the performative function behind the fictional becomes clearly visible. Action in the here and now is primarily determined by the chorus' own performance, by its dance, by the rhythmical singing of songs in honor of Dionysus Eleuthereus, by processional movements and others characteristic of the chorus, and by gestures of a nonverbal nature. Because of the vague and inaccurate concept of so-called illusion, indications of self-referentiality in tragedy have long been denied. Without being completely aware of it, scholars anachronistically projected back onto antiquity the dramatic rule of the naturalistic theater of the nineteenth century, namely that the action on stage should not be interrupted by any reference to its own theatrical nature. Yet later research has been able to detect this kind of self-reference in tragedy, in particular in the tragic chorus.[70] The difference between the dramatic genres is in this respect

---

[69] Calame 1989 successfully applies the model of a mimesis of distance to comedy as well. Even the comic mask, according to Calame, helps to fade out and conceal the performative "I" behind the "he" of the action, though the presence of the speaker's "I" continues to show through. He sees the distorting Dionysiac clothing of the potbelly and phallus as a kind of play that reveals the utopia of the stage; masking enables the umasking of social reality and also facilitates a distancing effect. Cf. also the remarks on the comic mask in Lohr 1986:78–79: "Das mangelhafte Trennungsvermögen von realem Schauspieler-Ich und darzustellender Rolle kann durch den Gebrauch einer *Maske* aufgehoben werden. Die Maske stellt einen 'Mehrwert,' einen 'mimetischen Zuschuß,' des agierenden Individuums dar, . . . Aber die Maske ist nicht nur Signifikant, darstellender Träger eines Anderen, sondern auch Signifikat, Dargestelltes ihres Trägers. . . . Die Maske wird zu einem Medium der Distanz, . . . Zugleich spaltete sich die Kultgemeinde in Darsteller und Zuschauer auf" ["The difficulty in distinguishing between the actual actor's 'I' and the dramatic role being performed can be done away with by the use of a mask. The mask represents an 'added value,' a mimetic 'subsidy' of the person carrying out the activity, . . . but the mask is not only a signifier, a sign-bearer that represents another, but also a signified, that represented by the sign-bearer. . . . The mask becomes a means of distancing . . . at the same time the cultic community is split into performer and spectator"]. But the chorus' mask also presents a possible transition from play to cult, thereby reducing the distance between it and the spectator; Henrichs 1994/95:70 draws attention to this.

[70] See inter alia Segal 1982:215–271, Goldhill 1986:244–264, Bierl 1991:111–226, Henrichs 1994/95, Batchelder 1995, Ringer 1998, and Dobrov 2001.

only one of degree, not of a fundamental nature, although in principle a different poetics and aesthetic obtain in comedy.[71]

Albert Henrichs has focused in several in-depth studies on the aspect of choral utterances about its own dancing in the orchestra and terms this phenomenon "choral self-referentiality." This however represents only one slice of a larger complex. I therefore suggest that in this case it is better to talk of ritual or performative self-referentiality, since all actions that are named in the *embrayage* fall into the realm of ritual and performative activity in the here and now.[72]

Relying in part on my studies of self-referentiality and metatheater, Henrichs is able to show how individual tragic playwrights managed to overcome the split that arose during the course of the transformation of theater into literature between choral dance, rooted in ritual and mainly concerned with translating cheerful vitality into bodily motion, and the tragic events of the plot. The festive mood arises either from a mistaken assessment by the chorus or when the members of the chorus project their dancing onto other positive choruses of myth and ritual, thereby being able to talk about their own ritual activity in an oblique fashion, but nevertheless remaining within the dramatic action and in harmony with their dramatic character.

The connection to the theater god Dionysus, who functions, like self-reference in performance, as a shifter, is crucial for the intrusion of the actual utterance situation.[73] In most cases, then, the performative element is coupled with ritual self-reference. Dionysus stands by synecdoche for the dramatic choral dance itself. The tragic chorus either refers to the *énonciation*, that is, to Dionysiac music, the *aulos*, and whirling, enthusiastic movement, or it associates its current ritual activity with other mythical transfigurations of a Dionysus who dances in an idyllic and ideal landscape with male and female members of his entourage. In this case too, myth and ritual enter into close interaction. Ritual frames the myth in the performance. The ritual chorus,

---

[71] See Möllendorff 1995. On the distinction between tragedy and comedy see also Seidensticker 1982:249–160 ("Appendix A: Zur Trennung von Tragödie und Komödie in der antiken Dramentheorie"; characteristically, this does not deal with the chorus).

[72] Cf. Henrichs 1994/95, Henrichs 1996, esp. 44–50, and Henrichs 1996a; Henrichs 1994/95:58–59 even refers in passing to the concept of ritual self-referentiality and calls for further study of this phenomenon, something which would however go beyond the limits of his less ambitiously defined project. Yet he defines the area of ritual too narrowly when he refers solely to the embedded rituals of lament, prayer, supplication, and summoning up of the dead.

[73] Cf. Bierl 1991:35–36, 83–84, 99, 106–107, 129, 155, 164, 190–191, 224, and references to choral dance in connection with Dionysus (242–243). On the performative as shifter cf. Johnson 1980:56.

which is present in the orchestra in honor of Dionysus, sees itself as a mirror of other Dionysiac choral circles that in turn take as their model the mythical constellation of Dionysus ἔξαρχος leading his Bakkhai. Euripides' *Bacchae* is characterized by this "metatheatrical" interplay of mythic and ritual techniques of interlocking and nesting.[74]

This type of "choral projection" onto other choruses is already one level removed from the actual here and now. The groups that are thereby presented are drawn from the ritual world either of the place of performance, Athens, or of other poleis that correspond to the locations where the plot is set or to other mythically imagined places.[75] In keeping with the prevailing anthropomorphism of the period, choral formation is attributed to the dance gods, in particular Apollo, Artemis, and Pan. The gods thus serve as model for dancing mortals.

While the application of the concept of self-referentiality in the field of tragedy has been met with relatively strong skepticism and opposition,[76] there have been fewer problems with this approach in comedy, since it has always been noted in connection with typical elements like the *parabasis* that the so-called illusion is here broken and that the poet and/or chorus speaks to the audience in his/its own right.[77]

The following argument is often made against self-referentiality from various sides: the concept of choral self-referentiality in drama is a *non sequitur*, because it is the poet and the poet alone who puts words and actions into the mouth of the chorus in the plot and it is not in the power of the dramatic chorus to determine its own utterances and movements. This also holds true,

---

[74] On choral self-reference in Euripides cf. Henrichs, "Dancing for Dionysos: Choral Performance and Dionysiac Ritual," currently in preparation for publication, extract in Henrichs 1996a.

[75] Henrichs 1994/95:68, 73, 75, 78, 88, 90 and 1996a talks of "choral projection."

[76] Cf. Kullmann 1993, Latacz 1993:294–295, 299–300 (critical appreciation), and Taplin 1986 in English. Taplin has now revised his opinion in the case of the *Oresteia*; cf. Wilson/Taplin 1993. Studies of the metatheatrical dimension, in particular of the *Bacchae*, despite their many excesses, cannot simply be dismissed as postmodern or poststructuralist, as skeptics are wont to do (Seaford 1996:32). Contrary to current opinion, there is no breaking of the illusion in this type of self-reference, rather it enables the audience with the help of references to ritual activity in the theater to identify itself with the ritual activity on the stage; cf. Bierl 1991:111–119. Kullmann 1993 unfortunately does not take these important qualifications into account. For the current state of scholarly discussion of metatheater, see Segal's lucid handling of the question in the new afterword (369–378, esp. 370–375) to the second and expanded edition (1997) of Segal 1982 and his excellent response (*BMCR* 98.5.26) to Seaford's critical review (*BMCR* 98.3.10). The recent harsh criticism in Radke 2003 is not convincing.

[77] See inter alia Taplin 1986, esp. 164n10 (with references), Bierl 1990, esp. 358–359, 370–76, 384–86, Bierl 1991:27–44, 172–176, Goldhill 1991:167–222, esp. 196–222, Dover, *Frogs*, 58–60, and Taplin 1993:67–78, 105–110.

naturally, for the passages in which the tragic or comic chorus refers to its own activity in the orchestra. To this kind of skepticism one may reply that these choruses are indeed created by an author, a poet who, following the principle of ancient mimesis, imitates ritual choruses, of which the theatrical chorus is a direct descendant. The dramatic role of the chorus evolved only gradually in a historical process, supplementing its performative role. The poet ultimately fashions his dance groups on this model and integrates them into a plot. Considered from the perspective of performance, the members of the chorus reenact other ritual dance groups through mimesis. Even though embedded in a mythic plot, from the spectator's point of view they resemble at the same time many other traditional choruses that dance and sing. It is precisely through self-referential signs that the poet is able to make the chorus appear as a mediating body between the action of the play and ritual, and between the fictional heroes of the then and there and the audience of the here and now.

Self-referentiality should be distinguished conceptually from metatheater to a greater extent than has so far been the case. While we understand dramatic self-referentiality as an expression by which one refers to one's own activity in the performance happening in the here and now, that is, to one's ritual action, metatheater has to do with problematizing and reflective speech in the theater about the aesthetic phenomenon of the theater.[78] Since the borders between ritual and theater are fluid, the two concepts overlap. Depending on whether one looks at choral dance, mask, and costume from the perspective of ritual and carrying out a performance or from the vantage point of theater as aesthetic event, either the term "self-referentiality" or the term "metatheater" is more appropriate.[79] Both are popular in the current literature. Yet it must be emphasized that the examination of the self-referential phenomena in this work is not an anachronistic transferral of contemporary (poststructuralist) theory to ancient texts, but that self-referentiality represents a characteristic of ancient dramatic poetry. This is connected with its specific closeness to ritual and to the oral nature of the medium. Eric Csapo's attempt to trace the still quite frequent references to the chorus' own dancing in tragedy (and comedy) back to the increasing influence of the new dithyramb, because these statements occur there with considerable frequency, is thus probably only partially correct.[80] Although the mutual influence of individual Dionysiac genres certainly cannot be denied, in my opinion the essence

---

[78] For this reason it is often equated with the concept of self-reflexivity.

[79] In my dissertation (Bierl 1991:190–191) I talk about the fact that when Dionysus is referred to, the cultic and ritual perspective tends to overwhelm the purely metatheatrical.

[80] Cf. Csapo 1999/2000, esp. 417–425 and, to a lesser degree, Csapo 2003.

of these frequent self-referential passages lies quite simply in the ritual nature of these genres themselves.

It is an inalienable part of the nature of a cultic and ritual action that during the ritual the participants refer on a verbal level to their own current activity. Generally speaking, each simple ritual in fact completes itself in the course of its performance. The utterances are limited to description of the action. The ritual framework, that is, the level of utterance, prevails over any narrative elements. Even in the case that a chorus in carrying out a ritual refers in addition to an accompanying myth, the ritual chorus, whose performance falls completely within a cultic frame, nevertheless tends to keep referring to this context and their present activity.[81]

The *Partheneion* of Alcman (fr. 1 *PMG* = Davies = fr. 3 Calame) represents an example of this phenomenon from early Greek choral literature.[82] The song was composed in the seventh century BCE for an annually recurring cultic celebration in Sparta. The occasion is a festival of Orthria-Aotis, at which girls probably completed their change in status from maidenhood to womanhood in a ritually marked nocturnal festival.[83] Its fit within the framework of the

[81] Braungart (1996:91–101) equally stresses the self-referentiality and self-contained nature of rituals. He focuses mainly on their performance and demonstration. He quite rightly asserts (91), in contradistinction to Frits Staal's thesis of the meaninglessness of rituals (Staal 1979): "Selbstbezüglichkeit schließt auch die Kommunikativität und Symbolizität des Rituals nicht aus" ["Self-referentiality does not exclude the communicative and symbolic nature of ritual"]. A little further on he adds (92–93): "Rituale sind nicht primär poietisch und zweckhaft, sondern »praktisch«. Sie zielen nicht primär auf ein faßbares Ergebnis. Insofern *machen* Rituale keinen Sinn, sie *haben* ihn" ["Rituals are not primarily poetic and directed towards an end. To the extent that rituals *make* no sense, they *possess* it"]. Braungart does not however make the connection with speech act theory. Furthermore, he does not investigate specific self-references in the performance of rituals, particularly on the verbal level.

[82] P. Louvre E 3320. Calame II 1977 is fundamental for the interpretation of the song in the context of an initiation ritual. From the substantial bibliography I mention here only the most important recent work: Page 1951, West 1965a, Puelma 1977, Calame 1977, Calame 1983:28–49 (text of fr. 3 Calame) and 311–349 (commentary), Segal 1983, Clay 1991, Pavese 1992, Robbins 1994, Clark 1996, Stehle 1997:30–39, 73–88, and Too 1997. Further bibliography in Gerber 1994:16–32.

[83] The ritual anchoring also remains controversial: Calame I 1977 argues for initiation, esp. 439–449 (Engl. trans., Calame 1997, esp. 258–263); Calame II 1977, esp. 138–146 (on the internal plot level Agido is leaving the choral group after the conclusion of her education), Calame 1983:312–313, Carter 1988, Nagy 1990:340, Nagy 1996:53, and Clark 1996; Griffiths 1972, Gentili 1976 (= Gentili 1984:101–109 [2006⁴:138–145]), and Gentili 1991 (homosexual initiatory wedding of Hagesikhora and Agido in a women's *thiasos*) read the *Partheneion* as an *epithalamion* or wedding song. These two theories are not mutually exclusive, since marriage is the goal of the initiation. Because of the poem's all-too concrete and immediate embedding in its pragmatic context the precise circumstances can no longer be reconstructed. The common denominator of most interpretations remains a female puberty initiation ritual, which can be combined with two other central paradigms in the study of religion, that of fertility (cf. the polysemy of *pharos*, 'plough' in line 61: φάρος [schol. A] or 'cloak,' 'garment': φᾶρος) and the annual festival

festival is, as in the case of other similar poems—such as, for example, Pindar's *Daphnephorikon* (fr. 94b S.-M.)—so complete that its meaning and the references to individuals are clear only to the insider, that is, to the female performers and to the Spartan community participating in it, through cultural identity and convention.[84] For the later reader, however, the references in a poem that is transmitted purely by oral means from generation to generation in an intact song culture remain highly cryptic. Because of the many open questions and references, the song is among one of the most often discussed texts in classical philology.

After the obligatory, almost completely lost mythical *narratio*,[85] the members of this female chorus refer again and again to their current ritual activity of dancing and singing in a choral dance song.[86] The girls refer repeatedly to their own chorus, and in one passage they may even name their own names (64–77). They sing about their magnificent get-up and their ritual activity that is contained both in dance and in performance. They sing about their own choral leader, who interestingly bears the speaking name Hagesikhora 'chorus

---

(cf. the *pannykhis*). Cf. also Stehle 1997:73–88, interpreting the poem as a ritual model, in which the entire population of Sparta is prepared, through the exemplary Hagesikhora, for the harvest and for marriage. Here she rightly opposes Calame's overly narrow (in parts) interpretation of initiation, which means that the chorus is involved primarily with itself. For a much wider, new cosmic reading cf. Ferrari (2008). Clark's thesis (1996), which builds on Cowan 1990—which asserts that in choral line dance gender role is socially constructed on the female body—overlaps substantially with my observations on the chorus of the *Thesmophoriazusae* (chap. 1). On the construction of the female gender role see now also Stehle 1997:78–88, esp. 85–87 (the strategy of alienation of the girls from their bodies by means of emphasis of their inferiority compared to their beautiful leader creates a double message in accordance with the taste of the male audience, namely that they are sexually desirable without being aware of it themselves).

[84] Cf. Kannicht 1989:47–51, esp. 50.

[85] The myth of the Hippokoontidai perhaps forms an aetiology for the ritual and is at least closely connected with it. Cf. Robbins 1994, who thinks that the eleven sons of Hippokoon correspond to the eleven members of the female chorus; Castor and Polydeuces, who along with Heracles attack the sons of Hippokoon, also compete with them as suitors over the same women, the Leukippidai Phoebe and Hilaeira (schol. Clem. Alex. *Protr.* 27, 11 [p. 308, 3ff. Stählin] = Euphorion fr. 29 Powell . . . μέμνηται καὶ Εὐφορίων ἐν Θρᾳκὶ τῶν Ἱπποκόωντος παίδων τῶν ἀντιμνηστήρων τῶν Διοσκούρων), who may correspond in turn with the two leaders of the chorus, Hagesikhora and Agido. According to Nagy 1990:346, in the ritual the two girls by means of mimesis reactualize the Leukippidai, whose priestesses have the same name and are also called πῶλοι. In the dance ritual the girls/"fillies" are tamed for the male order. The *Leitmotiv* of eros and the correct marriage ceremony (γαμῆν, 17) clearly connect the myth of the first part (lines 1–39a) with the detailed self-description in the second part of the poem (lines 39b–101). On *khoreia* as expression of the order of the Spartan polis, see Too 1997, who interprets the myth as the working out of chaos and inner discontent and as a contrast to this.

[86] Puelma 1977 is fundamental for this aspect of self-description. On *deixis* and the chorus' reference to its own performance in this song see Clay 1991:63–67 and Peponi 2004.

leader,' and about Agido, a second exceptional figure, whose name similarly plays on the idea of "leading." In their ritual activity the girls of Sparta simultaneously complete the ritual act of honoring the goddess Aotis.

ἐγὼν δ' ἀείδω
Ἀγιδῶς τὸ φῶς· ὁρῶ   40
F' ὥτ' ἄλιον, ὅνπερ ἇμιν
Ἀγιδὼ μαρτύρεται
φαίνην· ἐμὲ δ' οὔτ' ἐπαινῆν
οὔτε μωμήσθαι νιν ἁ κλεννὰ χοραγὸς
οὐδ' ἀμῶς ἐῆ· . . .   45
. . .
ταὶ Πεληάδες γὰρ ἇμιν   60
Ὀρθρίᾳ φᾶρος φεροίσαις
νύκτα δι' ἀμβροσίαν ἅτε σήριον
ἄστρον ἀυηρομέναι μάχονται.
. . .
  [χο]ροστάτις,
Fείποιμί κ', [ἐ]γὼν μὲν αὐτὰ   85
παρσένος μάταν ἀπὸ θράνω λέλακα
γλαύξ· ἐγὼ[ν] δὲ τᾷ μὲν Ἀώτι μάλιστα
Fανδάνην ἐρῶ· πόνων γὰρ
ἇμιν ἰάτωρ ἔγεντο·
ἐξ Ἀγησιχόρ[ας] δὲ νεάνιδες   90
ἰρ]ήνας ἐρατ[ᾶ]ς ἐπέβαν.

(Alcman fr. 1 Davies, lines 39–45, 60–63, and 84–91)

But I sing of the light of Agido: I look upon her as the sun, which Agido calls to appear as witness for us. That I either praise or blame her the famous chorus leader (Hagesikhora?) forbids me utterly.

For they, the "Pleiades" (or "Doves"), compete with us, because we bring Orthria a garment (a plough), while they rise up (dance gliding) through the ambrosial night like Seireios, the Dog Star.

Chorus leader, I would say, I alone a maiden, in vain I screech from the rafter, an owl. But I long to please Aotis especially, for she is our healer of troubles. Because of Hagesikhora the maidens have reached lovely peace.

33

The clear references to the chorus' own performance have been underlined in the text. In the foreground stand the "I" and "we" of the maidens, whose perspective lies completely in the here and now of the choral performance of the moment. In typical fashion, number switches between singular and plural. In the singular, the collective speaks as one group; in the plural, it regards itself as an association of several individuals. The maidens emphasize their singing (ἀείδω, 39), address themselves to their renowned chorus leader, possibly to Hagesikhora, and to Agido. Their activity arises entirely in the present of the performance. They underscore the situation of dance competition (μάχονται, 63),[87] in which both choral leaders whirl with them, and the ritual occasion, in which young girls, that is to say, the performers themselves, are contrasted with already ripe, beautiful, and adult dancers, who possibly lead them along the symbolic road of festive transition from childhood to womanhood. "Flying up" in dance (ἀυηρομέναι, 63) provides the staging point from which the maidens in a metaphorical and metonymical movement playfully transfer their maidenly identity of being "themselves" in the here and now (ἐ]γὼν μὲν αὐτὰ | παρσένος, 85–86) to birds and project their ritual activity onto the feathered creatures.[88] The collective of speaking and dancing performers competes with the two "primadonnas." The metaphoric mention of birds, who are likewise distinguished for their rhythmic movement, song, and their marginal position in the animal world, helps them express their subordinate position to the chorus leaders. In a direct comparison, they feel like an ugly owl on a rafter (86–87) compared to beautiful doves.[89] The goddess of the dawn, Aotis,

---

[87] The verb form μάχονται (line 63) has not only erotic but also choral-agonistic connotations; see Puelma 1977:36n66, Clay 1991:58–63, esp. 60, and Henrichs 1994/95:83 with 108n117.

88 See below chap. 1, n512. In ritual animals are a welcome level of projection that effects the cognitive transformation of the actors. Cf. Tambiah 1985:169–211 ("Animals Are Good to Think and Good to Prohibit"). Bowra (1934:41), followed by West (1965a:200), in fact suggests that the members of the chorus wore bird costumes.

89 "Pleiades" (Πεληάδες, 60) can equally mean "doves" (schol. A, lines 60ff.) and the constellation of the same name; stars also lend themselves well to choral projection: cf. Soph. *Ant.* 1146–1147, Eur. *Ion* 1078–1080, *El.* 467. Most interpreters see a second, rival chorus in the Pleiades; I, however, in company with schol. A, connect this expression with Agido and Hagesikhora (cf. among others Puelma 1977:34; Pavese 1992:71–76 connects this description of the choral leaders with a personal name derived from Peleus or Peleia that expresses local or genealogical origin; Clay 1991:61 by contrast sees a divine projection and mythical model of dancing girls). Astymeloisa, the chorus leader in the other Partheneion fragment of Alcman, is compared to "a star falling through the shining heavens" (ὤ] τις αἰγλά[ε]ντος ἀστήρ | ὠρανῶ διαιπετής, fr. 3, 66–67 Davies). It is interesting that the Pleiades are in fact credited with the invention of choral dance (Callim. fr. 693 Pfeiffer = schol. [K] Theocr. *Id.* 13.25): . . . φησὶ Καλλίμαχος, ὅτι τῆς βασιλίσσης τῶν Ἀμαζόνων ἦσαν θυγατέρες αἱ Πλειάδες, αἳ Πελειάδες προσηγορεύθησαν. πρῶτον δ' αὗται χορείαν καὶ παννυχίδα συνέστησαν παρθενεύουσαι. Their virginity is thus brought to the fore (παρθενεύουσαι). In the catalogue of the group of

in whose honor the ritual activity takes place, overcomes the exhaustion of agonistic dance (πόνων, 88). From the use of the aorist aspect in the final verses one can infer the reperformance of such songs. The goddess Aotis (and perhaps also Orthria) "becomes" their "healer" (ἰάτωρ, 89), because through Hagesikhora's (and/or Agido's) intercession, who following the model of the divine chorus leader presents herself as her human incarnation year after year, she gave meaning to the effort of other girls (νεάνιδες, 90) at this same festival. As always, the girls find "longed for peace" (ἰρ]ήνας ἐρατ[ᾶ]ς, 91) on this occasion too.[90] The completion of the dance ritual is consequently equated with their change of status. After a marginal phase, realized in a nocturnal dance under the educational direction of their chorus leader using symbolic movements partially resembling those of birds, the girls come to rest in the

---

seven maidens that follows, one is called Parthenia; another is named Lampado, which refers to the star's luminescence, associated with the radiant beauty of the maiden and the torchlight of the night festival. Their mother, who is described in the scholium as an Amazon queen, is probably Hippo (Callim. *Hymn.* 3.239–247), and as "horse" is thus semantically related to the "fillies." On the Amazons as mythical model of girls in initiation see Dowden 1997 and below chap. 1, nn284 and 369. The once widely circulated theory of the semi-chorus (with Agido and Hagesikhora as leaders of each chorus repectively) has lost some of its plausibility since Puelma 1977. At the center are cultic activity, social and performative context, and self-representation. The rivalry and competition appear to take place within the chorus.

[90] The identification of Aotis and/or Orthria is also controversial. Many interpreters identify Aotis with Orthria and Orthria with Artemis Orthia; Calame (II 1977:119–128), however, identifies her with Helen (associating the ritual with the festival of Helen in Platanistas; he sees Hagesikhora as representative of the goddess Helen); Griffiths (1972:24–27) identifies Hagesikhora as substitute for the marriage goddess Helen, who stands in opposition to Aotis-Artemis, the goddess of young girls. Gentili 1976:64–65 (= Gentili 1984:105–106 [2006⁴:141–142]) equates Orthria-Aotis with Aphrodite and points out that the "doves" (line 60; cf. above, n89) were regarded as her sacred animals (Gentili 1976:62–63 [= Gentili 1984:103n6 (2006⁴:139n6)]) and that the description thus expressions the connection of the choral leaders with their goddess. According to Garvie 1965 the reference is to Phoebe, one of the two Leukippidai, who is to be equated with the dawn goddess Eos (cf. Aotis). On the performative self-reference in the sentence πόνων γὰρ | ἆμιν ἰάτωρ ἔγεντο (lines 88–89) cf. Calame II 1977:116–117, Clay 1991:57, and Henrichs 1994/95:84. Calame (II 1977:118), however, connects the πόνοι with the "toils" of the initiation rite that manifest themselves in the activity of the chorus. Too 1997:27–28, in line with his overall interpretation, refers the πόνοι to the human concern to avert the threatening chaos in the myth by means of pious worship of the gods and correct completion of ritual, which also includes the present dance. On the connection of "peace" (εἰρήνη) with the status of the Spartan εἴρην, who has passed through the rite of initiation, cf. below chap. 1, n447. On εἰρήνη, Calame II 1977:118–119 with n141 and Clark 1996:166. Calame II 1977:102–103 compares the position of the choral leaders of the two *partheneia* (Alcm. fr. 1 and 3 Davies), Hagesikhora and Astymeloisa, with that of the εἴρην, who has already reached the goal behind the toils. The girls say that "perfection and completion" lie with the gods ([σι]ῶν γὰρ ἄνα | καὶ τέλος, 83–84). This τέλος is also connected with the "goal" or "end" of the initiation ritual and with the conclusion of its performance. On the word τέλος as expression of an initiation ritual see Nagy 1990:245–246.

traditional society of Sparta after their successful initiation in the fulfillment of their role as adult women.

The chorus' self-referentiality and self-description thus stand in the foreground of the remaining extract of the Louvre fragment. A similar picture presents itself in other purely ritual choruses. I suggest, therefore, that choral self-referentiality of this type in drama and dithyramb stems primarily from the dramatic chorus' ritual connections and only secondarily from the tradition of choral lyric, which is itself firmly embedded in the reality of ritual activity.

A performative perspective in the form of a further development of John Austin's speech act theory can shed light on these connections.[91] According to Austin, there are certain utterances that do not report, describe, or state anything and that are not subject to any pronouncement about whether the statement is true or false. He gives the following as one example: "I name this ship 'Queen Elizabeth.' " Such a statement is normally heard at a launch, at the moment when a bottle of champagne is slung against the ship's stern. Austin says that the uttering of this kind of sentence represents, at least partially, the completion of an action that is not in the conventional sense "only words." He calls this kind of utterance performative, because the act of speaking in this case, in contrast to statements, is joined with the performance of an action. In his own words, Austin explains the connection as follows: "The name is derived, of course, from 'perform,' the usual verb with the noun 'action': it indicates that the issuing of the utterance is the performing of an action."[92]

By means of this kind of utterance the speaker contributes to the performance of an action: in short, by saying it he completes it. In Austin's terms, alongside the locutionary act of the mere utterance "I name . . ." there exists an illocutionary act, in our case an explanation or descriptive notification with corresponding illocutionary force for the addressees. If the meaning is understandable for transmitter and receiver on the basis of social conventions and repetitive procedures, and if both fulfill the expected roles assigned to them in the given situation, then the speech act in this pragmatic communication situation may be successfully completed.[93] By uttering words, the speaker

---

[91] Cf. Austin 1975. The series of lectures *How to Do Things with Words* was given in 1955 as the William James Lectures at Harvard University and were published for the first time in 1962, after Austin's death. See inter alia Iser 1976:87–101, Johnson 1980:52–66, Culler 1982:110–128, and Petrey 1990. Classical philologists have only recently applied Austin's speech act theory; see inter alia Martin 1989, Nagy 1990, Prins 1991, Calame 1994/95, Nagy 1996, Calame 1999, and Schmitz 1999.

[92] Austin 1975:6.

[93] On "illocutionary force," "force of utterance," "force of locution," or simply "force" see Austin 1975:33, 72–73, 100, 104, 117, and 148.

or performer achieves a perlocutionary result. He produces a conviction in those taking part in the ceremony that the action of naming the ship has been carried out.

Although Austin limits his theory, derived from ordinary language philosophy, to the realities of the modern everyday world, he also makes a link to ritual through his examples drawn from ceremonies like the one above. In connection with the decisive criterion of convention,[94] which determines whether or not such an utterance with illocutionary potential is successful, Austin speaks explicitly of "ritual" and paraphrases it as *"conventional act."*[95] The leap to the world of ancient ritual is not quite as far as one might suppose, for each ritual action is completely rooted in the reality of everyday life and results in a real-life complex of activity.

In the fields of anthropology, ethnology, and the study of religion, only a few scholars so far have connected the concept of ritual with Austin's speech act theory.[96] As has been said above, ritual is a stereotyped, aesthetically and theatrically staged, and conventionalized action in an emotionally colored, multimedia, and symbolic performance used to communicate within a group.[97] Through reperformance this kind of activity may be continually renewed and reactualized independently of its original context. Socially accepted procedures, especially repetitive and formulaic utterances, are what make ritual possible. Performative action is successful because it continually recites fixed meanings or illocutionary roles over again. What has always possessed validity and consequently been codified in a traditional society in a marked form can be called upon at seasonally reoccurring festive occasions. It is not so much the intention of the participants[98] that is important for the success of this staged

---

[94] On convention and conventional action see Austin 1975:8, 14, 19, 81, 105, 107, 109, 119, 122, and 128. On conventional procedure as a criterion for reaching a conventional result, see Austin 1975:26–32.

[95] See Austin 1975:19. With the expressions "ritual," "ceremonial," "ritual act," or "ceremonial act" Austin presupposes a negative, exclusively heteronomous concept of ritual as compulsion. On ceremony and the ceremonial, which in distinction to ritual and custom are mostly confined to the secular sphere, see Braungart 1996:57–67, esp. 64–66.

[96] See Finnegan 1969, Bloch 1974, and Tambiah 1985:123–166; see above pp. 15–16 with nn41–42.

[97] The definition of ritual is built on the formulation of Burkert 1985:8 and Burkert 1979:37, also taking into consideration the modifications of Braungart 1996, esp. 74–118 and Tambiah 1985:123–166 (cf. his definition above, p. 14).

[98] Searle 1970 interprets Austin's speech act rather in the intentional sense and views it from the perspective of a regulatory system whose rules may also consitute the speech act; on regulatory and constitutive rules see Searle 1970:33–42. On the comparison of Austin and Searle see Petrey 1990:59–69 and 82–83. Intention as criterion for a successful speech act was already allowed for in Austin 1975:21, 40–45, 101, and 106. For criticism of intentionality cf. Culler 1982, 122–123; as Austin repeatedly underscores, what is decisive for the success of a speech act is its social context, not intentionality.

communication as the context and the authoritative convention of the group. This social agreement determines both the delivery (the utterance itself, locution) and the simultaneously occurring action of the address (illocution), which triggers a characteristic state of awareness necessary for reaction, and the effect of the action, i.e. its reception by those who receive the message. Let us take, for example, the chorus in Alcman's great *Partheneion* (fr. 1 Davies): when the girls make the statement "ἐγὼν δ' ἀείδω | Ἀγιδῶς τὸ φῶς" (39–40), they do more than simply articulate these words. They sing and, in addition, perform rhythmic movements that underscore their song. With the purely locutionary act "I sing" comes an illocutionary act. The actors describe their own activity, report on it, and give a retrospective guarantee of their piety. The manner of ritual speech, supported by its multimedia expression, and marked by rhythmic dance, obtains thereby a specific illocutionary form. Through utterance comes an effect, a perlocutionary act: the performers complete a ritual act—they honor Aotis. Or, viewed from the recipients' side: the maidens bring it about that members of the community watching and participating are convinced that honor has been shown to the goddess through song and that all come into contact with her because of this. The result of the communication process is additionally ensured through the maidens' emphasis of their intention and desire to please her: ἐγὼ[ν] δὲ τᾷ μὲν Ἀώτι μάλιστα | Ϝανδάνην ἐρῶ (87–88).

With the example above the connection to self-referentiality becomes more obvious. An utterance becomes performative precisely because it names and describes the act to be completed. When I say "I bet," the completed action of placing and making a bet results only from the fact that I use this formula. Performance thus always relates back to itself. When a chorus, as for example in Sophocles' *Ajax* (701), declares "νῦν γὰρ ἐμοὶ μέλει χορεῦσαι" ("now I want to dance"), it is at the same time making a performative utterance that refers to its own actual activity.[99] The action of dancing is completed simultaneously with the self-referential utterance. True, the desired action will not simply happen through the words alone. Rather, there must be indications that the choral dancers, the subject of the utterance, are really there. In their indexical dimension, with reference to the *énonciation* and the context, the speakers in the first person "I"/"we" represent an external point of reference, the presence of which is a necessary condition for the completion of the speech act.[100]

[99] Cf. Henrichs 1994/95:73–75. The expression with μέλει is here identical to a performative future; cf. below, chap. 2, n77.

[100] On the connection between performative utterance and self-referentiality, see also Johnson 1980:56–58.

Self-reflexivity is also of central importance for the deconstructionist and poststructuralist study of literature.[101] This type of literary theory is admittedly of relatively small value for the understanding of ancient texts, since Jacques Derrida, for example, does not consider the situational context, and consciously wants to expand into the infinite and indeterminate. While Roland Barthes, Paul de Man, and Jacques Derrida take a strong position against the present and the privileging of speech over writing in Western philosophy, archaic literature, because of its particular grounding in the everyday world, is founded on the present, on the orality of communication, and on the concrete background of the occasion. Even though Derrida derives much inspiration for his philosophy from Austin's evocation of the opposites word and deed and proves himself to be an Austinian in many ways, he problematizes the speech act as having immanence purely in its locution, its mere utterance, while Austin considers in addition illocution and perlocution as activities in the social context outside of speech. According to Derrida, every text stands at a distance from itself (*différance*). The alleged absence of the present on the level of signs and the total removal of limits from the context hinder, in his opinion, an unambiguous determination of meaning. Each reading rests on interpretative assumptions, and the text continually presents evidence that subverts these preconceived ideas and ruptures the given meaning.[102] For this reason, every text, according to Derrida, finds its meaning for the recipient in its own staging, i.e. in self-reference.[103]

Austin's theory is far better adapted for explaining self-referentiality in archaic Greek choruses because ordinary speech and ritual hymns and early Greek lyric, as well as in part Greek drama (and, in particular, Old Comedy), have in common the fact that they are completely bound up in the actual complex of actions in daily life and are carried out in an oral communication process. The self-referential utterance is created with performative verbs not, as in Derrida's theory, exclusively in the phatic act of locution; instead the self-referential part functions also in the illocutionary act as a necessary addition,

---

[101] In classical philology this trend mostly represents a point of departure for its application to antiquity. See e.g. Goldhill 1984, Gellrich 1995, esp. 50 (where she opposes the predominant tendency in literary criticism to consider the cultural context purely as an influence that lends meaning to the literary text). Cf. by contrast the balanced remarks of Segal 1992:444–450; he is of the opinion that deconstruction also has it positive sides; yet he is right to warn against completely neglecting the social and historical context.

[102] See Derrida 1976, esp. 101 and Culler 1982:214.

[103] On the comparison of Derrida and Austin and on the polemical exchange between Searle and Derrida, see Petrey 1990:132–165 and Culler 1982:117–128. On the philosophical backgrounds see also Frank 1984:476–519.

in order to ensure the execution of an action on a practical level. By means of reference to its own action ("I sing") Alcman's chorus of maidens seeks to bring about a desired consequence.[104] With the help of self-referential signals, the senders direct attention to themselves, and in so doing aim to ensure the receiver's comprehension ("securing uptake") and attempt to trigger the desired reaction ("inviting a response"). Nonverbal means of expression with specific referential character, such as dance movements, mimicry, and gesture, may additionally strengthen the appeal.[105] Through long-standing convention these illocutionary elements become effective as speech-action and produce results ("taking effect"), since both senders and receivers have a preexisting understanding. By means of the performative utterance of its self-reference, the chorus finally achieves the perlocutionary result they strive for: actors and spectators complete the act of worship in speech.[106]

Ritual acts are thus characterized by self-performative traits, since every ritual arises in one's own activity and comes into being therein. Admittedly, the goal here is not placing oneself on the stage, but demonstration and communication, which rest on the common agreement of the group and stand at the center of the performed action.

With the help of Austin's speech act theory the interconnection of self-referentiality, actual performance, and ritual can be more deeply understood. But using this as a foundation, how can one now apply such conclusions to the chorus of ancient theater, even if Austin expressly excludes the phenomenon of the theater and representation on stage as an object of research?

As has been seen, the situation in ancient drama is all the more complicated, because each dramatic chorus not only becomes absorbed into the utterance of the actual context of action, but further also undertakes a role in the fictional plot. The closeness of ritual and theater provide the point of depar-

---

[104] Cf. Petrey 1990:147–151; Austin thus considers external reference as part of self-referentiality and performativity; Derrida and poststructuralism look at the performative exclusively from the isolated text, without taking the context into consideration. For our perspective the example discussed in Petrey 1990:148 is extremely conclusive: following Roland Barthes, who highlights the "I sing" of ancient poets as example *par exellence* of the performative (Barthes 1977), she interprets Virgil's *arma virumque cano* in this context. According to her, the speech act is only successful because of the naming of the action of singing; following Barthes, "I sing" thus only refers to the locution in an internal sense, and not additionally to the external context. Cf. the summary in Petrey 1990:148: "In Austinian analysis, speech acts always perform themselves and something else as well. In deconstructive criticism, the concern has been with self-performativity alone."

[105] In Plutarch's symposium Ammonios, one of his guests, suggests "speaking dance" as a definition of poetry (Plut. *Quaest. conv.* 9.748a).

[106] On the three functions of the illocutionary act, "securing uptake," "taking effect," and "inviting a response," see Austin 1975:116–118.

ture. Ancient theater is based in large part on ritual conditions and is thus, as stated above, not fundamentally different from ritual. Historically speaking, drama seems to have developed out of this. Moreover, it is performed in a cultic environment and also relies in its narrative structure on ritual models. Mimetic representation of ritual sequences is identical with ritual. The difference from pure ritual is only one of degree, and so the points of transition are fluid. On the one hand, in ritual, too, one also brings the theatrical element of a staging to the fore for the sake of effect. On the other hand, rites do not always depend on the simple presence of reality, but many ceremonies contain disguise and masking. Both are based on repeatable practices. Like a ritual, theater works as a speech act only on the basis of conventions set up in the everyday world. It is only because of the fact that theater presents fiction as reality in a performative fashion that the event becomes able to be experienced in the first place.

Austin stressed the importance of convention for the functioning of the performative; since he emphasizes the direct presence of *ordinary*, everyday speech as further prerequisite of success, he excludes the theater and literature as a whole as a "parasitic" element.[107] He describes fictional speech from a pragmatic perspective as being of no account, an opinion that clearly depends on a later concept of mimesis modeled on Plato and that has nothing to with the period of classical drama.

But theater is particularly performative, since like other conventionalized acts it is performed in public. It is ironic that Austin's terminology seems to derive precisely from the theater.[108] Even though theatrical discourse as a kind of simulation is fundamentally distinct from external reality, drama should nevertheless be included in the theory of the speech act, because mimesis should be understood here not in terms of ontological truth content

---

[107] Austin 1975:21–22: "Secondly, as *utterances* our performatives are *also* heir to certain other kinds of ills which infect *all* utterances. And these likewise, though again they might be brought into a more general account, we are deliberately at present excluding. I mean, for example, the following: a performative utterance will, for example, be *in a peculiar way* hollow or void if said by an actor on the stage, or if introduced in a poem, or spoken in soliloquy. This applies in a similar manner to any and every utterance—a sea-change in special circumstances. Language in such circumstances is in special ways—intelligibly—used not seriously, but in ways *parasitic* upon its normal use—ways which fall under the doctrine of the *etiolations* of language. All this we are *excluding* from consideration. Our performative utterances, felicitous or not, are to be understood as issued in ordinary circumstances." Nagy rightly sees that the reason behind Austin's negative attitude toward poetry lies in his connection of poetry exclusively with writing, following modern assumptions ("for Austin, poetry is a matter of writing, not speaking" [1994/95a:12]).

[108] The infinitives "to perform" and "to act" in English normally refer to theater; see Johnson 1980:65.

as empty second-rank imitation, but as reenactment or reexperiencing of the contemporary real world.[109] Many words of the chorus, which is ultimately anchored in ritual, at the same time constitute an action. The moment of their utterance sets up and thus controls the action. At the moment of performance, the action is no less immediately experienced than a speech act that is based on the norms of everyday life.

The communicative situation is, as I have emphasized, more complex for dramatic choruses insofar as ritual, and therefore the pragmatic dimension, and plot are simultaneously present. Choruses are thus, like other ritual activities, much more connected to the present than other literature.

In Old Comedy mechanisms for distancing participants from the action of the plot and their dramatic role, as well as opportunities for participating in the action on stage, are much more frequent than in tragedy. The borders between the citizenry taking part in celebrating the festival, the entire pragmatic context, and the stage are consciously kept open. Moreover, in comedy there arises in particular the phenomenon of "ritual in ritual," that is, the performance anchored in the cult of Dionysus will also imitate rituals in its fictional action.

Using vocabulary from the illocutionary sphere, Austin establishes the structure that enables a successful performance: these same areas are also prominent in the speech of the dramatic chorus, whose conventions are equally determined by behavior patterns current in the real world. Austin's illocutionary groups—utterances that underscore the performance of an action (exercitives) and social interaction (behabitives), but also commissive, verdictive, and expositive utterances—can easily be expanded to include all manner of verbs denoting action in any series of ritual actions. The typical form in the first-person singular of the present active indicative, which emphasizes the presence of the speaker, is characteristic.[110]

---

[109] Before Plato, in a traditional society that relied solely on orality, mimesis had the meaning of continually reincorporating and reenacting a given model; see above, n60; Nagy (1996:55–56) thinks that the concept developed the sense of mere copying, as a result of a later destabilization of the absolute model. Iser 1976:96–101 (according to whom the convention changed in a horizontal fashion in the theater and literature, which led to a detachment from pragmatic context; in his opinion, the illocutionary role lies in its breaking of expectations [*Erwartungsdurchbrechung*, 101]), Johnson 1980:59–66, Culler 1982:116–123, Petrey 1990:86–110, and Nagy 1990:8–9 all argue against the exclusion of art and theater. Ohmann, for example, argues almost in Austin's sense that literature is only a "quasi-speech-act" (1971:13–14), which lacks an illocutionary role because it is only mimetic.

[110] On these lists see Austin's twelfth lecture, in Austin 1975:148–164. Austin himself says (1975: 150) that the list of possible verbs lies in the order of magnitude of 10 to the power of 3. Austin 1975:56–57 and 150 refers to the first person singular indicative present active.

By way of example, the following performative words indicating action may be brought under this expanded form of the performative, which includes ritual and drama: a) in ritual: "I pray," "I cry," "I sacrifice," "I pour," "I heal," "I celebrate," "I march"—in short, "I undertake" any form of ritual; b) in choral dance theater: "I sing," "I dance," "I go," "I jump," "I leap," "I stamp"—in short, "I carry out" any action that is an essential element of the performance of a chorus in the theater. But commands in the second-person singular and plural, as well as hortatory forms in the first-person plural, also fall into this category. In the realm of performative utterances the chorus frequently switches between the first-person singular and plural,[111] whether in the present or future tense. The speaker in the first person gives the impression, in a purely notional sense, that there is brief lapse of time between utterance and fulfilment. He may thus even place the announcement of his intention to transfer his speech into immediate action in the future tense, even when he is already performing the action for the observer *in the present*. The term "performative future" has recently been coined to describe this phenomenon. It is found chiefly in ritual texts, particularly in the field of magic, but also in self-references in every kind of performative action.[112] Here one speaks of one's own

---

[111] On the fluctuation of the choral "I" between singular and plural see Calame I 1977:436–439 (Engl. trans. Calame 1997:255–258), Calame II 1977:45–46, and Calame 1995:21n28, 39–40. According to Austin 1975:57 the "we" form is also performative.

[112] Austin (1975:55–66) talks extensively about grammatical features in his fifth lecture. Here the usual categories of first-person singular indicative present active are modified and expanded. Both commands (58, 59–60) as well as the second- and third-person are included (58–59), similarly "hereby" (57–58, 60–61). Cf. by contrast the clear distinction made by Benveniste 1966:267–276, esp. 274: "Un énoncé est performatif en ce qu'il *dénomme* l'acte performé, du fait qu'Ego prononce une formule contenant le verbe à la première personne du présent" ["An utterance is performative in that it *names* the performed act, on account of the fact that Ego pronounces a formula containing a verb in the first person of the present tense"]. On the performative future, which often appears in Pindar in the first person of verbs of singing, praising, and showing, but which clearly comes from the ritual tradition, cf. Faraone 1995 (with numerous examples), Henrichs 1994/95:80 (with 104n97), 87 (on tragedy), and Calame 1994/95:144 (with 152n25) (on ritual choruses); see now also D'Alessio 2004. On the model of the performative in magical texts cf. Poccetti 1991:194 (with reference to the illocutionary power of speech) and 198–204; cf. esp. the reference to the self-referentiality of magical and ritual speech (199): "L'enunciato performativo, in quanto costituisce in sé l'atto di ciò che si enuncia, è sui-referenziale, crea cioè da solo il proprio contesto di riferimento, dà implicitamente indicazione del canale comunicativo, che è contemporaneamente anche il canale e la forma della stessa *praxis* magica (in questo caso, la varietà dei *verba defigendi* del tipo καταδέω, καταγράφω, κατατίθημι, καταδίδωμι, *defigo, deligo,* ecc.) e fornisce, infine, mediante le categorie del tempo e della persona le coordinate del soggetto identificandolo automaticamente con l'agente magico" ["The performative utterance, inasmuch as it contains within itself the act to which the utterance refers, is self-referential, that is, it creates by itself its own referential context, gives an implicit indication of the communicative channel, which is simulta-

43

ritual action, which one is in fact already in the process of implementing, in the future. A performative command comes very close to this use of the future tense, because the intention is that action result from speech.[113]

Austin shows that in utterances the criteria of the descriptive and the performative are often simultaneously applied and cannot be distinguished precisely one from the other.[114] This is especially the case with explicitly performative verbs. He therefore comes to the conclusion that constative utterances may only treated as a subgroup and an exceptional case of the performative. Most verbs constitute and regulate an activity attached to them. The inherently illocutionary force of the utterance in a performance is at the same time self-referential. In a performance of a ritual or a drama, the main part of the locution is simultaneously performative. Verbs indicating activity refer back to their own action and in so doing support and determine this action. When a priest, for example, says, "Let us pray," the words introduce an action and determine it; with this utterance the speaker refers directly back to his prayer that is now being introduced and that is already partly being created by itself in this utterance.[115]

Every ritual and every performance is carried out by performative verbs of this type; the action, however, is also constituted by means of non-verbal actions, such as gestures, mimicry, and bodily attitudes. In addition to the underlying words with their illocutionary potential, the activity is also accompanied by other actions, which for their part already lie in the perlocutionary realm of the intended result and which rest on a specific convention.[116]

---

neously the channel and the form of the same magical praxis (in this case, the various *verba defigendi* such as καταδέω, καταγράφω, κατατίθημι, καταδίδωμι, *defigo, deligo,* etc.), and finally by means of the categories of time and person provides the coordinates of the subject, identifying it automatically with the magical agent"]. Cf. also Graf 1996:184–207, esp. 185–186.

[113] On ritual commands also in comedy cf. Kaimio 1970:121–129.

[114] Austin 1975:133–147, esp. 145.

[115] Cf. also Calame 1995:10–12 ("Enunciation as Action"), esp. 11, where he explores the imprecise boundary between the illocutionary and perlocutionary act of performative self-reference and refers to Oswald Ducrot's distinction between "self-referential acts of language that utilize the rules of discourse and those which introduce the causality of the 'exterior' world." A little later he continues: "This distinction is particularly pertinent for early Greek poetry in which the act of enunciation manifests itself in the utterance by way of performance verbs such as *to sing, to praise, to invoke*; it leads us again to those complex relationships which link the linguistic domain marked out by the utterance of the enunciation to the empirical domain corresponding to the enunciation/communication situation and its psychosocial protagonists."

[116] For the chorus the kinesic signs of performance—such as gesture, proxemics, and cheironomy—in combination with the level of linguistic signs are of importance; Fischer-Lichte 1983:31–93.

In sum, the performative, as has already been seen, is supported by the "I" of the speaker of the utterance by means of a string of deictic ("here," "this") and self-referential references and signals indicative of urgency ("now," "immediately" etc.), by which the actual frame of the utterance in the *hic et nunc* (*énonciation*) is brought to the fore.[117] The further the process of narrative distancing from the pragmatic situation advances, the more complex the identification and attribution of these signals becomes.[118] The choral "I," so important for speech acts, can in one and the same poem or dramatic extract assume quite different functions. The "I"/"we" of the singing chorus in its function as shifter can thus refer to the person of the performers, of the community, of the fictional dramatic characters, or even of the poet, and can fluctuate between these roles continually. In the case of Pindar, this unstable confusion of voices is particularly problematic, so that a considerable battle has blazed up in the scholarly literature about whether the "I" in the *Epinicians* can also refer to the chorus that is performing at the moment as speaker, or whether, in contrast to the more ritual forms of the paean and *partheneion*, the "I" should be limited solely to the epinician "I" of the poet in his laudatory function or to the autobiographical "I" of the historical Pindar.[119] In the

---

[117] For *deixis* cf. Rösler 1983a, Danielewicz 1990, F. de Toro 1995:13–22, and Felson 2004; for temporal indication with νῦν see Danielewicz 1990:11–12, Calame 1994/95:144–146, Calame 1995:41–42, and D'Alessio 2004:270–271; for "markers of urgency" (Calame) see Henrichs 1994/95:102n82.

[118] See Calame 1994/95 and Calame 1995:3–26 and 27–57, where he traces the development of a ritual chorus into the choruses of tragedy, which are embedded in the plot, and of simple addresses to narratively complex texts; the "I" and "you" assume in this process the authority of the speaker/author (*narrator*) and addressee/reader (*narratee*) in a fictional narrative. Cf. also Calame 1999.

[119] For the problem of the "I," see Rösler 1985, Gentili 1990:11–15, and Gentili 1990a:20–22. The theory of the clear distinction between paeans, dithyrambs, *partheneia* on the one side and epinicians on the other is advocated in Lefkowitz 1988 (= Lefkowitz 1991:191–201), Heath 1988, and Lefkowitz 1995. This schematic separation does not stand up to closer scrutiny; the opposite position to Lefkowitz and Heath is held by Carey 1991; Morgan 1993 and D'Alessio 1994 give a nuanced and balanced judgment; cf. also Krummen 1990:136–141, Nagy 1994/95a:20–25, and Calame 1997:228n78. Gentili 1990:15 characterizes the polyvalent role of the Pindaric chorus as follows: "Also eine mehrdeutige semiotische Verfassung, analog der des tragischen Chors, der bald die mimetische Darstellung einer dramatis persona übernimmt, wenn er die Funktion eines in die Dramenhandlung integrierten Akteurs ausübt, bald, in den strophischen Chorliedern, die Rolle des auf die Bühne projizierten Auditoriums annimmt oder auch die des inneren Zuschauers, der intellektuell und emotional am dramatischen Geschehen teilnimmt. Das ist ein Eintreten in und ein Heraustreten aus der szenischen Fiktion, das sich auf der gleichen Ebene wie das «Ich» der Chorlyrik vollzieht, welches sich nicht auf ein allgemeines einheitliches «Ich» reduzieren läßt, sondern von Fall zu Fall, in Beziehung auf den Kontext des Liedes, neu zu beurteilen ist" ["It is thus a polyvalent semiotic construction, analogous to that of the tragic chorus, that sometimes undertakes the mimetic representation of a dramatis persona when it exercises the function of an actor integrated into the plot of the drama, and sometimes in strophic choral songs takes on the role of the audience projected onto the

case of comedy, as we shall see, the multiplicity of choral roles is similarly complicated.

Before we come to the comic chorus, let us return to the problem of dramatic genre. Here too one may usefully apply speech act theory. Genre is formed from the traditional conventions of the group that performs the text. The resulting norms regulate the performance and the particular expectations of the recipients.[120]

The real world, the ritual connections of mythical drama in the festivals of Dionysus, but above all the particular conventions and repeatable procedures of the spectators define the norms of a particular genre through which they become speech acts. The atmosphere that is supposed to obtain in a particular context creates time and space for particular types of plays. It is entirely the same with rituals. On the basis of particular rules developed by the community, the sacrifice offered to the Olympian gods, for example, is different from practices directed toward to the chthonic gods, and there are both festivals of unrestrained joy and festivals of mourning.

In an early phase, in which ritual and myth are the dominant modes of expression of an original society and mimetic production is based on oral communication, occasion may closely coincide with genre.[121] Only when these ritual parameters gradually become weakened under the increasing influence of written communication and fictionalization around the middle of the fifth century BCE is there a gradual attempt to model occasion using rules of genre of a more fixed nature.[122] This explains why, despite the shared occasion of the Great Dionysia, comedy, tragedy and, attached to it, satyr plays, and dithy-

---

stage, or even that of the inner spectator that participates in the dramatic event intellectually and emotionally. It represents an entry into and departure from the plot on stage that occurs on the same level as the 'I' of choral lyric, and that cannot be reduced to an overall unified 'I,' but must be reevaluated on a case-by-case basis with reference to the context of the song"]. The same is true of the comic chorus, which Gentili ignores. Gentili (see also Gentili 1984/85, esp. 33–35) sees the hybrid creation of the dramatic chorus in its double function as a narrative and gnomic group and a mimetic group that takes part in the action; in the light of scholarship on performance I focus in addition on its performative and ritual function.

[120] Cf. Henkel 1988:513–525, esp. 519–520.

[121] Cf. Nagy 1990:9 and 362–363. and Nagy 1994/95a, esp. 11–14. According to Nagy's pregnant formulation (Nagy 1990:362), "The occasion *is* the genre." Thus the genre of the *thrênos* originally coincides with the occasion and act of lament.

[122] Nagy 1990:9 sees literary genre as compensation for the disappearance of the performative occasion. See Nagy 1990:362n127 on Hellenistic poems. Nagy 1994/95a:18–25 expands on the theory of the connection between genre and embedding in ritual and occasion by demonstrating in the case of Pindar's epinician odes that "genre can even absolutize the occasion" (18), which then becomes stylized as an exemplary and prototypical framework. Accordingly Old Comedy could also have transcended its ritual embedment into the idealized model of the comastic in order to allow the Dionysiac mood as moment to be experienced in its totality.

ramb are quite distinct. Comedy, like the satyr play, has a far more ritual character than tragedy. On the one hand, comedy was included later in the official *agôn*, and the older connection of the rural Dionysiac festival together with its carnival-like elements and *aiskhrologia* was preserved with the genre for a long time as performative frame. On the other hand, after the destabilization of this original occasional connection, comedy tries, possibly even consciously, to resurrect the actual ritual basis as a norm of the genre.

To summarize: the dramatic chorus occupies a dynamically mediating position between performing purely cultic activity and playing a consciously fictional role as *dramatis persona*. When one considers the chorus from the point of view of performance, it becomes clear that the two functions, the dramatic and the ritual, are analytically not easily separable, but are fused together through a rather lengthy historical process into an ambivalent unity. Both are there at the same time, yet one aspect appears more clearly than the other, depending on genre and perspective. In genres in which narrative and myth stand in the foreground, the ritual and performative side retreats further into the background. Choral self-referentiality does not occur in order to interrupt the action consciously but from the desire to integrate the ritual act, namely dance in the orchestra in honor of Dionysus, into the play. An important reason for this appears to lie in the long tradition of ritual choral song and dance: for illocutionary strengthening, the ritual moment clearly needs self-referentiality in order to be understood as such and to proceed successfully.

The Comic Chorus in Comparison with Tragedy and Satyr Play

While the tragic chorus has in recent times been thoroughly studied, in the field of comedy (and satyr play) there is no extensive study that focuses on the chorus from a performative-pragmatic point of view, applying new discoveries in anthropology.[123]

[123] The comic chorus has however been the subject of much research in the formal aspects of stucture and meter; see the survey of Zimmermann 1994; also, among others, Gelzer 1970, Zimmermann 1985, and Parker 1997. Just about all of the more recent studies that invesitgate the development from choral lyric to drama using performative or narratological perspectives generally look at tragedy alone. Comedy and satyr play remain almost entirely neglected; cf. above, n62; cf. also Gentili 1984/85, Segal 1989, Gentili 1990, Nagy 1990, Calame 1995, Baur 1997, and Calame 1999. For an exploration of Aristophanes' *exodoi* using these insights, see now Calame 2004. Ritual self-reference to Dionysus, which has received so much attention in scholarship on tragedy, has remained almost untouched in scholarship on comedy; see however Bierl 1990, Bierl 1991 (on Ar. *Ran.* and *Thesm.*, see brief remarks on 27–44 and 172–176), and most recently Riu 1999; it is noteworthy that at the excellent conference on Dionysus held in

What follows proceeds on the hypothesis that the chorus of the satyr play and of comedy, in comparison to the related genre of tragedy, is much more directed toward ritual. This has above all to do with its different practice with respect to the narrative structure of the genres. Tragedy, as has been shown, rests on fixed and repeatedly performed myths, while the comic playwrights construct their plots on the actualities of the real world, to which the realm of festival, religion, and the entire culture of ritual also belongs. The clumsy narrative confinement of many Aristophanic comedies, often criticized, is no shortcoming when viewed this way, but rather the expression of a specific relationship between the genre and its ritual function. The comic chorus should therefore not be considered solely from the viewpoint of tragedy, but as an autonomous, cultic form of polis discourse. Because of an extensive lack of "mythic" narrative material—in comedy, myth functions as plot only when it makes fun of myth—comedy has a fundamentally different poetics and aesthetic constitution. The openness of the borders of the stage to its "real life" context is an important characteristic. It is a convention of the genre that the comic chorus frequently and quite explicitly leaves the plot for the external and actual context of the play.

The interchange of choral function and dramatic role and the appearances of self-referentiality associated with this have now been profitably used in the interpretation of Old Comedy.[124] In keeping with the *communis opinio*, which assumes a strict separation of comedy and tragedy, the discovery that the comic chorus refers to its own activity in the orchestra has caused no difficulties, unlike the case of tragedy, because the comic genre in other respects as well plays quite readily with "metatheatrical" consciousness.[125] Nevertheless, another investigation is needed to present these phenomena with their ritual implications for the comic chorus.

Toward the end of the nineteenth century, all studies concerned with the chorus of Aristophanes revolved mainly around implicit production directions and problems of dividing up parts of the chorus. Scholars chiefly proposed

---

Virginia in 1991 (Carpenter/Faraone 1993 with review by Bierl, *Gnomon* 69 [1997]:389–398) there was space given to three papers on Dionysus and tragedy, while comedy received no treatment.

[124] Cf. Dover 1993 and Dover, *Frogs*, 58–60; the division of many passages is sometimes overly schematic; often both levels are involved simultaneously.

[125] See above, n77. Self-referentiality was here understood in particular as metatheatrical play with theatrical conventions and as the conscious breaking of the "illusion"; see the literature cited in Taplin 1986:164n10 and Bonanno 1987, esp. 150–167. On the self-awareness of the poet see in particular Hubbard 1991 and Müller 1992:135–141.

theories about possible semi- or subchoruses and attempted to illuminate the relationship between choral leader and the chorus as a whole and to answer the question whether certain lyric passages were performed by individual singers or by a chorus.[126] These studies fall under the category of the structure of comedy. Two main directions in the treatment of the comic chorus can be distinguished: analysis focused on action and plot and evolutionary-historical interpretation, directed toward the origin of comedy.[127]

As is well known, the more-or-less fixed building blocks of comedy, which are made up of the division of the chorus, for example into *parodos*, *agôn*, *parabasis*, and *exodos*, chart the course of a comedy.[128] Since Thaddeus Zielinski's seminal work, *Die Gliederung der altattischen Komödie* ["The structure of Attic Old Comedy"] (1885), scholars have turned to "the overall conception of the plot and the function of the plot elements in the overall framework of a given comedy."[129]

More recent studies mostly deal with the relationship of the comic chorus to the action on stage either within the typical structure of an individual comedy or in relation to the historical development of the genre. Thomas Gelzer sees the chorus in a plot structure that can be shaped in various ways, so that the chorus has a key role in the first part (from prologue to *agôn*) in the establishment of the desired new state of affairs. The actors involved, according to Gelzer, define their position according to their attitude to the chorus, which is largely responsible for the fantastic element of the plot: that is, they may act either as partisans or only as representatives of similar interests or as opponents of the dance collective in the orchestra. Gelzer maintains that the fierce confrontation is mainly about the achievement or exercise of power and control. In the *parabasis* the chorus then steps aside and out of the frame of the plot; in the second part, the participation of the chorus in the action and its significance decline drastically, and the fantastic situation, now that it has been achieved, is only safeguarded and defended in the remaining episodic scenes. Here the chorus in its intermittent songs is for the most part assigned only its traditional mocking function (often in the second *parabasis*) or the role of commentator and interpreter, and finally in the *exodos* helps shape the end in the form of a traditional celebra-

---

[126] Cf. among others Muff 1872 and Arnoldt 1873.

[127] For a long time many investigations pursued both goals at the same time.

[128] While earlier the ritual rigidity of the structure of the plot was emphasized (up to and including Gelzer 1960), today scholars are more disposed to see the poet's individual freedom and ability to circumvent these structural elements; see for example Gelzer 1993.

[129] Zimmermann 1994:1; for an overview of the scholarship, see 1–10 therein.

tion.[130] In a quite similar fashion, Bernhard Zimmermann treats the dramatic role of the comic chorus extensively from the viewpoint of whether it has a "plot-carrying" (*handlungstragend*) or "plot-interrupting" (*handlungsunterbrechend*) function. He sees "active participation in events on stage" and accompaniment of plot as subcategories of its "plot-carrying" function, while he distinguishes between explanation and preparation in the case of plot-interruption.[131]

Klaus-Dietrich Koch views the chorus within a process of historical development: from a position of limited autonomy in the earlier plays, it achieves a gradual integration and a closer participation in the action, until finally, at the beginning of the fourth century BCE, it is gradually forced out of the plot, evidence of this being the emergence of comedies in the manuscripts of which one encounters the χοροῦ notation with increasing frequency.[132] According to Koch, the chorus initially always stands in a definite and affirming relationship to the "comic theme" and assumes the function of a) "antagonist," b) "helper," or c) "field" or "foil." With the ensemble in the *Frogs*, the chorus increasingly becomes an accessory, and in both of Aristophanes' last plays the trend toward redundancy is clear.[133]

---

[130] On the *agôn* see Gelzer 1960, on the desire for control *ibid.* 196–197, and on the typical progression of the plot Gelzer 1970:1524–1527. On the structural elements see *ibid.* 1518–1524 and Dover 1972:66–72. Gelzer 1970:1520 sketches out a heterogenous evolutionary and historical reconstruction of comedy: "In der Komödie wurden wohl Elemente verschiedener Herkunft von verschiedenen anderen Festen zusammengestellt, als die beiden Theaterfeste in historischer Zeit neu organisiert wurden. Ihre jeweilige eigene ältere Tradition läßt sich nicht weit zurück verfolgen, und über den kultischen oder profanen 'Ursprung' dieser verschiedenartigen dramatischen und undramatischen Elemente wissen wir darüber hinaus nichts" ["In comedy elements of various origin and from various other festivals were probably assembled together when the two theater festivals were reorganized on a new basis in the historical period. Its own particular and more ancient tradition cannot be traced very far back, and we know nothing further about the cultic or profane 'origin' of these different dramatic and nondramatic elements"]. See also Gelzer 1966:55–70.

[131] See Zimmermann I 1985 (esp. his summary 242–261, particularly 242) and Zimmermann II 1985 (esp. the summary 221–234 ["Chor und Handlung"]); for *parodoi* see Zimmermann I 1985:6–149, *amoiboia* 150–241, for monody see Zimmermann II 1985:1–49, duets 50–72, and pure choral odes 74–220, which he again divides into *handlungstragend* (75–107) and *handlungsunterbrechend* (108–220) (*paraineseis*, songs influenced by tragedy, songs of ridicule, encomia, prayers and hymns, *parabasis* odes). See now also Zimmermann 1999. Parker's (1997) monograph on the Aristophanic chorus provides a metrical analysis of all the lyric parts and gives brief critical remarks on the state of text without going into these questions. On recent scholarship on single parts see Totaro 1999 (second *parabasis*) and Imperio 2004 (on some *parabaseis*). On aggressive derision and Aristophanic choruses see Treu 1999 and in general Saetta Cottone 2005.

[132] Koch 1968:94–98, esp. 94–96.

[133] Koch's scheme of "critical idea" to "comic theme" is ultimately valid only for political comedy.

Because there is no ongoing and continuous illusion in comedy, as the best (in my opinion) analysis of the comic chorus, by G. M. Sifakis, shows, it is questionable to evaluate the chorus solely according to the degree of the coherency of plot.[134] Sifakis has made it clear that one cannot speak of any real consistent division of plot and role identity of the chorus in any Aristophanic comedy. Because of the lesser importance of closed mythical narrative,[135] the constative, descriptive-narrative function does not really supersede the performative function of the here and now in this genre. In the simple plot sequences of Aristophanes that are based on ritual models, the chorus is chiefly a ritual actor; the dramatic role and the theatrical function are extensively fused together, so that now one, now the other aspect comes more clearly to the fore at different times, depending on the point of view. According to Sifakis, the boundaries of foreground within the plot are consciously kept open to the background of the external communicative frame of reference. Depending on the situation, the chorus fluctuates dynamically between being strictly rooted in the drama and expansion into the here and now. Just as the eye constantly adapts to given light conditions by expansion or contraction of the pupil, so the comic chorus is able from verse to verse to retract its specific connection to the action and broaden its standpoint, or conversely, to tune out the here and now and become more involved in its fictional role.[136] Sifakis

---

The theory does not apply well to parodic comedy, travesty of myth, *Märchen*-like comedy, or simple fantasy. Koch unequivocally denies the ritual dimension of the chorus; this attitude is among other things due to the fact that writing as he is in the 1960s he is predisposed to exclude any ritual explanations, since, as he sees it, the audience is no longer a cultic community (*Kultgemeinde*) but exclusively a theater audience (*Theaterpublikum*; 63), and the plays should be understood purely in terms of their contemporary reality—as if ritual would not have been part of contemporary existence at the time of Aristophanes. The ritual dimension can be undertaken even by a chorus that is less embedded in the plot. A lesser degree of integration is not necessarily equivalent to a development toward redundancy; the openness to the spectator is rather part of the genre's mode of play. As has already been said, in comedy a complete embedding is not desirable; a view of the here and now is always simultaneously attached.

[134] Sifakis (1971:7–14) is against the use of the concept of illusion, while Chapman (1983) continues to rely on this: metatheater is for him a conscious playing with illusion and the rupturing thereof.

[135] Cf. Warning 1976:283–294.

[136] Despite this in principle transgressive openness, the comic chorus is nevertheless, according to Gelzer's analysis, more of a fellow actor or player in the first half of the play up until the *parabasis*, while in the second half it is more of a mediator and go-between for the audience. Sifakis (1971) recognized this slipping back and forth between both levels years before the semiotic analysis of the tragic chorus by Calame (Calame 1994/95 and Calame 1999), who terms this the fading in and out of the *énonciation* framework. Calame nowhere refers to this important study of the comic chorus.

already emphasized the particular function of the chorus as mediator between players, performing citizens, and the public.[137]

On the other hand, scholars have long recognized the clearly ritual and pragmatic dimension of the comic chorus. Due to a one-sided view of dramaturgy that privileged the concept of a unified plot even for comedy, this characteristic could only be explained as a survival of predramatic and ritual elements.[138] This interpretation was widespread up to and including the time of Gelzer's dissertation (1960). Scholars made extrapolations back to comedy's origin on the basis of the conventional structure of its fixed constitutive elements. Typical of this tendency is Hans Herter's influential study *Vom dionysischen Tanz zum komischen Spiel* ["From Dionysiac dance to comic play"]. He argues for an organic development from Dionysiac phallic choral dances to Old Comedy. Comedy finally emerged from outgrowths of these, which attached themselves to original choral occasions and *kômoi* of traditional phallus singers, so that the actors developed as opposite numbers out of the chorus leader.[139] He considered the mocking, joking, and abusive speech of the chorus as a "relic of ritual."[140] In the case of the *parabasis*, in which deviation from the context of the plot is especially striking, and cult songs, dance, rebuke, laughter, and invective in a direct dialogue with the audience stand at the center, it was easy to find an explanation in the form of unassimilated remnants of ritual. The formulation of Gilbert Murray, an Oxford representative of the Cambridge ritualists, is well known: "The Parabasis is a nugget of unassimilated ritual embedded in the structure of the play."[141] Gelzer also sees the *parabasis* as a ritual remnant that is neither functionally adapted nor integrated into the plot. All in all, he views conventional elements as survivals whose real meaning has long since been forgotten.[142] In the course of the present study we will see that the style of the *parabasis*, because of its open-

---

[137] Möllendorff 1995a gives a brief interpretation of the role of the Aristophanic chorus. In his survey of modern scholarship he emphasizes the inclusion of the auditorium and intervention in the real world, but does not address the ritual dimension.

[138] On the survival theory of the Cambridge ritualists, see for example Cornford 1961[2]. Anything that contradicted the preconceived notion of an organic, closed plot could simply be explained away by the hypothesis of remnants of ritual.

[139] Herter 1947:38–42.

[140] Herter 1947:27.

[141] Murray 1933:12. The *parabasis* was accordingly seen for a long time as the actual core of comedy: see among others on this Herter 1947:31 and Sifakis 1971:15–20; see also below, chap. 2 n116.

[142] On the theory of survivals see Gelzer 1960:189n1; on the *parabasis* see Gelzer 1960:203–212; on the ritual popular substrate cf. also Gelzer 1966.

ness to the audience and to *énonciation*, is to a large extent typical of the comic chorus' ritual and transversal manner of speech, and is not only limited to the actual *parabasis* itself.

These two directions in scholarship, the one focused on the evolution and history of comedy, and the other on plot, have without doubt contributed much to the understanding of Old Comedy. The parts of the chorus that contribute to plot and those that are independent of plot are admittedly not as neatly separable as was originally assumed. Those choruses that cannot be fully and completely integrated into a fictional context should not be rejected as unimportant remnants of prehistory, but ought to be considered in connection with the performative viewpoints I have presented here of the blending in and out of *énonciation*. It is important here to recognize the ritual component of the performance in the here and now as well as the ritual make-up of the plot. The comic chorus thus not only reflects an original, conventional substrate of rituals that could certainly no longer be understood in the fifth century BCE, but to a large extent actually *is* ritual in the sense of the term we have established here.

Sifakis' study comes the closest to my analysis. Yet he too understands ritual rather as a primitive element from which comedy may have developed, while in my work the sociocultural context and elements that constitute the form and content of the extant comedies of Aristophanes are additionally classified as ritual in nature.

By way of a starting point one may accordingly summarize the ritual character of the comic chorus as follows:

1. The members of the chorus carry out a performative act, in which the performative should be understood as a speech act in the sense of a mimetic performance. In choral songs an activity generally stands in the foreground. By speaking, the members of the chorus bring about an action. They frequently refer to their own activity, that is, to their singing and to their ritual dance. Demonstrative self-presentation is at the center of this, corresponding to the ritual practice of self-display. Form and content form a unity. Redundancy, repetition, and compression are important elements of expression. The performance takes place using several media: speech, dance movement, gesture, music, and mask and costume—which emphasize the chorus' flashy exterior—all work together synaesthetically. The expressive quality of its speech, the sensory quality of the objects carried, and the clothing, together with the instrumental quality of its actions, combine to form a spectacular and aesthetically embellished complex of

artistic staging. Moreover, its words convey ideological value. Through associations, metaphors, and metonymy, speech moves objects and persons predicatively in a qualitative space. By means of mimetic actions and movements, these expressive impressions are fixed on a real level.

2. Because of its self-contained nature and its self-referential emphasis on the completion of the chorus' own action, other types of descriptions and constative utterances are reduced to a minimum.

3. In numerous choral songs contact is established with the gods in the here and now.[143] Hymns and prayers are prominent cultic forms. Choral lyric is incorporated in a way that is only partly parodic, and is equally characterized by its pragmatic-ritual function.[144] Beside the self-referential references to its own singing and dancing, the action of the chorus takes place at a festival. Ritual festive events are of great importance both in the fictional carrying out of action and in the here and now. In the social and cultural context of society choruses dance during initiation, at fertility festivals, and at new year's festivals. The ritual activity of the choral dance clearly is connected to the symbolic and dramatic enhancement of critical transitions. This social function is reflected in the dramatic integration of the chorus.

4. The ritual scheme of *pompê*, *agôn*, and *kômos* in the context of Dionysiac festival is copied in the course of the comedy. In the *parodos*, the chorus enters in a marching rhythm and is often engaged in a ritual acts. The *agôn* is often in the interest of the chorus and reflects the external competition of the comic playwrights and producers of the chorus for the victory prize. After completion of the actual plot, the ritual chorus often presents itself in the *parabasis* to the crowd. In the concluding *exodos*, the result of the comic experiment in thought is celebrated. Here the chorus anticipates the *kômos*

---

[143] While the tragic chorus can talk about its own performance only by resorting to the occasional device of projection onto other mythical or ritual choruses, the comic chorus has it easier in this respect as well. Of course, it can also act in this fashion. But its bearing is itself still largely ritual. The simple comic plot is arranged mainly about this chorus, whose actual identity continues to shine through the intermittent identity of its dramatic role. The masked members of the chorus form a representative cross-section of the community as a whole, and to a certain extent a microcosm of Athens. Through their activity they perform ritual practices and ceremonies of the polis as a whole, and in particular they honor the gods of their polis.

[144] On assimilation of the lyric tradition, see Kugelmeier 1996.

procession of the victory celebration and thus makes a transition into the external context.[145]

Wherein, then, does the difference between the comic and tragic chorus lie? In part its difference with respect to its aesthetic is fundamental, and in part this difference is also one of degree.

Contrary to tragedy, where the chorus tends to be made up of inconspicuous participants in the plot, such as old men or female bystanders, and is therefore rather straightfoward and predictable in terms of its role, the choruses of Old Comedy represent a considerable surprise and the central performative event for the audience. The financial expenditure for the rich decoration of the costumes and masks of this fantastic entity was far greater. Its conspicuously spectacular exterior is meant to be displayed and is directly connected to the development of the comic plot. While the rules of the tragic genre largely mask the framework of *énonciation* and attempt to embed the chorus in the action on stage, the chorus of Old Comedy tends to describe its role and its costume at first hand and to enter into contact with the audience. In tragedy one has a chorus that operates in a rather colorless fashion and that is far removed from the actual activity of the heroes. It interprets and comments on the events on stage from a different observation point while possessing a relatively stable role identity, and in its moralizing insistence on taking middle-of-the-road positions largely corresponds to the audience. Without completely obviously transgressing the boundaries between the here and now and the action on stage, in this role as inner or *idealized* spectator it remains palpably connected with the actual context. In comedy, on the other hand, the chorus determines action, and the distance from the everyday world of the spectator is immense because of the grotesque surroundings of the plot. But the distance is overcome by entering into direct contact with the audience. The role identity of the chorus members becomes so thin as a result of explicit references to the performance context that on the side of the recipient the boundary between it and the chorus appears equally transparent. In tragedy, the audience is thus drawn into the undertow of sorrow and lament on the stage through its implicit similarity to the chorus, while in comedy, by contrast, it assimilates itself to the viewpoint of the fantastic world, and it is through this that the desired

---

[145] For an interpretation of the *exodoi* involving an anthropological approach and the aesthetics of reception, see Pappas 1987. He thinks that the final structural element concludes the progression of ritual activity from νόσος to σωτηρία and achieves a catharsis in the ritual context of fertility festivals.

reactions of compassion (*Mit-Leiden*) or laughter (*Mit-Lachen*) respectively arise.[146]

All in all, the dramatic activity of ritual comic choruses should be measured against a naturalist-realist theater of total illusion even less than tragedy should be subjected to this approach. Rather, it is comparable to strongly conventionalized and expressive-symbolic theater like Japanese Kabuki, at the center of which one also finds demonstration, the display of metaphorical connections. Just as ritual mimetic groups attempt to do, in these forms of theater one presents oneself to the spectators, represents oneself and the role, and remains in a continuous exchange with them. The player acts here as a living sign that functions as a symbol. Simultaneously, behind this symbolic role one's reality as performing dancer is always allowed to filter through. Semiotically speaking, the chorus member dressed as a bird, for example, is at the same time signifier and signified. In Charles S. Peirce's terminology, the actor functions both as icon and as index, in the sense that he achieves a similarity with the actual object, which was intended to be *signified* by the external sign. Finally, as an iconicized index, the dancer also assumes the character of a symbol, since his body language, utterances, accessories, movements, and gestures can be interpreted as those of a bird, which in the Greek imagination is associated with experiences of crossing into another world.[147]

While the tragic chorus, being for the most part only a marginal group and connected to the figures and the action only through an external relationship, reflects in its songs experiences that largely pass it by or introduces

---

[146] On the comparison of comic and tragic choruses see the excellent observations in Taplin 1996:191–194. On the social marginality of the tragic chorus in its dramatic role, see Gould 1996. In his response Goldhill (1996, esp. 250–255) correctly notes that the chorus in its ritual role in the *énonciation* is anything but a marginal phenomenon, but possesses the authority of a mythic speech act of privileged fellow citizens.

[147] For the concepts icon, index, and symbol, see Peirce 1983:64–67; in connection with the semiotics of theater, see F. de Toro 1995:73–86. On the nature of Old Comedy as conventionalized and expressive-symbolic theater, see also Sifakis 1971:7–14, esp. 11: "Any conventional type of drama—or art for that matter—is by definition unrealistic and, in consequence, anti-illusionistic. It makes no demands on the credulity of the spectators, and no effort to appear true to everyday life. Thus conventional drama, be it Chinese opera, Noh drama, European ballet, or Greek comedy, is free to show in a symbolic way virtually anything the dramatist likes: tales of unlimited fantasy such as journeys to the underworld through lakes and strange landscapes, men riding beetles to heaven or building cities in the Birdland suspended between heaven and earth, and animals talking like men." On Kabuki see for example Pronko 1982. On the comic chorus' function of integrating and involving the audience in the comic plot, see also Möllendorff 1995a. On audience participation in ritual drama, see Turner 1982:31, 112, and Turner 1984.

mythical narratives as background information, the comic chorus is a ritual actant to a far greater degree.

In his detailed study, Jürgen Rode proceeds on the assumption that actual tragic choral song is constructed antistrophically and derives from an independent and nonmimetic choral lyric that contained gnomic elements, mythical narrative, interpretation, commentary, and description.[148] By contrast, the chorus of comedy and the satyr play has a considerable part in the action and in its songs represents action in the sense of speech act.

Nevertheless, one should not draw as sharp a distinction between the two genres as is usually done. Choruses that participate in the action can also be found in tragedy, particularly in the early plays of Aeschylus, for example the *Suppliants* and the *Eumenides*. Both of these choral groups stand at the center of the action and act in a largely ritual and performative fashion.[149] The entry of the Erinyes in particular is just as surprising and spectacular as a choral entrance in comedy.[150] But fundamentally they largely retain their role identity, and their pragmatic function is only visible at the edges, chiefly in the final procession, which is in many ways reminiscent of the Panathenaia.[151] There are many other tragic choruses that enact ritual as speech act.[152] This occurs primarily by means of the integration of cultic forms that are embedded in the tragic plot. Either this action happens autonomously and unannounced, or a dramatic announcement is followed by the performance of ritual in song.[153] In this context one may mention hymns, prayers, processions, sacrificial and

---

[148] Rode 1971; the structural description is certainly correct. It is nevertheless worth considering whether choral lyric might not also have developed out of ritual songs, to which gnomic elements and description were attached only secondarily.

[149] See the sound analysis of the *Eumenides* in Prins 1991, in which Austin's speech act theory is also applied.

[150] Taplin 1996:197–199 treats the *Eumenides* as an exception to the rule that there is a fundamental difference between tragedy and comedy, because the *Oresteia* in his opinion represents as kind of "aetiology for tragedy"; cf. Wilson/Taplin 1993. It remains questionable whether the *Eumenides* and the *Bacchae* are really fundamentally different from the other tragedies. On the unusual role of the chorus in the *Bacchae*, see Segal 1997; without going into the performative aspect, he describes among other things the loss of the function as authoritative voice of the citizenry in the light of the political transformation at the end of the fifth century BCE.

[151] Cf. Headlam 1906, Bowie 1993a (with further bibliography, 27), and Weaver 1996.

[152] On the integration of hymns and other cultic elements, see Kranz 1933:127–137. Supplication, sacrifice, prayer, invocation, the casting of spells, blessing, and marching to a song in a procession give rise to corresponding ritual actions through speech. On hymns in tragedy, see also Adami 1901 and Dorsch 1983.

[153] Rode (1971:101–103 and 111–113) somewhat schematically terms this form *Programmlieder* ["programmatic songs"], thus underplaying the amount of genuinely cultic material in tragic choral songs; see also 1971:114.

wedding rites, summoning of ghosts, laments, and blessings. Whether or not these cultic elements are in Rode's words "an original and necessary part of choral songs in general or tragedy" is, as Walther Kranz writes, hardly something that can be established, since this implies an overly fixed opinion about the question of origin.[154] Kranz does seem more likely to be right than Rode inasmuch as every chorus carries out a ritual action. It is of course important that in this case the tragic chorus, which in its narrative and descriptive parts is clearly anchored, just as comedy is, in the ritual of Dionysus, incorporates further ritual from the everyday world. Drama is simultaneously theater and ritual, and depending on one's point of view, emphasis may fall on one aspect at one time and on another at a different moment. Tragedy also employs parts of ritual that make up the *mythos*, that is the action of the plot.[155]

Astrophic songs in particular are strongly mimetic and so reactualize through word and deed all types of action that the poet brings into connection with the dramatic action on stage. Search scenes are typical of this in all three dramatic genres. In the verbal expression of searching, which is underscored by many other types of signs, the chorus bring about the corresponding action.[156]

Satyr choruses in particular—like the comic chorus before the *parabasis*, especially in the comic *parodos*—are often presented in actions or imitate actions in pantomime fashion with wild dance-like movements.[157] In the *Cyclops* the chorus refers in self-referential fashion to its own activity in the orchestra, just as is the case in the two other dramatic genres. In the *parodos*, while singing and dancing, it drives its flock to the cave of the Cyclops, and Silenos at the end of the prologue comments on the satyrs' activity and prepares the way for their actual entrance:

τί <u>ταῦτα; μῶν κρότος σικινίδων</u>
ὁμοῖος ὑμῖν <u>νῦν</u> τε χὤτε Βακχίῳ

---

[154] Rode (1971:114) considers these elements, contra Kranz 1933:127–137, to be merely secondary. On these ritual elements in tragedy, see the excellent contribution by Easterling (1988), who like me emphasizes the connection of ritual and tragedy. See now Easterling 1997, Seaford 2005, and Sourvinou-Inwood 2005.

[155] See for example Foley 1992, Zeitlin 1992, and the exemplary study in Wolff 1992.

[156] Cf. e.g. Soph. *Ichn.* (fr. 314 Radt) 64–78, 100–123, 176–202, Eur. *Rhes.* 675–721 (satyr play); Aesch. *Eum.* 254–275, Soph. *Ai.* 866–878 (tragedy) and Ar. *Ach.* 204–236, *Thesm.* 655–688 (comedy). See also Pöhlmann 1995.

[157] For the chorus in satyr plays see the excellent remarks of Seidensticker in 1979:236–238 (= Seidensticker 1989:338–340) and 1999:17–25, esp. 19–21. On choral self-referentiality in satyr plays see now also Easterling 1997:42–44, Kaimio 2001, and Bierl 2006, esp. 118–134.

κῶμοι συνασπίζοντες Ἀλθαίας δόμους
προσῆτ᾽ ἀοιδαῖς βαρβίτων σαυλούμενοι;

Eur. *Cyc.* 37–40[158]

What's all this? Is your stamping of the *sikinnis* now like it was when
as fellow shield bearers to Bakkhos you came in *kômoi* to the house
of Althaia, shaking yourselves about to the song of the lyre?

In the mimetic song action is completed through words: in the short, astrophic
interchange, the animals are herded (49–54) in a similarly gesture-filled
fashion as in comedy, and here, in addition to this action, the movements of
the chorus clearly imitate the *sikinnis*, the dance of the satyr play. Just as in
tragedy, here Euripides knows how to combine choral self-reference with
choral projection. The stamping of the *sikinnis* of the *énonciation* in the *hic et
nunc* is connected with dancing in the Dionysiac *kômos* once upon a time when
the satyrs and Bakkhos, carrying weapons, marched to Kalydon, where the god
fell in love with Althaia, the wife of his guest-friend Oineus. The ritual of the
current performance cites and in so doing makes present the mythical event
of the past.

In the same *parodos* the satyrs give a typically negative choral projection
that nevertheless functions as self-reference to their own dance, singing, and
music-making. While the bacchic dance is not shown on the grass in front of
the Cyclops' cave, it is performed in the Dionysiac orchestra with the utterance of the following verses:

οὐ τάδε Βρόμιος, οὐ τάδε χοροὶ
Βάκχαι τε θυρσοφόροι,

---

[158] The performative shifters have been emphasized here as well as in the passage of Alcman cited
above (p. 33) and in the further examples. With their help reference is made from the there
and then of the plot to the here and now of the current communication situation. Ludwig
Koenen has kindly sent me a copy of his unpublished lecture "Lustiges Spiel mit Theater-
Konventionen in Euripides' *Kyklops*," which he gave in the spring of 1999 at the colloquium
in Basel in honor of Joachim Latacz and from which I have profited. I have come to similar
conclusions independently of Koenen. Interestingly, he characterizes the shouts of the Satyrs
to Odysseus' men (Eur. *Cyc.* 654–662), who are blinding the Cyclops inside (i.e. offstage), as
speech acts. Nevertheless, the chorus exhorts itself here, in contrast to others songs in satyr
plays and comedies (cf. e.g. the searching song, below chap. 1, n261 and Ar. *Thesm.* 655–688, or
the work song in *Pax* 459–519), not to act, but with a shout of encouragement it informs the
audience about what is happening behind the stage. At most one could suggest that the Satyrs
are transforming their demands for action into dancelike movement in a dramatic fashion. See
now also Bierl 2006:130–134.

οὐ <u>τυμπάνων ἀλαλαγμοὶ</u>   65
κρήναις παρ' ὑδροχύτοις,
οὐκ οἴνου χλωραὶ σταγόνες·
οὐδ' ἐν Νύσᾳ μετὰ Νυμφᾶν
<u>ἴακχον ἴακχον ᾠδὰν</u>
<u>μέλπω</u> πρὸς τὰν Ἀφροδίταν,   70
ἂν θηρεύων <u>πετόμαν</u>
Βάκχαις σὺν <u>λευκόποσιν</u>.

Eur. *Cyc.* 63–72

Here there is no Bromios, here are no choruses and thyrsos-bearing Bakkhai, no thumping of the drums next to the water-pouring sources, no sparkling drops of wine: nor in Nysa with the Nymphs do I sing the song *Iakkhos Iakkhos* to Aphrodite, whom I flew after, hunting with the white-footed Bakkhai.

The negated deictic reference is ambiguous in terms of the performance situation, since the chorus really dances in the *hic et nunc* and Dionysus Eleuthereus is thereby imagined as being present. Even within the action of the plot the pronouncement represents an irony, since Dionysus, who throughout the *Cyclops* is equated with the drink sacred to him, is *de facto* right there in the next scene, namely as the wine of Maron, even though the Satyrs cannot taste it. One might compare the words with which the Cyclops upbraids the members of the chorus after Silenos together with Odysseus has traded the fabulous wine for food: ἄνεχε· πάρεχε· τί τάδε; τίς ἡ ῥαθυμία; | <u>τί βακχιάζετ';</u> οὐχὶ <u>Διόνυσος τάδε,</u> | οὐ <u>κρόταλα χαλκοῦ τυμπάνων τ' ἀράγματα</u> ("Stop! Make room! What's all this here, what's the meaning of this laziness? Why this Bacchic dancing? This is not Dionysus here, there are no bronze castanets and beatings of drums!" *Cyc.* 203–205). The Cyclops takes up the just-cited description given by the Satyrs and at the same time exposes it as false.

On the surface a gap, as it were, emerges in verses 63–72 between the actual performance of the chorus and the plot that slowly closes over the course of the piece. As far as the intrafictional setting of the play is concerned it can be fiercely negated, yet at the moment of the performance the sound of the drums resounds clearly, the members of the chorus raise the ritual shout in the Athenian theater of Dionysus, they sing and make wild movements. The central god, in whose honor the play takes place in the first place, through ritual self-referentiality establishes a bridge between the here and now and the there and then. Through his name both levels can be present alongside each other in the simplest fashion and be fused together.

Such examples of pure action in connection with self-referential utterances that relate to the carrying out of a simple action and simultaneously to the chorus' own ritual occupation of dancing and singing are commonly found in comedy. The relatively uncomplicated action of the plot is carried by the chorus and supported in an illocutionary fashion by references to itself.

In tragedy there are many other examples of astrophic songs that perform a speech act.[159] For example, in Aeschylus' *Suppliants* (825–835) the members of the chorus flee to the altars of the gods while singing words that correspond to their actions, the maidens of Argos perform a libation at the tomb in the *Libation Bearers* (152–163), and in the *Seven against Thebes* (848–860) the bodies of the brothers are carried in. In Euripides' *Heracles* the door to the palace is opened in the *astrophon* (1016–1038). The latter two passages simultaneously introduce a *kommos*, which is a perfect example of a speech act.[160] Lastly, a short prayer is enacted on stage in a brief choral song in Euripides' *Hippolytus* (1268–1281).

Sophocles *Trachiniae* 205–224[161] and Euripides *Bacchae* 1153–1164 represent spirited dance songs with choral self-reference as an expression of joy and celebration. *Astropha* of this sort that are dependent on extra-dramatic hyporchemes are extremely rapid, highly mimetic, and expressive choral interludes in which action is closely joined with speech, and in particular, the fictional plane with the external communication situation. The wild gestures and dance movements are enacted in a particular meter: they are partly in lyric iambics.[162] Cretics, dochmiacs, and anapaests are rhythmically especially suited to the mimetic presentation of emotions and small, rapid actions.[163]

---

[159] See Rode 1971:92–94 on this.

[160] Aesch. *Prom.* 687–695, Eur. *Supp.* 918–924, and Eur. *Ion* 1229–1243 represent brief laments without subsequent *kommos*.

[161] See Bierl 1991:135–137 and Henrichs 1994/95:79–84 on this; the self-referential, excited, and orgiastic choral language (esp. Soph. *Trach.* 216–221) is reminiscent of other hyporchemes. Cf. De Falco 1958, esp. 60–63; for Sophoclean hyporchemes see also Bierl 1991:126–127. On the question of the genre of Soph. *Trach.* 205–224, see Grandolini 1995 (with references to older scholarship).

[162] For iambics see below, chap. 2, n44.

[163] Iambic and cretic meters are especially typical of hyporchemes. Cretics and paeons are also characteristic of the paean and the hyporcheme; see Gentili 1952:139–149 and Gentili/Lomiento 2003:220–229.

A defining factor here is the participation of the choral "I," which may be split by the introduction of references to the song and the dance into a performer in the here and now and a role-player integrated into the plot.

Beside action-oriented songs of this type, ritual actions may also in strophic songs be simply attached in outward appearance to the sequence of events of a tragedy. Here one may mention prayers, as in the *parodoi* of Aeschylus' *Seven against Thebes* and Sophocles' *Oedipus Rex* and *Antigone*, or cletic hymns, such as the famous song to Dionysus in the fifth stasimon of the *Antigone* (1115–1154).[164] In the prayer to the gods, particularly with the pointed naming of Dionysus, the speech act of worship within the fiction of the play passes into the area of the here and now.[165] In uttering it, the members of the chorus in fact complete this action. The same is the case with oaths, curses, and blessings. So, for example, at the Persian chorus' insistent singing of "Come, come, come here, come to upper edge of the tomb, lift the saffron-tinged shoe of your foot!" (ἴθ' ἴθ' ἱκοῦ, | ἔλθ' ἐπ' ἄκρον κόρυμβον ὄχθου, κροκόβα-|πτον ποδὸς εὔμαριν ἀείρων, Aesch. *Persians* 658–660), Dareios really does return to the upper world. The perlocutionary result is ensured. The illocutionary force lies in the ritual and formulaic language with its dicola and tricola, which emphasizes the command. The lifting of the foot in the chorus' address to Dareios will have been imitated in the gestural language of the choral dance and strengthens the speech act.[166]

The famous "binding song" of the Erinyes in Aeschylus' *Eumenides* (321–396) is also comparable. Magical practices lie behind this: through their words, the chorus attempt to actually bind Orestes. The chorus' formation and its primitive diction aim at the desired effect of psychic binding. The chorus incites itself to join hands (ἄγε δὴ καὶ χορὸν ἄψωμεν, *Eum.* 307), and thereupon makes a magic circle around the victim at the altar. As phatic locutionary act, the ephymnion resembles an actual magical incantation that unleashes enormous illocutionary energy using assonance, alliteration, and the intense

---

[164] In the fifth stasimon of the *Antigone* (1115–1154) the combination of choral projection and self-reference also occurs; see Henrichs 1994/95:77–79 and already Bierl 1991:127–132; see also Scullion 1998, who interprets the song as a Dionysiac and cathartic dance to free Thebes of its "illness." For further ritual prayers, cf. *OC* 1556–1578 and Eur. *Hipp.* 61–72.

[165] In the *parodoi* of Soph. *OT* 209–215 and *Ant.* 147–154 Dionysus is invoked last. Once again Dionysus functions as a kind of shifter.

[166] Consider the opinion of Rode 1971:102n57 on the song in Aesch. *Pers.* 633–680: "Dies ist eines der wenigen Lieder, die man auch als 'echte' Kultlieder verstehen könnte, die also keine dem Kultlied fremden Elemente aufweisen" ["This is one of the few songs that could also be understood as 'real' cultic songs and that thus exhibit no elements that are foreign to cult song"]. For ἀείρων as a choral self-reference cf. Soph. *Trach.* 216 and the references in Henrichs 1994/95:106n105.

staccato rhythm of the "running" trochaics interrupted by a pherecratean. Repetition, redundancy, and the concentration of impressions give the song its insistency. The victim is, so to speak, put under hypnosis.[167]

> ἐπὶ δὲ τῷ τεθυμένῳ
> <u>τόδε μέλος</u>, παρακοπά,
> παραφορὰ φρενοδαλής,
> <u>ὕμνος</u> ἐξ Ἐρινύων,
> δέσμιος φρενῶν, ἀφόρ-
> μικτος, αὐονὰ βροτοῖς.

Aesch. *Eum.* 328–333 (= 341–346)

Over our victim this is our song: the blow of madness, mind-destroying frenzy, a hymn of the Erinyes, mind-binding, lyreless, withering for mortals.

In both examples the members of the chorus carry out a ritual with self-reference to the singing and dancing of the performance. In the refrain quoted above, this song (τόδε μέλος) is referred to deictically. The key concept of the ὕμνος δέσμιος is initially expressed briefly and in a pithy fashion (*Eum.* 306), to be then repeated in emphatic form in the magic formula. The chorus arranges its linear dance formation performatively (*Eum.* 307), using the hortative first-person plural form to order itself. The song's negative aspect as magic used to invoke and harness chthonic powers is emphasized in the plot, although as spectacular performance the hymn "binds" and enchants on the level of *énonciation*. The singers describe their song as "lyreless" (ἀφόρμικτος, *Eum.* 332–333 = 345–346) and "hated muse" (μοῦσαν στυγεράν, *Eum.* 308). Similarly, the chorus of the *Persians* refers to its own ritual activity as performer and talks of its own songs as ὕμνοι.[168]

The next two refrains testify in particular to the "I" of the speakers who complete the speech act. Throughout the whole song the "I"/"we" is emphasized. At the moment they utter their destructive words, the actors stamp on the ground and assert that the greatest glory of men will be struck down "by

---

[167] On the connection with magical practice see Faraone 1985. On the *Eumenides* from the perspective of choral self-reference, see also Henrichs 1994/95:60–65. For interpretation of the chorus of Erinyes in connection with Austin's speech act theory, see Prins 1991.

[168] Aesch. *Pers.* 625; Atossa does this already in her request for performance, *Pers.* 620. Cf. also Aesch. *Cho.* 475 (ὅδ' ὕμνος). For the mention of song and dance (as self-referential illocutionary intensification), see Kranz 1933:135 (with many other examples).

our dark-clothed attacks and the hate-filled dancing of our foot" (ἀμετέραις ἐφόδοις μελανείμοσιν, ὀρχη- | σμοῖς τ' ἐπιφθόνοις ποδός, *Eum.* 370–371). Again, the general self-reference to the "dance" of the *énonciation* prepares the way for the actual ritual practice of sympathetic magic, which is of significance for the progress of the plot.

The self-reference to the chorus' own performative presentation is taken up in the refrain immediately afterward. In a mimetic and highly charged dance, words about hunting, chasing, and attack with destructive foot stand at the center:[169]

> μάλα γὰρ οὖν <u>ἁλομένα</u>
> ἀνέκαθεν <u>βαρυπεσῆ</u>
> καταφέρω <u>ποδὸς</u> ἀκμάν,
> <u>σφαλερὰ γὰρ τανυδρόμοις</u>
> <u>κῶλα</u>, δύσφορον ἄταν.

Aesch. Eum. 372–376

> For jumping from up above I bring down the heavy-falling edge of my foot: unsure are the limbs of those who run at full tilt, a terrible destruction.

"Jumping" (ἁλομένα), the "foot" (ποδός), and "limbs" (κῶλα) emphasize in turn in quite immediate fashion the bodily action of dance that puts the chorus in a trance and connects the performers with their dramatic role. The whirling chorus' agonistic exertion practically brings it to the point of almost passing out. Like animals, the members of the chorus lunge at their victim and in mock combat make the limbs of other dancers under attack buckle.[170] One is here reminded of the animal choruses of Old Comedy. Only in tragedy, according to generic convention, the wildness and the uncivilized nature of

---

[169] See Henrichs 1994/95:64: "The feet of the Erinyes thus epitomize their choral identity as performers of the dance; at the same time, their feet function as instruments of destruction that physically perform the incantation in an act of sympathetic magic."

[170] Prins 1991:188–189 also emphasizes the relation of these lines to the performance going on in the present: she notes that the body of the dancer corresponds to the song, whose rhythmic properties are also called "feet" (πόδες) and "cola" (lit. "limbs, members," κῶλα). She refers (1991:188n14) to Svenbro 1984 (esp. 221) and the double meaning of μέλος as "song" and "limb." Dance is a ritual enacted on the body. At the same time as it is executed a transformation takes place. Svenbro 1984:220–224 refers in addition to the homology of sacrificial portions and rhythmic units. In a kind of sympathetic magic the attackers thus "dismember" their body and song into πόδες and κῶλα, which dancing by themselves are supposed in a gruesome sacrificial ritual to perform sparagmos on Orestes, rendered in turn into πόδες and κῶλα.

the animal, symbolized by the color of black, is emphasized as threatening contrast to the human, while in comedy this boundary is playfully removed.

Negative incantation can also be compared with positive blessing (εὐχὰς ἀγαθάς, Aesch. *Supp.* 626) in the *Suppliants* of Aeschylus (630–709), which is connected to the action on stage. This song is likewise a ritual speech act that attempts to influence reality through the illocutionary force and role of the wish. Even if the choral "I" retreats into the background in the wish expressed in the optative of the third person, the chorus is nevertheless present on both its levels through projections of a negative and positive nature. Twice the abhorrent Ares is degraded in lively dochmiacs as the negation of the choral dancing that is now taking place (τὸν ἄχορον βοὰν . . . μάχλον Ἄρη ["wild Ares, the shout hostile to the chorus"] and ἄχορον ἀκίθαριν δακρυογόνον Ἄρη ["Ares, hostile to the chorus and the lyre, source of tears"], Aesch. *Supp.* 635 and 682) and contrasted with the positive and desired state of Dionysiac harmony and festivity, which is identical with the present situation of the dancing chorus members in the orchestra (εὔφημον δ' ἐπὶ βωμοῖς | μοῦσαν θείατ' ἀοιδοί· | ἁγνῶν τ' ἐκ στομάτων φερέ- | σθω φήμα φιλοφόρμιγξ ["May the singers perform their work of the muse attentively at the altars; and from their pure mouths let a lyre-loving song stream out!"], *Supp.* 694–697).[171] Many other pointed oppositions may be explained on the basis of this constantly sought self-reference to the chorus' own performance for the sake of illocutionary intensification. Expressions such as "paean for the dead" (παιᾶνα τοῦ θανόντος, Aesch. *Cho.* 151) should not simply be dismissed as consciously sought after paradoxical figures of speech and oxymoronic periphrasis, or as theatrical genre-mixing.[172] Rather, attention is being drawn to the implicit contrast and opposing tension between tragic role and cultic function. The chorus tends to present its song in the orchestra as cheerful and exuberant, while within the frame of the plot it equally needs to assume severe aspects as well. Finally, by means of these dispositions the tragic poet is able to imitate the characteristic ambivalence of the Dionysiac mood and to incorporate it dramaturgically into the build-up of tension.

[171] On the paradoxical association of Ares and Dionysus see e.g. Eur. *Phoen.* 784–800; Bierl 1991: 154–157.

[172] Kranz (1933:135) proceeds from a fundamental opposition between the forms of the paean and the *kommos*, and thinks "es ist daher als Vereinigung des eigentlich Unvereinbaren zu deuten, wenn die Tragödie auch spricht vom παιὰν τοῦ θανόντος (vom Scholiasten getadelt)" ["This should accordingly be explained as the union of the essentially irreconcilable, even if tragedy speaks of the παιὰν τοῦ θανόντος, *Cho.* 151 (condemned by the scholiast)"]. He lists Aesch. *Sept.* 867, Eur. *Alc.* 424, *Supp.* 75, *Hel.* 175ff., and *Hipp.* 1373 among others as comparable passages. For the explanation in terms of a potpourri of genres in Plato's sense (*Leg.* 700d), see Rutherford 1994/95:122–124.

Connected with the dramatic incorporation of these ritual songs into the tragic events, rites connected with mourning and burial, especially the *thrênos* and the *kommos*, stand in the foreground.[173] Albert Henrichs speaks generally in this connection of an almost unbridgeable tension between the chorus members' dramatic role and their function as joyful dancers in the orchestra.[174] From an evolutionary and historical perspective this observation may be quite right. Nevertheless, the incorporation of dance ritual into the plot is so extensive that the breaking of this inner contradiction does not represent an unavoidable flaw or accident, but is sought out by the poet in order to intensify the speech act of ritual performance in illocutionary fashion. Otherwise the danger might arise that the ritual performance would remain exclusively hidden behind a dramatic "illusion," which would lead to the failure of one part of the performative speech action. After all, the aim of the chorus as an ensemble of citizens of the Athenian community at the festival in a ritual presentation in honor of the god Dionysus is to carry away the victory prize in choral song competition.

Tragedy thus has a much greater tendency to subordinate dance and ritual to the dramatic role or to combine both levels completely. The tragic chorus can also perform dance movements of mourning, thereby incorporating ritual traditions of *thrênoi*.[175] The verb χορεύεσθαι need not be taken to mean exclusively "to dance joyfully in the orchestra for cultic purposes," but in the course of the development of tragedy simply takes on the additional connotation "to move as chorus in response to tragic action on stage."

In tragedy, dance and direct *énonciation* gradually take a back seat to the course of events in the plot, gnomic utterance, reflection, and commentary or mythical description. Only now and then does its ritual and performative function surface next to the dramatic role. Here reference to actual activity is mostly also linked to ritual self-reference, that is, to the mention of Dionysus.

---

[173] See Kranz 1933:127–137. With regard to the sacred form of the integrated cultic song, Kranz lists as Aeschylean formal aspects religious formulaic language, repetitions, the repetition of sounds, refrains, alliteration, assonance, and the use of triadic structures. For *thrênoi* in Aeschylus, see Aesch. *Cho.* 306–478 (the long *kommos* at the tomb of Agamemnon; cf. the term γόος, *Cho.* 321, ἐπιτύμβιος θρῆνος, *Cho.* 334–335 [cf. θρήνων ἐπιτυμβιδίων, *Cho.* 342], and ἐφυμνῆσαι . . . ὀλολυγμὸν, *Cho.* 386–387 and in general Sier 1988:66–179) and *Sept.* 861–960 (cf. again the generic term θρῆνον, *Sept.* 863 and the contrast with the joyful paean, *Sept.* 866–970 [like *Cho.* 340–344]).

[174] Henrichs 1994/95, esp. 73. He rightly considers choral projection as a means of overcoming this gap.

[175] See Henrichs 1996:18 and 54–55, where the tension is viewed within the cultic framework.

The Comic Chorus

Play and Dance

In accordance with the conventions of the genre, the comic chorus is transparent in terms of its *Sitz im Leben* to a far greater extent than its tragic counterpart; its dramatic play constantly crosses over into its ritual function. Because of this, it possesses no continuous role identity; rather, its involvement in one single dramatic piece may go from direct participation in the action on stage to commentary from the sidelines to ritual presence in the here and now, and may freely float between these perspectives. The chorus' "coming forward" in the *parabasis*, where *énonciation* is so strongly blended in that its dramatic role is almost completely lost sight of, only represents an extreme case of stepping out of the plot, where the distance between agent and audience, as in every ritual, is almost entirely removed.[176]

Comedy seems to have developed from a joyful procession, the *kômos*. Unrestrained and exuberant behavior, eating, drinking, and ritual celebration are in the foreground. The occasion of the comic performance falls under the same festive auspices.[177] Over the course of a comedy one can detect the decreasing dramatic connection of the chorus. From relatively close participation in the *parodos* and *agôn*, the chorus moves almost imperceptibly after the *parabasis* and toward the end, in the *exodos*, into the ritual context of the performance, which is characterized by festive processions, sacrifice, and carousing for the victor of the *agôn*. For this reason the countless references to the *kômos* are primarily to be found in the closing parts of comedies. It will thus be important to trace this ambivalent swaying between dramatic role and performative and extradiscursive function in connection with the dramatic course of events by following the structural elements. We will see, however, in the discussion of the *Thesmophoriazusae*, that the essence of the *parabasis* as transversal manner of speech is not just limited to the *parabasis* itself, but fundamentally defines the chorus in all the traditional parts of comedy equally.

All in all, in comedy there are clearly no difficulties in enabling the chorus to make a connection back to its own activity, that is, to its singing and dancing

---

[176] In comedy, the performative function is largely subordinated to the comic plot, at least up until the *parabasis*, with the distinction that the verbal utterances and nonverbal gestures and movements themselves generally indicate a ritual action and, in contrast to tragedy, have no descriptive, narrative, or declaratory function.

[177] Cf. Cole 1993 and Peirce 1993.

in the orchestra. The so-called tension we spoke of in the case of tragedy does not exist here, because the exuberant nature of comedy's embeddedness in the real world corresponds to the mood of the play itself. Moments of ecstatic joy continually arise, which may, as in the case of tragedy, be connected to self-reference by the chorus.[178]

In a play on words Plato makes a connection between χαρά and χορός. Joy and cheerfulness are obviously part of any type of performative *khoreia* that is not too clearly subject to the demands of plot.[179] Choral dance in this genre is in large measure original "play" in which one experiences fun and which is not completely subordinate to deliberate action. Since Homer the Greek word has served as a circumlocution for carefree, joyful dancing.[180] On the oldest piece of evidence for Attic competitive dance culture, a Late Geometric oinochoe by the Dipylon Master (between 750 and 725 BCE), one already finds the following hexametric verse inscription: ὃς νῦν ὀρχηστῶν πάντων ἀταλώτατα παίζει, τοῦ τόδε ΚΑΙΜΙΝ ("Whoever of all the dancers now *plays* the most exuberantly, to him belongs this [vessel]").[181] One can easily recognize in this verb the substantive παῖς. Simple dance is to a certain extent "child's play." Greek cultural theory accordingly explains its origin in the unrestrained urge of children to move. By means of established forms and rules dance becomes παιδιά ('play'), and only afterward in an agonistic context and with hard training does it become a means of παιδεία ('education').[182]

Every ritual is always at the same time also play. What is definitive is the performative act. Play and ritual share the same "as-if" proper-

---

[178] In tragedy this occurs mainly in the so-called hyporchemes; these are songs of a joy that is deceptive. They function as a way of controlling reception within the drama, in order to heighten the contrast with the catastrophe that is to follow. Cf. above, p. 61 and below, 81–82.

[179] Cf. *Leg.* 654a; the gods gave morals choruses and by way of (folk) etymology named them χορούς, from χαρά ('joy'): . . . χορούς τε ὠνομακέναι παρὰ τῆς χαρᾶς ἔμφυτον ὄνομα.

[180] From the graceful ball-playing of the Phaeacian maidens, reminiscent of a dance, to the choral songs of drama, παίζειν is used as a verb indicating dance. See among others Hom. *Od.* 6.100, 8.251, 23.134 and 147; *Hom. Hymn.* 2.425 and 5.120; Hes. *Scut.* 277; Pind. *Ol.* 1.16 and 13.86; Ion fr. 27, 7–8 W.; Ar. *Av.* 660, *Thesm.* 947, 983, 1227–1228, *Lys.* 1313, *Ran.* 318–320, 333, 388, 392, 407b, 415, 452; Autocrates fr. 1, 1ff. K.-A.; for συμπαίζειν see Soph. *OT* 1109, Ar. *Pax* 816–817, *Av.* 1098, *Thesm.* 975 and Men. *Epitr.* 478. See Hommel 1949 (on Homer), Calame I 1977:165–166 (Engl. trans. Calame 1997:87–88), Burkert 1982, esp. 336–337, Dover 1993:173–179, Dover, *Frogs*, 57–59, 61, 236–237, Lonsdale 1993:1, 33–43, 67, 71, 80, 251, and Henrichs 1996:35–38. For play, dance, and satyr play see Bierl 2006.

[181] Athens, National Museum 192. For the inscription, see *IG* I² 919 = *CEG* 432 (pp. 239–240 Hansen, with scholarly literature; *IG* I³, p. 984 considers *IG* I² 919 as *"fictile"*). For reading and dating cf. Powell 1988 and Powell 1991:158–163; cf. Henrichs 1996:32–34 with table I.

[182] Cf. books 2 and 7 of Plat. *Leg.* and the anthropological basis derived from this by Lonsdale 1993:21–43, esp. 33–35. On παίζω, παιδεία, and παιδιά see among other passages Plat. *Leg.* 656c, 673a, 673d, 803e.

ty.[183] Apart from one's own identity one establishes a second presence in which one acts as if one were someone else. Ritual turns the spontaneous play behavior of children into a fixed, stereotyped, and repeatable context. Mimesis is thus again crucial:[184] Hermann Koller has shown how this Greek concept took root originally in the area of music and ritual dance.[185] In a performative culture of oral communication and mediation one may become involved with the Other through these marked forms of expression and restage and reactualize it. It is primarily gods and animals that are presented; humans have to distinguish themselves from them in terms of category from above and below, respectively. Seeing oneself in the collapsing of oppositions between the self and the other produces laughter and joy. Original choral dance is thus an instance of the phenomenon of the comic "tipping point" [*Kipp-Phänomen*] and is always connected with mimetic play.[186]

Plato interprets the chorus and the festival as the gift of the gods to mortals, as a kind of compensation for their adverse existence. Even though Plato incorporates choral dance and mimesis into a comprehensive state educational philosophy, one may still derive a kind of Greek "anthropology" from him. Most noticeable is the recognition of the play instinct as a requirement for the acquisition of culture.[187]

Modern play theory in the context of cultural anthropology and child pyschology can be remarkably well combined with these ancient views. Ritual play marks and dramatizes the transition of the collective conditions and so furthers group cohesion in the *rite de passage*. In the marginal phase all rankings and categories thus become blurred. All hierarchies and temporal and spatial boundaries are suspended, to be confirmed anew in the reintegration

---

[183] On the "as if" see Burkert 1979:57 and Burkert 1996:7.

[184] For the connection of play and ritual, see Braungart 1996:216–233, on the relationship to theater, 225–233; he sees as a fundamental distinction the fact that play is fundamentally open, while ritual is not; nevertheless, he does not here consider the complete openness of comic and exceptional rituals that place openness on the stage; for the connection of mimesis, art, and ritual, see his 234–253.

[185] Koller 1954, esp. 119–121.

[186] On the *Kipp-Phänomen* applied to the comic, cf. Iser 1976a.

[187] Plato explains choral dance on the basis of the instinct of every young creature to jump (πηδᾶν) and to romp (*Leg.* 673cd); children especially cannot keep still (653de). He thus sees the origin of dance in the urge to move and in the cradling of babies (even in the womb) to keep them calm. A concept of homoiostasis lies behind this: internal unrest may be overcome by movement (789e–791d). This model is applied to adults, who in ritual are viewed as the toy (παίγνιον, 803c; cf. 644de) of the gods. The gods gave mortals dance and festivals as relaxation (ἀναπαύλας) from everyday life and as compensation for inner disquiet (653cd); on the other hand, humans understood choral dance as an offering to the gods (791a); through play and dance they were able to gain the favor of the gods (803e).

phase. The chorus as microcosm and a group representative of certain gender-specific age classes has a special connection in initiations among traditional societies with these kind of staged passages from one state to another in which the foundation of a new identity is symbolically achieved. After the merging of self and other in the reintegration phase the changed self now emerges strengthened.

In connection with research on individual ontogenous construction of the subject, the British psychoanalyst Donald W. Winnicott developed the concept of the "intermediate area," which he saw as being of great importance for the infant's incipient capacity to distinguish between "I" and "not-I." According to this theory, during play the child makes use of so-called transitional objects such as a soft blanket or a toy that belong neither to the "I" nor the "other" of the mother. The field of play as phenomenon of transition or boundary becomes filled with images enriched by the child's perception of self and other that are neither completely "I" nor completely "not-I" and that simultaneously construct and deconstruct the "I"-boundary that may be developed from them. A positivistic boundary between true and false cannot be drawn; what is important here is rather the paradoxical nature of the transitory condition.

Drawing on Winnicott, Schechner applies these discoveries to the phenomenon of the theater. Here the role of a third figure is important, that of the mother in the case of the infant, and that of the spectator in the case of the theater. A precondition for this playful and creative process of representation is the suppression of skeptical questions.[188] Schechner considers the playful movement, the transition from presenter as "I" and represented as "not-I" into the paradoxical relation between "not-I" and "not not-I," and the typical double present, or "double negativity," as fundamental for the functioning of theater and ritual.

> During workshop-rehearsals performers play with words, things, and actions, some of which are "me" and some "not me." By the end

---

[188] Cf. Winnicott 1971, passim, esp. 1–25, on the role of illusion 10–14; cf. also the following (3): "I am here staking a claim for an intermediate state between a baby's inability and his growing ability to recognize and accept reality. I am therefore studying the substance of *illusion*, that which is allowed to the infant, and which in adult life is inherent in art and religion." Also (89): "I should like to put in a reminder here that the essential feature in the concept of transitional objects and phenomena (according to my presentation of the subject) is *the paradox, and the acceptance of the paradox*: the baby creates the object, but the object was there waiting to be created and to become a cathected object. I tried to draw attention to this aspect of transitional phenomena by claiming that in the rules of the game we all know that we will never challenge the baby to elicit an answer to the question: did you create that or did you find it?"

of the process the "dance goes into the body." So Olivier is not Hamlet, but he is also not not Hamlet. The reverse is also true: in this production of the play, Hamlet is not Olivier, but he is also not not Olivier. Within this field or frame of double negativity choice and virtuality remain activated.

Elements that are "not me" become "me" without losing their "not me-ness." This is the peculiar but necessary double negativity that characterizes symbolic actions. While performing, a performer experiences his own self not directly but through the medium of experiencing the others. While performing, he no longer has a "me" but has a "not not me," and this double negative relationship also shows how restored behavior is simultaneously private and social. A person performing recovers his own self only by going out of himself and meeting the others—by entering a social field.[189]

The famous definition of Johan Huizinga makes an extremely close structural connection between play and festival, and thus also with ritual.

Summing up the formal characteristics of play, we might call it a free activity standing quite consciously outside "ordinary" life as being "not serious," but at the same time absorbing the player intensely and utterly. It is an activity connected with no material interest, and no profit can be gained by it. It proceeds within its own proper boundaries of time and space according to fixed rules and in an orderly manner. It promotes the formation of social groupings which tend to surround themselves with secrecy and to stress their difference from the common world by disguise or other means.[190]

---

[189] Schechner 1985:110 and 111–112. On play see also Winnicott 1971, esp. 38–52, 53–64, Turner/Turner 1982:204–205, Turner 1982:20–88, esp. 30–35, 84–85, and Schechner 1993:24–36. Bateson 1972:177–193 views play in connection with "metacommunication" ("This is play") and for every game defines a "play frame" within which transgressions are allowed. But this sharp contrast between reality and play seems to be framed in too schematic a fashion. Bateson's categorization is connected among other things with the pejorative value placed on play in modern Western thought. Schechner contrasts this with an Eastern way of thinking where play, just as among the Greeks, is viewed as a worthy and serious interaction between gods and humans. In his opinion the world should be viewed as a permeable net through which play always finds access to serious reality. Play should accordingly be thought of less as the context of a time of exception or inversion, but rather as a mood or possible attitude to the world.

[190] Huizinga 1955:32. It is also important for Huizinga that the player is constantly aware of the fact that he is playing a role (32–33). For play in its connection with *agôn*, cult, ritual, sacred solemnity, festival, and religion, see Huizinga 1955:32–46.

Play is thus a creative and at the same time destabilizing activity. Huizinga in fact transferred his concept of play from ritual to poetry and to musical forms of expression.[191] Art, ritual, and performance are all in all barely distinguishable from play. Play represents not only an interruption of everyday life, but also an attitude with which one may again and again overcome the gravity and seriousness of civilization.

Peter von Möllendorff, in his dissertation on Aristophanes and Mikhail Bakhtin, has recently touched on these connections.[192] Unfortunately his investigation, which relies heavily on literary theory, leaves something to be desired in the area of ritual, although this theme is of central importance in Bakhtin's theory and in Old Comedy.[193] It is precisely in this genre that the interdependency of literature, theater, play, and ritual is important. It probably did not only develop out of impromptu play in a ritual context in which "the participants in the game became functionally separate and thus became author, actor (hero), and spectator."[194] Rather, even in Aristophanes' times comedy *is* play and ritual, in that with the help of the chorus it reactualizes this original unity in the festive context of license and inversion. By means of transversal openness the public is drawn in as fellow player and functional differentiation, as in ritual, is constantly suspended.

The chorus represents the central moment of this ritual play in comedy. In Greek its dancing activity, apart from being described by the specific verb χορεύειν, is also simply termed παίζειν. The members of the chorus behave like παῖδες, "children" at play,[195] because through mimetic processes they continu-

---

[191] Huizinga 1955:141: "*Poiesis*, in fact, is a play function." On poetry see 141–158, on art 182–197, esp. on dance 188–189 (Dance is "pure play"). On the relationship between play and comic theater, see Lohr 1986:18–24 and Braungart 1996:225–233.

[192] Möllendorff 1995:93–98. Möllendorff's view of an aesthetic poetics of Old Comedy is in general convincing; the digression on Bakhtin is superfluous if one takes the ritual component of comedy seriously. Bakhtin essentially provides only the impulse; Möllendorff's interesting analysis is ultimately based on the French reception of Bakhtin in the circle of Julia Kristeva and the *Telqueliens* (on this see Hempfer 1976, esp. 13–65), without Möllendorff being fully aware of this. Methodologically speaking, it seems naturally more advisable to explain these phenomena in terms of their own time than to derive them from postmodern and poststructuralist paradigms. On the concept of play that is fascinating to postmodern theory because of its fundamental openness, see Braungart 1996:217–218; he emphasizes that this background gets in the way of understanding the ritual implications.

[193] He touches on the area of ritual only in a footnote and refers only to Victor Turner; Möllendorff 1995:95n76.

[194] Möllendorff 1995:97.

[195] Lohr (1986:63–68) talks of the "comic fall" that he sees as characteristic of the genre, and connects this form with a regression into the state of early childhood; from the super-ego one moves rather quickly to a collective It as locale of the excluded, so that laughter is then "symbol and praxis of the earliest appropriation of the world" (65).

ally complete in their representational dance the movement from "not-I" to "not not-I." Schechner applies this scheme to all theatrical players; in the modern period the actor naturally stands in the foreground. He is thinking in particular of a modern performance, which in a certain sense comes far closer to the ritual choruses of Old Comedy than traditional theater.

The comic chorus cancels the historic split into choral leader, *khorodidaskalos*, poet, actor, and spectator at short notice in its *performance*; it always plays and dances in a role that is open to the pragmatic context. Thus when the members of the chorus appear as birds in Aristophanes' comedy of the same name, they take on, like children in a game or in ritual begging-processions, parts of the "not-I" (the bird) by means of costume and mask, without completely losing their "I." The performed bird becomes partly "I," and the performer speaks in this voice in the choral "I," but in so doing never quite gives up the "not-I" quality. The bird is thus simultaneously "not-I" and "not not-I," since behind the role of the bird the voice of the actually performing "I" filters through. This complex and paradoxical process of restaging a phylogenetically and ontogenetically early phase distinguishes the comic choral group. Like a child, each individual dances and plays while being conscious that he is at the same time someone else. Every playground, the orchestra or the χορός, where children or ritual choruses perform, is thus a place where the individual or collective identity is put into question and is continually created anew. The chorus of ritual, which dances at particular festivals, is in a certain sense the cultural institutionalization of child's play. From playful choral movements there finally arises the large-scale play of drama, which is founded wholly on an original mimesis and in its turn incorporates ritual elements from the real world.

To put it pithily, and to adapt the famous titles of the works of Johan Huizinga and Walter Burkert: in comedy, man is *homo ludens*, and in tragedy *homo necans*. The character of play and the dissolution of all temporal and spatial relations is really much more observable in comedy than in tragedy.[196] The

---

[196] In tragedy, as in comedy, the world in the actual plot is distorted in a Dionysiac fashion. In tragedy the point of view tends to be from above, from the sublime. Death and suffering in a royal family determine the story. In keeping with the tragic plot, sacrifice and ritual in general are mostly perverted into the horrific. The chorus of the community is seldom, however, directly involved in these gruesome acts. For example, the external ritual that constitutes sacrifice is distorted in such a way that a human being is torn apart in horrific fashion. In comedy, by contrast, the deformation takes place when figures are drawn down into the ridiculous and the grotesque. In this the chorus also plays a distinct part, even if it does not attain the comic dimensions of the actors. See on this Brelich (1975:111–112), who follows Arist. *Poet.* 1448a and 1449a (cf. also Plat. *Leg.* 814e) in associating tragedy with the superhuman and comedy with the subhuman. For the ritual and pragmatic poetics of the comic genre see now Bierl 2002a.

most important and original element for play is the chorus, which as it dances and plays constantly enters into contact with the audience, involves it in its game, and thus makes it become a potential fellow-player. Often the comic chorus refers quite explicitly to its own exuberant activity. This occurs most clearly in Aristophanes in the *parodos* of the chorus of initiates in the *Frogs*. Constant references are made to παίζειν and χορεύειν. It is in a certain sense the chorus' fundamental job to dance joyfully. The chorus' references to itself happen in a wonderful blending of two levels, that of the "player" in its function as ritual dancer in the orchestra, and that of the fictional performer in its role. They cannot be as neatly separated as Kenneth Dover in exemplary fashion tried to do.[197] It is the property of play to dynamize ways of perception and to make them become one. Fusion is ultimately achieved by the double ritual dimension; the ritual of the choruses of initiates in the plot in honor of the dance gods Demeter and Iakkhos is reflected in the Dionysiac chorus of the here and now. Both gods are called upon to watch over the dance and the choral performance (παῖσαί τε καὶ χορεῦσαι, *Frogs* 388; and παίζειν τε καὶ χορεύειν, *Frogs* 407b), both in the here and in the there.[198]

As in far eastern cultures, the gods enjoy entertainment and dance, and function as guarantors of a playful attitude to the world. Play does not have to be separated from everyday life by a clearly marked context, but for the Greeks extended in many ways into everyday experience. Delight at choral dancing and at mimesis are among their specific forms of expression. With comedy, on the other hand, a period of exception is certainly signaled in the Dionysiac context of the Great Dionysia and the Lenaia. As Gregory Bateson emphasizes, by means of the keyword παίζειν both spectator and participant in our passage receive the metacommunicative signal "This is a game," which introduces and sustains an experience of liminality in terms of Victor Turner's theory. It is only with the periodically determined complex of the ritual frame that the transitional phase comes to its end.[199]

[197] Dover 1993 and Dover, *Frogs*, 58–60. On dance, particularly round dance and figure dance as "the purest and most perfect form of play," see Huizinga 1955:188–189: "The connexions between playing and dancing are so close that they hardly need illustrating. It is not that dancing has something of play in it or about it, rather that is is an integral part of play: the relationship is one of direct participation, almost of essential identity. Dancing is a particular and particularly perfect form of playing."

[198] After the delivery of this choral *Leitmotiv*, Xanthias (or Dionysus; cf. Dover, *Frogs*, 247) also wants to παίζων χορεύειν (Ar. *Ran.* 415).

[199] See above, n189. The transitional phase in van Gennep's three-phase model, Turner's experience of liminality, and Bakhtin's concept of the carnivalesque correspond to this period of inversion or play. Lonsdale 1993:36–37 connects the playful and musical element in the reenactment in an agonistic context of an animal existence with the ritual activities of sacrifice and hunting.

According to Plato's *Laws*, comic, ecstatic, and bacchic dances and choruses represent a kind of exception and a deviation from the positive norm. In contrast to the other peaceful and warlike choral dance songs that by virtue of mimesis positively educate society in the values of the polis and that contribute to the maintenance of existing hierarchies and order, the obscenely sexual movements of the former transgress the values of civilized society.[200] Therefore these ridiculous and vulgar dance steps must not be carried out by full citizens—the mimetic embodiment of the ugly would in itself of course corrupt the citizens—but should be reserved for slaves and foreign professional performers. Citizens are of course advised to at least view these antidances and become acquainted with them as an alternative program to the code of respectable behavior (*Laws* 816d–e).

The practice of comedy in the fifth century is in contravention of Plato's moral and educational thought: the citizens put on a comic and grotesque chorus in which they often take on the shape of primitive and uncivilized creatures. The entire polis enters into a state of the ridiculous and the other and takes part in the ritual of inversion staged by fellow citizens, subsequently finding their way back to civilization in a somewhat purified state. Nevertheless, it emerges from the following discussion of the *Thesmophoriazusae* that the comic chorus not only constructs an anti-structure, but also in large part integrates the polis' cult of the gods and thereby has a simultaneously stabilizing effect. This happens among other reasons because positive dances, like the *pyrrhikhê*, that belong to the polis order are embedded as social reality in the chorus. Comic dissolution lies not outside but within the polis and its ritual practices, because these dances represent the marginal period of the youth during initiation.

Ritual Role

Finally, the comic chorus is especially comprehensible as ritual because of its structure. It usually devises metaphors against the background of which a plot can be expanded. In the time of Aristophanes, comedy is such a thematically rich field that it cannot be reduced to one fundamental scheme. One should

---

[200] Plato (*Leg.* 814e) makes a distinction in the case of dances that represent more beautiful bodies in a worthy fashion and uglier ones in a common fashion. He subdivides the first, serious group in turn into a peaceful and a warlike ὄρχησις. In the latter negative category he seems to include bacchic and other dances in which the performers undergo purifications and initiations while imitating drunken nymphs, Pans, Silenoi, and satyrs (815c). However, Plato does not explain what he means by this group, given his strict binary division. On *khoreia* and tribal initiation rites in Plato's educational theory, see Calame 1999b, esp. 299–307.

75

remember here its political, fantastic, and myth-parodying form. Even in political comedy, so important for Aristophanes, the chorus often comprises assemblages that either explicitly represent a ritual community or can be associated with such, such as groups of primeval gods and heroes or the famous animal choruses. First of all, one should recall comedies like Aristophanes' *Thesmophoriazusae* or *Frogs*, in which the action is set in a ritual context, namely the festival of the Thesmophoria and the celebration of the Eleusinian mysteries. Both the women who withdraw to the Pnyx from the men during the Thesmophoria and the initiates in the underworld show the ritual background on which the comic plot builds. Wherever sacred ceremonies are encountered in Greece there is most often dancing.[201] With the help of such ritual roles the chorus can thus very easily link reflexive references to its own performative action. The coincidence of role and function is thus guaranteed. Depending on the perspective, either of the two dimensions can move into the field of view to a greater or lesser extent. The festival creates an occasion, a "ritual within ritual" so to speak, on which the obligatory dances in honor of Dionysus can be held. Joyful and ecstatic choruses especially lend themselves to this, in honor of Dionysus first and foremost, but also Demeter and other gods who are associated with boisterous, chiefly agrarian festivals.[202]

Old Comedy also has a preference for composing its chorus from mythical and primordial groups of gods and heroes. Satyrs are here particularly favored, and have a similar ritual role in the related satyr play. Like their female counterparts, the maenads, they belong to the closest retinue of Dionysus, into whose cultic domain ritual dance in particular falls.[203] Among others may be mentioned Myrtilos' *Titanopanes* (Τιτανόπανες, *PCG* VII, 30–31), Cratinus' *Ploutoi* (Πλοῦτοι, *PCG* IV, 204ff.) and *Kheirones* (Χείρωνες, *PCG* IV, 245ff.), the *Heroes* (Ἥρωες) of Aristophanes (*PCG* III.2, 173ff.), Khionides (*PCG* IV, 72–73), Krates (*PCG* IV, 88ff.), Timokles (*PCG* VII, 764ff.), and Philemon (*PCG*

---

[201] See Osborne 1993, who treats festivals together with dramatic and musical competitions.

[202] Further ritual groups are represented among others by Philippides' *Women Celebrating the Adonia* (Ἀδωνιάζουσαι, *PCG* VII, 336–337) (the *Lysistrata* had this title in antiquity; see schol. *Lys.* 389), Aristophanes' *Banqueters* (Δαιταλῆς, *PCG* III.2, 122ff.) and Σκηνὰς καταλαμβάνουσαι (*PCG* III.2, 257ff.), Cratinus' *Delian Women* (Δηλιάδες, *PCG* IV, 134ff.) and Εὐνεῖδαι (*PCG* IV, 157–158), Phrynikhos' *Comasts* (Κωμασταί, *PCG* VII, 401ff.) and *Initiates* (Μύσται, *PCG* VII, 411–412); Plato com. composed *Women from the Rites* (Αἱ ἀφ' ἱερῶν, *PCG* VII, 436ff.) and Timokles the *Women Celebrating the Dionysia* (Διονυσιάζουσαι, *PCG* VII, 758–759), which may also be included in this category.

[203] Cf. inter alia the Σάτυροι of Cratinus (*PCG* IV, 232) and Kallias (*PCG* IV, 49), the Δημοσάτυροι and the Ἰκάριοι Σάτυροι of Timokles (*PCG* VII, 757–758 and 766ff.) and the Βάκχαι of Diokles (*PCG* V, 18–19) and Lysippos (*PCG* V, 618ff.). Extant tragedy can only produce the *Bacchae* of Euripides as an example. The Erinyes also function in a similarly ritual fashion in Aeschylus' *Eumenides*.

VII, 243), the *Centaurs* (Κένταυροι) of Apollophanes (*PCG* II, 520), the *Sirens* (Σειρῆνες) of Theopompos (*PCG* VII, 732–733) and Nikophon (*PCG* VII, 70–71), the *Amazons* (Ἀμαζόνες) of Kephisodoros (*PCG* IV, 63–64) and Epikrates (*PCG* V, 153), and Kallias' *Cyclopes* (Κύκλωπες, *PCG* IV, 42ff.). Their wild, primeval nature is brought onto the stage with comic and ecstatic gesticulation, so that here too *performance* can easily be brought into harmony with role. Song, equally important for the chorus, can be particularly well displayed with choruses of Sirens and Muses.[204]

Animal choruses are particularly characteristic of Old Comedy.[205] Numerous cultures have rites in which humans theatrically change into animals and perform choral dances. As lifeforms fundamentally different from humans, but which at the same time because of their close coexistence are quite near, animals are particularly well suited to reflect in playful fashion on important ideological relations in society, such as hierarchies and cosmogonies, and to stage them symbolically and expressively.[206] By means of projection onto the completely "other"—in Attic drama, as is well known, Dionysus himself represents this on the divine level—the polis is thus able to reflect on its values and norms. With the appearance of the animal other, which however at the same time confusingly resembles the self, namely the citizens of Attica, an inverted world comes to power for the duration of the comic play within the context of the festival of inversion. Significantly, the Dionysiac satyrs, Cratinus' *Cheirones* (Χείρωνες, *PCG* IV, 245ff.), Apollophanes' *Centaurs* (Κένταυροι, *PCG* II, 520), the

---

[204] Cf. the *Sirens* of Theopompos (Σειρῆνες, *PCG* VII, 732–733) and Nikophon (*PCG* VII, 70–71) and the *Muses* of Phrynikhos (Μοῦσαι, *PCG* VII, 409ff.).

[205] Cf. the following comedies with animal choruses: Magnes: *Frogs* (Βάτραχοι, *PCG* V, 628), *Birds* (Ὄρνιθες, *PCG* V, 630), *Gall Wasps* (Ψῆνες, *PCG* V, 631); Krates: *Beasts* (Θηρία, *PCG* IV, 91ff.); Krates II: *Birds* (Ὄρνιθες, *PCG* IV, 111); Pherekrates: *Ant Men* (Μυρμηκάνθρωποι, *PCG* VII, 161ff.); Eupolis: *Goats* (Αἶγες, *PCG* V, 302ff.); Aristophanes: *Wasps* (Σφῆκες), *Birds* (Ὄρνιθες), *Frogs* (Βάτραχοι), *Storks* (Πελαργοί, *PCG* III.2, 239ff.); Plato com.: *Griffins* (Γρῦπες, *PCG* VII, 438–439), *Ants* (Μύρμηκες, *PCG* VII, 468); Arkhippos: *Fish* (Ἰχθύες, *PCG* II, 542ff.); Kallias: *Frogs* (Βάτραχοι, *PCG* IV, 42); Kantharos: *Nightingales* (Ἀηδόνες, *PCG* IV, 57), *Ants* (Μύρμηκες, *PCG* IV, 59); Diokles: *Bees* (Μέλιτται, *PCG* V, 20ff.); according to Sifakis, Anaxilas' *Circe* (Κίρκη, *PCG* II, 282–283) should also be counted here, the chorus of which was made up of the companions of Odysseus who were turned into pigs. Perhaps they only imitated the animals, as in the parodos of Aristophanes' *Wealth*. Chorus members who ride horses or other animals played by other members of the chorus in costume in a way typical of comedy form an ambiguous unit that falls both under the category of animals as well as military formation: cf. the *Knights* (Ἱππεῖς) of Aristophanes and Antiphanes (*PCG* II, 368–369); further, the mounted *Amazons* (Ἀμαζόνες) of Kephisodoros (*PCG* IV, 63–64) and Epikrates (*PCG* V, 153). See in general Sifakis 1971:71–102 ("Animal Choruses"), esp. 76–77 and now Rothwell 2006.

[206] Cf. Tambiah 1985:169–211 ("Animals are Good to Think and Good to Prohibit") and Sperber 1996.

Sirens (Σειρῆνες) of Theopompos (*PCG* VII, 732–733) and Nikophon (*PCG* VII, 70–71), the *Titanopanes* (Τιτανόπανες) of Myrtilos (*PCG* VII, 30–31), or the *Ant Men* (Μυρμηκάνθρωποι) of Pherekrates (*PCG* VII, 161ff.) all present hybrid creatures that transcend the important categorical boundaries between god, human, and animal. It is precisely with the help of their ritual dance that the Attic audience is able to experience the distorted world order and the return of primitive conditions in an extremely lively fashion and on a nonverbal level. Against this background of the inverted world the use of barbarians, even women, for the comic choral role becomes understandable.[207]

Animal choruses appear quite early on vase paintings, and it is therefore likely that these choruses may already be connected at a very early stage with the evolution of Old Comedy.[208] Animals, like the comic chorus composed of twenty-four members, often represent a kind of social formation and so serve as metaphors for the communal life of humans in society. Their vital energy, which they also share with Dionysus and his retinue and other creatures from a primitive past—not coincidentally, wild animals such as panthers, deer, and goats are also found in his circle—expresses itself in wild jumps. On the comic stage this energy is artistically transformed into choral dance. Their group and herd formations and coordinated movements make many animals ideal projection surfaces onto which the human chorus can transfer its ritual activity. Fish and birds are prominent in this respect. In particular, the formation of accompanying dolphins is a favorite image in choral culture, as also in dithyrambs. Here one may recall the myth of the *Homeric Hymn to Dionysus*, in which the

---

[207] Particular ethnic groups are shown, for example by the *Egyptians, Babylonians, Carians,* and *Lydians*; see among others Magnes' *Lydians* (Λυδοί, *PCG* V, 629–630), Khionides' *Persians or Assyrians* (Πέρσαι ἢ Ἀσσύριοι, *PCG* IV, 73), Cratinus' *Thracian Women* (Θρᾷτται, *PCG* IV, 159ff.), and the *Persians* (Πέρσαι) of Pherekrates (*PCG* VII, 167ff.). See also Pherekrates' *Wild Men* (Ἄγριοι, *PCG* VII, 106ff.). Consider also the play on internal Greek prejudices in comedies such as Krates' *Samians* (Σάμιοι, *PCG* IV, 101ff.) and the *Spartans* (Λάκωνες) of Eupolis (*PCG* V, 398–399), Plato com. (Λάκωνες ἢ Ποιηταί, *PCG* VII, 460ff.), and Nikokhares (*PCG* VII, 45).

A subsequent stage of development could have been the transfer of the role of the comic chorus to personified objects and conditions; cf. Eupolis' *Cities* (Πόλεις, *PCG* V, 424ff.) and *Demes* (Δῆμοι, *PCG* V, 342ff.), the *Islands* (Νῆσοι) of Aristophanes (*PCG* III.2, 220ff.) and Plato com. (Ἑλλάς ἢ Νῆσοι, *PCG* VII, 440ff.) and the *Festivals* (Ἑορταί) of Plato com. (*PCG* VII, 443ff.; here ritual is of particular importance; for personified objects cf. e.g. the *Freighters* (Ὁλκάδες) of Aristophanes (*PCG* III.2, 226ff.). Here too the interchange between leader and company is important.

[208] See the overview of attempts at explaining animal choruses in Sifakis 1971:78–85; the interpretation I choose to follow here relies on ritual and symbol. For the principle of the alternate world that the different roles of the chorus present in variation, see also Seeberg 1995, who advocates the hypothesis that animals and other groups are only a secondary development and a replacement of the originally comastic choruses of potbellied dancers; they will have represented initial mimetic and plot elements in comedy (7).

pirates, who want to kidnap the god, are transformed into dolphins and then like a chorus follow the ship, as is shown on the Exekias cup (Munich 2044). The chorus of Euripides' *Helen*, for example, in the final, *propemptikon*-like song (*Hel.* 1451–1511) project their dancing successively onto dolphins and birds. On early vases armed warriors or Amazons are depicted riding on dolphins and peacocks. Dolphins as well as birds are closely connected with the Dionysiac and the musical and choral sphere. Both animals are equipped with a musical voice; a leader coordinates their group. In exactly the same way the chorus also pays attention to the lead dancer and the chorus leader and keeps in step with the music of the *aulos* player. The wings of the bird represent a metaphor for the lively and ecstatic dance in honor of Dionysus.

Further role vehicles for the comic chorus are military units, such as the *Knights* of Aristophanes.[209] Like the famous peacock and dolphin riders depicted on vases, they must also obey musical signals as a collective and follow the orders of a superior.[210] As in other ritual groups, in military formations defined segments and age classes of the whole population play a role. It is important for our topic that military display and fighting in formation were generally in antiquity very closely associated with ritual modes of behavior.[211] The famous weapon dances, in particular the *pyrrhikhê*, testify to the connection between ritual and military practice.[212] A fragment of Socrates (fr. 3 W.) cited in Athenaeus (628f) demonstrates this association quite beautifully: "Those who honor the gods most splendidly with choruses are the best in war" (οἳ δὲ χοροῖς κάλλιστα θεοὺς τιμῶσιν, ἄριστοι ἐν πολέμῳ). Athenaeus advances the explanation that the art of choral dance is practically compa-

---

[209] The following titles with connections to military groups are attested: there are the *Knights* (Ἱππεῖς) of Aristophanes and Antiphanes (*PCG* II, 368–369); Eupolis wrote a comedy called the *Squadron Leaders* (Ταξίαρχοι, *PCG* V, 452ff.), Telekleides (*PCG* VII, 681) and Hermippos (*PCG* V, 585ff.) composed plays called the *Soldiers* (Στρατιῶται); Hermippos' chorus members typically often seem to have an effeminate nature; hence his play was also possibly entitled the *Female Soldiers* (Στρατιώτιδες); Theopompos (*PCG* VII, 733ff.) also wrote a piece with the latter title; the plot seems to have been similar to that of Aristophanes' *Lysistrata*. The *Amazons* (Ἀμαζόνες) of Kephisodoros (*PCG* IV, 63–64) and Epikrates (*PCG* V, 153) also belong here.

[210] See the black-figure skyphos in the Boston Museum of Fine Arts 20.18 (ca. 480 BCE) (dolphin riders: Sifakis 1971, fig. 2; peacock riders: Pickard-Cambridge 1962, fig. 8b, Sifakis 1971, figs. 3 and 4) and the red-figure psykter by Oltos, New York, Norbert Schimmel Collection (ca. 520–510 BCE) (dolphin riders: Sifakis 1971, fig. 5). See also the riders seated on men dressed as horses on the famous Berlin amphora, Berlin 1697, Antikensammlung (ca. 550 BCE) (Pickard-Cambridge 1962, fig. 7 and Sifakis 1971, fig. 1).

[211] For archaic warfare as ritual activity, see Connor 1988a.

[212] On Greek weapon dances see Delavaud-Roux 1993; on the *pyrrhikhê* see Ceccarelli 1998 and my discussion below, pp. 207–217. On the connection between weapon dance and war, see Ceccarelli 1998:19–20.

rable with military drill, since both represent a demonstration of discipline in general, but also of control over one's body in particular.[213]

Comic soldiers of this type often appear as effeminate comasts; or conversely, women reach for weapons, like the mythical Amazons, to threaten the male order. The notion of the inverted world is expressed in this inbetween stage in which gender roles and other identity-bestowing characteristics are found next to each other without any distinction. This marginal counterworld can also be symbolically underscored by connecting it, for example, with a grotesque animal world. Young people who are not yet completely initiated are often connected with animals. They still jump around, wild and free, before being tamed and taken into the adult class. All comic distortions aside, a real-life dimension continues to be preserved in these dramatic roles too. The notion of the inbetween is thus also reflected in the combination of the communicative levels of plot and *énonciation*. In the example of the dolphin and peacock riders, despite all the reversals, the warrior component refers to the polis and its military institutions. The chorus and the *performance* in the chorus represent the element that connects them. It is the public place for social transitions. Here the two modes of communication are fused into their ambivalent and shifting unity. Beside the staging of a counterworld in the fictional role, which in its turn assimilates social practices, a new role identity as full citizens is created at the same time through dance and song in the transition. In the theater the chorus also dances and sings in its function as representative of its polis in honor of the gods, who ensure life in the city. The dissolution and the foundation of order stand dialectically side by side both in the plot and in the real-world context, and characterize the bewildering comic play.

Among other things the members of the chorus in their performance reactualize the initiatory transition from youth to hoplite status. As with comedy in general, this condition of marginality is characterized by a mixing and distortion of all practices of signification. The same thing occurs with the real-world weapon dance, the *pyrrhikhê*. The participants transport themselves back to the position of children (παῖδες) and symbolically become animals. The expressive side of this process is the dance. They move as is appropriate for children (παίζουσιν), they "play," hop, and jump like young, untamed animals.[214]

---

[213] Athen. 628f: Σχεδὸν γὰρ ὥσπερ ἐξοπλισία τις ἦν ἡ χορεία καὶ ἐπίδειξις οὐ μόνον τῆς λοιπῆς εὐταξίας, ἀλλὰ καὶ τῆς σωμάτων ἐπιμελείας.

[214] The verbs σκιρτάω, πηδάω, and ἄλλομαι are typically used to describe the chorus' dance movements in comedy and satyr play. Cf. also Naerebout 1997:281–282. They are characteristic of wild animals as well as maenads and satyrs.

The real-world chorus is thus the privileged locus of initiates. On a physical level, in the ritual dance and play they experience a social shaping that expresses itself in particular in gender role identity. Comedy assimilates in a joking form these critical transitions in particular. Naturally the paradigms of agricultural and new year festivals, at which choral dancing likewise takes place, are also transferable to comic choruses. The brief approach toward the other and the temporary dissolution of order make the world appear all the more stable when the period of reversal comes to an end. In the comic leap back to primordial days, the members of the chorus and the polis celebrating alongside them represent diverse phenomena of marginality; particularly in the reexperience of archaic initiation rituals, the polis gives expression to its tensions under the auspices of Dionysus, examines the current order, and after dissolving it, mentally reconstructs it.

According to a division that probably goes back to Aristoxenos, Athenaeus combines the choruses of the three dramatic genres with nontheatrical lyric dance forms. He compares the solemn *emmeleia* of tragedy with the *gymnopaidikê*, while the *pyrrhikhê*, because of its quick steps, is brought into schematic connection with the *sikinnis*, the dance of the satyr play, and the hyporcheme with the comic *kordax*.[215] Elsewhere, however, the *pyrrhikhê* is connected with the choral lyric genre of the hyporcheme.[216] The relations

---

[215] Aristoxenos fr. 103 Wehrli = Athen. 630c–e; cf. also Aristoxenos fr. 104–106 Wehrli. On this see Ceccarelli 1998:214 and 222–224. According to Aristoxenos (fr. 108 Wehrli) there was a kind of curriculum that led from the dances of boys in *gymnopaidikê* and *pyrrhikhê* all the way to choral dance in drama (= Athen. 631c): "Aristoxenos says that the ancients began first with the training of the *gymnopaidikê*, then moved to the *pyrrhikhê* before entering into the theater [πρὸ τοῦ εἰσιέναι εἰς τὸ θέατρον]." It comes as no surprise, then, that the two forms should be reflected in theatrical choral practice. Immediately before this passage Athenaeus reports (631b) that one should view the oskhophoric and bacchic forms as variation of *gymnopaidikê*. The Gymnopaidia, Oskhophoria, and the *pyrrhikhê* are connected everywhere in the Greek world with male puberty initiation. For dances at the Spartan Gymnopaidia in this social context, see below, chap. 1, n418; for the Athenian Oskhophoria, see Jeanmaire 1939:344–363, Brelich 1969:444–445, Calame I 1977:228–232 (Engl. trans. Calame 1997:125–128); naturally this no longer has anything to do with a classic three-phase initiation ritual (cf. Calame 1990:432–435); rather, the acceptance of youths into the society of men is celebrated in a ritual fashion and mixed with elements of fertility. As bearers of *oskhoi* (vine-branches) the young men display their readiness and are seen as bringers of agricultural and general welfare, symbolized in the branch. In Athenaeus (495ef) there is a fragment from Aristodemos' commentary on Pindar (*FGrHist* 383 F 9) in which we find a report of an ephebic running contest of the Oskhophoroi that took place at the Skira(?), but that probably happened at this festival (cf. Proclus *Chrest. ap. Phot. Bibl.* 322a13–30 [= 87–92 Severyns]); the winner received the pentaploa cup with the five elementary foods and celebrated with a *kômos* and chorus (κωμάζει μετὰ χοροῦ). This is clearly reminiscent of the *kômos* processions from which comedy developed. The comic chorus thus reactualizes these kinds of initiatory rituals in dance and song.

[216] See among others the scholia to Pind. *Pyth.* 2.127 and Athen. 631c.

between satyr play and comedy seem somewhat arbitrary and forced.[217] But they do confirm our conclusions: the comic chorus comes fairly close to the chorus of the satyr play. Both, like the hyporcheme, were especially marked by rapid mimetic movements with a performatively sung verbal accompaniment. While the tragic choral song comments, advises, analyzes, and narrates with its solemn step and serious tone, the chorus of the other genres is more active. In delivering its songs it does something: it searches, it runs, it hunts, it pursues, it flees, it curses, and it jumps and dances. But as soon as the tragic chorus lays aside its usual attitude and resorts to its very own dance, in the so-called hyporcheme it resembles the other two genres very closely.[218]

This barely plot-related, transversal form of discourse that transgresses the boundaries of the plot in the direction of the actual *performance* and the here and now is characteristic of ritual. We will likewise clarify the connotations of the highly mimetic weapon dance in the comic reflexes of initation rituals. In chapter 1, these connections will be examined using the *Thesmophoriazusae* as example. In chapter 2, our examination of choral culture will be expanded in a discussion of the Hellenistic songs of the Ithyphalloi and Phallophoroi, which are often referred to for questions of origin. All in all, the aim is to illustrate the clear rituality of these texts in as many different shades as possible with reference their linguistic structure as well.

---

[217] Cf. Wehrli 1945:81–83.

[218] For the hyporcheme see among others Diehl 1914 and Koller 1954:166–173. A precise definition of the genre is actually impossible. That which is characteristic of the hyporcheme, mimetic dance with performative verbal accompaniment as speech act, is typical of all choral genres of ritual, whether paeans, dithyrambs, or the like. Hence Wilamowitz (I 1895²:77) says of the hyporcheme: "Es ist ein schlechter Name; denn Tanzlieder sind sie ja alle" ["It is a bad name, for they are all dance songs"]. The classification is thus a scholarly act *post festum*. Originally, however, the occasion of the performance formed the sole generic criterion; Nagy 1994/95a. The boundaries between the hyporcheme and the *pyrrhikhê* and the *sikinnis* are open, because there were many dances that represented military practices, the pursuit of the enemy, and, projected onto the animal level, the hunt from the perspective of the hunters and the hunted. Cf. the explanation for the equation of *pyrrhikhê* and satyr dance in Athenaeus (630d): ἀμφότεραι γὰρ διὰ τάχους. πολεμικὴ δὲ δοκεῖ εἶναι ἡ πυρρίχη· ἔνοπλοι γὰρ αὐτὴν παῖδες ὀρχοῦνται. τάχους δὲ δεῖ τῷ πολέμῳ εἰς τὸ διώκειν καὶ εἰς τὸ ἡττωμένους "φεύγειν μηδὲ μένειν μηδ' αἰδεῖσθαι κακοὺς εἶναι" ["Both are fast dances. The *pyrrhikhê* seems to be a war dance, because youths dance it while bearing arms. Speed is needed in war for pursuit and for those defeated to 'flee and neither hold their position nor be ashamed to be cowardly'"]. Athenaeus ironically quotes the response of the Delphic oracle to Kroisos that he should flee as soon as a mule becomes king of the Persians (Hdt. 1.55.2), making an implicit reference to the animal role of the chorus in satyr plays and of many other ritual choruses.

Chapter 1

The Comic Chorus in the *Thesmophoriazusae* of Aristophanes

USING THE APPROACH DEMONSTRATED IN THE INTRODUCTION I should now like to analyze the *Thesmophoriazusae*, a work that has been relatively little discussed. This comedy is particularly well-suited for showing the non-.ristotelian, pre-dramatic, and ritual character of the comic chorus. The delib-rate, "ulterior" plot, or *sujet,* is not only overlaid by comic episodes on the part f the actors, but in particular by appearances of the chorus that make exten-ive reference to the pragmatic context and give way to an almost unbroken resence. Several songs appear to interrupt the action and deviate from it. ult, prayer, and dance are practically self-standing and are only very loosely onnected with the events of the plot. The utterances of the chorus are at the ame time independent actions in the here and now that support the polis cult.

As a point of departure I have selected the unusual dance song (947–1000) hat takes place almost completely in *énonciation*. The presentation of a choral pectacle for the pleasure of the gods and the spectators appears almost to tand independently and outside the plot. Because of its concentration on he actual activity of dancing and worship, this song is particularly suited to .lustrating the concepts of the performative and self-description as funda-1ental structural elements of a living ritual choral culture. In the course of 1y discussion it will be important to distinguish between the dramatic role of he members of the chorus in the fiction of the plot and their cultic and comic unction as actual actors. Particular attention will be given to the parabatic, hat is, the turning of the chorus toward the audience in the sense of a ritual tterance that partially transcends the events of the plot.

We will then feel our way forward from this central point to the end and rom there to the beginning in order to illustrate comprehensively the ritual .ature of the choral utterances in this comedy. From looking at the purely erformative as something that breaks up the plot we will carefully proceed to he chorus' simultaneously present function as supporter of the plot. My study hus focuses on the interdependence of the plot-bearing and plot-interrupting lements in the choral sections. The self-contained elements, directed at the rame of the here and now, are in a relationship of constant interchange with those elements that carry the plot, and in the performative form a kind of intersection. Depending on the predisposition of the observer, either the here of the actual ritual occasion or the there of the mimetic world being created will come more into the field of vision. The comic performance contains both perspectives, which were clearly simultaneously present for the original recipient.

The actual comic plot is at the same time only a vehicle or frame on which a complete, self-sufficient spectacle of laughter, dancing, and festivity is staged in the center of the polis. Within the simple events of the plot, which themselves developed from cultic and traditional celebrations and are wholly based on this real-world occasion, the troupe continually finds an opportunity to pass beyond the boundaries of plot in the direction of the actual and their simple role in the present.

The ritual nature of the comic chorus is to be found on both levels. The prayers, hymns, dances, and singing in the Dionysiac celebration that forms the occasion are just as much ritual expression as the reenactment of the festival of Demeter. From general and obvious forms of cult we will look at the progression of the dramatic events in various ways. All choral utterances, except those that are found in the *amoibaion*, or lyric interchange between characters and chorus, will be discussed. In focusing on the exchange between comic speeches and choral performance, we will finally arrive at a completely new ritual interpretation. The songs that appear at first glance almost independent and disruptive of the action on stage do in fact in subtle ways play a role in the development of the plot, which follows the ritual model of initiation of the youth into adult status.

The Chorus in Cultic Dance Song (*Thesm.* 947–1000) between Fictional Role and Comic Function: Ritual, Dance, Performance

Using the hymnic choral song at *Thesm.* 947–1000 as an example, I will show how a comic chorus refers to its own activity in the orchestra in a way that is characteristic of ritual. In scholarly literature this has generally been treated in a rather stepmotherly fashion purely as a choral song that interrupts the progress of the dramatic action.[1] From the point of view of the Aristotelian

---

[1] The best and most thorough interpretations of this song come from Thomsen 1973 and Zimmermann II 1985:191–200. Cf. also Parker 1997:428–437 (mainly on metre with some observations on the text). On the religious background of the *Thesmophoriazusae*, cf. Habash 1997, who also discusses the choral parts, although in a substantially briefer fashion. On this exclusive choral dance passage, cf. *ibid.*, 33–36. Cf. now Furley/Bremer I 2001:357–360, Furley/

tradition, this type of digression is to a certain extent thought of as something inferior. For this reason, the text has often been discussed merely as an instance of Greek choral art. Hardly anybody has appreciated these lines as an independent ritual performance that despite being the evocation of a living choral culture has been merged into the action of the plot in a meaningful way. What has been criticized as insufficiently lofty style and lack of reflection in content can be explained precisely by its ritual character, which is typical of the choral lyric of Old Comedy.

The members of the chorus sing the following song in the middle of the paratragic scenes between the *Helen* and *Andromeda* stratagems. Words in the text that refer to the fictional context of the play have been tentatively indicated in italics, while deictic references to the performance in the here and now—here the ritual activity of dancing stands at the center—have been underlined.

<u>ἄγε νυν</u> ἡμεῖς <u>παίσωμεν</u> *ἅπερ νόμος ἐνθάδε ταῖσι γυναιξίν*,   947
ὅταν ὄργια σεμνὰ θεοῖν ἱεραῖς ὥραις ἀνέχωμεν, ἅπερ καὶ
Παύσων σέβεται καὶ νηστεύει,
πολλάκις αὐτοῖν ἐκ τῶν ὡρῶν   950
εἰς τὰς ὥρας ξυνεπευχόμενος
τοιαῦτα μέλειν θάμ' ἑαυτῷ.

<u>ὅρμα χώρει,</u>   953
<u>κοῦφα ποσὶν ἄγ' εἰς κύκλον,</u>
<u>χειρὶ σύναπτε χεῖρα, ῥυθ-</u>   955a
<u>μὸν χορείας</u> ὕπαγε πᾶσα.   b
<u>βαῖνε καρπαλίμοιν ποδοῖν,</u>
ἐπισκοπεῖν δὲ πανταχῆ
<u>κυκλοῦσαν</u> ὄμμα χρὴ <u>χοροῦ κατάστασιν.</u>   958

ἅμα δὲ καὶ
γένος Ὀλυμπίων θεῶν   960
<u>μέλπε</u> καὶ <u>γέραιρε φωνῇ</u> πᾶσα <u>χορομανεῖ τρόπῳ.</u>

εἰ δέ τις
προσδοκᾷ κακῶς ἐρεῖν
ἐν ἱερῷ γυναῖκά μ' οὖσαν ἄνδρας, οὐκ ὀρθῶς φρονεῖ.   964/65

ἀλλὰ χρῆν

Bremer II 2001:350–359, and the new commentaries by Prato, 306–311 and Austin/Olson, 298–308 *ad* 947–1000.

ὥσπερ ἔργον αὖ τι καινὸν
πρῶτον εὐκύκλου χορείας εὐφυᾶ στῆσαι βάσιν.

πρόβαινε ποσὶ τὸν Εὐλύραν
μέλπουσα καὶ τὴν τοξοφόρον   970
Ἄρτεμιν, ἄνασσαν ἁγνήν.
χαῖρ᾽, ὦ Ἑκάεργε,   972a
ὄπαζε δὲ νίκην,   b
Ἥραν τε τὴν τελείαν
μέλψωμεν ὥσπερ εἰκός,
ἣ πᾶσι τοῖς χοροῖσι συμπαίζει τε καὶ   975
κλῇδας γάμου φυλάττει.

Ἑρμῆν τε νόμιον ἄντομαι
καὶ Πᾶνα καὶ Νύμφας φίλας
ἐπιγελάσαι προθύμως
ταῖς ἡμετέραισι   980a
χαρέντα χορείαις.   b
ἔξαιρε δὴ προθύμως
διπλῆν χάριν χορείας.
παίσωμεν, ὦ γυναῖκες, οἷάπερ νόμος·
νηστεύομεν δὲ πάντως.

ἀλλ᾽ εἶα, πάλλ᾽, ἀνάστρεφ᾽ εὐρύθμῳ ποδί·   985
τόρνευε πᾶσαν ᾠδήν.
ἡγοῦ δέ γ᾽ ὧδ᾽ αὐτὸς σύ,
κισσοφόρε Βακχεῖε
δέσποτ᾽· ἐγὼ δὲ κώμοις   988a
σὲ φιλοχόροισι μέλψω.   b

Εὔιε ὦ Διὸς σὺ   990
Βρόμιε, καὶ Σεμέλας παῖ,
χοροῖς τερπόμενος   992a
κατ᾽ ὄρεα Νυμ-   b
φᾶν ἐρατοῖσιν ὕμνοις,   993a
ὦ Εὔι᾽, Εὔι᾽, εὐοῖ,   b
‹ὦ Εὔι᾽› ἀναχορεύων.

ἀμφὶ δὲ σοὶ κτυπεῖται   995
Κιθαιρώνιος ἠχώ,
μελάμφυλλά τ᾽ ὄρη
δάσκια πετρώ-   998a

δεις τε νάπαι <u>βρέμονται·</u>　　　　　　　　　　　　　　b
<u>κύκλῳ</u> δὲ περί σε κισσὸς
εὐπέταλος <u>ἕλικι</u> θάλλει.　　　　　　　　　　　　　1000

Thesm. 947–1000

Come now, let us dance, as is the custom here for us women when we hold the revered mystery rites for the two goddesses in the holy seasons, and (that poor devil) Pauson observes the same rites and fasts as we do, (950) often praying to them with us that he too may celebrate such occasions from one year to the next.

Rise up, begin the dance, form the circle with light movements of your feet, (955) join hands with each other, let everyone take up the rhythm of the dance! Move your feet quickly! Let every eye watch over the circling array of our dance!

And let every one of you honor (960) the Olympian gods with song and with frenzied choral dance!

But if anyone thinks we as women are going to bad-mouth men in the sanctuary, (965) he is wrong.

But now we must first begin again the perfect dance-step of the beautiful round dance as if it were a new number.

Move your feet forward now and praise with dance and song the master of the lyre (970) and Artemis, bearer of the bow, chaste mistress! Hail, worker from afar, grant us victory! And let us praise Hera the matchmaker, as is fit, (975) who dances along with us in all our choruses and who keeps the keys to marriage.

And we call on Hermes, herdsman god, and Pan and the dear Nymphs, to smile on us with good will, (980) taking pleasure in our choral dancing. Lift up the double (?) charm of our choral dance! Let us dance, you women, as is the custom! But we keep to our fast strictly.

(985) Now come, leap, whirl with rhythmic foot! Turn the whole song! But you yourself be our leader, ivy-bearing Bacchic lord! And we shall honor you in dance and song in chorus-loving *kômoi*.

(990) O Euios, Bromios, son of Zeus and Semele, you who delight in choral dances and dance in chorus over the mountains to the lovely hymns of the Nymphs, o Euios, Euios, euoi, o Euios!

(995) All about you the echo from Kithairon sounds, and the dark-leafed bushy mountains and rocky glens rumble, and leafy ivy spiraling around you in a circle sprouts

Even for the skeptical reader who has become blinded by modern preconceptions it should be no problem to characterize a song like this as ritual. It has consequently always been classified in the scholarly literature as a prayer or hymn. There is no narration of myth or reflection of past or future events; rather, the chorus is totally concerned with its own ritual activity. Nevertheless, by confining themselves to the question of whether or not Aristophanes meant this as parody, scholars have long been blind to the value of these verses as an authentic expression of a living choral culture, anchored in the cultic life of the polis. The song can in fact claim to be considered as ritual in two senses. For the chorus completes a ritual act that is characteristic and constitutive of it; it sings and dances in its fictional role in the festival of the Thesmophoria as well as in its function as a company that has been appointed by the polis and that honors in a comic performance its divine patron Dionysus and other gods of the city.[2] The perspective oscillates in a way typical of comedy between this

---

[2]   On this distinction cf. already Zimmermann II 1985:192: "Auffällig ist in den beiden Hymnen-einlagen (947ff. 1136ff.) die schillernde Rolle des Chors als religiöse und politische Gemeinde der Frauen sowie als komischer Chor" ["The shimmering role of the chorus and religious and political community of women as well as comic chorus in the two hymnic interludes (947ff., 1136ff.) is remarkable"]. Following Dover, Sommerstein (*Thesm.*, 218 *ad* 947–1000) also refers to the ambivalence between function and role: "The chorus speak sometimes in their 'role' as women celebrating the Thesmophoria, sometimes in their 'function' as a chorus performing in a comedy (for these terms see K. J. Dover, *Aristophanes: Frogs* [Oxford, 1993], 57–60); the latter comes to the fore especially in 962–965, in 972, and in the choice of Dionysus (patron god of the dramatic festival) as sole addressee of the final section of the hymn." Cf. also already Horn 1970:117. On the distinction between figure and role on the level of actor, see Flashar 1996:86–87, who sets out the important differences from comedy in terms of the so-called suspension of plot using literary theory that proceeds on the premiss of the closed plot. According to the latter, it is not the "licence of the suspension of plot" in order to draw in the audience that is important, but the open manner of perception in ritual play, which is directed at an *identification*: "Das Herstellen der Identifikationsebene ist jedenfalls das primäre; am Anfang stand nicht die geschlossene Form des Spiels, das für die Komödie charakteristische Fiktionsbrüche zulässt, sondern die offene, das Publikum einbezie-hende Spielebene, wie sie von Anfang an in den präliterarischen Formen der Spott- und Rügelieder, den rituellen Begehungen der Phallophorien usw. vorgegeben waren und dann mit der Kunstform der Komödie die Bürgeridentifikation in der attischen Demokratie des fünften Jahrhunderts ganz zwanglos ermöglichte, um erst allmählich sich zu einer fiktion-alen Geschlossenheit zu entwickeln" (*ibid.,* 87) ["The construction of the level of identifica-tion is any case the primary; at the beginning lies not the closed form of play that makes for comedy's characteristic rupturing of plot, but rather a level of play that is open and draws the audience in, as appears to have been the case right from the beginning in the preliterary forms of songs of ridicule and blame and in the ritual occasions of the Phallophoroi etc., and then with the development of the art form of comedy made the citizen identification in the Attic democracy of the fifth century possible, in a completely incidental fashion, only gradually developing into a closed plot"]. For this reason I would like to consider preliterary forms of this kind and ritual *phallophoria* in connection with comedy in the next chapter (2).

internal and external view, and the characteristic performativity of the chorus thus contains both levels in the selfsame corporal action.

Because of this conflict concerning the position of the chorus as actants, there arises the bewildering constellation of "ritual in ritual" that is fundamental for the *Thesmophoriazusae*. The women's festival of Demeter becomes embedded in the frame of the principally male celebration of Dionysus, so that it becomes impossible to draw definite boundaries between the two areas and the recipient continuously switches between the there and the here, as in a mental kaleidoscope. The fact that the identity of the male citizen behind the female dramatic role of the chorus always remains visible also contributes to this situation. Furthermore, one role may be divided between several actors, and one and the same actor may also appear in several roles. Identity is established above all by the mask, which is immutable and goes through the whole play with the same expression. In contrast to naturalistic theater one cannot speak of a continuous illusion anywhere. Rather, the boundaries between the presenter, the person represented, and the audience are open. In this state of uncertainty between here and there, now and then, external frame and internal play, the chorus in the act of its spectacular display in song and dance performs a ritual in the sense of a speech act. In order to be understood as ritual celebrant, the chorus must thus refer to its own activity.

Contrary to the case of high choral lyric and many choral parts in tragedy, what is important, as has been emphasized, in this comic choral song is not the relation of previous events, still less the presentation of general thoughts and aphorisms or the artistic offering of an event from myth, but the concentration on the chorus' own current activity as a complex model of action. It is precisely by means of this that the dance song becomes the purest form of ritual. Thus Michael Silk's criticism of the lyrical quality of these verses, that they are "a mixture of elevated hymnody and rather flat comments on the proceedings,"[3] may be justified from a purely literary-historical point of view, but at the same time is inappropriate, since it does not take into account the ritual character of the song, which is based on the orality of the performance. For ritual speech demands precisely this self-referential commentary on the action that is taking place.

When the chorus turns to the audience, it demonstratively shows what is particularly characteristic for the performers of a ritual. In the past, this address was mainly viewed as a parallel to the *parabasis*, which was also generally treated as an interruption of the illusion. But as we have seen, a ritual act,

---

[3] Silk 1980:112n43.

in contrast to interpretation or narration, is accomplished by self-reference to the completion of one's own activity. The utterance is thus often a complete end in itself; for the current activity of dance and prayer is accomplished, according to speech act theory, both by and in the word. Furthermore, this kind of ritual is expressive and symbolic in nature and describes itself by means of a synaesthetic collaboration of different levels of expression. Dance, gesture, rhythm, and the accompanying song are brought to the fore and marked, that is, they stand in contrast to the unmarked forms of everyday discourse.[4] The repetition and formal conjunction of the same or similar elements in metre, melody, and diction aim at the recognition of continually returning models. Redundancy and fusion in this multimedia combination lead to a heightened perception and to the desired contact with the gods. Depending on each of these modes of choral play and perception, one will either focus on Demeter and Persephone, the protectors of the women's festival presented on stage, or on the other gods of the polis in the here and now.

The criterion of connectedness to the plot, anchored in the Aristotelian tradition, thus proves to be of little help in the assessment of the song.[5] Just like the hymn that follows (*Thesm.* 1136ff.), this praise of the gods also transcends the so-called illusion. In a spectacular pose directed at the audience and the gods, the simply-fashioned, directed plot is to a certain extent interrupted, if one looks at the continuum of plot from an Aristotelian perspective. For this reason, both hymns were often regarded as late and subsequently added *parabasis* odes that were not in their usual position. Once, however, one becomes

[4] On the distinction between marked and unmarked utterances, which goes back to Roman Jakobson, see Nagy 1990:5–6, 30–34, and further references in his index.

[5] Zimmermann II 1985:191 divides prayers and hymns into two groups: they are either "part of the plot construction, thus plot-conveying" (*handlungstragend*), or "they interrupt the development of the plot, but are nevertheless—in contrast to the odes of the *parabasis* and many comic songs—integrated into the dramatic action." He places our song in the second category. The ambivalent formulation already shows how vague this criterion is. Against such a distinction I would argue that any comic song that forms a part of the performance in any fashion is integrated into the action, even songs in a *parabasis* or certain satirical songs, but that on the other hand no choral song is completely absorbed in the plot. Zimmermann contradicts himself when he classifies *parabasis* odes purely as digressions, but then immediately thereafter describes songs (*Thesm.* 947ff., 1136ff.), to which he rightly ascribes a certain connection to the plot, as delayed *parabasis* odes (192). Difficulties are removed if one considers, in contrast to earlier scholarship, the *parabasis* not as a singular interruption of the action on stage, but the parabatic as an overwhelmingly ritual principle of Old Comedy. On the thesis of the delayed odes that are missing in the *parabasis* see Wilamowitz II 1893:349, Gelzer 1970:1473, Sifakis 1971:52, Thomsen 1973:42–45, and Parker 1997:397. Prato, 307 argues against this connection to a *parabasis* and sees the song simply as a tribute to the changed taste of the public, which now privileges dance and music over word and demands entertainment.

accustomed to the idea that in Old Comedy a rather different poetics and aesthetics obtain—something much closer to ritual and something fundamentally separate from the Aristotelian-based theater tradition that has been dominant in Europe since the Renaissance—then the essentially permeable nature of the boundaries between inner and outer frame no longer presents any problem. As soon as one leaves behind the modern fiction of a closed plot, then the judgment that this kind of spectacle interrupts the action of the plot becomes relativized. Instead, it becomes possible to recognize new kinds of reference to a plot-development that is delimited and open. Despite their independence, both these songs (*Thesm.* 947ff., 1136ff.) do evoke the ritual ambience of the festival of Demeter. The frame of the plot, which almost threatens to disappear because of the political and in particular poetological preoccupations, thereby receives support. The comic chorus in all Aristophanic comedies up to and including the *Frogs* is always the central authority. It participates in and helps direct the simple dramatic action by expressing the symbolic and graphic idea framing the plot, most often in the form of a metaphor that takes on a life of its own. Through every scene this synaesthetic element is inserted on the level of plot and the action on stage is thereby symbolically strengthened.

On the other hand, this song introduces the normally gradual transition to the perspective of performance (*énonciation*) that usually occurs after the *parabasis*. Considered purely in terms of staging, the choral part at *Thesm.* 947ff. functions as a scene-divider. The spectacular "interlude" bridges the time during which Euripides' relative is led away, chained to the board offstage, and finally brought in again. Yet this technical piece of staging does not completely explain the choral song here. The genre of Old Comedy also needs the ritual underpinnings of dance and song by a chorus. Despite its further development into dramatically more complex forms, and in addition to its presentation of a fictional event, the comic play remains always a *kômos*-like celebration by a chorus rooted in the real world of the polis, the wild, joyful romp of a boisterous, celebratory group through the city. Ritual verbal abuse, demanding, begging, and praying still remain a central fixture of Aristophanic comedy. The simple plot that twines around it lacks the syntagmatic stringency of a tragedy, because everything is aimed first and foremost at laughter. The audience's participation in the ritual action is enhanced through the chorus' stepping forward and out into the real-life frame. Beside their integration into the unpretentious, playful plot, the spectators must primarily become involved in the community-affirming ritual activities of derision, laughter, celebration, and making contact with the polis gods. The particular style of speech encourages participation. The choral "I" blends into a shifting unity that contains within it several voices—those of the poet, the performative group of citizens, and the chorus in its dramatic role. The gesture of self-presentation, characteristic of ritual, is thus also crucial for comedy's open manner of perception. With regard to the markings in the printed text, it must once again be emphasized that the boundaries are completely fluid and that the song cannot be divided up so definitively that the parts can be pinned down to function or role alone, as has been the assumption until now.[6]

The underlined self-references to the chorus' own presentation in dance and song represent a kind of intersection between comic function and dramatic role. This area of ritual activity, common to both levels, leads both chorus member in the here and now and performer within the plot together with the final product of the role, based on theatrical signs, to a unity that pulls in opposite directions, in which the dance movements and verbal utterances of the actor in the orchestra represent a praxis of signifiers that refers only indexically to the signified of the role.[7] For both in the cult of Demeter and in that of Dionysus, this type of dance song is performed precisely in the circular dance form that is repeatedly emphasized here. Circular choruses are a not infrequently found feature, especially when attention is to be drawn to the ritual aspect of dance, as in the hyporcheme in particular; otherwise, the formation in rows in the *stikhos* and the *zygos* is apparently the usual arrangement in the extended rectangular orchestra.[8] Aside from this the cross-shaped formation was also typical for the Dionysiac dithyramb. The discussion of the division of the chorus into chorus leader and chorus body, or into semichoruses, something that goes back to the nineteenth century, and discussion of the possible division into strophe and antistrophe, as well as questions of metre, cannot be explored in detail here.[9]

---

[6] Sommerstein *Thesm.*, 218 connects lines 962–965, 972, and 985–1000 (Dionysus hymn) with the function of the comic chorus; Zimmermann II 1985:192 by contrast connects lines 962–964 with the role of festive community (*Festgemeinde*) (also 947–952, 974, 983–984), while viewing lines 972–973 and 975 in terms of function. Two different interpreters then assign the same lines (962–964) first to the former, then to the latter category. For a list of Greek dance vocabulary see Naerebout 1997:275–289. The concepts adduced there all fall under the category of emphatic self-reference. One can therefore clearly see how closely the song is associated with the chorus' own performance.

[7] See Lohr 1986:77–78 on this.

[8] See Davidson 1986 (mainly on the tragic chorus); also Wiles 1997:63–86.

[9] I have here largely followed Thomsen's classification (1973:27–29). Because of the two anapaestic tetrameters (947–948) lines 947–952 are mostly interpreted as a *prokêrygma* delivered by the chorus leader (whether viewed as male or female) (Fritzsche, Enger, and Muff 1872:164, Arnoldt 1873:160–161, Mazon 1904:134, Horn 1970:116, Zimmermann II 1985:192, and Parker

Because of the countless references to the chorus' own dancing, the song has in fact also been called a hyporcheme.[10] Muff remarks quite appositely, but obviously without using performative and semiotic categories relating to deixis and self-referentiality:

> In diesem ganzen Liede ist fast von nichts weiter als von Tanz und Gesang die Rede, und namentlich geschieht des Reigentanzes in so bezeichnender Weise Erwähnung, dass man sagen kann, es wird hier förmlich mit dem Finger auf die Darstellung durch eine Mehrzahl von Personen hingewiesen.

> [In this entire song practically nothing else save dancing and singing is spoken of, and in particular mention of round dancing is made so distinctly that one may say that this performance by a multitude of persons is being formally pointed to.][11]

1997:428; Westphal 1869:53 treats them as a melodramatic speech). The lines could also have been sung by the chorus as a whole. The chorus leader is sometimes also assigned the melic lines 953–958 and the trochaic parts of lines 959–968 (Westphal 1869:53, 61), which is by no means convincing. Arnoldt 1873:161 distributes them as follows: chorus leader: 947–952, 953–958, 966–968, 985–989; semi-chorus a: 959–961, 969–976, 990–994; semi-chorus b: 962–965, 977–984, 995–1000. Mazon 1904:135 also splits the chorus into semi-choruses with the hymns to the gods (969–976 and 977–984); the semi-choruses would then have been united in the hymn to Dionysus (985–1000). But a complete chorus is usually assumed (Muff 1872:18, among others, argues for this because of the invocation of gods in common). The search for possible dance figures in this part remains rather speculative. Relying on a questionable term for a special dance called the διπλῆ (cf. 982) Lawler 1945:63–66 suggests in lines 981–984 a temporary division of the round dance into rows of semi-choruses facing each other, but overlooks the fact that Enger, 126 already associated line 982 with the *diple* dance (something already in fact considered by Biset, 820 *ad loc.* and Küster, *Notae ad Thesm.*, 223 *ad* 991). Thomsen 1973:31–34 and Zimmermann II 1985:195 argue against Lawler's interpretation; Coulon on the other hand accepts Enger's suggestion; cf. also my opinions on line 982, below, n90. Further discussion on divisions in earlier scholarship in Fritzsche, 383–386. Since Wilamowitz 1921:476, lines 987–1000, in which he saw a "dithyrambic invocation of Dionysus," have generally been separated as an astrophic entity; cf. criticism in Thomsen 1973:34–35. Parker 1997:428 returns to Enger's division in the programmatic passages (*proodos* [953–958] and *mesodoi* [966–968, 985–989]) and the strophic pairs (959–962 = 963–965, 969–976 = 977–984, and 990–994 = 995–1000). For metrical analysis see Zimmermann II 1985:191–200, Parker 1997:428–437, and my brief description below (pp. 257–259), based on Zimmermann.

[10] Cf. the reference in Muff 1872:164 (on the strophe *Thesm.* 985ff.).

[11] Muff 1872:24 (in connection with choral art as a reference to the participation of the whole chorus). The underlined portions given in my text of the song make it clear that the performative utterances about the chorus' own dancing appear here in considerably high numbers.

The First Part (*Thesm.* 947–968) —
The Chorus Forms a Round Dance

Overlaying of the plot (*énoncé*) occurs only to a slight extent and seemingly almost exclusively with the goal of maintaining the fictional frame of the Thesmophoria while preserving the independence of the performance. The ambience of the women's festival is thus sketched out using only a very few references. It was never the intention to bring to the comic stage a faithful copy of a ritual, that is, a prayer or dance in honor of the two goddesses Demeter and Persephone, not only because the women's rites were highly secret,[12] but also because the mainly male audience was excluded from the festival and could therefore in no way identify directly with the specific cult practices. But what does interest the men and what the poet sets great store by is the women's absurd transgression into the realm of political action. The male popular assembly on the Pnyx and the assembly of women at the Nesteia, the occasion of the dramatic plot, are intertwined.[13] The central practice of fasting, which gives its name to the second day of the Thesmophoria, and the *aiskhrologia* also practiced there are encapsulated right at the beginning like a heading, as is the description of the festival as "holy mystery celebrations of the two goddesses" (948). At the same time, the mocking of citizens is also one of the typical functions of the comic chorus, in particular in the songs of the second *parabasis*. Aristophanes refers to these two central practices through the use of key words (νηστεύει, 949; νηστεύομεν, 984; κακῶς ἐρεῖν, 963); they are, however, subjected to comic distortion.

The mood on this second day appears to have been especially eerie and grim,[14] which corresponds to Demeter's grief over the abduction of her daughter in the myth. The rites were correspondingly somber and strange. In particular the women evoked a primitive way of life on this day by fasting and lying on the ground on a bed (*stibas*) made of plants with anaphrodisiac effects.[15] Wreaths, with which the chorus normally loves to decorate itself,[16] were also not worn.[17]

---

[12] Cf. Zimmermann II 1985:191 and the remark of Burkert (1985:242): "When Aristophanes presents the comedy *The Women at the Festival of the Thesmophoria*, he is unable to give many particulars about the festival."

[13] Cf. esp. *Thesm.* 328–329 and 372–382, esp. 376–377. Two ἄρχουσαι head the women's organizations; cf. Isaeus 8.19 and *IG* II/III² 1184.

[14] Plut. *Demosth.* 30.5.

[15] Diod. Sic. 5.4.7.

[16] Cf. Blech 1982:208 and below, n110.

[17] Schol. Soph. *OC* 681, p. 37, 5–6 De Marco.

How, then, did the comic poet manage to incorporate this utterly noncomic occasion into his joyful play? On the one hand, choral dance is emphasized as unifying element; on the other, he comically reworks the motifs of the rites. The *aiskhrologia* directed against the men is now personally directed against the starving artist Pauson. In comic fashion he is said to participate in the celebration of the mysteries, to fast, and often to invoke the goddesses of the Thesmophoria from festival to festival, all so that he can get to enjoy these fasting orgies often (*Thesm.* 948–952). The humor of this mocking observation lies in the fact that the starving pauper celebrates a feast with the chorus that actually excludes any male participation, and that like the women he prays from year to year for the period of hunger and need to return cyclically, although he ought really to be pleading for wealth. While fasting represents for the women only a ritual of inversion and exception, of abstention and purification in preparation for the fertility that must be renewed annually and that is celebrated on the immediately following day of the Kalligeneia together with the return to normality and civilization, this ridiculous fool begs for times of fasting as often as possible.

Because of his poverty the ritual exception has become the rule for Pauson. In a pun on his name (Pauson = παύσων, fut. participle of παύω, "stop, cease") the chorus plays on the fact that he will never end this condition of need, in contrast to the members of the chorus.[18]

In paradoxical fashion the *aiskhrologia* against men that is mentioned here is immediately withdrawn (962–965), because it does not fit the ritual activity of the festive choral dance for one thing, and because for the male audience, to whom the festive mood is supposed to be imparted, it represents a clearly intended affront. The chorus then itself refers to the contrast between the

---

[18] Cf. παύσων in its meaning as the future participle active of παύω, "one about to end something." Borgeaud 1988:182 points to an ancient and now outdated etymology of the god Pan, who is invoked later on (*Thesm.* 978). There have been attempts to support the functional relationship between the Arcadian god Paon and the Vedic god Pushan, who in both cultures assume the role of nourisher in the polytheistic system, by means of a shared development of their names. W. Schulze suggested that Paon is derived from the root *Παύσων, with Pauson being retained in Illyrian and Messapian as a personal name. Cf. also Borgeaud 1988:181–182 and 186 (appendix) and 262nn42–48. In a play on words, Pauson the Athenian, according to this theory, is thus conflated with Pan, who really does join in the celebrations. In Arcadian myth it is Pan who helps deliver Demeter from fasting and anger, so that he is the one "who will end" the critical situation. The joke would then consist in the fact that the starving pauper is being compared to the nourishing god, the provider of meat. On the role of Pan in this song, see below, pp. 111–117.

somber rite of fasting and the joyful dance:[19] παίσωμεν, ὦ γυναῖκες, οἷάπερ νόμος· | νηστεύομεν δὲ πάντως ("Let's dance for joy, women, as is the custom! But we're still sticking fast to our fast," 983–984).

The ritual activity of dancing can be applied to a sad as well as a happy occasion. In comedy, however, the exuberant choral dance is particularly associated with playing (παίζειν). The gloomy nature of the fictional setting is left out as much as possible, while the joyful and cheerful nature of the Dionysiac celebration is for the most part included.[20] Like many other *parabasis* odes, this song has a further function. Viewed from the perspective of the male audience, it is to a large extent not a parody of a prayer or hymn, but the expression of genuine worship. The hymn represents a corrective to the comic period of inversion, during which many comic plays subject even the gods to ridicule and Olympus is threatened with collapse. The song reflects the existing polis cult and should be regarded as living lyric from actual cult practice. As in the odes of *parabaseis* and in the choral passages of other Aristophanic comedies, in the *Thesmophoriazusae* in particular the invocations of the various gods who protect and preside over the city are integrated into the performance, and the goddesses of the Thesmophoria in the plot actually play only a subordinate role.[21]

[19] On the dialectic relationship of fast and carnival, cf. Ginsburg 1989 (who sees fasting as an"alter ego" or "Zwillingsritual des Karnevals, sein bevorzugter dialogischer Widerpart" ["the twin ritual of carnival, its preferred dialogic counterpart"] *ibid.*, 26–27). The Thesmophoria as festival of inversion represents the ritual model of the comic plot, which is in turn embedded in the Dionysiac, inverted world of comedy. As a relational difference from the carnivalistic norm, fasting is also part of the complex construction of the festival, which cloaks itself with the plot of an Old Comedy in its succession of need and utopian, excessive abundance. On the Thesmophoria as a carnivalistic festival of license in the Bakhtinian sense, cf. Rösler 1986:36. The Kronia, Skira, Anthesteria, Lenaia, Dionysia, and Haloa are included in the same interpretative framework; cf. also Halliwell 1991a:294 and Möllendorff 1995:74n1 and 249n77. The privation of the fast is paradoxically juxtaposed with the sensual opulence of the Dionysiac dance. In this comedy, the comic excess of food is celebrated only at the end of the play, in a festival rooted in the here and now, with the renewal of fertility and plenty also representing the aim of the ritual complex in the plot and being celebrated on the third day of the Thesmophoria with a great feast of meat-eating.

[20] On dance and play as expressions in terms of body language of the carnivalesque, both in the Dionysiac festival at which the play is performed and in the plot-internal Thesmophoria, see Ivanov 1974:341 and 365n97; on "crossdressing," 338.

[21] Prayers involving a series of divinities are found in many songs in the *Thesmophoriazusae*: in the Agathon hymn (101–129) Apollo, Artemis, Leto, and once more Apollo are invoked, and in the *parodos* (312–330) Zeus, Apollo, Athena, Artemis, Poseidon, the Nereids, and the Nymphs are called upon. In the choral dance song just discussed (947–1000), the ensemble of choral members addresses the Olympian gods (960), in particular Apollo, Artemis, Hera, Hermes, Pan, the Nymphs (969–984), and finally Dionysus (985–1000), and in the following hymn (1136–1159), Athena and lastly Demeter and Persephone.

The song is thus mainly, *qua* speech act, pure ritual. The inevitable illocutionary emphasis on the chorus' own activity of dancing and praising leads to a perlocutionary result, to the *communitas* of internal and external spectator in a feeling of coming closer to the gods, which establishes a sense of community.[22] The role of the chorus thereby increasingly disappears behind its cultic function in the here and now. In what follows we will investigate the technique of self-referentiality in detail. Choral song and dance represent, as I have emphasized, the common denominator of function and role. Through emphasis on this ritual activity, the poet is consciously able to keep the connection to the external or internal hanging in the air.

Deictic concepts of time and place, commands, and in particular the "I"/ "we" of the chorus are characteristics of the performative utterance. In this song they appear with great frequency. By means of the combination ἄγε νυν ('come now!'), which conveys urgency, the request to dance is performatively intensified. The emphatic Greek pronoun ἡμεῖς ('we'), together with the key concept of playful dance (παίζειν, cf. παίσωμεν, 947), gives rise to an illocutionary command, by which the perlocutionary result that the speech act is aimed at is immediately attained. Here we are talking of the communal choral dance of the whole collective in which the choral leader is included.[23] It remains open to question whether the female choral leader speaks at all, as is often assumed. Despite the anapaestic metre, it would also be perfectly conceivable that the chorus as a whole spoke. With the order "Let us dance!" the group sets about its movements. It is noteworthy how the deictic signals "now" (νυν) and "here" (ἐνθάδε), which refer in their function as shifters to the frame of the dancing chorus made up of male citizens, includes the "then" and "there" of the plot level. Or in other words: in the performative context, the "here" and "now" of the plot, which naturally relate to the fictitious sanctuary at the Thesmophoria (ἐν ἱερῷ, 964) and the imagined women's festival, is mixed with the "here" and "now" of the performance, that is, with

---

[22] On the feeling of the unity of all social connections, which Victor Turner terms *communitas*, see Turner 1974:274 (definition) and passim (esp. 302, index with numerous citations) and Turner/ Turner 1982:205–206.

[23] The combination of ἄγε δή (or νυν) with subsequent hortative (cf. Aesch. *Eum.* 307) is a common introduction to a *prokêrygma*. Here the command to dance, customary in cult, is imitated; cf. Kaimio 1970:126 and Zimmermann II 1985:192–193. On παίζειν as a term for dance, cf. Ar. *Av.* 660, *Lys.* 1313, *Thesm.* 983, 1227–1228, *Ran.* 318–320, 333, 388, 392, 407b, 415, 452; συμπαίζειν: *Pax* 816–817, *Av.* 1098, *Thesm.* 975; cf. also the early inscription on the wine-cup (Athens, National Museum 192) of the Dipylon Master, *IG* I² 919 = *CEG* 432 (pp. 239–240 Hansen) . . . ἀταλώτατα παίζει; cf. Lonsdale 1993:33–43, Henrichs 1996:35–38 (on the *oinokhoê, ibid.,* 32–34), and above, Introduction, n180.

the theater of Dionysus and the festival of the Dionysia. Because of the fact that there is talk here of a "custom" or "ritual" (νόμος) of "women," that is, the reactualized role of the presenters, the festival of the Thesmophoria is constantly evoked in the play.[24] Yet, as is typical for ritual choruses, the male actors continue to be visible behind the women being portrayed.[25] Even the insertion ἅπερ νόμος ἐνθάδε ταῖσι γυναιξίν (947), "as is the custom here for women," where in the term *nomos* female ritual is being played on, contains an ambiguity, since dancing is also the *custom here*, i.e. in the orchestra of the theater of Dionysus.[26] Moreover, the word *nomos* naturally evokes the political dimension, which applies simultaneously to the men of the civic context and to the women of the plot. In line 983, immediately before the concluding hymn to Bakkhos, the diction of line 947 is taken up again using ring composition: παίσωμεν, ὦ γυναῖκες, οἷάπερ νόμος.[27] The chorus, made of men, in its mimesis of women does essentially the very same thing that is the theme of the play as a whole. Just as the two protagonists do, the members of the chorus transgress the strict borders separating the sexes in that they too penetrate the sacred preserve of the women.[28]

In typical fashion, the chorus switches back and forth between "I" and "we." At one moment the chorus sees itself as a collective unity in the singular, at another as a group that is composed of separate individuals, and accordingly speaks of itself in the plural.[29] The troupe in the orchestra gives itself

---

[24] On the concept of νόμος (and derivatives) cf. *Thesm.* 348, 361, 675, 685, 947, 983. The marked appearance of the word "women" supports the chorus' role in the plot and serves as a key concept for the problematics of the comedy; cf. *Thesm.* 371, 684, 947, 964, 983. The female role identity is also emphasized by feminine forms: πᾶσα, 955b, 961; μέλπουσα, 970; γυναῖκά μ' οὖσαν, 964.

[25] This is characteristic of Far Eastern types of play; cf. Pronko 1982. In principle it holds for all ritual choruses; see Schechner 1977:120–127, Schechner 1985:4–10, and Lohr 1986:77–78 (on folk theater). According to the theory of theater anthropology, the performer and dancer does not merge into his role completely, but rather into his nonverbal energy and his presence as a whole; he functions on the basis of a stylized, and marked, technique, distinct from the everyday world; instead of using a fictional psychological identity, the performer describes himself through a fictional body. Cf. Barba/Savarese 1991, passim, esp. 8–22.

[26] This is how it is expressed at the very beginning of the following song (1136–1137), the delayed antode of the *parabasis*: Παλλάδα τὴν φιλόχορον ἐμοὶ | δεῦρο καλεῖν νόμος εἰς χορόν.

[27] On νόμος see below, nn. 240, 274, 278.

[28] Cf. Zeitlin 1981, esp. 169–181 and 196–197.

[29] "We": ἡμεῖς, 947, ἡμετέραισι, 980a; "I": μ', 964, ἐγώ, 988b. Norden sees this phenomenon as an indication of the traditional seried (*gereihter*) prayer style, when the chorus talks of itself in the singular and the plural, and the second and first person are collapsed. Cf. Norden 1939:197 and Kaimio 1970:127–128, who cites as examples for self-commands to dance in the second-person singular *Lys.* 1279–1280, *Thesm.* 953–956, 961, 969, 981, 985–986 (in song *Thesm.* 947ff.), and *Ran.* 340, 372, 378 (in the *parodos*). It is therefore incorrect to take singular forms as indications of a single speaker (chorus leader); Kaimio 1970:128: "There is not the slightest reason to

commands using the second person singular of the imperative: form a round dance (953–954), take each other by the hand (955a), take up the rhythm (955b), while taking quick steps (956) be careful not to break the perfect circle (957–958). The commands occur at the same time as the body movements and represent pure performative speech acts. The action is brought about through speech. The ritual action, that is, getting into dance formation, is illocutionarily strengthened and accomplished through self-referential utterances. Speech is completely self-fulfilling in this activity.[30]

The parallels to the similarly framed speech act of the preceding search scene (659ff.), where the chorus similarly prepares itself for the round dance, are clear.[31] Kleisthenes hands over to them for safekeeping Euripides' relative,

---

think of delivery by single speakers or groups on the strength of the imperatives." The singular imperatives should in no way be understood here as commands from the *koryphaios* to an individualized addressee or from each individual singer to himself, but as a general address that is directed at all members of the collective involved with same choral dance; *ibid.*, 128–129: "The second person singular is predominantly used, meaning in an undetermined way anybody who is engaged in the same dance." On indifference to the use of person, see also Muff 1872:29–32 ("Person und Numerus"); he describes how many commentators depend on a rather narrow understanding of person and number to determine whether it is the chorus leader or the chorus as a whole that is acting. He correctly says (*ibid.*, 29): "Allein diese Voraussetzung ist irrig" ["It is incorrect to rely on this supposition alone"]. There is an extremely useful list in Norden 1939:193–199 ("Die Selbstanrede") and Kaimio 1970:121–137 of parallel passages which prove that the chorus can address itself in singular or plural as it sees fit: on the address in the second-person singular see inter alia Aesch. *Pers.* 571–575; Soph. *Trach.* 821, *OC* 118–122 (cf. esp. 121–122 προσδέρκου, λεῦσσέ νιν, | προσπεύθου πανταχῇ); and Ar. *Lys.* 302–303, 320–321, *Av.* 1720, *Thesm.* 663–667, *Eccl.* 293–295, 478–483, 486–487, 496–502; on commands in the second-person plural, see inter alia Soph. *Trach.* 210–213, *OT* 1524; Eur. *Supp.* 73–77, *Ba.* 83; and Ar. *Lys.* 1292, *Av.* 1721. Kaimio 1970:129 refers to the combination with πᾶς (cf. KG II.1, 85 and Schwyzer II, 245), which implies an unspecified number of individual performers. Cf. in song πᾶσα, *Thesm.* 955b, 961.

30 Zimmermann II 1985:193n16 also refers to this issue. Cf. Ar. *Lys.* 302–303, 320–321, *Thesm.* 663–667, *Eccl.* 293–295, 478–483; see also Wilamowitz 1921:475n2 and Parker 1997:429 with reference to Enger. Kaimio 1970:127 succinctly analyzes the ritual situation of this performative dance songs: "These imperatives accompanying the dance are not so subtly incorporated into the dramatic situation as the ritual imperatives occurring in tragedy, which are used by the chorus as an outburst of violent emotions, called forth by the events of the drama. The dance-imperatives in comedy are naturally sung by the chorus in a cheerful mood, but they are not used as a reaction to the events of the drama and embedded into an emotional or reflective context. They occur in songs where the dance is really represented as a ritual, into which the chorus are at present involved."

31 Cf. Zimmermann II 1985:193n14: κοῦφον . . . πόδα, 659 ≈ κοῦφα ποσίν, 954 (cf. also Pind. *Ol.* 14.16–17, κῶμον . . . κοῦφα βιβῶντα; Ar. *Lys.* 1303–1304, κοῦφα πᾶλον and *Lys.* 1309, 1316–1317; cf. Eur. *El.* 860–861, ὡς νεβρὸς οὐράνιον | πήδημα κουφίζουσα σὺν ἀγλαΐα and Eur. *Tro.* 325, πάλλε πόδ' αἰθέριον; cf. also Autocrates fr. 1.1–6 K.-A.: οἷα παίζουσιν φίλαι | παρθένοι Λυδῶν κόραι, | κοῦφα πηδῶσαι ‹ποδοῖν | κἀνασείουσαι› κόμαν | κἀνακρούουσαι χεροῖν | Ἐφεσίαν παρ' Ἄρτεμιν); διασκοπεῖν . . . πανταχῇ, 660 ≈ ἐπισκοπεῖν δὲ πανταχῇ . . . ὄμμα, 957–958 (cf. Soph. *OC* 122); τρέχειν . . . κύκλῳ, 662 ≈ ἄγ' εἰς κύκλον, 954.

who has just been exposed, so he can report the matter to the *prytanis*. The members of the chorus surround the criminal in a circle and using the same formation, they simultaneously occupy themselves with the search for other male intruders. In similar fashion, the chorus of the Erinyes encircle Orestes to "chain" him symbolically in a ὕμνος δέσμιος (Aesch. *Eum.* 321–396). The performative self-command ἄγε δὴ καὶ χορὸν ἅψωμεν (*Eum.* 307) corresponds to the imperative χειρὶ σύναπτε χεῖρα (*Thesm.* 955a),[32] which in its reciprocal syntactic relationship imitates the joining of the dancers to the circle of dance that is simultaneously created in the speech act of utterance. The Erinyes form a closed circle with their intertwined hands in order to put a spell on their victim using a magical speech act.

In metaphorical fashion at least Euripides' relative is also encircled as an evildoer in the choral dance song under discussion here. This is precisely why the members of the chorus put so much emphasis on the tightness of their formation; just as in the searching song, here too the chorus admonishes itself to be vigilant. Is there not a possibility that the relative is not actually led off by the Scythian henchman and brought back after the song,[33] but remains in the orchestra? The circle of dancers would then carry out the act of binding the captive to the board in a staged and gestural fashion.

Admittedly, stage convention and the fact that the songs (947ff., 1136ff.) as subsequent *parabasis* odes actually leave the chorus behind on the stage, alone, argue against this. Nevertheless, one can say that on the level of the

---

[32] The connection between Aesch. *Eum.* 307ff. and *Thesm.* 954ff. was already noted by Sommerstein 1989:136 *ad* Aesch. *Eum.* 307 and Henrichs 1994/95:95n38. Petersmann 1991:80, following Frisk II, 1112–1113, ventures an etymological connection between χορός and χόρτος, Lat. *hortus*, in the sense of "enclosure," so that chorus, following Frisk II, 1113, may be explained as "a row of dancers holding each other by the hand."

[33] On departure from the stage cf. for example the stage directions in Sommerstein's translation of *Thesm.* 109 and Henderson 1996:129. The only indication of this is the command δῆσον αὐτὸν εἰσάγων (930). On this point cf. Sommerstein's fine commentary, *Thesm.* 216 *ad loc.* "Leading/ bringing inside" in most cases certainly involves the stage building. But it is perhaps conceivable that the Scythian, by way of exception, actually leads his prisoner around the circle formed by the chorus, who then encircle him. Of course in this case the barbarian henchman would then have to have carried his plank, hammer, and nails with him. The relative reminds one of the magic voodoo-dolls that the ancients would "bind down" (καταδεῖν) in order to hand them over to the underworld powers and *daimones*, in particular the goddesses associated with the Thesmophoria, Demeter and Kore, but also Plouton and the Nymphs. As part of the procedure they would also be pierced with nails; on *defixiones* see Graf 1996:108–157, esp. 114–115, 122–124, 191. Bonanno 1990:257 interprets the scene as I do: "Rimasto invece sulla scena, legato alla σανίς in tunica color zafferano, assiste all'agile 'ballo tondo' nonché al 'paso doble' del Coro (vv. 936 [sic!]–1000)" ["Instead, remaining on stage and tied to the σανίς in a saffron tunic, he helps the nimble 'round dance' as well as the *paso doble* of the chorus"].

chorus, the activity of binding (930, 943), which takes place behind the scenes, is at the same time symbolically accompanied by body language. In sacrificial rites the round dance is in fact danced in the orchestra about the *thymelê*.[34] In a transferred sense at least, the relative is encircled like a sacrificial victim at the altar of Dionysus, or rather, Demeter, and the aggression against the intruder is transformed into dance. The almost tragic reversal is noteworthy here: Euripides' relative, who precisely in the parody of the *Telephos* sacrifices the "child" of Mika as a wineskin (*Thesm.* 733–764, esp. 753–759), now himself becomes a potential sacrificial victim for Dionysus. The reference to the polis gods becomes understandable, since the city of Athens punishes any violation of the ritual rules of the women's festival as an attack on its official cult. The whirling movements of the chorus members (in their actual identity as well as their dramatic role)[35] in honor of the gods, particularly the madness-inducing Dionysus, bring the relative, as well as the audience, under the spell of the order that the cultic dance as performance represents.

The introductory self-representation comes to a conclusion in three small strophes. In the first (959–961), the self-command is attached to a hymn to the Olympian gods, which is to be performed with dancing and the performance of which we will also see in the second part. Beside the χορεία, the second vocal and acoustic component of the choral dance song, the μολπή, is self-referentially thematized.[36] Praise of the gods accompanied by dance steps is a central cultic occupation of the Greeks. The song takes place in a high, lyric style, which also characterizes the marked manner of expression found in ritual. It produces a particular mood, which creates a solidarity among those praising and the spectators, who identify themselves with this, and on the other hand, through its arousing language, which underscores the wildly turning motion, arouses a feeling of proximity to the immortal. This "chorus-mad manner" (χορομανεῖ τρόπῳ, 961) anticipates in particular the μανία of the dithyrambic and Dionysiac conclusion, where

---

[34] On the altar in the theater see Poe 1989. On the altar of Agyieus in the *Thesm.* as a comic means of breaking the illusion *ibid.*, 131, on the *thymelê ibid.*, 138–139. See also Wiles 1997:63–86. On goat sacrifice on the *thymelê* and on bull sacrifice by the circular dithyrambic chorus, see also Burkert 1966a:101–102 with n32 (on the *thymelê*). On the performance of a κύκλιος χορός during animal sacrifice, see Furley 1993:36.

[35] The chorus members are simultaneously male in their function in the here and now as dancers in a chorus at a festival for Dionysus and female in their dramatic role as female dancers in a chorus at a festival for Demeter and Kore.

[36] On μέλπω/μολπή as the sign of choral performance see Cingano 1993:349–353; consider the strong concentration of instances μέλπω in this hymn: *Thesm.* 961, 970, 974, 989. On μολπή cf. *Ran.* 370, 384, and 1527.

the god of the performance clearly breaks into the realm of the Demeter plot (987ff.).[37]

In the second small strophe (962–965) the theme of the song is negatively defined. The women's *aiskhrologia* directed toward the men is not on the program, although one would expect such speech acts on the fast day (Νηστεία) represented in the plot. Admittedly, a comic twist lies hidden in the comment, since precisely this type of ridicule occurs in the case of the painter Pauson and malicious gossip is something fundamental to the chorus both in its comic function and in its role. Rather, it is exclusively connected with its very own activity. The choral dance song itself, designed to honor the Olympians, is the order of the day. The chorus thus commands itself in the third strophe to "begin next as something new the perfect step of the beautiful dance" (966–968).[38]

It is almost impossible to make a complete survey of the discussions of the details relating to choral dance in this song, in particular studies of possible changes in dance and pace. Most often there has been an attempt to deduce a succession of two or even three different dances on the basis of the performative diction of the chorus' utterances.[39] Yet it is in fact a characteristic of

---

[37] For χορομανεῖ τρόπῳ (961) cf. θυρσομανεῖ νεβρίδων μέτα δίνᾳ (coni. Hermann), Eur. *Phoen.* 791 (also with Dionysiac connotation), and *HF* 878–879. Cf. Bierl 1991:145, 154–158 (on both Euripidean passages). In comedy, joyful dance, particularly in a religious context, is often treated as harmless and beneficial *mania*: Ar. *Ran.* 316–459, esp. 332–333, 356–357; cf. also *Vesp.* 1474–1537, esp. 1486, 1496, and *Pax* 320–336.

[38] ἀλλὰ χρῆν | ὥσπερ ἔργον αὖ τι καινὸν | πρῶτον εὐκύκλου χορείας εὐφυᾶ στῆσαι βάσιν (text after Thomsen 1973:27–28). Contra Coulon's text ὥσπερ ἔργον, αὐτίκα (Dindorf) cf. Thomsen 1973:30. Blaydes I, 235 *ad* 967 translates ὥσπερ ἔργον as "*ut opus est, ut res fert.*" Zimmermann II 1985:194n22 interprets the passage correctly: "στῆσαι βάσιν χορείας ist eine poetische Periphrase für das gewöhnliche χορὸν στῆσαι 'einen Tanz beginnen'" ["στῆσαι βάσιν χορείας is a poetic periphrasis for the usual χορὸν στῆσαι 'to begin a dance'"]. The ingressive aspect of the aorist refers to the beginning of the performance of the round dance. Cf. the explanation of Blaydes I, 235 *ad* 968 (first found in Küster, *Notae ad Thesm.*, 223 *ad* 977), which does not go into the question of aspect: *Id est rhythmice et in numerum terram pedibus pulsare, quod* οἱ χορεύοντες *facere solent*. On χορὸν ἱστάναι ('to form, set up the chorus,' 'perform choral dance') cf. Aesch. fr. 204b.7 = 16 Radt; Soph. *El.* 280; Eur. *Alc.* 1155, *El.* 178, *IA* 676; Ar. *Av.* 219, *Nub.* 271; cf. further the derivatives χοροστάτις (Alcm. fr. 1.84 Davies; χορῶν κατάστασιν, Aesch. *Ag.* 23) and στάσις (Ar. *Ran.* 1281 [cf. Cingano 1986], *Plut.* 954). Cf. the name Stesikhorus and στησίχορος, fr. adesp. 938c *PMG*. Cf. also Calame I 1977:88n91, 94–96 (Engl. trans. Calame 1997:41n91, 45–46), Nagy 1990:361–369, and Henrichs 1994/95:95n36. The performative terminology of the speech act is of course particularly emphasized by the circumlocution. The substantive βάσιν is taken up in the immediately following command πρόβαινε ποσί (*Thesm.* 969). In dance, step and foot position are naturally of importance. On βάσις cf. Eur. *Ba.* 647 (βάσιν coni. Blomfield: πόδα LP; cf. Seaford 1996:203 *ad loc.*), where there may be an allusion to the language of dance.

[39] See Thomsen 1973:30–34.

literature that is pragmatic and completely rooted in the everyday world of literature that the details of a performance may often not be able to be reconstructed on a more exact basis. Many critics have made the same interpretative suggestions; they incorrectly take στῆσαι as meaning "stop" or "bring to an end."[40] From this they conclude that the round dance introduced in lines 953ff. comes to an end after line 968 and that the chorus begins a new dance in line 969.[41] Many interpreters even believe there is an additional *diplê* interlude (981–984)[42] before the bacchic dance begins in line 985.

Contrary to the *communis opinio* I believe that the round dance in close formation is never once stopped throughout the entire song. That is to say, neither in line 969 does the chorus begin a march in a straight line, nor does the collective divide itself up into opposing half-choruses in line 981; still less is the circular formation changed in line 985.[43] Thomsen has convincingly contradicted the theory that the tragic *diplê* dance (cf. 982), first attested in Hesychius, appeared here. In the following dithyramb (985ff.) the typical κύκλιος χορός is in fact continued.

On the basis, then, of the lines just cited (966–968) a change of step has erroneously been posited to have taken place. Using an incorrect inter-

---

[40] Cf. among others van Leeuwen *Thesm.*, 123 *ad* 966–968, Rogers *Thesm.*, 102 *ad* 967 (*sistere gradum*), and now Furley/Bremer I 2001:357 with Furley/Bremer II 2001, 354–355 *ad* 968 and Austin/Olson, 301–302 *ad* 966–968. Fritzsche, 390 interprets the passage as follows: "*sed cito te oportet— primum saltationis in orbem concinnum constituere gressum*, id est, sed cito te oportet primum in orbem saltare itaque novam praeparare choream." The meaning of στῆσαι (*constituere*) is thus made to hover between the correct interpretation "to begin the dance" (*saltare*) and the incorrect interpretation "bring to a halt" (or "end" [*finire*]), since he proceeds on the basis of a new step in line 969. Dover *Clouds*, 136 *ad* 271, on the other hand, correctly translates ἱστάναι with the object χορός as "bring into being." Thomsen 1973:31 and Prato, 104, 310 interpret στῆσαι βάσιν (968) in this sense.

[41] Fritzsche, 390, van Leeuwen *Thesm.*, 123 *ad* 966–968, Rogers *Thesm.*, 102 *ad* 969, and Mazon 1904:135n1, who, like Fritzsche, postulates a march because of πρόβαινε. Cf. also Sommerstein *Thesm.*, 111 (stage direction): "With a change of formation and rhythm" and Parker 1997:429. Blaydes I, 235 *ad* 969 thinks that it is only here that the dance begins. Fritzsche, 390 and Rogers *Thesm.*, 102 *ad* 969 assume a *diplê* dance between 969 and 984.

[42] Coulon and Lawler 1945:59–66. The *diplê* interpretation (cf. already Küster, *Notae ad Thesm.*, 223 *ad* 991 and Enger, 162 *ad* 982 [and see now also Prato, 310 *ad* 982]) is rejected by Thomsen 1973:31–34, using persuasive arguments; Zimmermann II 1985:195 follows him; διπλῆν (982) should be understood as a predicative adjective with proleptic meaning that belongs to χάριν χορείας and expresses "das reziproke Verhältnis zwischen menschlichem Tun und göttlicher Gnade und die gegenseitige Freude an diesem Tun" ["the reciprocal relationship between human action and divine favor and the mutual pleasure of this activity"]. Similarly now see Furley/Bremer II 2001:356–357 *ad* 982–983 and Austin/Olson, 304 *ad* 981–984.

[43] Lawler 1945:66 assumes an open circle in which the dancers do not hold each other's hands, but move freely as a *kômos*.

pretation of στῆσαι and Engers' conjecture ὡς ἐπ' ἔργον . . . καινόν, certain scholars[44] understood the passage to mean that the members of the chorus were exhorting themselves to stop their round dance and form themselves into a "new" formation for the subsequent hymn to the gods.[45] Yet precisely this κύκλιος χορός can be encountered particularly in the area of cultic worship of Dionysus and Demeter.[46] In the staging of a hymn to Dionysus within a fictional frame relating to Demeter there is thus no reason to change the arrangement at this passage in particular, once we point out the symbolic association of the scene with sacrificial ceremonies, at which the round dance was often performed around the altar.[47]

The expression ἔργον αὖ τι καινόν is thus not to be taken in the sense of a new dance to which the chorus now directs itself; rather, the circular formation continues in the following addresses to the gods. Because this is more

[44] Austin 1987:84 *ad* 967 conjectures ὡς πρὸς (accepted by Sommerstein); manuscript R has ὥσπερ.

[45] Thus the two most recent English translations of the passage. Cf. Sommerstein *Thesm.*, 111: "rather what we should now be doing, to proceed to another new task, is first of all to halt the graceful step of our circular dance" and Henderson 1996:130: "But now we should rather halt the graceful steps of our circle-dance and go on to our next number!" Cf. now also Furley/Bremer I 2001:357 with Furley/Bremer II 2001:354 *ad* 967. Thomsen 1973:30 (following Pickard-Cambridge 1968:239) sees it quite differently. He thinks that the chain is broken after lines 959ff. and that the chorus is now calling on itself to assume its previous arrangement. He also rejects ἐπ' or πρός, because no new dance is begun (Thomsen 1973:31n3). Johansen 1975:87 understands ἔργον αὖ τι καινόν as reference to the reintroduction of civilization, the dissolution and refoundation of which was reenacted in the festival of Demeter; see below, pp. 150–151. The dance would then correspond to an act of civilization. Ludwig Koehnen has correctly pointed out to me that in line 967 there is an uncertainty regarding responsion, since this line has one syllable more than the corresponding lines 960 and 964 (cf. Parker 1997:430–433). In his opinion it is striking that Aristophanes could easily have written αὖ νέον at the end, but that the poet clearly did not want this. Perhaps he intended to express something by his choice of the word καινόν.

[46] Ar. *Ran.* 440–442, 446–447. Beside the Erinyes in Aesch. *Eum.* (esp. 307ff.) there are other female choruses that form a round dance: Aesch. fr. 379 Radt (prayer); Eur. *IA* 1036ff., esp. 1054–1057, 1480–1481, cf. 1467–1472 (dance), *HF* 673ff., esp. 687–690 (cultic: Delian maidens), *Hel.* 1301ff., esp. 1312–1314 (Demeter and Kore!). On circular dances in tragedy see Davidson 1986. Round dances were connected with sacrificial ritual and were performed around the *thymelê* in the orchestra; see Rehm 1988:264–274 on the altar in the orchestra and Poe 1989. The altar as prop in the Thesmophoria festival becomes the tomb of Proteus in the immediately preceding parody of the *Helen* (*Thesm.* 885–888; cf. Rehm 1988:304–305 and Sier 1992:7n13); in the choral song (947ff.) the chorus dances around the altar, so that the dramatic action on the level of the actors and the ritual performance both in the women's festival and in the here and now become fused with one another on the level of the chorus.

[47] On hymnic performances by a chorus that groups itself about a sacrificial altar, see Bremer 1981:197–199; on the connection with animal sacrifice, see Furley 1993:36. For the connection between paean and sacrifice see Käppel 1992:44–47, 49–51, 55–56 (and test. 95), 58–63, 81, 285.

seldom encountered in the theater, the chorus keeps referring to it in a self-referential fashion. The κύκλιος χορός belongs essentially to ritual, and the continuous confirmation sets up the circular movement and regulates it in the sense of speech act theory.[48] The chorus, and also the poet, who in the *parabasis* in particular blends his own voice with that of the chorus, presents its dance song as "yet another new work," where καινόν should be understood in the sense of "innovative," "unusual," or "original." The poet's claim to originality is closely tied to his self-presentation in the *parabasis*, with which the song is continuously and formally placed in connection.[49] Nevertheless, the poet's utterance represents merely a variation or further development of the chorus' self-advertisement, which manifests its particular quality in the comic *agôn*.[50] Every comic chorus contains one original idea on which its iden-

---

[48] Cf. Searle 1970, esp. 33–42. Searle does not follow Austin's distinction between locutionary and illocutionary acts and prefers to subsume propositional characteristics under the illocutionary. On the other hand, he takes over Austin's idea of the perlocutionary effect as a separate category to be distinguished from the conventional effects of the purely illocutionary or performative act; see on this my Introduction, above, n98. On self-referential connections to the round dance see *Thesm.* 953–958, 966–968, and 985–986.

[49] On the poet cf.: Ar. *Nub.* 547, καινὰς ἰδέας and 561, εὑρήμασιν (with Hubbard 1991:103–105), *Vesp.* 1044, καινοτάτας . . . διανοίας, 1053, καινόν τι λέγειν κἀξευρίσκειν, Pherekrates fr. 84 K.-A., ἄνδρες, προσέχετε τὸν νοῦν | ἐξευρήματι καινῷ, | συμπύκτοις ἀναπαίστοις and Metagenes fr. 15 K.-A., κατ' ἐπεισόδιον μεταβάλλω τὸν λόγον, ὡς ἂν | καιναῖσι παροψίσι καὶ πολλαῖς εὐωχήσω τὸ θέατρον. Cf. Xenarchus fr. 7, 1–2 K.-A., οὐδὲ ἓν | καινὸν γὰρ εὑρίσκουσιν, Antiphanes fr. 189, 17–18 K.-A., ἀλλὰ πάντα δεῖ | εὑρεῖν, ὀνόματα καινά; cf. Henrichs 1993a:175 (with parallel adduced from Pind. Nem. 8.20–21). Cf. also Sifakis 1971:39 (C1: the content of *parabasis* and *pnigos* "explains the virtues and stresses the originality of his [i.e. the poet's] art as compared with the art of other poets or with the quality of comedy before him"). Outside the *parabasis* in the prologue: Ar. *Pax* 54–55, ὁ δεσπότης μου μαίνεται καινὸν τρόπον, | οὐχ ὅνπερ ὑμεῖς, ἀλλ' ἕτερον καινὸν πάνυ and other passages not related to καινός in Sifakis 1971:39. On the conventional idea of originality and innovation in hymns see Burkert 1985:103. Lohr 1986:175 emphasizes the element of the impromptu and novel for the provocation of laughter, a constituitive element of comedy: "Zur Aufführungssituation der theatralischen Form 'Komödie' gehört immer ein Moment unvorhergesehener Neuheit, mit dem sich die Schauspieler—für den Zuschauer meist nicht bemerkbar—den Raum der komischen Comunitas (sic!) schaffen; gerade auch in einem durchinszenierten Stück des modernen Repertoire-Theaters" ["Attached to the performance situation of the theatrical form 'comedy' there is always a moment of unforeseen novelty with which the actors—something that the spectator generally does not notice—create space for the comic *comunitas* (sic!); even in a scripted and staged piece of modern repertory theater"]. On the motif of novelty in the ritual song fr. 851b *PMG*, see below, chap. 2 nn90 and 93.

[50] On the identification of the poet with the choral leader (for example in *Nub.* 518–562, *Pax* 734–764) see Körte 1921:1244, Pickard-Cambridge 1962:198–199, Kranz 1933:26–27, Herter 1947:38, Dover 1972:50–53, and Sifakis 1971:52; on the identification of the poet with the voice of the actor cf. *Ach.* 496ff.; cf. Möllendorff 1995:222–266 ("Protagonist und Polyphonie"), specifically on the *Ach.*, *ibid.*, 222–235. Contrary to Lefkowitz 1991:24 and the *communis opinio* I do not believe that this form of the *parabasis* is older. Ar. fr. 30 K.-A., οἶδα μὲν ἀρχαῖόν τι δρῶν, . . . can

tity within the plot rests. In the competition it presents itself to the audience, which is celebrating alongside it, using self-descriptions that are also typical of ritual groups.[51] How deeply embedded in the ritual tradition this tendency to emphasize the newness and originality of one's own action is can also be seen in the equally bacchic song of the Hellenistic Phallophoroi, which will receive thorough investigation in chapter 2.[52] The similarity between the first part of this choral dance song and the popular song (fr. 851b *PMG*) just referred to is not simply limited to the foregrounding of personal achievement, but extends also to the performative situation. On both occasions, members of the chorus present their own current activity before they move on to the actual hymn.

---

hardly be taken in this sense. The fact that later *parabaseis* tend to remain in the dramatic role of the chorus could be an accident of transmission (cf. esp. *Av.* 685–722, *Lys.* 614–705, *Thesm.* 785–813). Even there one should rather speak of a state of fluctuation between different levels of utterance. Anapaests may be equally often used for the self-presentation of the chorus as for that of the poet; cf. Hubbard 1991:20: Cratinus fr. 105 K.-A. (the chorus of the *Malthakoi* speaks in its dramatic role about its garland); Eupolis fr. 13 K.-A. (the chorus of the *Goats* speaks in its dramatic role about its food); Ar. fr. 427–431 K.-A. (the chorus of ships in the *Holkades* takes an inventory of its cargo). Just as in Pindar's *Epinicians* the choral "I" may take on an autobiographical, epinician, social, and performative aspect, so the comic chorus unites various voices in itself; precisely in the *parabasis* the choral "I"/"we" may present itself to the audience as historical-autobiographical (as poet), generally political (as chorus in its real-world function), performative (as chorus in its role or function), and dramatic (as chorus in its role within the plot). The comic chorus can speak in several of these voices at once and can fluctuate freely between these manners of speaking. On different voices in Pindar see Segal 1995:180–181; in the tragic chorus *ibid.* and Calame 1999: 149–153.

[51] In Aristophanic comedies the chorus seeks to make its identity clear right at its first appearance by speaking self-referentially: cf. *Ran.* 209–214 (croaking of frogs), *Av.* 260–262 (twittering of birds), *Nub.* 275–290 and 298ff., and Eupolis *Aiges* fr. 13 K.-A.; on other animal choruses see Sifakis 1971:76; self-description of human choruses is found in *Ach.* 209–222; *Lys.* 254–265, 319–335; *Thesm.* 328–330; *Eccl.* 285–288; and *Plut.* 257–258. The wasps describe their stings only at a later stage, for dramatic reasons (*Vesp.* 403–407: up until this point the members of the chorus present themselves as old warriors at Marathon, 230ff.).

[52] The words of the song: σοί, Βάκχε, τάνδε μοῦσαν ἀγλαΐζομεν, | ἁπλοῦν ῥυθμὸν χέοντες αἰόλῳ μέλει, | καινὰν ἀπαρθένευτον, οὔ τι ταῖς πάρος | κεχρημέναν ᾠδαῖσιν, ἀλλ᾿ ἀκήρατον | κατάρχομεν τὸν ὕμνον (fr. 851b *PMG* [= carm. pop. 5b], carm. pop. 8 B., 48 D.). The claim to originality is practically hammered into the audience by means of an asyndetic and metaphorical series of attributes. This song is of particular importance since it has often been adduced as the possible ritual source of the *parabasis*, to which the song from the Thesmophoria (947–1000) also belongs. For interpretation see below, chap. 2.

Second, Hymnodic Section (*Thesm.* 969–1000)—
Danced Praise of the Gods

The second section of the song consists of a hymn to the Olympians (*Thesm.* 969–980), which becomes a further illocutionary confirmation of the real-life *khoreia* in the performative frame (981–984 and 985–989), and finally ends with a long praise of Dionysus, the god of the performative occasion. Pure hymns of this type directed to the various polis gods are characteristic of *parabasis* odes, with which this song has frequently, and correctly, been associated. The comic poet is free to decide what to do with these basic forms, to play with their structure, to double or shift parts. The *parabasis* odes of the *Thesmophoriazusae* are not to be found in their usual place, but come to some extent in the place of a second *parabasis* as two scene-dividing songs at a latter phase during the course of the play. The ode is thus inserted belatedly after the *Helen* trick, while the antode comes after the *Andromeda* tactic, in the form of hymns (947–1000 and 1136–1159), and this at the same time concludes the cycle of tragic parody.[53]

Perhaps they are original (ἔργον αὖ τι καινόν *Thesm.* 967) for this among other reasons, but certainly because the spectacular round dance in the theater represents a distinctive feature: hymns are generally staged as processions using the typical line formation. The dramatic chorus usually directs this sort of praise song to the gods when (in terms of the plot) it approaches a sanctuary.[54] The term *hymnos* seems to be used as a general overarching term for subgroups, as, for example, paean, dithyramb, *nomos*, or *prosodion*, and simply means a song in praise of the gods.[55] On the basis of a passage of Plato (*Leg.*

---

[53] Hubbard 1991:195n109 thinks the songs would have been out of place in the context of the women's self-justification in the *parabasis* of this play. Mazon 1904:134 and Gelzer 1970:1470 call *Thesm.* 947–1000 a "second *parabasis*," or "Nebenparabase." Cf. Wilamowitz II 1893:349, Gelzer 1970:1473, Sifakis 1971:52, Dover 1972:171n11, Thomsen 1973:42–45, Hansen 1976:184, Zimmermann II 1985:192, and Sier 1992:65n6. Schmid 1946:314n4 and Prato, 306–307, on the other hand, are sceptical.

[54] Cf. the *prosodion* in Ar. *Av.* 851–858 (cf. προσόδια, 853). Cf. e.g. the *parodos* hymns in Soph. *OT* 151–215 and *Ant.* 100–154, which culminate, as does this song, in an invocation of Dionysus (*OT* 209–215; *Ant.* 147–154).

[55] Proclus *Chrest. ap.* Phot. *Bibl.* 320a12–17 (Severyns 39) and Didymus *ap.* Orion, s.v. ὕμνος (pp. 155–156 Sturz). See the discussion in Furley 1995:31–32, which I follow here to a large extent. Furley thinks that the distinction between actual hymn and other genres of choral lyric has been wrongly introduced into studies of the history of literature, since the Alexandrians ultimately simply lumped everything that they could not unequivocally ascribe to a particular god and genre into the category of hymns. Against this view, Harvey 1955, for example, is of the opinion that the hymn represents a unique and separate genre from paean, dithyramb, and other hymnic forms. Käppel 1992, esp. 64 also believes that the paean was distinct from the hymn in terms of style and intention. On the differentiation of the target-group into gods and humans cf. Proclus *Chrest. ap.* Phot. *Bibl.* 319b33–320a6.

700b) and Alexandrian classifications into subgroups, a particular category, namely that of the actual *hymnos*, has nevertheless been deduced. According to a late-antique definition, this is distinguished by a specific performance mode: ὁ δὲ κυρίως ὕμνος πρὸς κιθάραν ᾔδετο ἑστώτων ["the hymn in the proper sense of the word was sung to the accompaniment of the kithara by those who had taken up their position"].[56] The practice of the members of the chorus in the Cretan Palaikastro *hymnos*, where they talk about their current activity using the typical performative "we," appears comparable to the women at the Thesmophoria, who move about the altar while dancing: γέγαθι μολπᾷ· | τάν τοι κρέκομεν πακτίσι | μείξαντες ἅμ' αὐλοῖσιν | καὶ στάντες ἀείδομεν τεὸν | ἀμφὶ βωμὸν εὐερκῆ (lines 6–10) ["Rejoice in the dance-song (*molpê*) which we play on the *pêktis*, mixing it with the *aulos*, and which we sing, taking up position around your well-fenced altar."].[57] On the basis of references such as this one usually speaks of a *standing* chorus, as if the chorus in a *hymnos* stands still and does not move.[58] In the light of the choral and dancing self-references in many songs, this widespread opinion must be revised.[59] Our *hymnos* in the *Thesmophoriazusae* clearly shows that the chorus dances to its song.

The verb forms derived from ἵστασθαι must be interpreted in the context of line 968 (πρῶτον εὐκύκλου χορείας εὐφυᾶ στῆσαι βάσιν).[60] Ἵστασθαι in refer-

---

[56] Proclus *Chrest. ap.* Phot. *Bibl.* 320a19–20. This sentence has invariably been cited as a definition of the proper hymn (cf. Harvey 1955:166 and Bremer 1981:197). For a precise explanation see Furley 1993:23n7 and Furley 1995:31–32. Immediately preceding this Proclus contrasts it with the *prosodion*, which was sung to the accompaniment of the *aulos* and during the procession to the altar or temple: ἐλέγετο δὲ τὸ προσόδιον ἐπειδὰν προσίωσι τοῖς βωμοῖς ἢ ναοῖς, καὶ ἐν τῷ προσιέναι ᾔδετο πρὸς αὐλόν (Phot. *Bibl.* 320a18–19 [Severyns 40 with comm., pp. 117–125]).

[57] Cited following West 1965:149 (= Powell 1925:160). In the case of this song too (*Thesm.* 947ff.) we may thus also speak of a παραβώμιον (cf. Bremer 1981:197), particularly since the altar used in the Thesmophoria, or the *thymelê* in the orchestra, has already been introduced into the play in the preceding parody of the *Helen* (885–888). Cf. above, nn34 and 46.

[58] Thus Harvey 1955:166 and Bremer 1981:197. See now also Furley/Bremer I 2001:10, who speaks of a "stationary chorus." On the performative mode of the chorus in the Palaikastro hymn (στάντες ἀείδομεν, 9) cf. West 1965:157: "Our hymn, sung by a choir standing round an altar (verse 9), may have been preceded or accompanied by a dance executed by others." *Ibid.*, n35 he also suggests the possibility that the chorus could later itself have begun to dance (referring to Jeanmaire 1939:432–433); see now Furley/Bremer II 2001:11 *ad* 6. On the dance of these chorus members in the sense of a "weaving process" (see now Furley/Bremer II 2001:11 *ad* 7) that symbolically introduces them as ephebes going through an initiation rite into the "web" of society, see Ceccarelli 1998:111–112.

[59] On the Proclus passage see Furley's sound remark (1993:23n7): "Emphasis should not be placed on ἑστώτων as indicating that there was no dancing at or round the altar during hymn-singing (thus Harvey); it is simply Proclus' antithesis to ἐν τῷ προσιέναι, 'during the procession.'"

[60] Cf. on χορὸν ἱστάναι above, nn38 and 40. Cf. however Austin 1987:84 *ad* 968, who, like van Leeuwen *Thesm.*, 123 *ad* 966–968 and Rogers *Thesm.*, 102 *ad* 967, argues that στῆσαι βάσιν here

ence to the chorus does not mean "place oneself" in the sense of "stand still," but "take up a position," "get into formation for a choral dance song." This is accordingly called a *stasimon*, except in the case of an entry or departure song. The chorus has thus arranged itself around the altar in circular formation and then dances in this formation in the *hymnos*.[61]

In the *Thesmophoriazusae*, immediately before and after the first *hymnos* to the various polis gods (969–980), the members of the chorus in self-referential fashion emphasize their movements in the round dance using speech (966–968 and 981–984).[62] In line 985 there is a clear break, but the choreography undergoes no fundamental change. To speak of a new dance, as many interpreters do, is thus not accurate; one could at most talk of a new rhythm for Bakkhos.[63] The round dance is characteristic precisely of the dithyramb, with which the ensuing cultic song of Dionysus (985–1000) may practically be equated.[64]

The impressive hymnic section is completely in the tradition of archaic cult lyric. As an expression of a living choral culture, it represents an authentic representation, in the sense of a reactualization, of existing ritual forms, but in no way is it a parody.[65] The prayer to a succession of polis gods is in fact a char-

---

means to stop. Cf. now also Furley/Bremer I 2001:357 with Furley/Bremer II 2001:354–355 *ad* 968 and Austin/Olson, 301–302 *ad* 966–968. More recently Habash 1997:34 similarly interprets χοροῦ κατάστασιν (958) as the "standstill" of the chorus members.

[61] On the ancient and modern misperception that the *stasimon* was a stationary song, see Henrichs 1994/95:93n21. On the correction that the *stasimon* included motion and dance throughout, cf. *ibid.*, 95n37 (with references). Cf. Nietzsche 1878/79:378: "Die στάσιμα drücken dem Namen nach nicht das Stehen aus; der Name heißt 'Standlieder,' nicht Stillstandlieder, weil der Chor seinen Standort erreicht hat, auf dem er wohl tanzen kann. Viele στάσιμα wurden getanzt" ["Despite their name στάσιμα do not refer to standing; they are called 'standing songs' because the chorus has reached the position in which it can now dance. Many στάσιμα were danced"]. In addition to the references cited in Henrichs see also Gentili 1984/85:31–32, Cingano 1986:141–142, and Grandolini 1995:249–250.

[62] It is not necessary because of the command πρόβαινε ποσί (969) to assume a march in 969–982 (*saltationem prorsus ruentium, quam vernacule dicimus* "Marsch," Fritzsche, 390). The members of the chorus could also while in a circle set one foot in front of the other emphatically at the moment they order themselves to perform a hymn. The imperative represents rather a further self-referential confirmation of the performance that regulates the round dance.

[63] Cf. above, nn9 and 43. Cf. for example Zimmermann II 1985:196 and Sommerstein's (*Thesm.*, 113) somewhat unclear stage direction: "As the rhythm and style of the dance change again."

[64] Cf. Zimmermann 1992:25–26, Ceccarelli 1995:292–293, esp. n17, and Ceccarelli 1998:123–124, esp. 124n10. On presentations of hymns around the altar see Bremer 1981:197–199. On the practice of circular dance in dithyramb, paean, and hyporcheme during sacrificial rites see also Furley 1993:35–36, and on the round dance in tragedy and comedy Henrichs 1994/95:95–96n38. See also above, n46.

[65] Cf. Thomsen 1973:42–43. Fraenkel 1962:213 unfortunately did not include the song in his treatment of the *parabasis* odes (*ibid.*, 191–215); however, in his article (Fraenkel 1931:5) following Wilamowitz II 1893:349, he did briefly include it in the context of the *parabasis*. Imitation of folk

acteristic of *parabasis* odes, as Eduard Fraenkel demonstrated fully. In similar fashion, different divinities are beseeched to come to the aid of the chorus and to participate directly in the chorus' own activity in the orchestra. In this passage, too, the double nature of the chorus in terms of its function and role is brought into play. It is significant that the majority of the gods named have a close connection with dance. In familiar fashion, and typical of Greek anthropomorphism, the idea of choral performance is applied to Olympos as well. According to the religious beliefs of the Greeks, humans become similar to the gods in hymnic choral dance songs of this type; conversely, taking pleasure in this, the gods participate in mortal round dances. The divine chorus represents the mythical frame for human ritual activity. The cultic dance thus reactualizes the model action of the gods, and in so doing, in the heightened state of perception of the ritual festive period, the boundary between god and human is removed, for both spectators and actors.

Apollo, addressed first, is the quintessential god of the Muses and in the Homeric *Hymn to Apollo* (*Hom. Hymn.* 3.186ff.) functions as the leader of the divine *thiasos*. As lyre player, he is also the divine founder of the musical accompaniment to the song of praise. He is also fundamentally the male polis god *par excellence*, with which the order of the chorus, the cosmos, and the harmony of the human and divine world are praised.

Because the deities Apollo, Artemis, and Hera (969–976), who are invoked first, are often connected in cult with female choruses, they are also to a certain extent drawn into the ritual framework of the plot.[66] Artemis is prayed to for victory, which can be understood as a reference to success aimed for by the comic chorus in the contest of comic plays. From the point of view of plot one may also associate this with the wish of the members of the dramatic chorus to triumph over the male intruder.[67] Hera, as marriage goddess, is

---

models can be detected, according to Fraenkel, in the musical and metrical composition, in structure, and in diction. On the rhythmic antecedent of the simple glyconics with which Aristophanes imitates the "religious poetry of the old days" (esp. *Equ.* 551ff. and *Nub.* 563ff., but also *Thesm.* 1136ff.), see also Wilamowitz 1921:242–243 (with reference to Philodamus' paean), Fraenkel 1931:3–5, Fraenkel 1962:191–194, and already Crusius 1894:21. Kleinknecht 1937:116 and Horn 1970:115 also take the hymn as nonparodic. On individual gods in the hymnic portion (969ff.) see also Habash 1997:34–36.

[66] The sources are collected in Calame I 1977 (Engl. trans. Calame 1997): on Artemis, 174–190 (Engl. trans. 91–101), 252–304 (Engl. trans. 142–174); on Apollo, 190–209 (Engl. trans. 101–113), 305–323 (Engl. trans. 174–185); on Hera 209–224 (Engl. trans. 113–123).

[67] Requests for victory in the dramatic *agōn* are found in *Ach.* 1224, *Equ.* 586–590, *Nub.* 1115–1130, *Av.* 445–447, 1102–1117, *Lys.* 1293, *Ran.* 390–393, *Eccl.* 1154–1162, 1182. Cf. on this Totaro 1999:168–170. Ἑκάεργε is a typical epithet of Apollo and Artemis; Horn 1970:117n223 sees it as referring to Apollo standing at a distance, since Artemis supposedly "mit musischem

particularly closely connected with the dramatic role of the women at the Thesmophoria, in which only married women could participate. Yet by referring to the fact that Hera enjoys dancing with all choruses,[68] the chorus also refers to itself and its own function in the here and now.

Hermes, Pan, and the Nymphs, who are called upon as the next group in the antistrophe (977–984), lead us into the outside and thereby represent a fluent transition to the concluding song in praise of Dionysus, who is often accompanied precisely by this retinue and whom the chorus also locates in wild nature. These are all dancing gods.[69] Hermes is addressed with the epithet νόμιος, which refers to the world of the pasture and the *eskhatiai* beyond the polis. At the same time, the adjective is a clever play on the musical dimension of the citharodic *nomoi*, which are sung mainly in honor of the previously mentioned Apollo. The seven-part *nomoi*, like for example the *nomos* of Terpandros, consisted of hymns to the gods, and had similar characteristics to the one discussed here. The shepherd Hermes is also a simple, pastoral musician (*Hom. Hymn.* 4.24ff.) and as νυμφηγέτης is imagined as "leader" of the group of nymphs, envisaged as a choral collective.[70]

Geschehen wenig zu tun hat" ["has little to do with musical activity"]. Cf. however Calame I 1977:174–190 (Engl. trans. Calame 1997:91–101), 252–304 (Engl. trans. Calame 1997:142–174).

[68] On Meineke's conjecture συμπαίζει (975) cf. Soph. *OT* 1109. Manuscript R transmits the reading χοροῖσιν ἐμπαίζει.

[69] On the connection of Pan, the Nymphs, Hermes, and Dionysus cf. Soph. *OT* 1098–1109 (in general the latter choral song, also characterized as a hyporcheme, is quite close to this hymn; see Bierl 1991:133–134). Pan is often the attendant of Dionysus or Hermes. As son of the pastoral god Hermes, Pan is often described as the friend of Dionysus; Borgeaud 1988:174–175. Pans, Nymphs, *silenoi*, and satyrs are combined in Bacchic dance (Plat. *Leg.* 815c). On the connection of Pan and the Nymphs see Borgeaud 1988:107–108, 140, 155, 173, and 227n102; on Hermes and the Nymphs see *ibid.*, 159 and 206n17. On Pan and Hermes cf. Borgeaud 1988:54, 66, 77 and 261n17 and on Pan's connection to Dionysus cf. *ibid.*, 54, 100, and 178 (with all references). On nymphs as female followers of Dionysus see Hedreen 1994:50–54, who argues for a distinction between nymphs and maenads. Dance also plays a role in the god's cult; in general, clapping (κρότος), laughter (γέλως), and cheerfulness (εὐφροσύνη) are essential parts of his ritual; Borgeaud 1988:150. On the origin of dance and its connection to *mania* and panic see the excellent observations of Borgeaud 1988:251n118. Pan is particularly connected with choral dance: in drama he is called in Aesch. *Pers.* 448 the god "who delights in choruses" (φιλόχορος). In the strophe of the hyporcheme in Soph. *Ajax* 693–705 he is summoned, as in the *parabasis* odes, to participate as "chorus master" (χοροποί' ἄναξ, *Ajax* 698) together with Apollo in the choral dancing now taking place (the song exhibits many Dionysiac associations and performative self-references; cf. Bierl 1986:53–54, Henrichs 1994/95:73–75, and Henrichs 1996:44–45). Cf. Pind. fr. 99 S.-M., Πᾶνα χορευτὰν τελεώτατον. Cf. the hymn to Pan fr. 936 *PMG*, where Pan's music and dance are praised. On Pan in drama cf. also Eur. *Ion* 492ff. and Ar. *Av.* 745–746 (the chorus of the *Birds* performs "holy tunes" for Pan and "festive choral dances" for the Great Mother), *Ran.* 230–231 (with Apollo); cf. Lonsdale 1993:261–275 (on Pan as χορηγός) and Henrichs 1994/95:101n79.

[70] In Aristid. *Or.* 53.4 Hermes is directly named as their choral leader (χορηγός).

The transition to the gods named in the antistrophe is smoothly made, since Apollo and Artemis are also particularly connected with the world of the outside. Like Hermes and Pan, Apollo is closely associated with the pastoral world and shares with both of them the epithet Νόμιος.[71] Apollo and Pan are similarly described as νυμφαγέται.[72] But Artemis is above all the choral leader of the Nymphs. It is she who is worshiped in the choral *thiasos* by young women on the threshold of adulthood, that is, brides (νύμφαι).[73] The nymphs thus represent in this function a bridge both to Hera and to Demeter and Kore, the goddesses of the cultic and dramatic context. Hera thus reaches into Artemis and Apollo's field of expertise in that she accompanies young maidens on the initiatory transition to marriage and leads them to the fulfillment of marriage, that is, the birth of children. For this reason Hera may also be invoked with the names Παρθένος and Τελεία (as in *Thesm.* 973).[74] But in particular Hera and the Nymphs belong to the ritual sphere of the festival of the Thesmophoria, since married women paradoxically represent themselves there as νύμφαι, and as a foil to the sequence leading from fasting (Νηστεία) to the production of offspring (Καλλιγένεια) they ritually reenact the transition from virginal abstinence to female fertility.

The nymphs called upon bestow fertility, just as Demeter does. Among other things they are responsible for human reproduction and growth, and are compared to chaste bees, which in the Greek imagination are brought into a metaphorical relationship with the status of the married woman. The women celebrating the Thesmophoria, separated from their husbands, also carry the name bees (μέλισσαι). Untamed female sexuality is thereby rendered acceptable for men, in that the wives are temporarily returned to the condition of chaste νύμφαι. As bees, they become symbols of a sexuality that is only to be found in expectation and that has not yet been consumed. Although all other norms of behavior are stood on their head in this festival of inversion, order

---

[71] Apollo: Apoll. Rhod. 4.1218, Theocr. *Id.* 25.21; Pan: *Hom. Hymn.* 19.5.

[72] *IG* IV².1, 130, 15–16 (1–2) (= fr. 936, 1–3 *PMG*) (Pan), *IG* XII.8, 358a (Apollo). Dionysus is also presented as a god involved in dance and play with the Nymphs (Soph. *OT* 1108–1109).

[73] Cf. also Larson 1997. A cult of Pan, the Nymphs, and Apollo Nomios is attested (*IG* I³ 974–981) in the cave of Vari on Hymettos (cf. Ael. *VH* 10.21). An inscription addresses Apollo Hersos (*IG* I³ 981). On the initiatory threshold position of νύμφαι between παρθένοι and γυναῖκες cf. Calame 1992:110–112 and also Calame 1999a:125–129 and 163. He refers in particular to the fact that νύμφη is also the term for the newly married young wife who has not yet had a child (127 with n. 34). The ambivalent status does not then abruptly cease with the rite of passage of marriage, but continues until motherhood, which counts as the actual boundary of womanhood. Cf. also Dillon 1999 (on sacrificial requirements on Kos for νύμφαι after marriage [Segre 1993: *ED* 178]).

[74] Cf. Calame I 1977:209–210 (Engl. trans. Calame 1997:113), who emphasizes that the cult of Hera Parthenos, the virgin, was never separated from that of Hera Teleia, the adult woman.

in matters sexual is supposed to be preserved.[75] This paradoxical oscillation between the dissolution and the preservation of the usual view of the world is a vital component of comedy. In particular, the juxtaposition of speaking parts, in which everything is topsy-turvy from the perspective of the plot,[76]

---

[75] On the myth of the "bees" and King Melisseus cf. Apollodorus of Athens, *FGrHist* 244 F 89 and Callim. *Hymn.* 2.110–111. On the women at the Thesmophoria as bees see Versnel 1993:251–254 (with ample sources and secondary literature); on the ideological implications and the explanation of the Thesmophoria as a festival of inversion see the excellent account in Versnel 1993:228–288, with whose conclusions I am in substantial agreement. Through the suspension of reproduction the wildness of female sexuality is tamed by marriage. It is generally assumed that virgins were excluded from the Thesmophoria. Callim. fr. 63.9–12 Pfeiffer is an important text here. Cf. among others Deubner 1932:53 and Versnel 1993:246 and 253. Still, the last word on the problem has not yet been said. Gerhard Baudy has kindly drawn my attention (*per litt.*) to this fact once more. The testimonium in Luc. *Dial. Meret.* 2.1 speaks explicitly in favor of participation by unwed girls. Yet given the comic context of this cynic of the imperial period, the seriousness of the statement may be placed in doubt. Baudy 1992:24n132 nevertheless maintains that the Callimachus testimony speaks only seemingly in favor of the exclusion of virgins, because in the same third book of the *Aitia*, from which the fragment comes, Callimachus tells the story of Akontios and Kydippe, which forms the *aition* of a prenuptial wedding ritual (of a κοῦρος and a παρθένος, fr. 75 Pfeiffer). Baudy (*per litt.*) adds that it is important to examine the context of fr. 63 more precisely, to determine whether it is spoken in the poet's voice or in a figurative way and how the banishment is grounded. Clearly the girls have "betrayed" Kore and broken a taboo. Narrated as the *aition* of the Thesmophoria, the exclusion would create expectations of its "repetition" in the structure of the festival. Baudy concludes on the basis of the two Callimachean fragments that there was also a symbolic pre-consummation of the marriage whereby the girls are switched into the category of married women (he also includes in this context the *aition* of the Thesmophoria on Paros, according to which Demeter brought the daughters of King Melisseus a weaving stool [see below, n350] and the mysteries, so that the women celebrating the festival are also called Melissai [Apollodorus, *FGrHist* 244 F 89]). This is the equivalent, then, according to Baudy, of a female rite of initiation (see now Kledt 2004:115–120); even though this view would support the interpretation that follows even further, I am careful to distance myself from it, because there is unfortunately no unambiguous evidence in support of it. Yet clear typological analogies to initiatory processes do seem to be there (see below, n398). For this reason talk of "mysteries" and initiatory rites (τελεταί) is not without grounds; cf. Burkert 1985:242 with nn9–10. There is in fact one indication that the sequence of *kathodos* to *anodos* and the myth of Demeter and Kore that frames the ritual structure was at times mimetically performed. This kind of performance would thus be reflected in Aristophanes' play. Cf. also Lada-Richards 1999:85; Kledt 2004 (a dissertation directed by Baudy in Konstanz) attempts to reconstruct the performance of the abduction of Kore using among other things the Thesmophoria (esp. 114–147). Of course this can only lead one to the well-known conclusion that the relative reenacts Kore's descent into Hades as a definite mythical pattern. Euripides accordingly corresponds to Demeter on her search for her daughter. Cf. among others Bowie 1993:214–216, Lada-Richards 1999:163, and below, nn120 and 404–407. Yet the indications in the play in relation to the plot are relatively few; rather, the play is loosely organized about the initiation, which the women at the festival and the men in the theater ritually reexperience.

[76] Here one sees the typical Aristophanic complex of the inverted becoming the normal. It is ultimately a reflection of the ritual inversion of order protected by the state.

and choral passages, in which, with a glance at the here and now, the holy, divinely sanctioned order of the gods is celebrated, reflects this comic tension. But this contradiction is also built into the choral song. Behind the cosmos there also appear elements of chaos and unfettered nature. The cultivating function of the grain goddess Demeter, who because of the chorus' role must always be kept in mind, stands at first in open opposition to the wild, unfettered ambience that Hermes, Pan, and lastly Dionysus represent.

The constellation of gods evoked is not merely a product of poetic imagination, for it also finds an actual correspondence in Athenian cult. For example, on a votive image from the Acropolis Demeter is clearly connected with Pan, the Nymphs, Hermes, Apollo, and Artemis.[77] Pan, son of Hermes and a nymph, particularly represents this wild, rustic, enthusiastic component of choral dance that finally culminates in the hymn to Dionysus (*Thesm.* 985ff.). It is *mania* that represents the important link between the female deities Artemis and Hera and the ecstatic world in which the Nymphs, Pan, and Dionysus have their home.[78] In particular Pan shares with Hermes and Dionysus an association with the phallic.

As goat-god, halfway between animal and human, Pan mediates between the different categories and incorporates impetuous male sexuality and fertility.[79] Most of all, he is also a wild dancer, who jumps like an exuberant goat and thereby constantly threatens to disturb the harmony of the Nymphs' round dance. His phallic and excessive sexuality directed toward the nymph Echo is opposed to the civilized encounter between Demeter and Iasion in the fields, from which Ploutos eventually arises as agrarian personification of prosperity and wealth.[80] As sacred child he symbolizes to a certain extent the Kalligeneia, the day of beautiful birth that is celebrated by women after the Nesteia. Yet in choral dance even a god like Pan may produce beauty, fertility, and wealth. Pan is sometimes (Aesch. *Pers.* 448), like Athena in the song following the one under discussion (*Thesm.* 1136), given the attribute φιλόχορος. His exuberance in dance is more reminiscent, however, of phallic songs, such as the somewhat later Hellenistic *kômoi* of the Phallophoroi and Ithyphalloi. According to Aristotle, comedy arose from the improvisations of the people who struck up these *phallika*.[81] The transition to the Dionysiac part is also prepared for

---

[77] Shear 1973; cf. Shear 1973a:168–170. On other evidence for the connection of Pan and Demeter see Borgeaud 1988:140–147.

[78] On nympholepsy cf. νυμφόληπτος (*IG* I³ 980), Borgeaud 1988:104–107, and Connor 1988.

[79] Cf. Borgeaud 1988:66 on the connection of Hermes as well: "In many respects, Pan is Hermes, only more so, and more exactly so."

[80] See Borgeaud 1988:84.

[81] Arist. *Poet.* 1449a9–13. On this see below, chap. 2, passim, esp. nn7–9.

by mention of the passion for choral dance associated with Pan, for in the bridging lines 985–989 the chorus refers once more to its own activity, singing now especially in its comic function. The self-referential speech act, which still reflects Pan's connection with the chorus, is completed in the chorus' performative announcement in the first-person singular that it will now celebrate Dionysus in song with "chorus-loving processions" (ἐγὼ δὲ κώμοις | σὲ φιλοχόροισι μέλψω, *Thesm.* 988–989).

As dancing goat, Pan is any case connected with the τραγῳδοί, the dancing singers for goat sacrifice who are linked with the development of tragedy.[82] The mention of Pan thus establishes the connection between the comic chorus and the material of the plot, for the other dramatic genre and its relation to comedy are thematized in the *Thesmophoriazusae* in a particularly intense fashion, precisely in the immediate context of this song. What Pan and Dionysus do in rural seclusion with their choruses corresponds to the singing and dancing of the comic chorus going on in the present in the orchestra under the leadership of its *koryphaios*. The gifts that he allows his worshipers to share, namely "laughter and cheerfulness," that is, "excess in correct form,"[83] are identical in effect to comedy.

In the myth, Iambe, the result of the sexual union of Pan and Echo (Philokhoros, *FGrHist* 328 F 103), cheers Demeter up and moves her to give up her withdrawal, the cause of the earth's infertility. In the figure of Baubo she is known for her gestures, which openly display sexuality and which characterize the Thesmophoria and comedy.[84] In addition, the *anodos* of Persophone is often represented on vases together with Hermes and jumping and dancing Pan figures, who with their wild movements apparently support her in the effort to overcome the boundaries of Hades.[85] Similarly, Pan appears as mediator in Demeter's return in Phigalia.

---

[82] See Burkert 1966a, on τραγῳδοί, esp. 92n11.

[83] See the inscription from a cave in Pharsalia (4th c. BCE): Πὰν δὲ γέλωτα καὶ εὐφροσύνην ὕβριν τε δικαίαν (*SEG* 1, 1923, 248, line 17, pp. 60–61).

[84] In an Athenian version that goes back to Philokhoros (*FGrHist* 328 F 103) and according to which Pan and Echo are Iambe's parents, Iambe combines indecent speech and self-gesture in comic play (παίζουσα) in front of Demeter. Παίζειν relates to the speech act and to the movement, which in a sense amounts to a dance. Cf. Olender 1990:89 and Borgeaud 1988:147. On the connection of the Iambe episode (*Hom. Hymn.* 2.192–205) with the *pannykhis* in Eleusis, where of course there was also dancing, see Borgeaud 1988:170.

[85] See the no-longer extant kalyx-krater Dresden 350 (*ARV* 1056, 95) (Persephone was securely identified by an inscription); on a skyphos from Boston, Museum of Fine Arts 01.8032 (*ARV* 888, 155), two Pan figures jump and dance about a goddess emerging from the earth; see in general on *anodoi* Bérard 1974; there is a good collection and interpretation of the most important *anodoi* vases in the context of Pan in Borgeaud 1988:145–146, 247nn75–82.

Hades' abduction of Persephone and Demeter's excessive mourning, which threatens the process of natural regeneration, form the mythical background to the ritual practices at the Thesmophoria. The breakdown of order is recreated by the women in the temporary cessation of sexual relations with their husbands, precisely during the Nesteia. At the end of the *Thesmophoria-zusae* the transition to the final day, the Kalligeneia, is introduced as the overcoming of this period of reversal. The mention of the lecherously leaping Pan prepares the way, among other things, for the comic finale and in this song also points to the inherent tension between harmony and chaos. Both his laughter and his ecstatic behavior effect a transition to the Dionysus hymn that follows and introduces the return to normality after ritual transgression. Pan's wild and animal-like skipping represents a challenge to the pure harmony of the divine dance.

Like Dionysus, he threatens the current order. Yet when ecstasy is shut out, society is in grave danger of becoming stuck in a sterile rigidity. By means of the comastic dance in the here and now of the performance a new harmony arises, just as in the Themophoria, and makes possible the regeneration of nature and fertility in a cyclical interchange.[86] The obscene gestures and movements of the women are homologous to the comic and Dionysiac dance in the orchestra, through which unity between the function and dramatic role of the chorus is restored.

The invocation of these gods of the outside does not occur, as it does mostly in *parabasis* odes, in the form of a *hymnos klêtikos* that calls for an epiphany to aid the chorus. Rather, they are here requested to "give a laugh" to the chorus and experience pleasure at the choral dance, which may be localized both in the plot and in the orchestra of the real world.[87]

With regard to the self-referential utterance of the chorus (*Thesm.* 979–982) Ole Thomsen makes a crucial observation: in line 982, as has been emphasized, we are not dealing with the tragic *diplê* dance, rather διπλῆν should be taken as a proleptic adjective with the phrase χάριν χορείας, which reflects the reciprocal relationship of joy between human worshipers and gods. By means of the repetition of προθύμως (979 and 981), as well as χαρέντα χορείαις (980b) and χάριν χορείας (982), this reciprocity is underscored. In

---

[86] On Pan, see similarly Borgeaud 1988:151.

[87] On the laughter of the members of the chorus in their role as women at the Thesmophoria see Winkler 1990b:188–209, who views the laughter at men in the context of *aiskhrologia* as the "laughter of the oppressed." In the sense of a social safety valve the festival of Demeter is suited to blowing off steam in order to then better resume social relations. Zeitlin 1982 also sees the Thesmophoria as a temporary relief for women from the frustrations of everyday life.

particular Pan, as divine choral leader, by means of his wild gestures induces γέλως in his *thiasos*,[88] which is in general characterized by cheerfulness and joyful play. The chorus in the orchestra is ultimately a reproduction of the divine round dance. Pan is precisely placed to experience sympathy toward the comic chorus in the theater, who, like him, dances exuberantly.[89] Therefore the members of the chorus order themselves to spur themselves on to joy over their dance in two ways,[90] for both men and gods, as well as dancers and spectators, take pleasure in this. As in many *parabasis* odes, through this specific ritual mode of address boundaries that normally exist between actors, audience, and gods, or that separate the poet from the human and divine choral leader, are removed.

Here we may remember the passage from Plato's *Laws* (653d–654a) cited earlier, where a pseudo-etymological connection is made between χορός and χαρά (654a).[91] The passage also mentions that the gods were given to men as companions in dance. Nevertheless, pleasure does not only exist in harmony and order, on which Plato places so much value in the context of cultic chorus. Playing with normal perspectives and the pleasure of the wild exuberance of the *kômos*, which in this genre forms a παλίντονος ἁρμονία with the round dance, are key elements in comedy. Joyful παίζειν is thus an especially suitable term for the comic chorus to use in reference to its own activity.

---

[88] In Soph. *Ajax* 698 Pan is in fact invoked as χοροποί᾽ ἄναξ.

[89] The participle χαρέντα refers possibly to Pan and not to Hermes, as has traditionally been assumed, or to both gods, since they are taken as a fixed unit of father and son. Cf. also carm. conviv. fr. 887.3–4 *PMG* (to the dancer Pan): γελάσειας ὦ Πὰν ἐπ᾽ ἐμαῖς | †εὐφροσύναις ταῖσδ᾽ ἀοιδαῖς ἀοιδε† κεχαρημένος. On γελάσαι cf. also Eur. *Ba.* 380 (Dionysus).

[90] Line 981, ἔξαιρε R: ἔξαρχε Meineke. Meineke's suggestion is a reflex of ἡγοῦ (987), where Dionysus is asked to become *exarkhos* of the dithyramb and thus the divine *khorêgos* of the chorus in the orchestra; ἔξαρχε is then a direct command to Pan to assume control of the chorus. Meineke was probably unaware of the dance imperative in the singular as an address by the chorus to itself. Still less should the addressee be thought of as one person; cf. Kaimio 1970:128 and Thomsen 1973:34n9. According to Lawler's view (Lawler 1945:63–66) ἔξαιρε represents a self-command to dance the *diplê*. One could of course assume a corruption of line 982: grammarians would mark a passage with the marginal notation διπλῆ in order to characterize the rejected verse as a suspected doublet. Perhaps they did so in this instance because they did not understand the reciprocal relation of lines 980b and 982 (for this see now Furley/ Bremer II 2001:356–357 *ad* 982–983 and Austin/Olson, 304 *ad* 981–984 and above, n42); in this way the indication could eventually have been incorporated into the text in expanded form. One possible version: ἔξαιρε δὴ προθύμως | πόδας, χάριν (χάριν Ellebodius, Biset: χαίρειν R) χορείας. Cf. the choral dance diction in Soph. *Ant.* 224, κοῦφον ἐξάρας πόδα. Cf. also the full presentation in Bierl 1999.

[91] See above, Introduction n179. One could therefore consider χαράν instead of χάριν in line 982. On the interchange of the two words cf. also Soph. *Trach.* 179. On the gods' enjoyment of the choral dance of men (or frogs!) see also *Ran.* 229–232.

The keyword χάρις (982) implies reciprocity and the important concept of reciprocal compensation.[92] God and mortal are connected with the help of this fundamental idea, which means that every favor from one side entails a moral obligation on the other side to reciprocate. The concept of χάρις means at once "thanks," "favor," "joy," and "grace, charm"; in Greek society, the balance of interests and cohesiveness among mortals and between mortals and gods is aimed at using χάρις. Walter F. Otto explains the concept as follows: "Χάρις ist nicht bloß das Erobernde, das andere in Besitz nimmt, ohne sich selbst mitzuteilen: ihre Lieblichkeit ist zugleich Empfänglichkeit und Echo, 'Liebenswürdigkeit' im Sinne der Gunst und Hingabefähigkeit" ["Χάρις is not simply the power to win someone over without giving anything oneself: its charm is at once receptivity and echo, 'loveliness' in the sense of favor and readiness to give oneself"].[93] With the key word "echo" the subsequent hymn to Dionysus (996) and adjoining Andromeda scene (1009–1135, esp. 1056ff.), in which Echo plays an important role in the comic effect, are foreshadowed. Just as humans and gods stand in a reciprocal relationship, so too untamed nature, which is under the protection of the gods invoked, including Dionysus, responds to the choral dance song of humans and gods, and the sound of it reverberates through the mountains and valleys (995–998).

With these reflections we have come to the crowning finale of the song. After the various polis gods Dionysus is finally summoned. By means of the naming of this central deity, in whose honor the chorus dances in its real-life function,[94] the change in perspective from the plot and its dramatic roles to the

---

[92] On the effect of exchange see Thomsen 1973:33. On the concept of reciprocity in ritual Seaford 1994, passim. On *kharis* in the relationship of gods to mortals in Aristophanes Bowie 1993:273–278. Consider Race 1982, esp. 8–10, who summarizes his findings on the reciprocal nature of *kharis* as follows (*ibid.*, 8): "No other word epitomizes so well the relationship which the hymnist tries to establish with the god—one of reciprocal pleasure and goodwill." Cf. also Meier 1985 (who shows among other things that Athena's political function of reconciliation in Aeschylus' *Oresteia* coincides with her gracefulness). The Kharites as personification of *kharis* embody the grace of the reconciliation of unequal individuals competing with one another. On song as *kharis* in the interplay of god and mortal in Pindar see among others Most 1985, esp. 60–95. Cf. also Χάρις in Pind. *Ol.* 1.30 and the definition in Nagy 1990:65n72: "'beautiful and pleasurable compensation, through song or poetry, for a deed deserving of glory.' This word conveys both the beauty ('grace') and the pleasure ('gratification') of reciprocity." Cf. also MacLachlan 1993, esp. 3–12, index s.v. "reciprocity," and Burkert 1996:129–155, who considers the facts of the matter more from the perspective of gift exchange.

[93] Otto 1970[6]:103.

[94] See Taaffe 1993:99: "It would be most appropriate to invoke Dionysus here: Dionysus presides over the festival that the women, as comic figures, have been created for, and so he makes possible their appearance and their speech in the first place. He is also the god of transformation and sexual ambiguity, an appropriately metatheatrical god." Cf. also Bierl 1991:172–176.

actual context of the Great Dionysia, at which this comedy was performed in 411 BCE, is achieved.[95] The transition to this Dionysus dithyramb is once again smoothly achieved. The performative self-affirmation (985-986) is linked to the many choral self-commands in this song. It is noteworthy that a new dance is not introduced here, as is often assumed, but the chorus' circular dance formation only affirmed. The imperative ἀνάστρεφ' (985) indicates at most a change in the movement of the round dance.[96] The next order, Bentley's conjectured τόρνευε (986), should also be viewed in this connection. The manuscripts have τόρευε πᾶσαν ᾠδήν, which means something like "Let the song ring out with full voice!"[97] The discussion about which of these two interpretative possibilities should be favored is almost impossible to survey. Both verbs are to be understood metaphorically here; they are derived from artisanal vocabulary and in both cases have to do with a turning motion.[98] Still, this nuance comes out substantially better in Bentley's conjecture. The chorus, dancing in circular formation, thus commands itself to produce its song,[99] the second component of its activity, while turning like a lathe. Χορεία and ᾠδή are here poetically combined, with ᾠδή standing for the whole through synecdoche.[100]

---

[95] Cf. other series in dramatic hymns in which Dionysus also receives the important final position. Cf. Soph. *OT* 151ff. (Apollo, Athena, Artemis, Apollo, Dionysus [209-215]), *Trach.* 205ff. (Apollo, Artemis, Nymphs, Dionysus? [216-220]); Ar. *Nub.* 595ff. (Apollo, Artemis, Athena, Dionysus [603-606]), *Lys.* 1279ff. (Dionysus is named in the center, 1282-1284, and Aphrodite at the end). The following invocations or mentions of the god do not represent independent hymns and are better integrated into the course of the plot: Soph *Ant.* 150-154 (Dionysus at conclusion to *parodos*), *OT* 1105-1109 (Dionysus at the end of song of joy); Eur. *Ion* 216-219 (Dionysus at end of strophe of *parodos*). Cf. also Habash 1997:36 in connection with Ar. *Thesm.* 969-1000: "This hymn demonstrates a movement from Demetrian to pan-Olympian, and finally to specifically Dionysiac elements. The Chorus begins its song as celebrants of Demeter, but ends it as Bacchants celebrating Dionysus. This final shift leaves the Chorus and audience in a Dionysiac mood that befits a Dionysiac, not Demetrian, festival."

[96] Cf. Wilamowitz 1921:475-476n2. On πάλλ' see Ar. *Lys.* 1303-1304 and 1309.

[97] On πᾶσαν cf. Thomsen 1973:37, on the whole discussion on τόρευε cf. Thomsen 1973:35-37. Cf. also schol. *Thesm.* 986.

[98] Τορεύειν = "drill"; τορνεύειν = "turn on a lathe."

[99] On the dithyramb as circular chorus *par excellence* see also Ar. *Nub.* 333, *Ran.* 366, μέλη ... κύκλια, *Av.* 917-918; on the dithyramb and κυκλιοδιδάσκαλος cf. *Av.* 1403 and *Av.* 1379 (comic treatment of the dithyrambic poet Kinesias, *Av.* 1372-1409; cf. also Ar. fr. 156 K.-A.). Cf. Ceccarelli 1995:292-293 and Ceccarelli 1998:42-44, 123-124.

[100] Cf. also Eur. *Cyc.* 661 and *HF* 978, where the conjecture τόρ‹ν›ευμα ... ποδός has turned out to be the transmitted reading. Wilamowitz 1921:476n2, using the same reasoning, is also in favor of this: "τορεύειν kann drehen wohl kaum werden" ["τορεύειν can hardly become turning"] (Thomsen [1973:35] does not understand Wilamowitz here ["his point escapes me"]). Bentley's conjecture τόρνευε was considered by Brunck (*Notae in Thesm.*, 136) and adopted by Coulon in his text; in any case, the decision does not have to depend on the verb τορνεύει (*Thesm.* 54) in the play, where it is reported that Agathon

Then follows a plea to Dionysus to lead the chorus. In a fashion typical of *parabaseis*, the god of comedy himself is asked to join the actors dancing in the orchestra for him, that is, to take over control of them.[101] Dionysus functions as divine model of the κωμῳδοί moving in the Athenian theater of Dionysus. In drama it is he most of all who is connected with choral dance.[102] The χάρις of the dancers in their dramatic role and function produces the same effect in the gods, and thus a direct participation of the gods becomes understandable in the imagination of worshipers. Beside the illocutionary confirmation of their own activity, the ritual action is also supposed to have perlocutionary consequences; it is supposed to delight the gods, in particular Dionysus as the god of the occasion, who, it is hoped, will then take over and lead the chorus. As with every *hymnos*, praise of one's own performance is closely linked with the assurance that one is thereby entering into a direct state of communication with the gods. The object of the chorus' ritual action resides in a double χάρις (cf. διπλῆν χάριν χορείας, 982). This desired reciprocity is ultimately supposed to have the effect of making the gods favorably disposed to their performance. The balance between god and human resides, then, in the ritual of hymnic and dance activity. The χάρις summoned up calls for a positive answer from the Olympians. According to Greek belief, the latter take part and involve themselves in the exuberant activity. At the very least the worshipers hope for divine approval and support, which also coincides in the performative context with victory in the *agôn*.

Choral self-representation must also be viewed in this connection. The more the chorus praises itself, the more intensely it seeks thereby to entice the god. The emphasis on its own activity in the orchestra is thus not merely an illocutionary confirmation that constitutes and regulates the activity. Self-description occurs with a perlocutionary aim as well, the intervention of the gods. In the religious imagination, a command of this nature also implies an action at the same time as its utterance: for in the actual hymn (990–1000) Dionysus then functions in the religious imagination of the dancers as their choral leader.[103]

---

is "turning" a new tragedy (cf. Fritzsche, 397–398 *ad* 986). Because of the difficulties Blaydes (I, 96 *ad* 986) conjectured χόρευε, adopted by van Leeuwen *Thesm.* in his text.

[101] On Dionysus as choral leader cf. Ar. *Ran.* 351–352, 396ff.; Soph. *Ant.* 1147; Eur. *Ba.* 115, 135ff., esp. 141. Lines 985–1000 have been briefly analyzed by me (Bierl 1991:174–175) from the point of view of metatheatricality. But the principally ritual element of these performative utterances had not yet been recognized at that stage, cf. esp. *ibid.*, 174n188. On the *khorêgos*, which the imperative ἡγοῦ plays upon, cf. Calame I 1977:92–143 (Engl. trans. Calame 1997:43–73) and Nagy 1990:345ff., 375–381.

[102] Cf. Bierl 1991:99n179.

[103] Gardner (1983) thinks that the performative approach in the study of ritual has been too

The attention of the divinity must be won by means of dance, and naturally also by means of the correct choice of words and suitable description of the place where the relevant god lives. Χάρις and τέρψις are the keywords with which a reciprocal relationship between god and human may be established.[104] The mythical narration, almost obligatory in hymns, the so-called *pars epica*, through which a precedent for the ritual behavior is generally described, seems to be completely absent here. In the actual hymn to Dionysus (990–1000) one cannot speak any longer of a prayer,[105] since the single, but central, request that he take over the chorus in an epiphany has already been uttered, right at the beginning (987). It represents the climax of an appeal, which in *parabaseis* is directed to the gods, to appear, hurry to the aid of the chorus, or even mingle with them.[106] The reciprocal relationship of χάρις

---

strictly confined to the illocutionary act and that it ignores the causal effect in the mind of the believer. Still, the boundaries do not have to be drawn so strictly. The request for perlocutionary consequences also of course implies that those praying already imagine this in terms of the religious inner perspective as having been realized. The command "Dionysus, lead the chorus!" can also be interpreted as a speech act: in its speech the chorus acts in such a way that in the imagination of the speakers Dionysus really does accompany them as choral leader. Furley 1995 refers to aspects of self-presentation and reciprocal communication by means of *kharis*, which are characteristic of every hymn (esp. 36 and 45).

[104] In defense of the transmitted χοροῖς τερπόμενος (992a) against Wilamowitz's conjecture χωρεῖς, which Coulon accepts, see Thomsen 1973:39–40; Thomsen (1973:40) correctly remarks that the relationship of ἡγοῦ in connection with χοροῖς τερπόμενος forms an analogy to κώμοις φιλοχόροισι σὲ μέλψω (sic!) in the reciprocal relationship that exists between lines 979–981 and 982; cf. also the names of the muses Terpsichore (Hes. *Th.* 78 and Corinna fr. 655–fr. 1.1 PMG) and Euterpe, or the name Terpandros; χαίρειν and τέρπειν "said of the gods" belong to ritual style; cf. Kleinknecht 1937:156 and Thomsen 1973:40 with n19; see also Norden 1939:195: "Denn bezeichnenderweise hat sie [i.e. Old Comedy] Reste alter Technik auch auf diesem Gebiet treuer bewahrt als die in gemessenerem Stilgewande schreitende Schwester" ["For it [Old Comedy] has significantly preserved the remains of old technique more faithfully in this area too than its sister with its more measured style"]. On χαίρειν/χάρις cf. in this song (*Thesm.* 947–1000) *Thesm.* 972a, 980b, 982, and Eur. *Ba.* 417–418, ὁ δαίμων ὁ Διὸς παῖς | χαίρει μὲν θαλίαισιν; Soph. *Ant.* 147–148, Νίκα | τᾷ πολυαρμάτῳ ἀντιχαρεῖσα Θήβᾳ. Cf. also Ar. *Nub.* 274, τοῖς ἱεροῖσι χαρεῖσαι; *Nub.* 311, Βρομία χάρις; *Av.* 1743, ἐχάρην ὕμνοις, ἐχάρην ᾠδαῖς (where Peisetairos is pretending to be a god); Alcm. fr. 27 Davies, Μῶσ' ἄγε Καλλιόπα θύγατερ Διὸς | ἄρχ' ἐρατῶν Ϝεπέων, ἐπὶ δ' ἵμερον | ὕμνῳ καὶ χαρίεντα τίθη χορόν; Aristonous, Paean in Apollinem (Powell 1925:162–164, 164 = Käppel 1992:384–386, 386–Pai. 42), line 45, χαρεὶς ὕμνοις ἡμετέροις, carm. conviv. fr. 887.4 PMG, †εὐφροσύναις ταῖσδ' ἀοιδαῖς ἀοιδε† [ἀοιδᾷ Page] κεχαρημένος; Ar. *Ran.* 231–232, προσεπιτέρπεται δ' ὁ φορμικτὰς Ἀπόλλων; *Ran.* 674–675, Μοῦσα, χορῶν ἱερῶν ἐπίβηθι καὶ | ἔλθ' ἐπὶ τέρψιν ἀοιδᾶς ἐμᾶς. On enjoyment by members of the chorus and mortals cf. Pind. fr. 75.2 S.-M. (the Olympian gods are to react to the χάρις by their arrival), Ar. *Ran.* 244, χαίροντες ᾠδῆς, and *Ran.* 358. Cf. also τερπόμενος . . . ἐρατοῖσιν ὕμνοις (*Thesm.* 992–993) and Philodamus, Paean in Dionysum (Powell 1925:165–171, 166 = Käppel 1992:375–380, 375–Pai. 39), line 9.

[105] Cf. Thomsen 1973:42 with references.

[106] Cf. Ar. *Ach.* 665–666, *Equ.* 559–564, 586–594; *Nub.* 563–565; *Pax.* 775–781; *Thesm.* 1136–1138, 1148–1159; and *Ran.* 326–327, 385a–388, 398–403, 674–675.

between human worshipers and the relevant deity is again evoked with the chorus' announcement in the performative future that it intends to celebrate Bakkhos in κώμοις φιλοχόροισι. Just as the chorus loves its own activity of dance, Dionysus, too, who has a special affinity for the χορός, takes pleasure in this.[107] With the repeated direct second-person singular address (σέ, 989; σύ, 990; ἀμφὶ δὲ σοί, 995; περί σε, 999) and the naming of the correct names (988, 990–991), Dionysus' attention is sought in ritual style,[108] so that the god may then react entirely in the desired fashion. At the center is the exuberant *kômos* song (988b),[109] which is essential for the chorus' performance in its comic function. Just as the members of the chorus often wear a wreath of ivy or other plants for the festive occasion, so too Dionysus himself is called "ivy-bearer."[110] Speech and gesture, in keeping with the pattern of the performance, become increasingly dithyrambic and enthusiastic. Here the comic element is also present. The chorus indulges, so to speak, in a Dionysiac balancing act between serious and exuberant elements.[111]

To arouse the desired χάρις, the chorus here celebrates its virtual choral patron with a hymn that emphasizes not so much a mythical event in the form of a narrative as the choral nature of the choral god *par excellence* in myth. The hymnic description thus gives the mythical frame of the ritual at hand. As divine role-model, Dionysus takes pleasure in the chorus' activity in the here

---

[107] On the reciprocal ambivalence of the word φιλόχορος cf. Sommerstein *Thesm.*, 220 *ad* 988–989.

[108] On the *Du-Stil* of predication in lines 987ff. see Norden 1913:158, who compares them with the hymn to Dionysus (Soph. *Ant.* 1115ff.). Thereupon follows the participial style typical of hymns (Norden 1913:166–168).

[109] On the *kômos* cf. below, chap. 2 nn29–30. The mention of the *kômos* functions as a performative switch to the performance currently going on in the here and now.

[110] Cf. Eur. *Cyc.* 620, φιλοκισσοφόρον Βρόμιον. On the Dionysiac epithet κισσοχαίτης cf. Cratinus fr. 361 K.-A., Ekphantides fr. 4 K.-A., Pratinas *TrGF* I 4 F 3, 16. On the ivy wreaths of the performers cf. Philodamus, Paean in Dionysum (Powell 1925:165–171, 167, 169 = Käppel 1992, 375–380, 376, 379–Pai. 39), lines 58–60 (Muses), 146–147 (performers); on the ivy wreaths of the worshipers of Dionysus in their fictional role cf. Eur. *Ba.* 106, 323, 342, 1055. Dithyrambic choruses were decorated with the ivy wreath in particular; on the dithyrambic chorus cf. Pickard-Cambridge 1968:75–77 (the part involving Dionysus [985ff.] approaches a dithyramb in tone). On the Pronomos Vase (Naples 3240 [*ARV*^{2} 1336, 1]) all participants in the satyr chorus wear an ivy wreath, except for two members of the chorus and the *aulos* player,. It is of course questionable whether the chorus of the *Thesmophoriazusae* (*Thesm.* 985ff.) or that of the *Trachiniae* (Soph. *Trach.* 216–220) actually danced wearing garlands of ivy. On the connection of garlands with cheerful music and choral dance cf. also Eur. *Alc.* 343–344 and *HF* 677.

[111] The *communis opinio*, which treats the song, in contrast to the comic action, as if it is entirely serious, should therefore be revised. Cf. MacDowell 1995:273: "It does include three hymns to various gods, which may have been impressive musically as well as poetically (312–330, 953–1000, 1136–1159); but the rest of the play is for laughs."

and now while being himself in the Dionysiac landscape of the mountains. Just as the chorus in the theater has wished, he cheerfully dances as choral leader (ἀναχορεύων, 994) of his mythical *thiasos* among the Nymphs, who honor him with their ecstatic cries of εὔιον εὔιον εὐοῖ.[112] At the same time, the Nymphs also represent the mythical examples of the chorus in its dramatic role as women at the Thesmophoria who are imagining themselves as νύμφαι. It is thus noteworthy that here the *pars epica* is described as a genre picture, with the emphasis thus being placed on the aspect of *khoreia* and accompaniment of the song, as in the chorus' self-referential commands (992a, 993–994).

Nevertheless, the chorus does not content itself with just this, but the projection of the Dionysiac choral scenery finally goes so far as to imagine, in a fashion typical of Dionysus, the whole environment also participating actively in the choral dance song (995–1000). In the famous *parodos* of the *Bacchae* the chorus strikingly describes this performative state of affairs: αὐτίκα γᾶ πᾶσα χορεύσει ("Now the whole earth will dance!" Eur. *Ba.* 114).[113] The transferral of the chorus' activity to nature equally confirms the cyclical formation of the performing troupe in its dramatic role and in its function as chorus. Choral self-referentiality and projection are here closely intertwined with one another. As Albert Henrichs has shown, this combination of choral speech occurs often in tragic choral songs.[114] In this passage the observation also holds true for the acoustic side of things, for in this setting the ecstatic sound of voices, drums, and *auloi* resound from the mountains and valleys all around Dionysus (ἀμφὶ δὲ σοί, 995), who thus also becomes the central ἐξάρχων of the auditory projection.[115] In the final image (999–1000), ivy is associated

---

[112] This the transmitted reading for 993b in manuscript R. In my text for reasons of responsion I adopt Hermann's conjecture ὦ Εὔι', Εὔι', εὐοῖ, which Zimmermann II 1985:198–199 and Sommerstein *Thesm.*, 112 also accept. Cf. now also Prato, 311 *ad* 993b and Austin/Olson 307 *ad* 994a–b.

[113] Cf. Philodamus, Paean in Dionysum (Powell 1925:165–171, 166 = Käppel 1992:375–380, 375–Pai. 39), lines 19–20, πᾶσα δ' ὑμνοβρυὴς χορεύ- | ε[ν Δελφῶ]ν ἱερὰ μάκαιρα χώρα.

[114] Cf. Henrichs 1994/95:73–90, Henrichs 1996a, and already Davidson 1986:39–41. Here, however, we see not so much the usual projection onto other dances, but rather a transference to nature. Henrichs 1996a:61n49 terms both passages just cited (Eur. *Ba.* 114 and Philodamus, lines 19–20) "pathetic fallacy." Cf. also choral projection onto the cosmos (Soph. *Ant.* 1146–1154, where Dionysus becomes χοράγ' ἄστρων); on this cf. Eur. *Ion* 1078–1080, *El.* 467, and Alcm. fr. 1.60–63 Davies.

[115] On κτυπεῖν see Eur. *Ba.* 129 and Soph. *OC* 1500, Ar. *Eccl.* 483, ἀλλ' ὡς μάλιστα τοῖν ποδοῖν ἐπικτυπῶν βάδιζε, *Eccl.* 545, κτυποῦσα τοῖν ποδοῖν, and *Plut.* 758–759; on βρέμειν see Eur. *Ba.* 156, 164. On the loud Dionysiac music during *oreibasia*, see Eur. *Ba.* 126–129, 155–165; cf. Ar. *Nub.* 311–313. His epithet Βρόμιος (*Thesm.* 991) derives from this; see Eur. *Ba.* 66, 84, 87, 115, 329, 375, 412, 446, 536, 1031, 1250; see Dodds 1960²:74 *ad* Eur. *Ba.* 65–67.

metonymically and metaphorically with the dithyrambic and cyclical dance form of the performance. Once again the god stands at the center as imaginary *koryphaios*; about him his sacred plant arranges itself in a round dance (κύκλῳ) and shoots up in spiral form (ἕλικι), which also plays on the circular motion of the chorus.[116]

The hymn on the one hand thus confirms in illocutionary fashion the present activity of the choral members, while on the other it is also intended to have a causal effect of a perlocutionary nature, namely the summoning of Dionysus as divine leader of the ritual performance, which includes both the dramatic plot involving Demeter and the actual performance involving Dionysus. The chorus thereby proceeds in an almost magical fashion. Through dance, speech, melody, and rhythm it attempts synaesthetically to get the attention of the god and the spectators. The circular dance is underscored by self-referential speech acts. The completed encirclement is supposed to enchant the gods, in particular Dionysus, so that they join the chorus. These circular dance movements in many respects resemble the effect of the *iynx*, the magic wheel used in erotic magic. The spinning wheel produces a penetrating sound that puts the beloved under the spell of the lover. Love affairs are also connected in the Greek imagination with χάρις and enchantment. Just as the members of the chorus attempt to make the gods subject to their will, so too does the ἐραστής in the case of the ἐρώμενος. The noise and intense

---

[116] Cf. now similarly also Austin/Olson, 307 *ad* 999–1000. Cf. Eur. *Hel.* 1331; Ar. *Ran.* 1321. On εἰλίσσω as an expression of choral dance, esp. in Euripides, see among others *Tro.* 2–3, *El.* 180, 437, *IA* 1055–1057, *HF* 690, *Phoen.* 234–236, 313–316; on this see Bond 1981:245 and Mastronarde 1994:221–222. Cf. *Ran.* 1314, εἰειειειλίσσετε (imitation of a Euripidean choral ode that Aeschylus performs monodically; note here the stretching out of this favorite verb of Euripides; parody among others of Eur. *El.* 436–437; cf. Dover *Frogs*, 352–353) and *Ran.* 1349, εἰειειειλίσσουσα. Cf. the idea in Eur. *Phoen.* 649–656 applied in *Thesm.* 999–1000, where the chorus tells of the birth of Dionysus. Ivy surrounds the newborn immediately: Βρόμιον ἔνθα τέκετο μά- | τηρ Διὸς γάμοισιν, | κισσὸς ὃν περιστεφὴς | ἕλικος (coni. Hermann; Diggle and Mastronarde adopt the transmitted ἑλικτὸς) εὐθὺς ἔτι βρέφος | χλοηφόροισιν ἔρνεσιν | κατασκίοισιν ὀλβίσας ἐνώτισεν, | Βάκχιον χόρευμα παρθέ- | νοισι Θηβαῖαισι | καὶ γυναιξὶν εὐίοις. Not only does Dionysus serve as inspiration for the Bacchic dance of the Theban maidens and rejoicing women—so that the abstract concept stands for the divine dancers themselves (so Mastronarde 1994:339 *ad* Eur. *Phoen.* 655: "By a variation typical of Eur., the abstract is used for a person, here the object rather than subject of the verbal action . . . : 'who is worshipped in dancing,' 'inspiration of dancing worship'")—but the scene of the ivy surrounding the baby can also be understood as a projection of choral formation onto Dionysiac nature. Thus Βάκχιον χόρευμα stands in apposition both to κισσός and the baby Dionysus, both described in terms of dance. Cf. esp. Soph. *Trach.* 219–220, εὐοῖ, ὁ κισσὸς ἄρτι Βακχίαν | ὑποστρέφων ἅμιλλαν. On this point see both the excellent discussion of Henrichs 1994/95:81–84 (who does not, however, investigate the special self-referential function of "ivy" and "turn" in connection with the round dance) and Bierl 1991:135–137.

motion of the magic wheel make the beloved give himself of his own free will (χαρίζεσθαι). Iynx, the mythological personification of this wheel, is considered, like Iambe, to be a daughter of Echo and Pan, who are both of importance in this song.[117]

In its dance the chorus thus whirls about the altar of Dionysus, the god of its desire, just like the magic wheel about the beloved. But encirclement is also found in the diction of μολπή and ᾠδή. Here one may mention in particular the arrangement of ring composition. Dionysus is approached in concentric circles. First, reference is made to a visual characteristic: the god is initially addressed as κισσοφόρε (988a), while at the end of the hymn ivy, which surrounds the god (999–1000), comes once more into the field of view. Then the focus shifts to the auditory dimension. Dionysus receives the epithet Βρόμιε (991), while the description of the noisy torrent of enchantment reaches a climax in the corresponding keyword βρέμονται (998b). At the center of the auditory attractions is the mention of the echo on Kithairon (996). Standing as it does almost at the midpoint of the Dionysus hymn, it reflects individual sensory impressions as on an axis of symmetry. The god is shown in *oreibasia* (κατ' ὄρεα, 992b) with his retinue of nymphs, and the mountains (ὄρη, 997) resound in the same way with the echo of the *kômos*. Moreover, the reciprocity of the multimedia relationship of χάρις between gods and mortals is emblematically mirrored. Dionysus, standing in the center, conducts a series of circles of dancers following one after another: in the mythical projection he leads the chorus of nymphs, in the world of the dramatic plot he leads that of the women at the Thesmophoria, who as νύμφαι relate themselves to these mythical nymphs, while in the here and now of the orchestra he is in charge of the chorus dancing in his honor.

This reciprocal connection is also manifest in the verbal concretization. Dionysus is pleased by ecstatic cries, wild music, and uninhibited movements of the "I" of the performer and by the internal chorus of the nymphs, and so he himself makes noise and dances (ἀναχορεύων, 994). Ultimately the entire surroundings—the idyllic landscape as well as the orchestra in the here and now, together with the assembled audience—are drawn into the activity.

---

[117] On the *iynx* cf. Callim. fr. 685 Pfeiffer (= schol. Theocr. *Id.* 2.17) and schol. Pind. *Nem.* 4.56a; cf. Borgeaud 1988:85 (with useful references). *Iynx* is also the name of a bird, the so-called wryneck, which can turn its head 180 degrees and emits shrill cries, which the Greeks compared with the pan flute or generally with the *aulos*; see Richter 1975. Among other reasons, the chorus members were frequently compared and equated to birds for the musical quality of their song (see above, pp. 78–79), esp. in the *Birds* of Aristophanes.

Echo and the Chorus of Maidens in the Further Course of the Play

In the mythological imagination of the Greeks, Echo is herself a nymph who defends her maidenhood, just like the women at the Thesmophoria, against the wild, ithyphallic attacks of the god Pan, who has fallen in love with her. In a version of the story in Longus (3.23) Pan drives the herdsmen mad and has them tear Echo limb from limb as a punishment. After this strange Dionysiac *sparagmos*, the earth, at the Nymphs' command, buries the far-flung, and still singing, parts of her body, thus preserving her music. The chorus of the *Thesmophoriazusae* combines in itself the part of Pan (as a group of comic performers) and that of the nymph (in the role of the women attending the Thesmophoria). The echo of ritual sound patterns spread over the hymn represents the dithyrambic and enthusiastic music that delights all gods, especially Pan and Dionysus, and performers and audience alike.[118] At the same time Echo serves as a symbol of maidenhood, which the women reactualize precisely on the fast-day of the Νηστεία.[119] The young women group themselves into a chorus during their initiation in exactly the same way as the choral members in their dramatic role of female choral members and worship the gods with dance and song.

Furthermore, Echo and the wild natural scenery anticipate the comic play on the echo-effect in the paratragic *Andromeda* scheme (1056ff.). It continues

---

[118] The myth of Echo, embedded in the plot of *Daphnis and Chloe* (Long. 3.23), is of great interest for understanding our song in terms of the relationship of *kharis* between gods and mortals. Echo is a maiden on the threshold of becoming a woman (παρθενίας εἰς ἄνθος ἀκμάσασα); her primary occupation consists of participating in the choruses of the Nymphs and Muses (ταῖς Νύμφαις συνεχόρευε, ταῖς Μούσαις συνῇδεν). After the virgin's limbs are gathered together and buried, the earth imitates (μιμεῖται) everything, even Pan as he plays his syrinx. "And he, when he heard the voice, sprang up and pursued it up into the mountains, not to catch it, but to find out who his hidden pupil was." The failed sexual relationship between man and woman, which also depends on *kharis*, thus here becomes sublimated to a musical relationship. Echo, now transformed into a natural phenomenon, imitates the musical activities of Pan and reactualizes them qua mimesis, at which the god experiences pleasure and even participates as dancer (ἀναπηδᾷ . . . κατὰ τῶν ὁρῶν) in order to discover the origin of the sound. Cf. Dionysus' *oreibasia* with the Nymphs (*Thesm.* 992); on πηδάω as choral term see *Lys.* 1316–1317, *Ran.* 1211–1213 (from Eur. *Hypsipyle* [fr. 752 N/Kannicht] on Dionysus as choral dancer): "Διόνυσος, ὃς θύρσοισι καὶ νεβρῶν δοραῖς | . . . | πηδᾷ χορεύων –"; *Vesp.* 1520 (on the dancing sons of Karkinos); *Equ.* 545, 599, 604 (in connection with the horses and riders of the chorus); Autokrates fr. 1.1–6 K.-A., οἶα παίζουσιν φίλαι | παρθένοι Λυδῶν κόραι, | κοῦφα πηδῶσαι ‹ποδοῖν› | κἀνασείουσαι› κόμαν | κἀνακρούουσαι χεροῖν | Ἐφεσίαν παρ' Ἄρτεμιν; and fr. adesp. 936.8 *PMG* (hymn to Pan), πηδᾷ. On the echo of the dithyrambic chorus, see also Pind. fr. 75.18 S.-M. On the echo as characteristic element of the bird chorus see Ar. *Av.* 215.

[119] Echo had a sanctuary on the Sacred Way to Eleusis (*IG* II/III^2 1011.8) and was thus closely connected with the cult of Demeter. Cf. also Philokhoros, *FGrHist* 328 F 103.

to be a contested point in the scholarly literature whether Echo appears in person to console the relative playing the role of Andromeda, or whether Euripides takes over the role of Echo and thus himself takes his Echo-idea in the *Andromeda ad absurdum*.[120] It is impossible to give a definitive answer. Aristophanes has clearly switched the two parodied parts of Euripides' *Andromeda*. In the tragedy there came first an anapaestic duet between Andromeda and Echo, then the *parodos* of the chorus of young female attendants, who enter into an *amoibaion* with Andromeda. Andromeda must first have ordered Echo to keep quiet in order to then be able to lament with the chorus.

The *amoibaion* also represents the basis of the introductory aria of the relative in his role as Andromeda in the *Thesmophoriazusae* (1015ff.). The subsequent grotesque interchange with Echo becomes the absurd highpoint of the scene, which explains the shattering of the Euripidean intrigue. Despite this reversal the relative turns to Echo in her cave: κλύεις, ὦ προσάδουσ' | αὐταῖς ἐν ἄντροις;[121] ("Do you hear, o you who answer me in song in your cave?" 1018–1019). The

---

[120] Heath 1987:51n106, Sommerstein *Thesm.*, 226–227 *ad* 1056–97 (with sound arguments) and Gilula 1996 argue for Echo's appearance as a separate person; see now also Slater 2002:175. Sier 1992:75–76 (with n41) on the other hand gives good reasons for thinking Echo was invisible, was reduced to her voice alone, and yet, as the scholia also maintain (schol. *Thesm.* 1056), was played by Euripides (see now also Prato, 321 *ad* 1056–64); similarly Bubel 1991:10n10. Van Leeuwen *Thesm.*, 133 apparatus *ad* 1056–1096 and Mureddu 1987:21–22 interpret Echo as an actual person, who remains invisible, however, performs behind the scenes with voice alone, and supposedly mimetically parodies the natural phenomenon thematized in the *Andromeda*. Klimek-Winter 1993:140–143, with Hansen 1976:182–183, believes Echo was visible to the audience and played by Euripides/Perseus, though she remained invisible for the parties affected, the relative and the Scythian (this seems to be the position of Austin/Olson). The report in the scholia probably means nothing other than that the momentarily released actor, who otherwise played the role of Euripides, here provided the voice of Echo. On the Echo part in general, see Mureddu 1987 for more detail. On the *Andromeda* parody cf. Rau 1967:65–89. As Iambe's mother, Echo could have been introduced by Aristophanes almost as a sort of sexually themed comic stand-in for the daughter, in keeping with the Thesmophoria as the context for the plot. Euripides finally transforms himself in the *exodos* scene into a procuress and resorts to the level of prostitutes, who adopt a vulgar speech similar to that of women during the ritual *aiskhrologia* of the Thesmophoria (Cleomedes 2.1, p. 166, 7 Ziegler). On prostitutes in the *parabasis* see below, nn312 and 324. In addition, in the comic Echo scene (1056ff.) one could also perhaps associate the so-called *êkheion* in Eleusis (τὸ καλούμενον ἠχεῖον, Apollodorus, *FGrHist* 244 F 110b), the sounding of a gong by which the lost maiden Kore was supposed to be summoned up from the depths. Cf. the explanation of Demeter's by-name Akhaia in schol. *Ach.* 708 and Etym. Magn., s.v. Ἀχαία (180.34–41). Cf. on this Bérard 1974:75–87, esp. 83–87.

[121] On the text of *Thesm.* 1018–1019: προσάδουσ' αὐταῖς, Sommerstein *Thesm.*, προσάδουσ' (Elmsley, Dobree) αὐτάς (Burges) Mitsdörffer 1954: 69–70, προσάδουσα (Elmsley, Dobree) τἄμ' (Willems) Coulon, προσαυδῶ σε τάν Bothe: προσαιδοῦσσαι τάς R and schol. *Thesm.* 1018. Cf. on this Austin 1990:28, who like Parker 1997:436 and 443 favors Mitsdörffer's solution; see now also Austin/Olson, 314 *ad* 1018–1019.

context of the *Andromeda* is in fact briefly introduced (1010ff.); Euripides clearly appears as Perseus. To understand the parody, the audience has to recall the tragedy together with the famous Echo-scene. Yet the just-cited verse becomes comprehensible from the reference in the immediately preceding choral song (996).[122] Echo reverberates in the wild Dionysiac landscape, in the cave that also defines the stage-setting of the *Andromeda*. Later on in the aria, the relative as Andromeda also refers to the chorus in an additional dramatic role (1029–1030): maidens, who form the chorus of the Euripidean *Andromeda*, are mentioned. The chorus of the comedy thus receives a tragic opposite, which in the parody makes sound fragments of the original resound over the cheerful stage. In the mock-aria Mnesilokhos behaves like an ἐξάρχων without a chorus. As in the parody of the *Helen*, through the unsuccessful rescue, which prevents a connection with the male, the relative approaches the ritual role of the women at the Thesmophoria, whom we know abstained from sex. Because of his failed marital reunion, the comic hero on stage regresses to the status of the lonely virgin unable to complete the initiatory transition to womanhood though marital consummation with Perseus/Euripides. In this respect he resembles the nymph Echo, who embodies the Νύμφαι of the chorus in its role as worshiper of Demeter. Echo becomes the *alter ego* of the relative, and for this reason she mimics him in the following scene (1056ff.) as well.

The relative's aria, which reworks the *amoibaion* of the original, also integrates words which the lamenting Andromeda originally directs to her choral retinue. At the moment of utterance the cliché "Dear maidens, dear and lovely" (1015), with which the tragic heroine addresses the sympathetic chorus, also becomes part of the address of the actual chorus of women at the Thesmophoria, who ritually reexperience the condition of παρθενία. The relative, like Andromeda and Echo, is threatened with death by a monster (Skythes, Ketos, Pan). In his moment of need, he laments that he has become separated from the chorus of his age-mates: ὁρᾷς, οὐ χοροῖσιν οὐδ᾽ | ὑφ᾽ ἡλίκων νεανίδων | κημὸν ἕστηκ᾽ ἔχουσ᾽ (1029–1031). The chorus of women celebrants oppose him of course, because he has trespassed as a male into a women's festival. His only hope of rescue is to associate himself with the women in the orchestra, as ultimately happens after the failed Euripidean schemes. Andromeda and Echo, like all young women before marriage, once indulged in beautiful dance and

---

[122] Sier 1992:74 speaks of the relative summoning Euripides as Echo in line 1019. Yet how can it be that Euripides, who in line 1011 is still named in the role of Perseus, now has supposedly slipped into the role of Echo without any occasion for doing so or any indication of transformation of identity? At most one may only draw this conclusion retrospectively, from his subsequent appearance (following schol. *Thesm.* 1056); for the audience, such a solution at this point could hardly have been comprehensible and for the actors, impossible to perform.

song surrounded by the circle of their age-mates as chorus in order to honor the gods.[123] The parodied orginal of Euripides makes this clear. Yet something new is mixed in here in a comic and grotesque form. The original context is adapted to the changed situation: Andromeda apparently laments that deprived of her age-mates she cannot celebrate with a *kômos* (κῶμον ἄγουσα; cf. 1031);[124] a typically masculine object, the voting urn, which serves to collect the voting pebbles, is introduced into comic context with slight sound change, so that the relative now says that he stands alone, without a voting urn in his hands (κημὸν ἔχουσα). Parody and the parodied thus enter into the characteristic reciprocal relationship of intertextual play. The *amoibaion* with the chorus becomes a monologic aria, the female ambience of the initiatory chorus is shifted by the change of some letters into the male realm of the public polis society. By means of the adopted lament of Andromeda that she will never experience marriage, the relative compares himself qua mimesis to the status of the female chorus as *nymphai*.[125]

At this point let us take a brief preliminary look at the series of events. In what follows dance continues to remain a *Leitmotiv* of the play. After the *Helen* scheme, the *Andromeda* trick also fails. Yet by means of the mimetic process of assimilation to the female figures and through the absurd intervention of Echo, Euripides and his relative gradually approach the position of the women celebrating the Thesmophoria. After this episode the chorus sings another hymn to the gods, to a certain extent the delayed *antode* of the *parabasis* (*Thesm.* 1136–1159), which separates the tragic schemes from the comic rescue brought about by the peace agreement with the women. After this assimilation to the female world, Pallas Athena and the goddesses of the Thesmophoria, the chorus' actual points of reference in its dramatic role, now stand at the center. As in the great choral dance song (947–1000), the goddesses are envoked in typical *parabasis* fashion to participate in the chorus of the performance in the here and now. First the chorus pronounces in almost prosaic fashion that it is its ritual duty to summon Athena to the activity at hand: Παλλάδα τὴν φιλόχορον ἐμοὶ | δεῦρο καλεῖν νόμος εἰς χορόν, | παρθένον ἄζυγα κούρην

---

[123] Cf. among others Eur. *El.* 178–180 (Elektra), *IT* 1143–1152 (chorus of Greek maidens serving as temple slaves in the land of the Taurians), and *Phoen.* 1265–1266 (Antigone); on Echo cf. Long. 3.23 and above, n118.

[124] Van Leeuwen *Thesm.*, 130 *ad* 1031 conjectures κῶμον ἔστηκ' ἄγουσ' and adopts it in his text; cf. Sommerstein *Thesm.*, 225 *ad* 1031.

[125] Cf. *Thesm.* 1034–1036: γαμηλίῳ μὲν οὐ ξὺν | παιῶνι, δεσμίῳ δὲ | γοᾶσθέ μ.' Here too the relative plays ironically on the situation of the ὕμνος δέσμιος in the previous choral ode (*Thesm.* 947–1000).

(1136–1139).[126] With Athena an even clearer reference to politics is established than is usual even for the *parabasis* (cf. 1140–47). Yet even here one cannot speak of a change of perspective and a move away from the mythical and ritual perspective, as Sommerstein thinks;[127] Athena is invoked above all because she embodies the state of maidenhood (παρθένον ἄζυγα κούρην) important for the women celebrating the Thesmophoria and because as goddess of the city she is responsible for the functioning of the democratic order together with its ritual requirements: the legal order (νόμος, 1137) of the men protects even the women's festival of inversion from violation. Interestingly, Athena is characterized as friend of choruses (φιλόχορον).[128] While the members of the chorus have until now used the expression "it is customary" (νόμος) mostly in connection with their ritual role as women at the Thesmophoria, it is now transferred to the ritual context of the chorus' activity in the here and now of the polis. We know nothing in fact of any direct participation of the goddess Athena in the Thesmophoria.[129] Rather, it is the scenery of the *pannykhis* at the central polis festival of the Panathenaea that is evoked, at which nocturnal choruses of maidens were conducted for Athena.[130] She is called upon to appear (φάνηθ', 1143), so that she may appoint longed-for "festival-loving peace" (εἰρήνην φιλέορτον, 1147) to her retinue. Here the reference is clearly both to the festival of the Thesmophoria as occasion for the dramatic plot and to the celebration of the Dionysia as occasion for the performance.[131] The

[126] On the invocation of Athena in *Thesm.* 1136ff. see also Anderson 1995:63–67. On the song cf. also Habash 1997:36–37.

[127] Sommerstein *Thesm.*, 231–232 *ad* 1143–1144.

[128] The chorus has already invited Dionysus and his κῶμοι φιλόχοροι in the previous ode to participate in the festive dance song (*Thesm.* 987–989). This epithet is not elsewhere attested in connection with Athena.

[129] Cf. however the reference to the Skira *Thesm.* 834 and below, pp. 196–206.

[130] On the *pannykhis* cf. Eur. *Hcl.* 777–783 and *IG* II/III² 334.30 and 32–33; on the nocturnal performances cf. Eur. *Hcl.* 780–783: there are choral performances by ephebes, νέων τ' ἀοιδαὶ χορῶν τε μολπαί (*Hcl.* 780). The place echoes with their cries (ὀλολύγματα, *Hcl.* 782) and resounds with the stamping of the maidens' feet in their nocturnal dance, παννυχίοις ὑπὸ παρ- | θένων ἰαχεῖ ποδῶν κρότοισιν (*Hcl.* 782–783). See in general Wilkins 1993:151–152, and on the *agônes* at the Panathenaia see Kotsidu 1991:35–62, esp. 59–60. On Athena as goddess worshiped by choruses of unmarried girls see Calame I 1977:232–241 (Engl. transl. Calame 1997:128–134). Pallas stands synonymously for παρθένος; see Fauth 1964:681. Furthermore, Athena is the goddess of the Arrhephoroi, who also perform choruses in her honor; cf. Eur. *Ion* 492ff.

[131] On further ritual and choral self-references see *Pax* 775–781: Μοῦσα, . . . | μετ' ἐμοῦ | τοῦ φίλου χόρευσον, | κλείουσα θεῶν τε γάμους | ἀνδρῶν τε δαῖτας | καὶ θαλίας μακάρων· | σοὶ γὰρ τάδ' ἐξ ἀρχῆς μέλει; *Nub.* 308–313: εὐστέφανοί τε θεῶν θυσίαι θαλίαι τε | παντοδαπαῖσιν ὥραις, | ἦρί τ' ἐπερχομένῳ Βρομία χάρις | εὐκελάδων τε χορῶν ἐρεθίσματα | καὶ μοῦσα βαρύβρομος αὐλῶν; Αν. 731–734: πλουθυγίειαν, βίον, εἰρήνην, | νεότητα, γέλωτα, χορούς, θαλίας, | γάλα τ' ὀρνίθων; and Eur. *Ba.* 417–418: ὁ δαίμων ὁ Διὸς παῖς | χαίρει μὲν θαλίαισιν. On the ἑορτή cf. *Ran.* 371: καὶ

Athenian people calls on its goddess (δῆμός τοί σε καλεῖ, 1145), who is accordingly further defined as "she who hates tyrants, as is fitting" (ὦ τυράννους | στυγοῦσ', ὥσπερ εἰκός, 1143-1144).[132] In this way the chorus evokes the political component of its role as *dêmos* in the popular assembly, which in the negotiation scene, as will be shown in more detail below, will become mingled with its identity as female celebratory community. With the postponed qualification γυναικῶν (1145-1146) this comic *mésalliance* of the women's *ekklêsia* in the *parodos* is restored.

The characterization as *dêmos* also refers to the chorus in its performative function. As chorus of citizens, the members of the chorus constitute a representative cross-section of all politically-enfranchised male inhabitants. The chorus speaks here for the people as a whole, who have gathered in the theater, and at the end of the comedy call on the patron goddess of the polis to come and bring peace to the Dionysia in the tense situation of 411 BCE.[133] Only after the postponed attributive genitive γυναικῶν (1145-1146) is the prominent dimension of the here and now reintegrated into the mimesis of the then and there. In the immediately following scene Euripides straightaway makes the decisive peace-offering to the women of the chorus (1160-

---

παννυχίδας τὰς ἡμετέρας αἳ τῇδε πρέπουσιν ἑορτῇ, *Ran.* 391, 398, 443-444, and *Pax* 816-817: Μοῦσα θεά, μετ' ἐμοῦ ξύμπαιζε τὴν ἑορτήν. The comparison with *Pax* 974-977 (prayer to Eirene for propitious reception of sacrifice): ὦ σεμνοτάτη βασίλεια θεά, | πότνι' Εἰρήνη, | δέσποινα χορῶν δέσποινα γάμων, | δέξαι θυσίαν τὴν ἡμετέραν is also of particular importance for this passage. In the *Peace*, the divine personification is also mistress of the chorus together with Dionysus as god of performance. Once again there is a typical fluctuation between performance and the fictional function of Eirene as founder of marriage (the wedding simply represents a metonymic extension of the peace accord).

[132] This scene makes Athena's role as protector of the *dêmos* clear; cf. Ostwald 1986:357-358. The frequent references to tyrants (e.g., *Thesm.* 338-339) in this work are of political importance given the historical situation in 411 BCE; on the other hand, they should not be overly interpreted as completely transparent statements of the politics of the day. Dover 1972:171-172 warns against excessive reliance on contemporary politics and views the references as a conventional means of expressing the *dêmos'* habitual fear of oligarchy. On the political background cf. Sommerstein *Thesm.*, 2-4, esp. on preparations for an oligarchic coup, cf. Ostwald 1986:337-358; Sommerstein (*ibid.*, 2) thinks the remarks directed against Persians and despots, which he interprets as exclusively political, were only integrated into the completed manuscript at a later stage, immediately before the performance at the Dionysia in 411 BCE; see now also Prato, 329 *ad* 1143-1144 and Austin/Olson, xliii. See below, n276 on the resulting ritual implications of the relative as intruder being compared to a tyrant. In a different performative perspective see now Slater 2002:150-180.

[133] Cf. esp. lines 317-319, corresponding to lines 1140-1142, and Anderson 1995:64: "When the women claim the practice of inviting Athena as their own, they are no longer just female celebrants at the festival, but stand-ins for those who would normally call on Athena at an assembly, namely the Athenian ecclesia." Anderson also does not see the performative dimension and the reference to the pragmatic context.

1161), who respond to it, since the men have come closer to their world and their comic mode of behavior. As city goddess Athena helps to polarize the Athenians' attitude to the Scythian barbarian and to act out racist comedy against him,[134] which builds solidarity and group cohesion among the spectators.

At the end of the song the fictional frame is strengthened by the appeal to the goddesses of the Thesmophoria, Demeter and Kore. They, too, are again and again implored to come and participate in the choral activity, with νῦν and ἐνθάδ' ἡμῖν (1158–1159) acting as a hinge between the *hic et nunc* and the "we" of the performers and the fictional "now," "here," and "we" of the chorus in its role as women celebrating the Thesmophoria and who uphold the command of abstinence.

> ἥκετ' εὔφρονες, ἵλαοι,
> πότνιαι, ἄλσος ἐς ὑμέτερον,
> ἀνδράσιν οὐ θεμίτ' εἰσορᾶν   1150
> ὄργια σεμνὰ θεοῖν ἵνα λαμπάσι
> φαίνετον, ἄμβροτον ὄψιν.
> μόλετον, ἔλθετον, ἀντόμεθ', ὦ
> Θεσμοφόρω πολυποτνία.   1156
> εἰ πρότερόν ποτ' ἐπηκόῳ
> ἤλθετον, ‹καὶ› <u>νῦν</u> ἀφίκε-
> σθον, ἱκετεύομεν, <u>ἐνθάδ' ἡμῖν</u>.

Thesm. 1148–1159

Come in friendly and gentle fashion, o mistresses, to your grove, (1150) where, a sight forbidden for males to look upon, you two reveal the holy mystic rites of the twin goddesses with torches, an immortal spectacle! (1155) Come, approach, we beg you, o much-revered Thesmophoroi! If ever before you heard our prayer and came, now too, we beseech you, come to us here!

The peace agreement may be considered as parallel to the end of *aiskhrologia* between the sexes (1160ff.). The comic intrigue of Euripides, who acts

---

[134] On this basis the chorus' anti-Persian attitude (337, 365) should also be read not simply as an extra-dramatic, political statement. On the friend-enemy complex that Athena establishes in the *Oresteia* by means of an association and dissociation of powers ("*Assoziation und Dissoziation der Kräfte*"), see Meier 1980:207–214, 218–222 (adopting the ideas of Carl Schmitt [30–33]) and Bierl 1996:29, 51–52, 64. Euripides and his agent (relative) as Athenians have the same interests as the chorus.

as a procuress, uses a young dancing girl called Elaphion.[135] As a result of her solo dance to the wild accompaniment of the *aulos*, played by Teredon, the Scythian becomes so sexually aroused that he is drawn into a rendezvous arranged by Euripides. The barbarian is thereby distracted from his assignment to keep watch over the prisoner, so that the relative can eventually be freed. Moreover, it may in fact be established that on the middle day of the festival, on which the plot of our play takes place, all prisoners were released from their chains.[136]

To the Scythian, the multimedia spectacle seems like a jolly, noisy *kômos* (βόμβο and κῶμο, 1176) *en miniature*, a mini-revel in the *kômos* which the chorus stages.[137] The latter stands for the cheerful, exuberant bustle of comedy,

[135] Euripides now humorously calls himself after Artemisia, queen of Halikarnassos in Caria (1200ff.), whose bravery in the naval battle at Salamis (480 BCE) caused Xerxes to exclaim (Hdt. 8.88.3): "My men have become women, my women men!" In the *agôn* in the *parabasis* of the *Lysistrata*, the male semi-chorus accuses the women of behaving like Artemisia (*Lys.* 675), since they endanger the traditional power of men through their behavior. On Caria as a locus of inversion, see Bierl 1994:31.

[136] Marcellinus *ad* Hermogenes, *Rhetores Graeci* 4.462.2–3 Walz. Cf. the orator Sopater, *ibid.* 8.67.4 Walz. The release of prisoners was also transferred to the Panathenaia and Dionysia (schol. Demosth. 22.68 [170b, p. 293 Dilts]); this could also form a basis for the invocation of Athena (*Thesm.* 1136ff.).

[137] Agathon's performance on stage is already described as an introverted solo *kômos* (see esp. *Thesm.* 104). Agathon here resembles the solitary *kômastaí* in vase paintings, who, following the Anacreon-like model of the poet, are shown with the *barbitos* (cf. *Thesm.* 137). Cf. Snyder 1974 and Frontisi-Ducroux/Lissarrague 1990; Agathon, however, does not have a beard, while the Anacreon figures retain this sign of masculinity. The onomatopoeic βόμβο (1176) is already anticipated by the *bômolokhos*-like comments of the relative at the entry of Agathon: he interrupts the *parousia* description of the servant with the insertions βομβάξ (45) and βομβαλοβομβάξ (48). The chorus, whose song (947ff.) becomes in a way a catalyst for the reconciliation in the final scene, has previously evoked the *kômos* (988b); the relative in his tragic mood parodically alters the term (1031); see above, n124. Here the comastic is now expanded, in contrast to the introductory Agathon scene. Euripides, dressed as a woman with harp (*pêktis*; on this instrument see West 1997; according to West 1997:50 a harp is meant in line 1217), and having a beard, now clearly resembles the figures on Anacreontic vases; at the same time the flute-player Teredon ('Woodworm') and the female dancer complete the musical side. The whole ensemble also resembles comastic vase paintings with an *aulos*-player (on the *aulos* as instrument of transgression see Wilson 1999) and a slave-girl as dancer (cf. for example the representation on a *kylix* from the Bareiss collection, Malibu 86.AE.293; Frontisi-Ducroux/Lissarrague 1990: ill. 7.32). In the comic finale the *hetaira* as sexual element in the *kômos* is also present in the person of the dancing-girl, and the phallic in the person of the Scythian. On the common presence of the *aulos*, which provides musical accompaniment for others, and of the stringed instrument (*barbitos*), with which the poet accompanies himself, see a fragment from the Agora, Athens, Agora P 7242 (*ARV* 566.4). The Anacreontic *kômos* scenes also usually display the type of the poet with parasol, an item of feminine apparel. The tableau in the *parabasis* (821–829) and the appearance of the relative form a bridge between the comastic scene of Agathon and Euripides. On the connection between weaving (cf. the female

which retains the upper hand over Euripides' tragic ideas.[138] After the barbarian has been made a fool of by the women several times and sent in the wrong direction after the fugitive,[139] the chorus ends the farcical game abruptly with a closing song, which at this stage of the plot in typical fashion switches over into the here and now:

confusion in the tableau 821–829) and dance with rhythmic beating on a string instrument, see Ceccarelli 1998:111–112; the πηκτίς, which Euripides carries (πηκτίδας, 1217), can be understood as a string instrument (cf. Anacr. fr. 373 and 386 *PMG*) as well as a loom. In the Palaikastro hymn (lines 7–8), which is connected, according to Lonsdale 1993:165 and Perlman 1995, with an ephebic oath, flute and *pêktis* are also combined as accompaniment. The dancing-girl Elaphion receives her name from the Dionysiac fawn, which is often connected with dancing maenads (cf. Eur. *Ba.* 866). On the deer (ἔλαφος, νεβρός) as choral metaphor cf. *Hom. Hymn.* 2.174–175, Ar. *Lys.* 1318–1319 (ἔλαφος); cf. Sappho fr. 58.16 L.-P., Bacchyl. *Epinik.* 13.86ff., Eur. *El.* 860–861: ὡς νεβρὸς οὐράνιον | πήδημα κουφίζουσα, *Ba.* 862ff., esp. 866 (νεβρός). The dancer jumps as lightly as a deer or flea (1180). The dance terminology, also used in lines 1178–1179 (ὀρχησομένη and ὄρκησι καὶ μελετῆσι), strengthens the dancing girl's activity on stage. The lascivious dance culminates in Elaphion winding herself about her victim with her lovely charms, to which the barbarian comments καλὴ τὸ σκῆμα περὶ τὸ πόστιον (1188). Σχῆμα refers to a dance position (Lawler 1964:25–27, 72, 83, 87, 114, 128, 133) and to the arrangement of her bottom, which is probably exposed. The play-within-play situation is emphasized by the fact that the flute-player is not the same as the *aulos*-player in the theater, who usually accompanied all musical choral parts and is elsewhere often addressed metatheatrically (Taplin 1993:105–110), but performs next to the latter; cf. Sommerstein *Thesm.*, 233 *ad* 1160–1175.

[138] Cf. Bierl 1991:175–176 and Bowie 1993:219–225.

[139] The comic chase-scene possibly alludes to the Chalcidian δίωγμα at the Thesmophoria. Cf. now Prato, xxx and 340 *ad* 1221. See the emphatic commands of the chorus, δίωκε and διώξεις (*Thesm.* 1223–1224), directed at the Scythian. The Χαλκιδικὸν δίωγμα or ἀποδίωγμα was a custom that is supposed to have consisted of a secret sacrifice. An *aition* reports that once, during a war, the women prayed for victory and the enemy thereupon fled and was pursued as far as Khalkis; Hesych. and Suda, s.v. and Versnel 1993:239. We are clearly dealing here in fact with a symbolic and mimetic pursuit of men by women, carried out in a kind of dance. In the inverted world the women play with the idea of besieging their male opponent by military methods as well. The idea of a female military dance fits well with the evocation of the *pyrrhikhê* in the tableau within the *parabasis* (821–829). The connection with the Thesmophoria is thus no coincidence, as Deubner 1932:60 thinks. Rohde 1870:554n2 (= Kl. Schr. II 1901:362n2) considers connecting the ritual with the dance of the women in Halimous (cf. below, n180). Deubner 1932:60 rejects Rohde's interpretation of a mimetic dance, although a few lines later he says that it must originally have been a mimetic chase. Mimetic action is achieved of course using expressive body language in dance; on this see in general esp. the thesis of Koller 1954. Dahl 1976:99 describes the practice, considerably more accurately, as "a symbolic act, to make sure that no men and nothing harmful was present" (here one may think of the search-song [*Thesm.* 655–688]). After the women have already actively and mimetically pursued their male enemies in the search-song, they entrust in grotesque fashion the task of pursuit to the police henchman at the end of the action, once the inverted world has been overcome. His departure will also have been in the form of dance.

ἀλλὰ <u>πέπαισται</u> μετρίως ἡμῖν·
ὥσθ' ὥρα δή 'στιν βαδίζειν
οἴκαδ' ἑκάστῃ. Τὼ Θεσμοφόρω δ'
ἡμῖν ἀγαθὴν
τούτων χάριν ἀνταποδοῖτον.

Thesm. 1227–1231

But there's been enough playing and dancing by us, so it's time for each and every woman to go home. May the two Thesmophoroi give us a good reward in exchange for our performance!

Even here it cannot be clearly established whether the chorus speaks in its role as women celebrating the Thesmophoria or in its function as comastic worshiper of Dionysus. The verb in the perfect passive πέπαισται characterizes the process of wild, comic dance (παίζειν) as having come to an end. The performative "we" and the deictic τούτων once more function as connecting elements between the Thesmophoria and the comic dance performances at the Dionysia.[140] The lines represent on the one hand a request within the dramatic plot by the women celebrating the Thesmophoria to their gods to reward their devotion; on the other hand, the male choral members, released from their occupations by the polis for this task, speak about their dancing now having come to an end and say that they expect a reward from Demeter and Kore for their pains, that is, help toward victory in the comic *agôn*. As in the great hymn (947–1000), the word χάρις, with its reciprocal implications, is here also of central importance. The women celebrating the Thesmophoria, that is, the members of the comic chorus, dance for the enjoyment of the two goddesses; now in exchange for this performance they hope for a return gift with which Demeter and Kore may refund joy as their "thanks." At the same time, the distance between the orchestra and the audience is also removed by these shifters. The "we" also includes the spectators, who in the shared laughter have found together with the goddesses a new, consolidated society. In the "we" the polis as a whole rejoices and wish for blessings from the mother and daughter in their function as agricultural goddesses as well as fertility in their fields and families.

---

[140] On the ambiguity between dramatic role and the function of the chorus in this passage cf. also Sommerstein *Thesm.*, 237 *ad* 1231: "[I]s this a prayer by women celebrating the Thesmophoria for the goddesses to accept and reward their worship, or is it a prayer by a comic chorus for blessing on, and for the success of, their performance?" See also Flashar 1994:67 and Totaro 1999:169.

The festival of inversion is now over; the married women, temporarily returned to being νύμφαι, now resume once more their married existence and pray for good offspring. The peace accord of the two men and the women anticipates the final day of the festive cycle, the Kalligeneia, and the end of the inverted world that the audience members also experience during the course of the Dionysiac comedy. At the end, after their fasting and abstinence, the women at the Thesmophoria await the resumption of normal married life and copious eating. After the toil of the dance the chorus in its comic function looks forward to the exuberant victory celebration with ample feasting and abundant drinking of wine. The men anticipate only natural and carnal behavior from their spouses, who have been celebrating separately according to the strict division of sexes. The comic poet projects this male attitude onto the basic structure of the comic plot, which is built on the simple concept that women object to the way they are depicted through the heroines of Euripidean tragedy, but during the period of separation in the festival in fact prove to be even worse than Euripides and men could ever have imagined. On the other hand, when it comes to the chorus, the ritual purity of the female agents in their dramatic role is taken into consideration. All in all, in the manner and custom characteristic of the paradoxical festival of the Thesmophoria, the women come across as ambivalent beings.[141] The unbridled and wild aspect of the chorus is restricted to the element of Dionysiac *kômos*, which is applied from the masculine world of the performers to the chorus of the dramatic plot.

Already in the songs before the caesura that the great choral dance song (947–1000) represents in the development of the plot, hymn, song, and choral dance are equally thematized in self-referential fashion. The lyric utterances in the *Thesmophoriazusae* represent, as will become clear in my analysis, a kind of counterpoint to what is happening on the stage.

---

[141] Cf. Versnel 1993:228–288, esp. 245–250 and 274–283.

The Song of Agathon (*Thesm.* 101–129) as Pseudo-choral Song and Its Lack of Connection with Actual Reality

The *kômos*, the exuberant procession and supposed original form of the comic chorus, is already reflected in the famous song of Agathon (101–129) with the same kind of parodic distortion as it is in the *Andromeda*-plot. The modern tragic poet, to whom Euripides turns for deliverance from his difficult situation, is shown working out a choral ode on the *ekkyklêma*. Agathon delivers the following lines:

ἱερὰν Χθονίαιν δεξάμεναι   101
λαμπάδα, κοῦραι, ξὺν ἐλευθερίᾳ
πατρίδι χορεύσασθε βοάν.

– τίνι δαιμόνων ὁ κῶμος;
λέγε νιν. εὐπίστως δὲ τοὐμὸν   105
δαίμονας ἔχει σεβίσαι.

– ἄγε νυν ὄλβιζε μούσᾳ,
χρυσέων ῥύτορα τόξων
Φοῖβον, ὃς ἱδρύσατο χώρας
γύαλα Σιμουντίδι γᾷ.   110

– χαῖρε καλλίσταις ἀοιδαῖς,
Φοῖβ᾽, ἐν εὐμούσοισι τιμαῖς
γέρας ἱερὸν προφέρων.

– τάν τ᾽ ἐν ὄρεσι δρυογόνοισιν
κόραν ἀείσατ᾽ Ἄρτεμιν ἀγροτέραν.   115/116

– ἕπομαι κλῄζουσα σεμνὰν
γόνον ὀλβίζουσα Λατοῦς,
Ἄρτεμιν ἀπειρολεχῆ.

– Λατώ τε κρούματά τ᾽ Ἀσιάδος ποδὶ   120
παράρυθμ᾽ εὔρυθμα, Φρυγίων
δινεύματα Χαρίτων.

– σέβομαι Λατώ τ᾽ ἄνασσαν
κίθαρίν τε ματέρ᾽ ὕμνων
ἄρσενι βοᾷ δοκίμων.   125

– τᾷ φάος ἔσσυτο δαιμονίοις
ὄμμασιν, <u>ἁμετέρας τε δι' αἰφνιδί-
ου ὀπός</u>. ὧν χάριν
ἄνακτ' ἄγαλλε Φοῖβον.

– χαῖρ', ὄλβιε παῖ Λατοῦς.

Thesm. 101–129

Take, you maidens, the holy torch of the two chthonic goddesses and sing and dance with freedom your song for your homeland!

– For which of the gods is the *kômos*? (105) Tell him! For my task is to
worship the gods piously.

– Come now, praise with song the archer with the golden bow,
Phoibos, who set up the walls of his land (110) in the Simois region!

– Hail and rejoice in the most beautiful songs, Phoibos, you who
bring to our musical performances in your honor the sacred prize
of victory!

– Sing too in praise of the virgin of the oak-covered mountains
(115–116), Artemis the wild!

– I follow, celebrating and praising the holy offspring of Leto,
Artemis, who knows not the marriage bed!

– (120) And Leto too, and the clashings on the strings of the Asian
lyre that make us move now out of step, now in step with the
rhythm, the whirling dances of the Phrygian Kharites!

– I give honor also to the Lady Leto and the lyre, mother of hymns
(125) famed for the shout of men.

– It is this that causes light to dart in the eyes of the god, this and
our suddenly lifted voice. Therefore praise Lord Phoibos with a
hymn!

– Hail, blessed son of Leto!

At the heart of the Agathon-scene is the question of mimesis. Because the poet
intends to compose a drama with a female chorus, he has dressed himself as
a woman. In contrast to the great choral dance song (947–1000), we here find
ourselves in the following paradoxical situation: an individual is imitating the
song of a collective. The spectator witnesses a pseudo-*amoibaion* between the

individual who initiates the song and a chorus composed of young women, with the poet undertaking both roles.[142] Through the distorting mirror of another poet Aristophanes thereby inserts into the dramatic plot the process of composition and coaching of a chorus before the actual performance. As modern scholarly directions in theater anthropology show, it is characteristic both of theater and of ritual to integrate events before and after the actual performance into the play.[143] Old Comedy has in common with ritual presentations the fact that the performance transcends the spatial and temporal frame of the plot in the direction both of the before and the after and of the here and now of the spectator's perspective.

The Agathon song is like a chorus *in statu nascendi*. As this process is revealed it becomes clear that the poet is ultimately in charge of leading the chorus and is in turn only a mirror image of an ideal, divine choral leader. Agathon acts like a parody of Dionysus, the god of the current perfor-

---

[142] Small changes in lines 102–103, 107, and 122 have been made in comparison with Coulon. Cf. in general the fine exposition in Zimmermann II 1985:22–29. The humor of the song lies according to Zimmermann II 1985:28 in the type of presentation; he terms it a "Pseudo-Amoibaion" (*ibid.*, 24). There is no space here to go into musical parody and the connection with the new Attic dithyramb and new music. See also Zimmermann 1993:45 and Kugelmeier 1996:271–297 (on the Agathon parody), esp. 277–280 (on the Agathon hymn). On the whole scene see also Rau 1967:99–114 (who [*ibid.*, 104–108] correctly rejects Kleinknecht's [1937:101–103, esp. 102] interpretation that the hymn is full of "nichtssagenden einzelnen Prädikationen" ["meaningless individual sentences"] and "übertriebenen Pathos" ["overblown pathos"], because the style, according to Rau, though caricaturing, nowhere oversteps the customary limit in hymns of this type), Horn 1970:94–106, Muecke 1982, Stohn 1993, and now Furley/Bremer I 2001:350–354, Furley/Bremer II 2001:341–346, and the new commentaries by Prato, 168–177 and Austin/Olson, 86–97 *ad* 101–129. Consider also the thesis advanced by Zeitlin (1981:177–178) that Agathon is not suited for the defense of Euripides because he is too well accustomed to the female role. Zeitlin 1981 goes into the problem of mimesis in the *Thesmophoriazusae* in detail and also addresses the function of Dionysus and Demeter in this comedy (194–200). For a detailed analysis of the play in terms of ritual see now also Tzanetou 2002; for the aspect of performance and body see now Stehle 2002 (both contributions to the special issue of *AJP* 123.3 edited by Gamel 2002).

[143] This inclusion of the frame, the before and after, has been emphasized in more recent approaches in performance studies and theater anthropology. Richard Schechner, applying the theories of Victor Turner, compares the theater together with the preparatory phase before the play with initiation and other such changes in status. The three-stage model of the *rite de passage* developed in van Gennep 1909 is thus transferred from rites of puberty in tribal societies to the theater: in both cases, actor and spectator undergo a process of transformation by means of theatricality; cf. Schechner 1985:117–150. On the integration of the rehearsal process into a performance cf. Schechner 1977:132–137. These connections will become gradually more meaningful in my analysis, since Aristophanes in the *Thesmophoriazusae*, as will become clear in the course of this chapter, thematizes the theater's mode of operation, using initiatory rituals as a basis.

mance.[144] Agathon's appearance draws on iconographic attributes from the real world. On the one hand, his outer appearance possesses a close likeness to depictions on vases of Anacreon, Ibycus, and Alcaeus in archaic Ionic gear (see *Thesm.* 160–163). The lyric poets are often represented as comasts with feminine accessories. With the *barbitos* in hand, the singer-poets lead the *kômos* of parasol-wielding dancers surrounding them, who in the din and musical ecstasy experimentally transgress the boundaries of the Other.[145] The poets' masculine self nevertheless remains continually present through the emphasis on their beards. Anacreon is not, however, portrayed as a real figure: instead, the poet is treated as an ideal type and a human manifestation of the leader of the *kômos*, Dionysus. It is for this reason that Agathon appears not as a reincar-

---

[144] On the Agathon hymn (*Thesm.* 101–129), see Rau 1967:104–108, Horn 1970:100–106, Muecke 1982:46–48, Zimmermann II 1985:22–29, Parker 1997:398–405, and now Furley/Bremer I 2001:350–354, Furley/Bremer II 2001:341–346, and the new commentaries by Prato, 168–177 and Austin/Olson, 86–97 *ad* 101–129. Zimmermann refers to the ritual embedding of the song. In the preparation the slave acts in the role of a *hierokêryx* who announces the epiphany of a god; on the sacrifice and prayerlike character of the preparatory scene (*Thesm.* 39ff.) cf. Kleinknecht 1937:151n1, Kleinknecht 1937a:300–301, and Zimmermann II 1985:22. The humor of the passage lies, according to Kleinknecht 1937:151n1 and Zimmermann II 1985:22, in the fact that this high-flown introduction does not, as in *Av.* 1719 and *Pax* 1318, announce a (supposed) divinity, but only a poet. Yet the ambivalence of the presentation extends at the same time to placing Agathon in the presence of gods. The fashionable poet is on many occasions connected with Dionysus. In terms of his external hermaphroditic appearance Agathon is in fact quite similar to him. He wears, as the in-law does later, a saffron robe (138) and carries a mirror (140) (see on this Seaford 1996:223 *ad* Eur. *Ba.* 918–919). On Dionysus in feminine garb see also Kenner 1970:116–129. Moreover, Agathon is addressed with quotations from the Aeschylean *Lykourgia*. Line 136 is a direct quotation from the *Edoni* (Aesch. fr. 61 Radt), and lines 137–145 could have been adapted directly from the scene of interrogation in which Dionysus is tried by Lycurgus. Cf. Sommerstein *Thesm.*, 167 *ad* 136; cf. also the reminiscence in Ar. *Ran.* 47. The metrical form with its ionic basis (but cf. the skeptical remarks of Parker 1997:402) makes one think of Dionysiac cultic poetry; cf. the *parodos* of Eur. *Ba.* 64–169, esp. 64–104 with the commentary of Dodds 1960²:71–72. The *ionicus a minore* was perceived as lascivious and soft (cf. Ar. *Eccl.* 882–883 and *Thesm.* 163). Further, the Phrygian harmony in which the song was probably composed also seems to point to Dionysus, since both harmony and god must have been particularly orgiastic and emotional, and is accordingly attacked by Aristotle (*Pol.* 1342b1ff.); West 1992:181. It also has its place precisely in the New Dithyramb, which also refers to Dionysus. On the New Dithyramb see Zimmermann 1992:117–132, and particularly in connection with the Agathon song (*Thesm.* 101–129) Zimmermann II 1985:28–29, Zimmermann 1988, and Kugelmeier 1996:279–280. On nearness to Apollo cf. below, pp. 146–148 (with nn166–169).

[145] Cf. Caskey/Beazley 1954:55–61 and Frontisi-Ducroux/Lissarrague 1990. Cf. also Muecke 1982:50. The audience may also have associated the *kômos* named in line 104, the imagined chorus, with the *kômos* of effeminate parasol-dancers. Cf. quite similarly Price 1990:169–170: "The nature of the chorus remains ambiguous, as played by Agathon in his long Ionian chiton. An Athenian audience, however, would have had no difficulty recognizing his 'chorus of maidens' as effeminate males costumed like Agathon, for the scenes on vases indicate that Anacreontic performances lasted at least until the mid-fifth century."

nation of Anacreon, as Snyder thinks, but rather as the comastic god himself.[146] On the other hand, this more archaic figurative scheme is comically exaggerated, since Agathon is clean-shaven and the masculine index of the beard thus disappears completely behind this effeminacy. In so doing Agathon assumes the practice, starting around 425 BCE and contemporary with the Aristophanic performances, of representing Dionysus as a beardless youngster.[147]

As we have already seen above, Dionysus is understood as the ideal ἐξάρχων (987), and as is well known, the poets themselves originally participated in the play as choral leaders. Furthermore, according to Aristotle (*Poet.* 1449a9ff.), drama arose from those "leading off" (ἐξάρχοντες) ritual songs. Through the imitation of another dramatic chorus in this lyrical passage, as I see it, the way is prepared for the chorus of the women celebrating the Thesmophoria. The latter chorus only appears in the *parodos*, of course, but this represents a similar prayer.

The performance situation is particularly complicated in this instance since Agathon in his song performs a scene of tragedy about Troy that cannot be precisely reconstructed. The imitated choral dance song is extremely polyvalent and shifting, in particular because no actual chorus performs, thereby giving rise to the paradox of a monody that reproduces a collective singing.[148] As in a kaleidoscope, depending on one's perspective, one clear image

---

[146] Snyder 1974. The scattered anacreontics (lines 104, 124 and variation in lines 117, 118 and 123; cf. Parker 1997:402), which represent the anaclastic form of the ionic dimeter, but which originally form a catalectic iambic dimeter (cf. Gentili 1952:21, 132, Gentili/Lomiento 2003:176, and Parker 1997:61–64), could also refer to the closeness to Anacreon. On the connection with Bakkhos cf. Frontisi-Ducroux/Lissarrague 1990:228–232, esp. the illustration 7.38 of Dionysus playing the *barbitos* (Paris, Cabinet des Médailles 576, *ARV* 371, 14), who in terms of type resembles the representation of the poet completely. Anacreon says of a bearded man clad in Ionian and eastern fashion, κωμάζει δ' ὡς Διόνυσος, fr. 123 Gentili (442 *PMG*). In fr. 82 Gentili (388 *PMG*) he makes fun in the symposium of just such an effeminate comast named Artemon, who carries a little parasol (σκιαδίσκην, line 11) with him; Price 1990:170–171. On the parasol in the tableau of the *pnigos* (*Thesm.* 821–829) see below, pp. 198–206. A speech-bubble–like inscription on a kylix in Erlangen (Erlangen 454, *ARV* 339, 49) confirms the theory of the comastic barbitos-player: ΕΙΜΙ ΚΟ[ΜΑ]ΖΟΝ ΗΥΠΑΥ[ΛΟΥ].

[147] Cf. Carpenter 1993. He interprets two exceptions, which already show in 470 BCE a beardless Dionysus (1993:186–187, ills. 7 and 8 [Private collection (*ARV* 605, 65*bis*), and Thessalonike, Archaeological Museum 8.54 (*ARV* 591, 28)]), as a reflex of stage practice; in his opinion, the vase paintings reflect the situation of the Aeschylean Lykourgia, in particular the *Edoni*, where Dionysus, as later in the *Bacchae*, appears as a masked man.

[148] Schol. *Thesm.* 101; van Leeuwen *Thesm.*, 21 *ad* 101–129, Rogers *Thesm.*, 14 *ad* 101–129, Coulon, Cantarella IV, 421, Rau 1967:106n19, Horn 1970:100–101, Muecke 1982:47, Zimmermann II 1985:22, Gannon *Thesm.*, 8 *ad* 101–129 (he thinks Agathon sings as Dionysus and the chorus of the Muses), and Sommerstein *Thesm.*, 164 *ad* 101–129 all correctly adopt the scholiast's explanation.

emerges, while other interpretative possibilities of the ambiguous picture must be kept in view.

The chorus in this fictional role seems to consist of Trojan maidens. The Apollo invoked is neither Delphic nor Delian, but the city god of Troy (109–110), who together with Artemis and Leto is on the side of the Phrygian polis (cf. 121) in the fight over Troy. In terms of plot the celebration of "freedom" (102)[149] can be associated with the departure of the enemy fleet. Sommerstein assumes that the solo singer who directs the responsive prayer of the community is ultimately to be identified with a priestess.[150] Yet the situation is even more complex than has hitherto been recognized. When in the introduction to this scene the slave of Agathon is compared to a *hierokêryx*,[151] an Eleusinian-Demeter layer is added to the Trojan location indicated in the song. Right from the start, with the call directed to Demeter and Kore (101–103), the song is brought close to the chorus of the women celebrating the Thesmophoria.

The mode of performance is also not clear from the text. Despite all the parodic elements directed against the style of Agathon, who follows the music of the New Dithyramb, the language throughout is suited to the ritual prayer style and shows definite similarities to the song already discussed (esp. 959ff.).[152] There, various Olympian gods, in particular Apollo and Artemis, as here, are invoked in a series of prayers. In the following *parodos* there is also a similar paean to Zeus, Apollo, Athena, Artemis, Poseidon and the Nereids, and the Nymphs (312–330). The song thus acts as a prefiguration for the chorus that will appear only later and which, as is well known, oscillates sharply between its dramatic role and function, and between the female cult of the goddesses of the Thesmophoria and the worship of the polis gods by the male chorus as representatives of the polis as a whole.

---

[149] On the text-critical result of lines 102–103 cf. ἐλευθερίᾳ, Hermann: ἐλευθέραι R and πατρίδι R: πραπίδι, Wecklein. Wecklein's conjecture would convey an unrestrained spirit in the choral ode, which is completely in keeping with the high-flown dithyrambic mood of the ode. Prato 1998:270–271 (cf. now also Prato, 170 *ad* 103a–b and Austin/Olson, 90 *ad* 101–103) follows the transmitted text of R because of the contemporary political events at the time of the first production (December 412/January 411 BCE). The hypothesis of a Trojan chorus put forward most recently after Cantarella (IV, 423 *ad* 101–129) by Sommerstein *Thesm.*, 164 *ad* 101–129 goes back to Bothe (III, 111 *ad* 101). Henderson 1996:223n38 follows Sommerstein. See now also Furley/Bremer I 2001:351–352 and Austin/Olson, 87.

[150] Sommerstein *Thesm.*, 164 *ad* 101–129. On the ancient ritual form of responsive song cf. Radermacher *Frösche*, 200 and Parker 1997:403 (with reference to Sappho fr. 140 L.-P.).

[151] Kleinknecht 1937:151n1.

[152] Cf. Rau 1967:104 and now Furley/Bremer I 2001:353 against Kleinknecht 1937:101–103 and now Prato, 169–170.

In particular, Agathon's connection to Dionysus brings to the fore the level of choral performance in honor of the god of comedy.[153] As is appropriate for comedy, the imaginary chorus is described as κῶμος (104). Naturally, the *kômos* may also be interpreted in a Trojan context as an expression of joy at being liberated from the Greek siege. The very term κῶμος thus functions as performative shifter, mediating between the here and now of the performance and the then and there of the plot.[154] Moreover, the mention of a "sacred gift of honor" (113) can be understood as a reference to victory in the comic *agôn*. Apollo and Dionysus, as divinities associated with the Muses, are responsible for success in the activity at hand.[155] Once again, the χάρις relationship of giving and taking seems to be decisive. The references by the imagined chorus to its own dance only spread to the level of performance in the imagination of the spectators, since in this instance the entire performative situation is purely presented as a recreation.

This quality, which cannot be comprehended in the here and now, stands for the fickle appearance of Agathon in general. The underlined passages are not realized in a choral performance. When mention is made of Leto's Asiatic lyre-playing, or of "the mother of glorious hymns with manly voice" (123–125), the goddess must here be taken as an ideal example for monodic performance of the hymn accompanied by the *kithara*. Like Agathon, a man who sings like a woman, the famous mother of Apollo and Artemis, her feminine stringed instrument, and the imaginary chorus of maidens represent a similar paradox, in that she lets the song ring out with "masculine voice" (ἄρσενι βοᾷ, 125).[156] In the choral allusions to playing the lyre the perversion of Agathon's performa-

---

[153] On the closeness of Agathon to the theater-god Dionysus see Hansen 1976:174, Muecke 1982:48, Saïd 1987:230, Zeitlin 1981:196, Gannon *Thesm.*, 8 *ad* 94, 101–129, and Taaffe 1993:82, 85.

[154] Cf. *Thesm.* 988b and above, n109 and below, chap 2. nn29–30.

[155] Cf. *Thesm.* 111–113, χαῖρε καλλίσταις ἀοιδαῖς, | Φοῖβ', ἐν εὐμούσοισι τιμαῖς | γέρας ἱερὸν προφέρων. The sense of the lines is equally ambivalent and illustrates the relationship of reciprocity. The meaning depends in particular on line 113; γέρας is interpreted by Austin 1987:74 and Sommerstein *Thesm.*, 31 as honorary privilege, namely of being mentioned first in the series before the others, which Apollo is entitled to and which he here receives through song, because he "produces it himself" (cf. Austin's explanation "*displays*" and now Austin/Olson, 92 *ad* 111–113). Cf. Sommerstein's (*ibid.*) translation: "Rejoice in our beautiful song, | O Phoebus, and be first to receive | this holy privilege in our fair tribute of music" (similarly Henderson 1996:102) and Sommerstein *Thesm.*, 165 *ad* 113 (with his proposal to understand προφέρων as "win before others"); elsewhere, however, προφέρειν means less "receive," "obtain," than (among other things) "give of oneself," "bring openly."

[156] There also seems to have been a comic element in this: Zimmermann II 1985:28; Wilamowitz 1886:156 suggests that Agathon used a falsetto delivery to emphasize this comic paradox. Tsakmakis 1997 thinks it probable that this role, which demands remarkable vocal and performative abilites, was played by the actor Nikandros, mentioned twice in Philodemos *On*

tive categories is also reflected. He praises Leto and the "blows on the Asiatic *kitharis* that are counterrhythmic and rhythmic, the whirlings of Phrygian Kharites" (κρούματά τ' Ἀσιάδος ποδὶ | παράρυθμ' εὔρυθμα, Φρυγίων | δινεύματα Χαρίτων, 120–122). Leto thus serves as the model for a monodic singer, whose tones recreate the choral dance song of a collective. The Asiatic element resides not only in the role, but above all also in the modern playing style of the new music and the New Dithyramb. The Kharites are more precisely characterized as Phrygians not only because of the plot locale, but also because of the mode in which the song is composed.[157] The mentions of feet, rhythm, and round dance clearly refer to the later self-references of the chorus, which emerge frequently in *Thesm.* 947–1000, as discussed in detail above.[158] Yet all these references to χορεία remain in a vacuum here, since no actual chorus performs and Agathon can hardly have accompanied his monody with dance steps.[159] The oxymoron παράρυθμ' εὔρυθμα, which describes the dances more precisely, reveals the performative paradox that while the rhythm is indeed suited for a choral presentation, in reality no chorus appears on stage.[160] There is no corresponding "we" of the collective to the "I" of the performing

---

Music (Περὶ μουσικῆς). Price 1990:170 interprets the "excellent masculine song" (*Thesm.* 125) as a reference to male comasts who present a distinctly feminine appearance in the *kômos*. She maintains (170n110) that Leto, associated with Lycia and Phrygia, is particularly fitting for the effeminate chorus and that for this reason she is not mentioned in the hymn to the Athenian polis gods (*Thesm.* 969–1000).

[157] On the stylistic and rhythmic interpretation of the song see Rau 1967:104–108 and Zimmermann 1988.

[158] Cf. esp. εὐρύθμῳ ποδί, 985 and above, Introduction n169, chap. 1 nn31, 38, 62, 90, and below, chap. 1 n269; διανεύματα is glossed in schol. *Thesm.* 122 by ὀρχήματα. Bentley conjectures, probably correctly, δινεύματα from δινεύω ('whirl'); Coulon himself later withdraws his defense of the transmitted διανεύματα, based on Hesych., s.v. διανεύει· στρέφει, κυκλεῖ (*pro* δινεύει); cf. Coulon, *REG* 50 (1937), 458. Parker 1997:400 and 404 also defends the transmitted reading. On δινεύω in a choral context with the meaning "move in a circle" cf. Hom. *Il.* 18.494, Eur. *Phoen.* 792, θυρσομανεῖ νεβρίδων μέτα δίνᾳ (on the choral implications of δίνη and the text [Diggle prints the transmitted †δινεύεις; δίνᾳ is a conjecture by Hermann] cf. Mastronarde 1994:380–382). Cf. however Fritzsche's conjecture διὰ νεύματα ('with nodding of the head') with the commentary *ibid.*, 37–38 *ad* 120–123; he suggests that for parodic purposes Aristophanes changed διὰ πνεύματα (cf. Eur. *Phoen.* 787) to διὰ νεύματα. Sommerstein accepts this conjecture, but for reasons having to do with the choral context, namely that the Kharites coordinated the chorus through nodding of the head, just as actual choruses were conducted by *aulos*-players (Sommerstein *Thesm.*, 166 *ad* 121–122). He follows here Wilamowitz 1921:341n1 and Austin 1990:16–17; see now also Austin/Olson, 95 *ad* 120–122.

[159] See esp. the command χορεύσασθε βοάν (103) and κῶμος (104); note also the important choral projection onto the Kharites, which remains without an actual counterpart and thus without effect: Φρυγίων | δινεύματα Χαρίτων (121–122).

[160] See Zimmermann 1993:45 and Mureddu 1982/83:83–84; see also Kamerbeek 1967:77–78 and Austin 1990:16.

Agathon. The effect of the expression ἀμετέρας . . . ὀπός (127) is purely artistic, since only a single persona sings and plays.[161] The solo singer merely imitates the "we"; on the practical level, the reference only emerges as a *pluralis maiestatis*. All in all, the self-referential allusions to the ritual activity of singing and dancing should not be taken here as pure speech acts, because no action corresponds to the utterance. One may at most refer to them as performative on a metaphorical level, since they describe the solo singer's mannered style of performance in a transferred sense.

Given the lack of actual performance information, a further hypothesis could be advanced. Over the course of the history of interpretation of this passage a second chorus of maidens or even of Muses that performs behind stage and interacts with Agathon has been constantly suggested.[162] Yet, as Newiger has rightly commented, these voices off-stage would be physically inexplicable to the audience.[163] Moreover, any actual effect that the mimesis of a chorus might have would be lost by a behind-the-scenes chorus of this type.[164]

---

[161] Austin 1987:74 *ad* 127 accepts by contrast Nietzsche's conjecture ὑμετέρας, which would thus lose the choral "we."

[162] This proposed solution is found mostly in the older editions, among others in Brunck, Bekker, Fritzsche, Enger, Blaydes (cf. also Blaydes I, 142 *ad* 101–129), and Hall/Geldart; see e.g. Beer 1844:79: "Dazu kommt noch als Paraskenion der Musenchor (Vs. 104–129), der nicht auf der Bühne, sondern hinter derselben von den erst Vs. 295 auftretenden Choreuten gesungen wird" ["To this the chorus of Muses is attached as a *paraskênion* (lines 104–129), which is sung by the chorus members, who only appear at line 295, not onstage but behind the stage"]. (It is mostly compared to the subchorus of the *Frogs*; but the chorus of frogs was probably visible: Dover *Frogs*, 57.) Fritzsche, 32–33, Enger, 24–25 *ad* 101–129, Enger 1846:62–70, Muff 1872:73, 113–114, 162, Arnoldt 1873:71, Wilamowitz 1886:157, Fraenkel 1962:112n1, and Austin 1987:73 argue for an off-stage female chorus of the Muses, whose members also assumed the role of the chorus at the Thesmophoria. Kleinknecht 1937:101 seems to assume that a chorus actually performed ("Wechselgesang zwischen Agathon und einem [Musen?-]Chor") ["Interchange of song between Agathon and a chorus (of Muses?)"]. Zielinski 1885:88–91 also sees a chorus of Muses; relying on a completely idiosyncratic train of thought, he theorizes that Aristophanes removed it as a semi-chorus (separate from the second semi-chorus of mortal women) from *another* version of the second *Thesmophoriazusae (B)* ("Kalligeneia")—which Zielinski regarded as preceding the present *Thesmophoriazusae (A)* ("Nesteia")—and adapted it for this version. In the "Kalligeneia," according to Zielinski, this semi-chorus of Muses supported Euripides and his relative.

[163] Cf. H.-J. Newiger's review of Fraenkel 1962 in *Gymnasium* 72 (1965), 252–254, esp. 253. Cf. also Rau 1967:106n19, Horn 1970:100–101, and Kugelmeier 1996:278.

[164] On the imitativeness of the New Dithyramb cf. esp. Ar. *Plut.* 290–321 (with Bierl 1994:38–41) and Zimmermann 1992:127–128. On the parody of Philoxenos in this passage (*Plut.* 290ff.) see Kugelmeier 1996:255–264. He establishes (262, 277) similarities between this passage and *Thesm.* 101ff., since there too a dialogue between chorus leader and chorus takes place—although the interchange in the *Wealth* is an actual one.

What sense would there in fact be in having the Muses at Agathon's command perform a choral song addressed to other gods? For while it is the Muses who usually inspire the poet, here they would ask the poet as ἐξάρχων whom they should honor with their song of praise.[165] Nevertheless, it might have been intended that the text be left open for even this possibility. Here I am admittedly assuming a completely different background from those who have so far supported the idea of the Muse chorus, for one might expect that this song too should clearly refer back to a divine model. In this case it may be seen in the arrangement of the gods grouped about Apollo, who leads off the singing in his capacity as κιθαρῳδός and ideal player of string instruments. The Muses take up as a refrain the song of praise directed at various deities, while the Kharites (122), Horai, and other female deities dance in the chorus. Apollo stands in the center as choral leader, and the female chorus surrounds him in a round dance (δινεύματα Χαρίτων, 122). This corresponds precisely to the situation in the *Homeric Hymn to Apollo* (*Hom. Hymn.* 3.179–206). There the Muses reply to Apollo's playing with beautiful voice (*Hom. Hymn.* 3.189: ἀμειβόμεναι ὀπὶ καλῇ; cf. *Thesm.* 127) and praise the immortal gifts of the gods (*Hom. Hymn.* 3.190: ὑμνεῦσίν ῥα θεῶν δῶρ' ἄμβροτα; cf. *Thesm.* 113),

---

[165] Cf. however the interpretation of Muff 1872:113–114, who does not take into consideration the dimension of the chorus' identity as women celebrating the Thesmophoria: "und nachdem er [Agathon] präludirt hat, fordert er in einem Liede die Musen auf, zu Ehren der unterirdischen Gottheiten die Fackeln zu ergreifen, zu tanzen und zu singen. Und diesem Wunsche willfahren die Musen; sie feiern in Liedern die Götter sowie das Spiel und den Tanz der Charitinnen. Dieser Gesang ist offenbar kein Theil des neuen Dramas, wie viele gemeint haben, sondern nur die Vorbereitung zu ihm, der Anruf der Götter" ["and after he [Agathon] has sung a prelude, he instructs the Muses in a song to take up torches in honor of the underworld deities, to dance and to sing. And the Muses comply with this wish; they celebrate in song the gods as well as the play and the dance of the Kharites. This song clearly forms no part of the new drama, as many have thought, but is only the preparation for it, the invocation of the gods"]. Beside line 41 (θίασος Μουσῶν) the only evidence for a subchorus of Muses in the Agathon song is the vocative Μοῦσαι (107), which is, however, based solely on a conjecture by Wilamowitz (ἄγετ' ὦ κλῄζετε, Μοῦσαι); R gives the reading ἄγε νῦν ὅπλιζε μοῦσα. Fraenkel 1962:111–114, esp. 113, following a splendid suggestion of Fritzsche, who had already combined Bentley's ὄλβιζε and Bergk's μούσᾳ, changed the text to ἄγε νυν ὄλβιζε μούσᾳ, with μοῦσα being used by way of metonymy for "song" (for this practice cf. fr. 851b, 1 *PMG* and below, chap. 2 n82). Sommerstein *Thesm.*, 30 follows this reading and, like Kugelmeier 1996:278 (the latter takes θίασος Μουσῶν [line 41] merely as "poetic metaphor"), also rejects the idea of a chorus of Muses. See also Van Leeuwen *Thesm.*, 22, who prints ἄγε νυν ὄλβιζε, Μοῦσα. But why should Agathon first address the Muses as κοῦραι (102)? How is a spectator supposed to identify these maidens as Muses? But see Austin 1987:73 *ad* 103: "The κοῦραι in 102 are clearly the Muses." He follows (73 *ad* 107) Gannon's conjecture ἄγε νυν ὀλβίζετε, Μοῦσαι (Gannon 1982:92 and in Gannon's text). Parker 1997:403–404 is skeptical about Fraenkel's μούσᾳ; but on metrical grounds this cannot fit Gannon's solution and so he places the passage in *cruces*. The difficulties in arriving at a clear answer perhaps point to the poet's consciously leaving the matter up in the air.

the Kharites form a circle with the Horai, Harmonia, Hebe, and Aphrodite, join hands, and dance in a circular formation (*Hom. Hymn.* 3.194–196, esp. 196: ὀρχεῦντ' ἀλλήλων ἐπὶ καρπῷ χεῖρας ἔχουσαι; cf. *Thesm.* 122). A divine chorus of this type praises the chorus leader Apollo especially, but also Artemis and Leto, who are particularly singled out in this hymn (*Hom. Hymn.* 3.197–199, 204–206). The choral constellation is further developed by an intertextual weaving of allusions in which Apollo is described in archaic lyric as leader of the chorus.[166] In Pindar (*Pyth.* 1.1–4), Apollo's lyre-playing gives the signal for the dance and song; the prelude-like *prooimia* have the function of directing the chorus' tempo and rhythm (ἁγησιχόρων . . . προοιμίων 4; cf. *Thesm.* 99).

In its reminiscences of the *Homeric Hymn to Apollo*, which itself functions as, and is called, a *prooimion* (Thuc. 3.104.3–4), the song as a whole thus has the character of a prelude that prepares the way for the later chorus of women celebrating the Thesmophoria, but also simultaneously represents its negative mirror image.[167] Agathon serves to a certain extent as a distorted image of the poet Aristophanes, who as *khorêgos* directs and leads his troupe. Yet while Agathon's chorus performs ritual actions only in an imaginary sense, the chorus of the women celebrating the Thesmophoria is real, mimesis aside, in that it sings and dances for the community and its gods.

Through reference to the Apollo hymn, the poet Agathon thus finds his divine model in Apollo alongside Dionysus as god of comedy.[168] The compar-

---

[166] Cf. Hom. *Il.* 1.603–604, Hes. *Scut.* 201–206, Pind. *Nem.* 5.22–25, and *Pyth.* 1.1–4. In the *Birds* Aristophanes integrates this situation into the hoopoe's call to the nightingale (*Av.* 209–222, esp. 216–219): as in *Thesm.* 101ff. at the center lies the ὀλολυγή, the loud ritual cry, particularly of women (*Av.* 222; after *Thesm.* 129 a scholiast has written ὀλολύζει in the margin).

[167] Enger, 25 *ad* 101–129 already recognizes the *prooimion*-like quality of the song. Cf. Aesch. *Ag.* 31, φροίμιον χορεύσομαι (the passage is not mentioned in the excellent study of self-reference in the *Oresteia* by Wilson and Taplin [1993], but *Ag.* 1216 is [*ibid.*, 172 and 179n23 (with reference to Hubbard 1992)]), Aesch. *Supp.* 830, φροίμια . . . πόνων, Eur. *HF* 753, φόνου φροίμιον, and Ar. *Equ.* 1343. On the *prooimion* see Nagy 1990:353–361 (at 356–366 Nagy shows that Pindar's stylized *prooimia* are idealizations); consider 353: "The *prooimion* or prooemium took the form of a prayer sung to a given god who presided over the occasion of a given seasonally recurring festival where the song was performed in competition with other songs." Since the song (*Thesm.* 101ff.) is addressed to Apollo in particular, it ultimately fails to achieve its goal, since Dionysus is the actual divinity who presides over the comic *agôn*.

[168] There is an important intertextual allusion in the reference to the spark in Apollo's eye. In lines 126–127 there is a high-flown description of how "light sparkles in the eye of the god" because of the lyre and "the suddenly lifted voices" of the singers. Chorus and choral leader are once more connected to each other through the typical *kharis* relationship. Music, voice, and dance please the god, making him shine and causing him to move and participate in the choral dance. Cf. Hom. *Hymn.* 3.201–206: αὐτὰρ ὁ Φοῖβος Ἀπόλλων ἐγκιθαρίζει | καλὰ καὶ ὕψι βιβάς, αἴγλη δέ μιν ἀμφιφαείνει | μαρμαρυγαί τε ποδῶν καὶ εὐκλώστοιο χιτῶνος. | οἱ δ' ἐπιτέρπονται θυμὸν μέγαν εἰσορόωντες | Λητώ τε χρυσοπλόκαμος καὶ μητίετα Ζεὺς | υἷα φίλον

ison of the two gods in a musical context is nothing unusual. Yet while Agathon accompanies his chorus on the *kithara*, the fact that the comic chorus is accompanied by an *aulos*-player is significant for its being anchored in the real world.[169]

Determining the change of speakers is a notorious problem in Aristophanes. The lack of actual χορεία has also led interpreters to search for various solutions about how to divide up the text. Most more recent divisions follow an opinion found in the scholia (schol. *Thesm.* 101) that in his solo song Agathon takes on the role of the chorus leader as well as that of the answering chorus. But it still remains unclear where the breaks should be made.[170] Person and

---

παίζοντα μετ' ἀθανάτοισι θεοῖσι. Apollo steps high and beautifully (202); βιβάς here already refers to his dance movements. A glow shines about him, sparks of light emanate from his feet and clothing (202–203). This shining is identical with the radiant expression of the chorus in the hymn fr. 851b, 1 *PMG* (cf. below, chap. 2 nn94 and 96); Apollo's feet refer to his dance, and his garment to his beautiful exterior. Agathon in our scene represents a parody of this; he too wears a long garment, which is here identical with saffron-colored clothing (*Thesm.* 138). The latter was normally worn by women, particularly at ritual celebrations (Ar. *Lys.* 44, 51, 644–645); the *krokôtos* is typical of Dionysus in particular; cf. among others Ar. *Ran.* 46, Cratinus fr. 40 K.-A., Pollux 4.117, and Dover *Frogs*, 40. In Ptolemy Philadelphos' famous procession, a ten-cubit high anthropomorphic figure of Dionysus wore a "purple *khitôn*, reaching to his feet, and on top of this a diaphanous *krokôtos* (κροκωτὸν διαφανῆ)" (Callixinus of Rhodes, *FGrHist* 627 F 2 in Athen. 198c). The relative will retain this saffron robe of Agathon as clothing (*Thesm.* 250, 253) in order to sneak into the festival of the Thesmophoria. In the hymn to Apollo, Leto and Zeus are happy that their son Apollo dances (παίζοντα, 206) among the gods. In our song, however, it is questionable whether Agathon actually dances, since his chorus is not really there. On the divine choral leader see Nagy 1990:361–365, esp., on Apollo, p. 361: "As the generalist of SONG, Apollo is the ultimate chorus leader of the Muses, their authority in the choral integration of singing, dancing, and instrumentation."

[169] On the closeness of Apollo and Dionysus, see Bierl 1991:91–99 and Bierl 1994a:82–83, Calame 1990:364–369, and Grandolini 1995:256–258. Because of its Apollonian description Rau 1967:104 terms the Agathon song a paean. On Apollo as a lyre-playing *khorêgos* see Calame I 1977:102–108 (Engl. trans. Calame 1997:49–53). On the presence of the *aulos*-player in representations of comic choruses see Taplin 1993:69–78, on metatheatrical *aulos*-players in comedy *ibid.*, 105–110. Reed and string instruments are largely complementary in their musical leadership function; Calame I 1977:126–133 (Engl. trans. Calame 1997:64–68) and Käppel 1992:80 (on the paean).

[170] In manuscript R αγαθ appears before lines 101 and 107 and before lines 104 and 111 χο; before lines 114, 117, and 120 there are παράγραφοι. Lines 101–103, 107–110, 114–116, 120–122 are thus assigned to Agathon, and lines 104–106, 111–113, 117–119 to the chorus. The attribution is less certain at *Thesm.* 122ff. In the old editions lines 123–129 are assigned to the chorus (or rather, Agathon speaking as chorus) (Brunck, Thiersch, Fritzsche, Bothe, Enger, Blaydes, Hall/Geldart, Rogers); so Horn 1970:104. Coulon, Cantarella, Gannon, Sommerstein *Thesm.* (now also Prato and Austin/Olson) give lines 123–125 and 129 to the "chorus," and 126–128 to "Agathon" (that is, Agathon as Dionysus or priestess). Van Leeuwen *Thesm.* assigns lines 123–127 (up until ὁπός) to the chorus, the command ὧν χάριν ἄνακτ' ἄγαλλε Φοῖβον to Agathon as *koryphaios* (his reason seems to lie in the singular form [!]; for this reason the transmitted imperative singular

number, we know, give no clear clues. Agathon could have sung a choral song with a completely different division of asides by the choral leader, particularly since self-exhortations by the entire collective are also found among those performing ritual actions.[171]

Aristophanes' criticism of Agathon is thus directed less at his style than at the lack of actual connection of his dramas to the real world. For this reason he cannot represent a mediation in the *Thesmophoriazusae*: dramatic action and choral songs are intimately connected with the ritual of the polis, that is, both in terms of the setting of the play at the Thesmophoria and in terms of its contemporary, real-life dimension in the polis cult of all the gods, but in particular that of Dionysus as patron of comic performance.

The Entrance of the Actual Chorus—The *Parodos* (*Thesm.* 295–371)

The real chorus of women celebrating the Thesmophoria enter the orchestra for the first time in silence and with smoking torches during Euripides' relative's prayer to Demeter and Persephone, goddesses of the Thesmophoria (280–294).[172] The hero's pious wish that his plan may succeed (282–283), the vow of sacrifice—a comic distortion of the *do ut des* formula—if he only be allowed to remain unrecognized by the women (284–288), his third request, for offspring for his daughter (289–291), and the dismissal of the slave-woman who carries the obligatory offering of cakes (285) because she is not permitted to attend the festival (293–294), all suit the dramatic role of the chorus as it assembles and enable the male intruder to sneak into the Thesmophorion without being noticed. For apart from his external resemblance to them because of his feminine attire, he now also successfully imitates the women in their festive context on the level of verbal utterance and of behavior. Like Dikaiopolis in the *Acharnians*, he also becomes part of the audience of a popular assembly; he

---

in lines 107 and 128 is changed into the plural; cf. Austin 1987:73 *ad* 107, where he suggests ἄνακτ' ἄγαλλε‹τε› Φοῖβον for line 128; cf. Parker 1997:405), and line 129 to the chorus.

[171] Cf. above, n170 on *Thesm.* 123–129. One could also argue that lines 101–103 should be given to the chorus as a self-command. Mazon 1904:127–128 argues precisely thus for the solution of the scholia, namely that Agathon is imitating a chorus in a monody; he does, however, divide the chorus into two semi-choruses; he interprets lines 101–103 as a command to dance given by one of these to the other (128).

[172] Cf. Zimmermann I 1985:112. The verb ἀνέρχεσθαι (281) may indicate the *anodos* onto the Pnyx as well as the first day of the festival, which bears the same name and on which the women ascended to the Thesmophorion, which lay on higher ground; see schol. *Thesm.* 585 and Deubner 1932:54.

takes a seat in the front row in order to hear the "speakers" (292) as clearly as possible.

The *parodos* in this way becomes a "play within a play" for the relative. The stage has thus already been set for the interplay of the two discourses, the female festival of Thesmophoria and the male *ekklêsia*. This constellation becomes a vehicle for comedy for the subsequent first real entrance of a chorus. One cannot sufficiently imagine the ridiculous nature of the scene: women gather to hold a popular assembly, something which lies wholly in the domain of the men. Only they have the right to take part in Athenian politics. Representatives of both sexes in this comedy thus encroach on spheres of activity allotted strictly according to gender-specific categories. The situation is made complicated in terms of gender identity by the third narrative authority. For over the mixture of female dramatic role with male political understanding arches the chorus of the performance, composed of male citizens. What connects the three modes of action is ritual. The citizen chorus honors the polis gods in the orchestra, the chorus of the plot prays to the deities of the Thesmophoria, and even the introductory ceremonies of a popular assembly use cultic epithets.

Furthermore, the intertextual blending of an *ekklêsia* into the context of the Thesmophoria is not as absurd as it might appear to a modern observer whose idea of the world has been completely shaped by the opposition between state and religion. Aristophanes succeeds in linking the two areas, since on the one hand the institutionalized political activity of the *dêmos* is closely interwoven with polis ritual and marked by festive occasions and appeals to the gods. On the other hand, even the festival of inversion of the Thesmophoria is arranged according to political points of view. The festival corresponds to an inverted world which, though in mirror image and with reversed conditions, nevertheless is organized in adherence to the usual norm. The women do not assemble against the wishes of the men: the male-dominated polis is in fact concerned that the women's festival proceed as it should.[173] It is by means of the ritual action of temporary separation from their *oikos* that the married women guarantee fertility and continuity of order.

The precise location of the Thesmophorion is controversial, but it is quite probable that the suggestion of the Pnyx is not entirely based on some comic idea of Aristophanes to bring about a combination of levels, but might have

---

[173] On the political character of the Thesmophoria see Detienne 1979:199–201, Loraux 1981:126, and Versnel 1993:251n80 (with further literature).

corresponded to reality.[174] For the few days of the festival of inversion in all its piquancy, the Pnyx, where the male popular assembly was traditionally held, would accordingly be precisely the place in which the women celebrated their holy rites without the presence of men. On these festive days the men ceased all political activity, and in particular the *boulê* and *ekklêsia* did not meet. By way of inversion, the women named two ἄρχουσαι corresponding to the male archons. These, together with the priestess, exercised overall supervision of the festival.

The day of the Νηστεία, the setting of the dramatic plot, provided ample opportunity for such an assembly. On this day of fasting, the women lay on beds of leaves in front of their camp city. In addition to the secret and strange rites performed by the ἀντλήτριαι—the "dipper-women" who fetched up the rotting remains of pig sacrifices that had previously been thrown into subterranean *megara*, placed them on altars, and mixed them with the grain for sowing—there was ample time for the women to come together because of the obligatory fasting and the accompanying cessation of all activities. On this occasion they could have all discussed questions concerning the festival and their situation. Diodorus (Diod. Sic. 5.4.7) considers the Thesmophoria overall to be a restaging of a primordial, primitive world.[175] According to Arnold van Gennep's scheme of the *rite de passage*, the Νηστεία is a day of marginality on which all current codes of the community are played through in inverted and distorted fashion. On the last day of the festival, the Καλλιγένεια, the city finds it way back to the normal order of things. In the male ideology of the polis the Thesmophoria is thus seen as a temporary return to a matriarchal stage of society that is imagined as preceding the current stage of civilization.

In what follows it will be shown how the three narrative perspectives interact. While attention has always been paid in the discussion of the *parodos* to the interweaving of *ekklêsia* and Thesmophoria, focusing on the simultaneous

---

[174] Cf. Henderson 1996:92–93, who considers that the women at the Thesmophoria referred to their place of assembly as the Pnyx in a kind of comic distortion because of the confusion of the levels. He nevertheless is inclined toward the earlier conventional interpretation that the Thesmophorion really was on the Pnyx (cf. *Thesm.* 658). Cf. Thompson 1936, who despite inadequate archaeological evidence tentatively located it next to the place where the men held their assemblies. Versnel 1993:240n40 has also more recently subscribed to this opinion. Following Broneer's influential article (Broneer 1942) the Eleusinion, the main sanctuary for Demeter and Kore in Athens lying southwest of the Agora on the northwest slope of the Acropolis, has generally been adopted as the locale for the women celebrating this festival. Austin 1990:20 and Sommerstein *Thesm.*, 196–197 *ad* 658 follow this theory.

[175] He reports that the Syracusans celebrated the Thesmophoria as μιμούμενοι τὸν ἀρχαῖον βίον.

performance of the ritual citizen chorus is something new.[176] Moreover, the relation to Agathon's song, which is not anchored in real life, needs to be examined.

The songs in the *Thesmophoriazusae* have in general little connection with the action in the plot. Rather, they deliver the necessary atmosphere, the ritual background to the comic play. At the same time the polis gods are honored from the standpoint of the male chorus, which as a representative cross-section of the community represents a bridge to the mainly male audience and to the polis. As internal observer, the comic chorus functions as a place of mediation for the audience, which is wholly marked by a male perspective. Since the men assembled in the theater could know, and were permitted to know, only a little about the women's festival of inversion, the members of the chorus also bridge the cleft between the female attitude in the plot and the male perspective of the audience. In order to address the spectators, the chorus chooses specifically male viewpoints which it extends onto its female role. Beside the representation of the ritual ambiance of the Thesmophoria, what we have here is laughter at the inverted world of the festival as viewed through the lens of the normal world of men, which at the City Dionysia, the performative occasion for comedy, likewise celebrates a festival of inversion and comic distortion.

In these types of songs the traditional function of the nondramatic choral song is blended into the development of the plot. Collective speech, worship, dance, prayer, expression of joy and comic festivity, criticism, ridicule, and praise are at the center. Nevertheless, the Aristophanic chorus has a more or less limited connection to the action on stage, up until the *parabasis*. It is in the *parodos* and *agôn* that debates between firm positions are often introduced and played out. In the case of the *Thesmophoriazusae* the plot-sustaining element admittedly seems almost negligible, for just as in the later songs, here too a pure prayer ritual lies close at hand.

Scholarship has treated the embedded hymn in the *parodos* (312–330), like the great choral dance song (947–1000), as a subsitute for the missing *parabasis* odes.[177] All four individual components of the entry song (295–311, 312–330, 331–351, and 352–371) have been compared with the *parabasis* on account of their prayer-like character, the cursing and blessing form, which reflects ritual praise and blame, and because of their political dimen-

---

[176] On the *parodos* cf. Wilamowitz II 1893:347–355, esp. 352–355, Kleinknecht 1937:33–40, Haldane 1965, Horn 1970:106–115, esp. 109–115, Zimmermann I 1985:112–121, Habash 1997:25–30, and Parker 1997:406–413.

[177] Cf. Horn 1970:111.

sion.[178] As is well known, Aristophanes plays with the building blocks of comedy. The ritual form of expression in the *parabasis* is thus not limited to this, but can ultimately be extended, as in this comedy, over the whole course of the play. This manner of speaking on the whole defines the comic chorus, which, in contrast to the more strongly narrative and commentative manner of its tragic counterpart, brings the traditional function of ritual to the fore. Yet despite the seemingly very loose connection to the plot, Aristophanes also places this *parodos* in the context of the story. The emphasis on the aspect of the *ekklêsia* is mainly responsible for this, for the women will after this decide on Euripides' sentence formally in an assembly.[179] By means of the speech act of the introductory prayers the entry song thus constitutes the collective organ that is of great importance for the progress of events on the stage.

Because of this plot-determining element the central expressive element of the round dance is almost left out by the members of the chorus, in contrast to the dance song (947–1000). For although dances are expressly attested at the Thesmophoria,[180] the element of body language is suppressed because it is not in keeping with the discourse of the popular assembly that is introduced here. One does not dance in a political institution. As a result, the emphasis is on resolutions and speeches rather than on a cultic festival. Only once the intruder is discovered is movement brought into play, which is expressed also on the collective level of the chorus. Nevertheless, the element of choral dance, which has already played a role in Agathon's song, is also implicitly present here.

Next, after the command for ritual silence (εὐφημία), obligatory both for the popular assembly and for any ritual activity, a woman, whose identity comically oscillates between a priestess of the Thesmophoroi and "heraldess,"[181]

---

[178] Cf. Horn 1970:111–115. On ritual blaming cf. Meuli 1975:33–68, esp. 33–41 ("Bettelumzüge im Totenkultus, Opferritual und Volksbrauch"), 177–250 ("Schweizer Masken und Maskenbräuche"), and 283–299 ("Der Ursprung der Fastnacht"), esp. among others 223 and 293.

[179] Up until line 530 the action consists of the presentation of the popular assembly of women. Lines 329 and 372ff. consitute an immediate reference to the deliberate "other action" (cf. Hartmann 1887:334); particularly after the relatively self-contained interlude of song and prayer we return to the actual plan (372ff.), that action be taken in this pseudo-political organization against Euripides for his hostility to women.

[180] See Plut. *Sol.* 8.4-5 (referring to the festival at Halimous on the 10th of Pyanopsion; on the day before the actual beginning of the Thesmophoria there was a visit to the local sanctuary of Demeter on Cape Kolias, during which the most prominent women of Athens would carry out a sacrifice and dance on the beach; the women of the chorus call themselves here εὐγενεῖς γυναῖκες, *Thesm.* 330) and Polyaen. *Strat.* 1.20.2.

[181] Cf. Horn 1970:109n203; contra Sommerstein *Thesm.*, 176–177 *ad* 295, who identifies the woman as Kritylla and thinks that the prayer to the divinities there named is only appropriate for a priestess of the Thesmophoroi.

corresponding to the blending of discourses, gives a command in prose form to pray to certain gods, a move designed to support the dramatic context, just as in lines 947 and following.[182] Because of the demands of plot development the cultic function in the women's festival has to be placed frontstage, while the herald aspect is introduced only secondarily. The deities named by the priestess have a more or less clear connection with the Thesmophoria.[183] Hermes in particular is named because in the myth he conducts Kore back to the world (*Hom. Hymn.* 2.334ff.). The Kharites are the personification of female charm and sexual attraction, which play an important role for fertility. They also naturally belong to the performance of a song, as has already been seen in the song of Agathon (121–122).[184] With Kalligeneia, the special goddess of "good birth," after whom the third and final day of the Thesmophoria is named,[185] and again with Ploutos and Kourotrophos, reference is made to the birth of noble offspring. The figure of the pure boy Ploutos embodies in the context of the festival both material wealth and the sexual fertility of the women. The name Kourotrophos is appropriate to many goddesses, but here represents Demeter herself in particular, who gives birth to and brings up the son of "Wealth" in his agrarian and human dimension.[186]

By concentrating on the specifically ritual element of this festival, Aristophanes also achieves a smooth transition to the previous prayer of

---

[182] Kleinknecht 1937:33–34 shows how the call for εὐφημία with subsequent prayer to certain polis gods introduces and sets up a popular assembly. The female speaker's prose is thus supposed to imitate the political ceremony in a way that is as unartificial and true to life as possible. The often-interrupted prayer of the priest in *Av.* 864–888 is comparable; cf. also *Av.* 1035–1057 and 1660–1666, where legal formulae are at the center.

[183] Cf. Deubner 1932:55. The less clearly associated divinities Kourotrophos, Hermes, the Kharites, and Ploutos may also be placed in the context of a festival of Demeter. An archaic inscription from Eleusis, *IG* I³ 5, mentions among the gods who are supposed to receive initial sacrifices at the Eleusinia the names of Ge, Hermes, the Kharites, and Plouton. Cf. Deubner 1932:55, 91n12 and Haldane 1965:40 with n3.

[184] Cf. *Pax* 796–797, *Av.* 782, 1320, *Lys.* 1279, and Ar. fr. 348 K.-A.

[185] In the second *Thesmophoriazusae* (*PCG* III.2, 182–200) she delivered the prologue, according to schol. *Thesm.* 298. Presumably this version was not set at the Νηστεία, but on the third day.

[186] Cf. a black-figure vase from Rhodes (London, British Museum 1906.12–15.1); Ashmole 1946 with ills. 2a, 3a, c, d, e. There the dance is performed by five women, who hold each other by the hand. The last woman holds a twig of *eiresiônê* (on *eiresiônê* as symbol of Ploutos and sign of wealth and fertility cf. Camps-Gaset 1994:77–87) and a naked dancing boy by the hand; the late arrival could certainly be Ploutos himself. Next to a priestess is a seated figure, probably the goddess Demeter, who watches the choral spectacle as onlooker. Simultaneously a phallus in the *liknon* is being revealed. On the image cf. Calame I 1977:133–134 (Engl. trans. Calame 1997:68–69). The naked παῖς ἀμφιθαλής perhaps embodies Ploutos, particularly typical of the day of the Kalligeneia. Lines 289–291 could be a comic reference to this kind of ritual content (phallus, Ploutos); the element of the dance is only hinted at in the following choral song and is only transformed into ritual action in the later choral dance songs (947ff. and 1136ff.).

Euripides' relative (280ff.).[187] Then three narrative "instances" are referred to with deictic signal words: the gods are to "grant the best and finest success for this assembly here and the ritual gathering now going on (ἐκκλησίαν τήνδε καὶ σύνοδον τὴν νῦν)" (301–302). The two juxtaposed categories of political assembly and women's festival have been sufficiently discussed in critical interpretations of the scene.[188] But "this ritual gathering" also means the gathering of the chorus members in the here and now and so the woman speaking is thus simultaneously the female leader of the chorus, who is concerned with getting the gods' help for her current activity.[189] The activity is to happen for the "use of the city of the Athenians, and for your (i.e. our) own happiness" (304–305).[190] These wishes are also precisely applicable to the current choral dance, which is intended both to serve the polis as a whole, in turn coming into closer contact with the gods, and also of course to bring the audience and the chorus luck, that is to say, success. The transmitted "we" refers to the typical

---

[187] Cf. *Thesm.* 280 and 285–286 with 295ff. On Ploutos cf. πλουτοῦντος, 290. As a male intruder, the relative renders the cultic contexts ridiculous. He prays (289–291) to Demeter and Persephone that his little daughter "Piggy-pussy" (line 289: χοῖρον R, εὔχοιρον Coulon, Χοιρίον Fritzsche) find a rich man (ἀνδρός . . . πλουτοῦντος) and be able to look after the "Willy-boy" (σαθίσκον; cf. schol. *Thesm.* 291, τὸν παιδαρίσκον) (cf. Austin 1990:20–21). In the ideology of the festival one really does encounter pigs, which symbolize fertility. In particular the married women are all symbolically transformed back into virgin genitalia that encounter the male sex for the first time in order to ensure good offspring. In the plot of the ritual, female and male genitalia made of dough where brought together. The relative takes up these suggestions in a humorous fashion and sees in Ploutos only a materially wealthy man who might get his little daughter pregnant. The textual situation of *Thesm.* 291—in opposition to the transmitted reading in manuscript R πρὸς θάληκον—involves the following conjectures: πρὸς φάλητα (Scaliger), Ποσθαλίσκον (Dindorf), πρὸς τὸ ληκεῖν (van Leeuwen), Ποσθάληκον (Rogers), and πρὸς σαθίσκον (Willems and Coulon). One has thus to make a decision whether "the Willy-boy (Ποσθαλίσκον/Ποσθάληκον) has intelligence" (cf. schol. *Thesm.* 291, τὸν παιδαρίσκον) or the girl ought to "pay attention to (πρός!) the phallus (or sexual act)" (νοῦν ἔχειν μοι καὶ φρένας, 291; cf. schol. *Thesm.* 291, ἀντὶ τοῦ κατωφερῆ τὸν νοῦν μου ποίησον). Austin 1990:20–21 and Prato 1993:696–698 argue for the corresponding diminutive forms Χοιρίον and Ποσθαλίσκον for a girl and boy (cf. schol. *Thesm.* 289 and 291). Sommerstein *Thesm.*, 48 and Habash 1997:25 also follow them. Cf. now also Prato, 38 and 215–216 *ad* 289, 291 and Austin/Olson, 15 and 147–148 *ad* 289, 291.

[188] See esp. Haldane 1965:40. He shows that σύνοδος is used to describe ritual meetings: cf. among others Thuc. 3.104.3, Plat. *Leg.* 771d3, and Arist. *Eth. Nic.* 1160a24 and 26.

[189] So too van Leeuwen *Thesm.*, 49 and *ad* 295–310, who correctly describes the woman as κορυφαῖος (ἱερεία), and Austin 1974:316–319.

[190] On line 305: Fritzsche's conjecture ὑμῖν is opposed to the transmitted ἡμῖν in manuscript R, which could also be interpreted in the sense of a wish that the current action might fall to "us ourselves" (i.e. the members of the chorus) (τυχηρῶς δ' ἡμῖν αὐταῖς, 305). In contrast to the reading ὑμῖν the chorus leader would then be included in the group. The comment in Horn 1970:110n208 is unclear, since the female speaker more than likely includes herself in the collective with the formula χαίρωμεν (311).

choral manner of speaking; the feminine αὐταῖς, however, which is emphasized by the pronoun, directs attention to the fictional part of the *énoncé*.

The next statement is also consciously left up in the air in terms of the
level of utterance. On the one hand, καὶ τὴν δρῶ- | σαν καὶ ἀγορεύουσαν τὰ
βέλτιστα περὶ τὸν δῆμον | τὸν Ἀθηναίων καὶ τὸν τῶν γυναικῶν, ταύτην νικᾶν
(305–307) clearly refers to the situation of the assembly: the woman who speaks
best will retain the upper hand. Once again the two areas are juxtaposed and
are then arranged chiastically; the δρώμενα of the ritual and speaking in the
assembly apply logically to the Athenian people and to their women,[191] and
ταύτην νικᾶν then brings both discourses together. Yet it has not been hitherto recognized that ταύτην νικᾶν also includes the communicative context of
the actual performance. The verb "to win" in Aristophanes can often refer to
victory in the contest at hand; the feminine form of the subject, ταύτην, which
completes ritual actions (δρῶσαν) and speech acts (ἀγορεύουσαν) for the polis
as a whole, could grammatically speaking apply equally to ἐκκλησίαν τήνδε
καὶ σύνοδον τὴν νῦν (301), which in fact is also identified with the chorus in
the here and now. Requests of this type by the chorus for victory in the comic
agôn are typical of the self-referential discourse of comedy, which transcends
the plot. This also characterizes the odes of the *parabasis*, which this play does
not have; for this reason, their attributes are transferred to the songs. This
manner of speaking is not confined to the *parabasis*, but is characteristic of the
genre as a whole.[192] Using ring composition, the female leader of the chorus
once more takes up the command to the group to begin the prayer (ταῦτ'
εὔχεσθε), and to pray for "good things for yourselves" (καὶ ὑμῖν αὐταῖς τἀγαθά,
310). This wish relates to the ἀγαθά that the Thesmophoroi bestow on women.
At the same time there is also a glimpse of the performative context here. The
formulation refers back to line 305 and implies that the deities named there
can come to the aid of the chorus in their current activity and have the ability
to assure their success.[193] The chorus then take up this suggestion in their cry
to the gods of ἐλθὲ δεῦρο (319).

---

[191] On gender differentiation in the pointed expression see Horn 1970:110 and Wilamowitz II
1893:349 and 352. For δῆμον . . . τῶν γυναικῶν cf. also *Thesm.* 1145–1146 and above, nn132–133.

[192] Cf. the antode of the *parabasis Equ.* 581–594, a *hymnos klêtikos* to Pallas Athena: ὦ πολιοῦχε
Παλλάς, . . . | . . . | (586) δεῦρ' ἀφικοῦ λαβοῦσα τὴν | ἐν στρατιαῖς τε καὶ μάχαις | ἡμετέραν
ξυνεργὸν | Νίκην, ἢ χορικῶν ἐστιν ἑταίρα | τοῖς τ' ἐχθροῖσι μεθ' ἡμῶν στασιάζει (*Equ.* 581–590).
The "victory" refers both to the great *agôn* against Kleon and to the contest of choruses in the
real world. Cf. also above, n67 on *Thesm.* 972b. Prayers for victory in the *agôn* of plays are not
confined to the *parabasis*: cf. *Ach.* 1224, *Nub.* 1115–1130, *Av.* 445–447, 1102–1117, *Lys.* 1293, *Ran.*
390–393, and *Eccl.* 1154–1162, 1182.

[193] Cf. the female chorus leader's wish for favor at the end of her second invocation (*Thesm.* 351)
and that of the chorus at the end of the comedy (1230–1231).

The singer's closing shout of *paian* equally reflects the complex narrative situation. On the level of performance the paean is associated with victory in the comic *agôn*.[194] A paean is normally sung in life-threatening situations, for example in war. On the dramatic level this cultic cry can thus be taken as a signal for attack and an expression of self-exhortation against the men.[195] The verb νικᾶν (309) could then to a certain extent be understood as a sign of the will to victory in a war of the sexes. Furthermore, the paean is sung at concrete cultic occasions, for example at sacrifices, weddings, processions, and to accompany prayers, all of which fit the situation of this *parodos*. We know too little of the modalities of performance to be able to construct a clear picture, but a song of this type normally seems to be performed by men.[196] There are of course choruses of young women for Artemis or Apollo.[197] The rule that choruses of young men sing the paean would be identical with the performative perspective of the citizen chorus. There can be hardly be a reflex here of actual women's cult practice.[198] The projection of the chorus of Theban elders onto the paean of Delian maidens in Euripides' *Heracles* (*HF* 687ff.) appears to be a poetic construct of the tragic artist. The poet thereby creates a point of comparison that makes understandable the sudden feeling of youthful power bestowed

---

[194] Cf. Ar. *Lys.* 1291–1294 and *Av.* 1763–1765 together with the τήνελλα καλλίνικος (cf. Dunbar *Birds,* 769 *ad* 1764–1765; cf. also *Ach.* 1227–1234). In the context of another literary contest, the dithyramb, cf. Timoth. *Pers.* fr. 791.202–205 *PMG.*

[195] Cf. *Pax* 453–458 (Hermes and the chorus encourage each other to drag Peace out against the will of the other gods). Haldane 1965:40 compares *Pax* 431–458 to *Thesm.* 305–311. On the paean as protection against disease and illness in connection with Apollo Agyieus in the pseudo-trial on the Pnyx, see *Vesp.* 863–874, esp. 868–874. Wilamowitz II 1893:354, because of *Thesm.* 748, imagines a statue of this divinity on the Pnyx and connects this with the typical appeal to Apollo. On *Vesp.* 863–874 see also Kleinknecht 1937:52–53; the call for εὐφημία is found here (*Vesp.* 868) and in *Thesm.* 295; on the wish for favor cf. *Vesp.* 869, *Pax* 453 with *Thesm.* 283, 305, and 310. On the performative situations of the paean see Käppel 1992:45–46 (war), 46–49 (general danger).

[196] See Calame I 1977:148 (Engl. trans. Calame 1997:77), Käppel 1992:81, and Rutherford 1994/95:114 (choruses of young men were the rule); on paeans sung by maidens, Calame I 1977:147–152 and 190–209, esp. 203 (Engl. trans. Calame 1997:76–79 and 101–113, esp. 109).

[197] These types of choruses of maidens, however, are the exception in the case of the male paean: see the comparison of the old members of the chorus with the Delian maidens, who perform the paean for Apollo (Eur. *HF* 687–700, esp. 687–694; cf. with this the description of the Deliades in *Hom. Hymn.* 3.146–164 and the comment in Calame I 1977:147 [Engl. trans. Calame 1997:76 with n204]), and the paeans directed at Artemis (Eur. *IA* 1467–1531, esp. 1467–1469, 1480–1484 and *IT* 1398–1405) and to Apollo and Artemis together (Soph. *Trach.* 205–224).

[198] Käppel 1992:61 mentions late attestations of paeans at sacrifices to Demeter and Kore in the Eleusinian mystery cult, which is naturally connected to the Thesmophoria. Yet here too (male) ephebes and *tekhnitai* perform the song (cf. *IG* II/III² 1078 and *IG* II/III² 1338.1–19). For dramatic reasons Helen sings a paean to Persephone as underworld goddess (Eur. *Hel.* 177; cf. Kannicht II 1969:70–71 *ad* Eur. *Hel.* 176–178 and Käppel 1992:48–49).

on the old men by Dionysus in their dance.[199] At this point in the *parodos* the female chorus clearly sings a paean in their dramatic role in order to facilitate the identification of the male audience with its (male) citizen chorus.

The chorus now replies to the command with a solemn *hymnos klêtikos*, which is, surprisingly, directed at completely different gods (312–330). It is not the divinities associated with the festival of Demeter that are invoked, but Zeus, Apollo, Athena, Artemis, Poseidon, the Nereids, and the Nymphs.[200] The ritual, hortatory formula χαίρωμεν (311) is answered by the collective's δεχόμεθα ("Let it be so!" 312). The group "takes up" the command in the performative "we" form; the gods whom the chorus wishes to address in the following prayer are grouped together in a kind of proem. We are dealing here with the θεῶν γένος (312), and not just the deities of the Thesmophoria, who belong specifically to the cult in the plot.[201] The song accordingly is a typical serial prayer (*Reihengebet*) to the polis gods that perhaps was uttered in the introductory ceremony of the *ekklêsia*. Yet apart from the explicit τελέως δ' ἐκ-| κλησιάσαιμεν (328–329) there is no trace of this dimension. Rather, it seems as if the chorus has completely drifted from its role into the utterance level of its function as citizen chorus. At the end it therefore has to summon itself back to its function within the drama (328–330).

The conventional character of this song, which is reminiscent of pure cult poetry, has been universally recognized by scholars.[202] But the conclu-

---

[199] Cf. Henrichs 1996a:60: "But, it is more likely that we are dealing with a poetic construct in which the poet assigns performance of the paean to the imaginary chorus of Delian Maidens in order to facilitate comparison with the male chorus of Theban elders in the orchestra."

[200] In the sanctuary of the Thesmophoroi on Thasos there were altars of Zeus, Artemis, Athena, and the Nymphs, to whom the families of the elite would offer sacrifices; cf. Rolley 1965.

[201] Cf. *Thesm.* 960, γένος Ὀλυμπίων θεῶν.

[202] On metrical grounds Wilamowitz II 1893:353 views the dactylo-epitrites that appear here as being "wie sie die wirklichen cultlieder boten" ["like ones found in real cult songs"]. Haldane 1965:41 comes close to this when he says: "the chorus . . . emerges as a party of worshippers at a religious festival." But he does not commit himself; the festival he speaks of must be the Great Dionysia of 411 BCE, and the worshipers are identical to the comic chorus of citizens. Silk 1980:112 in the throes of his literary criticism finds fault with the conventionality of the piece. But cultic poetry is never concerned with producing world literature; it is entirely grounded in the pragmatic. Zimmermann I 1985:116 makes a similar assessment, but his categories are concentrated on the course of the action. He approaches the song purely in connection with the conventional opening ceremony of a popular ritual and within the frame of the Thesmophoria, although these dimensions recede completely into the background in these lines. Horn 1970:111 has a similar approach: he sees a political element behind the invocation of Athena. He correctly observes: "Die komischen abrupten Übergänge vom Volksversammlungs- zum Frauengebet . . . fehlen diesem Lied fast völlig" ["Comic, abrupt transitions from the prayer of the popular assembly to that of the women . . . are completely absent in this song"]. Yet the political ought not be separated from the ritual task of the citizen chorus, since politics also determines polis ritual.

sion has thus far not been drawn from this that at this point the chorus also departs from its role and speaks in the here and now. Aristophanes thus does not imitate cult poetry for parodic purposes.[203] Rather, he composes this song of request within a living choral culture in order to fulfill a key ritual function of the chorus, namely honoring the gods of the city and giving them pleasure (cf. ἐπιχαρῆναι, 314).

The overcoming of boundaries between polis gods, cultic actors, and spectators is an important feature. The ritual of choral dance and prayer joins the groups in one communal activity, to which the gods are summoned. Following the logic of cult, they are expected to experience pleasure at their worship and to appear in person as a reaction to this (φανέντας ἐπιχαρῆναι, 314), in order to mingle with their worshipers. Clear connections can thereby be made to the song of Agathon, which is not grounded in any practical reality, and to the *parabasis*-like songs at 947ff. and 1136ff. Apart from support of the plot achieved by the naming of the goddesses of the Thesmophoria, there is also the real-world function of the worship of the patron gods of the city. One finds similar prayer series to the polis gods spread over the choral passages of the *Thesmophoriazusae*, so that this dimension behind the plot is not neglected.[204] Since the Agathon song is not performed by an actual group, one does not find there the usual request for epiphany and participation in the circle of the chorus. But these characteristics bring out all the more clearly the chorus' worship in the *parodos* and in the following choral dance songs.[205]

Zeus is named first as supreme principle of the cosmos (315). The popular assembly and the justice brought by order are after all under his control, and for this reason the invocation of him is taken up once more at the end

---

[203] Cf. Kleinknecht 1937:34: "Der herrliche Hymnus . . . ist durchaus auf ernsten Ton gestimmt und fern von jeglicher parodischen Tendenz" ["The magnificent hymn . . . is presented in a completely serious tone and is far removed from any kind of parodic tendency"].

[204] *Thesm.* 101ff.: Apollo, Artemis, Leto, and once more Apollo; 969ff.: Apollo, Artemis, Hera, Hermes, Pan, Nymphs, Dionysus; 1136ff.: Athena, Demeter, and Kore. See Haldane 1965:41, who analyzes the system behind the series and speaks of a "possible reminiscence of the state prayer" because of the gods mentioned.

[205] On the request for a divinity to appear cf. *Thesm.* 1136–1147, esp. 1143 (Athena), 1148–1159, esp. 1154–1155, 1158–1159 (Demeter and Kore); in other comedies cf. *Ach.* 665–675, esp. 665, 674 (the Acharnian Muse), *Equ.* 551–564, esp. 559 (Poseidon), 581–594, esp. 586, 591 (Athena), *Nub.* 263–274, esp. 266, 269 (Clouds), *Ran.* 323–336, esp. 326 (Iakkhos). On the δεῦρο-formula in cletic hymns cf. *Thesm.* 1136–1138 (Athena), *Ach.* 665 (the Acharnian Muse), *Equ.* 559 (Poseidon), 586, 591 (Athena), *Ran.* 394–399, esp. 395, 399 (Iakkhos). The request for the epiphany of a god is explicitly related to the chorus in the performance: *Thesm.* 1136–1138 (Athena), *Equ.* 559 (Poseidon), *Equ.* 586–594, esp. 589–590 (Athena with Nike and request for victory in the dramatic competition!), *Nub.* 563–565 (Zeus), *Pax* 775–777 (Muse), *Ran* 323–336 (Iakkhos), 385a–393 (Demeter), 394–413 (Iakchos), and 674–675 (Muse).

of the song by way of ring composition. As lord of the gods he is supposed to guarantee that the gods support the chorus members, even if they are only women (368–371). Once again, the chorus plays here with its double identity of dramatic role and function. The "we" refers to the performative context, to which the gods are summoned for support (ἡμῖν θεοὺς παραστατεῖν, 370), while the reference to female identity (καίπερ γυναιξὶν οὔσαις, 371) maintains the plot of an assembly of women. Although Zeus is less often connected with choral dance,[206] the gods subsequently named are very closely associated with it. Yet because the plot involves an *ekklêsia*, this dimension remains largely hidden. This fundamental element of the chorus thus establishes a connection to the Agathon song and the other choral dance songs, where choral divinities are equally invoked. While this motif is never really translated into action in the solo song of the new-fangled poet and in this hymn, which explains the lack of extensive references to the chorus' own dance, this central function does come to the fore after the popular assembly has gotten underway, especially since dance performance is also quite at home in the ritual ambience of the Thesmophoria.

The naming of Apollo (315–316) takes up the priestess' shouting of the paean (310–311). He is summoned in his function as inhabitant of the island of Delos.[207] The chorus implicitly views itself, as does the chorus in Euripides' *Heracles* (687ff.), as the embodiment of the Delian maidens, so that the female identity of the dramatic role can be blended in (330). This is all the more easily achieved by the invocation of Athena and Artemis (317–321), who as choral goddesses are equally responsible for the dances of young women. Furthermore, Athena, like Artemis, in particular oversees the condition of women before marriage, a state to which the married women at the Thesmophoria symbolically regress. Athena has of course a special connection with the city of Athens and its politically active citizens.[208] As particular choral goddess of young girls, Artemis again reflects the paean-motif, since this kind of song may also be addressed to her.[209] From the point of view of gender, Apollo, Athena, Artemis, and Poseidon are arranged chiastically; from the point of view of belonging together as sibling pair and gods who competed for power over the polis in a mythical battle, a parallel sequence can be observed

---

[206] Zeus is also invited in *Nub.* 563–565 to come to the chorus.

[207] Cf. *Nub.* 596 and *Ran.* 659.

[208] On the invocation of Athena (317–319), see Anderson 1995:58–62.

[209] Cf. Soph. *Trach.* 205–224 (Apollo and Artemis), Eur. *IT* 1398–1405, *IA* 1467–1469 (Artemis); cf. also schol. Soph. *OT* 173 (p. 147 De Marco) and Käppel 1992:35, 56–57 (paeans in honor of Apollo, Artemis, and Leto in Delos!).

here. This competition between Athena and Poseidon for patronage of the city
(πόλιν . . . περιμάχητον, 318–319) goes back to a cultural stage when women
still had a say in politics in the form of the right to vote.[210] The myth is evoked
because this prehistoric condition before the struggle is of importance for
the configuration of the dramatic plot of the Thesmophoria, which likewise
temporarily restages primordial matriarchal conditions. Athena and Poseidon
represent the integrated order that Demeter and the "noble women" need in
order to be able to guarantee legitimate sexuality, the fertility of the polis, and
the continuation of its offspring.

Poseidon may be less immediately associated with the chorus. Nevertheless, the appeal from *Knights* (551–564) in this connection may still have
been present in the audience's mind.[211] In this instance the *Du-Stil* address
particularly emphasizes the god and the traditional epithets unequivocally
connect him with his home in the sea. Instead of the expected participial
predication, the participal προλιπών is combined with the magical summons
(ἐλθὲ δεῦρο, 319) in a manner typical of cletic hymns:[212] he is asked to leave
the depths of the sea that teem with fish (προλιπὼν μυχὸν ἰχθυόεντα, 324),
and come straight to the chorus, right now, in the orchestra. The reference to
fish refers to Poseidon's "choral" retinue, which consists mainly of dolphins.
As with the previously named gods, he is also associated in the Greek imagination with the figure of "chorus leader," around whom the dolphins move in a
circular dance.[213]

---

[210] This configuration is in general suggestive of the Skira, which as another festival of inversion lends its character to the scenery in the *Ecclesiazusae*. Cf. Bowie 1993:256–258. During the
Skira women also had their own organizations and assemblies. The contest between Athena
and Poseidon concludes the prehistory of Athens. The *Knights* is influenced by this mythical
conflict; cf. Bowie 1993:66–74. Skiron is a place of license. At the Skira the priestesses of Athena
Polias, Poseidon-Erechtheus, and Helios traveled in procession to the temples of Athena,
Demeter, and Kore (!) in Skiron, near Eleusis. The women held a separate assembly (κατὰ
τὰ πάτρια [*IG* II/III² 1177.11–12]) and ate garlic in order to keep their men away from them
(Philokhoros, *FGrHist* 328 F 89).

[211] In this *hymnos klêtikos* the words ἐλθὲ δεῦρο (*Thesm.* 319) are directly connected to the chorus
of performers in the orchestra; cf. δεῦρ' ἔλθ' εἰς χορόν (*Equ.* 559) and above, n205. Poseidon
is also invoked of course because of the plot, since as horse-god he is the patron god of the
Knights.

[212] Cf. Haldane 1965:43.

[213] Cf. Hes. *Scut.* 209–212 and Arion 1 D. = fr. adesp. 939 *PMG*; cf. *ibid.*, 4–5, περί σε πλωτοὶ | θῆρες
χορεύουσι κύκλῳ; dolphins are called, *ibid.*, 8–9, φιλόμουσοι | δελφῖνες, i.e. they are associated
with the musical activity of choral dance. Like dolphins in the sea, so too the stars often serve
as projection surfaces for choral dance. On dolphins, cf. Eur. *El.* 435–437, *Hel.* 1454–1455 (the
Phoenician ship that is to take Helen to Sparta is addressed by way of apostrophe as χοραγὲ
τῶν καλλιχόρων | δελφίνων). See now Csapo 2003.

This self-referential context becomes even clearer with the address to the Nereids and Nymphs. Both groups of maidens serve as a divine model for the female collective that the chorus embodies in the plot. Once more the arrangement forms an artful chiasmus in which the Nereids relate to Poseidon and the Nymphs to the previously invoked Artemis as their χορηγοί. In addition to the dolphins, the daughters of Nereus represent the mythological example of a κύκλιος χορός, which is of great importance for the cultic dance of the chorus in this comedy.[214] The situation is identical in the case of the Nymphs, who make up Artemis' chorus.[215] At the same time, they represent a bridge in terms of content to the chorus' dramatic role since, as we have seen, in terms of the ideology of the festival the married women temporarily regress to the state of νύμφαι, that is, of brides and young women on the threshold of adulthood. The Nymphs in fact also bring us to the sphere of Dionysus, which is connected with the festive occasion of the performance.[216] They are invoked as "mountain wandering ones" (326), which refers to Dionysiac *oreibasia* and prepares the way for the later image (990ff.). The adjective οἰστροδόνητον (325) attached to μυχόν also reflects Dionysiac *mania*, which defines the chorus surrounding Poseidon.[217]

The first request in the concluding prayer (327–330) is also described by a verb that has Dionysiac connotations and is connected with the playing of music in the performance: "Let the golden *phorminx* resound to our prayers!" (χρυσέα δὲ φόρμιγξ | ἰαχήσειεν ἐπ' εὐχαῖς | ἡμετέραις, 327–329). By this is

---

[214] On the Nereids as a chorus (sometimes together with dolphins), see Bacchyl. *Dith.* 17.101–108; Aesch. fr. 150 Radt (from *Nereides TrGF* III, 262–264); Eur. *Andr.* 1267, *El.* 432–437, *Tro.* 2–3, *Ion* 1081–1086, *IT* 427–429, *IA* 1054–1057; in Soph. *OC* 716–719 the fifty Nereids are called ἑκατόμποδες (718) (with special reference to their feet, which are naturally of importance for dancing). Eur. *IT* 428–429 (χοροὶ | ... ἐγκύκλιοι) and *IA* 1055–57 (εἰλισσόμεναι κύκλια | ... ἐχόρευσαν) refer to the round dance. On their number, which corresponds to the fifty dancers in dithyrambic choruses, see Calame I 1977:78 (Engl. trans. Calame 1997:35) and Zimmermann 1992:26. On the Nereids and dolphins as divine escorts, see Wachsmuth 1967:100–112, esp. 103–106, 108–112, and Barringer 1995:69–94 (chap. 4: "Thetis, Nereids, and Dionysos") and 141–151 (chap. 8: "Marine Thiasos" [on Dionysiac associations]).

[215] Hom. *Od.* 6.99–109 (Nausikaa plays ball with the maidens and is surrounded by them, like Artemis by the Nymphs; cf. on this Calame I 1977:165–166 [Engl. trans. Calame 1997:87–88]), *Ant. Pal.* 6.57.7–8 (the Nymphs form a chorus together with the forest-dwellers), and Soph. *Trach.* 205–215. Cf. Larson 1997. The Nymphs are also invoked in *Ran.* 1344 and *Thesm.* 978.

[216] On nymphs and maenads see Hedreen 1994.

[217] Zimmermann I 1985:116 refers to the metaphorical use of the adjective, otherwise used only to characterize Io. Zimmermann connects the transferred use of οἶστρος with the New Dithyramb. The Nereids in particular, who are mentioned immediately afterward, have a connection with the dithyramb because of their number. Cf. above, n214. On the influence of the New Dithyramb on the song's metre and diction cf. Zimmermann I 1985:115.

surely meant the lyre of Apollo, who has just been invoked as χρυσολύρας (cf. 315). In the reciprocal relationship between human members of the chorus and the divine chorus, greater worth is thus bestowed on the musical accompaniment than on the dance.[218] But the Apollonian sound must here ring out in an almost Dionysiac fashion (ἰαχήσειεν, 328); the verb thus reminds one of the cry of *iakkhos* at the Eleusinian procession.[219] Yet at the same time the actual accompaniment of the song is meant, which in this case is not performed on the *aulos*, but on a stringed instrument. In the sense of a speech act the illocutionary role of the command refers to the event happening right now. In the very moment of the utterance of this request the musical accompaniment is completed, which actors and audience could interpret as the joyful reaction of the god Apollo.[220] It is clearly this instrument that the *kithara*, mentioned in the Agathon song (κίθαριν, 124), takes up. The player bases himself on the divine model of Apollo *kitharôdos*, who as χορηγός directs the song and the dance.[221] While the chorus in the Agathon song is only imitated, here it actually appears for the first time. The Apollonian dimension determines the ceremonial tone of this song as well, which is designed to convey the reverential mood of the hymn for the polis dominated by noble men.[222]

The cletic ἐλθὲ δεῦρο (319) applies to all the polis gods mentioned. The summons takes place both within and without the drama: on the one hand, the gods are invoked to ensure their assistance in the assembly, which is central to

---

[218] Cf. Ar. *Av.* 217-222, 776-784 (the gods make music in reply to a musical invocation in which they take pleasure).

[219] Cf. *Hom. Hymn.* 2.20; Eur. *Hcl.* 752, *El.* 1150, *HF* 349, *Tro.* 515, *Or.* 826, 965; Ar. *Ran.* 217. On ἰακχάζω as synonym of ἰαχέω cf. LSJ s.v. ἰακχάζω, II and Orph. *Lith.* 46 ἰ. ἀοιδήν (as in Ar. *Ran.* 213-217).

[220] Wilamowitz, who elsewhere generally includes the performative dimension of the chorus, here does not see this connection. He argues as follows (Wilamowitz II 1893:353-354) for a δέ instead of the transmitted τε (327): "Wie kann an die anrufungen angereiht werden 'und die goldene laute klinge zu meinen gebeten'? welche laute? es wird uns wirklich zugemutet, nichts hierin zu finden als 'und zu meinem liede soll der musicant die violine spielen.' Das wird der hoffentlich schon längst tun, sonst ist's zu spät. Aber eine goldene laute wird ihm der chorege schwerlich spendirt haben, die gehört nur dem χρυσολύρας, der eben angerufen war" ["How can 'and let the golden lute resound to my prayers' be attached to the invocations? What lute? We are asked to find here nothing more than the thought 'let the musician accompany my song on the violin.' That he should hopefully already have been doing for quite a while, otherwise [the instruction] comes too late. And the *khorêgos* would hardly have spent the money on a golden lute for him: that belongs only to the χρυσολύρας, who has just been invoked"].

[221] For Apollo as *khorêgos* and *mousagêtês* cf. Koller 1963:58-78. Cf. also Pind. *Pyth.* 1.1-4 and the passages collected above, n166.

[222] This is emphasized by the adjective εὐγενεῖς (330), which is, however, comically distorted in terms of the dramatic role by the attached substantive "women." At the same time the women at the Thesmophoria are considered as "well-born."

the development of the plot; on the other, they are also directly summoned to the activity going on in the here and now in the orchestra, which represents one part of their ritual worship. In so doing this song also takes over the function of the *parabasis* odes, which are absent in this play. Aristophanes seems to have incorporated the prayers extensively into the rest of the comedy, partly to convey the ritual ambience of the action and partly to provide validation, through the perspective of the performers, for the male majority opinion, which threatens to be drowned out in this play, so strongly molded by the women's temporary period of inversion.[223]

This ritual worship of the gods is in harmony with the positivity of comedy. Thus the comic playwright Phrynikhos says in his *Kronos* (fr. 9.1 K.-A.): ἀνὴρ χορεύει καὶ τὰ τοῦ θεοῦ καλά ("Men dance in the chorus and the affairs of the gods are in order"). The comic chorus of citizens do precisely this and worship the patron gods of Athens, even though in other respects comedy to a large extent stands the world of the polis on its head. The chorus dances for these gods and entreats them; in accordance with the Greek pattern of thought, the worshipers hope for a positive reaction from the divine side. The gods are envisioned as ideal chorus-leaders who are supposed to join the circular dance of their worshipers out of pleasure, thereby suspending the boundary between god and human for a short while. The audience, who knows from personal experience what being in a citizen chorus involves— every year about fifteen hundred young men danced in a public chorus, quite apart from the choruses that the demes and other micro-organizations of the polis arranged—identifies itself with the representative dancers and thus itself participates directly in the worship of the gods. It is true that in tragedy similar choral songs appear, but there the embedment in a fictional event is further advanced. Phrynikhos' maxim represents the comic opposite to the self-critical verse of the tragic chorus in the *Oedipus Tyrannus*, which asks itself, in the light of tragic developments, why it should continue to dance at all (τί δεῖ με χορεύειν; Soph. *OT* 896). Comedy, then, clearly has no problem in connecting the choral dance, a definitive element of the genre, with dramatic events using a generally much lower level of embedment. Tragedy, on the other hand, must deal with the difficulty of connecting tragic events, which may in extreme cases lead to doubting the existence of the gods, with the bodily expression of joy and unequivocally positive worship of them.[224]

---

[223] On the prayers in *parabasis* odes see the fundamental studies of Fraenkel (1931 and 1962:191–215).

[224] See Henrichs 1994/95:65–73.

In the following speech of the priestess-herald (331–351) in iambic trimeters, the parodic blend of the two areas of popular and Thesmophoric assembly comes strongly to the fore. Already in the entry prayer (331–334), the juxtaposition of male and female domains is projected in a comic and absurd fashion onto the world of the gods:

εὔχεσθε τοῖς θεοῖσι τοῖς Ὀλυμπίοις
καὶ ταῖς Ὀλυμπίαισι, καὶ τοῖς Πυθίοις
καὶ ταῖσι Πυθίαισι, καὶ τοῖς Δηλίοις
καὶ ταῖσι Δηλίαισι, τοῖς τ' ἄλλοις θεοῖς.

Pray to the Olympian gods, male and female, to the Pythians, male and female, to the Delians, male and female, and to all the other gods!

The priestess thus takes up the prayer of the chorus, which beseeches, after Zeus, male and female gods in alternate fashion. The formal invocation of the male and female Olympians first sums up the previous song in a meaningful fashion. In a false analogy to the formula Ὀλύμπιοι καὶ Ὀλύμπιαι the principal of equality is parodically extended to the Pythians and Delians, male and female, where no such female form exists as a separate category. Although the "Olympian" heaven of the gods may count as the central overarching term for all the divinities named, it becomes on the contrary downgraded to a local subgroup which stands on an equal level with the others.[225]

In what follows the emphasis is on the complementary ritual actions of blaming and cursing, as well as on those of praising and blessing, which are all of great importance for comedy. The passage is based on the traditional formula of execration of the enemies of the state and traitors that a herald would pronounce before the opening of the *ekklêsia*.[226] At the Thesmophoria a similar curse may have formed part of the ritual program. The comic effect again resides in the fact that the public discourse is intertextually embedded in the women's festival. Euripides and the enemies of women are thus indiscriminately thrown together with Medes and tyrants (335–339).

Horn thinks that Aristophanes is trying not to parody the curse formula, but to weave "political polemic against certain persons and groups" into the text.[227] Wilamowitz had already attempted to demonstrate political connec-

---

[225] The first position in the following line of the nonexistent female divine union (Pythian and Delian goddesses) makes the absurdity particularly apparent. Cf. Kleinknecht 1937:35 and Haldane 1965:3.

[226] See Kleinknecht 1937:34–37 (with evidence).

[227] Horn 1970:112.

tions between individual parts of this passage and events in the year of the performance, 411 BCE.[228] Given the public discourse of Old Comedy this political element was always present, but the references to a coup remain relatively unclear; ultimately, the mention of Persians and tyrants is one of the standard *topoi* of the genre. To talk of a political *parainesis* in this connection, however common this may be in *parabaseis*, is certainly an exaggeration.[229] The *parabasis*-like quality is emphasized several times, to be sure; still, the *parabasis* ought to be less strongly connected with serious political advice. Rather, the comic chorus' traditional role of carrying out speech acts of praise and blame, censure and blessing that are more or less connected to the action of the plot stands in the foreground in this structural element of comedy.

The joke depends on the intertextual use of official speech within the comedy. Together with the divine apparatus this form of utterance within a specific context "binds" the group of those involved, which is more precisely definied by the εἴ τις series (335ff.).[230] Within the drama, the sexual themes of possible female misbehavior, which later play a role in the speeches to the assembly, are already being prepared. The catalogue of negative female behavior—women like to drink wine, are sexually overactive, commit adultery, and even possibly foist their children on others—is introduced here for the first time. It reflects the fears of the men, who are not able to control their wives during the festival of inversion.[231]

The wives in fact uphold these male prejudices by cursing those who conceal these transgressions. Through the inclusion of masculine categories, their masculine ways of seeing are comically revealed and the spectator can identify himself with the male chorus members, who only represent women as far as the plot is concerned. In the act of uttering the curse the male intruder is condemned, while the women who are not affected by the curse formula, that is, the chorus in its dramatic role and all right-thinking Athenian women, are simultaneously blessed. The prolific expansion of the εἴ τις formula culminates in the following dichotomous expression, strongly reminiscent of traditional speech acts (349–351):

> κακῶς ἀπολέσθαι τοῦτον αὐτὸν κᾠκίαν
> ἀρᾶσθε, ταῖς δ' ἄλλαισιν ὑμῖν τοὺς θεοὺς

---

[228] See Wilamowitz II 1893:345–351.

[229] Horn 1970:113.

[230] Cf. the magical speech of the Erinyes in the ὕμνος δέσμιος, Aesch. *Eum.* 328–333; on this see above, pp. 62–63.

[231] Cf. the excellent interpretation in Versnel 1993:228–288 (particularly on the unrestricted drinking of wine, which is repeatedly mentioned in the *Thesmophoriazusae*, 264–268).

εὔχεσθε πάσαις πολλὰ δοῦναι κἀγαθά.

... a curse and destruction on this man and his house, but pray that
the gods will give all the rest of you women many blessings!

In her speech the herald-priestess calls for this binary distinction. Yet already
in her command—requests for prayer and blessing are pointedly placed at
the beginnings of lines—public condemnation and honoring are carried out.
Through comic refraction the ritual speech act naturally extends to the audience as well. Behind the parody lies the cultic reality: whoever disturbs the
women's Thesmophoria commits a crime against the polis as a whole, which is
the guarantor of the festival's orderly progress.

In the chorus' utterance (352–371) the speech act is confirmed by the collective using the performative "we" form ξυνευχόμεσθα (352),[232] while it simply
acknowledges the command εὔχεσθε in 351. Before the group repeats the
curses, a reference to victory in the assembly and in the comic context is
worked in (355–356) by referring back to lines 305–309.[233] The following repri-
mand (356–367) is admittedly of a highly explosive political nature, given
the historical situation shortly before the oligarchic coup, yet its meaning
should not be limited to this.[234] The chorus sings not only as a female popular

---

[232] Cf. Ar. *Vesp.* 885 and Thuc. 6.32.2.

[233] This occurs again in connection with motifs found in the *parabasis.* One ought not therefore
take as negative a view of these lines as Horn 1970:114 does: "Sieht man dieses überraschende
Motiv im Zusammenhang mit dem sicher verdorbenen Schluß des Liedes (s. u.), so wird man
sich fragen müssen, ob diese Strophe überhaupt noch viel ursprünglich Aristophanisches
enthält." ["If one views this suprising motif in connection with the end of the song, which is
certainly corrupt, one has to ask oneself whether this strophe actually contains much that is
genuinely Aristophanic"].

[234] Cf. Haldane 1965:44–45, esp. his statement (44): "The double image of the chorus falls temporarily into the background; whereas it was seen before as a party of women at a festival it
now emerges almost wholly as a debating society." Cf. also Zimmermann I 1985:117: "[Das
Lied], in dem der Chor ganz als δῆμος τῶν γυναικῶν singt" ["[The song] in which the chorus
sings entirely as δῆμος τῶν γυναικῶν"]; and *ibid.*, 120–121, esp. 121: "Die Parabase mit ihrer
Illusionsdurchbrechung ist für solche Worte nicht mehr geeignet; sie würde zu deutlich die
Meinung des Dichters zu erkennen geben. Durch das Einfügen von Parabasenthemen in den
kultischen Rahmen der Parodos bezieht Aristophanes die politischen Anspielungen und
Warnungen in die Handlung ein, läßt sie Teil einer dramatischen Szene, der Eröffnung der
Frauenvolksversammlung, werden" ["The *parabasis* with its shattering of the [dramatic] illusion is no longer suited for such words; it would reveal the poet's opinion too clearly. By means
of the insertion of *parabasis* themes into the cultic framework of the *parodos*, Aristophanes
incorporates political allusions and warnings into the plot, and has them become part of a
dramatic scene, the opening of the women's assembly"]. Cf. also the purely political interpretation in Banova 1994:153–158, esp. 156–157 and Prato 1995.

assembly: the festival of the Thesmophoria continues to be present as a reference. The political terms (παραβαίνειν τοὺς ὅρκους τοὺς νενομισμένους, ψηφίσματα καὶ νόμον ζητεῖν ἀντιμεθιστάναι, τἀπόρρητα τοῖσιν ἐχθροῖς τοῖς ἡμετέροις λέγειν; cf. 357–358, 361–362, and 363–364) are used ambivalently throughout, particularly since the Thesmophoria in terms of ritual "ideology" resemble a political institution and the name Thesmophoros itself was connected via folk-etymology with the term *thesmos* ('law'). The festival was also seen as a reminder of the fact that Demeter brought civilization, law, and order to humankind.[235]

Men were in fact not "usually" compelled to swear an oath in the popular assembly; rather, the forms of the oath appear to refer to the assembly at the Thesmophoria.[236] The concept of νόμος retains throughout the connotation of ritual and custom. The νενομισμένοι ὅρκοι are accordingly also ritual oaths that the married women at this festival give in order to ensure its successful performance. Their "ritual oath" also refers to the priestess' recent speech act, which subjects any act hostile to women and the polis to a curse.[237] A promise is implied in their confirmation of the instruction. Furthermore, the reference to ὅρκοι is reminiscent of the corresponding situation in the *Lysistrata*, where an inversion of gender roles is staged in the use of ritual performances and the heroine also makes the group of women take an oath, this time in connection with the sex-strike (*Lys.* 181–239).[238] The "resolutions" relate to the above-mentioned oath:

[235] Cf. Diod. Sic. 5.5.2, Callim. *Hymn.* 6.18, Serv. *in* Verg. *Aen.* 4.58; cf. Burkert 1985:246: "The Greeks finally interpreted Demeter *thesmophoros* as the bringer of order, the order of marriage, civilization, and of life itself, and in this they were not entirely mistaken." Similarly Wilamowitz II 1931/32:45 (repr. II, 44), Detienne 1979, 184 ("la Législatrice—celle qui donne à la cité ses «lois»" ["the legislator—she who gives the city its 'laws'"]); in reality *thesmoi* are primarily material objects, i.e. "what is put down" (cf. Burkert 1985:243); on the tension between these two meanings see Farnell 1907:77–81, Parke 1977:83, Brumfield 1981:70–73, and Camps-Gaset 1994:48.

[236] See Sommerstein *Thesm.*, 180 *ad* 359.

[237] On the oath in magical contexts see Faraone 1993 and Graf 1996:186–188. On the closeness between *defixiones* and ritual curses see Graf 1996:116–117. Graf sees magical *defixiones* in the context of crisis management. Without the nearness of the gods, which prayer seeks to achieve, the power to harm also becomes impossible.

[238] Cf. *Lys.* 183, 187, 191 (ὅρκος). Cf. Henderson *Lys.*, 90 *ad* 181–239. The oath accompanied by sacrifice (186–190a) here parodies the political and military oath of the *Seven against Thebes* (Aesch. *Sept.* 42–48). The speech act is described in great detail in the *Lysistrata*; Lysistrata pronounces the formula like a priestess, and the collective follows, repeating the words in unison. The oath is there accompanied by a sacrifice similar to that carried out by the γεραραί (or γεραιραί, Etym. Magn. 227.35) during the Anthesteria ([Demosth.] 59.73–78). Cf. also Faraone 1993 on the oath. On the mythic and ritual models in the *Lysistrata*, cf. Bowie 1993:178–204, whose analysis could be expanded considerably; cf. also Faraone 1997.

"resolutions"[239] and "laws"/"customs" may not be "altered." In the Greek scheme of things, a ritual clearly belongs to the ἄγραφοι νόμοι.[240] The ἀπόρρητα are not only state secrets or personal secrets: the word is also a technical term for any form of a ritual to which a particular group in a society does not have access, as is also the case for the Thesmophoria.

Even the punch line with which the chorus closes its long list of potential evildoers (male and female) demonstrates the interweaving of ritual relating to the Thesmophoria and political discourse: ἀσεβοῦσ᾽ ἀδικοῦσί τε τὴν πόλιν (367). Such people commit a religious outrage and crime against the city, for it is the polis that ensures the yearly performance of the festival and thus the city's continued existence. Crimes of a political and religious nature mean an attack against the law, but δίκη is equally determined by the gods. This sentence (367) is in no way anticlimactic, dull, and lapidary, as has too often been maintained, but firmly condemns opponents (both male and female). The two declarative indicatives in the speech act completely take over the place and function of the curse (cf. 350). The illocutionary role of command and the perlocutionary goal of cursing are easily derived from the context.[241] At the same time, the carrying out of this speech act is already a preparation for the condemnation of possible male intruders (667–686, esp. 670–671, 685). Even if the feminine forms (355, 356, 371, similarly also in 331–351) indicate that women in particular are being addressed, because the chorus speaks in its dramatic role and the participation of men in the assembly seems completely impossible, the censure nevertheless applies to the audience through the insertion of the political element.

This song, like the *Thesmophoriazusae* as a whole, is characterized by the opposing genres of praise and blame, which are quite characteristic of the

---

[239] The articles of association of a third-century BCE cult from Mylasa in Caria direct that the festival of Demeter Thesmophoros be conducted "as the women have decided" (ὡς ἔδοξε ταῖς γυναι[ξί . . ., Sokolowski 1955 [*LSAM*], nr. 61, 5). This corresponds to the formula normally used in popular assemblies conducted by men.

[240] Cf. ἄγραφοι νόμοι (Thuc. 2.37.3) and ἄγραφα νόμιμα (Demosth. 18.275, Plat. *Leg.* 793a10); cf. Soph. *Ant.* 454–455, ἄγραπτα κἀσφαλῆ θεῶν | νόμιμα. On the meaning of νόμος as ritual and social practice, see Leinieks 1996:244–254.

[241] Following Wilamowitz II 1893:354–355, Horn 1970:114–115 thinks that a curse would be expected instead of a statement (367); arguing against the use of conjectures introducing a curse formula, Zimmermann I 1985:118–119, correctly maintains, although he makes use of the argument criticized above, that "die feststellende, indikativische Form um so pointierter erklingt, ja, dem ganzen Lied noch mehr Parabasencharakter verleiht" ["the declarative indicative form sounds even more pointed, in fact gives the whole song an even more *parabasis*-like character"]. By this he understands only the political aspect. Austin 1987:78 *ad* 365–366 views the sentence as a delayed anticlimax, since the women would not have the heart to curse a fellow woman (followed by Sommerstein *Thesm.*, 181 *ad* 367).

comic chorus. Speaking well of someone (εὖ λέγειν) relates first and foremost to the gods of the city, while speaking ill (κακῶς λέγειν) relates to particular women and men of the community. The speech act of defamation in the formulary repertoire has its counterpart in the real world. As in several other festivals of inversion, particularly those connected with Demeter and Dionysus, verbal attacks aggressive in both content and gesture, *aiskhrologia* and *tôthasmos*, are particularly fundamental actions in this festival.[242] Crude, ridiculous, and mocking remarks are precisely a characteristic of Old Comedy. Its positioning in the Dionysiac festive context makes a connection between *aiskhrologia* and this dramatic genre highly likely.[243] Ritual ridicule is very often based on the battle between the sexes. In the upside-down world of the festival of exception and inversion it is therefore permissible to denounce the other sex. This license to defame individuals or whole groups also obtains in same-sex contexts, in which accusations of abnormal sexual practices are hurled. Wolfgang Rösler has shown in a seminal work that in the *Thesmophoriazusae aiskhrologia* has itself become the theme.[244] He shows how this aggressive act heightens collective experience in the group and fosters solidarity among women, who rely on a distinct separation between themselves and the opposite and other to define themselves as a community in their own right.

A connection has already been made between the sexual and erotic components of the chorus' curse upon women who act contrary to the interests of fellow members of their sex (339ff.).[245] The curse (331-351) is significantly directed against men and more so against outsider women, like slave-women or old women, who have been separated from the true group of married women of childbearing age.[246] While many attestations speak of *aiskhrologia* between

---

[242] Beside the Thesmophoria, one may mention the following as festivals connected with Demeter: the Stenia, closely connected in time with the Thesmophoria, the Haloa, and the so-called jokings at the bridge (*gephyrismoi*) during the procession to Eleusis; as festivals connected with Dionysus: the Anthesteria, Lenaia, and the Great Dionysia. On *tôthasmos* see Fluck 1931:11-33, Rusten 1977, and below, chap. 2 n66.

[243] Cf. Schmid 1946:13-42, esp. 13-26, Henderson 1991²:1-29, esp. 13ff., Degani 1987, Reckford 1987:461-467, Rosen 1988, Degani 1988, Halliwell 1991, Halliwell 1991a:294-296, and Degani 1993. Cf. now also Treu 1999 (for blame and praise, esp. 129-140) and Saetta Cottone 2005 (for *Thesm.*, esp. 285-344).

[244] Rösler 1993, passage 77.

[245] Cf. Haldane 1965:44 (who adopts an explanation common at the time, that *aiskhrologia* served to foster fertility; cf. Deubner 1932:53 and 57-56) and Zimmermann I 1985:117.

[246] Hence the explanation of Austin 1987:78 *ad* 365-366—that the chorus (like the priestess as chorus leader in line 349) also will not curse other women in line 366, so that the curse in line 367 ends up becoming a "lame statement of fact"—seems only in a very limited sense correct. Old women do not seem to have been excluded from the festival, but virgins certainly were. The situation regarding slave-women and *hetairai* is not clear; in lines 280ff. a slave-woman is present; before the relative enters the Thesmophorion, however, she is sent away (293-294).

individual groups in the assembly of women, mockery of the other sex, which is so important for this comedy, will certainly also have been present.[247] Our sources are ultimately quite sparse, but most attest to the practice of obscene invective among women themselves.[248] Aristophanes probably changed the function of the rites of the Thesmophoria, which for the most part took place among the women participating in the festival, for his own dramatic purposes and, through the application of structurally related practices involving ridicule, directed them against men in order to address the male audience.[249] Praise of one's own group represents the counterpart to disparagement, as is expressed in the *parabasis*. In this song the speech act of εὖ λέγειν is admittedly directed at the polis gods, since emphasis on one's own qualities would make little dramatic sense at this point. At the same time, the characteristics of women, who purely on the level of plot (i.e. in the context of Demeter) had to be described positively, are presented from the perspective of the male world of (Dionysiac) performance in such a way that they correspond to the prejudices of the citizen chorus performing and those of the spectators. The inverted world of the ritual thus, from the perspective of the polis, turns on itself.

---

[247] Burkert 1985:244: "[T]hey may split into groups and abuse one another, but there must also have been occasions on which men and women derided one another."

[248] On *aiskhrologia* at the Stenia cf. Hesych., s.v. Στήνια· ἑορτὴ Ἀθήνησιν καὶ . . . διασκώπτουσι καὶ λοιδοροῦσιν; *ibid.*, s.v. στηνιῶσαι· βλασφημῆσαι, λοιδορῆσαι; Phot., s.v. Στήνια· ἑορτὴ Ἀθήνησιν ἐν ᾗ ἐδόκει ἡ ἄνοδος γενέσθαι τῆς Δήμητρος· ἐλοιδοροῦντο δ' ἐν αὐτῇ νυκτὸς αἱ γυναῖκες ἀλλήλαις. οὕτως Εὔβουλος. Cf. Eubulus fr. 146 K.-A. with Brumfield 1981:79–82. On *aiskhrologia* at the Thesmophoria, cf. Apollod. 1.5.1, Cleomedes 2.1, Diod. Sic. 5.4.7; in Apollod. 1.5.1 ritual ridicule at this festival is derived from Iambe's derisive cheering-up of Demeter. Baubo, the Orphic equivalent of Iambe, is said to have exposed her genitalia for this purpose. Cf. Fluck 1931:28; on *aiskhrologia* in general cf. Fluck 1931, passim, West 1974:22–39, and Chirassi Colombo 1979:39n34. Cf. also in the context of the grain-goddess the cult of Damia and Auxesia on Aegina (and in Epidauros), where ten *khorêgoi* incited female choruses to mutual ritual ridicule (Hdt. 5.83); cf. on this Fluck 1931:20–22 and Nagy 1990:344 and 364–365. On mutual *aiskhrologia* by women in connection with beatings with a whip plaited from μόροττον (bark), cf. Hesych., s.v. μόροττον and Deubner 1932:58, who, like Versnel 1993:238 more recently, connects this action with the practice of being beaten with the *Lebensrute*. There is an account of men and women trading insults in Pellene (Pausanias 7.27.9–10); there were similar practices on the island of Anaphe, where male and female choruses who ridicule each other are attested (Apoll. Rhod. 4.1719–1730, Apollod. 1.9.26); cf. Fluck 1931:59–62.

[249] Here one must draw a distinction: ritual ridicule carried out directly in front of men can hardly have taken place at the Thesmophoria, since no men were allowed at the festival. The *aiskhrologia* of the other sex can thus only have taken place without the presence of the opposite party. Aggression against the Other that is not present, but remains outside, serves in this case purely as female self-definition. In the *Thesmophoriazusae* the masculine recipient of comic abuse and criticism is however included in the fictional festival in the form of the audience.

The Reactions of the Chorus to the Speeches in the *Agôn* (*Thesm.* 433–442, 459–465, 520–530)

After the opening ceremony of the assembly an *agôn* composed of three speeches follows. Each time the chorus adds its own opinion (433 [434]–442, 459–465, 520–530). Bernhard Zimmermann considers this one of the choral songs influenced by tragedy and categorizes it under the general concept of choral songs that interrupt the action of the play.[250] For here, in a manner typical of Sophocles and Euripides, a position is taken on the immediately preceding action on stage. One finds again to a large extent, then, the style of commenting on events that we established earlier as characteristic of the tragic chorus. Furthermore, this contest of speech is clearly reminiscent of the traditional structural element of the comic *agôn*. The actual *ekklêsia* and the assembly of women at the Thesmophoria are combined with the tragic *agôn* as we know it from Euripides, so that the so-called separating songs [*Trennliedchen*] clearly evoke the odes of the comic *agôn*.[251]

To the speech of the first woman (383–432)—who denounces Euripides' misogyny, reveals his influence on the male audience (with corresponding negative consequences for women), and ends with the plea to get rid of the tragedian by any means possible (430–431)—the chorus, full of admiration for her rhetorical ability, responds with the intermezzo (433–442). Such interjections by the collective resemble forms of agreement found in the everyday life of the polis.[252] This first, positive reaction ends in a personal attack against

---

[250] Zimmermann II 1985:141–145, who still includes only *Ran.* 814–829, 1251–1260, and 1370–1377 in the same subgroup. For criticism of the tendency to foreground the criterion of closed action too rigidly, see above, pp. 51–52 and n5. Under the category of choral songs that interrupt the action of the plot Zimmerman also treats parainetic choral odes (*ibid.*, 108–140), encomia (151–168), songs of ridicule (*Spottlieder*) (169–190), and prayers and hymns (191–220). The latter three subgroups clearly fall into the category of the ritual speech act of εὖ and κακῶς λέγειν, an essential element of the comic genre. The *parainesis* before the *agôn* exhorting one to do one's best is a traditional form. In a few lines the *agôn* is thus introduced, the contest presented, and the heroes spurred on and either praised or belittled, depending on the content. On the three elements of the chorus in the *Thesmophoriazusae* see also Parker 1997:412–417.

[251] See Zimmermann II 1985:141–143. He suspects that Aristophanes is here specifically using the *agôn* in Euripides' *Telephus* as a model (cf. Zimmermann I 1985:122 with n49). While in tragedy speech and counterspeech are generally separated by two lines sung by the leader of the chorus, we have here a song. Specific textual reminiscences (cf. Gelzer 1960:155n3) and the two catalectic iambic tetrameters (531–532; cf. also the introduction by the chorus leader in 381–382), which formally correspond to the *katakeleusmos*, point to the comic *agôn* (Gelzer 1960:154–155).

[252] Zimmermann (II 1985:142) comments: "Aristophanes dadurch, daß er jede Rede durch ein Chorlied abschließen läßt, den Eindruck eines 'Volksgemurmels' erwecken wollte und damit wieder

Xenokles, son of Karkinos (440–442). This practice of ὀνομαστὶ κωμῳδεῖν (comedy directed at a named figure) is part of the ritual license that allows prominent figures from politics and society to be ridiculed during the festival of inversion.[253] Thus once more an element that is often found in the *parabasis* plays a role here as well.

The speech of the second woman, who adds to the arguments of the first speech the further charge of atheism,[254] thus imitating the setup of an assembly much more vividly than any speech or counterspeech could, is also followed by a positive reaction from the chorus. Thanks to the schemes of Euripides, in whose tragedies the existence of the gods is again and again denied, she, a maker of garlands, is losing her livelihood (443–458). The chorus admires the speaker's fighting spirit (λῆμα, 459) and her convincing presentation. Finally, clear arguments are advanced for making Euripides pay for his hubris (465). The cultic context of this little song (459–465) has so far not been properly appreciated. When the woman maintains with comic exaggeration that Euripides "with his tragedies makes people believe that there are no gods" (450–451) (οὐκ εἶναι θεούς, 451),[255] he thereby becomes marked as the enemy of the chorus, who in the *parodos* and later songs worship the gods of the polis (θεῶν γένος, 312, cf. 960) with their song and dance. The statement that Euripides must be punished for this takes up the speech act of cursing (367) and already anticipates the next great song, in which the chorus searches the orchestra for other male intruders and continues these motifs word for word (667–686).[256] The chorus is thus also speaking here in a ritual sense, in that it takes Euripides' poetry as an attack on its ritual identity.

The chorus at first answers the counterspeech of Euripides' relative, who defends him by saying that women are in reality considerably more cunning and depraved than he depicts them in his tragedies (466–519), with surprise

---

die Ebene der Volksversammlung ins Spiel brachte" ["By having every speech end with a choral song, Aristophanes wanted to give the impression of the murmuring of a crowd and thus brought the environment of the popular assembly back into play"].

[253] Cf. Sommerstein 1996. Xenokles was, like Euripides, a tragic playwright and apparently also had political ambitions. On Xenokles see Sommerstein *Thesm.*, 170 *ad* 169, Sommerstein 1996:349, and beside this passage *Vesp.* 1508–1511, esp. 1510–1511, *Pax* 782–795, 864, *Thesm.* 169, *Ran.* 86, Pherekrates fr. 15, and Plato com. fr. 143 K.-A.

[254] On Euripides as atheist see the titles listed in Winiarczyk 1989:144–145, esp. Lefkowitz 1987 and Lefkowitz 1989.

[255] Cf. the sound remarks of Sommerstein *Thesm.*, 186 *ad* 451.

[256] Cf. δοῦναι δίκην (*Thesm.* 465) with δώσει τε δίκην (668) and the double appearance of ὕβρεως (465 and 670). The statement also possesses here the illocutionary role of a command.

and horror (520–530).[257] Yet his words seem to have reached their target, for the collective, in a tetrameter couplet (531–532) in the closing part of the song, now actually affirm by way of conclusion, "Yes, in comparison to those women who are completely shameless by nature there is nothing in the world that could be in any respect more despicable—except for women!"[258] Aristophanes the rhetor here conceals himself behind the relative and underneath the proverbial "stone" (529). He thereby pours his "biting mockery" over the female sex (cf. 529–530). The supposed κακῶς λέγειν of the women against Euripides is now directed against themselves. For the chorus in its dramatic role this agreement is completely surprising;[259] behind it also lies the criticism that the people believe any kind of fancy rhetoric. But the chorus' utterance, given its function as a collective of male citizens responsible for a comic presentation in honor of Dionysus, makes complete sense. The men take up the ritual form of *aiskhrologia*. The audience's prejudices about women are thereby served, which must have given rise to loud and unrestrained laughter.

All three *intermezzi* not only express a reaction of comment, but in each case fit skillfully into the ritual speech category of disparaging *aiskhrologia* and elevating eulogy that runs through the piece like a *Leitmotiv*. Once again, the form derives from public debate in an *ekklêsia*, the pretext which gives the scene its character. Echoes of tragedy may also play a role here, yet even in this group of short songs the speech of comedy is quite distinct from the dominant discourse of tragedy. Insofar as tragic choral songs do not integrate ritual speech into the action in the same way, they represent not only a reaction to what precedes, but often also a reflection, with or without the citation of mythical exempla, whereby the preceding events are reworked and the way is prepared for subsequent events.

---

[257] There is an approximate responsion between lines 433–442 and 520–530 (on this see Parker 1997:414–417), while the reaction of the chorus to the second woman forms an *astrophon*.

[258] The chorus reads Euripides' *Melanippe Desmotis* into its song intertextually: τῆς μὲν κακῆς κάκιον οὐδὲν γίγνεται | γυναικός (fr. 494, 27–28 N/Kannicht). The ridicule is thus directed against women as well as Euripides. Lines 531–532 are regarded by Taaffe (1993:91) as a key passage in the *Thesmophoriazusae*.

[259] On the internal level of the Thesmophoria, ridicule of one's own sex lies behind the pseudo-woman's counter-oration. For analysis of how this passage functions comically in the role-playing of the sexes, see Taaffe 1993:91 and Ferris 1989:23.

The Search Scene of the Women Celebrating the Thesmophoria (*Thesm.* 655–688)

Euripides' rescue plan to have his relative, disguised as a woman, influence the assembly of women in his favor by means of a speech is unpredictably confounded by the entry of the effeminate Kleisthenes (574ff.),[260] who interrupts the agonal speeches before the *ekklêsia* (381–573) with his paratragic messenger speech and as comic spy of the other side delivers a report about a secret informant. A search is immediately mounted, a suspect is quickly found, and a rough interrogation leads to his unmasking and arrest. Before the women's darling Kleisthenes departs to report the case to the *prytaneis*, he places the convicted relative in the custody of just two women, namely Mika and her wet-nurse. He does not include the chorus in the guard explicitly, following the conventions of tragedy.

The chorus now begins an impressive choral dance song that mimetically represents a lively search for further male intruders. Here, for the first and last time in this play, the chorus becomes a moving force in the dramatic action, even though this scene has no actual consequences for the further development of the comedy, since the search efforts produce no results. Search scenes of this type belong to the repertoire of the dramatic chorus;[261] Aristophanes integrates them into his comedy, "at the same time taking the active role that the chorus is deprived of in the *parodos* because of the particular structure of this comedy and transfering it to another part of the drama."[262]

These passages, in which the chorus keeps a lookout for someone, are particularly characteristic of the satyr play.[263] The chorus in so doing translates word directly into action: it performs a speech act, since the group simultaneously carries out the typical self-instructions for the search. We have already come to the conclusion in the Introduction that the chorus of Old Comedy, like that of the satyr play, very often speaks in this active form and

---

[260] In contrast to the relative and Euripides, who only resemble women in terms of their dress, Kleisthenes is a *kinaidos*, a man who has lost all his masculinity and thus effectively become a woman (cf. Winkler 1990a:194). He no longer counts as a man and can therefore penetrate the female realm with impunity; see Winkler 1990b:193 and Versnel 1993:245n58.

[261] Cf. Ar. *Ach.* 204–236, *Av.* 1188–1198, *Eccl.* 478–503; Aesch. *Eum.* 254–275; Soph. *Ai.* 866–890, *OC* 117–137, *Ichn.* fr. 314 Radt, 64–78, 100–123, 176–202; see Kaimio 1970:134–137.

[262] Zimmermann II 1985:104. On the whole song see *ibid.*, 104–107 and Habash 1997:32–33. Westphal 1869:36 and 61 sees the song as a *parodos* because of the strong plot elements it contains.

[263] See above, Introduction n156.

supports the dramatic action, which to a large extent is itself dependent on basic ritual forms, while the tragic chorus also admits elements of narrative, reflection, and commentary into its discourse. Speech in a speech act may, however, be directed not so much at the external action of the play but may rather be particularly related to the chorus' performativity in its function as a citizen chorus. The rituality consists, then, as has already been described, mainly in self-referential speech about the current activity of dancing and singing, which defines the ritual performance of the chorus.

The search song (655–688) is on the one hand integrated into the course of events; on the other hand, however, the action also simply affords an occasion for choral dance so that the scenes may thereby be divided. At the same time, as the chorus members perform in the orchestra, their words also apply implicitly to the relative and take up the central motif of cursing.

The anapaestic *prokêrygma* of the chorus leader (655–658) is reminiscent of the *kommation* of a *parabasis*, which is actually lacking in the actual *parabasis* (785ff.) of our play.[264] The keyword is the participle ἀποδύσας (656). Removing the outer garment as well as girding the undergarment high up frees the women for their searching activity translated into dance form.[265] The "we" (ἡμᾶς, 655) as subject accusative stands in the emphatic line-beginning position and gives us, together with the further adverbial qualification that they should conduct the search "in a good and manly fashion" (εὖ κἀνδρείως, 656), a view of the *énonciation* of the male performers. It is only through the feminine participles that the female role is referred to.

The first accompanying action, that is, the lighting of torches, connects the pronouncement with the plot explicitly, in which the members of the chorus mainly take over the function of worshiping Demeter and Kore. The torchlight and night are evoked in all songs as a kind of *Leitmotiv* to maintain a connection to the plot. Even Agathon, by mentioning the torches (101–102), makes a loose connection to the cultic context of this comedy right at the beginning of his pseudo-choral song. Similarly, in the *parodos* reference is made to the fact that the chorus has entered with burning torches that provide light for the nocturnal dances at the Thesmophoria (280–281).

The torches have clearly gone out in the meantime and are now lit again in this passage to place the cultic character more in the center once again after

---

[264] Cf. Gelzer 1970:1473.

[265] Cf. also *Ach.* 627 and *Lys.* 663, 687–688. Undressing (ἀποδύεσθαι), in the sense of the removal of the mask and costume associated with the dramatic role, is not, however, as was often maintained in the past, a necessary condition of the *parabasis*; cf. Sifakis 1971:106–108. The setting aside of clothes normally occurs before the dance (*Ach.* 627, *Vesp.* 408, *Lys.* 615, 637).

the intertextual assimilation of the *ekklêsia* and to give the torch its function as instrument of the mimetic search. With this light the chorus seeks to illuminate the surroundings in the fictional darkness of the *pannykhis* in order to find out whether any other man has intruded (ἐσελήλυθε, 657).[266] The instruction with the χρή formula culminates in the command to "run through the whole Pnyx and inspect the tents and the throughroads" (περιθρέξαι | τὴν πύκνα πᾶσαν καὶ τὰς σκηνὰς καὶ τὰς διόδους διαθρῆσαι, 657–658). Here the three performative levels—the actual performance in the orchestra, the male *ekklêsia* on the Pnyx, and the female cultic organization during the Thesmophoria—are collapsed into each other. In the plot of the play the male Pnyx also represents the place of assembly, which stretches in front of the women's tent city (σκηναί) and its pathways. With reference to the performative space, the Pnyx that must now be searched corresponds to the orchestra, which is located front of the stage building (*skênê*) with its side entrances (*parodoi*).[267]

In what follows the chorus as collective or the *koryphaios* switches to catalectic trochaic tetrameters (659–662),[268] but resumes commands to itself with χρή and the accompanying infinitive. Here explicit reference is also made to the chorus' own movement in dance: εἶα δὴ πρώτιστα μὲν χρὴ κοῦφον

---

[266] On Handley's decision to emend the metrically problematic εἰσελήλυθεν (R) to ἐπελήλυθε, "has come against us," see Austin 1987:80–81; the emendation ἐσελήλυθε was proposed by Faber.

[267] Cf. also Sommerstein *Thesm.*, 196–197 *ad* 658. On temporary accommodations in σκηναί in Bitalemi, see Kron 1992:620–622.

[268] The fact that choral self-commands typically occur in the singular does not allow for the establishment of a criterion for the separation of chorus and chorus-leader; see Kaimio 1970:134. Metrical considerations argue perhaps for the *koryphaios*. Van Leeuwen *Thesm.*, 87 assigns lines 659–662 already to the group; contra Kaimio 1970:134, Zimmermann II 1985:105, and Sommerstein *Thesm.*, 82–83, who assign them to the (female) chorus leader. Fritzsche, 244 assigns the song from line 659 onward to a semi-chorus; he makes the following divisions (on the proposed rearrangement see below): 655–658: leader of the whole chorus; 659–662: leader of the semi-chorus; 663ff.: semi-chorus. Rossbach/Westphal 1889³:172 assign 655–658, 659–666 and 687 to the chorus leader; Muff 1872:49–50, 61, 163 assigns 655–662 to the female chorus leader and 663–666 to the chorus; Arnoldt 1873:109–114 idiosyncratically assigns 655ff. to six separate members of semi-chorus (2 στοῖχοι): 655–658, 659–662, 663–666, 667–676/7, 678–686, 687–688; van Leeuwen *Thesm.*, 88 again assigns 667–674 to the *koryphaios*. Formerly the general tendency was to construct an antistrophic system with the subsequent hostage-scene (667–686, or –688 ≈ 707–725, or –727); cf. Fritzsche, 243–244 (who does not actually subscribe to this and suggests placing lines 659–662 after 663–666, so that the resulting strophe corresponds with 699–706 [with the exception of the tetrameter missing after 706]; see *ibid.*, 244–245 and 256), Rossbach/Westphal 1889³:172, Muff 1872:163, Arnoldt 1873:109–114 (divided among a further six speakers!), and van Leeuwen *Thesm.*, 88 and 91. Cf. now Parker 1997:422. Conversely, Hermann unconvincingly proposed a responsion between the *astrophon* in *Thesm.* 459ff. and lines 663ff.; cf. Parker 1997:417.

ἐξορμᾶν πόδα | καὶ διασκοπεῖν σιωπῇ πανταχῇ (659–660) ["Come, first lift up your foot lightly and search everywhere in silence!"]. For a chorus, searching in the orchestra can only mean choral dance. The command "lift up your foot lightly" (659) is a self-referential utterance;[269] while pronouncing the words the chorus puts them into action, dancing and searching at the same time.

The search operation is supposed to be conducted quietly, yet the chorus in fact sings and dances throughout the scene. This is not simply to be taken, as Sommerstein thinks, as making fun of the conventions of dramatic theater, tragedy in particular, where the chorus always sings, even when silence is commanded.[270] Rather, the linguistic mechanisms of choral performativity are also here being exposed. In a drama, a chorus can only express an action that must be completed in silence as a speech act. The sung words are connected to the chorus' own execution of the movement in the present, so that steps and gestures, as well as utterances in song pertaining to them, must be presented loudly and clearly in order for the audience to be able to perceive them as a speech act that underpins the mimesis of an action. After the command to make haste, reference is again made to the formation of the round dance (κύκλῳ, 662),[271] characteristic in this ritual context, in which the members of the chorus are supposed to move quickly in the orchestra (τρέχειν, 662).

The chorus then takes up the recited trochaics with lyric trochaics and continues its self-commands to inspect the place in the imperative singular (ἴχνευε ... μάτευε ... ῥῖψον ὄμμα ... ἀνασκόπει) (663–666).[272] The resulting search action is then accompanied by a longer, astrophic, and polymetric section (667–686). At first glance, the chorus seems here too to introduce an extended reflection, as is more usual for tragedy. Yet even this extract accords with the ritual mode of expression that is typical of the comic chorus. While the chorus of the *Thesmophoriazusae* in all its important songs brings the ritual background of comedy to the fore chiefly through prayer, there are no such

---

[269] Cf. *Thesm.* 954, κοῦφα ποσίν; Soph. *Ant.* 224, κοῦφον ἐξάρας πόδα; Eur. *Tro.* 342, μὴ κοῦφον ἄρῃ βῆμ' ἐς Ἀργείων στρατόν; cf. also above, n31. Feet naturally constitute the principal body part to which the chorus makes particular reference in its self-referential utterances. Cf. in the great choral dance song (947–1000) κοῦφα ποσίν, 954; βαῖνε καρπαλίμοιν ποδοῖν, 956; πρόβαινε ποσί, 969; and ἀνάστρεφ' εὐρύθμῳ ποδί, 985.

[270] Cf. Sommerstein *Thesm.*, 197 ad 660.

[271] Cf. *Thesm.* 954, 957–958, 968.

[272] Cf. Kaimio 1970:134–137 and 127–129. In terms of choral self-referentiality the parallels to lines 947ff. are striking; cf. above, n31. "Inhaltlich wiederholt er (i.e. der Chor) zunächst die Anweisungen des Prokerygmas" ["In terms of content the chorus at first repeats the directions of the *prokêrygma*"], rightly remarks Zimmermann (II 1985:105), yet he overlooks the fact that the chorus needs these performative directions to support its own activity.

appeals directed to Demeter and Kore or the other polis gods. This is clearly connected directly with the present activity of searching and keeping watch.

But even if hymnic speech does not occur in this passage, this song does have a religious character, for the chorus—whose cultic range of functions in the contest of speeches is extensively mixed with the political—now sees itself increasingly as an agent of the divine. In the case of a citizen chorus this is naturally comprehensible only in the context of polis religion. During the intensive search for further men who might have sneaked into the assembly and the festival, the women of the Thesmophoria paint an imaginary picture of such an enemy. In long, conditional periods the consequence of this sort of godless behavior is demonstrated; the gods will punish it. As with the priestess' curse formula, introduced by εἴ τις (335ff.), so too must the future less vivid conditionals (ἢν γάρ με λάθη[273] δράσας ἀνόσια, 667; κἂν μὴ ποιῶσι ταῦτα τοιάδ' ἔσται, 678; and αὐτῶν ὅταν ληφθῇ τις ὅσια ‹μὴ› δρῶν, 679) be interpreted as a speech act, whereby the illocutionary role represents a threat and curse. The closeness of the group to the gods has already been shown in the prayer of the *parodos*; now the destructive curse and κακῶς λέγειν against those who are enemies and have different thoughts are shown on stage.

The women do not intend to exercise any violence themselves if they should capture somebody, but deliver their curses in a form that implies that the gods will themselves take vengeance. This corresponds completely to the passive role of the chorus in this play. Kleisthenes hurries away just before the song with the women's agreement that he will report the infringement to the *prytaneis* (654). The male-dominated polis thus intervenes in the name of the women, since it is guarantor of the orderly course of the women's festival. The gods are in turn the patrons and guarantors of the city. It is therefore no surprise that the Thesmophoria, despite its inverted nature, is in accord with

---

[273] On the text of line 667: με λάθη Bergk: μὴ λάθη R (unmetrical!), ληφθῇ Reisig. Wilamowitz 1921:590 opts for ληφθῇ: "με λάθηι ist lächerlich: wenn er sich verstecken kann, wird er kein warnendes Exempel" ["με λάθηι is ridiculous: if he can hide himself, then he cannot be any kind of warning example"]. See also Zimmermann II 1985:106, Sommerstein *Thesm.*, 82, Austin 1990:23, and Parker 1997:423; now also Austin/Olson, 240 *ad* 667. In the company of Fritzsche, 246 *ad* 667, Rogers *Thesm.*, 71 *ad* 667–686, and Coulon and Gannon, I nevertheless prefer με λάθη. There is nothing "ridiculous" about this: the relative does after all infiltrate the assembly secretly; the curse is aimed at him and other disguised intruders. This does of course involve a leap of thought, but one that is quite understandable given the highly emotional situation. The women after all set out with the goal of capturing still more men on their search, and for this reason the action of seizing is here left out. Prato 1998a:73–74 defends με λάθη using similar arguments; see now also Prato, 268–269 *ad* 668. He correctly sees a *Leitmotiv* in this secret infiltration (cf. *Thesm.* 184, 589, 599–600, 664). Cf. however 679, where ληφθῇ is transmitted; an infelicitous repetition of this verb would occur in 667. The predicate λάθη δράσας (667) refers back to λέληθεν ὤν (664). On μὴ λάθη cf. Aesch. *Eum.* 255–256.

the official ideology of the city. Into the curse that accompanies the search is woven a layer of religious and ideological argument that forges connections to the choral utterances preceding and subsequent. The transgression of these boundaries set up by the polis is considered as an impious act (ἀνόσια, 667, 685 [cf. 679]; παράνομα, 685), as hubris, as actions contrary to what is right, and as signs of an atheistic character (ὕβρεως ἀδίκων τ' ἔργων | ἀθέων τε τρόπων, 670-671). The gods, threatens the chorus, will assuredly punish such an intruder harshly (δώσει τε δίκην, 668) and make an example (παράδειγμ', 670) of him. He will henceforth no longer doubt the existence of the gods (672) "and will soon teach all mankind to honor the divine powers, to respect rightfully that which is holy, and concerning themselves with law and ritual, do that which is fair and noble" (δείξει τ' ἤδη | πᾶσιν ἀνθρώποις σεβίζειν δαίμονας | δικαίως τ' ἐφέπειν ὅσια καὶ νόμιμα | μηδομένους ποεῖν ὅ τι καλῶς ἔχει, 673-676/7).[274] The assertion in line 672 is clearly aimed at Euripides, accused in the assembly of having suggested to the audience in his tragedies that the gods do not exist (450-451).[275]

The ideological key concepts in this passage are reminiscent of contemporary tragedy, especially that of Euripides, who throughout the play is a target of ridicule and *paratragôidia*. The final lines, in particular, describe the intruder being searched for as a criminal who has been struck by madness and driven to this awful sacrilege (μανίαις φλέγων λύσσῃ παράκο- | πος, 680-681).

---

[274] For metrical reasons Parker 1997:423 does not adopt Hermann's conjecture ἐφέπειν (*Thesm.* 675) and places the transmitted ἐφέποντας in *cruces* (p. 420). I have construed the clause ὅ τι καλῶς ἔχει as an indefinite relative clause that forms the object of ποεῖν, and not, as in Sommerstein *Thesm.*, 83-85, as a statement (ὅτι) governing the infinitive and dependent on δείξει (although in his commentary Sommerstein *Thesm.*, 197-198 ad 674-677 does refer to the possibility I have adopted here). Another consideration is whether ὅσια καὶ νόμιμα, in contrast to most translations (cf. the alternative solution of Sommerstein *Thesm.*, 198), ought not both be taken as objects of ἐφέπειν; in this case μηδομένους would have to be taken as a circumstantial participle upon which the infinitive ποεῖν depends (cf. Wilamowitz 1921:590). Thus: "He will show all men that they should worship the gods, uphold divine and human law, and be sure to do that which is good." Henderson 1996:120 construes this the same way. On the ambivalence of the word νόμος, which has religious as well as political connotations, see above, n240. The division of lines made by van Leeuwen *Thesm.*, 88-89 and earlier editors between choral leader (667-674) and entire chorus (675-686) makes little sense. On this passage cf. *Thesm.* 356-367, 465, 715-716, 718-725, esp. νόμον (361) ≈ νόμιμα (675) (cf. παράνομα [685]), ἀσεβοῦσ' (367) ≈ σεβίζειν (674), ἀδικοῦσι (367) ≈ ἀδίκων τ' ἔργων (670) ≈ ἀδίκοις ἔργοις (716) (cf. δικαίως [675]), ταύτης τῆς ὕβρεως (465) ≈ ὕβρεως (670) ≈ ἐνυβριεῖς (719), δοῦναι δίκην (465) ≈ δώσει τε δίκην (668), ἀνόσια (667, [679; cf. Prato 1998a:74], 685) ≈ λόγους τε λέξεις ἀνοσίους (720) (cf. ὅσια [675, 679]), ἀθέων τε τρόπων (671) ≈ ἀθέοις ἔργοις (721).

[275] Cf. the relation of οὐκ εἶναι θεούς (451) to φήσει δ' εἶναί τε θεοὺς φανερῶς (672). It seems as if the women also credit Euripides with the sacrilege of penetrating a secret sanctuary, since in his tragedies he reveals women's secrets. On the charge of atheism leveled against Euripides see above, n254.

Such an individual bears the characteristics of a tragic hero. This type of tyrant is well known to the audience in the form of Creon and Oedipus, Lykos, Lycurgus, and Pentheus.[276] *Mania* and *lyssa* breed hubris, an offense against divine *dikê* and all conceivable values and norms. The women are searching for a θεομάχος. The idea of a deed that is inspired by madness refers quite clearly to the Dionysiac dimension.[277] This world is hardly unfamiliar to the chorus as a group that is performing a comedy in Athens in honor of Dionysus. For this reason there is much that is reminiscent of Euripides' *Bacchae*, particularly the choral songs *Ba.* 863-911 and 977-1023.[278] This tragedy was of course only

---

[276] On the τύραννος cf. e.g. Soph. *Ant.* 60, 1056, 1169, *OT* 873 and, among other places, 514, 799, 925, 939, 1043; Eur. *HF* 809 (Heracles), *Ba.* 776. On the role of the tyrant in Soph. *OT* and *Ant.* see Bierl 1991:58n41; on Pentheus Seidensticker 1972 and Bierl 1991:68-70. It becomes even clearer on the basis of this passage that the mention of tyrants in the curse (*Thesm.* 338-339) not only has political implications, but is also extensively connected to the ritual and religious.

Apart from violent anger, hubris, greed, and sexual lust, it is impiety in particular that belongs to the image of the tyrant; cf. Plat. *Rep.* 571a-576b. On Pentheus as θεομάχος, cf. Eur. *Ba.* 45, 325, 635-636 and also 544, 789-790. On Creon as a θεομάχος, cf. Bierl 1991:63.

[277] On hubris cf. Soph. *OT* 873 (Oedipus) and Eur. *HF* 261, 313, 459, 708, 741 (Lykos). On the *mania* of attackers cf. Aesch. *Sept.* 343-344 (Ares), 497-498 (Hippomedon), Soph. *Ant.* 134-137 (Polyneices); on *mania* and *lyssa* cf. among others Soph. *OT* 1258, 1300, 1318 (Oedipus), *Ant.* 765, 955-965 (θεομάχος) (Creon); on the madness of Heracles and on *lyssa* see Eur. *HF* 822-1428, esp. 875ff., and Bierl 1991:84-87; on the analogy of *lyssa* and Dionysus cf. Aesch. *Xantriae* fr. 169 Radt and Eur. *Ba.* 851, 977. On *mania* in tragedy see Padel 1995; in Euripides in particular Schlesier 1985.

[278] Cf. in particular Eur. *Ba.* 997-1010. On Pentheus in connection with hubris cf. Eur. *Ba.* 375, 516, 555; at the same time Pentheus regards Dionysus' behavior as hubris (*Ba.* 247, 779); Cadmus and Agave are also connected with this kind of behavior in *Ba.* 1297, 1311, 1347; on hubris cf. generally Fisher 1992, passim, on the *Bacchae ibid.*, 443-452 and Leinieks 1996:214. According to the chorus, Pentheus is ἄνομος (*Ba.* 387, 995, 1015), ἄδικος (*Ba.* 995, 997, 1015, 1042), ἀνόσιος (*Ba.* 613), ἄθεος (*Ba.* 995, 1015), ἄσεπτος (*Ba.* 890), and παράνομος (*Ba.* 997); in the chorus' opinion, Pentheus is insane: hence the occurrence of concepts such as μαίνομαι (*Ba.* 399-400, 887, 999), λυσσώδης (*Ba.* 981), παράκοπος (*Ba.* 1000), and ὀργή (*Ba.* 51, 537, 647, 997, 1348). For the positive alternative, cf. the Dionysiac καλόν (*Ba.* 881, 901, 1007) with the remarks of Henrichs 1969:239-240 and Merkelbach 1988:124-125. In Euripides, ἡσυχία is part of the positive Dionysiac worldview (*Ba.* 389-392); μανία and ὀργή represent its opposite (*Ba.* 386-401, 647); concepts such as εὐσεβεῖν (*Ba.* 1009) and δίκη (*Ba.* 992ff., 1011ff. [as punishment!, cf. *HF* 739]); δώσει δίκην, *Ba.* 847 (cf. *HF* 740 [Lykos!], 842 [Heracles]) ≈ *Thesm.* 668, δώσει τε δίκην remind one of utterances of the chorus in the *Thesmophoriazusae*; on *dikê* see Schlesier 1985:33n127; on the concept of the ὅσιον: the personification Ὁσία, whom Pentheus violates, is invoked in *Ba.* 370-374); on this cf. Hose II 1990/91:356-358; the attribute ὅσιος is attached to the Dionysiac sphere (*Ba.* 70, 77, 114); on the concept of νόμος, see νόμοι (*Ba.* 891) and νόμιμον (*Ba.* 895); cf. τὰ δ' ἔξω νόμιμα | δίκας ἐκβαλόντα τιμᾶν θεούς (*Ba.* 1009-1010); on the meaning of νόμος as religious practice, cf. *Ba.* 331, 484, 891, 895 (cf. 201) and Leinieks 1996:244. τιμᾶν θεούς (*Ba.* 1010) also appears in a similar fashion. Self-revelation is also important: Dionysus wants to reveal himself to mortals as god: *Ba.* 22, ἵν' εἴην ἐμφανὴς δαίμων βροτοῖς ≈ *Thesm.* 681-683, πᾶσιν ἐμφανὴς ὁρᾶν | ἔσται γυναιξὶ καὶ βροτοῖς (where this is, however, said of the enemy: it will be revealed to him that god "punishes injustice and impiety" [*Thesm.* 684-686]; *Ba.* 47, αὐτῷ θεὸς γεγὼς ἐνδείξομαι [said of Dionysus] ≈ *Thesm.* 673ff., δείξει ... [said of the enemy]).

performed several years later, yet in the *Lysistrata*, likewise performed in 411 BCE, there are also allusions to the ideas that later characterize the *Bacchae*.[279] These may clearly be traced back to a common Dionysiac model[280] that influences all of tragedy as an ideological context and that in late Euripides assumes more and more importance as a system of reference.[281]

For the comedies centered around women, ritual role-reversal and the idea of women on top is decisive. The chorus is therefore comparable to the chorus of the *Bacchae* in many respects.[282] These, too, restrain themselves and leave punishment to the god; they speak in a manner that is equally quite ritualistic and carry out speech acts that imply an action. The Bakkhai curse and despise Pentheus' sacrifice, they worship the god with song and dance, and the chorus in so doing often refers to its own performance.

Behind this relatively peaceful facade men must be on the lookout for a real outbreak of violence.[283] Male anxiety about what the women in their

[279] Cf. Levine 1987. On the structural connection between the behavior of Pentheus and that of the relative, who both spy on women in their secret cults and thereby transgress gender boundaries, see Zeitlin 1982:146–147. She observes the closeness in the structural relation between Bacchic rites and the Thesmophoria, which function as "ideological opposites" (132); see in particular Zeitlin 1981:194–200. On the intertextual connections between the *Lysistrata* and the *Thesmophoriazusae*, see generally the sound remarks in Hubbard 1991:186–199 and Taaffe 1993:101.

[280] On the predecessors of the *Bacchae*, see Bierl 1991:11–12. Aeschylus' tetralogy the *Lycurgeia* seems to have had a great influence on Euripides. Cf. the reference in *Thesm.* 134ff. to Aesch. fr. 57–67 Radt, particularly the quotation from the *Edoni* (Aesch. fr. 61 Radt) in *Thesm.* 136. Cf. also Seaford 1996:223 *ad* Eur. *Ba.* 918–919 (esp. on the mirror of *Thesm.* 140).

[281] Bierl 1991, passim, on Euripides 137ff., esp. 219–226.

[282] The Dionysiac description of the enemy as μανίαις φλέγων (*Thesm.* 680) is completely ambivalent, insofar as the women are themselves associated with fire because of the torch light (280, 655). In their function as citizen chorus the dancers are also Dionysiac. Their glow is a metaphor of the enthusiastic behavior that they express in song and dance in honor of the gods, particularly Dionysus. Madness is ultimately overcome by madness; cf. *HF* 822ff. and *Ba.* 977ff. Cf. also Schlesier 1985:11n44 on the ambivalence of Dionysiac madness. On the Dionysiac (and Demetrian) role of the chorus, cf. also Zeitlin 1981:196: "This ambiguity also means that the women must, in turn, play a double role, as followers of Demeter *and* as Bacchants of Dionysus." The subsequent hostage-taking of the wineskin (689ff.) clearly takes the women into the sphere of the Dionysiac. Violence now seems to break out; the women want to set fire to the altar (726ff.) to which the relative flees. The woman who is summoned to help in lines 728 and 739 is, significantly, named Mania. On the positive, idyllic, and Dionysiac projection of the chorus, cf. *Thesm.* 985–1000.

[283] In the case of Euripides' *Bacchae* the violence is projected onto the Theban maenads and seen as *mania* sent by Dionysus as a punishment. Yet the Lydian Bacchants also show substantially violent tendencies in their choral speech acts. Cf. in particular the disputed reading of the *ephymnion* in the third stasimon, 877–881 = 897–901; contra Seaford 1996:218–220 and Leinieks 1996: 370–372, which invert the meaning with the help of Blake's conjecture in order to remove the simultaneous contradiction from Dionysus and his chorus. I, along with Dodds 1960²:186–188 *ad* Eur. *Ba.* 877–81 and Hose II 1990/91:373–374, support the interpretation that the Bakkhai, in accordance with Greek ethics, here call for brutal revenge against the enemy; cf. Bierl 1991:

secluded festival community, which separates them for a time from the male-controlled *oikos*, might be getting up to manifests itself in the concern that the women might really take over the power of the polis for good or might use force. This male fantasy finds its symbolic expression in the myth of the Amazons and the Bakkhai.[284] In the case of the women celebrating the Thesmophoria, the spectator also never knows whether their dances might not actually turn into violence. In myth there are frequent reports of this happening in cases of male transgression. According to Aelian (fr. 44 Hercher), King Battos of Cyrene, absolutely determined to observe the *arrhêta* of the Thesmophoria, was attacked by the *sphaktriai*, the women who, quite unusually, were given responsibility for carrying out sacrifices.[285] With hands and faces smeared with the blood of the sacrificial victim, they brandish their swords[286] and try to castrate the spy.[287] Similarly, at the unmasking of the male intruder, the comic playwright does not deny himself the opportunity of having the women cast an aggressive eye on the infiltrator's phallus (*Thesm.* 643–648).

206; see also *Ba.* 977–1023.

[284] On the myth of the Amazons and the *Lysistrata*, see Bowie 1993:184–185. Detienne 1979:210 already connects the women at the Thesmophoria with Amazons; he is followed by Zeitlin 1982:146 and Versnel 1993:250.

[285] For a more complex view of the sacrificing women, see Osborne 1993a. He attacks Detienne's (1979) overly schematic and structuralist approach, which sees women as fundamentally excluded from the action of sacrifice, in keeping with their political role, and which views the Thesmophoria as an exception to the rule. Conversely, according to Osborne, the opinion widely held before Detienne's work, that women generally took part in sacrifice, is also incorrect. He argues for distinctions drawn on the basis of specific cults. Instead of the apparent homology of politics and sacrifice, he emphasizes the differences between the two areas; in certain cases, sacrificial occasions could also bring women into public life, from which they were otherwise excluded in political contexts. Detienne's model of exception for the Thesmophoria does thus have a certain validity.

[286] In Eur. *Ba.* 993 Dike carries the epithet ξιφηφόρος, which is traditional (cf. however Shapiro 1986:390–391, who withholds the designation of Dike from several representations of winged women [ills. 10–12]). The women at the Thesmophoria are accordingly enforcers of *dikê* in addition to their function as female sacrificers.

[287] Cf. Detienne 1979, Burkert 1985:244, Bowie 1993:213, and Versnel 1993:250. Cf. also the Spartan setting of the episode of Aristomenes, the hero of the Messenian resistance (Paus. 4.17.1); he tries to capture the women in the temple of Demeter in Aigila, but the celebrants of the Thesmophoria defend themselves with sacrificial knives and spits. He is tied up and beaten with torches, and only manages to escape because the priestess of Demeter falls in love with him. The relative is also tied up and anybody who wants to set the prisoner free is threatened with a torch by the Old Woman (*Thesm.* 916–917). For similar stories see the list in Bowie 1993:212–213. In the following hostage-taking and sacrificial scene (*Thesm.* 689–761) ritual is again parodied. The relative assumes the role of the σφαγεύς, the only man allowed to attend the festival, while the women participate actively in the sacrifice and catch the blood (*Thesm.* 750–755). Cf. Detienne 1979:193–194 and 208.

The actual events on stage are important for these generally observed procedures against a further possible intruder. The actions of threatening and cursing are aimed directly at the relative, who remains onstage with his guards. The chorus may possibly have encircled him while singing their song, something that corresponds to a magical and symbolic "binding," a so-called κατάδεσμός.[288] The relative becomes the comic surrogate for Euripides, whom the song and the play as a whole intertextually monopolizes and parodies.[289] This choral song thus fits excellently into the development of the plot. And the immediately following scene demonstrates that the relative considers himself directly addressed by the speech act. He reacts to the women's threatening behavior with a comic hostage-taking (689ff.). This parodies the kidnapping in Euripides' *Telephus* and brings the Dionysiac dimension of the women to the foreground through the fact that the stolen child is represented as a wineskin.[290]

The search song ends abruptly with the following two verses (687–688):[291]

ἀλλ᾽ ἔοιχ᾽ ἡμῖν ἅπαντά πως διεσκέφθαι καλῶς.
οὐχ ὁρῶμεν γοῦν ἔτ᾽ ἄλλον οὐδέν᾽ ἐγκαθήμενον.

But I think we've searched everything quite thoroughly.
In any case, we don't see any other man sitting here.

---

[288] Cf. also Sommerstein *Thesm.*, 198 *ad* 689–758. He thinks that when Mika calls on the chorus for help after the child is stolen (696ff.) this means that the relative flees not to the altar of Apollo Agyieus on the stage, but to the *thymelē* in the middle of the orchestra. Possibly he had already been encircled previously; after the song he takes the supposed baby and hurries to the center.

[289] The κηδεστής as relative by marriage acts as Euripides' representative; Bonanno 1990:253 views the relative as the tragic poet's double. According to Hubbard 1991:185 the choice of the figure of the κηδεστής shows how much Euripides follows traditional attitudes to women. In particular, he argues, it should be noted that Euripides thereby honors the institution of marriage, of central importance for the Thesmophoria. The *Thesmophoriazusae* thus thematizes not Euripides' misogyny, but rather popular misconceptions about him and his handling of female roles, just as the *Clouds* is not directed at Socrates, but builds on popular prejudices against Socrates and other intellectuals.

[290] Cf. also Ar. *Ach.* 325–351, where the "baby" is a charcoal-basket. On wine, not otherwise permitted to women, as characteristic indication of a women's festival of inversion, see Versnel 1993:262–268; sexual desire thereby unleashed is kept in check by antaphrodisiac plants (λύγος, κόνυζα, κνέωρον). Despite all these liberties, wine must be concealed, hidden, and renamed in order to reduce any scandal; cf. *Thesm.* 733–761 and Versnel 1993:268. He considers the fact that sacrifice and access to wine is exceptionally granted to the women during the festival as a ritual processing of the anxiety that troubled Greek males. They must have still been concerned that their oppressed wives, despite all security measures, would break their chains and give full expression to their desires (284).

[291] Like lines 659–662 immediately following the *prokērygma*, these concluding words are also catalectic trochaic tetrameters.

These concluding verses clearly mark the fact that the time for searching is over. The chorus thereby shows that the speech act that set up and guided the action in the orchestra is coming to an end.[292] At the instant of uttering line 687, the chorus members stop their dance movements. The negative result that they have not found any further men (688) acts as a hinge to the following hostage scene. The words have an effect on the relative, who is the sole ad-dressee of the chorus' torrent of words and who in reaction to this speech act moves to defend himself. From the perspective of the performance now going on outside the plot, the statement in line 688 (οὐχ ὁρῶμεν γοῦν ἔτ' ἄλλον οὐδέν' ἐγκαθήμενον) is of course ridiculous since in the audience there are thousands of men sitting and following the action.[293] In a manner typical of ritual the chorus infringes on the participants that it represents.

The choral dance song thus constitutes the action of searching. Apart from the intensification of the chorus' own dance movements, the long-winded periods and the associative and redundant ordering of the repetitive contents, expressed now negatively, now positively, imitate the up and down motion of people intensively searching.[294] Since the interplay of content and form ultimately constitutes the action, Sommerstein's criticism of the quality of the poetry in this passage seems to miss the point.[295] For this song is not

---

[292] Cf. Zimmermann II 1985:107: "Die Frauen würden kein Ende ihrer Verwünschungen finden, wenn nicht die Chorführerin in den Versen 687f. die Suche für beendet erklären würde" ["The women would not cease their cursing if the chorus leader in lines 687–688 did not declare the search ended"]. He sees the performative aspect without, however, making use of the concept. It remains questionable whether it is really the *koryphaios* who puts a stop to the chorus' endless talk, or whether it is not actually the chorus, or the chorus leader, who speaks the lines, since the search has come to an end at precisely the same time. Both the search and the dance are completed by this utterance.

[293] Cf. Dionysus' question to Pentheus—if he wishes to see the women sitting together in the mountains (συγκαθημένας ἰδεῖν, Eur. *Ba.* 811)—which (along with *Ba.* 816) is interpreted by Segal 1982:226 and Bierl 1991:212 with n97 as a reference to the situation of the audience in the theater. Taaffe 1993:94 comes to a similar conclusion from the perspective of gender-role identity: "In another joke on gender identity, they find no men, when it is clear that many men have in fact infiltrated this secret meeting and the men are just where you might expect to find them, too: in the audience."

[294] Cf. the repetition and parallelism in expression ἦν γὰρ - κἂν - ὅταν. For purposes of clarity I reproduce here once more the repetitive and winding thread of the argument: when someone commits an impiety (*negative*), he is then punished (*passively, by humans*) and serves as an example to show the necessity of piety (*positive*) (667–677); if he does not do so (*negation of the positive*), then the following will happen (*declaration of the negative*) (678): if someone is caught committing a crime (*negative*), he will become an example of how the god punishes wrong-doing (*positive, actively, by god*) (679–686).

[295] Cf. Sommerstein *Thesm.*, 197 *ad* 663–686: "Much of the diction and most of the sentiments of this song are tragic, but its stylistic quality as poetry is mediocre, its most notable feature being a high degree of repetitiveness."

poetry, but the direct expression of a living choral culture. The ritual choral dance song is characterized precisely by the redundancy and repetitiveness found fault with by Sommerstein. It expresses here a completely concrete and simple action, namely searching, which is based on repetitive models and which as a fundamental biological program of action has been ritualized and processed into cultural codes.[296]

The *Parabasis* (*Thesm.* 785–845)

The *parabasis* of the *Thesmophoriazusae* separates the *Palamedes* stratagem from the *Helen* stratagem, and as a result of deviations from the traditional structure its form is very free.[297] Because of the absence of odes, the character of the choral dance song retreats far into the background. The ritual elements of hymns to the gods and concern with the chorus' own dance, which are characteristic of the lyric parts of the *parabasis*, are, as has been discussed, transferred to the other songs, in particular to the two later choral scenes (947–1000 and 1136–1159). The chorus of the *Thesmophoriazusae* is thereby marked by a relatively limited engagement in the action of the plot, but by an intensive rituality.

Because of the expansion of the mood and tone of the parabatic, the actual *parabasis* itself does not represent any real break in dialogue of the characters in comparison to the other songs. This is even more striking in that this *parabasis*, as with that of the *Birds*, fits more clearly into the context of the plot than in the other comedies. The *communis opinio* has generally evaluated the *parabasis* in general—at least the part containing the anapaests—as a digression from the action in the play and as a breaking of the "illusion," since the chorus leader, or the chorus as a whole, addresses the audience directly, praises or censures individuals by name, discusses the matter of the poet and his work, focuses on and praises the author while attacking his rivals, strives for success and recognition among the audience and the judges, and/or talks about politics and dispenses advice.[298]

---

[296] Cf. the sociobiological theory of Burkert 1996. One could perhaps think here of the hunt for a natural enemy that invades one's own territory. On fear of death and concern for survival as a background of religion see Burkert 1996:30–33, on territorial and boundary concerns *ibid.*, 45 and 165–166.

[297] There is no *kommation*, or rather it is integrated into the anapaests. Ode and antode, as well as *antepirrhêma*, are missing. The structure is as follows: 785–813 are anapaests (catalectic anapaestic tetrameters); 814–829, *pnigos* (anapaestic dimeters); 830–845, *epirrhêma* (catalectic tro-chaic tetrameters). On the *parabasis* of the *Thesm.*, see Moulton 1981:127–135, Zeitlin 1981:185–186, Bonnette 1989:240–248, Hubbard 1991:195–199, and Taaffe 1993:76–78.

[298] On the contents of the actual *parabaseis* of the first five extant works and numerous fragments cf. Sifakis 1971:38–41 (with tables 45–51).

Here, in any case, the chorus goes on to talk about itself, as is in fact normal with *epirrhêmata*.[299] The fluctuation between role and function takes an only apparent step back in the anapaests. Nevertheless, παραβῆναι here does at least partially involve an even further movement away from the chorus' dramatic role—which up until this point has been that of a chorus of ritually celebrating women—and toward a general commentary on womanhood. The clearly male identity of the chorus in its comic function, which remains ever present behind the female masking, gives rise to greater comic effect the more the chorus concentrates exclusively on its fictional femininity.[300] One can just imagine the hearty laughter among the mainly male audience: male citizens appear before the spectators and attempt to teach them that women are better than they are!

In terms of its strongly argumentative speech the *parabasis* is comparable to a public appearance before a court or before the *dêmos*. In this way it becomes like the speeches delivered before the women's assembly.[301] All in all, the interlude functions like a defense against the charges brought against women. The dramatic role thus remains present, even behind the discussion of the general question as to which sex is morally superior, since the presentation, designed to prove the supremacy of women over men, is linked to the *Leitmotiv* of *aiskhrologia* between the sexes, which is an ingredient of the Thesmophoria and is thematized in this comedy.[302] The emphasis on the superior qualities of the women functions as a counterpart to the putting down of men. Censure and praise, which belong to the fundamental speech acts of Old Comedy and are particularly characteristic of the *parabasis*, are here integrated into the ritual context of the plot. The actual *parabasis*, which the comic poet evidently developed only at a late stage to praise himself or defend himself against attacks, using the chorus leader as his representative in the first- or third-person, here becomes reshaped into the comic chorus' usual self-presentation.[303]

---

[299] Sifakis 1971:43 mentions that the contents of the *epirrhêmata* have spread into the actual *parabasis* of the *Thesmophoriazusae* and have therefore changed the usual situation.

[300] Taaffe 1993 discusses these connections using insights from feminist performance criticism.

[301] See Moulton 1981:128 and 135.

[302] See Rösler 1993.

[303] See Hubbard 1991:19–20, rightly remarking that anapaests were used for choral self-presentation almost as frequently as they were to defend the claims of the poet. The anapaests of the *Birds* and the *Thesmophoriazusae* should therefore not be treated as a later development followed by the poet in order to free himself from the "undramatic" form of the actual *parabasis*; examples of self-description *ibid.*, 20n17: Cratinus fr. 105 K.-A. (chorus of *malthakoi* speaks in its role about wreaths of flowers), Eupolis fr. 13 K.-A. (chorus of goats talks about its fodder), and Ar. fr. 427–431 K.-A. (chorus of freighters talks about its cargo). On the themes actually typical of *epirrhêmata* in the anapaests of the *Thesmophoriazusae*, see Sifakis 1971:43.

The chorus delivers the keyword of the *Leitmotiv* right in the first line, which here in abbreviated fashion incorporates the usually two-versed *kommation* into the speech as a whole. The question of whether the chorus leader or the chorus as a whole spoke or sang cannot be determined unequivocally. The metre points to a recitative quality, while the *kommation*-like style suggests song and dance.[304] The argumentative style of delivery argues against collective speech, while the specifically ritual element and the intrusion of the epirrhematic argues for it.[305] The first line (785) is in any case programmatic:

ἡμεῖς τοίνυν ἡμᾶς αὐτὰς εὖ λέξωμεν παραβᾶσαι.

Let us step forward in the *parabasis* and praise ourselves!

The "we," placed in emphatic first position, and the reflexive "ourselves" emphasizes the group. The (female) chorus leader can of course speak for the whole using the plural form. From a performative and pragmatic point of view, much speaks in favor of this line being emphatically sung and danced by the whole chorus as a kind of *kommation* marking a transition. First, the "we" in line-initial position leaves it open as to whether the chorus speaks in its dramatic role or whether it speaks in its function as chorus; the feminine forms of the reflexive pronoun and participle stress its female role. The performative hortatory subjunctive εὖ λέξωμεν refers in clear-cut fashion to the εὖ λέγειν of women, which corresponds to the κακῶς λέγειν of men. The self-command clearly shows the ritual aim. The participle παραβᾶσαι self-referentially mirrors the technical term *parabasis*. Its literal meaning refers to the chorus' movement: that is to say, the group wheels and now steps forward to address the audience directly. The figurative meaning, to step out of the frame

---

[304] Rossi 1978:1149–1155 (cf. Nagy 1990:46 on this) argues for the performance style of the παρακαταλογή, a musical "recitative" by the chorus leader, which falls between song and speech and is accompanied only by the mimetic dance figures (σχήματα) of other actors; for discussion as to whether the *kommation* was sung or recited by the chorus or chorus leader, see Muff 1872:86–88. Pollux 4.112 talks of the song of the *kommation*: τὸ μὲν κομμάτιον καταβολή τίς ἐστι βραχέος μέλους. The *kommation*, according to Hubbard 1991:18, was thus sung and apparently also accompanied by dance. Scholars long debated whether the *parabasis* in the stricter sense might not also have been sung (and danced?) by the entire chorus; it was largely assumed that the chorus stood motionless during this part; cf. the discussion in Muff 1872:89–90. Today the unanimous opinion is that the *koryphaios* recited it; Hubbard 1991:19.

[305] The manner in which *epirrhêmata* were performed is also disputed. For earlier theories see Muff 1872:91–95 (he himself believes, 94–95, that the whole chorus sung and danced) and the summary in Hubbard 1991:21n27. Westphal 1869:48 even proposed a connection to the wild and "obscene" *kordax*. Hubbard (21) represents the *communis opinio* that the *epirrhêmata* were also recited by the chorus leader (cf. similarly, for example, Dover 1972:50), so that the chorus could have accompanied his words with gestures and dance figures.

of the plot in order to praise oneself in a form of digression, as Sifikas defines the concept,[306] appears to be not quite correct, since Old Comedy, as he himself stresses, never constructs a strictly consistent illusion of plot. New investigations have on the contrary shown that the *parabasis* does not interrupt the action, but is an integral part of the play in which the central themes are collected.[307] The *parabasis* is clearly connected with a ritual mode of speech in which *énonciation* is emphasized while *énoncé* retreats into the background.[308] Through direct contact between audience and chorus members, the distance between performer and spectator is bridged, a situation characteristic of any ritual performance. This immediate involvement turns theatergoers into active participants. In any event, this manner of speaking is by no means confined solely to the *parabasis*, but is typical of the genre of Old Comedy.[309]

This finding has considerable consequences for the interpretation of this self-praise. Through the address of the male audience by the chorus, whose identity varies between role and function, the praise of the female sex is relativized and deconstructed. The winking and nudging of the male players directed at the male spectators more or less reduces the grand defense of women to a farce. The reaction probably consisted not of open agreement with the arguments put forward, but of laughter shared with the male performers at the women whom they played.[310]

From a plot-internal point of view, the speech is closely connected with the cultic context of the Thesmophoria. The counterattack to the claims advanced by the men is a further reflex of ritual *aiskhrologia*, which becomes a theme

---

[306] The verb παραβαίνειν appears explicitly in five passages: Ar. *Ach.* 628–629 (629), *Equ.* 507–509 (508), *Pax* 734–735 (735), Plato com. fr. 99 (V. 2) K.-A., and *Thesm.* 785. For a precise discussion with evaluation of the other sources, see Sifakis 1971:62–68. Sifakis excellently demonstrates how the *parabasis* is connected with self-praise (65). For its definition as a digression, cf. *ibid.*, 66, 69 and below, chap. 2 n118. Although Sifakis has clearly refuted the so-called illusion of the closed plot in Old Comedy (7–14), he here remains under the influence of the older scholarship. For the *parabasis* see also the discussion below, pp. 310–314.

[307] Cf. among others Bowie 1982, Harriott 1986:20–36, Reckford 1987, and Hubbard 1991; see now also Imperio 2004:13–14. Koester 1835:15–16 had early on attempted to find points of contact between the *parabasis* and the rest of the action in the play, but this view was only taken up again much later.

[308] Direct confrontation with the audience finds a correspondence in the attitude of certain figures on the Pronomos Vase who do not communicate with the other figures involved in the plot of a dramatic performance (as depicted by means of profile view), but rather enter into contact with the viewer frontally, that is, with the authority of the pragmatic context; Calame 1995:116–136.

[309] See Flashar 1996:86–87 and Purves 1997 (who also relies on Schechner's theater, *ibid.*, 6–7).

[310] See Hubbard 1991:197, who characterizes the *Thesmophoriazusae* as play "about men's attitudes toward women," and Taaffe 1993:74–102. See now also Stehle 2002.

throughout the play. The men's position is based on the well-known premise that women are the root of evil for humankind (πᾶν ἐσμὲν κακὸν ἀνθρώποις, 787) and on the piling up of negative conditions that are associated with the female sex (κἀξ ἡμῶν ἐστιν ἅπαντα | ἔριδες, νείκη, στάσις ἀργαλέα, λύπη, πόλεμος, 787–788).[311] The women counter that the evil (κακόν) cannot be all that great if men marry them and guard them like a treasure (788–799). As a logical consequence of this refutation, they then propose the thesis that they are far better than men (800). Since no one represents an absolute κακόν, the argument now revolves around the comic contest as to which of the two is worse by comparison (χείρους, 801, 820; ἥττων, 804; χείρων, 805), that is, which is relatively speaking the greater κακόν. Although the women insist on their moral superiority (βελτίους, 800, 810; ἀμείνων, 808), they concede with an implicit nod and a wink that they, too, are to some extent bad.

They comically try to prove their superiority by comparing speaking names that express abstract virtues in the political and military spheres with the names of contemporary leaders (802–809). The aristocratic speaking names of the εὐγενεῖς γυναῖκες, such as Nausimakhe, Aristomakhe, Stratonike, and Euboule, represent instances of success in contrast to the actual disasters of the politicians Kharminos, Kleophon, and Anytos.[312] To the archaic way of thinking, names are metaphors for the identity of the name-bearer, and in them the claim to realization of the content of the name is emphasized. It is precisely in ritual that women contribute to the construction of ritual reality, that is, to founding and securing the noble status of their social identity.[313] By inserting the names of well-known prostitutes, the women's declaration of their superiority is clearly rendered suspect, inasmuch as the symbolic content of the name is at odds with the reality, as in the case of Nausimakhe. The women's claim to superiority (810) is thus once more demonstrated as

[311] Cf. Hom. Od. 11.427, Hes. Th. 562–612, esp. 590–602, Op. 54–99, Semonides (on the different types of women) fr. 7 W., esp. 94–118, and reflexes in Eur. Hipp. 616–633, Med. 573–575, and in Old Comedy, esp. in Sousarion fr. 1.3–5 K.-A.: κακὸν γυναῖκες· ἀλλ' ὅμως, ὦ δημόται, | οὐκ ἔστιν οἰκεῖν οἰκίαν ἄνευ κακοῦ | καὶ γὰρ τὸ γῆμαι καὶ τὸ μὴ γῆμαι κακόν. For concentration in the parabasis of the Thesmophoriazusae on the κακόν that is woman, cf. Thesm. 786, 787, 789, 791, 796, 797, 799.

[312] The whoremonger Kleophon is inferior to the famous hetaira Salabakkho (805), whose name is reminiscent of the word for trumpet signal. Nausimakhe, according to schol. Thesm. 804, is also supposed to have been a prostitute (πόρνη). The claim to sophrōsynē, upon which ritual places such great importance with respect to women as guarantors of legitimate offspring (cf. Brulé 1987:342–343), is contradicted by their actual behavior.

[313] See the excellent remarks in Calame 1995:174–185. Euboule is reminiscent of the cult name of Artemis Aristoboule. On this scene see also Möllendorff 1995:250–251, who speaks of a mixing of the level of signified belonging to male discourse and the level of signifier belonging to female discourse.

in no way serious, and the men take some pleasure at the comparison. At the same time the chorus as chorus of citizens is here able to bring its role of deliverer of criticism to bear against powerful individuals. Finally, the women show that they are only relatively better, since in accordance with the division of roles between the sexes they commit only small crimes at home, while the men commit great ones in the state: women only pinch a little wheat from the storage cellar, but men embezzle public funds (811-813).

In the *pnigos* (814-829) the audience is in typical fashion included in the attack: "We could prove that many of them do this" (ἀλλ' ἡμεῖς ἂν πολλοὺς τούτων | ἀποδείξαιμεν ταῦτα ποιοῦντας, 814-815). With the deictic τούτων the members of the chorus once again point clearly at the spectators and intensify the *parabasis'* direct manner of speech. Then follows the statement "that, beside this, they are more often gluttons, clothes-thieves, tricksters, and kidnappers than we are" (καὶ πρὸς τούτοις γάστριδας ἡμῶν | ὄντας μᾶλλον καὶ λωποδύτας | καὶ βωμολόχους κἀνδραποδιστάς, 816-818). The women do not exclude themselves categorically from the group of evildoers; men are simply more likely to become bad. Women are certainly tricksters (βωμολόχοι) themselves, as can be established precisely in the case of ritual *aiskhrologia*. Yet as a comic citizen chorus, the male players tell these sorts of dirty jokes accompanied by appropriate gestures, thus meeting with the audience's approval.[314]

Finding fault with men (μεμψαίμεθ' ἂν, 830) is certainly continued, but the women remain entirely within their traditional role and within the area of competency alloted them. The fact that the mother of a bad man such as Hyperbolos is accorded the same honor as that of the mother of the successful general Lamakhos (830-845) is decried as deplorable. The mocking of men in general here returns once more to the traditional ὀνομαστὶ κωμῳδεῖν of powerful politicians.

The men in the audience thus feel ultimately confirmed in their chauvinistic attitude, despite the direct attacks on them, and come away with the following message after the speech act of self-praise by the women: women are utterly bad, as they themselves admit; comparatively speaking, they are only a little less bad, because they cannot undertake any public tasks. Men are actually good; only a few are guilty of public crimes. It is therefore the citizen chorus' task to subject these to censure.[315]

---

[314] On the derivation of comedy from impromptu scenes played by clowns of this type, see below, pp. 280-282.

[315] On the freedom to criticize and deride, see Gelzer 1970:1528, Edwards 1991:168-179, and Gelzer 1992:31-35; on the connection of *iambos* and comedy, see Degani 1987, Degani 1988, Rosen 1988, and Degani 1993; see now also Treu 1999:129-140 and Saetta Cottone 2005:143-151. Blaming (μέμ-

The ritual nature of the scene does not manifest itself only in praise and blame, which are just as much a part of Dionysiac license as the *aiskhrologia* of the Demeter festival: the dramatic role of the chorus as women at the Thesmophoria also has an extensive effect on this part too. One should not, then, read this *parabasis* simply as a political statement against certain politicians or as a parody of a courtroom speech. The ritual nature is shown especially on the level of content. The men, dressed as women, here thematize the mixed feelings they experience toward women at the Thesmophoria. The temporary loss of control over women causes all kinds of suspicions to arise in the men. For men, women at this festival in particular are a "beautiful evil" (καλὸν κακόν), something the chorus explains in its opening demonstration (785–799). The festival is supposed to further female and agrarian fertility. The polis, which with the exception of ritual occasions completely excludes women from public life, needs the married woman as mother of legitimate male offspring in order to ensure its own continued existence.[316] Marriage is the institution by which the city is able to regulate reproduction.[317] The sexuality necessary for this goal is ritually renewed by the separation of the sexes in the festival cycle. The Thesmophoria reenact a cultural relapse into matriarchal conditions and a reentry into civilization, which is founded anew at the Kalligeneia with marriage and the desire for good offspring. In their segregation, the married women preserve a certain ambivalence. The wild sexuality necessary for survival and the fundamental inversion of the normal order are experienced as a threat to the male world and thus filled with contradictory signs. Lascivious, unbound sexuality is simultaneously overlaid with signals of chastity in order to make the intolerable tolerable.[318]

Aristophanes knew how to depict this paradoxical mixture of layers by using intertextual connections in the speech of the women; Euripides receives particular attention as the target of literary parody. The starting position of

---

φεσθαι, λοιδορῆσαι) and praising (ἐπαινέσαι) are central themes of the *parabasis*; cf. *Ach.* 676–691 (esp. 676), 702–718, *Equ.* 565–580 (esp. 565), 595–610 (esp. 595–596), 1274–1289 (esp. 1274–1275), *Nub.* 575–594 (esp. 576), 607–626, *Vesp.* 1015–1050 (esp. 1016), 1275–1291, *Av.* 753–768, 1072–1087, *Lys.* 626–635, 648–657, *Thesm.* 785–813, 830–845 (esp. 830), and *Ran.* 686–705, 718–737.

[316] The constant concern about spurious infants in the *Thesmophoriazusae* (339–340, 407–408, 502–516, 564–565) is also based on this.

[317] On marriage as a central institution that exercises control over the legitimacy of masculine offspring, see des Bouvrie 1990:44–50.

[318] On mechanisms for control over the Athenian woman, see des Bouvrie 1990:50–57. On the role of the Athenian woman in general, see *ibid.*, 35–59; see also Gould 1980, Foley 1981 (on the role of the woman in Attic drama), La Matina 1987 (on women in Aristophanes from a semiotic point of view), and Versnel 1993:276–288.

the defense rests partly on the particular situation of the *aiskhrologia* by men, which clearly responds in *iamboi* to the attacks delivered by women at the festival of Demeter.[319] In the first part of Semonides' *iamboi* on women (fr. 7.1–93 W.) it is told how Zeus created the different types of women from eight animals, earth, and sea. A negative characterization is constructed using parallels between the behavior of animals and women. The bee (83–93), which also functions as the symbol of chaste and noble women at the Thesmophoria, represents a significant exception.[320] In the second, general part of the poem (94–118), the image of woman is unrelentingly negative. The fragment of Sousarion (fr. 1 K.-A.) directed against women, which is often cited in connection with the development of Old Comedy,[321] might have stood in a similar ritual context:

ἀκούετε λεῴ· Σουσαρίων λέγει τάδε,
υἱὸς Φιλίνου Μεγαρόθεν Τριποδίσκιος.
κακὸν γυναῖκες· ἀλλ᾽ ὅμως, ὦ δημόται,
οὐκ ἔστιν οἰκεῖν οἰκίαν ἄνευ κακοῦ
καὶ γὰρ τὸ γῆμαι καὶ τὸ μὴ γῆμαι κακόν

Listen to me, you peoples! Thus speaks Sousarion, the son of Philinos from Tripodiskos in Megara: women are an evil. But even so, my fellow citizens, it is impossible to have a house without evil, for both marrying and not marrying are evils.

What is important here, on the one hand, is the direct address to the people (1, 3), which is identical to the address of the audience in Old Comedy, especially in the *parabasis*.[322] On the other hand, the fragment also possesses much in common with the *parabasis* of the *Thesmophoriazusae* in terms of the theme of

---

[319] Cf. Wilamowitz I 1895²:58n17: "Auch das Weibergedicht des Semonides, eine Predigt über ein hesiodisches Thema, welche an sich ohne rechten Zweck erscheint, erhält als Replik auf die Spöttereien der Weiber am Demeterfeste Sinn und Salz" ["Semonides' poem on the types of women, a sermon on a Hesiodic theme that appears without a real purpose of its own, also gains sense and humor as a reply to the ridicule by women at the festival of Demeter"]. Cf. Rösler 1993:83 on this, who also associates the Semonides poem and the fragment of Sousarion with the *Thesmophoriazusae* (*ibid.*, 80–86).

[320] Women at the Thesmophoria were called μέλισσαι. Cf. Apollodorus, *FGrHist* 244 F 89 and Detienne 1979:211–212; on bees, see esp. Detienne 1971 and literature cited in Versnel 1993:251n82; now also Kledt 2004:119–120.

[321] See the testimonia in *PCG* VII, 661–663 (and pp. 147–148 W. [with text]), esp. Marm. Par., *FGrHist* 239 A 39.

[322] The words ἀκούετε λεῴ seem to have been a traditional Athenian formula of proclamation and public address that is reflected in Old Comedy; cf. Ar. *Ach.* 1000, *Pax* 551 and *Av.* 448. For the vocative ὦ δημόται cf. *Ach.* 319 and *Nub.* 1322; cf. also ὦνδρες δημόται (Ar. *Plut.* 322; cf. *Ach.* 328).

marriage with the evil that is woman.[323] For although the speech is conceived as a riposte to this kind of attack, the male point of view remains detectable through the Athenian players, who emphasize the female character as a κακόν. In the *parabasis*, as in the fragment of Sousarion, the fundamental ambivalence in the attitude of men to women is at the center. Woman is a κακόν, but a necessary one for the house and for the continuation of the family line. This explains the concentration on marriage and the comic paradox that both being married and not being married amounts to a κακόν (5): for in the marriage partnership one lives together with a κακόν, yet life without marriage is "bad," because the continued existence of the polis is thereby endangered.

Hesiod's Pandora as καλὸν κακόν (Hes. *Theogony* 585) equally explains the paradox of woman at the Thesmophoria. Without sexual attraction, a Καλλιγένεια can hardly come to pass, but from beauty, to be sure, arise jealousy and discord between men, particularly when the woman cannot be placed under the direct oversight of the husband, as is the case at the festival of Demeter. Despite the emphasis on their virtues and chastity, in the eyes of men women are potential whores precisely during the inverted world of the festival.[324] Hence the insertion of Salabakkho among the glorious and noble names (804ff.), which in turn mark the female infringement on politics and war that the Demeter festival represents.[325] The claim to female superiority is also inserted intertextually.[326] Both in Euripides and in the *Lysistrata* this is based on the role of the woman as keeper of the marital household and on her prominent ritual function in the polis.

From the male standpoint, they emphasize their superior ability to watch over the patrimony (τὰ πατρῷά γε | . . . σῴζειν, 819–820). Safeguarding the patrimony ranks equally with patrilineal inheritance from father to son, which does, however, necessitate woman as bearer of children. For this reason, τεκεῖν becomes the *Leitmotiv* of the *epirrhêma*.[327] Quite in keeping with male expecta-

---

[323] For γαμεῖν see *Thesm.* 789.

[324] Cf. Versnel 1993:282, who views sexuality, which is displayed but never consummated, as a fundamental paradox of the women celebrating the Thesmophoria (*ibid.*, 254). To the same category belongs the fact that the women espouse a lofty ethical claim to chastity, but on the other hand are compared with prostitutes. See above, nn120 and 312.

[325] See myths about martial conflicts in connection with the Thesmophoria in Bowie 1993:212–213 and above, n287.

[326] *Thesm.* 810 ≈ Eur. *Melanippe Desmotis* Pap. Berol. 9772 = Suppl. Euripideum fr. 6 (p. 32 v. Arnim), esp. line 3 (cf. fr. 499.3 N/fr. 494.3 Kannicht): αἱ δ' εἶσ' ἀμείνους ἀρσένων. δείξω δ' ἐγώ; cf. also Hom. *Il.* 4.405.

[327] On τεκεῖν cf. *Thesm.* 832, 836, 839, 845. The Thesmophoria have a double function, the increase of natural fertility as well as that of women, in order to ensure the continued existence of humanity; consider the famous scholion to Lucian *Dial. Meret.* 2.1 (276.14–15 Rabe): περὶ τῆς τῶν καρ-

tions, giving birth to men who are good and useful for the continued existence of the city as a whole occupies the central position.[328] The concluding play on the words τόκος/τεκεῖν together with the accompanying alliterative piling-up of concepts (840–845) underscores this ideological core. The mother of the evil politician Hyperbolos is put in the spotlight and faulted for her practice of lending money at extortionate rates of interest. The semantically related Greek homonyms "interest" and "male offspring" (τόκος) are comically mixed, which gives rise to a meaningful comparison between the exchange of money and intercourse in marriage.[329] Procreation is like a loan of money; a mother is simply a kind of bank. She is removed from her bodily connection to her son, since she functions only as an abstract carrier that ensures the transaction of payment and repayment. A male child is considered as interest or profit from this exchange between the sexes, which ensures the well-being of the polis from generation to generation in the male line.[330]

At the same time there is a connection between this comparison and the commensurable claim of a woman who has given birth to a capable son to receive a better place at the women's festival than the mother of a bad son. The mention of *proedria* (834) at the women's festivals of the Skira and Stenia is also a metatheatrical reference to the current order of seating in the theater.[331] Here the demand for privilege has of course a particularly comic effect,

---

πῶν γενέσεως καὶ τῆς τῶν ἀνθρώπων σπορᾶς; cf. *ibid.*, 20–22: the throwing of piglets into an underground chasm happens διὰ τὸ πολύτοκον εἰς σύνθημα τῆς γενέσεως τῶν καρπῶν καὶ τῶν ἀνθρώπων. See now Kledt 2004:132, 135–136.

[328] The formulation εἰ τέκοι τις ἄνδρα χρηστὸν τῇ πόλει (*Thesm.* 832) is reminiscent of both the goal expressed by the chorus in the *parabasis*, χρηστὰ τῇ πόλει | ξυμπαραινεῖν καὶ διδάσκειν (*Ran.* 686–687), and in particular of the *epirrhêma* of the women in the *parabasis* of the *Lysistrata* (648–651), which is related intertextually to the *Thesmophoriazusae*. In the *Lysistrata* the connection is made—via a useful piece of advice (χρηστὸν τῇ πόλει παραινέσαι, *Lys.* 648)—to women's central usefulness for the city; they bear sons, who as future men guarantee the continuity of the system: τοὐράνου γάρ μοι μέτεστι· καὶ γὰρ ἄνδρας εἰσφέρω (*Lys.* 651). Here too female reproductivity is compared to a monetary contribution.

[329] On this play on words, cf. *Nub.* 1156–1159, Plat. *Rep.* 507a, 555e, and Arist. *Pol.* 1258b4–7.

[330] The personification of Ploutos' agricultural wealth also plays a great role in this festival; cf. *Thesm.* 296 and above, nn186–187; in society Ploutos is also equated with monetary wealth; the plot of Aristophanes' comedy of the same name is based on this polyvalency. In the Thesmophorion of Bitalemi dedications of metal used for bartering have also been found: see Kron 1992:633–635. On Ploutos in the Euripidean *Helen*, parodied in the *Thesmophoriazusae*, cf. line 69 (Theoklymenos' palace is Πλούτου [L: Πλούτῳ Nauck] . . . ἄξιος); at the same time, Theoklymenos is also connected with Pluto-Hades, who is of central importance in the myth of the Thesmophoria as Persephone's husband; see Foley 1992:136.

[331] On *proedria*, the right to sit in the first row on festive occasions, see Sommerstein *Thesm.*, 209 ad 834: this privilege was normally reserved for selected officials or priests, but could by way of exception be extended to those who had rendered a service to the state.

since women, if allowed in the theater at all, always sat at the back.[332] With the mention of the first row, the distance between performance and plot is bridged in a way typical of Old Comedy. As in any ritual, the spectator thereby becomes in turn active participant.

The Central Image of the *Parabasis* as Symbolic Expression (*Thesm.* 821–829) and the Initiatory Interpretation of the *Thesmophoriazusae*

The *tableau vivant* with which the *pnigos* comes to its comic end is also based entirely on ritual concepts of the chorus in its role. The motif of better management of paternal capital retreats into the background behind the play with mention of the semantically related homonyms of the symbolic concepts κανών (822, 825) and σκιάδειον (823, 829),[333] which may describe gender role identity on both sides. Figurative speech that operates using simple objects from the immediate living environment is characteristic of ritual discourse.

The concentration of polyvalent signifiers in this instance is also related to the ritual of the Thesmophoria, which provides the frame for the plot, and to the Stenia and Skira (834), which are mentioned immediately afterward and which also have a connection to this festival. The *parabasis* constantly returns to elements of this festival in an associative and redundant fashion and thus focuses on themes and motifs that are of importance for the work as

---

[332] On the question of the presence of women in the theater, see Henderson 1991a; women apparently sat in the rows at the back (*ibid.*, 140–144); he shows that a distinction needs to be drawn between a purely male "notional audience," which was clearly viewed politically, and an "actual audience," which encompassed all participants in the festival, certain women included; on καθῆσθαι (838) as metatheatrical term, see above, n293. On *proedria* in the theater of Dionysus, cf. Pöhlmann 1981. On the mention of the *proedria* of the priest of Dionysus in the *Frogs* (297), cf. Bierl 1991:37. Cf. also the priest's invitation to Dikaiopolis in *Ach.* 1085–1094 to take part in the Khoes. It is clear from both passages that the priest is taking part in a festival in his official capacity, that is, that the ritual of performance directly flows into another ritual event. Cf. also Dover *Frogs*, 230 *ad* 297.

[333] On the symbolic see among others Turner 1967:19–47, Turner 1969, Geertz 1973:87–125 ("Religion as cultural system"), Lewis 1977, Foster/Brandes 1980, Jensen 1986, and Braungart 1996:108–113; see particularly the comments of Jensen 1986:112–113 ("Ritual as Condensed Action"). On its application in the field of drama, des Bouvrie 1990:70–77 and des Bouvrie 1993:87–92 (with copious references). Cf. also Moulton 1981:131–135, who similarly treats the passage as the "imagistic center of the *parabasis*" (131). On the concept of initiation in the study of religion, see the general overview in Grohs 1993. As a *rite de passage*, it always requires symbolic dramatization; see van Gennep 1909 and Turner 1967:93–111. For initiation as puberty ritual in classical and religious studies, see the key works listed above, Introduction n61. On the use of the interpretative paradigms of *ephêbeia*, initiation, and structurally determining *rites de passage* for plot structure in tragedy and Old Comedy, see below, n481.

a whole.[334] The self-referential connection to the Stenia (ninth of Pyanopsion), which comes immediately before the actual Thesmophoria (eleventh to thirteenth of Pyanopsion) and which forms together with the festival at Halimous (tenth of Pyanopsion) a larger five-day complex, seems to be drawn here particularly because of the *aiskhrologia* that usually took place there. Details of this picture (821–829) yield a further meaning when they are linked to the mention of the Skira, a festival that also has a heortological connection to the central practices of the Thesmophoria. At the Skira, which took place at the height of the summer, women threw "piglets" and other fertility-inducing objects, such as cakes in the form of snakes and male genitalia, as well as pinecones and twigs into subterranean pits (μέγαρα); the "decomposed" remnants of all these things were then brought up at the Thesmophoria in October to be added to the earth at the sowing of crops.[335] The Skira belong to the rites of the Arrhephoria and have a structural connection to the Thesmophoria as an anticipation of the latter.[336] In particular, women gathered together both at the Skira and at the Thesmophoria, with men being excluded in both

---

[334] Here I am in agreement with more recent scholarship, which generally regards the *parabasis* as a focal point for the themes appearing in that particular comedy; Hubbard 1991:11 and 17n5.

[335] Given the highly unclear nature of the scholion to Lucian *Dial. Meret.* 2.1 (275.23ff. Rabe) there is still a debate about which festival of Demeter this rite of casting down was performed at. Relying on Clem. Alex. *Protr.* 2.17, the following scholars (among others) argue for the same Thesmophoria: Brumfield 1981:77, 159–161, Burkert 1966:7–8 (= Burkert 1990:43–44), Burkert 1983:257n5, and Burkert 1985:242–243; see now also Kledt 2004:134 and 186n4. At the previous year's festival: Harrison 1922³:123 and Clinton 1992:63n203. Clinton 1988:77–78 refers to a similar practice at the Eleusinia (but with the qualification [Clinton 1992:63n203] that *megarizein* at the Mysteries was not synchronized with the Thesmophoria). Simon 1983:19–20 argues for the Stenia, which took place only two days before the Thesmophoria (according to her the "bailing" thus occurred on the day of the Kalligeneia). Rohde 1870:554–556 (Kl. Schr. II 1901, 361–364) considers the day of the procession to Halimous, one day after the Stenia, while placing the activity carried out by the ἀντλήτριαι only several days after the festival. Skira: Robert 1885:363ff., Deubner 1932:40–44, 50, Parke 1977:83, 159–160, and Baudy 1992:22ff. According to Baudy 1992:23, the putrescent piglets and live snakes mentioned in the description are simply a ritual fiction: piglets and snakes were symbols for female and male genitalia, and in ritual reality only imitations made of dough were thrown down into the chasm. Cf. now also Kledt 2004:128–132. On the piglet as vulva, cf. *Thesm.* 289 (with schol. and above, n187, and below, n471), *Ach.* 792 (with schol.) and the remarks of Versnel 1993:256–257.

[336] Cf. Harrison 1922³:131–135, Baudy 1992:22–23, and Camps-Gaset 1994:142–144. Schol. Luc. *Dial. Meret.* 2.1 (275–276 Rabe) incorrectly collapses "Arrhetophoria/Arrhephoria/Skirophoria and Thesmophoria" into one, which clearly goes back to an abbreviated comparison based on an analogy of summer and autumn rituals. On the Skira see also Calame 1990:339–354 and in general (in connection with the structure of the festival and symbolic spatial partitioning of Attica) *ibid.*, 289–396; see now also Kledt 2004:152–187.

cases.[337] The Arrhephoria, as did the Thesmophoria, restaged the myth of the abduction of Kore, the young maiden *par excellence*, by Hades.

Let us turn next to this image and then to its connections with the ritual. The chorus of women show that the objects relating to weaving and wool-working and typical of their house-bound role—that is, the loom (ἀντίον, 822), the shuttle, or the rod with which the layers of woven thread are pushed together (κανών, 822), and the woolbaskets (καλαθίσκοι, 822)—are looked after carefully and not lost. The parasol (σκιάδειον, 823) comes as the climax at the end of the series. It is also an important accessory for women, not for their work, but rather for their external appearance: it protects their pale, genteel complexion from exposure to the sun. Like the mirror (cf. *Thesm.* 140), it relates to the external characteristics of feminine vanity and toilette.[338] Among the men, these objects, which have the same names, but a different meaning—κανών (825) as the wooden frame which keeps the shield taut (cf. Hom. *Il.* 8.193) and σκιάδειον (829) as metaphor for the shield itself here refer to their role in warfare—are poorly cared for, because men just throw them away out of cowardice.[339]

---

[337] Cf. *IG* II/III² 1177 = Sokolowski 1969 (*LSCG*), nr. 36.8–13 (Thesmophoria and Skira are named as festivals at which separate assemblies of women were held). In Ar. *Eccl.* 18 the women plot their takeover while assembled at the Skira. The place of assembly at the Skira in Piraeus is the Thesmophorion. Mommsen (1864:289–299) incorrectly thought, on the basis of schol. *Thesm.* 834 (τὰ δὲ Σκίρα λέγεσθαί φασί τινες τὰ γινόμενα ἱερὰ ἐν τῇ ἑορτῇ ταύτῃ Δήμητρι καὶ Κόρῃ [i.e. Θεσμοφορίοις]), that the Skira mentioned in line 834 were different from the Skirophoria. He wanted to connect the assembly at the Skira directly with the Thesmophoria, and placed them on the day of the *anodos* (ibid., 298–299).

[338] The parasol in comedy is invariably the mark of an effeminate character; cf. Eupolis fr. 481, Pherecr. fr. 70, and Strattis fr. 59 K.-A.

[339] There is no further evidence for σκιάδειον with the meaning "shield." Schol. *Thesm.* 823 offers as an explanation σκέπασμά τι ἐπὶ τῆς κεφαλῆς βαλλόμενον or "part of the sail" (μέρος τοῦ ἱστίου) (clearly as a reaction to the other instruments, which are all connected with weaving). The scholiast probably relates the sail to Athena's *peplos*, which was fixed to a wagon and brought up onto the Acropolis at the Greater Panathenaia; cf. Deubner 1932:32 with reference to (n4) Strattis fr. 31 K.-A.: τὸν πέπλον δὲ τοῦτον | ἕλκουσ' ὀνεύοντες τοπείοις ἄνδρες ἀναρίθμητοι | εἰς ἄκρον ὥσπερ ἱστίον τὸν ἱστόν; on the *peplos* in connection with this image, see below, n348. A comic play on words might lie behind the fact that Strattis in his *Psykhastai* fr. 59 K.-A. connects σκιάδειον with ῥιπίς ('fan,' from ῥίπτω [cf. *Thesm.* 829]; cf. Frisk II, 658); thus Pollux 10.127: ὁ δὲ Στράττις ἐν Ψυχασταῖς προειπὼν ῥιπίδα ἐπήγαγεν εἴτε σκιάδειον. Kock (I, 728 ad Strattis fr. 56) thinks the following: *Fallitur enim Pollux, cum ῥιπίδα et σκιάδειον idem esse dicit.* The objects were certainly not identical, but Strattis seems to have associated them comically because women used them both to protect themselves from the summer heat. For the parasol as particularly characteristic of women, and also in particular of effeminate men, cf. also Dion. Hal. *Ant. Rom.* 7.9.4; there, as in this passage from the *Thesmophoriazusae*, it is reported that Aristodemos, tyrant of Cumae, made the young people soft: ἠκολούθουν τ' αὐτοῖς . . . παιδαγωγοὶ γυναῖκες σκιάδεια καὶ ῥιπίδας κομίζουσαι. The connection with female handwork could equally reside in the association with ῥίψ "wickerwork made from young

τοῖς δ' ἡμετέροις ἀνδράσι τούτοις
ἀπόλωλεν μὲν πολλοῖς ὁ κανὼν
ἐκ τῶν οἴκων αὐτῇ λόγχῃ,
πολλοῖς δ' ἑτέροις ἀπὸ τῶν ὤμων
ἐν ταῖς στρατιαῖς
ἔρριπται τὸ σκιάδειον.

Thesm. 824–829

But as for our men here, for many of them their *kanôn* has gone missing from the house, along with their spear, others have had their
skiadeion fall from their shoulders while on campaign.

The deictic pronoun once again includes the audience. The transition from
the immediately preceding part relating to women is smooth: for many men
"their *kanôn* has gone missing from the house" (825–826)—men are worse
housekeepers than women, it seems, because they are incapable of watching
over possessions, which also lend them a womanly appearance and effeminacy. The chorus, Agathon, and the relative have assumed only external signs
for their mimesis of the female role,[340] behind which their male identity still
shines through. They have only to divest themselves of these signifiers to
become completely male again. Many men in the auditorium will have had a
similar experience in the course of their lives.

Only on hearing the lines does one understand the metonymous shift of
meaning, which is finally accomplished with the uttering of αὐτῇ λόγχῃ: men
are worse in the political and military arena, because out of cowardice they
throw away (ἔρριπται) the wooden shaft[341] together with the spear and the
"sunshade," the shield, with which they protect their head, thus wasting their
patrilineally passed down inheritance (ἐκ τῶν οἴκων).[342] Such a man is like

---

twigs or shoots or rushes," a word that is also etymologically related to ῥίπτω (Frisk II,
659–660). The parasol was probably "woven" or "plaited." Our passage *Thesm.* 829 would then
have the following comic connotations: on campaigns, the woven screen/shield was waved
over the head "from the shoulders" like a fan, to be then suddenly cast off from the upper arm;
ὦμος is often connected with weapons (Hom. *Il.* 5.41 and 15.544); the word can also mean the
"shoulders" of a garment worn by women (LSJ s.v. I.3).

[340] The relative (*Thesm.* 140) asks in puzzlement how mirror and sword go together for Agathon.
Here one encounters the same paradoxical association of effeminacy and manliness that ultimately characterizes Dionysus as god of the members of the chorus.

[341] Cf. schol. *Thesm.* 825: τὴν κάμακα τῆς λόγχης λέγει. οἱ μέν φασι κανόνα αὐτὸν λέγειν τὸ ξύλον
τῆς λόγχης, οἱ δὲ τὸν κανόνα τῆς ἀσπίδος.

[342] In the ephebic oath the young men swear to uphold the fatherland as it was and not to allow
anything to be lost, that is, "to hand it down to the next generation not diminished, but bigger
and better" (9–10: καὶ ο‹ὐ›κ ἐλάττω παραδώσω τὴν πατρίδ-| α, πλείω δὲ καὶ ἀρείω); cf. Tod II, nr.

the much-ridiculed "shield-abandoner" (ῥίψασπις), who abandons the male code of behavior (κανών, cf. Eur. *Hec.* 602, *El.* 52) together with his spear (αὐτῇ λόγχῃ), the sign of aristocratic birth.[343] The verb form ἔρριπται clearly harks back to the *Palamedes* parody (770-784) just before the *parabasis*; the relative wants to write on oar blades and cast them into the sea. When he finds out, however, that there are none around, he decides to take votive tablets from the sanctuary of Demeter, inscribe them with a call for help to Euripides, and "throw" (ῥίψω, 771; διαρρίπτοιμι, 774) them overboard.[344]

204, pp. 303-307, Merkelbach 1972 (= *Philologica* 88-94), and Siewert 1977 (here the inscription is reproduced as it appears on a stele from Akharnai from the fourth century BCE, following Tod II, 303-304 and Siewert 1977:102-103; the text is also attested, with slight deviations, in literary sources in Pollux 8.105-106 and Stob. 4.1.48; Siewert 1977:104-109 shows that fifth-century writers already referred to it). The ephebic oath is a typical speech act in the Austinian sense (note the speaking "I"). Aglauros was the goddess of young men as a group. On the heortological connection with our tableau see Baudy 1992:18-19 (twelfth Skirophorion).

[343] On the ῥίψασπις cf. Ar. *Nub.* 353 and Dover *Clouds*, 148 *ad loc.*; cf. also Ar. *Pax* 1186 (with Olson *Peace*, 294-295 *ad* 1185-1186), Plat. *Leg.* 944b7-c1, and Archil. fr. 5 W. (with *Pax* 1298-1301). On the spear as symbol of the aristocracy, cf. Trag. adesp. fr. 84 N/Kannicht = Carcinus, *TrGF* I 70 F 1, λόγχην ἦν φοροῦσι γηγενεῖς.

[344] Lines 776ff. are anapaestic dimeters. In earlier scholarship the lines were seen as a substitution for the missing *kommation*. Cf. van Leeuwen *Thesm.*, 101 *ad* 776-784: "*ceterum* commatii *loco sunt hi anapaesti, parant enim transitum a diverbio ad chori parabasin.*" Accordingly, the chorus would already have taken up position with the performance of lines 776ff. Bothe (III, 151 *ad* 741) in particular argues that the *parabasis* was accompanied by the throwing away of the tablets, which is, however, extremely unlikely (cf. Fritzsche, 291; he assigns lines 778-780, ἄγε δὴ - μόχθων, and 783-784, βάσκετ' - ταχέως χρή, to Euripides [MS Monacensis 492 assigns the whole set, 776-784, to Euripides]; Rogers *Thesm.*, 81 *ad* 776 correctly argues against this). In favor of the *kommation* hypothesis is the emphatic χώρει, χώρει (782), which apart from being an address to the writing tablets he casts away (Fritzsche thinks that the relative here writes "Euripides, come, come!"; Rogers *Thesm.*, 82 *ad* 781, following Enger, 136 *ad* 782, interprets the imperative as a command to the stylus [σμίλη] to inscribe the wood carefully) could also be an address to the chorus, who are often ordered to form up in just this way: *Thesm.* 953, *Ran.* 372, *Eccl.* 478 (cf. χωρεῖτε, *Ran.* 440). In all cases it is clear how Aristophanes' chorus continually picks up and processes the references like weaving a fabric. On the *Palamedes* parody see Rau 1967:51-53. DuBois (1988:77-78) compares the inscribing of the tablets to taking possession of the female body sexually, often compared in Greek culture to plowing. Precisely these two levels, human sexuality and agriculture, were synchronized and ritually strengthened at the Thesmophoria; cf. esp. also Baudy 1992. DuBois refers to the αὖλαξ (furrow) made by the plow (phallus) on the δέλτοι (tablets). There may in fact even be a play on the word δέλτα, which also refers to the female pubic triangle (cf. Henderson 1991²:146; duBois 1982:98-99 considers this possibility in another context [Soph. *Trach.* 680-683]).

After the Battle of Salamis the Greeks brought the wrecked ships to Cape Kolias; Hdt. 8.96 cites in relation to this an oracle of Lysistratos: "The women of Kolias shall one day roast their barley with oars." There was a sanctuary of Aphrodite on Cape Kolias, south of Phaleron; on the day of the procession to Halimous, the tenth of Pyanopsion, just before the Thesmophoria, there was ecstatic dancing on the beach; the connection between Cape Kolias and the Thesmophoria could explain the mysterious oracle: women celebrating the Thesmophoria in Eretria

The comic *mésalliance* of male and female signs thus induces laughter. The most diverse connotative strands from all over the entire play are brought together in this image as a focal point. Ritual speech and poetry weave in associative fashion various individual elements into the web of connections. According to representatives of the Prague school of linguistics, in particular Roman Jakobson, motifs constantly move in a simultaneous and reciprocal process along a syntagmatic, horizontal axis of combination using metonymy, and along a paradigmatic, vertical axis of selection using metaphor. Eventually they return with slight change in a sort of loop. Poetry is in fact often traditionally associated with spinning, sewing, and weaving.[345]

The complex image of the sunshade in combination with instruments relating to women's woolworking only becomes fully comprehensible through a later recurring reference to the Skira (834).[346] In the complex festive cycle that extends from the Arrhephoria to the Panathenaia and that Walter Burkert has interpreted as a new year's ritual connected to female and male initiation, woolworking also plays a central role.[347] At the Khalkeia, in late autumn, on the thirtieth of Pyanopsion, two young girls at the tender age of between seven and eleven, representing all maidens, enter into the service of Athena on the Acropolis. Up until the Arrhephoria in the following summer, they are chiefly concerned as *ergastinai* with the making of the *peplos* for the goddess, which is then presented to her at the subsequent Panathenaia at the end of July (twenty-eighth of Hekatombaion). The great polis festival thereby seals the return to the normal order of things after the preceding reversals, celebrated during the course of the transition from the old to the new

---

(Plut. *Quaest. Graec.* 31.298bc) rediscover the technique of roasting as part of a restaging of a primitive lifestyle (Diod. Sic. 5.4.7). They do not roast meat over a fire, but in the sun. Perhaps in this place on the sea there took place the special rites with oars to which Aristophanes here refers. In *Lys.* 1–2. Aristophanes also alludes to the rites at Cape Kolias on the day of the festival at Halimous, on which women, from the male perspective, took every opportunity to take pleasure in sex, dancing, and wine. The relative realizes that the requirements on the day of the Nesteia have nothing more to do with oars and grasps for what lies at hand.

[345] Spinning is described in Latin as *filum deducere* (Ov. *Met.* 4.36); *ducere* or *deducere* is often combined with *carmen*, which means something like to compose a song; see Nagy 1996:49. On "stitching" a song cf. the verb ῥάπτω (preserved in *rhapsôdos*) and Nagy 1996:61–64; on the weaving (ὑφαίνειν) of songs and texts (Latin *texere*; on the word *textus* see Scheid/Svenbro 1996:131–155, 209–216), see Nagy 1996:64–65. For all three aspects of woolworking in the context of combining and weaving together of elements to produce a new "fabric" or "weaving," which is subject to continuous alteration in the process of reperformance, see Nagy 1996:66ff.

[346] Moulton (1981:134) is the only commentator to indicate a connection between the parasol and the Skira. See now also Prato, 291 *ad* 823.

[347] Burkert 1966 (= Burkert 1990:40–59), Burkert 1983:135–161, and Burkert 1985:227–234.

year.[348] The Skira, held on the twelfth of Skirophorion, to which the rites of the Arrhephoria belonged, were celebrated both for Athena and for the Eleusinian Kore. The Arrhephoria, as has been demonstrated above, structurally anticipate the Thesmophoria, at which weaving and woolworking are also of central importance. Numerous loom weights and jewelry were found in the Thesmophorion at Bitalemi.[349] The dedications do not necessarily indicate the presence of looms and the making of garments in the sanctuary, but at the very least the votive offerings represent symbolic conditions that point to the central female activity in the *oikos*, and using the myth that accompanies the ritual one may posit a connection to weaving.

Apollodoros of Athens (*FGrHist* 244 F 89) relates that Persephone as νύμφη prepared herself for her impending marriage by, among other things, weaving costly clothes. After her abduction by Hades and disappearance, Demeter, her mother, entrusts the basket (κάλαθος) that contained these clothes to the

---

[348] After the Arrhephoria the Arrhephoroi were discharged. There were two maidens, not four (as Deubner 1932:12 thinks). Cf. Burkert 1966:3–5 (= Burkert 1990:41–42). The two girls also belonged to the εὐγενεῖς. On the Arrhephoria see now also Brulé 1987:79–123 (esp. on discussion of sources, 79ff.) and Donnay 1997 (with criticism of the initiation theory, 201). On the basis of Etym. Magn. 149.19 Brulé 1987:392 assumes that there were two groups of Arrhephoroi: two girls who enter into yearlong service, and another two who for three years and nine months are responsible for the *peplos* presented every four years to the goddess at the Greater Panathenaia. The young maidens are first-fruit offerings for Athena, representatives of feminine *eugeneia* (cf. *Thesm.* 330), which must reproduce itself; on the function of introduction into the female role cf. Camps-Gaset 1994:136. On Athena's *peplos* and weaving on the Acropolis, cf. Brulé 1987:99–116 (also on the Plynteria and Kallynteria). Agraulos is the first mythical laundress of the cloth; the washing festival also took place shortly before the Skira/Arrhephoria on the twenty-ninth of Thargelion; Burkert 1970 (= Burkert 1990:77–85, esp. 78). The Kallynteria were celebrated much earlier, in Anthesterion or Maimakterion; on the *peplos* and weaving in general, see Barber 1992:106–112 ("The Greek Terminology of Cloth Making"). A papyrus in Cologne (inv. nr. 264) contains the hypothesis to Euripides' *Auge*; Telephos, who also plays an important role in the *Thesmophoriazusae*, as has been seen above, is her son. The editor of the papyrus, Ludwig Koenen, shows the connection between the myth of Auge and the ritual of the Plynteria; just like the mythical maidens who dance in a chorus on the Acropolis during the Arrhephoria, the beautiful and virtuous Auge in the service of Athena Alea in Tegea is also the leader of a chorus of maidens; Koenen 1969. Girls on the threshold of initiation dance in choruses and are here prepared for marriage. The papyrus then mentions the washing of a garment. Washing is also connected with preparations for marriage, the goal of female initiation. Nausikaa, who at Athena's behest washes clothing at the river (cf. πλυνοί, *Od.* 6.40 and 86), also represents a reflex of this ritual practice (Hom. *Od.* 6.1ff.). She too dances in a chorus after this, and as chorus leader is even compared to Artemis, another goddess of virginity. Artemis and the Nymphs (*nymphai!*) dance in a circle; the choral dance of Nausikaa and her companions is at the same time a ballgame (*Od.* 6.100), just as the Arrhephoroi also danced on a space used for ball playing (cf. Eur. *Ion.* 492ff. and see below, n351). Consider the emphasis on the verb παίζειν in the sense of playing and dancing (*Od.* 6.100 and 106) and above, Introduction n180.

[349] Kron 1992:621.

Nymphs. She herself goes to Paros, to King Melisseus, and gives the Kore's bridal clothing to the sixty royal daughters as a guest-gift and also reveals to them the mysteries of the Thesmophoria. Since then, as Apollodoros aetiologically explains, all women celebrating the Thesmophoria are called "bees" (*melissai*).[350]

The *kalathiskoi* named in line 822 and the tools of female woolworking thus recall the objects with which important female rites were accomplished. The little baskets are a symbol of feminine identity and are passed on from year to year in sacred rites. Through these actions initiation into marriage, which is to say the reproduction of the polis, is ensured. As at the Thesmophoria, so too at the Arrephoria choruses of young women performed. *Kalathiskos* itself can refer to a special form of tragic dance. One might suggest that the chorus leader refers in the *pnigos* to the accompanying dance movements of his chorus.[351] In the *Lysistrata*, which was performed at the Lenaia of the same

[350] Clem. Alex. *Protr.* 2.17, Ov. *Met.* 5.393, and Claudian *Rapt. Pros.* 2.138–139 also mention the κάλαθος. Cf. also the naming of the κάλαθος in Callim. *Hymn.* 6.1ff., 120ff. and the festive introduction of a κάλαθος at the festival of Demeter by Ptolemy Philadelphos in Alexandria in imitation of the Athenian rites (schol. Callim. *Hymn.* 6.1, Pfeiffer II, 77). On the connection of weaving, birth, and sowing at the Arrhephoria and Thesmophoria, see Moret 1991:236–242. Carrying baskets was part of the secret rite of the Arrhephoria; in addition, there were also maiden basket-carriers (Kanephoroi) at the Panathenaia. Baskets are symbols of fertility: the basket of the Arrhephoroi contained symbolic objectsthat were used in the introduction to sexuality in the form of "ritual play-activity" (Baudy 1992:12); the covered baskets carried down into subterranean passages contained, according to Baudy 1992, twelve phallic snakes with the heads of children, simultaneously representing procreation and birth. What the girls brought back from their journey into the underworld was, Baudy thinks, exactly the same: after the initiatory learning experience the cult object simply underwent a change, now representing an infant.

[351] On the *kalathiskos* as a dance form see Athen. 467f and Pollux 4.105. On basket dances in the cult of Demeter and Artemis, see Lawler 1964:109–110; for a comic phlyax basket dancer with artificial breasts and phallus, much as we imagine the participants in the chorus might have looked, see *ibid.*, 89 with ill. 35. See also Brommer 1989:485–486 (with a list of illustrations on vases) on this dance. For dancing boys and girls with broad wreaths of this type at the Spartan Karneia, see Burkert 1985:234. According to Eur. *Ion* 492–506, the three daughters of Aglauros dance in front of the temple of Pallas and near a cave of Pan on the north slope of the Acropolis. The daughters of Kekrops possibly represent the mythic model for ritual choruses of girls (cf. also Lee 1997:212 *ad* Eur. *Ion* 496: "There may also be a reference to the reenactment of their story in the ritual of the summer festival known as the Hersephoria or Arrephoria"), upon which the tragic chorus projects its current performance. Dance in the here and now is reflected in myth and in ritual, which has a close connection to the plot, since Ion is viewed as the reincarnation of Erichthonius. Luc. *Salt.* 39 reports that the myth of Erichthonius, the incarnation of King Erechtheus resurrected as baby, was danced mimetically. Ritual dances of this kind could be practiced on the area used for ball playing by the Arrhephoroi (Plut. *Vit. X or.* 839c). In the deme of Phlya, Athene Tithrone (Paus. 1.31.4) was associated with sexually charged dances; Petersmann 1990. Tithrone simply means "the jumper," according to Petersmann 1990:47–48; jumping and dancing belong together, as both activities promote fertility and offspring. Athena is herself

year, 411 BCE, the woolworking of the women equally stands at the center as reflex of the rites of the Arrhephoroi; consider in particular Lysistrata's extensive woolworking metaphor (*Lys.* 567ff.), which comically reworks the preparation of Athena's *peplos*. In the immediately preceding *pnigos*, the Proboulos is comically dressed up as woolworking woman (*Lys.* 532–538). In addition to this costume he also receives a woolbasket (*Lys.* 535).[352]

The repeated mention of the sunshade (σκιάδειον, 823, 829) and, in particular, the not otherwise attested synonymy with "shield" become more understandable when taken in connection with the Skira and Panathenaia. In the context of the reversals of the normal order at the end of the year in June, on the day of the Skira (twelfth of Skirophorion) the priestess of Athena Polias, the priest of Poseidon-Erechtheus, and the priest of Helios, under the cover of a white canopy carried by one of the Eteoboutadai, march in procession from the center of the polis, the Acropolis, to the periphery on the border of Attica, to Skiron, located near Eleusis, just before the Kephisos River. Here there was a sanctuary of Athena Skiras and one of Demeter and Kore, where according to Pausanias (1.37.2) Athena and Poseidon were also worshiped. The canopy was known uniquely as the σκίρον, from which the name of the festival was apparently later derived. The word means nothing more than a large σκιάδειον (Harpocr., s.v. σκίρον and Suda, s.v. Σκίρον; schol. *Eccl.* 18).[353]

On countless vase paintings of the late sixth and the fifth centuries one finds representations of several enthusiastic bearded parasol-bearers and of whole *kômoi* similarly outfitted, which cannot, however, as Ernst Buschor in

---

Pandrosos (schol. *Lys.* 439), the all-bedewing. Pandrosos is also one the daughters of Kekrops, who form the mythic model for the Arrhephoroi. On leaping gods, see also Petersmann 1991; on Tithrone, *ibid.*, 85. Pausanias (5.3.2) reports that women in Elis were immediately impregnated by their husbands after a prayer to Athena and that the latter was worshiped there as Μήτηρ. Weaving and dancing are also at the foreground for the initiation rites at Brauron, located on the border of Attica in the peripheral zone of the Outside, where Attic girls were dedicated to (significantly) Artemis; Cole 1984:238–244 and Brulé 1987:177–283, esp. 225–240, and particularly 227–229 ("Artémis fileuse") and 250–260. On the Arkteia, see also Sourvinou-Inwood 1988, and on dance at Brauron, Calame I 1977:186–189 (Engl. trans. Calame 1997:98–100). On the rites in Brauron in general see now Gentili/Perusino 2002.

[352] For interpretation of the wool metaphor, see Moulton 1981:48–58; on the motif of weaving in this comedy, see Dorati 1998:44–50; I am planning a detailed study of the ritual backgrounds of the *Lysistrata*. On the basket, cf. Henderson *Lys.*, 137 *ad* 532–538, and in the wool metaphor *Lys.* 579. On the metaphor of woolworking and spinning in connection with female initiation see now also Ferrari 2002:11–60.

[353] Deubner 1932:50 sees in the large σκιάδειον of which Lysimakhides, *FGrHist* 366 F 3 (in Harpokration, s.v. σκίρον) speaks not a parasol but rather a canopy. See also Parke 1977:157 and Simon 1983:23 (although protection against the sun is recognized as its practical and immediate purpose, they stress the status and dignity that such an array lends priests).

a famous article claimed, be associated with the Skira. Rather, they seem to be connected generally with male transvestism in the circle of Dionysus.[354] Did the members of the chorus, clad perhaps in similar fashion to these feminine-looking comasts, accompany these lines with dance? The image would certainly have been most impressive from a theatrical point of view. Our performers increasingly experiment with the other sex in this comedy, so that they certainly would not have worn any (false) beards simply on the basis of their dramatic role as women. The chorus was possibly made up of ephebes on the threshold of manhood. We will discuss the implications of such a symbolic *tableau vivant* further below.

Sunshades were clearly also held over the Kanephoroi at the Panathenaia to protect the honorable maidens from the effects of the sun.[355] A Dionysiac element is also blended in this passage with elements of Demeter and Athena. The associative combination of ritual patterns thus reworks various examples from the contemporary world of the audience, among which the components of the Skira are here prominent. The latter is above all a harvest festival. On

---

[354] On the Anacreontic vases see Caskey/Beazley 1954:55–61 and Frontisi-Ducroux/Lissarrague 1990; for arguments against connecting the red-figure vase paintings (Buschor 1923/24) with the Skirophoria, or Skira, see Deubner 1932:49–50, who assigns them speculatively (132–133) to the Lenaia. On the difficulty of drawing an unequivocal connection between a visual sign and a ritual referent, see Durand/Frontisi-Ducroux 1982. The Skira, at which the decision in *Ecclesiazusae* 18 has been taken, have nothing to do with women dressing in men's clothing; this is why the women do not have the important idea of putting on men's attire. Bowie 1993:257–258, following many other commentators (e.g. Kenner 1970:130–131), connects this reversed transvestism in the *Ecclesiazusae* with the Hybristika of Argos, which fell in midsummer and at which women also put on beards. Aristophanes always makes use of ritual models in pastiche-like free association. Female comasts carry parasols in the following illustrations in Frontisi-Ducroux/Lissarrague 1990: ills. 7.3 (Paris, Louvre G 285; *ARV* 380, 170), 7.5 (Paris, Louvre G 220; *ARV* 280, 11), 7.9 (Copenhagen, Nationalmuseum 13365; *ARV* 185, 32), 7.24 (Palazzolo Acreide), 7.25 (Bologna 234; *ARV* 524, 20), 7.27 (Cleveland 26.549; *ARV* 563, 9), 7.28 (Vienna 770; *ARV* 576, 33), 7.29 (formerly Rome, Cippico collection; *ARV* 291, 25), 7.30 and 7.31 (Chiusi C 1836; *ARV* 815, 2), 7.34 and 7.35 (Madrid 11009). On the history of the scholarship, see Kenner 1970:113–116 and Frontisi-Ducroux/Lissarrague 1990:213–217; the use of the term "Anacreontics" stems from Beazley, who took it from an inscription on a krater by the Kleophrades Painter (ca. 500 BCE, Copenhagen, Nationalmuseum 13365), on which similar comasts are depicted, and transferred it to the entire group. On a further oriental context, see Price 1990. On the Madrid stamnos (Madrid 11009) eight female comasts of this type are represented with small parasols. Next to them is also a wool basket (see above, n350), which refers to women's woolworking. On the parasol and Anacreontic vases, see also Miller 1992 and Delavaud-Roux 1995, who place the groups of female comasts in a Dionysiac context. See now on the Anacreontic vases Miller 1997:193–198, Miller 1999, Neer 2002:19–23, and Bundrick 2005:84–87, 90, 166.

[355] See the discussion in Deubner 1932:31n14, arguing that parasol and stool do not represent any special cultic equipment, but are simply carried for the comfort of the Kanephoroi. See also Miller 1992:103–105.

the sacred Skironian field, where the harvest was officially ended with the reaping of the crop on the twelfth day of Skirophorion, the canopy that had previously served the high representatives as protection from the sun was also erected as a roof for the fieldworkers, who began the threshing there.[356] The day of the Skira also brings with it, however, the desired connection with masculine war. In myth the legendary battle between Athens and Eleusis, in which the Athenian king, Erechtheus, was killed by Poseidon, took place on the Skironian field.[357] On this day too, Agraulos, a daughter of Erechtheus, sacrificed herself for her homeland because of an oracle, and her sisters shared her lot. According to Euripides' *Erechtheus*, the Athenians worshiped the maidens under the name of the Hyakinthidai with yearly rites and festive dances (fr. 65, 68–80 Austin). Their sacrificial death corresponds to the fall of the daughters of Kekrops from the Acropolis, which serves as the *aition* for the practices of the Arrhephoroi.[358] It was at the sanctuary of Agraulos/Aglauros that ephebes would take their oath to defend the fatherland bravely, as symbolized in its agrarian fruits.[359] As Gerhard Baudy has shown, the mock battles of ephebes on the Skironian field correspond to the mythical model. The death of Erechtheus and his warriors is paralleled by the harvesting of the sacred crop there and is analogous to the death of the ephebe, who rises once more, like Erechtheus in the form of Erichthonius. Beside the conflict between Athens and Eleusis, there were other mythical and historical battles that served as possible *aitia* for ritual two-sided "wars."[360] In particular, the ephebes believed they were reenacting the most famous of all wars, the Trojan conflict. The epoch-making

---

[356] See Baudy 1992:29n161.

[357] The priest of Poseidon proceeding from the Erechtheion represented Poseidon and his opponent Erechtheus in the same person.

[358] See Philokhoros, *FGrHist* 328 F 105.

[359] See the text in Siewert 1977:102–103 and above, n342. For this reason a woman, Mika, curses the women's cowardice in the name of Aglauros (*Thesm.* 533); she wants to remind her comrades of their "ephebic oath" sworn by the name of Aglauros (the "rustic"), to be brave and defend the *nomoi* of their institution, which forms a counter-polis. Mika presents the virtuous handworker Penelope as the model on whom the women should base their actions (*Thesm.* 547). The ephebic oath sworn by the various crops of Attica also evokes the *panspermia* of the Thesmophoria.

[360] Baudy 1992:18–20; see now also Kledt 2004:160–163. Baudy (14–17) convincingly does not date the Arrhephoria, as does Burkert 1966:5n2 (= Burkert 1990:54n8), on the basis of a sacrifice in Erkhia which fell on the third day of Skirophorion, but also dates it to the twelfth of Skirophorion. For as Baudy says, the birth of Erichthonius, which was celebrated at the Arrephoria, could hardly have been before the death of Erechtheus (12th Skirophorion), whose symbolic reincarnation Erichthonius after all represents. See now also Kledt 2004:169–173. On the rituality and symbolic nature of expression in Greek warfare of the archaic period, see in general Connor 1988a.

conquest of this city was dated to the twelfth of Skirophorion (Clem. Alex. *Strom.* 1.104), as was the historical battle at Mantinea (Plut. *De glor. Athen.* 7.350a).[361]

For this reason the *tableau vivant* (823–829) also evokes Homer in its diction. All in all, the Trojan War provided a generally recognized explanatory myth for the *pyrrhikhê*, which Neoptolemos-Pyrrhos was thought to have instituted. Troy is supposed to have been destroyed by this dance, the so-called Trojan leap.[362] This spectacular dance with weapons was performed in Athens at the Panathenaia by choruses that represented the three age-classes of men, not their *phylai*.[363] This qualifies it as a time-honored ritual reaching back to before the reforms of Kleisthenes. Like many ritual actions, the *pyrrhikhê* is a highly complex and shimmering phenomenon which simultaneously conveys not only one but several meanings and to which justice cannot be done using simply one model of development. The main function of the dance appears to be preparation for war. This type of weapons dance clearly accompanied the transition of the male youth to adulthood, and represents a ritual practice that underscores in festive mode the *rite de passage* of initiation at puberty.[364]

---

[361] Cf. Baudy 1992:19 and Burkert 1983:158; significantly, the Spartans placed the sack of Troy at the time of the Karneia. In ritual, during the time of dissolution the Acropolis was seized by men from Eleusis, the Kerykes, who were also involved in overseeing the Bouphonia at the Dipolieia (see, however, the reservation expressed in Burkert 1983:139n17), while the protectors of the Acropolis, Poseidon-Erechtheus and Athena, departed with the sun god Helios.

[362] Luc. *Salt.* 9. Another *aition* (schol. [B] *ad* Hephaestion, p. 299, 1 Consbruch) maintains that Pyrrhos was the first to jump from the Trojan Horse (further references in Borthwick 1967:18–19), described by Homer (*Od.* 4.277) as a λόχος. On the connection of λόχος with birth and ambush, see Lonsdale 1993:150–168 and below, n372. On the Trojan leap and its reflex in Eur. *Andr.* 1129–1141, see Borthwick 1967. On the *lusus Troiae* and the *pyrrhikhê* as metaphorical weaving movement in the social web see Scheid/Svenbro 1996:35–49, esp. 47–49, and 184–188 and Ceccarelli 1998:149. In Fronto *Ad M. Aur. Caesar* 1.5.4, the metaphor of weaving in connection with the *pyrrhikhê* is applied to the written discourse of Latin and Greek poetic verse.

[363] On the *pyrrhikhê* in general, see Ceccarelli 1998; on its appearance in Athens, *ibid.*, 27–89. Cf. esp. the inscription *IG* II/III² 2311, esp. 72–74 = *SIG*³ 1055 (cf. *SEG* 37, 1987, 129) from the fourth century BCE, which gives information about the prizes at the Greater Panathenaia; cf. the photograph and brief illustration of the inscription in Neils 1992:15–17, Kotsidu 1991:100–103 (with tables 6–7), Ceccarelli 1995:296–297, and Ceccarelli 1998:32–33. The presence of the *pyrrhikhê* at the Panathenaia is also attested in Lys. 21.1–4 (*agôn* of dancers of the *pyrrhikhê* at the Lesser and Greater Panathenaia). Osborne 1993:30–31 maintains that the *agôn* of the *pyrrhikhê* was also an event involving the *phylai*.

[364] On this see Baudy 1992:20n111. On the *pyrrhikhê* as preparation for war, see Athen. 630d–631a. On initiation and Troy, see Bremmer 1978. It has even been suggested that the *pyrrhikhê* is connected with the conferring of weapons and the Attic ephebic oath sworn by the name of Aglauros; cf. Vidal-Naquet 1986:136 (*pyrrhikhê* as equivalent to the ephebic oath) and Lonsdale 1993:162–166, esp. 164. On the connection of the *pyrrhikhê* with the *ephêbeia* and initiation, see Ceccarelli 1998: index s.v. "Efebi," "Efebia," "Iniziazione," "Rito di passaggio," and "Transizione."

Beside being performed by choruses, this dance may also be performed by solo dancers and by women. In a panhellenic context the occasion of the dance is not limited to festivals in honor of Athena, but also plays a role at festivals of Dionysus and Artemis. Apart from Pyrrhos, it is the polis goddess Athena who is credited in Athens with the invention of the *pyrrhikhê*, but Zeus, Artemis, the Kouretes, Dioskouroi, satyrs, and Amazons are also involved. What links this ambivalent spectrum of references is clearly an initiation ritual for male and female youth, who by means of mimetic and acrobatic movements prepare themselves for adulthood, that is, for war and marriage.[365] Visual representations of performers of this dance show mostly naked or lightly clothed male or female dancers who, arrayed only in a helmet and carrying a shield in the left hand, a javelin or spear in the right, take up wild offensive and defensive positions. They protect themselves and jump up, swinging their shields up and down above their heads and brandishing their spears.

In Athens Athena herself represents the divine model, since in paradoxical fashion she combines these male and female signifiers simultaneously in her own person.[366] She forms both the *aition* of the *pyrrhikhê* and the divine center of the sequence of rites that stretch from the Arrhephoria up to the Panathenaia and that relate to the turn of the year. In a tradition that is attested in Lucian and that probably goes back to the fifth century BCE, the birth of the goddess is tied to this dance. Hephaistos, who facilitated this birth from Zeus' skull by means of an axe, in a conversation with Zeus explains the event, saying that she jumped out dancing the *pyrrhikhê* and swung her shield

[365] On the structural similarity of war and marriage as goal of initiation, see Vernant 1990:34: "Here again both the link and the polar opposition between the two types of institution are noticeable. Marriage is for the girl what war is for the boy: For each of them these mark the fulfillment of their respective natures as they emerge from a state in which each still shared in the nature of the other"; see in general *ibid.*, 29–53. For the connection of dances in armor with female initiation, see also Bron 1996. The *skiadeion* is also distantly reminiscent of the σκιάδες at the Spartan Karneia. Demetrios of Skepsis reports (in Athen. 141e–f) that the festival was staged as an imitation of military training; nine such *skiades* were erected, and nine men at any one time ate together in one *skias*, three from each phratry. Demetrios thinks they were so called because they resembled tents (σκιάδες δὲ οὗτοι καλοῦνται σκηναῖς ἔχοντες παραπλήσιόν τι). On the basis of this characterization one could even make a connection in our passage to the well-known tents (σκηναί; cf. *Thesm.* 658) of the women at the Thesmophoria. In this case, the women's festival would be imitative of a male military structure. In *Thesm.* 624 there is an allusion to the camaraderie of the tent. While the women treasure their ritual camping at the annual celebration of the Thesmophoria, the men part with it quite casually.

[366] On Athena and the *pyrrhikhê* cf. Dion. Hal. *Ant. Rom.* 7.72.7 (invention of the dance after Athena's victory over the giants); Plat. *Leg.* 796b–c (Athena does not dance this dance empty-handed, but in full armor); *Crat.* 406d–407a (the name Pallas is etymologized from πάλλειν in the context of a dance in armor, admittedly without specifying any particular dance).

and shook her spear like one possessed (Luc. *Dial. Deor.* 13 [8], 17–18: ἡ δὲ πηδᾷ καὶ πυρριχίζει καὶ τὴν ἀσπίδα τινάσσει καὶ τὸ δόρυ πάλλει καὶ ἐνθουσιᾷ).[367]

The ecstatic dance movement with its jerking back and forth of objects might also form the background for our image (*Thesm.* 819–829). The spear in the right hand "has been lost" (ἀπόλωλεν, 825) and the shield in the left hand "has been cast away" (ἔρριπται, 829) because the movements of the weapon dance have perhaps been too violently carried out by many male ephebes, as opposed to the way the women perform it. In a fragment from Pherekrates' *Kheiron* (fr. 155, esp. 8–12 K.-A.), Kinesias is personally charged by Music with having perverted "and so destroyed" it (ἀπολώλεχ' οὕτως, 10) that in his dithyrambs, "as in his shields" (καθάπερ ἐν ταῖς ἀσπίσιν, 11), left seems right to him. Perversion in connection with the notion of the shield-abandoner here implies a loss.[368]

The ambivalence of gender roles (which, as has been seen, also describes the theme of the *Thesmophoriazusae*) and the interplay of male and female signs, of weapons and weaving instruments, as well as the paradoxical connection of war, birth, and marriage, are made concrete in the goddess Athena. As arms-bearing virgin, she stands between the strictly defined social roles of man and woman. As warrior goddess, she is responsible for the initiation of the male youth. As permanent virgin, she is simultaneously, like Artemis, symbol of women in transition from maiden to mother, which the participants in the Thesmophoria as νύμφαι also experience. Both male and female youth

---

[367] On the mad tossing back of the head in connection with the death of the Gorgon as the σχῆμα τῆς Ἀθηνᾶς, see POxy 2738 (vol. 35, 1968, 46; the fragmentary commentary on a comedy, possibly by Eupolis) and Borthwick 1970; on *kheironomia* and the swinging of Neoptolemos' shield in defensive fighting as *pyrrhikhê*, see Eur. *Andr.* 1131: ἐκεῖσε κἀκεῖσ' ἀσπίδ' ἐκτείνων χερί, and 1135: δεινὰς δ' ἂν εἶδες πυρρίχας. See below, n372.

[368] Reckford 1977:288 observes that ἀποβαλὼν ὅπλα (Ar. *Vesp.* 27) contains a double meaning: "losing one's weapons" and "losing one's genitalia." Kleonymos the shield-thrower has just been mentioned (Ar. *Vesp.* 15–23). On the word-play on ὅπλον in the further meaning of phallus cf. *Ach.* 592, also Henderson 1991[2]:110, 123, 248, MacDowell *Wasps*, 131 *ad* 27 and 242 *ad* 823, as well as Sommerstein *Wasps*, 154 *ad* 27 and 207 *ad* 823. Kinesias is also associated in Aristophanes with the dithyramb and κύκλιοι χοροί (Ar. *Av.* 1379, 1388, 1403); in *Ran.* 152–153 he is named as the composer of a *pyrrhikhê*. He apparently combined the *pyrrhikhê* and the dithyramb; κύκλιοι χοροί were also performed on Kos (Segre 1993: ED 52 and 234) at the Dionysia and described as *pyrrhikhai* (κυκλίων τᾶι πυρρίχαι); cf. Ceccarelli 1995 and Ceccarelli 1998:121–123; on the Pherekrates passage Ceccarelli 1995:295–296 and Ceccarelli 1998:44 with n83; on Kinesias Ceccarelli 1995:293–296 and Ceccarelli 1998:42–44, 124; on the switching of right and left cf. Borthwick 1968:62–65. One may also perhaps think of a mirror image, as Ar. *Ach.* 1128–1131. The verb ἔρριπται (*Thesm.* 829) could be a reflection of the fact that Pyrrhos' dance leveled Troy to the earth. Luc. *Salt.* 9 puts it as follows: ἡ ἐκείνου ὀρχηστικὴ καθεῖλεν καὶ εἰς ἔδαφος κατέρριψεν (where the second verb also implies the rapid movement of the shield).

on the threshold of adult status may be represented as human reflections of the polis goddess.

As with all *rites de passage*, the initiation ceremonies also proceed along the lines of van Gennep's three-phase model. After the obligatory separation from the normal world, the initiates undergo a time of transition until they reach the stage of reintegration into society in a new social identity. The stage of marginality is characterized by a fundamental reversal, or mixing, of the gender roles. In the period of transition men demonstrate female types of signification and behave contrary to the male, hoplite code of honor, in that they retreat to the periphery and live according to the rules of ambush (λόχος), theft, and deception (δόλος). Girls, conversely, temporarily assume masculine traits, exercise in athletic competition, and hunt in the wild. In myth Artemis and her retinue of nymphs reflect these modes of behavior. According to Callimachus' hymn to Artemis (*Hymn.* 3.237-247) the Amazons form themselves into cyclical choruses under the leadership of Hippo and perform weapon and shield dances, the so-called *prylis*, in honor of the goddess.[369] On the other hand, the mythical Kouretes (Callim. *Hymn.* 1.52) and male age-groups undergoing initiation put on quite similar dances.

In the phase of marginality both sexes, then, assume characteristics of what represents in each case the opposite. In contrast to the briefly experienced Other, the formation of a gender-specific social role identity is designed to be concluded in a symbolically definitive and impressive manner. Athena as goddess of war and weaving represents the mythical model of male and female youth in the liminal transition period of initiation, which Victor Turner describes as a "betwixt and between" condition.[370] In addition to

[369] The Ephesian *prylis* dance attested in Callimachus is the *aition* for the annually performed weapon dances of Lydian maidens at the Ephesia, the subject of the well-known fragment of Autokrates from the *Tympanistai*. See Calame I 1977:178-183 (Engl. trans. Calame 1997:93-96), Dowden 1997:122, and Ceccarelli 1998:135-136. In this fragment the characteristic self-referential terminology of choral dance appears frequently: παίζουσιν, κοῦφα πηδῶσαι, ἐξαίρουσα, ἄλλεται. On the Amazons as a mythic model for girls in initiation, see Dowden 1997. On the Amazons as mythic image of the lack of differentiation in signs, see duBois 1982. For Amazons dancing the *pyrrhikhê*, see Bron 1996:78-79 and Ceccarelli 1998:22-23, 98-99, 135, 211, esp. ills. 72-79 (depictions on Athenian vases). For female initiatory choruses, see Calame I 1977 (Engl. trans. Calame 1997) and Lonsdale 1993:169-205.

[370] See Turner 1967:93-111. On a distinction in the initiatory model concerning ritual transvestism in the case of the Cretan Ekdysia, see the sound observations of Leitao 1995:136-142. In particular he attacks what he sees as the overly abstract scheme of the structuralists (Vidal-Naquet and Turner). In his opinion, what is at issue is not only an inversion of signs (for example, masculine and feminine), but also a ritual dramatization aimed at the differentiation of social gender roles. When, for example, boys are given feminine clothing in an initiation, the social context needs to be taken into account, namely the fact that youths are closer to women in

their symbolic confrontation with the structural opposite, the boys and girls are of course simultaneously familiarized with their future role by means of ritual games and action. The girls practice their area of social responsibility as future housekeepers and mothers with woolworking and with introduction into feminine sexuality, while the youths have to concern themselves with the craft of war and athletic fitness.

The paradoxical arrangement in the *Themophoriazusae* of homonymous objects that describe the male as well as female sphere of action is thus taken from ritual practices in the real world. The chorus, in its role as women dancing at the Thesmophoria who retrospectively become maidens on the threshold of sexual maturity, consequently projects its presence onto other female choruses within the field of initiation. Weapon dances play with sexual ambivalence, which is reflected in the liminal state between (female) role and (male) function.[371] Reflexes of homonymous linguistic play with opposites is in fact something found in ritual. The *pyrrhikhê* builds on elements of the male and female λόχος, which may refer to ambush in war and the process of lying in and giving birth.[372] The festival of the Panathenaia in particular brings the two

---

terms of their social gender role and status than are men. In the transition, these characteristics are emphasized purely in ritual terms, to be then discarded in a celebratory fashion.

[371] It is possible that male youth undergoing initiation also provided the personnel for Athenian theatrical choruses; cf. Winkler 1990 for the case of tragedy, which is in fact the object of parody in this comedy. See also Graf 1998:25–27 (also with extension to comedy: 27). Winkler 1990:55ff. furthermore makes a connection between the *pyrrhikhê*, the theatrical chorus, and the hoplite formation. On the *pyrrhikhê* as initiatory practice of the male youth, see Lonsdale 1993:137–168, Leitao 1995:134, and Ceccarelli 1998: index s.v. "Efebi," "Efebia," "Iniziazione," "Transizione"; on Sparta and Crete, Ceccarelli 1998:99–115; on initiatory elements in the mythical realm, Ceccarelli 1998:187–218; and on the *pyrrhikhê* in the theater, Ceccarelli 1998:37–45, 219–225.

[372] See Loraux 1981a, Lonsdale 1993:150–152 with nn58–72, and Ceccarelli 1998:202–204 (λόχος as ambush), 204–206 (λόχος as birth). Artemis and Athena are called Λοχία. Evidence for Artemis Lokhia, who protects initiated girls up until the birth of their first child, can be found in Cole 1984:243n62. Athena as Lokhia is implicitly attested in Eur. *Ion* 452ff. (see Lee 1997:209 *ad* Eur. *Ion* 452). The *lokhos* of the Trojan Horse is like a "birth" from its interior (Lonsdale 1993:150). Orestes' company, which ambushes and attacks Neoptolemos, is described in Eur. *Andr.* 1114 as a ξιφήρης . . . λόχος; Orestes is called Κλυταιμήστρας τόκος in the following line, which forms an end-rhyme with the preceding one. On the emphasis on τόκος in *Thesm.* 843–845, see above, pp. 194–195 and n329; λόχος, like χορός, depends on the locale and on the group that carries out the activity (Lonsdale 1993:139). For a description of Pyrrhos' fight as *pyrrhikhê*, see Eur. *Andr.* 1114–1146: cf. the excessive movement of the shield as *kheironomia* (1130–1131) and the movement of the feet (τὸ Τρωικὸν πήδημα πηδήσας ποδοῖν, 1139); he is in fact explicitly associated with this (δεινὰς δ' ἂν εἶδες πυρρίχας φρουρουμένου | βέλεμνα παιδός, 1135–1136). The hostile band (λόχος) lies in ambush and is "shaded by laurels," δάφνῃ σκιασθείς (Eur. *Andr.* 1114–1115), which may represent a further connection to the σκιάδειον (*Thesm.* 823, 829). Orestes is the leader of the *lokhos* and is described as "scheme-knitting" (μηχανορράφος, Eur. *Andr.*

sexes together with the performances of male πυρρίχαι and affords an occasion for choosing a wife, a precondition for the birth of the next generation.[373]

The images on Attic vases of maidens dancing the *pyrrhikê*, who are shown in the women's quarter of the house and accompanied by a female *aulos*-player, represent a complex play of equivalences between the weapon dance, marriage, birth, and woolworking.[374] Women in the transition phase are associated with weapons; the Amazons, to whom the women in the *Lysistrata* refer, are the mythical exemplum of this.[375] In ritual, both in the vase paintings and in the compressed verbal image of the *pnigos*, one finds a hybrid network of heteronymous systems, a simultaneous overlapping of male and female signifiers. They are clearly designed both to express the liminal situation of the fluid transition between maidenhood and being fully a women and to refigure in symbolic fashion the preparation for marriage.

On the lid of a pyxis from the Kanellopoulos Collection in Athens dated to the fifth century BCE one finds, for example, the following configuration:[376] there is a column, clearly representing the interior of an *oikos*; from right to

---

1116); this adjective also points to the connection between the *pyrrhikê* and woolworking. On Orestes as a symbol of the male initiate who during the marginal phases operates using deception and ambush, see Bierl 1994a. Orestes and his men attack Neoptolemos in a circle (κύκλῳ, Eur. *Andr.* 1137; on *pyrrhikê* as a circular choral dance see above, n368); the latter reacts with the "Trojan leap" (Eur. *Andr.* 1139) and further elements of the weapons dance. He thus replies to one *pyrrhikê* with another *pyrrhikê*. On the widespread idea of a connection between the dance and warfare, cf. carm. pop. fr. 857 *PMG* and Luc. *Salt.* 14 (the Thessalians used to call their fighters in the front ranks προορχηστῆρες).

[373] See Baudy 1992:44. Choruses of maidens joined the male dancers of the *pyrrhikê* and the ephebes singing the paean (Eur. *Hcl.* 777-783). On the communal marriage of all ephebes after completion of the *agelê* in Crete, see Ephorus, *FGrHist* 70 F 149 = Strabo 10.4.20, C 482.

[374] There is scholarly debate on whether scenes of this type represent a reflection of actual cultic practice or simply a parody; Lonsdale 1993:148 with n43. Epithets from the realm of domestic labor and housekeeping are remarkably frequent on the graves of women; see Brulé 1987:343.

[375] See Bowie 1993:184-185; for other mythical and ritual models, 178-204 therein. On women and war, see Graf 1984. Cf. esp. the *sphagia* and oath scene in Ar. *Lys.* 181-239, where the *aspis* is also central (*Lys.* 185, 188, 190). Lysistrata later boasts that she has four *lokhoi* of armed women inside (τέτταρες λόχοι | μαχίμων γυναικῶν ἔνδον ἐξωπλισμένων, *Lys.* 453-454); see Henderson *Lys.*, 126 *ad* 453-456, who thinks that women in full armor, apart from depictions of Athena, were only to be seen on the stage or in the *symposion*, where there were allegedly *hetairai* who danced the *pyrrhikê* in this outfit as a diverting interlude. He relies here on Poursat (1968:586-609, esp. 607-609), whose theory of the symposium has now rightly been subjected to reconsideration. For other feminine *lokhoi*, cf. Aesch. *Eum.* 46 (Erinyes) and Eur. *Ba.* 916 (Maenads).

[376] Schauenburg 1976:50 ill. 21 (discussion p. 43) and Ceccarelli 1998: nr. 72, pl. X (discussion pp. 62-63). On waterbirds see Autokrates fr. 1 K.-A. (because of their violent movements, the Lydian female dancers of a weapons dance in honor of Artemis are compared to a waterbird [οἷα κίγκλος, line 10] that rapidly moves its tail to and fro like a wagtail [Ael. *Nat. Anim.* 12.9]; cf. κιγκλίζω and LSJ s.v.).

left one sees an unidentifiable object on the floor, perhaps a ball of wool, a seated female *aulos*-player, and a female dancer of the *pyrrhikhê*, practically naked save for coverings wrapped around her loins and breasts. She is armed with spear and shield, but the usual helmet is missing. Her hair is therefore visible, surrounded by a band. Then there is a woman, who is clearly watching the performance. Next to her is a *kalathos* for the wool, beside which another woman is kneeling. Finally, we see a winged Eros and a water bird.[377] The wool-basket and the Eros refer to domestic life and sexuality in the marriage, for which maidens prepare under the influence of Athena. Another image shows a female dancer of the *pyrrhikhê*, who completely resembles her model, Athena, with a female *aulos*-player, whose presence indicates that this is a performance; behind, the Parthenon is represented in miniature.[378] Paola Ceccarelli in her study of the *pyrrhikhê* refers to an extremely interesting parallel. A later commentary on Aristotle's *Rhetoric* by the Byzantine grammarian Stephanus, probably written c. 1150 CE, mentions that apart from referring to the acrobatic weapons dance performed by soldiers "against and with swords," *pyrrhikhê* also designates a "dance with the σπάθη at wedding games."[379] Like the object named in the *pnigos*, σπάθη has a twofold meaning: it may mean either a sword with a long blade or a "flat wooden blade used by weavers in the upright loom (instead of the comb [κτείς] used in the horizontal), for striking the threads of the woof home, so as to make the web close."[380] Athena as goddess of weaving and war is able to embrace this polarity in the *pyrrhikhê*.[381]

---

[377] Ceccarelli 1998:60–62 discusses similar representations; for depictions of female dancers of the *pyrrhikhê* in general, see 60–67 therein.

[378] Bell krater Vienna 732, Pothos Painter, ca. 420 BCE (*ARV* 1190, 30; Poursat 1968: nr. 41, 592 ill. 45, Ceccarelli 1998: nr. 41, pl. XII with discussion pp. 65–66).

[379] Stephanus, *In Artem Rhetoricam commentaria* 3.8 (Arist. 1408b36) (in *Commentaria in Aristotelem Graeca* 21.2, p. 317 Rabe): πυρρίχη ἡ ἐνόπλιος, ᾗ χρῶνται οἱ στρατιῶται κατὰ ξιφῶν καὶ μετὰ ξιφῶν κυβιστῶντες καὶ οἱ ἐν ταῖς γαμηλίοις παιδιαῖς παίζοντες μετὰ σπάθης. See Ceccarelli 1998:63 and 208. For παίζειν and παιδιά as concepts belonging to choral dance, see above, Introduction n180.

[380] LSJ s.v. 1. Cf. also Aesch. *Cho.* 232 and Moret 1991:243n110. For a feminine sword dance cf. the red-figure depiction of a girl, attributed to the painter Makron, on a fragmentary vase (Malibu, J. P. Getty Museum 86.AE.315); see on this Bron 1996, who also views the scene in an initiatory context. While female dancers of the *pyrrhikhê* are consistently shown with shield and spear, the sword in this connection is practically unique.

[381] Ceccarelli 1998:207–208 also connects the passage in Stephanus of Byzantium with the κούρειον, the hair-offering made to Artemis by boys of ephebic age, and with the γαμηλία, which probably was a sacrifice performed on the day of the Koureotis during the Apatouria by the husband for his young wife upon her acceptance into his phratry. See on this Deubner 1932:232–234 and Parker 1996:105 with n12. Brulé 1987:402–404 interprets Pollux 8.107 differently and argues that the γαμηλία was a very early sacrifice made by the father in front of the phratry in honor of his daughter (aged 5 to 7) as future bride, and could have coincided with

This passage especially illustrates the ambivalence of homonymous signs and the symbolic polysemy in the central tableau of the *pnigos*. Here, too, there are men and women who in their dance concern themselves with objects that bear the same name and come from the fields of weaving and warfare. The κανών corresponds to the σπάθη. "Those who dance at wedding games with a sword/weaving rod" (οἱ ἐν ταῖς γαμηλίοις παιδιαῖς παίζοντες μετὰ σπάθης) correspond to the comically described men in the *makron* (*Thesm.* 824–829). After their successful initiation, women retain the objects that define their role. Men, however, give up the weaving instruments at the end of their dance, just as women give up the instruments of war. Only thus can the marriage they aspire to and the regulated education of the new generation in accordance with the idea of the Καλλιγένεια come about. But when men throw away the homonymous male instruments, then in terms of symbolic content they are men no longer, but are like women. The continued existence of the polis would also thereby be endangered. The structural similarity of the Athenian Thesmophoria and Amazon society, which is reenacted in the female *pyrrhikhê*, is described by Ken Dowden:

> This same pattern is exhibited, for instance, by the Athenian Thesmo-
> phoria: breaking off of sexual contact; segregation of the sexes;
> establishment of magistrates by the women as they take up resi-
> dence on the Pnyx (γυναικοκρατία). The Pnyx is not very far, either,
> from where the Amazons drew up their battle-lines—in front of the
> Areopagos, which mediates between Pnyx and Acropolis.[382]

The ambivalent construction of the *pyrrhikhê* and similar rites of transition also illuminates the comically distorted encroachment of women on the

---

her being entered into the list for the Arkteia. One could also simply call a wedding feast for the bridegroom a *gamêlia*. Bruit Zaidman/Schmitt Pantel 1992:70 remark that it is no coincidence that the ceremony took place exactly nine months after the marriage month, Gamelion, at the Apatouria, which concluded the legal act of marriage. According to Proclus' commentary on Plat. *Tim.* 21b, a rhapsodic contest among the young men took place on this day of the Koureotis; perhaps there were also choral dance competitions. Although the transitional phase would already have been concluded, the *pyrrhikhê* coming at the successful completion of the *rite de passage* would once more have evoked the dangers of marginality; see Lonsdale 1993:162ff. On the *koureion* see Cole 1984:233–238 and Schmitt 1977. The belt (see the depiction of a female dancer with belt on the Kanellopoulos pyxis; Schauenburg 1976:50 ill. 21, Ceccarelli 1998, nr. 72, pl. X) is also an ambivalent sign of masculine weaponry and feminine chastity; the dedication of the premarital belt is the symbolic act of preparation for marriage; Schmitt 1977:1062–1064. Women have to lose their first girdle in order to become a wife; after consummation of the marriage they wear the girdle of the married woman; men have to wear a belt as warrior. Ephebes receive the weapon belt as sign of their manhood.

[382] Dowden 1997:127.

areas of politics and warfare that was discussed in the immediately preceding section and that in the case of the *Lysistrata* defines its plot.[383]

Σπάθη has yet a third connotation. It is used synonymously with the word πλάτη, which refers to the broad, lower end of an oar (Lycoph. *Alex.* 23). Oarblades have a close connection to the *parabasis* of the *Thesmophoriazusae*, as we have seen. Immediately before this, the relative mentions them, playing on Euripides' *Palamedes* (770–773), but has to make do with sacred tablets from the sanctuary.[384] Just as the man in his imitation of a woman would like to cast a πλάτη into the sea, and finally does so, but using a different piece of wood, so too in the *pnigos* the chorus sings of men who lose their σπάθη, while women keep theirs safe.

The poet thus harnesses the symbolic polysemy of the *pyrrhikhê* and the objects that are swung during its performance. In the *pnigos* the members of the chorus in their role or the chorus leader alone reaffirm the ambivalence of women at the Thesmophoria,[385] who as νύμφαι reexperience the initiatory transitional stage. Standing between the worlds of man and woman, the members of the chorus may have imitated a weapon dance with their gestures and movements. The mixing of male and female realms, the comic theme of the whole *Thesmophoriazusae*, is underscored by the conscious blending in of the external communications context. Behind the female masks and costumes it is male performers who emerge and who in the *pnigos* sing of polyvalent objects. Possibly these were shaken in the air by some members of the chorus at the same time as the orgiastic movements of the *pyrrhikhê*. As Dionysiac group they simultaneously become Dionysiac dancers of the *pyrrhikhê*, a *kômos* of wild dancers, whose spears may be associated with the *thyrsos* or phallus.[386]

---

[383] See among others Rosellini 1979, Loraux 1981:157–196, Zeitlin 1981:169–181, Foley 1982 (also on *Eccl.*), Graf 1984 (on other ritual models, with reference to the *Lysistrata*, 245 and 254n59), and Bowie 1993:178–181, 205–207. Cf. in general Vernant 1990:29–53. On weaving as metaphor for integration into the "social fabric," i.e. the citizen body, see Calame 1997:57 with n145 and Ceccarelli 1998:111, 113, 149, and 157.

[384] See above, n344.

[385] On the participation of the whole chorus, see Koester 1835:6 and Hubbard 1991:20 with n21. Normally, however, no motion of the chorus is assumed when it sings. The association with weaving could also be understood as a self-referential reference to choral dance. On the chorus' weaving, cf. Nonnos' χοροπλεκής ('chorus-weaving') (Nonn. 6.49 and 14.33), Naerebout 1997:278–279, Calame I 1977:77–78 with n63 (Engl. trans. Calame 1997:34–35 with n63 [and 57 with n145]), Restani 1995 (on the relationship between music, dance, and weaving), Nagy 1996:65 (on weaving of song), and Ceccarelli 1998:111–112 with n104.

[386] On the symbolic and visual dimension of choral dance, see Golder 1996. Golder even goes so far as to describe individual poses by the chorus on the basis of the art of the day. The dance *skhêmata*, like synaesthetically translated *tableaux vivants*, intensify the symbolic message (esp. *ibid.*, 11). On the Dionysiac *pyrrhikhê*, cf. Athen. 631a–b and Ceccarelli 1998:67–72. On the

By means of the pointed reference to the shield the tableau may have triggered in the audience's mind a memory of the well-known *kômoi* of parasol-dancers depicted on contemporary vases. The Dionysiac performers, who overlay their male identity with feminine accessories and who through wine, dance, and music transport themselves into the ambivalent condition of otherness,[387] emerge from their female dramatic role, which is conversely overwritten with male signs. In this ambiguous border region of the contradictory definition of gender roles, role and function overlap in a comic way.

The ambivalent sign of the sunshade is connected, as has been seen, both with the Skira and with the Panathenaia, which has connections to the former. Aristophanes also draws on this symbol in the *Birds*. The Titan Prometheus approaches Peisetairos with a σκιάδειον to tell him the secret of how to depose Zeus. He asks him to hold the parasol over his head so that he may not be seen by Zeus (*Av.* 1508–1509).[388] He then takes up the parasol again and sets off, in order to give Zeus the impression that he is an attendant holding the parasol for a Kanêphoros at the Panathenaia (*Av.* 1550–1551).[389] In this scene one can recognize the rhythm of the Athenian cycle of the new year, and one sees the following elements in a comic reworking: the procession under the canopy at the Skira; the temporary inversion of the world; the threat to the Olympian cosmos;[390] the Promethia as model for the bringing of the new fire to the Pan-

---

performance by choruses of *pyrrhikhê* dancers in circles at the Dionysia on Kos (Segre 1993: ED 234), see Ceccarelli 1995. There is also a similarity in terms of rhythm and metre between the *pnigos* and the *pyrrhikhê*, whose most common form used the catalectic anapaestic dimeter with numerous resolutions and in terms of rhythm remained open to the dactylic in order to make use of the κατ' ἐνόπλιον (cf. Ceccarelli 1998:167–177). The catalectic anapaestic dimeter concludes the *pnigos* (*Thesm.* 829) with the central term τὸ σκιάδειον, which in line 823 already forms a monometer and is thus brought to the fore.

[387] Cf. Frontisi-Ducroux/Lissarrague 1990. They describe the *kômos* as a dance in which the collective acts in completely uncoordinated fashion and each carries out his own ecstatic movements (227).

[388] Bowie 1993:162 also sees in the *skiadeion* an allusion to the procession under the canopy at the Skira. On the parasol see also Dunbar *Birds*, 698 *ad* 1508–1509.

[389] Cf. the connection with the Panathenaia: Peisetairos ends the dialogue by adding that Prometheus should also take the δίφρος as *diphrophoros* (*Av.* 1552). Cf. Dunbar *Birds*, 709–710 *ad* 1550–1551 and 1552 with list of sources; Harpocr., s.v. σκαφηφόροι, quotes Demetrios of Phaleron (*FGrHist* 228 F 5), who thinks that according to a legal provision metics had to carry σκάφαι and their daughters water vessels (ὑδρεῖα) and parasols (σκιάδια); Ael. *VH* 6.1: τὰς γοῦν παρθένους τῶν μετοίκων σκιαδηφορεῖν ἐν ταῖς πομπαῖς ἠνάγκαζον [i.e. οἱ Ἀθηναῖοι]; cf. Pollux 3.55 and 7.174. In the following song by the chorus of birds about the realm of the Shadowfeet, the word σκιάδειον is possibly taken up by association (so already Rogers *Birds*, *ad. loc.*); cf. Dunbar *Birds*, 711 *ad* 1553–1555.

[390] The cutting off of the Olympians from their supply of sacrificial victims is additionally compared with fasting at the Thesmophoria (*Av.* 1519).

athenaia; finally, the return to order at the great festival of Athena accompanied by the victory over the Titans.[391] Immediately before this parasol scene, in a song (*Av.* 1470–1493) in which the chorus of birds tells of the wonders seen on its flights, the Kleonymos tree, which loses its shields, and an exchange of blows with Orestes, the ephebe *par excellence*, are at the center. Prometheus, like Kleonymos and Orestes, acts with cunning and in the dark, in a marginal world of fantasy and the horror of the realm of shadows. These sign complexes express the symbolically comparable transitions of the new year and initiation. Kleonymos also seems to lose his shield in a weapon dance (*Av.* 1481).[392] Orestes, who is here comically confounded with the contemporary clothes-thief of the same name (*Av.* 712), operates, as in Euripides' *Andromache*, by lying in ambush in the dark and, like Prometheus, under something that provides shade (cf. Eur. *Andr.* 1115, σκιασθείς);[393] whosoever encounters the hero Orestes at night is surprised by a blow to his right side and stripped naked. The formulation in Greek γυμνὸς ἦν πληγεὶς ὑπ' αὐτοῦ | πάντα τἀπὶ δεξιά (*Av.* 1492–1493) is reminiscent of a possible duel in the *pyrrhikhê*. The initiate fights naked, as does the dancer of the *pyrrhikhê*, during the phase of marginality and with his shield attempts to ward off the spearthrusts of his opponent by lunging to the left and right. But Orestes still hits him on the right, all over his side.[394]

---

[391] On the Panathenaia as festival of the new fire, see Robertson 1985; on the Promethia as an original procession by torchlight that departed from an altar in the Akademia and served as the model for the torchlight run at the Panathenaia, Robertson 1985:259–260 and 281–288.

[392] For Kleonymos as "shield-abandoner" see the testimonia in Dunbar *Birds*, 238 *ad* 289–290.

[393] See above, n372. Prometheus goes underneath a parasol (cf. Dunbar *Birds*, 695 *ad* 1494–1509) and is also "wrapped up" (συγκαλυμμός, *Av.* 1496; cf. ἐκκεκαλύψομαι, *Av.* 1503) (see Agosti 1987/88). For a good mythical and ritual interpretation of the *Birds*, see Auffarth 1994 (he connects the comedy, as Craik 1987 already does, with the Anthesteria and interprets Prometheus as a trickster figure [76ff.]); cf. also Bowie 1993:151–177.

[394] I reproduce here Coulon's text. Cf. the quite different interpretation of Dunbar *Birds*, 692–693 *ad* 1490–1493. With MSS. AMS she reads τἀπιδέξια, "paralysed all down his right side," and connects this with attacks by certain heroes who could give their opponents a stroke (so also Hofmann 1976:205); in Ar. *Heroes* fr. 322, esp. 4–7 K.-A., they release as ταμίαι | τῶν κακῶν καὶ τῶν ἀγαθῶν (4–5) all manner of illnesses upon evildoers (such as κλέπτας καὶ λωποδύτας, 6; cf. *Thesm.* 810–818, esp. λωποδύτας, 817). On the question of whether the figure of Orestes (as in *Ach.* 1162ff. and *Av.* 712) is meant to be the mythical hero of the festival of Khoes or a historical and notorious highwayman, see Hofmann 1976:200–206, who wants to separate the two figures and sees in this Orestes "einen ganz und gar unheroischen Wegelagerer, der dank seines mythologischen Gattungsnamens zum Heros emporstilisiert wird" ["a completely unheroic highwayman who owing to his mythological generic name is elevated to the status of hero"] (205). With Henrichs 1991:192n67, I assume a comic and associative overlapping of both figures. One could also understand lines 1492–1493 in the following way: "unprotected all down his right side, he was hit by him," or: "completely naked/unprotected, he was hit by him with a blow to the right" (perhaps also "on the right side," ἐπὶ δεξιᾷ). On nudity in the *pyrrhikhê*, cf. Ar. *Nub.* 989 and Ceccarelli 1998:49 and 51–52.

The catalogue of elements that the ritual and festival prescribe for the polis reflects the whole span of disintegration and refoundation from the Skira to the Panathenaia. The decomposition and restoration of fertility at the Thesmophoria, which has to do with agriculture and human sexuality, are thematically enriched by references to the upcoming festival cycle, which synchronizes the three paradigms of agriculture, initiation, and new year. The temporary return to the stage of being a girl on the threshold of adulthood is connected with the Skira, Arrhephoria, and Panathenaia, at which young men and women are confronted with initiation rites. Overcoming the period of inversion is the goal of the ritual complexes. The marginal phase of separation culminates in the unification of both sexes. At the Panathenaia the completion of the girls' and boys' initiation is celebrated by a meeting of choruses at which contacts arise that lead to marriage, the ultimate goal. The temporary isolation of the sexes at the Thesmophoria and the playing out of a primeval *gynokratia* that threatens the world of men come to a conclusion with the Kalligeneia and the reinstatement of the normal order and with the return of women to their *oikos*. They are underscored by the above-mentioned rites from the realm of Athena, which structurally anticipate the Thesmophoria.

The key themes of the play—the absence of role identity, the marginal area between man and woman, the phenomena of transvestism and mimesis, as well as the dissolution of order—are illuminated by means of further rites drawn from the real world. The *Thesmophoriazusae* reflects the central questions of the polis ideology, which are also dealt with in ritual. The reversal of all codes in ritual play and the chaotic mixing up of all structures are preconditions for coming to know the prevailing values and norms. Under the auspices of Dionysus, at whose spring festivals the normal world also becomes perverted, the polis enacts the critical transitions of new year, harvest time and change of status in summer (June to August), and the decisive turning-point in autumn, when the sowing of crops determines hunger or nourishment, death or survival.[395]

[395] In the case of the *pyrrhikhê*, beside the aspects of initiation, which stands unequivocally in the foreground, and of the new year, which is completely peripheral, the increase of agricultural fertility can also be observed. In the description of the six weapon dances performed by Xenophon's soldiers at a reception for Paphlagonian messengers (*Anabasis* 6.1.5–13), in second place comes the harvest dance (καρπαία) of the contingents from Ainis and Magnesia. The mimetic dance concerns a confrontation between a robber and a farmer, who defends himself while he is sowing and plowing with a team of oxen (Xen. *Anab.* 6.1.7–9). All six presentations are staged by people from Greek marginal areas and represent to a certain extent only a marginal Greekness; the performance of the Thracians, that of the Ainians and Magnesians (i.e. Thessalians), both dances by the Mysian, and the entry of the people from Mantineia and Arcadia culminate in the *pyrrhikhê* danced by a slave-girl owned by an Arcadian. Cf. Ceccarelli 1998:20–21.

On the basis of these heortological connections, the invocation of gods such as Athena, Poseidon, Artemis, Pan, the Nymphs, and Hera—who at first glance have little to do with Demeter and Kore, the controlling deities of the Thesmophoria—becomes understandable. Athena and Poseidon are connected with these goddesses at the Skira.[396] The central position afforded Athena next to Demeter and Kore is not explained solely by her function as polis deity *par excellence.* Up until now the mention of her name has generally been seen only in connection with the overlapping of male and female discourses, in which the chorus of women assume a political position as popular assembly. The political intervention of the chorus as male group of performers in the here and now has also been discussed in this chapter.[397] Yet Athena is also of central importance from a cultic and inner-dramatic point of view, since she, like Artemis (though the latter is situated on the periphery, unlike Athena), as eternal and armed virgin represents the initiatory model for girls (and youths) during the transition to marriage.[398] Weaving and choral dance are preparations for married life, which is ritually celebrated in the Thesmophoria, during which mothers would temporarily experience the ambivalent transition phase in an imaginary sense.[399] The swaddled baby Erichthonius as rebirth of the dead Erechtheus is the mythic exemplum for the male initiate who attains manhood at the Panathenaia. The rite of the Arrhephoria is in symbolic play form a representative initiation of prepubescent girls into the mysteries of sexuality

---

[396] See above, p. 204 and Deubner 1932:47.

[397] Camps-Gaset 1994:140–142 particularly stresses the political character of the Thesmophoria, in the sense of the conveying of Athenian citizenship. Before marriage, she emphasizes, it is Athena who protects the citizen status of girls. Demeter takes over this function after marriage: "En revanche, les fêtes de Déméter représentent la confirmation—et l'affirmation—de ce statut civique qui comporte la sécurité et la garantie pour la cité qu'il y aura toujours des Athéniens et que la femme—ce mal ambigu, donné par les dieux—se maintient dans un ordre civilisé, celui d'Athéna et de Poseidon, celui de la famille et de la sexualité légitime" ["On the other hand, the festivals of Demeter represent the confirmation—and the affirmation—of the civic status that means security and the guarantee for the city that it will always have Athenians and that women—that ambiguous evil given by the gods—will abide by the civilized order, that of Athena and Poseidon, that of the family and lawful sexuality"] (142).

[398] Certain commentators in fact insist on the idea that the Thesmophoria was also a festival of initiation; see Jeanmaire 1939:269–282, 296–307, Johansen 1975, Lincoln 1979, and Baudy 1992:24 with n132; now also Kledt 2004:114–147, esp. 115–120. For a critical discussion of the initiation theory, see Versnel 1993:253–254 with n88. Sfameni Gasparro 1986:280–283, esp. 282, sums up the state of affairs: she thinks it is in fact incorrect to speak of an actual initiation in the case of the Thesmophoria, but that there are clear typological analogies to initiation throughout. See above, n75.

[399] Pan is connected with these rites of Athena through the cave of Pan on the precipitous north face of the Acropolis, down which the Arrhephoroi descended with their baskets. Cf. Eur. *Ion* 492–494.

and agriculture. The Erichthonius baskets form the model for the plant beds through which the functions of sowing, harvest, procreation, and birth are experienced in a preparatory fashion.[400] These contents are then confirmed by the married women at the Thesmophoria. It is thus not surprising that the last song of the chorus in the *Thesmophoriazusae* (1136–1159) is directed at Athena and the goddesses of the Thesmophoria, for Athena also has connections with marriage. When a girl married, at the Proteleia she was taken one more time by her parents to the Acropolis, where they would perform a sacrifice for Athena.[401]

The *Helen* and *Andromeda Paratragôidia* and the Subsequent Plot from an Initiatory Perspective

In the previous section we examined how the plot depends on a development that leads, in harmony with the fictional framework of the separation of the sexes and their undefined condition, to the unification and reestablishment of the differentiation of roles. After the *parabasis*, the relative attempts to escape from his hopeless situation by an imitation of the Euripidean *Helen*, because he thinks that the successful rescue of this heroine by Menelaos from the hands of the Egyptian barbarian Theoklymenos may serve him as a plan of action. He therefore takes on her role in order to be brought to safety by her husband, a role which Euripides plays. This richly comic scheme, reminiscent of the cunning of an initiate,[402] ultimately has to fail, like the relative's attempt to be rescued by staging the situation of the *Andromeda*. The intertextual interplay of quotations from the two Euripidean tragedies, which were performed a year previously, in 412 BCE, has a parodic effect, the comic side of which has been thoroughly explored.[403]

---

[400] Cf. Baudy 1986:9–48 and Baudy 1992:31–40.

[401] Suda, s.v. Προτέλεια· ἡμέραν οὕτως ὀνομάζουσιν, ἐν ᾗ εἰς τὴν ἀκρόπολιν τὴν γαμουμένην παρθένον ἄγουσιν οἱ γονεῖς εἰς τὴν θεὸν καὶ θυσίας ἐπιτελοῦσι. According to Deubner 1932:16 it remains questionable whether by "goddess" Artemis is meant. After a wedding the priestess of Athena visited the newly married wife (Suda, s.v. αἰγίς). At the birth of a child the priestess received a *khoinix* of barley, a *khoinix* of wheat, and an obol—likewise when an inhabitant died. On other connections between Athena and the blessing of marriage and child, see Deubner 1932:16–17. The connection with agriculture is further attested by the Prokharisteria. At the end of winter, when the grain began to sprout, this sacrifice, associated with the return of Kore (see Suda, s.v. Προχαριστήρια), was made to Athena.

[402] Cf. μηχανορράφος, Eur. *Andr.* 1116; on cunning and deception in initiation, see Vidal-Naquet 1968:111–113, 120 (*PCPS* n.s. 14 [194] [1968], 53–54, 61–62), Moreau 1992:210–211, and Bierl 1994a:89–90 with 154–155 nn47–50.

[403] Cf. Rau 1967:53–65 (*Helen* parody), 65–89 (*Andromeda* parody). On parody of the four Euripidean

The ritual implications of these two parodies, however, have so far only been analyzed to a small extent; Froma Zeitlin has referred to the connection of ritual and drama in the *Thesmophoriazusae* in an important study in which she outlines to what extent the two tragedies can be related in terms of their deep structure to the two goddesses important for the Thesmophoria, Demeter and Persephone.[404] The transformation of the figure of Helen into faithful wife is especially connected to the ideology of the Thesmophoria, and here Zeitlin introduces as evidence the explicit connections between Helen and Persephone (Eur. *Hel.* 175, 244ff.) and the blending of the central myth of Demeter and Kore into the choral song addressed to the Great Mother (*Hel.* 1301–1368).[405] She notes that Andromeda especially underscores the theme of the maiden Kore. As far as can be determined from Zeitlin's nuanced presentation—she reads the comedy as well as its mythical background mainly as an expression of marginality, as a metatheatrical or even metaritual statement about the threshold between festival and theater, Dionysus and Demeter, tragedy and comedy, man and woman—she does not draw any clear connection to the transitional phase between maidenhood and womanhood in female initiation rites.[406] The construction of the Aristophanic plot has an effect, as we have seen, not only on the central myth, which is connected with the ritual

---

dramas *Telephos, Palamedes, Helen,* and *Andromeda,* see Zeitlin 1981:181–194. She remarks that the relative plays a masculine role in women's clothing in the first two scenes, while after the *parabasis* he assumes feminine roles and thereby ultimately entices Euripides for the desired *sotêria*; Zeitlin (1981:182) interprets the "successive insertion" of parodies as "metatheatrical variants" of the comic intruders who are ridiculed and driven out by the comic hero. See now also Tzanetou 2002:339–351.

[404] Zeitlin 1981:194–200. Gruber 1986 (esp. 14 [study of situations of social conflict], 19–20 [threshold situation and "metatheater"], and 37 [playing out of conflicts between the sexes in the *Thesmophoriazusae*]) and Bowie 1993:205–227 are extensively based on Zeitlin's findings. On the "metatheatricality" of the *Thesmophoriazusae,* see also Bonanno 1990:256–261 (on the *Helen* and *Andromeda*) and Bierl 1991:172–176. Bowie 1993:212–217 emphasizes the myth of Demeter and Kore as reference model; he does not go into other heortological connections. He treats (*ibid.,* 215) the relative as a comic Persephone, and sees Persephone's role as divided between the dancer Teredon (sic!) and the relative, who is freed by Euripides in the form of Demeter (216). See now also Tzanetou 2002:339–359.

[405] Zeitlin 1981:199. On Eur. *Hel.* 1301–1368 see Bierl 1991:163–172. On Helen as Kore/Persephone see Guépin 1968:120–122, 128–133, 137–142 and Foley 1992.

[406] Disputes about ritual, in particular the relationship of the Kore myth to initiation (also in the reception of theories in Bowie 1993:205–227) are simply not discussed further in Zeitlin 1981. See, however, her contemporaneous piece (Zeitlin 1982), which concentrates on ritual and in which the structural and dialectic connection of the Thesmophoria to the Arrhephoria is discussed (150–153). Harrison 1922³:131 already calls the Arrhephoria "the Thesmophoria of the unmarried girl." On the contested initiatory interpretation of the Thesmophoria, see above, nn75 and 398; on the myth of Persephone in the sense of a female initiation and as aetiology for the Thesmophoria and Haloa, see Lincoln 1979. See now also Kledt 2004:34–36, 38–57.

in the plot, but, as in the other comedies, further mythical and ritual references arrange themselves about the center. In associative fashion individual elements are isolated, reassembled, and linked to a complex plot.

In what follows the theme of the threshold state, so important for the *Thesmophoriazusae*, will be connected with the liminal state in the ritual process of female and male initiation. This critical phase becomes, as we have seen, a *Leitmotiv* in this comedy, since the married women project themselves back to their former status of *nymphai*. In the *tableau vivant* of the *parabasis* (821-829) the chorus strikingly realizes these connections in the form of image and dance.

As long as Euripides' relative as comic hero is provided with the external signs of the female sex, he is located in a transitional stage between clearly defined roles. He may be compared metaphorically with Erichthonius, the ephebe *par excellence*, whose *rite de passage* is connected with the ceremonies under discussion and is concluded at the Panathenaia.[407] The mortal dangers, torments, and enchainment comically reenact the symbolic death of the initiate and his rebirth as fully adult man; on the level of myth it is thus possible to associate the relative's fate with the death of Erechtheus and his renewal as Erichthonius.

In order to be able to infiltrate the women's festival, the man has to put on women's clothing. Yet this mimesis, as in the case of the comic chorus, is further complicated. While playing this additional role the performer remains present for the audience in the original role. Agathon, who rejects the defense of Euripides, although as effeminate figure he would be suited for this, combines male and female indications, like the hero after his dressing-up scene. The question the astonished relative asks in reaction to the appearance of Agathon, "What on earth have a mirror and a sword to do with each other?" (τίς δαὶ κατόπτρου καὶ ξίφους κοινωνία; 140), is of importance for the image under discussion in the *parabasis* (821-829). The combination of objects

---

[407] The *Telephus* parody, together with the abduction of the baby, may also be connected with this; the relative while still in his role as woman parodies the role of the man Telephos; he wants to steal the baby Orestes (the model for male initiation), who is here in the women's festival presented as a girl, but turns out to be a wineskin (*Thesm.* 733-734: ἀσκὸς ἐγένεθ' ἡ κόρη | οἴνου πλέως), which is finally sacrificed. Here all levels of meaning have been comically inverted. As Arrhêphoros he steals the "female" baby Erichthonius, whom the hero, as he undergoes initiation and oscillates in the liminal space between Orestes and Kore, finally himself becomes. The diachronic structure and relations have become distorted. On wine at the Thesmophoria, or at the analogous Roman festival of Bona Dea, see Versnel 1993:262-268. The abduction has so far generally been read as a reflex of the abduction of Kore; Zeitlin 1981:197.

corresponds exactly to the paradoxical combination of the sexes. In this line (140) the general state of liminality in this comedy is condensed into a symbol through these two contrary objects.

This motif emphasizes the liminality of the transition from youth to adulthood in what follows. The married relative leaves wife and child behind and assumes Agathon's womanly accessories in order to play his female role. In so doing, he resembles Agathon and young men undergoing initiation, who in the phase of separation from their previous condition decorate themselves with both male and female signifiers. In this way he also resembles structurally the women celebrating the Thesmophoria, who, conversely, as married women project themselves back to the transitional phase of being a bride and thereby also temporarily combine elements of male and female discourse.

The feminine saffron-colored robe, a ritual tunic designed to emphasize the beauty and sexual radiance of the young woman with its dazzling color, here plays an important role. The beautiful and alluring costume stands therefore in diametric contrast to the precept of chastity, to which the virgins are subjected in accordance with the expectations of the men. The κροκωτός thus symbolizes a profound sexual ambivalence and the condition of abnormal inversion.[408] The relative receives the κροκωτός of Agathon (253; cf. 138), who according to Hansen and Zeitlin is celebrating a private Thesmophoria.[409] In accordance with its ritual polysemy this yellow garment characterizes Mnesilokhos as a follower of Demeter, as a girl in the service of Artemis Brauronia, and as a fellow Dionysiac player.[410]

In this passage, however—and contrary to the approach of Zeitlin and Bowie—it is the aspect of preparation for marriage and the motif of the initiatory isolation of prepubescent girls at Brauron that should in particular be emphasized. This sojourn on the periphery of Attica in honor of Artemis goes hand in hand with the representative initiatory service of the two Arrhêphoroi on the Acropolis. In the famous section of the *parabasis* in *Lysistrata* 642–647, both these cults are combined with other rites involving young girls. The service of a girl who is there called ἀλετρίς evokes Demeter and the Thesmophoria, the goal of female fertility, and once more indicates the struc-

---

[408] See Sourvinou-Inwood 1988:128, in general 119–135.

[409] See Hansen 1976:170 and Zeitlin 1981:196.

[410] On Dionysus and the *krokôtos* see above, n168; on Dionysus in women's clothing, see Kenner 1970:119n460 and Bremmer 1992:189–194 (in connection with initiation, 194–198). On Artemis and the girls at Brauron wearing the *krokôtos*, see Sourvinou-Inwood 1988:119–135. On Demeter and saffron, see Bowie 1993:215n51.

tural connection between preparation for marriage and revisiting of this transitional phase at the Thesmophoria.[411]

After the relative has been revealed as a male intruder, he then, as a man dressed in the feminine *krokôtos*, plays the role of two Euripidean heroes, Telephos and Oiax, in order to induce Euripides to intervene. But Euripides does not react to this. He is obviously waiting for a signal from a female figure, seeing that it is female figures who determine the action in his romantic rescue tragedies.

The chorus at this point performs its *parabasis*, in which the position of the women is laid out. The central *tableau vivant* paradoxically combines the male and female realms in the dance of the *pyrrhikhê*. It is only after this that the comic hero tries out his imitation of Helen (τὴν καινὴν Ἑλένην μιμήσομαι, 850) because he becomes aware of his feminine attire (γυναικεία στολή, 851). In Euripides' version she is the epitome of the faithful wife. Because of her abduction by Paris she has become separated from her husband, Menelaos. For ten years she lives a life of chastity in Egypt, while her *eidôlon*, the symbol of a wicked and lascivious woman, resides in Troy. The relative responds to the ideology of the Thesmophoria through this splitting up and separation of the negative component of the female. He has been asked previously in the assembly why it is that Euripides enjoys putting female monsters like Phaidra or Melanippe on the stage, but never figures like the chaste Penelope as we know her from Homer (547–548; cf. also the misogynous reply at 549–550). Yet even a Penelope has her negative side, for in another tradition she is characterized as a *hetaira* and prostitute.[412] The women naturally prefer to remain silent about this.

With his *Helen*, Euripides placed just such an exemplary wife in the center, completely brushing away all her morally questionable characteristics in the mythic tradition. Theoklymenos states after the intervention of the Dioskouroi that Helen is without doubt the best and purest woman (ἀρίστης σωφρονεστάτης θ' ἅμα, Eur. *Hel.* 1684) and presents an extremely noble mind

---

[411] On *Lys.* 642 (or 641)–647, see esp. Sourvinou-Inwood 1988:136–152, on the ἀλετρίς, 142–146. On the basis of the scholia this office is normally associated with Athena (Brelich 1969:238–240 and Henderson *Lys.*, 156 *ad* 643–644).

[412] In Lycoph. *Alex.* 771–773 Penelope is described as a whore (ἡ δὲ βασσάρα, | σεμνῶς κασωρεύουσα, 771–772). According to Duris of Samos, *FGrHist* 76 F 21 (= schol. Lycoph. *Alex.* 772), she gives herself to all the suitors and so gives birth to the shady god Pan (already in Pind. fr. 100 S.-M. he is the result of the union between Apollo and Penelope; according to Hdt. 2.145–144 her sexual partner is Hermes). Tzetzes attempts to rationalize away the negative characterization by going on to say in the scholion that this was about another Penelope (Πηνελόπης ἄλλης). As in the case of Helen, the contradiction experienced as a paradox in the Greek image of women is here done away with by means of a doubling. On Penelope see Papadopoulou-Belmehdi 1994 and Ceccarelli 1995a:181.

(εὐγενεστάτης | γνώμης, Eur. *Hel.* 1686-1687). Both Penelope and Helen, whom the relative now embodies, thus correspond precisely to the ideal of the married women at the Thesmophoria, who refer to themselves as "well-born women" (εὐγενεῖς γυναῖκες, *Thesm.* 330).[413] Her ambivalent appearance on the stage and in life is determined by, among other things, the male perspective. In completely similar fashion to Penelope in Homer's *Odyssey*, Helen is purified by Euripides and stylized into an incarnation of all that is pure and positive, while the tragic poet projects the objectionable part of the Helen figure onto a phantom-like false double.

Helen is not only a reflex of Persephone, the main figure in the central mythologeme of the Thesmophoria, but also a heroine responsible in Spartan cult for the initiation of young girls, which Euripides also emphasizes in his tragedy.[414] At the end of the play, the chorus in a *propemptikon* imagines Helen after her return to Sparta. In its vision, she dances a nocturnal dance with the Leukippidai, who also represent a model of female youth just before marriage,[415] and Hyakinthos, in front of the temple of Athena Khalkioikos. Here the members of the chorus in typical fashion project their own current activity onto the Spartan ritual choral dance (Eur. *Hel.* 1465-1470). Helen is connected in the rite with the festive marriage of girls, with which the critical

---

[413] Des Bouvrie 1990:289-313 interprets the tragedy as the " 'symbolic' establishment of marriage, marital fidelity and female chastity" (313). In her opinion, Dionysiac tragedy dissolves the institution of marriage; *anagnôrisis* brings the separated partners together once more, and the successful flight to Sparta refounds the marriage.

[414] Foley 1992, following Zeitlin, explores connections between Helen as she appears in Euripides' play and Persephone and the cult of Demeter, while at the same time also viewing Helen as a figure of initiation (145-146). On Helen's initiatory function see Calame I 1977:333-350, 354-357, 443, 447 (Engl. trans. Calame 1997:191-202, 204-206, 260, 262). For Helen as *khorêgos* who outshines her companions because her initiation has been concluded, see Calame I 1977:92, 127n170, 136, 345-346, 397-398 (Engl. trans. Calame 1997:42-43, 65n170, 70, 199, 229-230). Theocr. *Id.* 18 gives an *aition* for a Spartan tree cult in which maidens celebrate Helen; Gow II 1950/52:358 *ad* 43-48. At Platanistas on the Eurotas Helen was celebrated with a running race and dances as the embodiment of a maiden who has completed the initiatory phase and is ready for marriage; in Therapne, however, the aspect of the married woman and goddess had central place; her husband Menelaos was also honored there; cf. Calame I 1977:333-350 (Engl. trans. Calame 1997:191-202) and Larson 1995:80-81.

[415] See Kannicht II 1969:381-383 and Calame I 1977:323-333 (Engl. trans. Calame 1997:185-191); Larson 1995:64-69 has reservations about this theory (esp. 67-68) and thinks that the cult of the Leukippidai had to do with the initiation not of maidens but of ephebes. Penelope (mentioned in *Thesm.* 547-550) like Helen fluctuates between the faithful wife and the chaste virgin who prepares herself for marriage; the weaving of the *peplos* and her scheme in the *Odyssey* (Hom. *Od.* 19.137ff.) can be linked with the activity of the *ergastinai*. On the trick at the loom and on Penelope's name see Hölscher 1989²:46 and 325n6; see also Brulé 1987:35, 116, 344; for a connection between the Leukippidai and ritual weaving, the manufacture of a *khitôn* for Apollo in Amyklai as preparation for the Hyakinthia, see Paus. 3.16.2 and Pettersson 1992:40.

transition phase of the ritual process of initiation comes to a successful end. The *telos* of the days of the women's festival and the choral dances at night in the month of Pyanopsion also represents marriage and the confirmation of marriage as cultural institution. Just like the women at the Thesmophoria, Helen thus unites the condition of the married woman and the young bride just before marriage.

The same semantic ambiguity also marks the relative: he is married and only temporarily separated from his wife, yet returns to the liminal state of initiation when he assumes his role. This marginal state together with the assumption of feminine markers predestines him for the role of Helen.[416] In view of the lack of so-called illusion, the relative oscillates between various identities. The spectator is confronted with a *mise en abyme* that has mimesis in the theater as its theme. As Helen, the relative becomes a player who is yet one step further removed from the staged reality of the Thesmophoria plot, which is why Kritylla refuses to play along in the role of Theonoe and the rescue ultimately fails.[417] The removal of the separation of the sexes and the bringing together of man and woman as goal of the festival of Demeter cannot be achieved here since the assembly of the ritual, which is articulated along structurally similar lines, does not correspond to the comically enacted reworking thereof. Ultimately it emerges that this Helen is a man. The point of the joke lies in the fact that in this second level of tragic mimesis the tension

---

[416] On the one hand Helen and Menelaos are a married couple; on the other, the plot as mythical preparation for marriage leads toward the successful completion of female initiation. The barbarian locale of Egypt refers to the condition of marginality. The streams of the Nile are significantly referred to as καλλιπάρθενοι, "virgin-beautiful" (*Thesm.* 855). Perhaps the cultic Helen could also renew her virginity symbolically, as she does in Euripides; on Helen's *loutron* cf. Paus. 2.2.3 and Foley 1992:158n71. The καλλιπάρθενοι ῥοαί (*Thesm.* 855) are possibly an allusion to this. In Eur. *Hel.* 543 Helen regards herself as δρομαία πῶλος ἢ Βάκχη θεοῦ when she sees Menelaos for the first time; cf. Ar. *Lys.* 1307, and for the filly as metaphor for young woman undergoing initiation, see Calame I 1977:340, 411–420 (Engl. trans. Calame 1997:195, 238–244), Henderson *Lys.*, 221 *ad* 1307–1308, and Versnel 1993:278n168. The comparison with a bacchant could come from the Dionysiadai, who are connected with the Leukippidai; cf. Calame I 1977:323–333 (Engl. trans. Calame 1997:185–191); the priestesses of the Leukippidai, also termed πῶλοι, are associated with Dionysos Kolonatas. On the role of Dionysus in initiation, see Foley 1992:157n62 and Seaford 1988:124–128. On the metaphor of taming the woman through the act of marriage, as if she were a wild beast, see the collection of verbs in Seaford 1987:111. This idea reflects the fundamental ambivalence of women, whose wild side is domesticated by marriage; see Versnel 1993:276–288.

[417] On the role of the maidenly Theonoe, who represents the righteous matter of marital fidelity, see des Bouvrie 1990:311–312. As Nereus' granddaughter she is just as maidenly as the Nereids and Nymphs (cf. *Thesm.* 325–326) who serve as a model for the chorus. Kritylla is however completely grounded in the reality of the festival; her role as *thesmophoriazousa* who is temporarily taken back to maidenhood is of course completely identical to the status of Theonoe.

between the male identity of an actor and the female identity of the role also remains constantly present.

The scene imitates the recognition of a separated married couple. The successful rescue of the "wife" would correspond to a new wedding. Despite the failure of the plan on the level of the comic plot, the successful end of the comedy, which has to coincide with the end of the ritual in the fictional context, is already being prepared for. As the embodiment of seductive beauty, Helen stands, as do the women at the Thesmophoria and the relative, between Artemis, goddess of the liminal transitional phase, and Aphrodite, Hera, and Demeter, the goddesses of consummated marriage.[418]

The scene is rudely broken off by the entry of the prytanis summoned by Kleonymos, who orders his Scythian policeman-henchman to fasten the offender to a wooden board and to guard him. This intervention reflects the

[418] See Calame I 1977:344–345 (Engl. trans. Calame 1997:198–199). In terms of his second level of identity as male ephebe, the relative is also associated through the Spartan perspective with the Spartan cycle of the Hyakinthia/Gymnopaidia and Karneia. The festive cycle is comparable to the Athenian new year cycle in July/August; in particular, the central *khoreia* may be compared with the current performance of the Athenian citizens. At the Hyakinthia, choral dance served as preparation for marriage and the selection of a bride (Polykrates, *FGrHist* 588 F 1, cited in Athen. 139c–f); at the Gymnopaidia, it is a symbolic expression using body language of the marginality of the transitional phase (Plat. *Leg.* 633c, Plut. *Ages.* 29.2–3, Paus. 3.11.9); at the Karneia, by contrast, the activity of the chorus members underscores renewal (Eur. *Alc.* 445–451) and collective marriage (choruses of men and women dance together in Cyrene; Callim. *Hymn.* 2.71–87). On the festive cycle on Sparta, see Pettersson 1992, passim, esp. on choral dance at the Gymnopaidia, 45–55; at the Karneia, 77. Athenaeus (631b) says the *gymnopaidikê* was performed naked and that variations thereof represented oschophoric and Bacchic dances. This form is thus ultimately traceable back to Dionysus, the god of comic performance. For choral dance as expression of initiation, see Calame I 1977:439–449 (Engl. trans. Calame 1997:258–263), Harrison 1927[2]:23–25, Jeanmaire 1939:182ff., 531–540, Brelich 1969:32, 38–39, 75n71, 94n128, 108n152, 139–140, 171–173, 187–191, Moreau 1992:208–210, and Pettersson 1992:48–51. Among others *neaniskoi* danced at the Hyakinthia. The *eirenes* (twenty-year-olds) received a red cloak and a shield (!) as token of their new military status (Xen. *Lac.* 11.3). The mimesis of Helen with the emphasis on feminine characteristics points to the fact that, on the fictional level at least, the transgressions of women into the preserve of the male warrior (*pyrrhikhê*) are thereby overcome and the women at the Thesmophoria now concentrate solely on imminent wedding as the aim of the comedy and of the festival. Pettersson 1992:38–40 also connects the Hyakinthia with female initiation rites: he associates the triad Demeter-Kore-Pluto on the altar at Amyklai, as described by Pausanias (3.19.3–5), with Polyboia's transition from the status of maiden to adult (death of the maiden!). He interprets Hyakinthos as Polyboia's father; he then plays a similar role to Kepheus in Andromeda's initiation. The *gymnopaidikê* as well as the *pyrrhikhê* were of course also performed in Athens. According to Athen. 630e, the *gymnopaidikê* is comparable with the tragic *emmeleia* because of its ceremonial and solemn movements. This means that in tragic parodies the initiatory hero is brought close to the tragic mode of dance. The chorus is also drawn into the tragic sphere through its interaction with the hero.

interest of the polis in having the course of the festival undisturbed. Kritylla applauds this intrusion by the state and comments that an ἀνὴρ ... ἱστιορράφος (934–935) almost snatched the relative away from under her nose when she was watching over him. This man is Euripides, of course. The polysemy of this epithet has passed almost unnoticed. The scholia (schol. *Thesm.* 935) connect it with Egypt, the setting of the *Helen* plot, where linen and papyrus were in fact produced. Euripides/Menelaos would accordingly be a miserable Egyptian. Van Leeuwen sees in this passage yet another comic allusion to the epithet μηχανορράφος.[419] Euripides' μηχανή is paralleled by the μηχανή of the ephebe, who thereby himself becomes sewer/weaver. The "sail" in fact has ritual connotations as well, which allude to the weaving of the sail for the Panathenaia. Through his intrusion into feminine space Euripides is also brought under the spell of feminine signs.[420]

Even the relative's plea to the prytanis to be tied to the board naked, as opposed to in his saffron costume, is not an incidental or unplanned touch (939–942). Rather, the theme of female intiation is thereby underscored through the mention of the ritual saffron-colored clothing, which becomes a key motif in the plot.[421] As has already been seen above, the saffron garment is a symbolic signal of the maiden in the transitional stage of becoming a woman, particularly in the cult of Artemis Brauronia. The sexually attractive clothing symbolically prepares the virgin for marriage and sexuality.[422] The end of the preparation and segregation phase of the Arkteia is marked by the celebratory throwing off of the garment. The act of presenting oneself naked indicates a definitive turning point in the life of the girl. At the same time, the surrendering of her body to her husband on the wedding night is thereby anticipated and practiced.[423] The relative's plea to be bound naked is thus also a reference

---

[419] Van Leeuwen *Thesm.*, 121 *ad* 935. Sommerstein *Thesm.*, 217 *ad* 935 further interprets "a sail-stitching fellow" as a shabby man dressed in sailcloth stitched together in makeshift fashion. Presumably he has in mind Euripidean figures such as Telephos.

[420] The reference to Egypt in the scholion to *Thesm.* 935 could also be connected with the inverted world there as described by Hdt. 2.35. The women go to the agora, while the men sit at the loom. This corresponds precisely to the upside-down world of comedy, of the ritual attached to the Thesmophoria, and to states of inversion during initiation.

[421] Cf. *Thesm.* 138, 253, 941, 945, 1044, and 1220.

[422] Sourvinou-Inwood 1988:127–130.

[423] Sourvinou-Inwood 1988:130–134; she refers to the parallels in *Lys.* 644–645 (in R's reconstruction καταχέουσα) and Aesch. *Ag.* 239 (κρόκου βαφὰς δ' ἐς πέδον χέουσα). On the state of scholarship, see Sourvinou-Inwood 1988:68n1; in *Lys.* 644–645 the transmitted reading χέουσα (καὶ χέουσα, Stinton) stands in opposition to the conventional interpretation of Γ κατέχουσα, or the emendation of Ellebodius and Bentley κᾆτ' ἔχουσα. Cf. also Henderson *Lys.*, 156 *ad* 645, who adopts Stinton's καὶ χέουσα for his text. Iphigenia is in particular the archetypal bear of Artemis, cf. schol. *Lys.* 645 and Brelich 1969:242ff.; on the aetiology and on the Bra000ronia in

to the fact that he wishes to get past his transitional phase. When the prytanis refuses, the relative cries out in pointedly comic form, "O saffron clothing, what have you done! There is no longer any hope of rescue!" (945–946). Only the taking off of the garment would have represented a sign that the time of marginality, suffering, and testing could soon come to an end. Only as bride could this "Helen" have been snatched away to Sparta by her "Menelaos." The intervention of the prytanis and the Scythian prevents the successful transition to marriage, which would have amounted to being rescued from a precarious situation. The Helen theme is often presented with particular emphasis on the bodily level,[424] and for this reason the comic playwright dwells on this point. Helen's naked body was believed to have a completely disarming effect: her husband Menelaos is said to have dropped his sword at the sight of her naked breast (Ar. *Lys.* 155–156 and Eur. *Andr.* 629–630).[425] The refoundation of the marriage partnership is thereby alluded to. In terms of the plot of our play Menelaos must of course not be moved to return to his "spouse." Rather, Kritylla and the entry of the prytanis stand in the way of the "married couple." The relative as Helen thus would dearly have loved to have disarmed the power of the state, the Scythian policeman in particular, with the removal of his dress in order to ensure the transition to marriage. The comedy of the situation of

general, see Brelich 1969:241–268 and Brulé 1987:179–283, and on Iphigenia in the context of initiation, Dowden 1989:9–47. Iphigenia, like Helen, is also the model of the maiden undergoing initiation immediately before marriage. On Helen, who is abducted as a young pretty girl by Theseus, see Brulé 1987:98, 289–290, 297 and Sourvinou-Inwood 1988:52–53. The girl is represented as a sexually mature woman on the threshold of marriage, despite her tender age of seven years. For the Greek conception of woman in general, see Carson 1990. A woman's bloom coincides with the transition to marriage (Carson 1990:146–147). For the *anakalyptêria* on the wedding night as an opening up of female borders and of making oneself available, see Carson 1990:163–164.

[424] For the staging of the Helen myth on the bodily level, see Worman 1997. On the body as a central area of play with the opposite sex, see also Zeitlin 1990:71–75. On the body in general as the place where ritual as the ideological praxis of society is enacted, see Bell 1992:94–101 and 197–223, esp. 201–204. Here Bell draws particularly on Michel Foucault; cf. in particular Foucault 1979:1–69, esp. 32–69 ("The Spectacle of the Scaffold"), where execution is presented as a communal festival, a spectacular performance, and a ritual that is carried out on the body of the condemned.

[425] See Worman 1997:161–162 and Henderson *Lys.*, 86 *ad* 155–156. This may also be read as a further reference to the central image of the *parabasis* (*Thesm.* 821–829). Women are better than men because their attractiveness enables them to cause men to throw away their weapons. On the *krokôtos* in the *Lysistrata*, cf. lines 42–48 and 219–220. The garment has the power of sexual attraction; as ambivalent sign it is worn both by prostitutes and by chaste virgins. From a male perspective one could also say that the Spartan relative/Helen perhaps alludes to the Gymnopaidia with his reference to nudity; cf. n418. Nudity here, as in the case of the girls, means a lack of identity. The dancers are still in a liminal status, which will be overcome only with the Karneia and their marriage.

course lies in the fact that in addition to the feminine marker of the *krokôtos* and *mitra* the previously concealed phallus is clearly visible.[426]

The interruption of the scene by the entry of the chorus (947–1000) underlines the anchoring of the comic hero in the time and space of the ritual festival of the Thesmophoria. The song serves not merely, as is the case with tragic songs, as a method of structuring and of condensing time; rather, the context is symbolically focused once more on the *Leitmotiv* of initiation.[427] Through their dance the members of the chorus intensify their reenacted marginal condition of women undergoing initiation. The relative with his saffron garment is thus part of the whole: he also symbolically becomes a "maiden" on the threshold of marriage, which would be the outcome of his rescue. While carrying out this dance the chorus members (both male and female, depending on role and function) change from enemies to companions in this critical transition.[428]

After the choral dance song, the relative, bound to a plank, stands at the center together with the Scythian. The arrangement gives Euripides the idea of now rescuing the relative with the help of his *Andromeda*, also performed in 412 BCE. According to this scheme, the shackled relative in saffron gown corresponds to Andromeda, the Scythian to the sea monster, and the tragic poet to the hero Perseus.[429]

---

[426] On the word "weapon" in the sense of phallus, see Henderson 1991[2]:110, 123, 248 and above, n368.

[427] On dance as a characteristic element in initiation, see Jeanmaire 1939:182ff.; he sums up the connection succinctly in the following pregnant expression: "Etre initié, c'est «être dansé»" ["To be initiated is to be 'danced'"] (183). This also holds for the relative. See also Moreau 1992:208–210 and the further literary citations above, n418.

[428] The chorus thus also emphasizes that this is still during the Nesteia, the day of fasting (947–952). The transition to the Kalligeneia, on which day the institution of marriage is once more instituted, is not yet complete. The relative's remark that as an old man in this disguise he will become an object of laughter for the crows, which he ceremoniously feeds (ἑστιῶν, 942), stands in humorous contrast to this. He thereby presents himself in paratragic fashion as a human sacrifice that will be served up to the hungry crows—who in this case are the wild women. On *diasparagmos* by birds in tragedy, cf. e.g. Aesch. *Supp.* 801, Soph. *Ant.* 1017–1018, and Eur. *Ion* 504–506, 902–904, 917. Van Leeuwen *Thesm.*, 121 *ad* 942 notes that Θεσμοφόρια ἑστιᾶν (cf. Isaeus 3.80) might have been a term for the sacrificial meal at the Kalligeneia. In the second *Thesmophoriazusae* of Aristophanes a catalogue of tasty dishes is recited (fr. 333 K.-A.). And every comedy ends with a celebration involving eating and drinking. In addition, the curse ἐς κόρακας is comically reworked (κόραξιν instead of οἰωνοῖς). Line 942 is taken up again in the lament (1026–1028): the Scythian has hung him/her (Andromeda) up as a baneful and joyless meal for the crows.

[429] On the scene see Mitsdörffer 1954, Rau 1967:65–89, Zeitlin 1981:190–194, Zimmermann II 1985:7–13, Hall 1989, Sier 1992, and Parker 1997:436–445. On the *Andromeda* of Euripides, see Bubel 1991 (with the critical review by Bierl, *BMCR* 3.6 [1992], 429–434) and Klimek-Winter 1993:55–315. On the parody in the scene on the visual level, see Golder 1996:10–11.

Yet even this *paratragôidia* is not simply defined by the external situation. As in the case of the *Helen*, the *Andromeda* is in turn chosen for its symbolic mythical content, which clarifies the condition of the comic protagonist. Since he is not allowed to remove his *krokôtos*, he once again plays a virgin in transition to becoming a married women. The entire staging of this tragedy is clearly based on the model of a female initiation. Ethiopians, like Egyptians, represent a barbarian no-man's-land, the landscape of marginality. The borderline situation immediately preceding marriage is dramatized by the deadly threat of the barbarian, who corresponds to Hades in the case of Kore. The potential disaster develops the idea of death and rebirth in initiation, which mythically represent change of status. Perseus/Euripides plays the role of the bridegroom who falls in love with the virgin and wants to marry her.[430]

It is thus also important that in this scene we do not simply have a literary parody; Aristophanes incorporates the text in his comedy because of its symbolic content. Modern research on parody indicates that this is never a one-way process designed to denigrate the text being parodied, but that both texts, both the parodying and the parodied, mutually illuminate each other and stand in a productive dialogue with each other that provokes laughter.[431] The intertextual reading of one discourse in another engenders an open attitude of perception. The concept of parody in this case needs to be expanded from a purely literary one to a cultural phenomenon. The integration of the *Helen* and the *Andromeda* is effective for the very reason that as symbolically similar actions they are able to illuminate in a comically

---

[430] On the *Andromeda* as typical initiatory situation, see Bierl, *BMCR* 3.6 (1992), 431–432 (with references). The threat of being devoured by a monster is a characteristic indication of initiation: cf. Moreau 1992, esp. 221–225, on Andromeda and the κῆτος *ibid.*, 224; cf. also the comparative morphology of initiation in Brelich 1969:37 and 90n 116. On the topos of marriage with Hades in tragic marriage, see Seaford 1987. On the possible resolution of the Danaid trilogy by the institution of the Thesmophoria, see *ibid.*, 110–119, esp. 115–116; Herodotus (2.171) says that the festival was founded by the Danaids from Egypt. On the Danaids and the Thesmophoria, see also Detienne 1988 and Zeitlin 1992:234–238. Mourning, death, and antisexual impulse configure the sequence from abstinence to fruitful sexual union. On Andromeda as bride of Hades, cf. *Thesm.* 1019 (?) (on the basis of many conjectures, cf. Klimek-Winter 1993:154–155), 1040, 1055. On the association of funerary lament and lament before marriage, see Alexiou 1974:120–122 and Seaford 1987:113–114. Conversely, Perseus' action is also interpreted as an initiatory trial; cf. Burkert 1992:82–87, esp. 85 and Bremmer 1994:62. Perseus' *monosandalismos* can equally be seen as an indication of marginality in initiation; on this see Henderson *Lys.*, 159 *ad* 667–669. Ginzburg 1989:239–242 presents another interpretation, associating Perseus with shaman-like figures of myth. The signifier of *monosandalismos* is characterized by a polysemy, and refers only indirectly to a signified. Signs of initiation and underworld thus do not contradict each other, acccording to Ginzburg: both refer to marginality and liminality. Cf. *ibid.*, 235–295 (on the characteristic sequence of the asymmetric gait).

[431] Cf. Rose 1993, who stresses the metafictional quality and comedy of the moment.

distorted manner the crisis-prone stituation of the hero in the liminal phase of initiation.[432]

The relative's monody arranges the elements of the *Andromeda* next to the actual situation, and the comedy and the tragic action of the virgin thus become merged into a unity. All in all, Mnesilokhos here glides back and forth completely freely between his new role and his actual situation, so that the fluctuating assumption of male and female gender in grammatical terms is in no way synchronized with this.[433] The impression thereby arises of a comic,

---

[432] Cf. Möllendorff 1995:262–263: "Die moderne Parodieforschung ist sich weitgehend darin einig, daß die parodistische Bezugnahme eines Textes auf einen anderen keineswegs ausschließlich satirisch funktionalisierbar, also einseitig ausgerichtet ist; vielmehr problematisiert die Parodie die naive Auffassung, ein Sprecher könne mithilfe der Sprache die innere oder die äußere Wirklichkeit mimetisch abbilden, indem sie das sprechende Subjekt in die Äußerung hereinzieht und es gewissermaßen aus der Sicht des parodierten Textes betrachtet: denn sie integriert in ihre aktuelle Äußerung ein fremdes Wort mit einem fremden sprechenden Subjekt, so daß die hierarchischen Positionen von Autor und Held der parodistischen Äußerung aus der Sicht des Rezipienten potentiell vertauschbar sind, also auf eine Ebene gesetzt werden" ["Modern scholarship on parody largely agrees on the fact that the parodic reference of one text to another does not function exclusively as satire and is thus not configured as a one-way process; rather, parody problematizes the naïve approach that a speaker using language is able to picture the inner or outer reality in mimetic fashion by incorporating the speaking subject into the utterance and by considering it in a sense from the point of view of the parodied text; for it integrates into its current utterance a foreign word with a foreign-speaking subject, so that the hierarchical positions of author and hero of the parodic utterance are potentially interchangeable from the point of view of the recipient, and are thus placed on the same level"]. This is however viewed in terms of a polyphonic, postmodern discourse that is in large part foreign to Bakhtin himself. In this connection it is worth noting that there were attempts in the former Soviet Union to explain parody as a ritual and cultic phenomenon; see Freidenberg 1974. Freidenberg (275–276) also turns his attention to Aristophanes and in fact discusses the parody of the Thesmophoria (*Thesm.* 295ff.). In his opinion (and following Aristotle), tragedy and comedy go back to a shared orginal form: the comic forms a double to the high-brow. The relative thus here also forms a comic discourse with the ritually elevated quality of Euripides' tragedy. Nesselrath 1993 relies on the traditional concept of parody; in so doing he shows how strongly influenced the development of comedy was by the element of mythic parody or travesty (see also Nesselrath 1990:188–241); comedy thus always represented a dialogue with elevated myth: the comic double is clearly based on the same narrative and ritual plot elements. On parody and intertextuality, see also Verweyen/Witting 1982 and Glei 1992 (from the perspective of classical philology).

[433] See the good analysis by Sommerstein *Thesm.*, 224 *ad* 1015. With Euripides too, who immediately thereafter perhaps even takes over the wide-ranging and playful role of Echo (cf. however the reservation expressed above, n122) and leaves the conventional discourse completely (Rau 1967:84), as with the relative, it is striking that both, in contrast to the case in the previous *Helen* parody, partially lose sight of the direction of the plot in the sense of a logical and syntagmatic development, as is characteristic of tragedy. This is caused by the absence of role identity and by paradigmatic interludes typical of comedy. Although the Scythian disappears off-stage for rather a long time in order to get himself a mat, the escape, the releasing of the bonds, is not simply translated into action. Cf. Möllendorff 1995:251. Nevertheless, in contrast to earlier scholarship, I see throughout this entire passage a meaning that goes beyond mere parody.

uncoordinated, triply-encoded, and mutually connected, while at the same time chaotic, juxtaposition of two roles, behind which the actual player remains present. The comic hero thus only partially assumes the role of the girl. Behind the imperfect, theatrical imagining the male identity continues to shine through, just as the chorus also switches between their plot-internal role and their plot-external function.

The lament about the suffering inflicted by her relatives (συγγόνων, 1039) and the man who put her into the saffron robe[434] is extremely expressive (1036–1044). The *krokôtos* is emphasized with the deictic pronoun as costume of the here and now (κροκόεν τόδ', 1044). Perseus/Euripides, in his later conversation with the Scythian in the presence of the relative, in turn problematizes in a metafictional fashion the phenomenon of mimesis (1098ff.). Because of the interplay of the two discourses, the person he speaks to is both Andromeda and Mnesilokhos. Within the Andromeda plot Euripides addresses him as "virgin" (ὦ παρθέν', 1110). For the Scythian, who, like Kritylla before him, will not be drawn into this game without illusion, it is only the real dimension that counts. He says the person being addressed is no virgin, but rather an old sinner, a crook, and a scoundrel (1111–1112), to which Euripides retorts that she is Andromeda, daughter of Kepheus (1113). The Scythian then in a comically factual manner uses the primary sex-marker, the relative's dangling phallus, as proof for his argument (1114). The contrast between tragic plot and comic disillusionment gives rises to laughter. In any case, the failure of the Euripidean scheme is once more ensured. Euripides continues in the role of Perseus. He claims to have been seized by love for the virgin, and expresses his wish to lie down with her on the bridal and marriage bed (πεσεῖν ἐς εὐνὴν καὶ γαμήλιον λέχος, 1122).[435] This would mean marrying her and successfully overcoming the transition stage. Thus if the Scythian were to agree to the request, then Euripides would be allowed to release the bride from her chains and saffron robe and take her home. This would mean the successful rescue of the relative.

But the Scythian does not play along with the staging of the *Andromeda*. In his eyes, the advances of Euripides remain simply weird and tragic-sounding nonsense. When Euripides attempts to untie his beloved, he intervenes. Like the audience, he perceives the two actors as actual, male performers. Since

---

[434] The word συγγόνων (1039) in the text of the *Andromeda* refers to the father, Kepheus, and his family; in the comedy it refers to Euripides.

[435] This wish refers back to the maiden's lament that she will die without the wedding paean (γαμηλίῳ μὲν οὐ ξὺν | παιῶνι, 1034–1035); the marginality of the immediately prior situation could be overcome through marriage.

Euripides declares his love for the prisoner, the barbarian guard interprets this on the level of pure reality in the here and now as a homosexual relationship, which he does not want to stand in the way of. He says he can certainly turn the man around and tie him to the plank with his head facing toward it; or in a pinch, he will even allow Euripides to drill a hole through the wood so that he can service his lover from behind (1119–1120, 1123–1124). The audience would certainly have broken into hearty laughter at these coarse remarks. Still, these are not just dirty jokes pandering to the tastes of simple folk, but actually intensify the message on the symbolic level. Because of the women's clothing and the apparently pederastic relationship, the relative is simultaneously equated to a young man in the liminal phase of initiation. Euripides becomes in the eyes of the Scythian the ἐραστής, and the relative his ἐρώμενος. In fact, in terms of the Spartan context introduced into the immediately preceding scene of the *Helen* parody, this homosexual relationship becomes understandable. In an epoch-making work on pederasty in Sparta, Erich Bethe emphasizes that the physical relationship between ἐραστής and ἐρώμενος played an important role and should be interpreted in the context of initiation rites, which represent a precondition for entry into the world of the hoplite society of adult males.[436] The connection between a twenty- to thirty-year-old man and twelve- to twenty-year-old youth constituted an institutionalized relationship and formed a part of the *agôgê*, which structured the system of age-classes on symbolic and ritual basis. At age thirty a Spartan could marry and only then would he receive citizenship. If one considers the relative in terms of his male identity, then he, just like the adult women at the Thesmophoria, is temporarily transported, in a symbolic and ritual act, back to the threshold situation of young people before marriage. It is only at the conclusion of the Thesmophoria and toward the end of the comedy, which for its part is based on ritual structures of action, that the women, as well as the men, turn back to their usual socially defined role relationships and the separation of the sexes is removed.

Reference has already been made to how the relative and the chorus resemble each in terms of their status as *nymphai*, which is also comically mediated via the figure of Echo.[437] This connection deserves a closer look. In contrast to the previous *Helen* stratagem, which is separated from the *Andro-*

---

[436] Bethe 1907. Cf. Calame I 1977:421–427 (Engl. trans. Calame 1997:245–249), Cartledge 1981, Bremmer 1980, and Bremmer 1990. Xen. *Lac.* 2.12–14 admittedly emphasizes that according to Lycurgus the relationship between *erastês* and *erômenos* should not be sexual in nature, yet everything points to the fact that in reality it was in fact built on this. On the phenomenon of Greek homosexuality in general, see Dover 1989[2], passim, and on the Dorians 185–196.

[437] See the brief preview of the plot, above, p. 129.

meda parody by the great choral dance song (947–1000), it is here particularly remarkable that the relative now comes into contact with the chorus as Andromeda. This happens because of the reading in of parts of the Euripidean text, which in this passage originally consisted of an interchange in song between the heroine and the chorus composed of virgins. In particular, the words uttered at the beginning of the monody, φίλαι παρθένοι, φίλαι (1015), are not simply integrated into the comic text for the pure fun of the process of intertextuality. This typical address to the tragic chorus shows a close emotional connection between Andromeda and the maidens who accompany her.[438] In mutually interconnected encoding of the parody the base text also has meaning in the new situation. The relative turns to the members of the chorus, who in terms of the ideology of the festival reactualize in mimetic fashion, as does he, the state of παρθενία. Zeitlin differentiates between two levels of audience in this parodic game: the Scythian, on whom it has no effect, and the nearby chorus, who is perhaps even pleased by it, since it is subsequently very quick to make peace with Euripides.[439] The chorus thus acts here once more as a kind of "inner spectator" in comparison to the audience in the theater, which also enjoys the comic virtuoso interlude. The Euripidean text enters into a reciprocal tension with the situation in the comedy. Up until now, the chorus was hardly "dear and trusted," but was downright hostile to the relative. Through his presentation of the exemplarily chaste Helen of Euripides' tragedy the relative approximates the chorus' disposition more and more closely. Andromeda, another exemplary maiden on the threshold of marriage, once again constitutes a mythical reworking of the ambivalent and critical situation of the change of status from maiden to married woman, something that the members of the chorus must also undergo in the ritual of the Thesmophoria. The relative's address to the chorus thus sets out their commonality and tries to enlist sympathy. For the relative, the successfully completed *rite de passage* means that he can go home again to his wife (1020–1021). The women also strive for the *telos* of the festival, namely reunification with their husbands. The paradoxical situation of diametrical opposition simultaneously combined with congruity provokes laughter. Even the addressee of the "you" (sing.) form (1018, 1020, 1029) remains undetermined, and could refer equally well to Euripides, the Scythian, and the chorus. Since on the one hand Euripides as winged Perseus has apparently just disappeared once more, perhaps in order to appear as Echo immediately afterward—his visual appear-

---

[438] See Klimek-Winter 1993:153 and Mitsdörffer 1954:67.
[439] Zeitlin 1981:190–191.

ance remains completely unclear—and since on the other hand the Scythian has also left the stage at the time of the performance of the song to fetch a mat (1006–1007), the only actual person remaining to interact with is the chorus.

Against this background, the relative's address, ὁρᾷς, οὐ χοροῖσιν οὐδ' | ὑφ' ἡλίκων νεανίδων (1029–1030), appears all the more absurd. Although he is standing right in front of the chorus, he says that he finds himself without the accompaniment of a chorus of maidens of the same age.[440] In the monody he is not of course accompanied by them in song, but he is standing in the orchestra right in their midst. The chorus members in their female identity are of approximately the same age as the maiden Andromeda, since the women are also presented as being transported back to their youth.

The chorus of maidens is in fact particularly *à propos* in the context of female puberty rites. Many heroines, Helen in particular, are abducted in the prime of their youth and from the dance circle of their contemporaries, which mythically reworks the crisis-ridden *rite de passage* of marriage. The χοροί have their institutional place in the life of young maidens. In the ritual activity of song and dance they take the step toward adulthood.[441] In any case, the comic Andromeda's transition is to be unsuccessful, since the Scythian returns with his mat in line 1083 and confronts the stage Perseus.

The "basket" (κημόν, 1031) that the relative is missing in his monody is also quite ambivalently encoded. On the one hand κημός refers to the voting basket: "the notorious litigiousness of the Athenians merrily continues to assert itself παρ' ὑπόνοιαν even in the face of fictitious death."[442] This meaning, which is directed at the male hero as Athenian citizen, is partially overlaid by the connotations the basket has regarding woolworking (cf. 822), the central

---

[440] In line 1018 in the original Echo is of course addressed (cf. schol. *Thesm.* 1018); line 1029 (ὁρᾷς) is according to Rau 1967:73 still directed at Echo; according to Klimek-Winter 1993:179–180 ὁρᾷς is however a "mere colloquialism." He thinks that it is here superfluous to try to determine the addressee. But when it comes to the Euripidean *Andromeda* he maintains that ὁρᾷς is not colloquial, but should be taken as an apostrophe to the chorus (*ibid.*, 180). In my opinion, one cannot separate out the function quite so neatly; in the parody the connection is flexible, especially since the address to the chorus here becomes particularly paradoxical.

[441] Cf. among others Calame I 1977, esp. 439–449 (Engl. trans. Calame 1997, esp. 258–263). Therefore the lament in the Euripidean text is not simply about "[d]ie wehmütige Erinnerung der tragischen Heldin oder des weiblichen Chores an die Reigenspiele der Jugend" ["the tragic heroine or female chorus' sorrowful reminiscences of childhood dancing and playing in a circle"] (Mitsdörffer 1954:77). Klimek-Winter 1993:181–182 (with many parallel passages) correctly reckons that what is at issue here is the loss of what for a Greek woman represents the world that both determines and is necessary for existence. Nevertheless, he too does not recognize the dramatization of the critical moment of marriage as a death-experience.

[442] Rau 1967:74 with n133, where the meaning of κημός as feminine ornament (following Hesychius) is rejected as "incorrect."

occupation of young maidens and women.[443] The paradoxical intertwining of a typically masculine and a typically feminine object (Hesychius even explicitly describes κημός as feminine ornamentation) graphically emphasizes the transgression of the boundaries of male and female gender identification during the transitional phases of initiation.

The relative's command to lament for him is unambiguously directed at the members of the chorus (γοᾶσθέ μ', ὦ γυναῖκες, 1036). They are now addressed as women, since they represent the period of youth only temporarily. Paradoxically, they are asked to represent the chorus whose absence he has only just pointed out. Through lament the women at the Thesmophoria are supposed to undertake the central function of the *hymenaios*, that is, dramatically accompany the *rite de passage* of wedding, a critical period for the bride, with songs of mourning.[444] The plea for sympathy directed at the women is comically undermined by the relative's complaint that Euripides has sent him right into the sanctuary, in the midst of women (τόδ' ἀνέπεμψεν | ἱερόν, ἔνθα γυναῖκες, 1045–1046). Elements both hostile and friendly to the chorus are thereby directly juxtaposed.

The *Andromeda* plan naturally also has to fail. Yet the chorus appears to move closer to its former enemy: for now the women call on Pallas Athena, first as παρθένον ἄζυγα κούρην (1139), to join the dance (1136ff.). It becomes more and more clear that escape from the entanglements can be achieved only through the chorus. The chorus in its interaction with the hero thus also takes on the dramatic role of mediator.[445] After the *parabasis* the chorus almost imperceptibly changes into a dance group that has as its model the initiatory choruses of real-life Greek ritual. Athena is the divine example for both Athenian maidens and ephebes. The chorus finally invokes her using the

---

[443] The feminine form ἔχουσ' (1031) makes the contrast with the masculine voting basket particularly grotesque; at the same time the female significance of the object asserts itself over the male. On the probable change παρὰ προσδοκίαν from an original κῶμον to κημόν, see Mitsdörffer 1954:78 and Rau 1967:74.

[444] See above, n430 and Contiades-Tsitsoni 1990:112, 124. Death is often presented as marriage in Hades. Many funerary laments resemble wedding songs that sing of the separation of the girl from her parental home. See also Danforth 1982:86 and further Rehm 1994, esp. 11–42, with the critical review by Zeitlin, *BMCR* 5.7 (1994), 612–618, esp. 614: "What R.[ehm] might have noted, however, is that these similarities are not just conflations but derive from the parallel nature of two *rites de passage*, whose function in each case was to assure separation from a previous status and incorporation into a new one." Rehm's (1994:121–127, esp. 126) analysis of the *Helen* in this connection as criticism of the Sicilian expedition (cf. also Rehm 1996:57–58) is disappointing.

[445] On the interaction of the chorus with the hero and the chorus' presence and absence as dramaturgical tool, see Rehm 1996. See also Gruber 1986:37–38, who observes (37) that the hero has to get the chorus on his side and that this can happen only by using a clever piece of acting.

epithet κληδοῦχος (1142), "key-holder," which should be interpreted not only politically, but also as having cultic implications.[446] In the *Thesmophoriazusae* Aristophanes brings together in associative fashion many rituals that have to do with the transition of young people to adult status, both within and without Athens, and embeds them in the context of the Thesmophoria. In his mimesis of Helen and Andromeda, who exemplify the figure of the young woman immediately before marriage, the relative comes close to the idea of the women celebrating the Thesmophoria, who in parodic play gradually assume the role of his guide. As Alcman describes in his Great Partheneion (fr. 1 Davies), the girl that awaits her wedding stands out in the chorus of her age-mates. This intrigue does not work in any direct fashion: rather, through the symbolic discourse of female initiation, the relative gradually becomes a kind of secret chorus leader without himself being aware of it.

For this reason even the chorus' rapid coming to terms with Euripides immediately after the second hymn-like song (*Thesm.* 1136–1159) does not come as quite the surprise it has generally been assumed to be. With the offer of peace, the end of the festival of inversion, mutual *aiskhrologia*, and division of the sexes are simultaneously agreed upon. Comedy and the Thesmophoria have in common a delight in abusive speech. After the failure of his tragic intrigues, Euripides now makes the women an offer: never again will he make them the victim of his defamatory speech (ἀκοῦσαι μηδὲν ὑπ' ἐμοῦ μηδαμὰ | κακὸν τὸ λοιπόν, 1162–1163; οὐδὲν μή ποτε | κακῶς ἀκούσητ', 1166–1167). But

---

[446] See Sommerstein *Thesm.*, 231 *ad* 1142. In Eur. *IT* 1462–1463 Athena in her function as *dea ex machina* orders Iphigenia as priestess to exercise her key-holding function (κληδουχεῖν) for Artemis in Brauron. Iphigenia is the mythic model for the "bears," who prepare themselves by weaving and dance in the periphery during their service to Artemis, just as the Arrhephoroi on the Acropolis do in the service of Athena. Iphigenia is also practically synonymous with Kalligeneia, "the beautifully born one"; see Dowden 1989:46. The personification Kalligeneia is of course celebrated as Demeter's wet-nurse on the third day of the Thesmophoria, which bears the same name. Beauty is the most important prerequisite for marriage. Young girls and boys interact both at the Tauropolia at Halai and at the Arkteia at Mounikhia and Brauron. The choruses at the *pannykhis* at the Tauropolia bring together women and girls, who are accepted into the community of women in a ceremony by torchlight: see Dowden 1989:33–34. The festival of the Thesmophoria exhibits similar traits, with the distinction that here mature women relive their initiatory experience. In Brauron and at the Tauropolia the *pyrrhikhê* was also perhaps danced for Artemis by the women. See Brulé 1987:313–314 and Ceccarelli 1998:77–78; on the ephebic *pyrrhikhê* at Halai and other places in Attica, *ibid.*, 83–87. On the *prylis*, see above, n369.

[447] Hesych., s.v. εἰρήνη glosses the word with κόρος τέλος. At age twenty the εἴρην did not yet have full citizenship; this he obtained only at thirty, at which age he could marry. From the perspective of the play the marriage (i.e. the return of the relative to his wife) will take place only after the completion of the actual plot. On the *eirên*, see Pettersson 1992:82–85 and 88–89.

if the women do not release his relative from the plank, then he will continue his *aiskhrologia* against women. Once again, the actual cultic context is wittily played upon; Euripides again incorporates male suspicions about women separated from their husbands during the festival. As in the *Lysistrata*, the isolation of the women is explained by the fact that the men have left their families because of war. Therefore he finally utters the comic threat that if the women do not accept his offer, he will tell the men, as soon as they have returned from the campaign, what havoc the women have caused during the Thesmophoria (1167–1169). The chorus agrees to these conditions without much hesitation, partly out of fear and partly because its action in the orchestra has already prepared the way for the conclusion of this condition of inversion.

The overcoming of the separation of sexes and the liberation of the relative can be compared to marriage, the *telos* of initiation. The chorus calls on Athena in the immediately preceding song to come and bring "festival-loving peace" (εἰρήνην φιλέορτον, 1147). With this the end of the unstable phase of marginality, thoroughly comparable to an internal war, is simultaneously indicated. In Sparta, a young man who has successfully come through the ἀγωγή at the age of twenty is called an εἴρην. Hesychius associates the term with εἰρήνη, explaining that "peace" indicates the *telos* of male education.[447] The chorus in Alcman's Great Partheneion (fr. 1 Davies) says (90–91) that "because of Hagesikhora the girls have set out on the path of lovely peace (ἰρ]ήνας ἐρατ[ᾶ]ς)." They approach this desired condition because they have learned correct behavior through contact with the chorus leader in dance and are thus on the way to passing successfully through the *rite de passage*. With the help of the χάρις that has accrued to them through the process they have undergone, they gain beauty as precondition for the goal of marriage.[448]

---

[448] See Calame II 1977:118–119 with n141, Clark 1996:166 and above, Introduction n90. Elektra laments that in this impoverished, peasant anti-world she is ἀνέορτος ἱερῶν καὶ χορῶν τητωμένη (Eur. *El.* 310). Immediately prior to this she complains that she does not dance at joyous festivals (οὐκ ἐπ' ἀγλαΐαις, Eur. *El.* 175; on choral dance and ἀγλαΐα see below, chap. 2 nn94 and 96) in the circle of Argive girls (οὐδ' ἱστᾶσα χοροὺς | Ἀργείαις ἅμα νύμφαις | εἱλικτὸν κρούσω πόδ' ἐμόν, Eur. *El.* 178–180). Choral dance is to be equated with a festive atmosphere; despite her marriage to a Mycenaean farmer she has remained a maiden; she is still waiting for her *telos*; marriage with Pylades, which, like the preparation in the chorus of maidens, will give her "peace," is only announced at the end of the play. In heortological terms the worship of Eirene is also closely connected with Athena and the Panathenaia, which is important for the *Thesmophoriazusae*. At the Synoikia, celebrated on the sixteenth of Hekatombaion, there was perhaps already in Aristophanes' time a sacrifice to Peace personified. The cult is however only attested with certainty from 374 BCE onward; on this see Deubner 1932:36–38 (who thinks it does not exist in the late fifth century).

Euripides' comic scheme has already been briefly explored in terms of its dance-related aspects.[449] We shall now look at them from an initiatory perspective. Through his participation in the *Helen* and *Andromeda* parodies, Euripides enters more and more into contact with the feminine realm, particularly since he actually enters the cult sanctuary of the Thesmophorion. It is noteworthy that Euripides, who up until this point has refused to put on women's clothing, now assumes the female role of the procuress Artemisia, though without shaving off his beard.

After the Scythian has been duped, the relative can swiftly be freed of his chains. Euripides orders him to run off home like a man (ἀνδρικῶς, 1204) to his wife and children (1204–1206).[450] Return to married life may be compared to its renewal, which is also the ritual goal of the Thesmophoria. The relative probably casts off his saffron-colored robe as soon as he is freed; ambivalent sexual status, which was important in playing through the initiatory phase of youth, is thereby brought to an end.[451] Now the relative is once again a real man, and his escape proceeds without problem. His wife, from whom he has been separated over the course of the entire play, stands symbolically for all Athenian women who withdraw themselves from the οἶκος during the festival. Admittedly, the construction of the comedy avoids having a meeting between the relative and his wife in the Thesmophorion, and for this reason she is treated in the plot as having been at home all the while. Meanwhile, offstage, a sexual union takes place between the Scythian and the dancer. "Marriage," the goal of the plot of Old Comedy and of the Thesmophoria, is here used dramaturgically for a successful outcome of the entanglement within the plot, in order to facilitate the relative's return to his legitimate marital relationship.

When the Scythian returns to the stage from his sexual encounter, he looks for the prisoner and once again mentions his saffron-colored garment (1220). The barbarian cannot find him, because the clothing has been taken off. Moreover, the chorus, which has now completely gone over to the side of the men, sends him in the wrong direction; after the festival of inversion the women now subject themselves to the men once more.

---

[449] Cf. above, pp. 132–136.

[450] The expression "get out of here as quickly as possible like a man" (ὅπως ἀνδρικῶς | . . . τάχιστα φεύξει, 1204–1205), is of course still meant ironically; through such behavior the relative continues to remain effeminate and resembles men who cast off their shields in battle. See Sommerstein *Thesm.*, 236 *ad* 1204–1205; he refers to the connotation Euripides intended, namely that ἀνδρικῶς means "resolutely." The expression ὡς τὴν γυναῖκα (1206) is already prepared for in the *Andromeda* parody (1020–1021): ἔασον ὡς | τὴν γυναῖκά μ' ἐλθεῖν.

[451] On the comparable initiation ritual of the Cretan Ekdysia, in which initiates also took off their female clothing in a festive fashion, see Leitao 1995.

Just like the women, the men now reclaim their sexual identity. Unmanly behavior is now projected onto the barbarian, whose stupidity causes much laughter. In the role of procuress Euripides relieves the Scythian archer of his quiver (συβίνη, 1197) as payment for the transaction with the dancer. The stranger, who up until now was the only real man, now behaves like the Athenian "shield-abandoners" previously criticized by the women (824–829).[452] Even so, a certain confusion in the code prevails right up until the conclusion; it is only at the end of the Dionysiac staging of inversion that is comedy that the festival, on which the plot of the play is based, is definitely over.

As we conclude this discussion of the *Thesmophoriazusae* we should take another look at the plot structure in order to reply to a criticism frequently made, namely that the lengthy middle section (210–1159) is ultimately sense-less and superfluous from a dramaturgical point of view, especially since the third section (1160–1231) can be joined almost seamlessly to the introduction (1–209). First, as Möllendorff, for example, has recently put it,[453] it is Euripides' intention to oppose the threatening judgment of the women. Yet he avoids sneaking into the women's realm himself, because he is afraid of being swiftly revealed as a man (189–190). With Agathon's refusal to put in a good word for him with the women, Euripides' plans seem to have been shat-tered (209). It is only then that the relative presents himself. The main action

---

[452] On the text of line 1197: συβίνην Brunck (in -νη corr. Blaydes): συβήνην schol. R and Suda, συμβήνην R. Given the sexual word play in line 1215 on βινεῖν (συβίνη· καταβεβίνησο) I accept Brunck's emendation. Van Leeuwen *Thesm.*, 149 *ad* 1197 cites passages in support of the idea that Artemis Brauronia received this kind of συβήνη as votive offering. See also Sommerstein *Thesm.*, 235 *ad* 1197 and Wilson 1999:72 with n59, who also see this humor in the variant συβήνην. The word play also depends on the etymology of the substantive, which combines συ- (from σῦς, "pig") and βιν- (from βινεῖν, "copulate"); in the case of the reading συβήνην an iotacizing pronounciation may already have been present. The myth has it that the swineherd Eubouleus pastured his animals in the area where Pluto abducted Kore into the underworld; the pigs also fell into the gaping earth. This was the reason, then, that the ritual of throwing piglets into the *megara* was introduced (schol. Luc. *Dial. Meret.* 2.1 [275.26–276.3 Rabe]). In Greek "piglets" may be used as a circumlocution for the genitalia of girls on the threshold of marriage. According to Henderson 1991²:132, ὗς (= σῦς) is identical to δέλφαξ, which describes the genitalia of mature women. When the barbarian thinks that he has "banged" (1215) a συβίνη in the truest sense of the word (ὀρτῶς), this is then playing on the fact that the return from χοῖρος to σῦς has been completed and that the women are now seen once more in their adult and fertile condition; ὀρτῶς can further be connected with the erect phallus with which the Scythian completes his work (Henderson 1991²:112). On the interpretation of *Thesm.* 1215 see also Henderson 1991²:152 and now Prato, 339–340 *ad* 1215. As the relative is being shaved, he compares himself to a piglet (οἴμοι κακοδαίμων, δελφάκιον γενήσομαι, *Thesm.* 237); with these words he introduces his staged phase of female initiation. See in general also Versnel 1993:256–260, esp. 256–257.

[453] Möllendorff 1995:246–247.

in the plot, which revolves around the comic hero dressed as a woman, does not achieve its goal: the relative is also discovered. And the rescue attempts are also unsuccessful. But as soon as Euripides takes the matter into his own hands he manages forthwith, in an astonishing way, to conclude peace with the women on a long-term basis. The freeing of the relative is then just a small matter.

For critics who simply look at the syntagmatic structure, almost all of this comic to-ing and fro-ing revolving about the relative's adventures seems unnecessary. This is the opinion of Wilhelm Süss, for example:[454]

> Who can doubt that all this could continue in this style for a good long while? But the play has to come to an end eventually, and it comes to a very surprising one. A very drastic and clumsy tactic: a girl sent by Euripides, who is dressed up as a procuress, manages to distract the policeman to such an extent that the rescue succeeds at long last. Of course, a precondition for this is the involvement of the women of the chorus in the plan. Surprisingly, this presents not the slightest difficulty after Euripides has agreed not to write anything nasty about them in exchange for their help in freeing his in-law. And in so doing Aristophanes has pulled the wool over his audience's eyes.
>
> If the two parties were so minded, they could easily have come to an agreement a lot sooner and avoided all this expenditure of malice.

In any retelling of the plot, in whatever form, one comes across these kind of "incongruities," with which scholars have long struggled.

If one applies Rainer Warning's analysis of comedy, one rightly sees that in this middle section we are dealing not so much with progress on the syntagmatic level, but with episodic and comic play on the paradigmatic level.[455] Meaning in what appears to be syntagmatically meaningless has been sought in literary parody,[456] in reflections on mimesis,[457] and in play with gender

---

[454] Süss 1954:158–159.

[455] See Möllendorff 1995:252n85.

[456] See among others Gelzer 1970:1469, Tschiedel 1984:41–46, and Sier 1992:63; Gelzer 1993:84 also speaks of the ineffectual nature of the Euripidean scheme, but nevertheless treats it as "Aufhänger für die Tragödienparodien" ["a peg on which to hang the parodies of tragedy"].

[457] See Zeitlin 1981:171–211, Paduano 1982:115–127, Gruber 1983:106–110, Gruber 1986:19–41, Sier 1992:63, and Sommerstein *Thesm.*, 7. On reading the *Thesmophoriazusae* as metatheatrical play, see Zeitlin 1981:181–194, esp. 182, Paduano 1982:115–127, Bonanno 1990, Bierl 1991:172–176, Hubbard 1991:182–199 (metatheater and intertextuality), and Sommerstein *Thesm.*, 4–6, 8–10;

roles.[458] Finally, by applying poststructuralist theories some have seen that the "discursive state of boundaries" is a characteristic of this main part of the plot: the actual theme is accordingly polyphonic representation without any particular aim, that is, the simultaneous unfolding of polyphonic discourses in alternate agreement and disagreement.[459]

The aim of this discussion has been to show that this rich middle portion of the play is not simply paradigmatic comic play, but also works in a symbolic, ritual, and performative fashion on the syntagmatic dimension of plot. The action of the comedy runs parallel to the course of the festival of inversion, the Thesmophoria, which imitates a *rite de passage*. At its center is the reversal of the male and female worlds in the liminal phase of transition. It is only at the festival's end that one finds one's way back to the normal order of things. What has rightly been called the threshold state, in particular the reversal and mixing of gender roles in the main part of the play, is thus not some kind of postmodern end in itself, but an expression of the transitional phase of initiation, which the festival of the Thesmophoria also reactualizes. It is played out paradigmatically in a ritual and symbolic way in order to make the conclusion understandable on a syntagmatic level by association. The ritual chorus supports the development of the plot, which in accordance with the tripartite model recalls separation from the given norm, the state of marginality, and the return to the normal order of things.

In this connection Michael Vickers' interpretation—which focuses exclusively on the historical and on contemporary politics, and which I largely distance myself from because it seems highly contrived—here offers an interesting parallel to my ideas in terms of the carrying out of the plot.[460] His interpretation also proceeds on the basis of a syntagmatic connection between the parodies and the action of the play as a whole. His contention that the play must date to 410[461] in order to incorporate the events of 411 is only tenable in any sense because Vickers takes a sequence of events, namely the critical return of a political leader to Athens from exile, that is only seemingly similar in structure and imposes this upon the ritual framework of the imitation of an

---

on the metatheatrical statement that comedy is better than tragedy, see Bierl 1991:175–176, Hubbard 1991:186, Bowie 1993:219–225, and Sommerstein *Thesm.*, 10. See now also Tzanetou 2002:355–359.

[458] See Zeitlin 1981, esp. 171–174, Taaffe 1993:74–102, Høibye 1995, and Sommerstein *Thesm.*, 4, 7–8.

[459] See Möllendorff 1995:247–254 following Gruber 1986:11–41 and Zeitlin 1981, esp. 170–171 (she also addresses the connections between myth and ritual [194–200]).

[460] Vickers 1989.

[461] See Vickers 1989:42 with n5; this dating goes back to Dobree; cf. the telling criticism in Sier 1992:63n1.

initiatory *rite de passage*. In Mnesilokhos he sees a comic cipher of the effeminate Alcibiades. Vickers also treats Palamedes, Menelaos, Helen, and Andromeda as further aspects of this prominent personality, who as the target of the satire establishes a notional unity in this comedy. Between the Euripides interlude and the rest of the plot one may, according to his completely fantastic explanations, detect a syntagmatic connection. Euripides, according to Vickers, is targeted because he supposedly wrote material sympathetic to Alcibiades and appeared to collaborate with the oligarchy.[462] His role at the end reflects Peisandros' efforts to bring Alcibiades over to the side of Athens. Mnesilokhos in chains and his tragic reflexes represent, says Vickers, Alcibiades at the court of the barbarian Tissaphernes, so that the play's conclusion corresponds to Alcibiades' hoped-for return to Athens. The modern historical prejudice of this interpreter sees in the *Thesmophoriazusae* an experimental playing through of politics.[463] Such an interpretation can of course hardly do justice to Old Comedy as ritual performance, even though this genre is certainly no stranger to political allusion. Vickers attaches contemporary references to the text in too one-sided a fashion, without paying attention to the symbolic world of images and the unfolding of a specific rituality in the course of the plot.

Mnesilokhos—Name as Program of Action

Once again I present my thesis as an alternative approach. At the center of the lengthy main section of the play (210–1159) stands the relative, who, dressed as a woman for his role, undergoes the puberty rites of a girl, but in terms of his male identity undergoes the initiation of an ephebe.[464] In this "betwixt and between" condition the comic hero is, significantly, nameless.[465] Anonymity is an expression of a critical transition, often associated with death and rebirth with a new identity. The familiar name Mnesilokhos is never used in the play

---

[462] On one-sided interpretation of tragedy in terms of the history of the time, see the critical remarks of Bierl 1991:22n61.

[463] Cf. Vickers 1989:65.

[464] Thiercy 1986 does not see the reminiscence of initiatory features in the *Thesmophoriazusae*, although he does consider the structure of initiation as fundamental in a number of comedies (305–327). He views the *Thesmophoriazusae* only in terms of its erotic structure (335–337).

[465] Cf. Barton 1990:22–23 and Olson 1992:307 (who does not consider the connection between function and meaning); Möllendorff 1995:241–242 thinks that Euripides represents tragedy, and his relative comedy, in particular the voice of the author Aristophanes; Cratin. fr. 342 K.-A. (εὐριπιδαριστοφανίζων) is usually cited in support of the connection between the two writers.

itself and seems to have been bestowed by the scholiasts only at a later stage.[466] It is usually concluded that the scholiasts transferred this name to the relative from Euripides' similarly named father-in-law.[467] Taking over an opinion already current in antiquity (schol. *Thesm.* 74) many critics have therefore taken the view that the relative is identical with the father-in-law. This is in fact rather improbable, as Hiller showed, since the hero—particularly given the international audience at the Great Dionysia—would scarcely have been recognizable to all spectators simply on the basis of a portrait mask. Moreover, one would have to imagine a κηδεστής as being a man belonging to the same generation as Euripides.[468]

It is clear that some of the scholiasts call the relative Mnesilokhos simply on the basis of the Euripidean *Vita*.[469] The question is what kind of evidence led the Alexandrian compilers to do this. It is known that a playwright's biography was mainly reconstructed from his work and from citations in other contemporary dramaturges. The Euripidean *Vita* in particular presents a hodgepodge of comic attacks against the tragedian as fact. It knows of two Mnesilokhoi: the one is Euripides' father-in-law, father of his second wife, Khoirile (*Vita* 5 [5, 5 Schwartz]; cf. *Vita* 2 [2, 12 Schwartz]); his second son from this marriage is the actor Mnesilokhos (*Vita* 2 [2, 13 Schwartz]). The older Mnesilokhos, the father-in-law, is generally identified with the relative, since the title υἱός

---

[466] Cf. Hiller 1874:449–453. In the play he is only described as κηδεστής (*Thesm.* 74, 210, 584, 1165) or γέρων (*Thesm.* 63, 585, 1111, 1123, 1199, 1212, 1219–1220). It is only one group of scholiasts who give him the name Mnesilokhos; cf. the beginning of the scholia: προλογίζει Μνησίλοχος κηδεστὴς Εὐριπίδου, schol. *Thesm.* 603, 1065 and schol. *Ach.* 332; in the scholia to *Thesm.* 129, 469, 633, 756, 760, 1064 (κηδεστής) and 1031, 1090, 1199 (γέρων) the name is not mentioned. Brelich 1969:102n143 notes that fellow initiates are often seen as "relatives." The characteristic solidarity between age-groups being initiated together might also explain the spontaneous readiness with which the relative undertakes Euripides' case among the women.

[467] On Mnesilokhos, father-in-law of Euripides, see *Vita* 5 (p. 5, 5 Schwartz), Suda, s.v. Εὐριπίδης (ε 3695 II 468, 22 Adler; here, however, the daughter is the first wife and is called Khoirine) and van Leeuwen *Thesm.*, 1n2.

[468] See Hiller 1874:452. The father-in-law would have been about ninety years old in 411; he was probably long dead. It is quite unlikely that he still had small children (*Thesm.* 1206). See Hiller 1874:453, Wilamowitz I 1895²:7n12, van Leeuwen *Thesm.*, 1–2, and Sommerstein *Thesm.*, 157 ad 1.

[469] On the *Vita* see Wilamowitz I 1895²:1ff.; he thinks (12–13n18) that the basis for identifying this *genos* originates from one of the Alexandrian compilers from the period 230–130 BCE; see also Lefkowitz 1981:88–104 and 163–169. Beside the *genos* there are also papyrus fragments (*POxy* 1176 [vol. 9 (1912) 124–182]) of a biographical dialogue about Euripides dating from the third century BCE and composed by Satyros that also largely presents the gossip of comedy, particularly the *Thesmophoriazusae*, as historical fact; see Lesky 1972:275.

would otherwise have been used if the son were meant to have been identified with him.[470]

The biographers also seem to have taken the father-in-law Mnesilokhos simply from the *Thesmophoriazusae*. They could have proceeded on the following assumptions: they had in front of them reports from comedy, such as fragment 41 K.-A. of Telekleides, where in order to ridicule Euripides it is claimed that Mnesilokhos and many others helped the famous tragedian compose. This comic gossip they then incorporate as historical fact into the *Vita* (ch. 2 [1.10–2.2 Schwartz]) (συμπεποιηκέναι). Like the later scholiasts, they saw the connection with the *Thesmophoriazusae*. For in a transferred form here too the relative supports Euripides, who himself has no idea what to do. On the one hand he declares that he is ready, in place of Agathon, who refuses to help, to sneak into the women's sanctuary in women's clothing to undertake Euripides' case there. On the other hand, the initiative for the attempt to rescue him with Euripidean parodies is also his. When Euripides at first does not react at all, he introduces the *Helen* and helps to realize the "reperformance" of the *Helen* and *Andromeda* within a comedy.

Following the biographical method he then becomes the father-in-law through the following thought-process: in the *Thesmophoriazusae*, the comic hero is described as a relative by marriage (κηδεστής); moreover, he enters with his little daughter. Aristophanes is perhaps reacting to ridicule from other comedians who gave her the name Χοιρίλη when he associates her with the piglet (289): the diminutive form Khoirile plays in particular on a colloquial term for the female genitalia, which perfectly suits the ritual humor of Old Comedy in general and the cultic context of the Thesmophoria in particular.[471] If the κηδεστής has a daughter who was eventually identified in

---

[470] On the basis of the discussion in the *Thesmophoriazusae*, Hiller 1874:452 connects the testimony in *Vita* 2 (1.10–2.2 Schwartz), taken from Telekleides fr. 41 K.-A. (Μνησίλοχός ἐστ' ἐκεῖνος <ὃς> φρύγει τι δρᾶμα καινὸν | Εὐριπίδῃ, καὶ Σωκράτης τὰ φρύγαν' ὑποτίθησιν), that Sokrates and one Mnesilokhos collaborated in the composition of the Euripidean tragedies because of the discussion in the *Thesmophoriazusae* with the father-in-law. Kassel-Austin *PCG* VII, 683 do the same. Telekleides belonged to the generation of comic playwrights immediately preceding Aristophanes; his first victory at the Dionysia occurred shortly after 446 BCE. His criticism of Euripides has an immediate temporal connection to Aristophanes' works between the *Acharnians* and the *Thesmophoriazusae*. It is at least also probable that the aging Euripides was criticized for receiving help from his son, especially since the latter was himself involved in the profession as an actor. Cf. also the talk of Kephisophon's collaboration (cf. Lefkowitz 1981:89). All in all, however, the entire *Vita* consists only of wild speculation.

[471] See above, nn187 and 335. Manuscript R reads χοῖρον in line 289. Wilamowitz 1875:149n3 correctly sees a sexual joke in the name Χοιρίλη. Cf. Wilamowitz I 1895²:7n12 on the metaphorical meaning of the name, already explained by Philokhoros (schol. Eur. *Hec.* 3 = *FGrHist* 328 F 90): "Daß der Name Χοιρίλη wirklich als Eigenname vorkommt, ist eine triviale Wahrheit,

grotesque fashion with Euripides' wife, then, according to the type of reconstruction used in a *vita*, the relative by marriage, connected with the co-author
Mnesilokhos, can only have been his father-in-law.

Aristophanes could thus quite possibly have had the intention in the
Thesmophoriazusae of targeting Mnesilokhos, the generally known co-pro-
ducer of Euripidean tragedies (Telekleides fr. 41 K.-A.), and of intertextually
reworking the comic attacks of others. The *genos* compilers would accordingly
seem to have grasped Aristophanes' comic intentions very well. But the question immediately arises as to why he then avoids mentioning this name explicitly. A combination of two reasons suggests itself:

1. A prominent political figure among the oligarchs, who at the time of
the production were preparing to launch a decisive blow against Kleisthenes'
constitution, had the same name. At the very beginning of the rule of the Four
Hundred, a Mnasilokhos, one of their number, had the chairmanship for two
months (411/10).[472] At a time that was extremely tense for the democracy,
Aristophanes quite deliberately avoided naming the name directly in order
not to anger its opponents any further and in order not to bring the current
political climate to boiling point. Perhaps for this reason, too, possible references in the *parodos* to the threatening rule of tyrants were disguised in ritual
garb to the point of being almost unrecognizable.

2. Above all, Aristophanes wanted to prevent the play from being understood as a political statement in the sense of taking up a position either for or
against the oligarchy. The unequivocal connection with the powerful oligarch
of this name would have destroyed his ritual game completely. Many associations were supposed to be detected, but in the comedy he wanted first and
foremost to continue a favorite discourse about Euripides and against tragedy
and at the same time bring to mind another Mnesilokhos.

---

mit der nur ein Geck etwas kann ausrichten wollen" ["That the name is attested as an actual
personal name is a trivial fact that only a fool would attempt to make something of"]. Zielinski
1885:83 here sees further evidence for his theory that the *Thesmophoriazusae* that we have is a
reworking of the so-called Θεσμοφοριάζουσαι δεύτεραι. In the supposed allusion to Khoirile
(*Thesm.* 289) he sees proof of the fact that her father, Mnesilokhos, must have performed in
the Θεσμοφοριάζουσαι δεύτεραι ("Kalligeneia"): "In the 'Nesteia' [i.e. in the *Thesmophoriazusae*
we have] the poet substituted a beloved 'cousin' of Euripides for him—presumably because
Mnesilokhos had died in the interim."

[472] Arist. *Ath. Pol.* 33.1; cf. *IG* I³ 373.2. Cf. Vickers 1989:44, who nevertheless argues for a performance in the year 410. He views the connection with the archon Mnasilokhos merely as an
"extraordinary coincidence" (44); the target, he maintains, is Alcibiades, who at the beginning
of 411 was flirting with the Oligarchs. On the distribution of the name, see Fraser/Matthews I,
316 and 318; II, 315 and III.A, 303 (s.v. Μνασίλοχος and Μνησίλοχος).

Because of other comic performances many spectators were in a position to associate the relative with this name even without any name being used. As is well known, Greek poetics readily uses speaking names as program for action in the plot.[473] Comedy in particular is especially partial to this.[474] In this instance Aristophanes refrained from explicitly applying this dramaturgical device. Nevertheless, the plot, which is based on ritual complexes, is in continual etymological connection with Mnesilokhos. If the author really did have Mnesilokhos in mind when he composed the comedy, which is quite likely, then here he proceeds using implication and disguise. For the relative does indeed carry out an action as a μνησί-λοχος—he is a comic hero who recalls, i.e. imitates in playful form, the time of the λόχος, the marginal phase of initiation that is marked by a mixture of masculine and feminine symbols.[475]

[473] See above, p. 190; on this Greek idea in general, see Calame 1995:174–185, esp. 183 (on comedy and Archilochus). On the power of names, see also Pulleyn 1994.

[474] On the use of speaking names in comedy, see Steiger 1888 (who thinks that proper names must be speaking names [13]), Marzullo 1953, and the extensive bibliography in Di Marco 1981:163n19. On the names of Aristophanic heroes and the question of how they were introduced into the plays, see Barton 1990:13–27, esp. 22–27, and Olson 1992.

[475] For memory in grave-cult images of the important stage of being an ephebe, see Blech 1982: 341 with n46. In his historical and political approach to the play, Vickers (1989:44) also considers the possibility that Mnesilokhos could be a speaking name. But for the term λόχος the only possibility he considers is the unit in the Spartan army, which he then connects with Alcibiades' stay in Sparta. The deverbative compound name Mnesilokhos could additionally be an allusion to his comic function as *bômolokhos* (on Mnesilokhos as *bômolokhos*, see Whitman 1964:222, Wit-Tak 1968:363, Gruber 1986:24, and Henderson 1991²:87): a βωμο-λόχος is "one who lies in wait for a person at an altar" and in so doing hurls aggressive and vulgar speech at the person sacrificing; on this form of malicious speech cf. Ar. *Equ.* 902, *Pax* 748, and *Ran.* 358. On the semantics of the word, see Nagy 1979:245n3, who also sees Arkhi-lokhos as being possibly linked with this etymology. The case of this figure of the iambic poet (cf. Nagy 1979: 243–252) is of particular interest, especially since he was worshiped as a hero in connection with Dionysus and Demeter: on the cult aetiology of the Mnesiepes inscription, cf. Archil. fr. 251 W. (Dionysos Oipholios) and West 1974:25; the structural similarity with the *aition* of the Great Dionysia (schol. *Ach.* 243) is striking; Archilochus is the archetypical χορηγός of the city (fr. 120 W.) who looks after the fertility and welfare of the community; on the poet's cultic worship of Kore, Demeter, and Dionysus at the festival of the Iobakkhoi, cf. Archil. fr. 322 W.; see now also Clay 2004 and Compton 2006:41–58. On the connection of iambic poetry with the cults of Dionysus and Demeter, see West 1974:23–25 and in general Nagy 1990:395–397; on the association of iambic poetry and comedy, see Nagy 1979:249–252, Degani 1988, and Rosen 1988; cf. Nagy 1979:301–308 (Archilochus in connection with Apollo and the Muses). Mnesilokhos is the comic-iambic "hero" of comedy and the social representative of the "chorus-leader" Euripides; finally, a comparsion with the chorus, which feels itself connected to the same cults, can also be made through the relative via Dionysiac and Demetrian components. Agathon is, like Archilochus, a "servant of the Muses"; cf. Archil. fr. 1 W. θεράπων . . . Μουσέων and the epiphany of Agathon in the *Thesmophoriazusae* (39ff.; on the comically exaggerated divinity of the poet, see Kleinknecht 1937: 151n1; the passage is reminiscent of the parody of human divinity, esp. *Av.* 1706–1765 [see Kleinknecht 1937a]), in particular because of his close relationship to the Muses (*Thesm.* 41 and 107).

On many occasions Aristophanes will not provide a character with a name immediately upon his first appearance, but will delay his naming up until a point when releasing the name will have a particular effect in the dramatic context. In the *Thesmophoriazusae* we have an exceptional case in which the anonymity of the hero is maintained over the entire course of the play, but in which the actual name of a historical figure is eventually alluded to.[476]

Certainly not everyone in the audience could have caught the possible play on the name Mnesilokhos and the subtle etymological humor. But the ritual dimension of this comedy was understandable to all original recipients. In the synaesthetic spectacle it will have been symbolically quite clear that the relative is undergoing a *rite de passage*. The hero, as woman in his second-level fictional role, and as man in reality, is retrojected into the conditions of the undifferentiated and inverted world of the transition. The chorus here helps, in particular in the *tableau* of the *parabasis* (821–829), to make this condition, which is expressed in the *lokhos* and in the *pyrrhikhê*, clear in symbolic fashion. The chorus also has a critical role in preparing the way for the return to normality.

Concluding Remarks on the Role of the Comic Chorus in the *Thesmophoriazusae*

The *Thesmophoriazusae* is thus not merely a literary representation, and still less is it about contemporary politics. Rather, against the background of the Euripidean parodies, the projection surface of an Attic festival, in which the female sex phylogenetically undergoes a primordial and precivilized stage and ontogenetically a threshold state between being a virgin and an adult woman, is used to handle the male identity of the Attic citizen in a playful fashion and as a comic and Dionysiac experience.

The chorus is given an important role in this. It is the bearer of the ritual ambiance, and it constructs the festive background on which the plot feeds. The collective interacts with the comic hero and with the audience. The chorus

---

[476] See Olson 1992:306–307. He refers to another extreme case, in the *Knights*; the Sausage-seller comes onstage in line 146, but only receives the name Agorakritos in line 1257. The anonymity of the relative in our play is mentioned by Olson, but not further explained (1992:307). Aristophanes could certainly have had dealings with Mnesilokhos, as with other Athenians of his day (Olson 1992:316–318). But then, as already mentioned, he would have centered his interest on another Mnesilokhos; Mnesilokhos the helper of Euripides was too insignificant a figure to have a whole comedy explicitly constructed upon him, something which could only have been done with a portrait mask.

is thus above all a mediator.[477] In its function as Dionysiac chorus it speaks of its own activity, and thus self-reference as speech act underpins ritual dancing and the worship of all the gods of the polis. In its fictional role too, the chorus performs purely ritual tasks that the festival as context of the play predetermines. At the center here stands *aiskhrologia* and the hymn to the gods, which coincide with the comic chorus' traditional function of praising and blaming, the complementary κακῶς λέγειν and εὖ λέγειν.[478] As fellow actor in the drama its speech is also often identical to its action. We have seen that in the *Thesmophoriazusae* in particular the comic chorus has a ritual nature, since its utterances are entirely translated into action and contain no general reflections or narratives. The construction of a ritual background and its speech against, about, and with the comic hero construct a syntagmatic connection with the structure of the plot, which is entirely based on a ritual model.

The realization that both the comic hero and the chorus of the *Thesmophoriazusae* reactualize the initiation of girls and youths in a ritual, symbolic, and multimedia spectacle contains an even deeper significance if one connects it with John J. Winkler's thesis, already discussed in the Introduction, that the tragic chorus is equivalent to the initiatory experience of young men.[479] Gregory Nagy has performed a great service in modifying this initially surprising and controversial theory in Attic tragedy. According to the latter, the choral tradition, which can be connected very clearly with rites of initiation in the real world, was so radically monopolized by the polis theater that these practices can be found only as remnants in the fifth-century chorus. The theatrical chorus is thus not actually identical to ephebic

---

[477] Steiner 1988:208 considers the chorus in a certain sense as a variably expanding connector between stage and audience. He gives the following striking characterization of the function of the tragic chorus: "So wirkt er als eine Art Zugbrücke, die der Dramatiker mit metrischen und choreographischen Mitteln nach Belieben hochziehen und senken, verkürzen oder verlängern kann. Über den Chor läßt sich der Zuschauer an die Bühne heranziehen oder von ihr distanzieren; er kann praktisch in die szenische Situation verstrickt, ihm kann aber auch (naiver) Zugang zu ihr versperrt werden" ["It functions thus as a kind of drawbridge that the dramatist using metrical and choreographic means can raise and lower or shorten or lengthen as he sees fit. Through the chorus the spectator can bring himself closer to the stage or distance himself from it; he can almost involve himself in the situation on stage, but he can also be barred from (naïve) access to it"]. Cf. also the definition of the tragic chorus' role in Goldhill 1986:271 as "commentator, expander, mediator between the actors and the audience."

[478] On praise and blame in poetry see Nagy 1979:213–275; on the ritual connection of iambic poetry and comedy, 249–252. West 1974:34–37 and Nagy 1979:242–243 consider *iambos* as a particular dance step; that is, the comic chorus also in its dance fulfills this ritual dimension of praise and ridicule. See below, chap. 2 n44.

[479] Winkler 1985 and the reprint Winkler 1990. Independently of Winkler, Seiterle 1984, esp. 138–139, has expressed the thesis that original rituals involving goats were part of initiation celebrations. Cf. also Seiterle 1988:7–11.

service, but it notionally imitates in a ritual way a chorus of young men on the threshold of adulthood in the imagination of the presenter and recipients. The chorus members in the orchestra form a bridge to an audience that in its ideal composition consists of adult full citizens. In the performance the chorus mediates between the dramatic action and the spectator first by acting ritually as if it were in the ephebic transitional phase as citizen-to-be. Second, the members of the comic chorus in their function as actual dancers appear in all respects as full citizens, who as microcosm form a representative part of the polis as a whole. The initiatory status manifests itself in tragedy through the fact that the chorus here is almost exclusively made up of socially marginal groups such as girls, old men, women, and prisoners-of-war. Even though the actual historical and archaeological "hard" facts put forward by Winkler can in no way prove his thesis beyond doubt,[480] he does concern himself with the figurative level of evidence in the text and shows how many tragedies play out ephebic experiences and how the chorus made up of marginal figures reflects them.[481] Nagy extends this theory in a consistent fashion. He interprets the

[480] For criticism of Winkler's thesis, see Csapo/Slater 1995:352. Winkler 1990:48-49 did, however, offer a convincing reply to the argument that there could hardly have been an exemption from military service for members of the chorus if the chorus had formed part of military training: he sees the reason as lying in a symbolic equivalence of the two civic duties. Goldhill 1987:74-75 and Graf 1998:25-27 are also positively disposed to Winkler's position. It is much more questionable whether the representation of the chorus members as ephebes on the Pronomos Vase (nn110, 308 above), upon which Winkler relies, should be taken as fact. For a narratological analysis of the vase, see Calame 1995:116-136.

[481] It is interesting, however, that he omits the important observations of the original piece (Winkler 1985:32-38) in the 1990 reprint (but see Winkler 1990:57). He does see Perseus in the Euripidean *Andromeda* as a typical ephebic hero who has to undergo an adventure in the Outside (Winkler 1985:33-34), but he does not recognize Andromeda's initiatory status. On Orestes see Winkler 1985:35 and Bierl 1994a. On the direction in scholarship that connects Attic tragedy with *ephêbia* and rites of puberty, see the bibliography in Goldhill 1987:74n70 and Zeitlin 1990:68n12. Cf. in particular the application of interpretative scheme in the sense of an "initiatory" process in Zeitlin 1990:86-87; this she understands as a temporary questioning, with subsequent confirmation, of masculinity. On the mixing of images and metaphors of the mysteries and ephebic initiation in Sophocles' *Philoctetes*, see more recently Lada-Richards 1997 and Lada-Richards 1998. On the use of the interpretative paradigm of the *ephêbeia*, initiation, and structure-determining *rite de passage* for plot structure in Aristophanes (for the *Knights*, *Wasps*, and *Clouds*) see Bowie 1993, esp. 45-58, 78-101, 102-112. Here however he is constantly forced to postulate inversions of the standard model to take into account the usually older hero. Cf. the critical comments in reviews by A. H. Sommerstein (*JHS* 114 [1994]: 188-189, esp. 188), D. M. MacDowell (*CR* 44.2 [1994]: 263-265, esp. 264), J. F. McGlew (*BMCR* 94.10.10), and R. M. Rosen (*BMCR* 94.10.11). For this reason I shall here follow the path of theatrical reactualization of these experiences of the liminal, a reactualization that is also to be found in the ritual structure of festivals. The reflex of the puberty rites of young girls and the synchronization with male initiatory ceremonies in Aristophanes have so far not received attention. The closest to my approach is Loraux's interpretation of the *Lysistrata* (1981:157-196, esp. 173-179).

tragic chorus of nonprofessionals as an instrument that using a ritual recollection of the initiation stage conveys to the audience in an "intersubjective" way the pathos experienced there.[482]

From this we may establish the following conclusions concerning the *Thesmophoriazusae*: both comic hero and chorus are connected with initiatory symbolism. Here too, the marginal chorus of women mediate the process of transition for the audience; both actors and chorus are retrojected as adults in a comprehensive ritual process of reversal into a pubertal and marginal situation. In contrast to tragedy, here it is not pathos that is conveyed; rather, the reversals experienced in rites of puberty and striking cultic experiences are transmitted to the polis gathered in the theater by means of dance and symbolic action as comic passions, laughter, and an atmosphere of festivity. In the penetrating synaesthetic experience of the *communitas* the feeling of connectedness among all participants becomes stronger in both dramatic genres.

So far these reflections on the initiatory quality of the tragic chorus have not been applied to comedy.[483] There are two possibilities for the special case which the *Thesmophoriazusae* represents in terms of its *paratragôidia*. First, in parodying the other genre the tragic setup is imitated. Second, one may recognize these traits in the comic chorus in general, but in a comic transformation. In comedy, reception is not guided by way of commentary delivered by a chorus that is only marginally involved in the action.[484] There is also here little of the tension between the authoritative voice of the chorus in its real world function as educator and the limited speech of the chorus in its inner-dramatic role as outsider, as Simon Goldhill correctly maintains in the case of

---

In this study she employs female initiation as well as the return to this marginal condition as structural interpretative categories. It is no coincidence that the *Lysistrata* is closest to the *Thesmophoriazusae*. See above, nn. 279, 284, 328, and 375. For the *Frogs* see also the extensive monograph by Lada-Richards (1999), who again sets out the ritual character of the play as *rite de passage* and the interpenetration of ephebic and Dionysiac or Eleusinian mystery initiation (esp. chap. 2, 45–122: " 'Separation', 'Limen', 'Aggregation': The *Frogs* as a 'Rite of Passage' "). The comic chorus is however almost completely ignored in all initiatory interpretations to date. For some indications, see now Lada-Richards 1999:220–229, who pursues a similar direction independently of this work.

[482] Nagy 1994/95:48–52.

[483] Winkler 1990:21 refers to the relations in comedy only once in passing. But there can be no talk in comedy of an ordered exercise in rank and file. Even in tragedy the round dance is far more common than Winkler suggests. See Davidson 1986 and Wiles 1997:63–86 on this.

[484] On the social marginality of the tragic chorus in its fictional role and on its collective otherness, see also Gould 1996. Barlow 1971:25 talks of a "different focusing perspective." On the focusing function of the tragic chorus, see also Goldhill 1986:273.

tragedy.[485] The Aristophanic performers in the orchestra hardly possess an authoritative and gnomic attitude, and even less to be seen is the almost deconstructivist tendency of members of the tragic chorus to place all advice under question by adding an opposing viewpoint.[486]

On the contrary, in comedy the chorus performs simply as a ritually speaking and acting group that helps fashion the comic play as it oscillates between the plot and the here and now. The confirmation and simultaneous dissolution of the norm happens almost exclusively in cultic dance and in hymns to the gods. Precisely like a tragic chorus, the women celebrating the Thesmophoria *qua* festival chorus still allow their Dionysiac and theatrical-performative dimension to shine through and provide an audience for the hero.[487] Festivity and unrestrained pleasure are given full expression and trans-lated into action, so that all can participate in this. The choral-lyrical gestures of gnomic instruction and mythical narrative as context are absent, since they are diametrically opposed to the comic.[488]

But ritual play even of this type has a distant connection with initia-tion. Both the comastic Dionysiac activity of the male youth and the fictional involvement of a comic chorus in an inverted world ritually represent limi-nality, a state beyond all norms and categories and situated on the threshold between childhood and adulthood. Even if participation in a comic chorus cannot simply be equated with a rite of initiation, the experience is at least structurally similar to an initiatory experience. For this reason the comic playwright is able to superimpose other rites of passage as contexts for the plot on top of the ritual scheme of collectively reactualized initiation. In this connection, annually reoccurring polis festivals of inversion, which may be interpreted both as new year's and agrarian fertility festivals, are of particular importance. In the *Thesmophoriazusae* the members of the chorus in terms of both their role and their function take themselves back to the initiatory stage, and the two other liminal aspects are simultaneously present.

[485] Goldhill 1996:254. Cf. also Goldhill 1986:267–271.
[486] Goldhill 1986:271 terms this dialectic connection "play of *difference*," significantly following Derrida's *différance*.
[487] See now also Baur 1997:40–44 and Baur 1999a:23–26. Baur (1997:44–47; 1999a:26–28) empha-sizes the "separate status" (*Sonderstatus*) of the dramatic chorus; in contrast to the actors, it represents an entity without a signified that always remains simply the theatrical institution of "chorus"; its fictional characterization is accordingly merely an accidental property. The historical evolution from citizen collective to theatrical institution occurs according to Baur only in the realm of the signifier.
[488] The felicitous observation by Lehmann (1991:47) that the tragic chorus aids expression, not communication ("dem *Ausdruck*, nicht der Mitteilung") is even more applicable to the comic chorus, since it preserves the ritual element to a much greater degree.

Beside the chorus' purely ritual role in the here and now, which is attested in the *parabasis*-like manner of speech, it also contributes somewhat to the deliberate action set "elsewhere." Through its ritual action the chorus on the one hand constructs the background that forms the context for the action on stage in a fairly independent fashion. The comic play is also, on the other hand, implicitly propelled by the chorus' interaction with the actors, since the chorus in its role in front of an internal audience shapes and characterizes the relative.[489] At first, within the plot of the trial at the Thesmophoria he is made out to be the enemy of the women. After his uncovering, he is symbolically and visually presented in the *tableau vivant* of the *parabasis* as a male/female inititiate. During the choral dance song (947–1000), he is assimilated to their initiatory status in terms of role and function. This ultimately, in parallel to the conclusion of the women's festival in the plot, enables the comedy's "happy ending."

Rituality in the Microstructure

In conclusion to my discussion of the *Thesmophoriazusae* I would like to enlarge on the concept of ritual seen in the comic chorus, particularly in aspects that are not related to the plot. Here our point of departure at the beginning of the chapter, the great choral dance song (*Thesm.* 947–1000), will serve once more as example. In what follows rituality will also be shown as it occurs in the microstructure. It must be stressed again that form cannot be separated from content.

Stanley J. Tambiah's theory of performative ritual yields important conclusions, particularly in the context of theater. The cultic side should not of course be limited to the illocutionary side, which one might assume following John Austin, as if one were only concerned with a speech act without perlocutionary consequences. For what is first and foremost in the mind of the worshiper is

---

[489] Gruber (1986:37–39) is so far the only scholar to put forward ideas about the role of the chorus in relation to its performative interaction with the hero and the audience. The chorus of the *Thesmophoriazusae* has up until now been too strongly disqualified as "nondramatic." But even Gruber subscribes to a false dichotomy of ritual and theater: "Far from being a ritual 'element' that identifies Aristophanes' debt to archaic predramatic structures, the chorus of Old Comedy is a supremely *theatrical* instrument that in this play as well as in others is capable of great sophistication" (1986:37). It has been shown in this chapter that ritual belongs to the theatrical speech of the chorus, whose structure can therefore largely be described as predramatic, since the comic playwright in a ritual performance does not so much intend to place emphasis on the creation of a total illusion, but rather to draw the audience and the everyday world into the production.

making contact with the gods through this kind of prayer, something Tambiah often refers to. In his opinion, one may consider songs of this type as performative in three senses: as speech acts in the sense of Austin and Searle; as dramatic spectacle; and finally in the sense that they problematize and define hierarchical values and positions in performance. These criteria are tightly interwoven and are not susceptible to separate investigation. As a culturally determined system of symbolic communication, the choral song is also based on fixed models and an ordered series of actions and words. Expressiveness is enhanced by a synaesthetic manner of performance, the content and form of which is primarily characterized by conventionality and stereotypical formularity, compression, and mixture of expression (fusion) or redundancy based on repetitive phenomena.[490]

What is distinctive about the presentation of a choral dance song is the simultaneity of various media. The *opsis* of the spectacle, the external appearance enhanced by costumes and masks, contributes especially to the typical demonstrative attitude in ritual. The round dance in the rectangular orchestra, with its rhythmically repetitive movements that lead to ecstasy, brings about a collective unity through the use of the same sequence of movements by a representative group of individual citizens. The rhythm, the movement, or κίνησις, and the powerful accompanying music produce a socially unifying experience in both body and spirit. Then there is also song (μολπή), a mode of expression based on words and language in which a myth often gives the context for the ritual being performed. The occasion of these ritual performances generally presupposes the participation of a group. In the case of Greek drama and dithyramb, which are dedicated to the worship of Dionysus, a large part of the polis as a whole is gathered in the theater. The choruses are a distinctive element in a performance that joins audience and actors in a particular experience. The ritual and its mythical treatment impart in symbolic form the system of norms and values held in common by the community, thereby creating contact with the cosmos and the gods who protect the city. The fictional plot of comedy is based on myths, which are in turn drawn from the community's ritual repository of experience. At the same time, the reality of the performers and the crowd involved is always visible behind this game. The chorus itself is an important shifter between the inner and the outer, the here and the there.

The discourse of choral dance songs, as is the case in many ritual performances in other cultures, is distinct from everyday speech, echoing the sepa-

---

[490] Tambiah 1985:123–166, esp. 128.

rate state of the festival. Everyday speech is, however, roughly imitated in the speaking parts. The stylistic level of the chorus members is elevated, and their language is of a conventional rather than an intentional nature. Since we ultimately find only an imitation of human intention in songs of this kind, the performers lack any free emotional expression and spontaneity.

Our song is marked by a great formal regularity, despite modulations in voice (φωνῇ, *Thesm.* 961). Yet it never depends on purely stereotypical convention, but presents above all "aesthetically arranged, symbolic and expressive actions" and "phatic acts," "which emphasize their own performance and make reference to themselves."[491] Despite all this uniformity, the chorus makes contact with the gods in this festive tone using lively, creative metaphors in an uplifting and intensified form of communication.[492] Repetitive examples, stereotyped streams of identical or similar sounding words—such as, for example, the brief invocations of the gods, reference to χάρις or in particular to the chorus' own dance formation—are of great importance. The self-referential and self-limited manner of referring to the round dance should at the same time be understood as a performative speech act, which translates typical self-representation into action.

The formulaic nature of prayer, invocations in *Du-Stil*, the enumeration of names and cultic places, and the catalogues of several divine addressees are also reflected in the course of the melody and in the rhythm. The creative function of fixed units of recycled song has been emphasized in Homeric studies by Albert Lord and Milman Parry in particular.[493] Lord explained how for a singer in a purely oral culture the moment of composition coincides with performance.[494] On the basis of memorized formulae and by the use of small variations, such as, for example, expansions, contractions, rearrangements, substitutions, and recursive new combinations, the poet continually composes new verses according to need, context, and the nature of his audience.

One ought not view the stylized technique in the Aristophanic choral song as the result of a stereotyped ossification that was necessary for the mnemonic technique of oral poetry because of the gradual disappearance of

---

[491] Braungart 1996:108 and 117–118; for explanation of the connections see 108–118.

[492] Tambiah 1985:142. He reports that the tribe of the Chamulas in the high country of Mexico calls formalized, ritual diction "hot" speech (in contrast to everyday, "cold" speech).

[493] Parry 1971 (the book includes Parry's relevant works [1902–1935]) and Lord 1960. See Nagy 1990:51, however, for the differentiation caused by the development of spoken poetry from a song culture (SONG). Nagy thinks that the formulaic nature of oral poetry was only a result of the suppression of melody and dance.

[494] On orality as a cultural mode of presentation that in the telling of a tragic myth functions on the level of the emotions, see des Bouvrie 1990:89–92.

melody and dance. Since music and *khoreia* play a central role here, the characteristic style depends on the fact that the comic poet is restaging a ritual mode of performance in a living choral culture, a mode that is reflected in the phraseology, metrics, and melody.[495] The choral dance song of lines 947–1000 is thus of a ritual nature, because Aristophanes does not simply imitate the metre and diction of choral lyric as literature, but in the process of mimesis productively reactualizes forms of expression which are anchored in ritual and in which Greek society handed down its values and norms through communal song.

Let us now take a brief look at the formal structure, which is closely connected with the content. One can easily follow this ritual technique of variation of the song in its rhythmic and metrical structure.[496] The transition from everyday modes of expression to the marked choral style is fluid. First comes an anapaestic prelude (947–952) that as a steady recitative (*parakatalogê*) falls between song and speech. The song then moves via an ambivalent and brief anapaestic period (953) consisting of four long syllables (two syncopated trochees, an anapaest or two spondees) to a trochaic section (954–956). The lekythia (954, 956) as catalectic trochaic or acephalous iambic dimeters pave the way for the iambic period (957–958).[497] The following three small trochaic strophes (959–961, 962–965, 966–968) refer back to lines 953–958. After a cretic, which may also be interpreted as a catalectic trochee (962, 966; paeon 959),

---

[495] These three categories correspond to the tripartite division of λόγος, ἁρμονία, and ῥυθμός, which constitute μέλος, according to Plato (Plat. *Rep.* 398d); cf. Arist. *Poet.* 1447a21–23 (not however used by Aristotle). *Logos*, continues Plato, forms the basis; tone (ἁρμονία) and movement (ῥυθμός) have to follow this as subordinated levels. In what follows, only λόγος and ῥυθμός can be analyzed, since the musical framework has been completely lost. Even in the area of ῥυθμός, only the metrical form can be discussed, since the actual movements of the dance, which is what the term really designates (cf. Plat. *Leg.* 664e–665a: τῇ δὴ τῆς κινήσεως τάξει ῥυθμὸς ὄνομα εἴη; *Rep.* 400c: τὰς ἀγωγὰς τοῦ ποδός), can also no longer be reconstructed. The three categories that make up μέλος are also important for the analysis of the phallophoric songs in chap. 2.

[496] For the metrical analysis here I largely follow Zimmermann II 1985:192–200. See also Parker 1997:428–437. All in all, the short periods are largely variations on the original Indo-European verse of the dimeter with twelve *morae* (περίοδος δωδεκάσημος); see Gentili 1952:15–19 and now Gentili/Lomiento 2003:13–14 and 53–54.

[497] Coulon, following Wilamowitz 1921:475n2, uses a different division. He puts the anapaestic colon together with line 954 to form a catalectic trochaic tetrameter, followed by a trochaic trimeter (χερὶ σύναπτε χέρ', <ἱερᾶς> ῥυθμὸν χορείας), a trochaic tetrameter (ὕπαγε πᾶσα. βαῖνε καρπαλίμοιν ποδοῖν. ἐπισκοπεῖν δέ), and a catalectic tetrameter; see the criticism in Parker 1997:431. Sommerstein *Thesm.* also reads 957–958 purely trochaically, while taking 957 as trochaic trimeter (βαῖνε καρπαλίμοιν ποδοῖν· ἐπισκοπεῖν δέ) and 958 as Coulon does. Parker 1997:428–431 interprets 953–958 as a sequence of iambic and choriambic cola; he takes 956, βαῖνε καρπαλίμοιν ποδοῖν, as a glyconic.

follow a lekythion in 960 and 963, or a complete trochaic dimeter (967), and a catalectic tetrameter. The trochee is considered particularly animated and fits the comic chorus' quick movements. Aristotle (*Rhet.* 1408b36) tells us that the comic and orgiastic *kordax* was also danced in this rhythm. The antistrophic hymnic section directed to the Olympians is introduced by two iambic dimeters, to which a catalectic form is attached (969–971, 977–979). Two reiziana form the midpoint, where the transition once again occurs seamlessly through its iambic beginning (972a/b, 980a/b).[498] Then follow once again two catalectic iambic dimeters (973–974, 981–982) and the concluding periods (975–976, 983–984), which consist of a combination of iambic trimeter and the clausula of the catalectic dimeter. The transition to the Dionysiac section is made up solely of short periods with no enjambment (985–989), and again happens smoothly. An iambic trimeter is again followed by a catalectic dimeter; now follow an iamb with a molossus, an iamb with spondee (988a) as a catalectic form of the preceding line,[499] an aristophaneus (988b), that is, a combination of choriamb and baccheus,[500] and finally the clausula of the catalectic iambic dimeter. The spondaic element in particular refers to a simple cultic form that is also favored in *carmina popularia* (fr. 863, 865, 871, lines 2 and 5 *PMG*). The concluding antistrophic hymn to Dionysus (990–994, 995–1000) starts with an aristophaneus (990, 995), already used for the invocation in line 988b. The choriambic element is taken up in the following pherecratean (991, 996). Lines 992a–993a (= 997–998b) begin with an aeolic short verse, the so-called dodrans B, which joins a iambic foot with a choriamb;[501] a single iamb forms the connection to the following aristophaneus. The end of the strophe consists of two catalectic iambic dimeters (993b–994, 999–1000). The predominant short periods emphasize the repetitive metre, which has the effect of orchestrating and integrating the song. We have already talked above about ring composition, which emphasizes the cyclical motion in this song.

Repetitions, parallelisms, and series also mark diction on the level of content. Self-exhortations to dance come thick and fast. Rhythm also accom-

---

[498] For the reizianus, see Gentili 1952:73–78 and now Gentili/Lomiento 2003:199 and 203–204. It appears with both forms of the beginning (long, two shorts) together with a pherecratean in the famous Rhodian swallow song, which as a folk song demonstrates rhythmic structures typical of orality (fr. 848 *PMG* [= carm. pop. 2], carm. pop. 41 B., 32 D.).

[499] Zimmermann II 1985:197–198 interprets the conjunction of iamb and molossus or spondee as syncopated iambic dimeter.

[500] The aristophaneus can be analyzed as a catalectic anaclastic choriambic dimeter and also represents a *dôdekasêmos* in shortened form. The character of the choriamb is significantly described as κύκλιος (Choeroboscus *in* Heph. p. 218.23 Consbruch); it is thus perfectly suited for this dance.

panies content. The four longs in ὄρμα χώρει (953) set the dance in motion slowly, and the resolutions of the second trochaic foot in the following κοῦφα ποσίν, ἄγ' εἰς κύκλον (954) with the resulting four shorts accompany the gentle and nimble movements of the chorus' feet. The catalectic form of the trochaic dimeter forms the clausula-like short period that ends in the cretic εἰς κύκλον, thus underscoring the formation of the circle as closed system.

The serial invocation of the Olympian gods (969ff.), for example, is also of importance. The self-command πρόβαινε (969) stands at the important initial position of the short period, with the object τὸν Εὐλύραν forming the end (969) and being connected to the participle μέλπουσα (970). The two lines begin with πρόβαινε and μέλπουσα, thereby addressing the central aspects of the performance of a choral dance song. Artemis' title (970), and her actual name with a two-member apposition that only appears in the following line (971), is syndetically joined to this. The two reiziana form the central greeting (972a) and plea for victory (972b) together with the command at verse beginning. Then follows the name of Hera together with an epithet (973), then a variation of a choral self-command with a change from second-person singular imperative to first-person plural hortative (974), and finally a relative clause in which it is said she participates in the performance (975) on the one hand and has a role in the plot (976) on the other. The antistrophe invokes in varying fashion a series of gods from beyond the city (977–978) with the request to smile upon the chorus of the here and now (979–980). Finally, through repetition in diction, we circle back via the reciprocal relationship of performers and gods (981–982) to the choral self-command to dance.[502]

The fusion of word, music, and rhythm achieves both an emotional intensity and an insidious loss on the level of signification. Because of the "poetic" and aesthetic formation using hyperbaton, rhythm, and alliteration, both performers and spectators receive an impression of an integrative unity and inner meditative centering as grammatical sense units blend into each other and lose their unambiguous contours. At the center point is rhythmic motion,

---

[501] The dodrans is ultimately a choriambic dimeter with double *akephalia*, i.e. a further variation of the dimeter or the short period of twelve *morae* (σημεῖα).

[502] For the principle of repetition and rhythm ("Wiederholung und Rhythmus") as the aesthetic form of ritual and ritual texts, see Braungart 1996:166–186. Braungart's further categories of festival and celebration, cult, play, and mimesis ("Fest und Feier" [187–199], "Kult" [200–215], "Spiel" [216–233], "Mimesis" [234–253]) are also relevant for our example. On the function of repetition in ritual, see Baudy 1998, esp. 21–99.

the recognition of rhythmic patterns: in short, *khoreia* as self-presentation and the motor function of cult.[503]

By means of the free interchange of variation, the working of paradigmatic and syntagmatic relations in concert, and the dynamic embedding of metaphoric and metonymic dimensions, a new, cohesive message comes into being. It conveys to performers and participants the subjective impression of being included in a greater whole: for this redundant and repetitive orchestration engenders a feeling of oneness with the cosmos. It is precisely the even, repetitive movements of the dance in a similarly varying rhythm, distinct from the iambic trimeters of the speaking parts based on everyday speech, that on a fundamental and corporeal level underscore this function, whose effect is to bring about social proximity.[504]

Eugene G. d'Aquili, Charles D. Laughlin, and their research group have demonstrated the integrative effects of ritual in neurobiological experiments. They have shown how in so-called spillover effects the flow of stimuli from parts of the central nervous system in which the cognitive and intentional abilities as well as analytical thought are located are diverted to other regions of the system that are thought to contain vegetative and sensory centers as well as centers responsible for integrated thought and imagination. The exchange can also occur in the opposite direction. The total effect of these

---

[503] Cf. Tambiah 1985:164–166; in this connection he cites Bateson 1974:161: "When words are set to music, spoken in unison or both danced and sung, only the high-level boundaries are likely to match perfectly, and therefore the structure is only fully intelligible at the highest levels with lower-level segmentation destroyed." He also discusses (Tambiah 1985:389 nn51–52) Jakobson's famous treatment of the poetic function (cf. Jakobson 1960, esp. 358 [cf. Selected Writings III, 27]). The Marxist theory of choral dance developed by Bloch 1974 maintains that the repetitive, redundant, and fusionistic characteristics of formalized ritual cause a lack of propositional power in speech and a loss of creativity. Bloch sees dance as an instrument of political power, a kind of opium for the people designed to bring about complete control of the bodily functions of the subjects. For criticism of this view, see Tambiah 1985:154–155.

[504] Cf. also Nagy 1990:30–48. He contrasts SONG with speech, where SONG is every speech act distinguished by dance and music from everyday speech. Myth and ritual represent the festive context that separates the dance song mode (SONG) from normal speech. The mode of expression in song culture occurs in marked, stylized, and stereotyped speech, characterized in morphology and syntax by isocola, rhyme, alliteration, and other stylistic devices. Nagy 1990:33 connects the structures of this original choral speech with Jakobson's poetic function. In his opinion, poetry is only a later offshoot of this original song culture. *Khoreia* is a typical expression of this song culture; as indicated above, Nagy also emphasizes the tendency toward formalization and stylization that is only to be compared with metrics in poetry in a diachronic sense (*ibid.*, 38–51). Nagy puts forward the hypothesis that the rhythmic cola of song are related to the stichic metres of lyric, but that dactylic hexameter, elegiac distichs, and iambic trimeter, which are actually spoken poetry, represent a further derivative of this (*ibid.*, 48–51).

sudden distributions of stimuli in the individual is an overwhelming feeling of wellness, security, and joy.[505] The ritual agent or individual involved in the action experiences for a short while a feeling of harmony with the self and with the world. Transcendent powers, the cosmos of *daimones* and Olympian gods, seem to work benevolently upon the ritual performers. The performers (as well as the gods) thus become transmitters and receivers of a message.[506] This paradoxical communications situation is reflected in the relationship of χάρις that characterizes hymnic discourse.

This biological analysis of ritual thus proceeds, in simplified terms, on the basis of two mutually complementary and asymmetrical systems. Laughlin mentions by way of example the exchange between the frontal cortex of the brain and the sensory centers of the cerebral cortex, whereby each form of perception in cognitive terms is first brought under control through a process of symbolization, then the reciprocal relationship of the left and right hemispheres of the brain, and finally the interchange between the hierarchically constructed levels of cortical and subcortical, endocrinal and immunological structures. D'Aquili and Laughlin had earlier attempted to group all biological oppositions as either energy-creating (ergotropic) or energy-retaining (trophotropic).[507] In terms of this theory, ritual activity throws the nervous system into complete uproar.[508]

Dance, rhythmic accompaniment on the *tympanon*, the shrill sound of the *aulos*, and song belong inalienably to ritual performance. In the same way as figurative speech, which has a particular impact on the imaginitive and spatial center of the right hemisphere, they have a strong stimulatory effect on the endocrinal and immunological system. There, ecstasy-inducing chemical substances are released that give rise to *enthousiasmos*, the feeling of being filled with a divinity. At the same time, cognitive centers are also stimulated

---

[505] See the collection of d'Aquili/Laughlin/McManus 1979, esp. d'Aquili/Laughlin 1979, and the overview of biogenetic structural theory in Laughlin 1990. Ritual is defined as a human cultural technique; with its help *homo sapiens* learns in symbolic fashion how to come to an understanding with others of its type about cognitive centers. Moreover, during the course of phylogenesis, ritual came to have the function of getting different somatic subsystems within an individual to interact and synchronize with one another. See also the corresponding definition of ritual (Laughlin 1990:25): "Ritual is a special case of formalized behavior that usually involves group members in a reciprocal performance that is highly structured, repetitive, and stereotyped, and results in the coordination of the behavior, perception, cognition, and experience of individual group members relative to some social goal or purpose."

[506] See Tambiah 1985:145 and 154. On the gods as the ultimate causal impetus behind phenomena experienced in the ritual process, see d'Aquili/Laughlin 1979:170-171.

[507] D'Aquili/Laughlin 1979:172-180.

[508] Laughlin 1990:29-31.

by the invocations to the gods, for apart from the musically intensified perception of the word, its linguistic dimension also has an effect on the analytical consciousness of intentional sensual perception in the left hemisphere. But one may also consider cognitive stimulation through language as activation of the ergotropic system. The resulting tension is ultimately set in motion, so that dance becomes both trigger and result in a ritual cycle. In our song, this connection is clearly visible in the performative and illocutionary self-commands and self-references. When these commands are voiced, action arises. The chorus dances, which in turn causes stimulation, which in turn keeps the dance going.

Like animals, humans also seek to control their environment through motor behavior.[509] Problem-solving strategies of this kind extend far back into the phylogenetic past of mankind. Rituals possibly reflect absolutely fundamental biological programs of action, such as, for example, the search for food, flight, pursuit, and aggression. The bodily realities of life itself, such as sexual maturation, menstruation, or distinctions in status, are often reflected in ritual. The biological kernel is generally embedded in social contexts in a hidden fashion. Ritual transforms basic realities into a new program of action, which in turn may be clothed in a complex mythical narration. Religious rituals create images and symbols for the common orientation of a group. The link between the mental world and the natural environment is the human body. Rituals represent strategies that attempt to channel simple somatic modes of behavior after mental processing for group stability. The spiritual process then manifests itself once more in formed and formalized sequences of bodily movement.[510] Repetitive motor functions generally predominate, while visual and acoustic signals function as triggers, causing the ergotropic system to be strongly stimulated. As soon as oversaturation of rhythmic stimuli occurs, activation of homoeostatic, energy-conserving nerve centers takes place, which then causes a feeling of oneness.

In traditional societies organized along tribal lines, choral dances are attested for various occasions: they are carried out, for example, during hunting, in war situations, at initiations, at sexual presentation, at harvest, when influencing nature through magic, and, of course, when worshiping the gods and *daimones*. One could assume a biological kernel for the comic chorus as well. Presentation of the phallus is certainly a possible motive for action; concerns about natural and human fertility and strategies of hierarchic differentiation, among other things, also seem to lie behind this. According to

[509] See d'Aquili/Laughlin 1979:177 and Burkert 1996.
[510] See Burkert 1996:166.

Burkert's theory, this biological program of action was then soon overlaid by social and cultural motifs. The two sign systems, purely ritual bodily movement in dance and its symbolic refiguring in song, enter into a fruitful union, undergo expansion, and form the mental infrastructure and the cultural memory of a society,[511] which are important for the cohesiveness of the group. The central cultural contents of this group are learned in the repetition of both word and movement. Turning to the gods gives the feeling of unassailable stability and security in the face of the uncertainties of biological life. Dancing creates joy, which is strengthened through words, and eventually transferred to the gods, who are ideal participants in the same activity as the human chorus members. Through this reciprocal construction the cosmos as a whole, that is, the performers, the community involved, and the gods protecting them, is united under the sign of the *khoreia*.

The emotionally loaded language converts cultural knowledge, which is also supposed to be absorbed during initiation, into dance movement. The gods are worshiped, and through physical means of accompaniment the distance between them and humans is narrowed, until finally from the perspecitve of the performers and spectators they appear as fellow and lead dancers. Tambiah correctly observes that in many cultures spectacular dances particularly associated with divine epiphany represent the most effective and central medium of communication. Following Radcliffe-Brown, he thinks the reason for this is that dance performers when involved in their communal activity experience a temporary feeling that they can transgress the laws of gravity and soar up to the gods just like birds. It is therefore also no coincidence that many Greek choruses make use of the creative metaphor of flight.[512]

The round dance in this passage of the *Thesmophoriazusae* is equally sensational and involves the gods in the current *khoreia* through embedment strategies, so that the spatial and hierarchic divisions of the world are temporarily set aside.

[511] On the concept of cultural or collective memory, see Assmann 1991 and Assmann 1992.

[512] See Tambiah 1985:149–150: "Dance is a superb vehicle for realizing the sense of force and power through 'ritual gesture,' through physical motion that gives the illusion of the conquest of gravity, and through movements that create spatial tensions between the dancers." Cf. ἀείρομαι, αἴρομαι, or αἴρω in choral language: Alcm. fr. 1.63 Davies: ἀυηρομέναι μάχονται (see above, Introduction nn88 and 166), Soph. *Trach.* 216 (consider also the upward motion intensified by ἀνα- 205, 210–211, 218), Eur. *Tro.* 545–546 (cf. also 325), Ar. *Nub.* 266, 276–277, *Lys.* 539, 1292, and *Eccl.* 1180. On a red-figure *astralagos* vase by the Sotades Painter (British Museum E 804, 460–450 BCE), three groups of women from a female chorus are depicted sweeping over the ground as if equipped with wings; see Robertson 1992:189–190 (ills. 199–202) and Lonsdale 1993:xvi and xxi, ill. 1 (a and b).

Moreover, in a ritual performance, hierarchies, sometimes those between choral leader and chorus, sometimes those between the gods invoked and their human worshipers, are defined. Already existent distinctions in status are confirmed. In the hymnic genre in particular, relationships of super- and subordination, which are otherwise partially suspended in the ritual inversion of comedy, are stabilized.[513] At the same time, the strict delineation of the boundary between god and human is transcended, as with sacrifice. The human chorus members praise the gods in dance and song; the latter take pleasure in this and transform themselves from recipients to transmitters, having an effect on the ritual group in turn. Dancers become facilitators between human spectators and the gods and in the festive atmosphere of their ritual occupation experience the feeling that the gods involve themselves directly in their play and assume the leadership of their activity.

To sum up, then, a tension between the dissolution and the establishment of order can be observed in the comic chorus and in its reception by the audience. The countless signs of an inverted world, seen in the act of self-retrojection into the transitional phase between youth and adulthood and in the realization of yearly reoccurring festivals of inversion both in the plot and in the ritual context of the Dionysia, are contrasted by means of ritual forms of affirmation of the cosmos, as in hymns to the gods and in prayer. Symbolic inversion in synaesthetic performance creates *communitas* and gives rise in the contrastive process of boundary definition to an overarching and emotionally based appreciation of the inherited cultural values and norms of the polis. The chorus brings together all the contradictory components of this multimedia experience and focuses them upon themselves. On the one hand, as part of the plot, it is directly involved in constructing and controlling the action as ritual process and in emotionally conveying its inverted effect to the audience by means of laughter and comedy. On the other hand, it functions simultaneously as a chorus of citizens that conveys the transcendent embodiment of the polis to its fellow citizens using the medium of rhythmic body language.[514] The anti-illusionist chorus thus becomes the central means of expression of a ritual and symbolic performance that has little to do with naturalistic, Aristotelian theater and its primacy of unbroken role and plot.

---

[513] On hierarchy in ritual see Burkert 1996:80–101; on the allocation of power and meaning in ritual using indexical means, see Tambiah 1985:156–161.

[514] According to des Bouvrie 1990:94–99, the dramatic chorus serves mainly to incite the audience emotionally during the ritual process.

In the next chapter we will extend these connections to non- and predramatic choruses. The question of to what extent the specifically ritual nature of the Aristophanic chorus may be derived from choral culture in general will be investigated. Aristophanes' songs clearly stand in a continuum that extends from pure worship to ritual play. Because of its high reflectance and the seriousness of the themes it treats, archaic choral lyric can be adduced as a parallel only to a limited degree. However, because it is rooted in a ritual occasion one may find traces of ritual speech even there. Once its mythic narration and its serious, gnomic nature are set aside, one can get at the lyric of everyday cult practice. Self-description and self-referential speech there in the speech act simply support the action being currently performed and turn the presentation into a spectacular event. The mythic is only introduced as a framework. Aristophanes reveals himself to be a poet who is attached more to this everyday, "lower" choral tradition. Yet he does allow the solemn, sublime, and authoritative to enter his work in a comic, intertextual process.

Limited dramatization is characteristic of Aristophanes' ritual form of utterance, since the chorus is integrated into the comic play only in a belated and secondary fashion. As in the *Thesmophoriazusae*, the specifically ritual appears in other comedies and in choruses with their *Sitz im Leben* in a *parabasis*-like mode of expression directed at the participant.

Most of all I wish to demonstrate again how in synaesthetic performances of this kind central ritual meanings are combined together on various levels of expression.

Chapter 2

Kômos and Comedy

The Phallic Song between Ritual and Theater

The Choral Culture between Literature and Ritual: Origin or Structural Commonalities?

When one talks today in a scholarly context about ritual and theater, a culturally preformed association usually asserts itself. Under the influence of Aristotle's theory of *entelekheia*, which is also expressed in his *Poetics*, under the influence of the Enlightenment, and especially as a result of the historical and genetic interest of nineteenth-century scholarship, which even today continues to shape the kind of questions our scholarship asks, we normally consider Attic drama as a historical development. Its origin, according to this approach, lies in primitive ritual, from which tragedy or comedy gradually freed itself, until eventually, in the course of the fifth century BCE, in a matter of decades, it became in an almost miraculous fashion the aesthetic and poetic cultural artefact we call "theater."

In this chapter we will be concerned with leaving behind this teleological mode of thought and will instead emphasize the structural connection of theatrical and ritual forms. The diachronic genesis from ritual beginnings to developed theatrical production is thus replaced by a relationship of interdependency. The two phenomena are accordingly to be understood neither as a "not yet" nor as a "no longer," but may both be present simultaneously. Their commonality is based on their performativity: both theater and ritual are staged in a spectacular fashion in front of the whole polis.

In the case of the genre of Old Comedy in particular, there are many facts that argue clearly in favor of this paradigm-shift. The dramatic productions take place in a cultic context, in honor of the god Dionysus. Certain comastic celebrations take place both before and after, so that the complex as a whole appears as a ritual continuum.[1] By means of typical strategies of embedment,

---

[1] On the cultic context and roots of ancient theater, cf. Graf 1998; for tragedy see now Easterling 1997, Seaford 2005, and Sourvinou-Inwood 2005; against the *communis opinio* of a connection with Dionysiac ritual see now the vehement attacks of Scullion 2002 (for tragedy) and of Stark 2004:11–102, esp. 97–102, 322 (for Old Comedy). Stark's sociohistorical approach is

the ritual and tradition of choral culture are also integrated into drama. The plot structures of Old Comedy are, as has been mentioned, to a considerable extent constructed on the foundation of ritual models that constitute the communal life of the citizens, for the ancient polis defines itself largely through ritual practice.

Ancient drama is first and foremost a public spectacle. A major part of the citizenry actively participates in it. The chorus of the drama forms a representative segment of the entire community and often acts in a ritual fashion. In Aristophanes' choral songs the members of the comic chorus pray to the gods, for example; they praise them in a hymn, or ask them to appear and mingle with them and take part in the activity being carried out in the here and now. Furthermore, the comic chorus often carries out actions that have little to do with its theatrical role in a naturalistic sense. As in ritual, in comedy there is an absence both of the total merging of the players with their roles that is usual in civic veristic theater and of the clear differentiation between performers and spectators, with the chorus intervening as connecting link. And so the chorus scolds and ridicules people present in the theater, pelting them with rude and obscene expressions, even throwing sweets at their heads. *Aiskhrologia* and references to festive events and to the ritual calendar are prominent. In particular, the members of the chorus laugh, dance, and sing, which is in itself an expression of *choral culture* and represents the very essence of ritual action.[2] This property of the chorus is characteristic of those societies that communicate extensively in an oral fashion despite the presence of writing and take their identity primarily from myth and ritual.[3] Beside its real-world function as comic chorus in the here and now, this internal group also experiences a condition of ritual inversion in its dramatic role.

The comic chorus is thus, as has been emphasized several times already, not only derived and descended from ritual, but *is* to a large extent ritual as well.[4] This thesis is distinct from the scholarly approach that considers ritual

---

highly reductive and questionable, as she does not refer to Greek culture in all its aspects. On the complex program of the City Dionysia, cf. Pickard-Cambridge 1968:57–125, Goldhill 1987, Connor 1989, and Cole 1993, esp. 25–29; cf. also the latest attempt at reconstruction in Sourvinou-Inwood 1994 and now in detail Sourvinou-Inwood 2003:67–200. On the comic play as continuum, see also Sfyroeras 1992, esp. 3–8.

[2] On choral dance as ritual action *par excellence* see Burkert 1985:102: "Rhythmically repeated movement, directed to no end and performed together as a group, is, as it were, ritual crystallized in its purest form."

[3] Cf. the remark of des Bouvrie 1990:89–92 on Greek theater as an oral medium.

[4] On ritual theatricality, see also Lanza 1983, esp. 107–108 and 115–116. Lanza sees ritual as incorporated into the theater in the form of lament, laughter, and fear. He especially recognizes the relationship of spectacle and ritual. Cf. esp. 107: "Ogni rito è dunque in qualche modo spet-

in comedy solely from the aspect of origin. Moreover, this theory enables us to set the aspect of literary parody in Aristophanic choral songs, which has until now been considered as central, in context. Even when Aristophanes receives, adopts, and parodically reworks cultic lyric,[5] he is still able to fashion choral performance in a completely new and productive way. *Mimesis* of a choral culture that resides in the pragmatic is not the equivalent of fundamentally literary *imitation*, but can mean authentic reenactment, a re-*experiencing* and recalling of model choruses, which in a society of this nature are omnipresent in mythic imagination as well as in ritual practice. A choral song by Aristophanes is thus part of a cultic choral tradition that was still alive in his own time and that by means of emotional involvement mediates the symbolic connections of a community of people living together.[6] The only difference between pure and dramatic cultic lyric resides of course in the fact that the playwright attempts to embed the ritual substrate in a plot sequence to a greater or lesser degree. Since Old Comedy lacks a syntagmatic dramatic unity, the choral song often remains at the same time tangible as an independent ritual song.

There are two indisputably ritual and predramatic texts, cited by the travel-writer and antiquarian Semos of Delos (ca. 200 BCE), that are of great interest precisely in terms of the concept of performance referred to above. In

---

tacolo. Si potrebbe allora distinguere tra rito, nel quale chi si esibisce e chi osserva non sono distinti, e spettacolo vero e proprio, nel quale attori e spettatori sono istituzionalmente separati. Ma anche questa distinzione è difficile: i confini appaiono labili: la stessa messa, per rifarci a un esempio relativamente familiare, può apparire da questo punto di vista volta a volta rito o spettacolo. Dipende dai margini di coinvolgimento degli intervenuti; e lo stesso si dica anche per le processioni, le laudi con responsorio, talune forme 'sperimentali' di teatro contemporaneo ecc" ["Every ritual is then in a certain sense spectacle. One may thus distinguish between ritual, in which performer and observer are not distinct from one another, and spectacle in the correct and proper sense, in which actors and spectators are institutionally separated. But this distinction also has its difficulties: the borders appear to be slippery. The very same Mass, to use a relatively familiar example, may appear from this point of view to be now ritual, now spectacle. It depends on the limits of involvement of those attending; the same can be said for processions, praises with responses, certain 'experimental' forms of contemporary theater, etc."]. This is strongly reminiscent of the theories of theater anthropology and performance studies; consider e.g. Schechner 1977 and Schechner 1985.

5   See Fraenkel 1962:191–215 (on the *parabasis*; he sees cultic lyric, in addition to Stesichorus and Alcman, as an influence on Aristophanes), Gelzer 1972 (*parabasis* odes and Alcman), Mastromarco 1987:83–93 (on the *parabasis*; he focuses on the phraseology connected with the motif of originality and superiority to other poets), and Kugelmeier 1996 (general monograph).

6   For anthropological studies on tragedy based extensively on Turner's concept of the experiencing of a liminal and marginal phase (corresponding to the three-phase model of *rite de passage* proposed by van Gennep 1909), see des Bouvrie 1990, passim (on the chorus esp. 94–99) and Aronen 1992; on Dionysus in particular, see Hoffman 1989 and des Bouvrie 1993 (as god of symbolic inversions).

his work *On Paeans*, which we know from the *Deipnosophistae* (622a–d = *FGrHist* 396 F 24) of Athenaeus (ca. 200 CE), he introduces as examples of the genre one song associated with the Ithyphalloi (fr. 851a *PMG*) and another with the Phallophoroi (fr. 851b *PMG*). As ritual texts, they have been more or less exclusively discussed using the traditional historical-genetic approach and in terms of the origin of comedy. Aristotle had in fact identified (though rather in passing) the latter as lying with the early singers of phallic songs, which were still customary in his own time (*Poetics* 1449a9–13).[7] With the phallic songs of Semos it was thought that a link to the origins of comedy had now been discovered.[8] Apart from the parallels to the *parabasis* the evidence is actually rather scanty, and only a few still subscribe to the theory that the performance of compositions of this nature could only represent a point of departure for Old Comedy.[9] One of the chief difficulties in connecting the two phallic fragments of Semos with the origins of the comic genre is the fact that they come from a period later than Aristophanes. The only way out of this dilemma is to assume that they are survivals, an approach that Aristotle had already demonstrated. A folk practice, so the theory goes, continued to exist in other places as a substrate, while in a local phenomenon limited to Athens it developed into world literature. In principle this cannot of course be excluded, but because of the lack of sources one cannot reach any final conclusion or indeed any proof: everything remains ultimately in the realm of speculation. And the songs of Aristophanes are too complex to be derived from this kind of phallic song alone.

I shall therefore follow a different path here. In what follows, I intend to show how the texts enable us to see the simultaneity of ritual and theater, the common denominator of which is formed by the concept of performance. *Phallophoria*, an activity quite removed from everyday events, is carried out as a sacred ceremony on the one hand, while on the other it is a ritual action conspicuously located in the theater. The passage of Athenaeus is particularly fruitful for this performative approach, since the quotation from Semos gives a detailed description of the performative context: the realm of visual signs,

---

[7] For discussion, see Leonhardt 1991; his theory of the reversal of relations that links comedy with dithyramb and tragedy with phallic songs has meanwhile been conclusively set aside by Patzer's review (*Gnomon* 67 [1995]:289–310).

[8] Kolster 1829:51–61 was the first to do this. The connection to the *parabasis* has always been critical; see below, nn116–117.

[9] Cf. Leonhardt 1991:15–16; Radermacher *Frogs*, 12 and Pickard-Cambridge 1962:147, 150–151 were already decisively opposed to this idea; both argue for searching for the origin in popular, agonistic begging- and blame-κῶμοι performed in animal costume (Radermacher *Frogs*, 4–36, Pickard-Cambridge 1962:151–162); Gelzer 1966:57–70 sees the point of departure for the development of Old Comedy in countless traditional festivals and folk customs. On the question of origin, see now also Rothwell 2006.

otherwise almost entirely lost, the ὄψις of the spectacle, that is, the costuming or external decoration, as well as the actors' sequence of movements in the theater and the action after the actual entrance of the song, are all described.

In order to avoid any misunderstanding, it must first be said that those predecessors who sought the origins of comedy certainly recognized the connection between ritual and the theater of Aristophanes; yet they mostly proceeded on the assumption that the comic genre gradually freed itself from its ritual beginnings and that at the latest stage Aristophanes was already creating a higher literature. The ritual element is thus dismissed as something inferior and primitive and accepted only as a remnant. As an alternative to this evolutionary hypothesis, I offer the idea of a combination of theater, "literature," and ritual that continues on the diachronic level and that in terms of the time axis is at some no longer determinable starting-point valid both for the time of Aristophanes and for even a much later period. If one leaves aside as an exceptional phenomenon the relatively brief interlude of the modern European theater, purely oriented toward Aristotle, this close interaction of levels can be observed from the spectacle-like performances of most tribal peoples all the way to postmodern theater, which is rediscovering precisely this choral dimension and which is abandoning the "dramatic" in the sense of a closed action in favor of a return to predramatic and pre-expressive forms.[10]

In what follows the two fragments of Semos will be considered as documents of a living choral culture. Even though explicit references to the performers' own dance are not found here, in contrast to the central passage in the *Thesmophoriazusae* (947–1000), the songs are also performed by a chorus, a *kômos*. Procession (fr. a) and hymn (fr. b) belong accordingly to the realm of choral presentation, if one understands by chorus a cultic group that performs movements while singing at or in a ritual.

In the case of the hymn, on the basis of a misunderstood description by Proclus (in Photius 320a20), who characterizes the performers as ἑστῶτες, a stationary bodily attitude has been assumed. Recent scholarship tends no longer to separate the "real hymn"[11] from the paean, dithyramb, or *pros-*

---

[10] Cf. Lehmann 1991:2 and more recently Baur 1999a:3–4; on the chorus in twentieth-century theater, see Baur 1999 and Baur 1999a. Cf. now Lehmann 1999, esp. 233–238. On the return to pre-expressive forms in contemporary theater, cf. the approach of so-called theater anthropology, in particular the theoretical and practical works of Jerzy Grotowski and Eugenio Barba; on this see Ruffini 1991 (with bibliography). On postmodern theater, see A. de Toro 1995. On postdramatic theater, see now Lehmann 1999.

[11] Proclus *Chrest. ap.* Phot. *Bibl.* 320a19–20 (Severyns 40): ὁ δὲ κυρίως ὕμνος πρὸς κιθάραν ᾔδετο ἑστώτων ["A hymn in the strictest sense is performed to the *kithara* with the chorus standing/having taken up their formation"].

271

odion,[12] but rather to establish the relationship of these separate genres to hymn as the relation of subspecies to species. The subgroups are thus combined with the generic concept.[13] Immediately preceding this description, Proclus (in Photius 320a18–20) makes a distinction between a *prosodion*, which is sung while moving toward the altar, and a hymn. The latter, as is well known, is generally performed around the altar. Just as with the *prosodion*, a hymn may also be accompanied by a dance. In any case, the performers did not sing while rigidly "standing" about the altar; ἑστῶτες must on the contrary be interpreted as meaning that they have formed a formation and now, often in a κύκλιος χορός, and using gestures and body movements, are performing the hymn in honor of the god.[14] The setup possesses a strong similarity to the *stasimon*, which should not under any circumstances be interpreted as a "standing-still song," and to the *parodos* in developed drama. One could describe fragments 851a and b *PMG* as *parodoi in nuce*, and the subsequent improvisation in ridicule as a *stasimon* (στάδην δὲ ἔπραττον, Athen. 622d) or *epirrhêma*.[15]

The central element of comedy is the chorus, through which the dramatic genre is also connected with Greek choral culture. Walter Burkert in a ground-breaking study brings together the concept θεωρία, the "display" of the festival, and the development of theater. He lists three types of spectacular θεωρία incorporated into ritual that represented extensive and emotional events for the archaic citizen: the festive procession, or πομπή; the athletic contest (ἀγών); and presentations by χοροί, which were performed with dance and musical accompaniment and also for the most part in an agonistic context. In the ritual context of the festival a sacrifice was often offered to

---

[12] For a different view, see Harvey 1955 and Käppel 1992:64–65, 83 (on the paean, in which he sees a particular style of addressing the divinity in contrast to the general hymn).

[13] Didymus *ap.* Orion, s.v. ὕμνος (pp. 155–156 Sturz) and Proclus *Chrest. ap.* Phot. *Bibl.* 320a12–17 (Severyns 39). See now also Furley/Bremer I 2001:10–13.

[14] For discussion see above, pp. 108–109 and Furley 1993:23n7, Furley 1995:31–32, Bremer 1981:197–199, Bernadini 1991, esp. 85–89, and, on the *prosodion* in particular, Grandolini 1991, esp. 132.

[15] Cf. the remark in Muff 1871:6n3, who reports on the view in scholarship that the Ithyphalloi represent a *stasimon* (because they come first to the center of the orchestra and sing only once they have done so), and the Phallophoroi a *parodos*. He relativizes this theory and also refers to στάδην ἔπραττον. Cf. also Navarre 1911:249, who translates στάδην ἔπραττον in a similarly one-sided fashion as "ils jouaient en place fixe (loco stantes agebant)" ["they perform while standing on the spot"]. Kolster 1829:58–60 sees it the opposite way round: the song of the Ithyphalloi is a *prosodion*, and that of the Phallophoroi a *stasimon* ("Erat igitur ithyphallus carmen ἐμβατήριον, phallophororum vero στάσιμον" [58]). He thinks the song was originally accompanied by dance and violent movement and that in being transferred from the street into the theater it was changed into a standing song, so that the original movement can still be observed in the entry procession (58–59).

the gods, which at the same time provided the meat to feed the festive crowd. Within the context of the Great Dionysia, which were first instituted by the Athenian polis at the time of the Peisistratidai on the basis of older, more rural festivals and which also included procession, sacrifice, *agôn*, and choral performance, Attic drama developed, according to Burkert, as a *Gesamtkunstwerk* that synaesthetically reconfigured ritual elements.[16]

Not every "display" or "show" attained the level of Attic stagecraft. The songs of Semos do of course combine the same ritual elements: the spectacle (θέα) takes place in the permanent structure of the polis' θέατρον, which historically replaced as the site of performances the *agora*, the marketplace, where the players and choruses had previously entertained the spectacle-hungry people. The term χορός, as I have already emphasized in the Introduction, refers simultaneously to the place where a chorus performed. Procession and musical presentation were offered alongside animal sacrifice in honor of a deity. Choral culture is thus just as closely connected to ritual and its ritual occasion as drama, which arose from it. One may pursue the question whether certain songs ought to be regarded as literature rather than ritual in the case of choral lyric as well.

The deficient role identity of the dramatic chorus as *dramatis persona* and the fact that the actual performers are not completely concealed behind the plot—that is, the narrative complex which is determined within the communication system as a whole and which does not clearly distinguish between inner and outer, between the there of the plot and the here of the current performance—can all be explained by the inherited ritual function of choruses and their social presence and function.[17]

The traditional, purely literary-historical approach points to Alcman's Great Partheneion (fr. 1 Davies = fr. 1 *PMG* = fr. 3 Calame) or the epinicians, pae-

---

[16] Burkert 1987, esp. 29–35. Cf. also Goldhill 1999:2–10.

[17] Baur 1997:45n48 (= Baur 1999a:27n45) emphasizes, as do I, that one should not overestimate the historically determined difference that Calame 1994/95 brought out between the chorus of choral lyric and that of drama. Seen from the point of view of the performative there is clear continuity: independently of my conclusions Baur (*ibid.*) also thinks that "wer den Tragödienchor verstehen will, muß weniger die Unterschiede zur verwandten Chorlyrik als vielmehr die zum unser abendländisches Theaterverständnis so stark beeinflussenden aristotelischen Modell betonen" ["whoever wishes to understand the tragic chorus should emphasize to a lesser extent the differences between it and the choral lyric related to it and rather emphasize its differences from the Aristotelian model, which has had such a strong influence on our Western notion of theater"]. Though he correctly defines the special status (*Sonderstatus*) of the ancient chorus (Baur 1997:44–47; Baur 1999a:26–28)—"[d]er Chor spielt immer einen Chor" ["the chorus always plays a chorus"] (1987:44 = 1999a:26)—he does not locate this in its continued ritual function the way I do here.

ans, and dithyrambs of Pindar as written monuments of archaic lyric, thus effectively detracting from their practical performative context. Despite their indisputably artistic form, these poems continue to remain anchored in their *Sitz im Leben*. On the other hand, in the case of so-called simple cultic lyric this aspect is never contested. Chance epigraphic finds of ephemeral, customary occasional poetry such as the Palaikastro hymn (see below) or songs connected with folkpractices cannot, however, be neatly separated from so-called high literature and reduced exclusively to their cultic value. These songs too possess the aesthetic trademarks of ritual style, which have been described as follows: repetition, fusion, redundancy, metaphor, alliteration, chiasmus, *homoioteleuton*, and rhythmically shaped speech. These are all characteristics normally associated with lyrical literature. On the other hand, as modern studies on the orality of archaic literature have in particular made clear, even "high" choral lyric, such as the Great Partheneion of Alcman (fr. 1 Davies), is completely tied to a ritual occasion. A song like this is absorbed to a large degree in its concrete connection to its current context and occasion, which is evident to the local festival audience. For a later reader, of course, the precise circumstances remain unclear.[18]

Festive spectacle only really becomes literature in the time of the Alexandrians with its separation from a ritual performative context, which is a result of the phenomenon of textual transmission. Aristotle is the first to make this decisive step with respect to Attic drama by considering it primarily as a text.[19] Both brilliant choral poetry, such as Alcman's Louvre *Partheneion*, and more pedestrian customary songs of ritual practice or popular songs could quickly transcend the ephemeral nature of the one-time performance by being repeated at a later time. The reperformance of choral cultic poetry takes place mostly in the ritual context of seasonally reoccurring annual festivals.[20] Yet one may possibly recognize in this the point of departure of the development that with the introduction of the book trade would ultimately lead to the complete separation of texts composed in writing from festive occasions.

[18] Kannicht 1989:47–51, esp. 50. Claude Calame (*per litt.*) correctly draws my attention to the fact that in investigating this one ought also to consider the status of poetry (ποίησις) in Greece during the classical period. Ritual songs exist ultimately only in poetic form, and the distinction between songs that can be ascribed to authors and *carmina popularia* (as with that between Homeric, anonymous, and inscriptional hymns) is somewhat illusory in this connection.

[19] In an important article Massenzio (1972) discusses the fact that Aristotle consciously separated tragedy from its ritual and sacred context and reduced it to the text.

[20] In the same way dramas could also be staged anew: consider Aeschylus' *Oresteia* or the *Frogs* of Aristophanes. This is not so much an instance of ritual repetition as a theatrical interest in the same public ambience.

On the Performative Manner of Speech and Self-Reference in Ritual Choruses

I have already described in the previous chapter the extent to which ritual depends on the illocutionary confirmation of its own action, in what way cultic action results from a jussive manner of speech, and how contact with the deity is established. In the actual process of utterance the group or the individual does something. The insistent call invokes the god in a sympathetic fashion and creates a closeness to him.[21] The locating of a ritual in its occasion also causes the chorus to refer to its own activity, to its singing, dancing, and action in the here and now. The emphasis on the chorus' own rhythmic and musical presentation supports its implementation and is supposed to trigger a heightened state of attention in the deity being called upon. The chorus praises its own performance and its spectacular skill in the display; the spectators become convinced of this by the immediate impressions acting on their senses, and the divine addressee is thought to be addressed directly. The gods as archetypal choral members are sympathetically drawn in through the χάρις of the performance and are invited to reciprocate in turn.[22]

The chorus' self-description and self-reference to its own dancing in the here and now run right through the whole tradition of choral song. Self-referentiality is also a characteristic of rituals. The carrying out of an action needs verbal confirmation: it is in the utterance that the action is completed.[23] In his semantically and thematically oriented analysis of choral lyric, Carlo Odo Pavese has shown that this motif seldom appears in epinicians, but is prominent in the dithyramb, hyporcheme, *partheneion*, and paean.[24] This is clearly

---

[21] See, for example, Preisendanz II 1973/74:245–246, hymn 11 (where someone attempts to obtain a prophetic gift from Apollo at night). The example is discussed in Furley 1995:39–40. On the magic hymn, see Poccetti 1991 (who also applies the performative model, 194, 198–204).

[22] Cf. above, chap. 1 n92 and in general pp. 116–125, also Furley 1995:36.

[23] See Jensen 1986:112–113, 119–121 and Braungart 1996:91–101.

[24] Pavese 1968, esp. 416–417 and Pavese 1979. Pavese marks the theme with *cho* (*chorus*) or *dcho* (*descriptio chori*). The subdivision into individual motifs seems overly complex. For references by the chorus to its own activity, cf. Alcm. fr. 1.39–101 (cf. above, pp. 32–36), fr. 3–fr. 1.7–10, fr. 27, fr. 32, fr. 33 Davies; Pind. fr. 52b.96–102, esp. 99–100: ἱστάμεναι χορόν | ταχύ]ποδα . . ., fr. 52d.2: χορε]ύσομαι; fr. 52f.18: ποδὶ κροτέο[ντι; fr. 52m (a).10–11: χορὸν ὑπερτατ̣[| . . .]χάριν; fr. 70b.25: Μοῖσ' ἀνέστασ' Ἑλλάδι κα[λ]λ̣[ιχόρῳ; fr. 70c.16: πόνọι χορῶν; fr. 75.1–2: δεῦτ' ἐν χορόν, Ὀλύμπιοι, | ἐπί τε κλυτὰν πέμπετε χάριν, θεοί; fr. 94b.6–15, 33–39, 66–70; fr. 94c; fr. 107a–b S.-M.; *Nem.* 3.1–12; *Isthm.* 3/4.90b and *Nem.* 9.1 S.-M. (*kômos* and song combined); Pratinas fr. 708, esp. lines 1–5 and 14–16 *PMG*; cf. also the performative self-description in the first-person plural, without explicit mention of the χορός, in the folk songs fr. 848 *PMG* (Rhodian swallow song), 870 *PMG*, and 882 *PMG* (Sicilian song of the *boukoliastai*) and in the begging song of the Samian *eiresiônê*, carm. pop. fr. 1 D. The phenomenon is also found in the so-called song of

not simply a random semantic characteristic of certain genres. In his structural approach Pavese does not actually recognize the fact that these choral genres include this theme precisely because of their being anchored in ritual. And it is in dramatic choral lyric also, in particular in the songs of Aristophanes, that numerous instances of self-referentiality and descriptions of the chorus' own performance appear.[25] On the basis of the above it becomes clear that the treatment of this theme by no means constitutes an anachronistic application of poststructuralist interests: rather, the motif has its roots in the ritual nature of the chorus.

But one should not fail to make the observation here that self-referentiality can also of course be indicative of the growing self-awareness of the poet. Although instances of drawing attention to one's own artistic achievement are generally found in the work of later practitioners of a developed

---

the *koronistai* by Phoinix, fr. 2 D. = Powell 1925:233–234, lines 15ff., which is however not an authentic folk song but rather a Hellenistic imitation; see Schönberger 1980:50–56 and Furley 1994. As in the Callimachean hymns, the performative cliché is inbuilt, although the work is aimed at a reading audience; cf. *ibid.*, esp. 25–31. Cf. furthermore the self-referentiality in customary hymns: the Palaikastro hymn, West 1965:149–151, 149 = Powell 1925:160–162, 160, lines 6–10; Macedonius, Paean in Apollinem et Aesculapium (Powell 1925:138–140, 138 = Käppel 1992:383–384, 383–Pai. 41), lines 1–5; Paean Delphicus I (Käppel 1992:387–389, 388–Pai. 45), lines 14–16 = Powell 1925:141–148, 141, lines 12–13; Limenius, Paean Delphicus II (Käppel 1992:389–391, 390–Pai. 46), lines 15–17 = Powell 1925:149–159, 149, lines 13–15.

25 A similar self-presentation of the chorus, also in connection with choral performance (cf. the switching between performative and dramatic function) is found particularly in Ar. *Ran.* 209–220, esp. 212–214: ξύναυλον ὕμνων βοὰν | φθεγξώμεθ' εὔγηρυν ἐμὰν ἀοιδάν, | κοὰξ κοάξ, 229–235: ἐμὲ γὰρ ἔστερξαν εὔλυροί τε Μοῦσαι | καὶ κεροβάτας Πὰν ὁ καλαμόφθογγα παίζων, | προσεπιτέρπεται δ' ὁ φορμικτὰς Ἀπόλλων | ἕνεκα δόνακος, ὃν ὑπολύριον | ἔνυδρον ἐν λίμναις τρέφω. | βρεκεκεκὲξ κοὰξ κοάξ, and 240–250; on the song of the Frogs and the *parodos* of the Mystai (*Ran.* 316–459) in the switching between performative and dramatic role cf. Dover *Frogs*, 57–60 and Dover 1993. The self-description is entirely comparable to the chorus of swallows, carm. pop. 848 *PMG*. Cf. Lefkowitz 1991:21–22. She correctly states: "These choral swallows, like the Wasps and Frogs of Aristophanes' comedies, preserve some of their human characteristics, and only with their final words do they reveal their true identity." Comic choruses always present their appearance and action in verbal terms as well. Comparable with the passage in the *Frogs* are the parabasis odes in the *Birds* 737–752, esp. *Av.* 745–752: Πανὶ νόμους ἱεροὺς ἀναφαίνω | σεμνά τε Μητρὶ χορεύματ' ὀρείᾳ, | τοτοτο τοτοτο τοτοτο τίγξ | ἔνθεν ὡσπερεὶ μέλιττα | Φρύνιχος ἀμβροσίων μελέων ἀπε- | βόσκετο καρπὸν ἀεὶ | φέρων γλυκεῖαν ᾠδάν. | τιο τιο τιο τιο τίγξ, and *Av.* 769–784, esp. 769–773: τοιάδε κύκνοι | τιο τιο τιο τιο | συμμιγῆ βοὴν ὁμοῦ πτε- | ῥοῖσι κρέκοντες ἴαχον Ἀπόλλω, | τιο τιο τιο τίγξ. Cf. also the self-presentation at the entry of the Clouds, *Nub.* 298–313, esp. 308–313 with the ritual self-referentiality to the here and now of the festive context in Athens: εὐστέφανοί τε θεῶν θυσίαι θαλίαι τε | παντοδαπαῖσιν ὥραις, | ἦρί τ' ἐπερχομένῳ Βρομία χάρις | εὐκελάδων τε χορῶν ἐρεθίσματα | καὶ μοῦσα βαρύβρομος αὐλῶν. The Dionysia represent the current occasion for the dramatic competitions (in song, round dancing, and *aulos*) and the sacred offering. On the performative choral "I" in comedy and tragedy cf. Lefkowitz 1991:22–25.

genre,[26] one in fact already encounters this phenomenon in the first preserved examples of Greek poetry. It can increasingly be seen with the expansion of written expression in the fifth century BCE, and in the reading culture of the Hellenistic period this form achieves special significance. But a self-referential procedure of this sort seems to represent only a secondary phenomenon that actually rests on the basis of the illocutionary confirmation of a verbally realized performance situation in the process of written composition. The splitting into ritual and artistic self-reference is almost impossible in a performance, since the "I" of choral lyric can hardly be separated from the voice of the poet. Conversely, from the mixed and polyvalent voices of the speaking "I"/"we" it becomes possible to trace the claim to originality all the way back to the authority of the composer, thereby removing the actor from the picture, in terms of both his actual and his possible fictional identity.

In his hymns Callimachus as literary and self-aware *poeta doctus* also refers back to this old form of self-referentiality. Although these were never intended for choral performance, only for reading, he reverts to the illocutionary self-reference of traditional performance, following the trend of extensive re-ritualization and strategies of cultic embedment in order to maintain the fiction that these songs of praise are being danced and sung by choruses.[27] Hymnic presentation, which in fact occurs in Semos' second song (fr. 851b *PMG*) in a type of prelude to Dionysus, does not therefore stand in opposition to choral dance presentation. Even the Homeric hymns, which function as *prooimia* to epic/rhapsodic performance, occasionally point back to the ideal performance of an imaginary chorus.[28]

---

[26] See my observations in Bierl 1991:111–119, 225–226. On Aristophanes, see Hubbard 1991, passim (on intertextual self-references) and Bremer 1993:160–165.

[27] For reference to choral dance song, cf. Callim. *Hymn.* 1.52–54; 2.8, 12, 28–31, 85–87, 93; 3.3, 170–174, 180–181, 240–247, 266–267; 4.79, 279, 300–315; in general on the interplay between traditional generic conventions and artistic freedom, see Henrichs 1993, esp. 129–130 (on the cultic framework and association with a ritual performance that is connected with group solidarity). On the connected problem of the so-called mimetic hymns that reconstruct the conditions of the *énonciation* within the song itself, which are undoubtedly unconnected to the extradiscursive reality, see Calame 1992a:55–58, esp. 57n19 (with further references).

[28] Cf. Calame 1995a:16–17 (on the dances and songs of the Delian Maidens, i.e. the choral embedding of Hom. *Hymn.* 3.146–173): "Est-ce à dire que les *Hymnes homériques*, dont la fonction introductive ne devrait plus faire de doute, étaient chantés par un chœur? Ou, sinon par un groupe de choreutes, en tout cas par un aède entouré d'un chœur, selon le mode citharodique illustré par de nombreuses descriptions de performances épiques dans l'*Iliade* ou l'*Odyssée*?" ["Does this mean that the Homeric hymns, whose introductory function should now be beyond doubt, were sung by a chorus? Or, if not by a chorus, then in any case by a bard surrounded by a chorus, in the citharodic fashion illustrated by numerous descriptions of epic performance in the *Iliad* or the *Odyssey*?"]. See also Furley 1993:24–29.

Self-reference to activity in the here and now marks Semos' songs of the Ithyphalloi and Phallophoroi as popular songs connected with ritual custom, anchored in the real world. They can thus be classified as part of the tradition of ritual and communal choral poetry. At the same time, they should be viewed as an artistic representation in the Hellenistic sense. This phenomenon of being on the border between a ritual utterance, a serenade performed in a Hellenistic theater constructed of stone, and a minor artform handed down as literature makes these quotations of particular interest. Yet poetic composition and ritual use, as in the case of Aristophanes, are not mutually exclusive.

In what follows the classification of these songs as part of choral song culture, which is connected with Old Comedy, is based on the *kômos* in particular. A *kômos* is a mobile, riotously celebrating choral group[29] that generally stages a carnevalesque world. More recent discussions have seen the *kômos* as the origin of all dramatic forms.[30] It is true that there is no explicit self-reference to choral dance, but the group does however refer to its song and its movements. The members of the chorus march in more-or-less coordinated fashion into the theater. The choreography stages a controlled "otherness" consisting of a group of young people whom the festive community engages for the purpose of performance.

The *kômos*, from which Old Comedy apparently developed, represents, like ritual, a particular practice of signification by a group of actors,[31] where there

---

[29] Cf. Adrados 1975:40: "*Komos*, I say, was the generic term for every type of chorus which changes place in performing ritual actions accompanied by dance, and eventually song, whether mimetic or not." Similarly Heath 1988:182: "It is not only the revelry after a symposium that could be described as a κῶμος—any mobile celebration will do."

[30] Cf. Adrados 1975:37–49, who originally argues for a broad meaning that extends beyond the later restricted use of the term to the more or less comic (37–38). He thus thinks that "[a] *komos* can perform all the genres of the Dionysian contest, besides various others." Ghiron-Bistagne 1976:207–297 is the best modern discussion of the *kômos*. On the *kômos* as origin of all dramatic genres see 265–297; she divides the *kômos* historically into three areas: a) the carnevalesque festive procession of people going to and returning from a festival (208–225); b) the chorus that dances and sings (225–231); and c) the *kômos* after a symposion (231–238); cf. also Kuithan 1808:44–76, Lamer 1922:1286–1304, Reckford 1987:443–451, and Heath 1988; Hoffman 1989:97 also quotes the passage from Semos as indication of the inverted world. See now also Pütz 2003:156–191 ("The Komos in Aristophanes") (with my critical review in *CR* 55 [2005]:422–424) and Schmitz 2004:280–320, who classify the *kômos* among the *Rüge*- and *Heischebräuche* of peasants and young people in the countryside and villages, later transferred also to city life. These customs have according to Schmitz a function of social control. On comasts in archaeological research see now Bron 1999, Smith 2000, Smith 2003, Isler-Kerényi 2004, Steinhart 2004, and Rothwell 2006 (I thank Erich Kistler, Zurich, for these references).

[31] On the praxis of signifiers, see Lohr 1986, passim, esp. 1–28, who is here is strongly influenced by the *Telqueliens* of the French poststructuralist school, in particular Julia Kristeva. For a radical critique of Kristeva's positions proceeding from the structuralist concept of know-

is only occasional indexical reference to the corresponding signified.[32] In the *kômos* and in comedy one expresses oneself first and foremost through signs and gestures that indicate a transgression of norms (ὕβρις), the inversion of the world, and a return to a primordial and chaotic past.[33] The *kômos* is constituted as a central network of signs that surrounds and connects the individual significatory phenomena. This choral form explains the motifs of sacrifice, wine, phallic sexuality, and aggression, as well as its connections to Old Comedy. In the archaic symposiastic *Männerbund* initiation is an important factor. The noisy procession staged at an annual festival represents in particular a reactualization of the ritualized transition from male youth to adulthood in the form of a choral presentation. The dramatic and critical transitional phase in initiation is experienced as an inverted world.[34] Remnants of the archaic initiation of the aristocracy are found in the Athens of the late fifth and the fourth centuries BCE, the time of Aristophanes, in comastic associations of young men formed from aristocratic circles. As an expression of the transgression of norms they are often arranged around the sign of the phallus. The notorious aristocratic gangs of rowdy youths with the scandalous names of Ithyphalloi, Autolekythoi, and Triballoi who make the streets of Athens unsafe after their wild binges are well known from Demosthenes' oration *Against Konon*. The Athenian drinking brotherhood of the Ithyphalloi is directly reminiscent of the group of the same name in Semos, so that the Ithyphalloi assume a key position in Hans Herter's organic theory of the origin of comedy, which is based on Aristotle.[35]

---

ledge, see Hempfer 1976:13–65. In one of the more recent books on ritual Bell also works intensively with the concept of practice, drawing on Bourdieu's (1977, esp. 72–158) concept of practice; see Bell 1992, passim, esp. 74–88, 140–142, and index s.v. *practice*.

[32] See Lohr 1986:74–80.

[33] Lohr 1986:63–68 calls the phenomenon "comic fall" (*komischer Sturz*).

[34] On the connection between initiation and symposium, see Bremmer 1990.

[35] See Herter 1947, esp. 16–18. The description of the Autokabdaloi is also reminiscent of the Autolekythoi. The Ithyphalloi, Autolekythoi, and Triballoi have a special tie to the phallus. Demosthenes 54.16–17 reports that the Ithyphalloi dedicated themselves to Ithyphallos in a kind of initiation. For the Autolekythoi and Triballoi as phallus gangs, see Whitman 1969 and Griffith 1970. The name τριβαλλοί has been interpreted as τρίφαλλοι; Herter 1938c:1681. On the Athenian aristocratic drinking clubs, see Parker 1996:335–336 and Murray 1990. In Athens it appears that the Ithyphalloi also danced in the theater to rhythm (Hyperides fr. 50 Jensen): οἱ τοὺς ἰθυφάλλους ἐν τῇ ὀρχήστρᾳ ὀρχούμενοι. The theater is thus an important gathering place for these ephebic groups; in the trial of the Hermokopidai, Diokleides (Andoc. 1.37–38) makes the final statement that he saw about three hundred of the aristocratic conspirators in the orchestra of the theater of Dionysus and that they were arranged (ἑστάναι δὲ κύκλῳ) in groups of six or seven, some in groups of up to twenty. Might he have been thinking of the Ithyphalloi, who normally gave small performances in the orchestra in a chorus of varying size? In Semos the Ithyphalloi also perform in the orchestra (Athen. 622b): ὅταν κατὰ μέσην τὴν ὀρχήστραν γένωνται.

Besides initiation, however, are festivals of fertility or transition or inversion, in particular new year's festivals, that can be adduced as a possible *Sitz im Leben*. The three central interpretative categories in the study of the history of religion (fertility, new year, and initiation) do not lend themselves to a neat separation between them, but as in the case of the *Thesmophoriazusae*, all play a role in the arrangement of this comically distorting practice of signification.

Ritual Analysis of the Songs (fr. 851 *PMG*)

An in-depth ritual and performative interpretation of the Semos texts will show that the songs, by using redundancy and fusion, expand the synaesthetic occasion of the choral presentation into a sensory ritual experience involving the consumption of wine, sexuality, and sacrifice, and blend this into a "thick" discourse with allusions to the chorus' own performance.[36] In what follows, the text as transmitted will be considered in its performative context. The form and content of the choral song cannot here be separated: optical and visual, gestural, and kinetic signals in the description of the performance make up a "thick" unit of expression and communication together with its rhythmic form and verbal signs, the content of the linguistic message.

In his entertaining conversations over dinner, Athenaeus presents the extract (Athen. 621d–622a) using the following introduction: κωμικῆς παιδιᾶς ἦν τις τρόπος παλαιός (621d) ["There used to be an ancient style of comic *paidia*"]. In the Greek imagination, as has already been shown, dance and play were often associated with one another. There is an attempt to enact the pleasure of play using movement of the body. In comedy *paizein* is thus often used synonymously for dance.[37] The Spartan Sosibios (ca. 300 BCE) who is quoted by Athenaeus (*FGrHist* 595 F 7) subsumes under the Spartan term *deikêlistai*, which means something like performers in a mimetic presentation, all sorts of popular comic actors who are called different names in different cities.[38]

---

[36] For a similar synaesthesia, consider in particular Pindar's dithyramb to Athens, fr. 75 S.-M. In a cletic hymn Dionysus is summoned to the Dionysia and the dithyrambic performances currently underway. Precisely as in the description of the heavenly Dionysia (Pind. fr. 70b S.-M.), Pindar in his picture of the Bacchic spring festival (14–19), where reference is made to its own occasion and performance, fuses together impressions of color, sound, movement, and smell in a manner characteristic of ritual speech; see also Zimmermann 1992:53–60, esp. 54. On "thick" description, cf. Geertz 1973:3–30 ("Thick Description: Toward an Interpretative Theory of Culture" and Jensen 1986:119–120 ("'thick' performance").

[37] Cf. above, Introduction n180.

[38] Their name seems to be derived from δείκηλα, which Hesychius glosses as, among other things, "masks"; further explanations and passages in Pickard-Cambridge 1962:135. On ἀποδείκνυμαι and ἀπόδειξις in the sense "present publicly" and "public presentation," see Nagy 1990:217–224 and 515 (in the index, with numerous further references). For ἐπίδειξις, see Goldhill 1999:3–4.

In this cultural and historical deipnological context the statement that Sosibios enumerates all kinds of expressions for mimes of this type suits Athenaeus' antiquarian and collector's interests: they are called Phallophoroi in Sikyon, elsewhere Autokabdaloi ('improvisers'), in southern Italy Phlyakes, in many places Sophistai, and in Thebes Ethelontai.[39] While these types of improvised scenes drawn from everyday life—Sosibios mentions a theft of vegetables or the burlesque entry of a strange and boastful doctor who uses a strange dialect—are more reminiscent of the speaking parts in Attic comedies,[40] it is possible to connect the following description by Semos with the chorus of Old Comedy.[41] Throughout the whole passage (621d–622d) Athenaeus seems

---

[39] ἐκαλοῦντο δ' οἱ μετιόντες τὴν τοιαύτην παιδιὰν παρὰ τοῖς Λάκωσι δεικηλισταί, ὡς ἄν τις σκευοποιοὺς εἴπη καὶ μιμητάς. τοῦ δὲ εἴδους τῶν δεικηλιστῶν πολλαὶ κατὰ τόπους εἰσὶ προσηγορίαι. Σικυώνιοι μὲν γὰρ φαλλοφόρους αὐτοὺς καλοῦσιν, ἄλλοι δ' αὐτοκαβδάλους, οἱ δὲ φλύακας, ὡς Ἰταλοί, σοφιστὰς δὲ οἱ πολλοί· Θηβαῖοι δὲ καὶ τὰ πολλὰ ἰδίως ὀνομάζειν εἰωθότες ἐθελοντάς (Athen. 621e–f). In Thebes they are known as Ethelontai, volunteers, because they are not organized by the state. In Athens, too, as Aristotle reports (*Poetics* 1449b2), comedies were performed by *ethelontai* until 486 BCE; that is to say, comic performance was not yet under the control of the polis, and so at this stage amounted to a kind of freeform farce without any overarching or structured plot, which was only introduced by Krates. Improvisation privileges the paradigmatic level, while the syntagmatic level of action appears only secondarily and is never carried through in a consistent fashion. On improvisation as spontaneous use of signifiers and precondition for the comic, see Lohr 1986:172–175. On reflexes of improvised theater, especially that of Oscan Attelan farce, in Plautus, see Vogt-Spira 1995, whose conclusions may be applied to Aristophanes as well. On the Ethelontai, see Kranz 1933:8. Cf. now on Athen. 621d–f Stark 2004:34–40, esp. 34–35.

[40] A passage from Alexis' *Mandragorizomenê* (Alexis fr. 146 K.-A.) is quoted by way of illustration: see Arnott 1996:430–434; on the introduction to the play, 419–421. On the role of the doctor in Greek and Roman comedy, cf. *ibid.*, 431–432. The act of stealing food is a fundamental motif in farce and a typical source of low humor; fruit and wine may also be associated with Dionysus, to whom they are in fact supposed to be offered. On the stealing of food, cf. Ar. *Equ.* 418; on stealing fruit, Epich. fr. 239 Kaibel. Robbery and theft stand in opposition to the code of civilization; the motif also belongs, for example, to the staged counterworld of Spartan initiation, where the initiates are supposed to steal cheese from the sanctuary of Artemis and are subject to a whipping if caught. There is also the Spartan mimetic dance called the *tyrbasia*, in which people caught in the act of stealing meat are imitated (Pollux 4.104–105). The Athenian young men's association of the Triballoi is charged with the sacrilegious action of stealing and eating offerings to Hekate (Demosth. 54.39). The simple transgression of norms induces raucous laughter in the group. The doctor can be associated with the *alazôn*, and the fruit thief with the *bômolokhos*. The division into the types *alazôn* and *bômolokhos* can already be seen in Aristotle. The *eirôn*, the ironic and cynical wise man, is also often mentioned in addition to these. Cf. Arist. *Eth. Nic.* 1108a21–25 and 1127a13–1128b4 (detailed distinction between *alazônes* and *bômolokhoi*); cf. also the *Tractatus Coislinianus* (in Kaibel 1899:50–53, here 52 [§6] and Koster 1975:63–67, here 66, lines 38–39); cf. generally also Hubbard 1991:2–8. On the passage of Sosibios in particular (Athen. 621d–622a), see among others Pickard-Cambridge 1962:134–137, Koller 1954:44–45, Breitholtz 1960:114–122, and Taplin 1993:49–51 (on the *phylakes*).

[41] Reich 1903:274–280 sees comedy as a conglomerate of nonchoral mimes and choral members (Autokabdaloi, Phallophoroi, Ithyphalloi); Sosibios is influenced here, Reich thinks, by Aristote-

to have thematized the connection of choral celebration and the subsequent improvisation of the performers, which manifests itself in the ritual ridicule of the spectators drawn into the ritual and in other entertaining little gags taken from the everyday world.[42]

Athenaeus changes his informant from this point on and quotes both of our comastic songs, using Semos as his source.[43] Like Sosibios, Semos also speaks of Autokabdaloi, who make speeches in improvised form (σχέδην) while crowned with ivy, and says that these choral actors and their "poems" were later termed *iamboi*.[44] The ivy is already a clear reference to Diony-

---

lian and peripatetic theory, which characterized *mimos* and *phallikon* as original comic forms (*ibid.*, 254 and 280). Breitholtz 1960:116–117 emphasizes that Sosibios' report says nothing about dance. Webster in Pickard-Cambridge 1962:136 thinks that this involved small, popular scenes that were originally danced—he makes a connection with the potbellied dancers, *phlyakes*, and the Spartan dance of men caught in the act of stealing meat (Pollux 4.104–105)—and that later, under the influenced of developed comedy, became fossilized as a spectacle without dance.

[42] On the passage as a whole, esp. on the fragments of Semos, see among others Muff 1871:5–7, Thiele 1902, Reich 1903:274–280, Cornford 1961²:106–111, esp. 106–109, Radermacher *Frösche*, 12, Körte 1921:1218–1219, Pickard-Cambridge 1962:134–151, Wilamowitz I 1931/32:200–201 (= repr. I, 196–197), Herter 1938b:1678–1680, Herter 1947:18–35, Pohlenz 1949:35–39 (= Kl. Schr. II 1965:501–505), Gelzer 1960:210, Händel 1963:107–109n17, Gelzer 1966:68–69, Sifakis 1971:20, West 1974:23, 36–37, Adrados 1975:307, Ghiron-Bistagne 1976:208–212 and 245, Blech 1982:208–209, Reckford 1987:487, Leonhardt 1991:37–38, Cole 1993, esp. 32–34, Csapo/Slater 1995:94, 97–98, and Csapo 1997:264. See also the discussion in the literary histories Müller II 1857:197–198, Schmid 1929:635, and Lesky 1971³:271–272. Breitholtz (1960:114–122) is extremely skeptical about any conclusions relating to the possible origins of comedy. He concludes (122): "Wir haben es hier mit einer der von der Theatergeschichte am meisten missbrauchten Textstellen zu tun" ["We are dealing here with one of the textual sources most abused by scholars of the history of theater"]. Athenaeus is not interested in the precise distinction between chorus and the individual mime; rather, in his dinner conversation he is clearly only concerned about the effect of the behavior of performers of this type. In Hellenistic theater the choral song becomes considerably less important as the aria becomes favored and as solo-ists take over the choral parts as entertainment in the theater. Cf. Gentili 1977:11–22 (2006²: 41–49).

[43] The two texts can be found as fr. 851 (a and b) *PMG* (= carm. pop. 5 [a and b]) (= *PMG*, pp. 452–453), carm. pop. 7 and 8 B. (= Bergk III 1882⁴:657), carm. pop. 47 and 48 D. (= Diehl II¹ 1925:206–207), also in Kaibel 1899:73–75, Jacoby III, 290–291 on Semos, *FGrHist* 396 F 24, and Tresp 1914:201–203 (fr. 165).

[44] Σῆμος δ' ὁ Δήλιος ἐν τῷ περὶ Παιάνων (*FGrHist* 396 F 24) οἱ αὐτοκάβδαλοι, φησί, καλούμενοι ἐστεφανωμένοι κιττῷ σχέδην ἐπέραινον ῥήσεις. ὕστερον δὲ ἴαμβοι ὠνομάσθησαν αὐτοί τε καὶ τὰ ποιήματα αὐτῶν (Athen. 622ab). Here, too, a later dramatic development seems to be conflated with an earlier choral stage: after the dance the choral performers seem to transition in a clearly improvisatory way into a speech and ridicule the audience in true iambic fashion, so that the performances as a whole are accordingly called *iamboi* after the meter. On impro-visation and ridicule, see Vogt-Spira 1995:81–84. On the *iambos* as ancient choral form, see West 1974:34–37 and Nagy 1979:242–243. West 1974:35 correctly sees the Syracusan ἰαμβισταί, who are compared to the Dionysiac round-dancing chorus of Athens (Athen. 181c), as dancers who clearly correspond to the Athenian performers of the dithyramb. The dance of the *iamboi*

sus.[45] Then, before the actual texts of the songs of the Ithyphalloi and Phallophoroi, Semos gives an extensive description of the ritual and performative context of the occasion that includes their wreaths, masks, costume, and entrance into the theater. In a semiotic code that operates on various levels, individual redundant signifiers are added together with the help of fusion to form a complex symbolic image, which together with the practice of signification in the performance and the verbal concretization of the songs blends into a comprehensive synaesthetic unity of signs. The comic dissolution of the everyday order of things or the inversion of the world is thus indicated as a message or signified in the process of communication.[46] As is clear from the description of the players, the central sign of the celebration is the massive erect phallus[47] that is carried in by an especially prominent actor, the phallus-bearer, accompanied by the choral group. In the biological world the phallus has a particular use in demonstrative behavior. Primates use their erect member for sexual display and to mark out their territory.[48] Humans

---

will also assume a central position in my interpretation of the songs in Semos. According to West, *iambos* may represent a choral address as well as a speaking verse, and may also describe the combination of chorus and individual speaker that develops from the *exarkhos* of the choral group. *Iambos* thus does not, he maintains (West 1974:22), consist of the specific verse form, but the style of vulgar invective characteristic of *iamboi*, which is connected in particular with Dionysus and Demeter (*ibid.*, 23–25 and Richardson 1974:213–217). On the ribald ridicule in the *Thesmophoriazusae* that is sandwiched between the Demetrian role and the Dionysiac function of the chorus, see above, pp. 169–171. On the combination of *iambos* and comedy, see Degani 1987, Degani 1988, Degani 1993, and Rosen 1988. See now also Treu 1999, esp. 129–140 and Saetta Cottone 2005, esp. 143–151.

[45] On ivy as a Dionysiac characteristic, see Blech 1982:185–210.

[46] On the inversion of the world in Dionysiac ritual, see Hoffman 1989.

[47] In contrast to Herter 1938b:1679 and Herter 1947:21, and because of the song that follows, I follow Pohlenz 1949:35 (= Kl. Schr. II 1965:501) in the view that neither the Phallophoroi nor the Ithyphalloi were themselves equipped with an erect phallus. Herter 1938b:1679 thinks this must have "been visible through the see-through Tarentine clothing." Elsewhere he even says (1947:21): "vielleicht hob er sich aber auch plastisch ab oder wurde geradezu exhibiert" ["perhaps it stood out prominently or was simply exhibited"]. A fetish carried by the Phallophoros need not of course exclude the presence of other phalli in the group, especially since as a kind of chorus leader he encompasses the characteristics of the whole ensemble. Blech 1982:209n133 connects figurative representations with the highly decorative headgear of the Phallophoroi; on a fragment of black-figure pottery from Segesta, a man with a cap covered in phalli can be seen, and on a fragment of red-figure pottery there is a depiction of a man with an ivy wreath with phalli fixed to his forehead and nose (Athens, Acropolis 702; *ARV* 213, 238). This is strongly reminiscent of grotesquely extended bodies in carnival rites.

[48] Burkert 1983:24, 58, 69–70, Fehling 1974:7–38, and Burkert 1979:39–41, 45; for more on the phallus, see Burkert 1983:58–72, esp. 69–72, and Burkert 1985:104 (in processions), 244 (phalli made of dough at the Thesmophoria). On the phallus, see Herter 1938c. In earlier work the phallus was seen to have a mainly apotropaic function, but Herter interprets it as an indication of fertility in particular. Yet the connection to death and the world beyond is also emphasized

transform this ethologically ritualized behavior in an expressive fashion into complex ritual forms such as the phallus procession.[49]

The phallus is enlarged for purposes of clarification and becomes an independent iconic symbol, detached from the body. Phalli of this type have for example been found on Delos in a shrine to Dionysus near the theater. Two giant erect marble phalli on stone pedestals have now been installed in this monumental complex, which was constructed by the successful *khorêgos* Karystios at the end of the fourth century BCE; on the pedestal of the rightmost one a winged phallus-bird has been carved in relief.

Delos, with its famous *phallophoria* at the Dionysia, has recently been considered by Susan Guettel Cole as a possible *Sitz im Leben* for these songs, since Semos came from there.[50] Relying on the sequence of procession (*pompê*) with *phallophoria*, sacrifice, and procession of revellers (*kômos*), which precede the actual theatrical *agôn* at the Great Dionysia in Athens, she interprets the ceremony that lies behind Semos' description as a ritual activity too, which symbolically marks as an inversion of the normal the transition from everyday life to the festival and to the theatrical competitions that took place there. The location of the rites in a fully formed Hellenistic stone theater is more than clear from the context transmitted along with the songs. Even if their setting on Delos cannot be proved unequivocally, Guettel Cole's suggestion nevertheless represents an excellent working hypothesis. Joint ritual components that are also expressed in the text of the songs, namely *aiskhrologia* and *tôthasmos*, phallic presentation, the drinking of wine at the symposium, sacrifice, marching in a procession accompanied by song, and the comastic proces-

---

(*ibid.*, 1728–1733); cf. also Leonhardt 1991:32. Ghosts from the otherworld and *daimones* also have erect phalli. But one should on the contrary, though without completely losing sight of the traditional aspects, also emphasize in particular the moment of inversion, the mixing of all categories, and the grotesque, carnivalesque body that attracts attention to itself, thereby marking the Other; cf. similarly Graf 1998:15. Csapo 1997:259–260 also criticizes the traditional pattern of interpretation that views the phallus as symbol of fertility, aggression, and something apotropaic; he considers the Dionysiac phallus from the perspective of Turner's "interstructure" (in contrast to the "antistructure," which Csapo defines as a clear exception to the norm; Turner uses both concepts without drawing a clear distinction between them), the total confusion of all standards, so that a contradictory function is fulfilled, namely returning society, vulnerable to social divisions, to normality without bringing these social differentiations themselves into question. Cf. Csapo 1997, esp. 253–254 and 287–288. Instead of "interstructure" I use the phrase "betwixt and between," which also goes back to Turner and comes close to the concept of liminality (Turner 1967:93–111; cf. above, chap. 1 n370). In my view, the *kômos* as wild choral procession reactualizes in accordance with the rules of the comic genre the inverted, chaotic world of initiatory rites during the marginal phase.

[49] For the biological and ethological derivation of ritual, see Burkert 1996 and Baudy 1998:67–99.

[50] Cole 1993, esp. 30–34.

sion, may be connected with the entrance into a theater of a chorus, which, as in Old Comedy, oscillates between Dionysiac ritual and artistic theater.[51] Exuberant pleasure at the festival appears next to grotesque transgressions of normal boundaries, to tokens of the Other, the marginal, and death. Dionysus, as addressee of the second song and embodiment of the phallus in the person of Phales, unites these positive and negative aspects.

In Semos' description further visual features redundantly accompany the central phallus:[52] the Ithyphalloi wear masks of drunkards. Yet the chorus does not here enter wholeheartedly into a fictional role, such as that of satyrs; rather, the simple mask allows the real identity of the citizen chorus honoring the god of wine to shine through clearly.[53] This happens even more obviously in the case of the Autokabdaloi and Phallophoroi, who wear no mask at all, but are visually characterized as worshipers of Dionysus by their headgear and costume, as are the other groups. The Autokabdaloi wear the typical garland

[51] For the joyful, comastic aspect of sacrifice, see the pictorial analysis in Peirce 1993, who emphasizes the positive traits of ritual as opposed to the darker aspects of guilt that Vernant as well as Burkert and Meuli accentuate. She shows that πομπή, ἑορταί, χοροί, κῶμος, victory, joy, celebration, laughter, and *symposion* are often combined with sacrifice into a visual network of signs.

[52] οἱ αὐτοκάβδαλοι, φησί, καλούμενοι ἐστεφανωμένοι κιττῷ σχέδην ἐπέραινον ῥήσεις. ὕστερον δὲ ἴαμβοι ὠνομάσθησαν αὐτοί τε καὶ τὰ ποιήματα αὐτῶν.

οἱ δὲ ἰθύφαλλοι, φησί, καλούμενοι προσωπεῖα μεθυόντων ἔχουσιν καὶ ἐστεφάνωνται, χειρῖδας ἀνθινὰς ἔχοντες· χιτῶσι δὲ χρῶνται μεσολεύκοις καὶ περιέζωνται ταραντῖνον καλύπτον αὐτοὺς μέχρι τῶν σφυρῶν. σιγῇ δὲ διὰ τοῦ πυλῶνος εἰσελθόντες, ὅταν κατὰ μέσην τὴν ὀρχήστραν γένωνται, ἐπιστρέφουσιν εἰς τὸ θέατρον λέγοντες --- ἀνάγετ', εὐρυχωρίαν . . .

οἱ δὲ φαλλοφόροι, φησίν, προσωπεῖον μὲν οὐ λαμβάνουσιν, προσκόπιον δ' ἐξ ἑρπύλλου περιτιθέμενοι καὶ παιδέρωτος ἐπάνω τούτου ἐπιτίθενται στέφανον [τε] δασὺν ἴων καὶ κιττοῦ· καυνάκας τε περιβεβλημένοι παρέρχονται οἱ μὲν ἐκ παρόδου, οἱ δὲ κατὰ μέσας τὰς θύρας, βαίνοντες ἐν ῥυθμῷ καὶ λέγοντες --- σοί, Βάκχε, τάνδε μοῦσαν ἀγλαΐζομεν . . . (Athen. 622bc).

[53] On the lack of consistent illusion (in terms of how the spectators react to the fictional role of the player) and "inlusion" (in terms of how the players behave toward the spectators with respect to a subjective knowledge of their role identity) in folk plays and in ritual performance, see Lohr 1986:53–58, 74–80. In contrast to the veristic theater of the eighteenth and nineteenth centuries, actual performers and the bearers of fictional roles never overlap completely. On the mask *ibid.*, 78–79; like Calame 1989, Lohr treats the mask as a means of achieving distance between performer, role, and spectator. Cf. Lohr 1986:78: "Die Filterwirkung der Maske schwächt die eindringenden dämonischen Kräfte im archaischen Ritual ab, die ursprünglich im *enthusiasmos* vollkommen vom Ich Besitz ergriffen hatten. Diese Funktion der kultischen Maske wird in einer Art phylogenetischem 'Maskensprung' in die säkulare Darstellung des Mythos transponiert" ["In archaic ritual the filtering effect of the mask alleviates the threatening, demonic powers that in the process of *enthusiasmos* had originally completely taken possession of the I. This function of the cultic mask is transposed in a kind of phylogenetic 'mask leap' into the secular presentation of the myth"]. The qualification μεθυόντων refers of course to wine-drinking associated with the cult of Dionysus and the symposium. Kugelmeier 1996:154n269 is wrong not to see a reference to drunkenness in fr. 851 *PMG*.

of ivy that dramatic choruses in Athens also at times wore.[54] In the case of the Ithyphalloi, the type of garland is not given any further description. The mask that is absent in the case of the Phallophoroi is replaced with a lavish headgear that characterizes the players as wild men of the Outside. A visor-like frame woven from *herpyllos* (wild, creeping thyme), an evergreen plant sacred to the Muses,[55] and twigs of the *paiderôs*, whose red flowers had aphrodisiac and sexual connotations, frame their faces;[56] in addition, they wear over this the obligatory "thick wreath," here made of ivy and violets, which are also appropriate in the context of sacrifice, drinking, and the symposium.[57]

The marking of the period of inversion is further underscored by the long, effeminate robes that are typical of Dionysus, who is often character-

---

[54] The ivy-wreath was worn as decoration by Attic citizen choruses, actors, participants in Dionysiac processions, the victorious poet, and the *khorêgos*; see Blech 1982:208. On ivy as decoration, cf. also above, chap. 1 n110.

[55] Cf. Ar. *Pax* 168; Theocr. *Epigr.* 1, 2; Nic. *Ther.* 67. Blech 1982:209 identifies ἕρπυλλος with thyme, LSJ, s.v. and Olson *Peace*, 99 *ad* 166–169 with *Thymus sibthorpii*.

[56] According to LSJ, s.v. παιδέρως, this plant is *Quercus ilex*. A special kind of rouge appears to have been extracted from its berries. According to Paus. 2.10.6, the παιδέρως grows only in the sanctuary of Aphrodite in Sikyon. Despite the fact that Phallophoroi are mentioned just before in the quotation of Sosibios (Athen. 621f), these Phallophoroi are not necessarily connected with the ones in Sikyon, although most commentators admittedly for this reason associate Semos' Phallophoroi with Sikyon; cf. Herter 1947:19 and 50n83. The fact that the two plants are attested for Sikyon in particular is not sufficient, since the plants are of such a general type and so widely distributed that their appearance can hardly be limited to one place alone. Delos is again a more likely candidate, since Semos came from Delos and also writes about cults of Delos in his own work. In particular Dionysus and *phallophoria* play a prominent role there, as Cole 1993, esp. 32ff., argues. The following also argue for Delos: Wilamowitz 1921:266, Wilamowitz I 1931/32:160 with n3, 201 (= reprinted ed. I, 156 with n4, 197), Käppel 1992:54 and 330 (test. 100). In the general introduction to his commentary on the fragments in Semos, Jacoby remains undecided (204): "Dieses buch [Περὶ παιάνων] gehört ins gebiet der real-philologie und vielleicht der literarhistorie; es war sicher nicht musiktheoretisch und nicht auf Delos beschränkt oder auch nur von delischen zuständen ausgehend" ["This book [Περὶ παιάνων] belongs to the realm of *Realphilologie* and perhaps to literary history; it was certainly not concerned with musical theory, nor was it confined to Delos or exclusively concerned with Delian matters"]. Shortly thereafter he then comments on F 24 in particular (208): "Alle diese formen kann es auch auf Delos gegeben haben" ["All these forms could also have occurred on Delos"] (in the separate volume of notes by Jacoby (135n49) with reference to Vallois 1922). Bruneau 1970:312n2 disagrees with Marcadé 1969:189n3 and does not see the connection with Delos. The language of the extant songs corresponds to the language of Attic drama, with only slight Doric coloring; there is no Sicyonian Doric to be found, at any rate. But the songs are not ancient either (cf. Wilamowitz I 1895²:59n19), and are influenced by *koinê*. West 1982:148 considers the possibility of an Athenian origin for the Ithyphalloi (fr. 851a *PMG*).

[57] E.g. Plat. *Symp.* 212e; cf. Herter 1947:19 and 50n85. On the crown of violets as sign of the spring, the time of the occasion for Bacchic performances, cf. also Pind. fr. 75.6 (and 17) S.-M. For the chorus who talks about the fantastic garland of flowers it wears on its head, cf. Cratinus fr. 105 K.-A. Cf. further fr. 852 *PMG* ("flower" dance). The head decoration also acts as source of visual meaning.

ized as androgynous.[58] The comic inversion of the world is emphasized by the following signs of transvestism:[59] over a *khitôn* with white middle-section and flowered sleeves—with the Ithyphalloi indications of plants are generally absent—the Ithyphalloi wear a Tarentine wrap made of a fine, thin, transparent material, which is belted at the waist and which reaches to their ankles.[60] Conversely, the anomaly of the Phallophoroi is strikingly demonstrated by the *kaunakê*, the Sumerian-Babylonian hairshirt made of sheep's wool, which transports the actors from the fabric of civilization to the realm of slaves, barbarians, and the animal.[61]

The performative description of these choral entries is of great importance for the fluid transition from theater to ritual. Despite the brevity of the ritual songs, which are grouped with the traditional *carmina popularia*, Semos surprisingly places the choruses that perform them in the context of the theater. The Ithyphalloi proceed in silence through the entryway of the theater, and when they have reached the middle of the orchestra, where the chorus normally sings and dances, they take up position, turn to the audience (ἐπιστρέφουσιν εἰς τὸ θέατρον), and sing their phallus song, perhaps

[58] On the effeminate Dionysos *thêlymorphos*, see Casadio 1987:227–228 (= Casadio 1999:115–117).

[59] On Dionysiac transvestism, see Casadio 1987:227–234 (= Casadio 1999:115–123) with list (1987:229n69 [= 1999:117n69]) of interpretative categories (agrarian magic, reintegration into a state of paradise, transitional rites in the marginal phases of initiation of youths). On the Ithyphalloi and Phallophoroi in this connection, see Kenner 1970:112 and Casadio 1987:229 (= Casadio 1999:118).

[60] Tarentine cloth is transparent and thus particularly arousing. It is doubtful, as I have said, whether the Ithyphalloi actually wore an erect phallus on their body (though their name might suggest this) that, as Herter thinks (Herter 1938b:1679 and Herter 1947:21), shimmered through this garment. The Spartan *gypones* dancers also wear the *tarantinidion* (Pollux 4.104); cf. also Casadio 1987:231 (= Casadio 1999:120). For the transparent garment with girdle as aphrodisiac enticement, cf. Ar. *Lys.* 46ff., esp. 48, διαφανῆ χιτώνια. On the feminine appearance achieved by the long ankle-length garment, cf. the dress of the tragic actor, the god Dionysus, and Agathon in *Thesmophoriazusae* 130ff. The six bearded, bald-headed transvestite dancers on the Sabouroff red-figure vase (ca. 460 BCE) from Malibu (Malibu, J. Paul Getty Museum 86.AE.296; *ARV* 837, 10; ill. Price 1990, pl. 10b and Csapo 1997, pl. 1C), who also wear the long *khitôn*, have often been compared to the Ithyphalloi, especially since they are also associated with a *thyrsos*-like phallus-staff; for an extensive description of the exterior of this vase, see Reich 1903:276n2; cf. also Price 1990:164 and Csapo 1997:264. The grotesque, bearded dancers wearing long feminine garments on an Attic black-figure vase (Amsterdam 3356) from the middle of the sixth century BCE have also been compared to the Ithyphalloi; see Webster in Pickard-Cambridge 1962:81, 141, 304 and ill. 21 (pl. 6b).

[61] On the *kaunakê* see Herter 1947:20, Starkie *Wasps*, 332 *ad loc.*, MacDowell *Wasps*, 278–279 *ad* 1137, Sommerstein *Wasps*, 222 *ad loc.*, and Pickard Cambridge 1962:141n6. The Thracian nickname τριβαλλοί (for τρίφαλλοι) for an Athenian drinking club should also be viewed in this context: the Thracians represented the quintessence of the wild barbarian for the Athenians; Herter 1938c:1681.

accompanying it with dance.[62] The second choral group performs similarly: the collective divides itself up, one part proceeding into the theater through the side-entrances (*parodoi*) and the other through the middle doors, and in a rhythmic procession (βαίνοντες ἐν ῥυθμῷ) they sing their hymn to Dionysus as a phallic *prosodion*. The circumstantial participle λέγοντες (agreeing with the actors) used to introduce the text of both songs is, however, problematic. Ought one then to interpret this to mean that the Phallophoroi and Ithyphalloi only "spoke," and did not sing, the text? As will emerge from the following analysis, body movements and music are naturally closely linked to other forms of ritual expression. Because of his literary interests Semos apparently had no interest in the performative self-references and so introduced the quotations with the unmarked, everyday verb "to say, speak." This simply conveys the information, then, that the text of the songs, which consists only of their *logos*, "goes as follows."[63]

The formation, as well as the pragmatic context, is reminiscent of entries in Old Comedy through the *parodos*. It is almost as if we have in front of us stage-directions for entry songs of the chorus in a particular role. Yet it follows from the small songs of four to five lines that here we do not of course have the description of a dramatic *parodos*, but a purely ritual action, the entry of a phallic procession. In the first case (fr. a), both diction and gesture draw attention to the arrival of the gigantic phallus, which is probably, as in fragment b, carried in by a Phallophoros. The audience, perhaps also a part of the chorus, which enters into contact with the spectators and perhaps mingles with them,

---

[62] For dance accompanying the φαλλικόν, see Pollux 4.99–100. A φαλλικόν is always a song to the phallus; cf. Suda, s.v. φαλλικά, φαλλάκιον = Etym. Magn., s.v. φάλαικον (786, 57–58), Phot., s.v. φαλλικόν, and schol. Ar. *Ach.* 261.

[63] As to whether the texts were spoken or sung, most scholars opt for the latter, despite the introductory λέγοντες; see, among others, West 1982:148, "the chant of the (Athenian?) Ithyphalloi"; Wilamowitz I 1931/32:160n3 (= repr. I, 156n4), "Delisches Kultlied" ["Delian cult song"]; Nilsson I 1967³:592, "charakteristisches Lied" ["characteristic song"]. Neither the meter of the first text nor that of the second offers a decisive answer to this question, but the song hypothesis does seem to be justified from a performative point of view. Other Ithyphalloi, who greeted Demetrios Poliorketes in Athens (cf. below, n70), are clearly connected with *kômos*-like choral dancing: Demokhares of Athens, *FGrHist* 75 F 2 (quoted in Athen. 253cd) describes the performative situation as follows: προσοδιακοὶ χοροὶ καὶ ἰθύφαλλοι μετ' ὀρχήσεως καὶ ᾠδῆς ἀπήντων αὐτῷ καὶ ἐφιστάμενοι κατὰ †τοὺς ὄχλους ᾖδον ὀρχούμενοι καὶ ἐπάδοντες. See also the glosses in the Suda and in Phot., s.v. ἰθύφαλλοι· . . . καὶ ποιήματα δὲ καλεῖσθαι, ἃ ἐπὶ τῷ ἱσταμένῳ φαλλῷ ᾄδεται μετ' ὀρχήσεως. The Athenian Ithyphalloi will have danced to an ithyphallic rhythm in accordance with their nature; cf. the grammarian's quotation, repeating a quotation from Hypereides' speech again Arkhestratides (Hyp. fr. 50 Jensen): οἱ τοὺς ἰθυφάλλους ἐν τῇ ὀρχήστρᾳ ὀρχούμενοι. For further dancing Ithyphalloi, cf. Athen. 129d; the Phallophoroi mentioned by Antheas of Lindos also performed a *kômos* (Athen. 445ab).

is ordered in this movement to make way for the living epiphany. In the second scenario (fr. b), the god Dionysus is praised in hymnic form by the entering Phallophoroi as divine personification of the fetish object.[64]

In the case of the Phallophoroi, there is even a description after the hymn of a further ritual action by the chorus members: they run to the audience and pull them in, making them participants in the ritual by ridiculing them.[65] *Tôthasmos* and *aiskhrologia*, censure and ridicule combined with an attack on the audience, are also part of the inventory of Aristophanic comedy.[66] This ritual ridicule under the protection of a mask that only partially obscures one's identity also belongs to the group of signs that mark a transition from the normal world to that of the festival. Semos says the chorus members make fun of whomever they choose from the audience. They do so standing (στάδην), presumably in contrast to the processional march of the hymn. They have set up their formation (στάσις) in the orchestra, but this does not mean they stand still, but as in the *stasimon*, they are now free to make fools of selected citizens through dance and vulgar gestures. This is accompanied by loud laughter, but at the same time this is also a deadly serious occasion, as the ancient debates about ὀνομαστὶ κωμῳδεῖν in comedy show us.[67] Under the cover of the state of

---

[64] It must be emphasized that the two juxtaposed passages should not be interpreted as a unique ritual sequence in the sense of a diachronic narrative, although Semos, or perhaps even Athenaeus, could to some extent have manipulated the juxtaposed variants in this direction.

[65] εἶτα προστρέχοντες ἐτώθαζον οὓς [ἂν] προέλοιντο, στάδην δὲ ἔπραττον· ὁ δὲ φαλλοφόρος ἰθὺ βαδίζων καταπασθεὶς αἰθάλῳ (Athen. 622d).

[66] On *tôthasmos* see Fluck 1931:11–33 and Rusten 1977, who emphasizes the exhibitionist element in addition to the ribald and aggressive ridicule. The Phallophoroi possibly opened their cloaks in a kind of *anasyrisis* or lifted them high so that the strapped-on erect member concealed underneath would appear. Herter had already suggested this concealment of the phallus under the cloak in the case of the Ithyphalloi. Cf. above, n47. Of course both the bearer's object and the accompanying group could be phallic. Cf. the reverse of the so-called Heydemann cup (Florence 3897), which depicts a phallic procession at the rural Dionysia (illustrations in Deubner 1932, pl. 22:2, Ghiron-Bistagne 1976:211 fig. 66, and Csapo 1997, pl. 4). The cloak may have been removed for the *tôthasmos*, which is reminiscent of the (aggressive) scenes in the transition to the *parabasis* in Old Comedy; cf. also *Ach.* 626–627, *Pax* 729–730, *Lys.* 615, and *Thesm.* 656. With these passages the ancient opinion (schol. *Pax* 729) is generally reproduced that the cloak was removed in order to be able to move freely while dancing. Only at *Wasps* 408 do we find the removal of the long cloak (together with the exposure of wasp's sting, reminiscent of a phallus) not at the transition to the *parabasis*; cf. also Sifakis 1971:86–88, 98, and 103–108.

[67] See Sommerstein 1996. Nagy 1979:243–252 shows the complementarity of praise and blame in *iambos* and indicates how *kômos* and comedy, which developed from the latter, have a similar function. Just as the *iambos* uses ritualized aggression against an ἐχθρός and thereby creates a group solidarity among the φίλοι at the symposium, so too the ridicule of individual citizens in *ad hoc* fashion in the marketplace serves to increase the cohesiveness of the whole community (249–252).

ritual inversion, the less privileged are by way of exception given the chance to attack the powerful, to the amusement of all. Only the Phallophoros leads the way, his faced covered with soot.[68] Preparation and postlude both belong to a performance in ritual and theater. The actual entry is never clearly separable, but reaches into the before and after, just as in Aristophanic comedy.

Tôthasmos corresponds in many ways to the improvisations of the speaking Autokabdaloi and Iamboi (Athen. 622b). The iambic rhythm of the choral song changes to the rhythm of improvised ridicule. In the retrospective of the literary and cultural historians Sosibios and Semos, whom Athenaeus quotes in his learned discourse, what emerges is the rhêsis, in Aristotelian terms, of the actors, which to a certain extent is understood as the original proliferation of actual choral performances. From direct ridicule of the audience we move to small dramatic scenes, such as the appearance of a boastful doctor (alazôn) or a vegetable thief (bômolokhos), while the chorus continually oscillates between ritual function and fictional role.

The entire passage has accordingly been adduced, with some justification, as a possible explanation of the origin of comedy: yet in the final analysis this does not take us beyond Aristotle's speculations. I shall therefore attempt to interpret the songs themselves in their verbal dimension as meaningful, aesthetically articulated ritual that is in accord with the elements that have so far appeared from the description of the context and that possesses a completely similar meaning and function to that of certain choral songs in Old Comedy. But here there is a complete absence of any participation in a plot that has dramatic roles. What we have here, then, is a kind of re-ritualization in a developed Hellenistic theater. The performance may also of course, as has been seen, have functioned as prelude to the theatrical agôn.

Fr. 851a PMG

As they move forward with rhythmic steps, the Ithyphalloi in fragment a give the order in song to make way for the entrance of the phallus, the god.[69]

---

[68] Black soot, white gypsum, or yeast as original makeup help to create a distancing and symbolic emphasis, an effect also produced by masks; cf. Pickard-Cambridge 1962:74–80. The color black is also a particular marker of the Attic ephêbeia and other rites of puberty; see Vidal-Naquet 1968, esp. 112.

[69] The god here is probably Phales, the personification of the phallus in the procession at the rural Dionysia, but also connected with Dionysus. Cf. Pohlenz 1949:35 (= Kl. Schr. II, 1965:501): "die Ithyphallen melden den Einzug ihres Gottes, der wohl eher Phales als Dionysos ist" ["The Ithyphalloi announce the entry of their god, who is probably Phales rather than Dionysus"]. In the phallic procession at Acharnians 241–279, discussed in greater detail below, Phales is described as "companion and fellow-comast of Dionysus" (Φαλῆς, ἑταῖρε Βακχίου, ξύγκωμε,

Simple ritual rhythms—associated in particular with Phales-Dionysus, or with Ἰθύφαλλος, the personification of the phallus in the fourth century BCE, but also with Demeter as goddess of fertility—regulate their speech and body movements. We are dealing with an ithyphallic meter, appropriate for the choral group of Ithyphalloi, that follows a lyric iambic trimeter.[70] The performers sing the following song (fr. 851a *PMG*):

263-264). On the phallus in the cult of Dionysus, see Herter 1938c:1701-1710. On Phales, see Herter 1938. In Methymna on Lesbos, Dionysus has the additional name Phallen; Herter 1938a. For the theme of *parousia* in the entry procession, cf. the German Advent song "Macht hoch die Tür, die Tor macht weit, es kommt der Herr der Herrlichkeit!" ["Make high the door, make wide the gate, here comes the master of magnificence!"] and generally Weinreich 1929:34–286, esp. 59-63.

70 The text is contested. The meter is normalized following Bergk or Tyrwhitt's conjecture (3ia|ith||3ia|ith||). It would thus be identical to the hymn of Hermokles, also preserved in Athenaeus (253d-f) (Duris of Samos, *FGrHist* 76 F 13, carm. pop. fr. 46 B. [= Bergk III 1882⁴:674-676], Poetae Melici II D. [= Diehl II¹ 1925:249-251] and Powell 1925:173-175), which was composed for Demetrios Poliorketes when he entered Athens in Dionysiac costume in 291 (?) BCE. A further parallel can be found in the small song by Theokles (Athen. 497c, Poetae Melici III D. [= Diehl II¹ 1925:251] and Powell 1925:173). On the Theokles song: Athenaeus connects the drinking vessel described as a *dikeras* with Ptolemy Philadelphos, who is supposed to have decorated statues of Arsinoe with it. The fragment is rich in performative information; performance in the here and now is emphasized; cf. σήμερον, the first-person singular and plural, *sôtêria*, the Tekhnitai, a king, and the symposium. As with the other fragments of Semos preserved in Athenaeus that concern the Ithyphalloi and Phallophoroi and are introduced with λέγοντες, the means of performance is also here much debated. Fraser I 1972:232-233 discusses the text and thinks it is not clear who the *speaker* is. Contra Wilamowitz I 1924:166n2: "offenbar bei einer Prozession der Techniten vor Philadelphos gesungen. Ich hatte Theokles früher falsch unter Philopator gesetzt" ["Apparently sung at a procession of the Tekhnitai in front of Philadelphos. I had previously incorrectly placed Theokles under the reign of Philopator"]. Here he refers to Wilamowitz 1921:127n2, where he dates Theokles to the time of Philopator.

On the hymn to Demetrios Poliorketes: Tresp 1914:203 compares Semos' Ithyphalloi with the singing and dancing Ithyphalloi, who according to Demokhares of Athens, *FGrHist* 75 F 2 (with paraphrase of the hymn, which is attested in Duris' version), greeted Demetrios (Athen. 253c). Cf. Habicht 1970²:50-55 and 232-233, Habicht 1995:94-103, Parker 1996:258-263, and Stehle 1997:42-46. For information about the Theokles and Hermokles text I thank Albert Henrichs; cf. also Henrichs 1999, in which the hymn to Demetrios is also addressed (243-247). Anacreon fr. 78 D. (= 431 *PMG*) already uses the combination 3ia|ith||. On this cf. also Gentili 1952:95–96 (now also Gentili/Lomiento 2003:124), and West 1982:148 (without Anacreon fr. 78 D.). Rossbach/Westphal 1889³:306 also mention Ar. fr. 425 K.-A. (with the conjecture δάπτοντα, so that the first verse forms a trimeter); cf. K.-A. in *PCG* III.2, 233.

In the form adopted by Page (*PMG*) and West 1982:148, the first verse is a lekythion (trochaic dimeter catalectic), which easily admits variations; the ithyphallic represents the catalectic form of the lekythion. Wilamowitz's division (Wilamowitz 1921:266n5) into four trochaic dimeters is not convincing. Once again, underlining indicates the performative element, and italicization here and in the following examples indicates matters specific to the phallus cult.

ἀνάγετ᾽, εὐρυχωρίαν
τῷ θεῷ <u>ποιεῖτε</u>·
θέλει γὰρ ὁ θεὸς ὀρθὸς ἐσφυδωμένος
διὰ μέσου <u>βαδίζειν</u>.

1 <ἀνάγετε πάντες,> ἀνάγετ᾽, εὐρυχωρίαν Bergk ἀνάγετ᾽ <ἀνάγετε κῶμον>,
εὐρυχωρίαν coni. Tyrwhitt (denuoque Porson) 2 ποεῖτε τῷ θεῷ A, ποιεῖτε
(om. τῷ θ.) E, transp. Porson 1sqq. ἀνάγετ᾽ εὐρυχωρίαν ποι- | εῖτε τῷ θεῷ·
θέλει γὰρ | ὀρθὸς ἐσφ., deleto ὁ θεός, coni. Wilamowitz <ἀνάγετ᾽> ἀνάγετ᾽ |
εὐρυχωρίαν ποιεῖτε | τῷ θεῷ, θέλει γὰρ ὁ θεὸς Wilamowitz 1921:266n5 prob.
Diehl 3 ἐθέλει AE, corr. Meineke ἐσφυρωμένος A, em. Meineke[71]

Come on, up, make plenty of room for the god! For the god, upright
and at bursting point, wants to march through the middle.

Despite the detailed description, the following questions of choreography
remain unresolved: 1.) Was the phallus carried a) in front or b) behind the
comastic group as it entered? 2.) a) Does the chorus address the audience as it
enters, which is most likely given the context (ἐπιστρέφουσιν εἰς τὸ θέατρον),
b) does a chorus-leader direct these words to his group, or c) does the group
order itself to move aside, as is also entirely possible given the use of the
imperative in performative speech? Option 1.a, which may be justified on the
basis of the model of the famous *phallagôgia* of Dikaiopolis (Ar. *Ach.* 241–279)
and on the basis of visual representations, implies an address to the spectators (2.a). Yet the command to make way, if given to fellow members of a
community seated in a permanent theater of stone, can be seen only as a relic
of an earlier stage of development when the spectators, simply standing in
the marketplace, would crowd around the actors. Of course, if the phallus is
carried behind the group (1.b), then options 2.b and c would be conceivable.
The chorus would then be pushed to the side to enable the entry of the god
and the arrival of the phallus with the phallus carriers in a choreographically
impressive manner. If a section of the chorus were to have stationed itself
in front of the area of the spectators, then solutions 2.b and c together with
option 1.a would be conceivable. Thus a semi-chorus and the audience could
certainly have been addressed, so that the firm boundary between stage and
spectator would be broken, just as in ritual.

The urgency of the order is underscored by the three short syllables at
the beginning (ἀνάγετ᾽).[72] With their spondaic beginning, the ithyphallics

---

[71] There is the mistake in the apparatus to line 1 in Page (*PMG*, 453): he prints ἀνάγετ᾽ <ἀνάγετε>
κῶμον, εὐρυχωρίαν coni. Tyrwhitt.

[72] On ἄγε or ἄναγε as a performative signal of urgency in ritual, cf. above, chap. 1, n23. Cf. also Ar. *Av.*
1720–1721: ἄναγε δίεχε πάραγε πάρεχε· | περιπέτεσθε . . . (self-address in fight songs); cf. Dunbar

alternating with iambic trimeters (or at first with the lekythion) imitate the penetration of the erect member.[73] The god is the phallic symbol; he enters and participates in the sacred activity of the chorus.[74] The god wishes to enter, and the circle of the community, who in the ritual using a typical metaphor joins their divinity in a sexual act, is opened to him. In accordance with Austin's speech act theory, the action of the comastic procession is completed in the simple performative utterance.[75] With this self-command the entry of the group onto the dance floor is brought about: εὐρυχωρίαν refers to the here and now of the orchestra, to which Semos refers in his introductory text. This is a wide open space (χῶρος) suitable for the performance of the χορός, so that χορός can also refer to the dance floor. Areas are often described with the adjective εὐρύχορος, which refers to the breadth necessary to accommodate

---

Birds, 753 *ad* 1720: "This series of orders must have produced excited chorus-movements in the *orchestra*." *Ibid.* and in Dunbar *Birds*, 284 *ad* 383, as well as 290 *ad* 400, Dunbar notes that ἄναγε should here be understood as a technical military term. On the connection between ephebic military and choral service, Winkler 1990; the imperative is admittedly rather general and can be connected with any specific performance of an action: cf. Eur. *Tro.* 325: <ἄναγ'> ἄναγε χορόν (cf. in this connection Tyrwhitt's supplement ἀνάγετ' <ἀνάγετε κῶμον> in line 1); for the completion of a sacrifice or festival: LSJ, s.v. I.5; in particular the striking up of a song may be introduced in this way: e.g. Soph. *Trach.* 210–211 and LSJ, s.v. I.7.

[73] The ithyphallic meter is so called because of its use in the Dionysiac φαλλαγωγία; see the sources in West 1982:97–98 with reference to Semos' Ithyphalloi. On the ithyphallic see West 1982:97–101, 146–148 and Gentili 1952:94–105 (now also Gentili/Lomiento 2003:123–128); Aristophanes' use of the asynartetic combination with a iambic dimeter (the euripideus), as in Ar. *Equ.* 756–760 and 836–840, *Nub.* 1114, *Vesp.* 248–272, *Ran.* 396–397, 443–447, Pherecr. fr. 2.3 and fr. 195 K.-A., is interesting; like Euripides, Aristophanes uses the ithyphallic as a clausula, cf. Gentili 1952:104–105 (now also Gentili/Lomiento 2003:127–128). On the ithyphallic in Aristophanes, see also White 1912:73–74 (§ 203). West 1982:146–148 especially emphasizes the use of iambs and ithyphallics in traditional and ritual songs, which speaks in favor of the song hypothesis. Cf. *ibid.*, 148, the combination of the ritual τήνελλα καλλίνικε Archil. fr. 324 W. and the refrain of the Palaikastro hymn with fr. 851a *PMG*. As is well known, Aristophanes incorporates much material from popular song (Silk 1980:124–129). One could also argue that Aristophanes himself did not make many distinctions in rhythmic structure from current ritual forms. The conventionality, repetition, and simplicity that Aristophanes is criticized for in his lyrics (Silk 1980) may well be grounded in the characteristic ritual nature of choral song, which emphasizes the here and now of the performance. Cf. Mathews' (1997) response to Silk's criticism, which refers to the ritual and performative dimension, esp. to dance (*ibid.*, 32–42).

[74] The gods are often invoked in cletic hymns to observe and participate in choral dance. This occurs especially in the odes of the *parabasis*.

[75] Cf. Aesch. *Cho.* 942: ἐπολολύξατ' (cf. the commentary of Sier 1988:289 *ad loc.*: "Die Aufforderung zur Ololyge ist schon Artikulation des Jubels, die den Schrei ersetzt" ["The command to pronounce the *ololygê* is already an articulation of the rejoicing and takes the place of the actual shout"]). The word represents the action, and so the command already amounts to the chorus' moving apart. Cf. in another context Ar. *Nub.* 127 with Dover *Clouds*, 109 *ad loc.* (with reference to Austin).

ecstatic Dionysiac dance.[76] In the form of a notional *paronomasia* the members of the chorus thus implicitly also order themselves to form a "wide chorus," which is also supposed to be beautiful (εὖ) for the worship of their god. Yet in terms of meter, the form with omega is required here, so that the focus is in particular on the space (χῶρος) to be created for the chorus. The chorus sings of how the god as phallus wants to enter, and the phallus does just that, being carried in by the bearers. The use of θέλει with the infinitive is equivalent to the use of the performative future in Pindar as well as in dramatic, ritual, and magical texts,[77] with βαδίζειν representing a self-referential expression for the performative activity of the phallic procession in the here and

[76] *IG* I³ 1178.1 = *CEG* 12 (pp. 10–11 Hansen) (funerary inscription for Silenos from Rhegium, 433/32 BCE): εὐρύχοροι . . . Ἀθῆναι, cf. Corinna fr. 655–fr. 1.8 *PMG*: γῆαν εὐρού[χορον, fr. adesp. 934.20 *PMG*: πόλιν εὐρύχορον. Cf. LSJ s.v.: "with broad places, spacious," Hom. *Il.* 2.498, 9.478; *Od.* 13.414, 15.1; *Anth. Pal.* 7.99.5; roads broad enough for choral dance: Pind. *Pyth.* 8.55, Eur. *Ba.* 86–87 (and the Delphic oracle at Demosth. 21.52); for roads: Philodamus, Paean in Dionysum (Powell 1925:165–171, 169 = Käppel 1992:375–380, 379–Pai. 39), lines 145–146 and Eur. *HF* 783. Cf. also Seaford 1996:159 *ad* Eur. *Ba.* 86–87: "εὐρύχορος often seems to imply χῶρος (place) rather than χορός (dance and song)"; and LSJ s.v. "Prop. *with broad dancing-places*, cf. χορός; then a conventional epithet, perh. connected by poets with χῶρος." For the etymological connection of χῶρος and χορός, see Boedeker 1974:85–91. For the epithet "with beautiful chorus" (καλλίχορος), cf. Eur. *HF* 690, *Hel.* 1454–1455, *Phoen.* 786, *Cresphontes* fr. 453.7–8 N/Kannicht, Corinna fr. 669 *PMG*, Ar. *Ran.* 451; ἤϋχορος *Appendix nova epigrammatum* 2, 520, 7 Cougny; εὔχορος Phot., s.v. εὔκυκλος. Cf. also εὐρύνω, "to clear the arena for dance," Hom. *Od.* 8.260. For εὐρυχωρία: cf. Com. adesp. 257 K.-A., εὐρυχωρίας σε δεῖ. The word refers metaphorically to free space for performing some action: [Plat.] *Min.* 315d3–4 εὐρυχωρία τῆς ἀποδείξεως; for *apodeixis* as public performance, cf. Nagy 1990:162, 217–224. In keeping with the strong sexual coloring of the song, εὐρυχοιρίαν ('broadness of vagina') could also have been used in this passage (line 1) or could at least have occurred to the audience. A similar textual suggestion is made by Bowie 1990:35–36 in connection with Ar. *Vesp.* 834; instead of the transmitted φιλοχωρία he conjectures φιλοχοιρία; one could construct εὐρυχοιρία as a parallel to the frequent word εὐρυπρωκτία ('broadness of anus'), Ar. *Ach.* 843, *Vesp.* 1070: cf. on εὐρυπρωκτία Henderson 1991²:77, on the corresponding adjective εὐρύπρωκτος *ibid.*, 77, 195, 210, 213–214, 218. For the name Χοιροψάλας used of Dionysus in the Sicyonian mysteries, see Herter 1938c:1702 and Henderson 1991²:132n128.

[77] On the performative future, see Calame 1994/95:144 with 152n25, Faraone 1995, and Henrichs 1994/95:80 with 104n97; cf. already Norden 1939:199–201 (on the future in prayer). The concept of the performative future and performative verb forms will here be transferred to the third person, although it has hitherto been applied generally to the first and second persons only. Cf. above, Introduction n112. For θέλω with the infinitive in the sense of the more commonly used future, cf. Pind. *Pyth.* 9.1–3 ἐθέλω . . . Πυθιονίκαν . . . ἀγγέλλων Τελεσικράτη . . . γεγωνεῖν, Pind. *Isthm.* 1.15–16 ἐθέλω . . . ἐναρμόξαι νιν ὕμνῳ; Thummer I 1968/69:128 classifies such constructions as examples of the "'enkomiastische' Futur, das die gegenwärtige Intention des Dichters ausdrückt und niemals über das Gedicht hinausweist" ["'encomiastic' future, which expresses the poet's current intention and never refers beyond the poem"]; it is identical to the performative future.

now.[78] With the two asyndetically arranged attributives ὀρθὸς ἐσφυδωμένος, the divinity is transformed into a phallic symbol using metaphor in a tropological fashion typical of ritual. The perfect participle also forms a link to the feast: just as symposiasts burst with drunkenness and overeating,[79] so too does the erect phallus as expression of excitement. Both areas stand *pars pro toto* for Dionysus and his ecstatic affirmation of life. The entering phallus, the exuberant *joie de vivre*, the inversion of the world, and grotesque corporality are constantly associated with carnival and fertility.[80] The connecting link between all ritual phenomena is the *kômos* that is here being staged.

---

[78] The expression ὀρθὸς ... βαδίζειν corresponds to the formulation in the description of the Phallophoroi that follows, where it is said of the *phallophoros* that he enters thus (ἰθὺ βαδίζων); Semos' choice of vocabulary here is probably influenced by the song of the Ithyphalloi. On βαίνειν (cf. βαίνοντες ἐν ῥυθμῷ in the preceding performative information provided about the Phallophoroi), which is synonymous with βαδίζειν, as a term in common parlance with sexual connotations, cf. Henderson 1991²:19n70 ("fuck"), 27, 136, 147, 155 ("mounting"), and 194n10. For μέσος cf. *ibid.*, 156. For its use in combination with the *kômos*, cf. Ar. *Plut.* 1040: ἐπὶ κῶμον βαδίζειν (*kômos* of the young man about whom the old woman complains; like the Ithyphalloi, he wears a garland and is drunk and out of control). For βαδίζειν as self-referential expression of the chorus cf. inter alia *Thesm.* 1228–1229: ὥρα δή 'στι βαδίζειν | οἴκαδ᾽ ἑκάστῃ (in reference to the chorus' departure at the end of the play).

[79] Cf. Timokles fr. 31.2 K.-A. *ap.* Athen. 246f, δειπνοῦσιν ἐσφυδωμένοι. The transmitted ἐσφυρωμένος probably slipped into the text because of the words μέχρι τῶν σφυρῶν in the preceding description of the Ithyphalloi. If the god (ὁ θεός) is fitted out with ankle bands or some kind of foot covering ("mit Knöchelbinden oder sonst einer Fußbekleidung," Pape II, s.v. σφυρόω) or, something that would make more sense, with a garment that reaches all the way to the ankles, this does not refer to the phallus being carried in, but to the cult statue or the person representing a divinity such as Dionysus. But this would deprive the fragment of its ambiguity. Cf. Herter 1938b:1678: "Ob Dionysos oder der Phallos als solcher mit diesem θεός gemeint war, läßt das Lied nicht erkennen" ["It cannot be determined from the song whether Dionysus or the phallus as such was meant by the term θεός"] (with a list of the commentators who argue for the one solution or the other *ibid.*, 1678–1679). In any case, the solution appears to lie not in an either-or, but rather in a both-and framework. Bursting and swelling (σφυδοῦν) applies equally to both Dionysus and the phallus. For Dionysos Φλεύς (from φλέω, "be full of, teem with"), see Graf 1985:283–284, who considers (Graf 1985:284n10) the suggested connection with φαλλός and φαλήν to be problematic. On the adjective ὀρθός in a vulgar sense, see Henderson 1991²:112. Cf. in particular the φαλλὸς ὀρθός in Dikaiopolis' phallic procession (Ar. *Ach.* 243, 259–260) and Csapo 1997:284. On Orthos as name for Dionysus, see Herter 1938c:1702; on the ancient *daimônes* called Orthanes worshiped in Attica, *ibid.*, 1693.

[80] One may compare the aetiology for the *phallagôgia* at the Athenian City Dionysia (schol. Ar. *Ach.* 243): The Athenians did not honor the god imported from Boeotia to Athens. The male population subsequently fell victim to a disease of the genitals. The Athenians were only freed from this after they introduced a ritual that consisted of Dionysus being brought phalli as a gift. The inversion of order is restored to equilibrium with a renewal of fertility for the community.

Fr. 851b *PMG*

Even more interesting for its ritual and performative meaning is the following song (fr. 851b *PMG*) of the Phallophoroi, which introduces a hymn to Dionysus:[81]

> σοί, Βάκχε, <u>τάνδε μοῦσαν ἀγλαΐζομεν</u>,
> <u>ἁπλοῦν ῥυθμὸν χέοντες αἰόλῳ μέλει</u>,
> καινὰν ἀπαρθένευτον, οὔ τι ταῖς πάρος
> κεχρημέναν <u>ᾠδαῖσιν</u>, ἀλλ' ἀκήρατον
> <u>κατάρχομεν τὸν ὕμνον·</u>

For you, Bakkhos, we give this shining musical presentation, pouring out a simple rhythm with changing melody, [a presentation] new, virginal, one that uses songs never before used, but as something unmixed and pure we begin this hymn.

The singers introduce themselves and refer to their own activity. In a speech act they bring about and complete the ritual action of the performance of a praise song. Characteristic performative expressions in the "we" form are foregrounded. Reference to the here and now of the current performance is made using the deictic pronoun. "This musical performance" (τάνδε μοῦσαν, 1) happens in honor of the god of the festive occasion, and consists of the following three levels: the rhythm of body language (ῥυθμόν, 2), the melody of the musical "song of the limbs" (μέλει, 2), probably determined by an *aulos*-player, and the content of the song sung (ᾠδαῖσιν, 4).[82] Melody, movement, and

---

[81] The god addressed in the previous text (fr. a), who through a kind of fusion is equated with the phallus, is sometimes also associated with Dionysus in his appearance as Phales. See above, n79. As "proem" the fragment is naturally, as in Aristophanes, also already part of the whole song of praise that the chorus sings as an ensemble. It would be incorrect to assume that the *iamboi* (3ia|3ia|3ia|3ia|2ia cat.) are here, in contrast to an actual hymn, only spoken or performed in a *parakatalogê*. On the sung and danced *iamboi* of the Phallophoroi, see West 1974:36. On iambic trimeters in traditional and ritual chants, West 1982:147. He cites fr. 847, 851b, 860, 870, 883 *PMG* as examples of iambic trimeter; fr. 861, 868, 876b, 879.2, and 881 *PMG* as examples of slightly shortened forms of the trimeter (*ibid.*, nn23–24). Actual *prooimia* are kitharodic, rhapsodic, or choral-melic depending on the context; cf. Calame 1995a:3 with n5 and Nagy 1990:353–360. Of course the movement of the *evocatio* (e.g. "Sing for me, Muse, of Apollo, who . . . ") that one finds in the Homeric Hymns with its particular function as proem should not be interchanged with the *invocatio*, the direct appeal to the divinity in cult hymns.

[82] ᾠδή is here somewhat synonymous with μολπή, i.e. the unity of song and dance (cf. Nagy 1990:94); in any case ᾠδή seems to mean in particular the diction of the song. Rhythm, *melos*, and *ôidê* give rise to the μοῦσα, the hymn as musical *Gesamtkunstwerk*. Hymns and dance performance often belong together: see e.g. Burkert 1985:102–103. Processions also often stop along the way and perform hymns and dance. In the theater, as in our case, the stopping is abbreviated because of

the lyrical words of the song, which are distinct from everyday speech, in addition to the previously described *opsis* of the actors as they enter, thus create the synaesthetic performance of a prayer. Form and content stand in an immediate connection to one another. Through their explicit self-presentation, the members of the chorus bring about a demonstrative and attentive attitude in themselves and in the spectators, who are drawn into an imaginary collective. The performance completes the act of praise, while the individual semiotic components, in particular the word of command, constitute and regulate this minimal hymn. There is no actual prayer or mythical narration. In terms of Ausfeld's famous tripartite division of the hymn (*invocatio* – *pars epica* – *preces*), only the *invocatio* with its presentation of the chorus' own performance, so characteristic of ritual, actually appears in our case.[83] This means that perlocutionary consequences, such as the appearance of the divinity, are aspired to implicitly, but the song contents itself with concentrating on its own activity of song and dance using gestures of self-display. Dionysus is supposed to be attracted sympathetically and magically by the self-referential emphasis on musical activity.[84] Using the *Du-Stil* of predication Bakkhos is addressed as the addressee of the song,[85] which creates an immediate contact with the

---

spatial limitation. The procession could also of course have endlessly circled in the orchestra.

The *prosodion* is here performed by an entering *kômos*, whose movements could in the broadest sense be deemed equivalent to a "dance." We have unfortunately lost the dimension of melody and choreography. They may perhaps also have underlined the abnormal character of an inverted world; one can imagine the noisy and shrill sound of *auloi* and obscene sexual gestures. All that is left is the λόγος of the ᾠδή, in which the description of the performative context does, however, allow us to make conclusions about the other semiotic levels. Nagy 1990:51 likewise distinguishes three dimensions: diction, the rhythmic structure of movement, and melody. Here he applies the threefold division of lyric poetry (μέλος) into *logos, harmonia,* and rhythm found in Plat. *Rep.* 398d and Arist. *Poet.* 1447a21–23: ἅπασαι [sc. ποιήσεις, the genres of epic, tragedy, comedy, dithyramb, and lyric] μὲν ποιοῦνται τὴν μίμησιν ἐν ῥυθμῷ καὶ λόγῳ καὶ ἁρμονίᾳ . . . For the triad, cf. already Alcm. fr. 39 Davies and above, chap. 1, n495. In the song of the Phallophoroi, dance (ῥυθμός), words, and melody are thus fused together in the μέλος, with the last two levels mentioned being subsumed under the concept ᾠδή. For μοῦσα in the sense of a concrete song, generally in self-referential form (τάνδε μοῦσαν 1), cf. Aesch. *Eum.* 308 μοῦσαν στυγερὰν (immediately after the similarly self-referential χορὸν ἄψωμεν [*Eum.* 307]; cf. on ὕμνος δέσμιος above, pp. 62–65), Aesch. *Supp.* 695, Soph. *Trach.* 643, and Ar. *Thesm.* 107 (with chap. 1 n165); Pind. *Nem.* 3.28 Μοῖσαν φέρειν; cf. also in prose Plat. *Leg.* 829d.

[83] Ausfeld 1903. Bremer 1981:196 prefers the division *"invocation, argument,* and *petition"* for actual cultic hymns. On form and composition of hymns see now Furley/Bremer I 2001:50–64.

[84] Cf. Furley 1995; on the Greek hymn in general see, among others, Wünsch 1914:156–170, Keyßner 1932, Burkert 1985:102–103, Bremer 1981, Lattke 1991:13–79, Furley 1993, Burkert 1994, Calame 1995a:2–5, and now Furley/Bremer I 2001:1–64. On the place of the hymn between ritual and literature, which here occupies a central position, see the collective volume Cassio/Cerri 1991.

[85] Cf. Norden 1913:143–163.

god.[86] It remains an open question whether the fragment should be viewed as a paean, since it is after all transmitted in Semos' book Περὶ παιάνων.[87]

As I have pointed out, this song has up until now been treated almost exclusively in connection with the question of origins. In the context of the question of to what extent Attic comedy reworked and incorporated archaic and contemporary lyric, Christoph Kugelmeier considers the songs as a possible model for the scene of *phallophoria* in the *Acharnians* (241–279).[88] He characterizes the song of the Phallophoroi (fr. b), in comparison to what he terms the "traditionally observed" song of the Ithyphalloi, as "reflective in a literary fashion." He bases his opinion on the fact "that it expressly distances itself from the πάρος . . . ᾠδαί" (he also compares the formulation καινὰν ἀπαρθένευτον) "and in a skilful antithesis to the thus far simple rhythm characterizes itself as an αἴολον μέλος."[89] This claim to innovation is almost hammered into the ears of the audience in an asyndetic and metaphorical series of attributives. The Muse is "new," "virgin," "uses songs unheard before"; the members of the chorus begin an "unmixed hymn." Behind the chorus as it performs the voice of the artist seems to appear, who like Pindar and Aristophanes enters into a dialogue with his public.

The song has in fact the effect of polished poetry of the sort one would expect of Aristophanes or even Hellenistic poetry. Just as in an Aristophanic *parabasis*, with which it is often connected, it seems to engage with predecessors and to insist on its own originality.[90] A conscious poetic construction can

[86] Together with two satyrs, who have been connected by Cole 1993:31–33 with the comastic performers of this song, a naked and enthroned Dionysus also appears on the Karystios monument on Delos. Like his priest in Athens in the theater of Dionysus, on Delos the god himself had the right of *proedria* and was thus imagined as being present in an immediate sense.

[87] Cf. Käppel 1992:54 and 330 (test. 100) on Delos. This could also perhaps be assumed for fr. b because of the intensive style of speech, which Käppel emphasizes as a characteristic of the genre. He does not, however, consider the text a paean. Sacrifice and symposium could also be made out to be possible connecting links in terms of occasion, although the important generic characteristic of the *epiphthegma* is not present. The metrical structure, but more particularly the framework of the inverted world, the element of the phallic and ridicule, are unusual for a paean. To sum up, one can say that this catchy folk song of the Hellenistic period integrates elements of the paean. Ghiron-Bistagne 1976:208–209 and 245 call the phallic songs paeans.

[88] Cf. Kugelmeier 1996:152–154. The question continues to be posed; Kugelmeier follows the majority of scholars in thinking that the scene in the *Acharnians* cannot be viewed as a copy of a phallic procession. For an approach to the problem using another formulation, see below, pp. 314–325.

[89] Kugelmeier 1996:154.

[90] Bing 1988:22–23 connects the insistence on innovation with literacy and shows that the motif is especially typical of the Hellenistic period. But the topos goes back all the way to the archaic period. Among the older evidence he cites fr. 851b *PMG* besides Hesiod, Pindar, and Timotheos. Hellenistic poets introduced innovation in the category of the book in particular. Bing

further be seen in the fact that metaphor, antithesis, asyndeton, alliteration, homoioteleuton, parallelism, chiasmus, and enjambment appear frequently and in a sentence with a relatively complex construction.[91]

Yet poetic diction and references to originality should not be compared without qualification to an art that is sophisticated and detached from ritual. A judgment of this sort may be based entirely on the teleological assumptions already mentioned. Composition of a poetic and aesthetic nature does not necessarily represent a diametrical opposite to ritual. Rather, rhythmically repetitive form together with poetic stylistic features and insistent claims to innovation are also entirely characteristic of a ritual text.[92] In sum, rituality and classical as well as Hellenistic tendencies toward artistic self-awareness are fused together in this fragment.

In what follows the choral song will thus be treated as the expression of a traditional choral culture, the foundations of which lie in the myth and ritual of a society based on oral communication. Rituality ought in no way to be understood as the stereotyped, unreflective repetition of fixed texts and formulae with no adaptation, change, or renewal, although the recent and widespread use of the word "ritual" in this sense might make one think so. Quite the opposite: the idea that a performance ought to bring a god pleasure necessitates a continuous change in expression. Just as the worshiper wishes

---

mentions Meleager's *Garland*, *Anth. Pal.* 4.1.55, where the author calls his poems ἔρνεα πολλὰ νεόγραφα; similarly Philippos' *Garland*, *Anth. Pal.* 4.2.3; Boiskos of Kyzikos *Suppl. Hell.* 233.1: καινοῦ γραφεὺς ποιήματος; and Philikos of Corcyra *Suppl. Hell.* 677: καινογράφου συνθέσεως (the last two poets thereby foreground their metrical innovations). On the emphasis of the new in the living choral culture, see below, n93. Henrichs 1993a:175–177 also refers to the ancient tradition of this topos, which goes back to Pindar and Aristophanes; *ibid.*, 176–177n12. He also includes fr. 851b *PMG* in this context, following Bing 1988:22. For Aristophanes see now also Bierl 2004a:1–8. For the motif of superiority, self-promotion, and originality in choral lyric, see Maehler 1963:93–101 and Mastromarco 1987:83 with n17. For emphasis on innovation in Hellenistic poetry, see Parsons 1993:163–166.

[91] The accumulation of "a" sounds is striking, as is the alliteration of κ and α, the homoioteleuta in -ον and -αν, the chiasmus stretching over five lines, τάνδε μοῦσαν ἀγλαΐζομεν and κατάρχομεν τὸν ὕμνον, the prominent antitheses and parallelisms: σοί, Βάκχε, τ<u>άνδε μοῦσαν</u> ἀγλαΐζομεν, | ἁπλοῦν ῥυθμ<u>ὸν</u> χέοντες αἰόλῳ μέλει, | <u>καινὰν</u> ἀπαρθένευτ<u>ον</u>, οὔ τι ταῖς πάρος | <u>κεχρημέναν</u> ᾠδαῖσιν, ἀλλ᾽ ἀκήρατ<u>ον</u> | <u>κατάρχομεν τὸν</u> ὕμν<u>ον</u>. The song uses forms from Attic drama, in which Doric coloring in lyrical sections is characteristic (especially α for η). The doricisms do not go as far, for example, as using the Doric first-person plural ending -μες that is typical for Sikyon. The fragment is associated with this city because of the Phallophoroi mentioned immediately before this in Athenaeus (*Athen.* 621f). Perhaps the fragment is even a quotation from a contemporary Attic comedy (from the fourth century [?]; see below, n123).

[92] On the poetic structure of ritual, see Tambiah 1985:165 (with reference 389n52 to Jakobson's "poetic function," Jakobson 1960:358 [cf. Selected Writings III, 27]). Nagy 1990:33 rightly also connects song culture (SONG) to this ritual speech.

to make a fresh and unused offering to the god, this too is the goal in the area of aesthetics. This concept and the agonistic context in which many musical presentations are arranged allow the voice of the poet, the manufacturer of the composition (ποιητής), to appear behind the voices of the actors, even when the performance takes place in a communication situation dependent on orality, as is usual in forms of traditional society.[93] Written composition for

---

[93] Cf. Burkert 1985:103: "Although the names and basic rhythms of the dances are traditional, the cult in no way demands the repetition of ancient, magically fixed hymns. On the contrary, the hymn must always delight the god afresh at the festival; therefore for dance and hymn there must always be someone who makes it, the poet, *poietes*." Cf. also Herter 1947:26: "es steckt darin auch schwerlich die Spekulation auf die Neugier des Publikums, die schon späteren Rhapsoden nicht fremd war, oder auch die Originalitätssucht, die seit Pratinas, Kinesias und Timotheos das Programm so vieler Dichter bestimmt hat. Zwar haben sich gerade die attischen Komiker etwas darauf zugute getan, wenn sie eine 'neue Idee' vorbringen konnten, aber ihre kultischen Vorläufer empfinden noch ganz unmittelbar, daß der Gottheit etwas Frisches und Unberührtes als Weihegabe gefällt" ["this is unlikely to represent an attempt to gain the audience's curiosity, which was already a concern of the later rhapsodes, nor the quest for originality that had shaped the program of so many poets since Pratinas, Kinesias, and Timotheos. While it was advantageous for Attic comic playwrights if they could present a 'new idea,' their cultic predecessors still had a direct sense that the god is pleased by an offering that is fresh and untouched"]. The one need not of course exclude the other. The interest of the spectators clearly also had to be awakened. Pickard-Cambridge 1962:141 seems to indicate the connections in the following statement, when he says that singers wanted to give the impression of improvisation ("no doubt supposed to be improvised on the spot"). All the same, he continues on the basis of the thesis that the text has a strongly Hellenistic form. But the improvisations only actually start after the song. For innovation as a requirement for comedy (cf. now also Bierl 2002a) and for novelty in Ar. *Thesm.* 967 as a *parabasis*-like statement (with comparable passages), see above, chap. 1 n49; cf. also the relative's remark about Euripides' "new" *Helen* (*Thesm.* 850: τὴν καινὴν Ἑλένην μιμήσομαι), in which Euripides' claim to originality shines through in comic fashion; but Aristophanes' approach in this passage, namely to have the relative perform the *Helen*, is especially new. For Aristophanic self-advertisement, see Bremer 1993:160–165. For borrowings in *parabaseis* of metaphor and vocabulary in connection with personal originality and superiority in choral lyric, in particular in Pindar's epinician odes, see Mastromarco 1987:83–93.

   The topos of innovation in song is not a Hellenistic invention, but begins at a very early stage: Hom. *Od.* 1.351–352: τὴν γὰρ ἀοιδὴν μᾶλλον ἐπικλείουσ᾽ ἄνθρωποι, | ἥ τις ἀϊόντεσσι νεωτάτη ἀμφιπέληται; Hesiod (fr. 357.2 M.-W.) reports how he and Homer sang songs on Delos: ἐν νεαροῖς ὕμνοις ῥάψαντες ἀοιδήν; Alcm. fr. 3–fr. 1.1–2 Davies: Ὀλ]υμπιάδες περί με φρένας | ἱμέρῳ νέα]ς ἀοίδας (with Page's supplement *CR* 9 [1959]:16); Alcm. fr. 4–fr. 1.5–6 Davies: γαρύματα μαλσακὰ [| νεόχμ᾽ ἔδειξαν; Alcm. fr. 14a Davies: Μῶσ᾽ ἄγε, Μῶσα λίγηα πολυμμελὲς | αἰὲν ἀοιδὲ μέλος | νεοχμὸν ἄρχε παρσένοις ἀείδην; Terp. fr. 6 Loeb (= 4 Gostoli) (*PMG*, p. 363): σοὶ δ᾽ ἡμεῖς τετράγηρυν ἀποστέρξαντες ἀοιδὰν | ἑπτατόνῳ φόρμιγγι νέους κελαδήσομεν ὕμνους; Pind. *Nem.* 8.20–21: πολλὰ γὰρ πολλᾷ λέλεκται, νεαρὰ δ᾽ ἐξευρόντα δόμεν βασάνῳ | ἐς ἔλεγχον, ἅπας κίνδυνος; Pind. *Ol.* 3.4–6: Μοῖσα δ᾽ οὕτω ποι παρέ- | στα μοι νεοσίγαλον εὑρόντι τρόπον | Δωρίῳ φωνὰν ἐναρμόξαι πεδίλῳ | ἀγλαόκωμον; Pind. *Ol.* 9.48–49: αἴνει δὲ παλαιὸν μὲν οἶνον, ἄνθεα δ᾽ ὕμνων | νεωτέρων; Bacchyl. *Dith.* 19.8–10: ὕφαινέ νυν ἐν | ταῖς πολυηράτοις τι καινὸν | ὀλβίαις Ἀθήναις; Eur. *Tro.* 512–513: Μοῦσα, καινῶν ὕμνων | ᾆσον σὺν δακρύοις ᾠδὰν ἐπικήδειον;

a one-time performance places the stress on originality, and with the spread of writing this trend is only increased. The simple rhythmic structure of the folk song, transmitted not by accident among the anonymous *carmina popularia*, shows that here we have the product of a living choral culture that has been influenced by contemporary literary tendencies.

Ritual speech is a form of discourse that has a festive tone and that is particularly based on a tropology of central metaphors in order to make distinctive and expressive signals accessible to the observer through redundancy and fusion. The song of the Phallophoroi attempts to extend in tropic fashion the synaesthetic experience of the choral dance ritual to the sensory experience of wine consumption, sacrifice, sexuality, and festivity, while on the linguistic level of signification blending it into a "thick" discourse of self-referential allusions. These areas have a close ritual connection to the divine addressee, Dionysus. Elements relating to the inversion of the natural order are found on an equal level with a confirmation of the cosmos in the sense of the worship of an important polis god: negative and positive elements are evoked at the same time in order to attract the attention of the theater god.

The predicate ἀγλαΐζομεν is a performative expression in the "we"-form that creates a self-reference to the musical and rhythmical singing and dancing. The phatic utterance contains in particular the cultic act of providing Dionysus with renown and honor. This poetic verb is derived from the substan-

---

Xen. *Cyr.* 1.6.38: ἐν τοῖς μουσικοῖς τὰ νέα καὶ ἀνθηρὰ εὐδοκιμεῖ. This motif appears particularly clearly in Timotheos fr. 796 *PMG*: οὐκ ἀείδω τὰ παλαιά, | καινὰ γὰρ ἀμὰ κρείσσω· | νέος ὁ Ζεὺς βασιλεύει, | τὸ πάλαι δ᾽ ἦν Κρόνος ἄρχων· | ἀπίτω Μοῦσα παλαιά. Cf. also Timotheos in his *Persians*, where he talks of how the Spartans brought him to account "because I dishonor the older muse with new hymns" fr. 791, 211–212 *PMG* (ὅτι παλαιοτέραν νέοις | ὕμνοις μοῦσαν ἀτιμῶ); cf. the invocation of the paean that appears shortly before this, Timoth. fr. 791, 202–203 *PMG*: ἀλλ᾽ ὦ χρυσεοκίθαριν ἀέ- | ξων μοῦσαν νεοτευχῆ. Cf. also carm. conviv. fr. 917c, 3–4 *PMG*: ἄρτι βρύουσαν ἀοιδὰν | πρωτοπαγεῖ σοφίᾳ διαποίκιλον ἐκφέρομεν (as in fr. 851b *PMG* the *skolion* also belongs to the poetry of everyday use; it is performed in the symposium as an expression of a living song culture by a group that appears in the performative verb form in the first-person plural). Cf. also the insistence on originality in Pratinas fr. 710 *PMG*: οὐ γᾶν αὐλακισμέναν | ἀρῶν ἀλλ᾽ ἄσκαφον ματεύων, and Kinesias in Ar. *Av.* 1376: . . . νέαν (i.e. ὁδὸν) ἐφέπων and *ibid.*, 1384–1385: καινὰς . . . ἀναβολάς.
After Pindar and Aristophanes one may observe in Timotheos, Kinesias, and Pratinas, parallel to the transformation of culture by writing, a radicalization in the construction of artistic consciousness that leads to the Hellenistic practice. But the transitions are fluid; in performance the motif is additionally seen as a self-referential confirmation of the ritual. In comedy, with Aristophanes we are still partly on the side of ritual, while similar utterances in Middle and New Comedy refer also to Hellenistic practice. Yet the theme of innovation is also part and parcel of the comic: one can laugh only about something that is new. Cf. now also Bierl 2002a. Because of the inversion of the world on the level of signs in the situational context it is even conceivable that comic elements appeared in the actual hymn.

tive ἀγλαΐα ('shining,' 'beauty,' 'joy'), which is a characteristic of every form of celebration. Aglaia personified, together with Thalia and Euphrosyne, make up the *thiasos* of the Kharites (Hes. *Theogony* 907–909; Pind. *Ol.* 14.13–17), who incorporate in mythic fashion the *kharis* necessary for performance.[94] In their speech the members of the chorus create this *kharis* in a twofold and reciprocal fashion. Male performers identify themselves with these mythical female dancers.[95] The grace and charm of their performance create pleasure for the divinity being worshiped, which is returned to the chorus as thanks. Aglaia is especially responsible for victory in the contest, which is possibly carried out with the participation of other choruses after this preparatory ritual in the theater.[96] In similar fashion, as in many passages of Old Comedy, victory in the coming *agôn* of comic performances is thus contemplated. In Solon, the adjective ἀγλαός is in particular connected with the Muses,[97] whose musical substrate (the actual song, μοῦσαν, 1) the chorus thematizes in self-referential form in the *carmen populare*.

This "we"-form relates to the transmission of the performance to the audience and implies furthermore the occasionality of the festival. The splendor (ἀγλαΐα) results from the interplay of all signifiers: speech, movement, music, the external presentation, and the festive context. The diction shifts the boundaries of perception toward that which may be experienced in concrete terms, to a sensory shimmer. The deep-red reflectivity of wine has

---

[94] Cf. Pind. fr. 75.7–8: Διόθεν τέ με σὺν ἀγλαΐα | ἴδετε πορευθέντ' ἀοιδᾶν (in the self-referential and performative combination of song, dance, and music of the *aulos*, lines 18–19) and fr. 148 S.-M.: ὀρχήστ' ἀγλαΐας ἀνάσσων, εὐρυφάρετρ' Ἄπολλον (for Apollo as dancer), here in connection with dance. For the *kharis* of choral dancing, cf. above, chap. 1 n92. On ἀγλαΐζω: the verb appears with the same meaning in Theocr. *Epigr.* 1.4. Cf. Etym. Magn. (9.52), s.v. ἀγῆλαι· τιμῆσαι θεόν, ἀγλαΐσαι (= among others Lex. Bachm. [11, 18]); cf. K.-A. on Eupolis fr. 131. Cf. ἐπαγλαΐζω in Ar. *Eccl.* 575 ("praise"), and Ar. fr. 700 K.-A., Cratin. fr. 334 K.-A. ("make pure"); according to LSJ, s.v., ἀγλαΐζω never appears in Attic prose, which fits the song theory.

[95] The Kharites dance at the weddings of both Cadmus and Peleus (Quint. Smyrn. 4.140). Furthermore, the verb is also reminiscent of Aglauros, who together with the other daughters of Cecrops also represents a dancing *thiasos*.

[96] Cf. Bacchyl. *Epinik.* 3.5–6 (in connection with Nike): σεύον]το γὰρ σὺν ὑπερόχῳ τε Νίκᾳ | σὺν Ἀγ]λαΐᾳ . . . Splendor and the personification Aglaia are necessary elements for victory and are central aspects of the victory celebration; hence the importance of the word in epinicians. The three Kharites are addressed in self-referential form as the appropriate guarantors of the subsequent *kômos*: cf. Pind. *Ol.* 14.13–17: <ὦ> πότνι' Ἀγλαΐα | φιλησίμολπέ τ' Εὐφροσύνα, θεῶν κρατίστου | παῖδες, ἐπακοοῖτε νῦν, Θαλία τε | ἐρασίμολπε, ἰδοῖσα τόνδε κῶμον ἐπ' εὐμενεῖ τύχᾳ | κοῦφα βιβῶντα. On the poetically-shaped names of the Kharites, see also Kannicht 1989:31. On the shining of the *kômos*, cf. Pind. *Ol.* 3.5–6: φωνὰν . . . ἀγλαόκωμον. *Kômos* and victory are also of importance in this song. On dancing and splendor, Pind. *Pyth.* 1.2: βάσις ἀγλαΐας ἀρχά.

[97] Solon fr. 1.1 G.-P.: ἀγλαὰ τέκνα.

precisely the same effect on the observer.[98] The dimension of wine-drinking and drunkenness, which in contrast to the Ithyphalloi is not emphasized on the level of ὄψις, is accordingly integrated through the words of the song. The members of the chorus "pour out" (χέοντες, 2) a "simple rhythm" (ἁπλοῦν ῥυθμόν, 2), the trimeter of the *iambos* sung in cultic contexts, to which the ἰαμβίζειν of ritual ridicule in the improvised portion represents the logical continuation.[99] To this they add a "scintillating melody" (αἰόλῳ μέλει, 2), transferring the glittering of colors to the iridescence and rich variation of sound as well as to the quickness of movement.[100] In addition, the hymn is

[98] Cf. the adjective ἀγλαός, "shining," "glowing," "shimmering"; cf. the epithet in connection with the liquid nature of water, ἀγλαὸν ὕδωρ (Hom. *Il.* 2.307); ἀγλαΐζω thus extends beyond the meaning "give as an honour" that LSJ, s.v. ἀγλαΐζω I.2 assign it in this passage (on the meaning "praise," "honor," see above, n94), which Campbell 1993:239 translates accordingly as: "To you, Bacchus, we give glory with this music." It also implies in a quite concrete sense the splendor and glow of the song, the performance, and the Dionysiac drink. For the combination with offerings that decorate the sanctuary, cf. Isyllus, Paean in Aesculapium (Powell 1925:132–136, 133 = Käppel 1992:380–383, 381-Pai. 40), line 28: θυσίαις ἠγλάισεν τέμενος.

[99] For ῥυθμός as the ordering of movement (ἡ τῆς κινήσεως τάξις), cf. Plat. *Leg.* 665a: τῇ δὴ τῆς κινήσεως τάξει ῥυθμὸς ὄνομα εἴη, τῇ δὲ αὖ τῆς φωνῆς, τοῦ τε ὀξέος ἅμα καὶ βαρέος συγκεραννυμένων, ἁρμονία ὄνομα προσαγορεύοιτο, χορεία δὲ τὸ συναμφότερον κληθείη. In connection with movement in dance, cf. Ar. *Thesm.* 955a/b: ῥυθ- | μὸν χορείας; Plat. *Leg.* 670b: βαίνειν ἐν ῥυθμῷ; Xen. *Cyr.* 1.3.10: ὀρχεῖσθαι ἐν ῥυθμῷ. Without indicating parallels Thiele 1902:409n3 thinks that the expression ῥυθμὸν χέειν is "gut und alt" ["good and old"]. Cf. the passages in LSJ, s.v. χέω III.1 "of the voice"—e.g. Hom. *Od.* 19.521: χέει πολυδευκέα φωνήν; Pind. *Isthm.* 8.58: ἐπὶ θρῆνόν τε πολύφαμον ἔχεαν; Aesch. *Supp.* 631–632: κλύοιτ᾽ εὐκταῖα γένει χεούσας; and especially Ar. *Vesp.* 1020 (parabasis): κωμῳδικὰ πολλὰ χέασθαι. On the metaphorical combination ὕμνους οἰνοχοεῖν, see Dionysius *Eleg.* 3.1 G.-P. (for the combination of wine and poetry, see also Dionysius *Eleg.* 1.1–2).

In Anaphe, men and women indulge in mutual ridicule during sacrifice to Apollo Aigletes (Apoll. Rhod. 4.1713–1730); Apollo and Dionysus are particularly connected with splendor and the *kômos*. Ritual ridicule, sacrifice, emphasis on shining appearance, and elements of an inverted world are also found in a ritual context in the *Thesmophoriazusae* and our fragment. Cf. the remarks on *Thesm.* 101–129 above, pp. 137–149; on Apollo's splendor and performance, cf. esp. *Thesm.* 126–128; the self-command ἄγαλλε is identical with the performers' ἀγλαΐζομεν. Cf. Etym. Magn. (9.52), s.v. ἀγῆλαι· τιμῆσαι θεόν, ἀγλαΐσαι (= among others Lex. Bachm. [11, 18]) with the form ἄγαλλε *Thesm.* 128; cf. further K.-A. on Eupolis fr. 131 (*PCG* V, 371). Κωμαῖος is also a name given to Apollo in Naukratis; see also Ghiron-Bistagne 1976:273, who identifies the Apollo (*ibid.*, 275) on a Laconian cup (*ibid.*, fig. 127, Museum of Tarento 20909) as this Komaios.

[100] For αἰόλῳ μέλει cf. Lycoph. *Alex.* 671; cf. Telest. fr. 806.3–4 *PMG*: αἰολομόρφοις (coni. Wilamowitz, adopted by Campbell 1993, 128) | . . . καλάμοις. "Quickly moving": Hom. *Il.* 19.404: πόδας αἰόλος ἵππος; "glittering": of objects, e.g. τεύχεα, Hom. *Il.* 5.294–295; esp. of music and dance: Eur. *Ion* 499: ὑπ᾽ αἰόλας ἰαχᾶς; in the context of choral projection *Ion* 492ff. (on the Makrai rocks, where the Aglauridai perform their choruses in front of the temple of Athena); Ar. *Ran.* 247–248: ἔνυδρον ἐν βυθῷ χορείαν | αἰόλαν ἐφθεγξάμεσθα (in the song of the Frogs, which bears a great similarity to fr. 851b *PMG* in terms of performativity; on the self-referential word χορεία, cf. also Ar. *Ran.* 336, 396–397; cf. also *Thesm.* 980b and 982). Kugelmeier 1996:154 sees in the "bunt-

described with the epithet "unmixed" (ἀκήρατον, 4).[101] The song under way
is thus like pure wine; it is offered to the god of wine like a poured offering

---

schillernden Melodie" ["brightly shimmering melody"] an antithesis to the simple rhythm.
Admittedly the composer of the song had no other choice but to use *iamboi*; the traditional occasion, in particular the element of ridicule that follows, determines the genre; the musical framework in comparison with everyday speech is always festive. Variation does not necessarily have
to be equated with artistic intention as seen in the Hellenistic period, but is also a recognized
element of ritual style.

[101] Cf. the synonymous ἀκηράσιος in connection with the word wine in Hom. *Od.* 9.204–205:
οἶνον . . . | ἡδὺν ἀκηράσιον, θεῖον ποτόν. The adjective ἀκήρατος can be derived both from
κεράω = κεράννυμι (i.e. meaning "unmixed"; cf. Aesch. *Pers.* 614–615: ἀκήρατόν τε μητρὸς
ἀγρίας ἄπο | ποτόν; the passage occurs in a clear description of χοαί [*ibid.*, 607–622]) and from
κηραίνω (i.e. meaning "unharmed," "unadulterated," "untouched," "pure"; cf. Hom. *Il.* 24.303
and Theocr. *Id.* 22.38 in connection with ὕδωρ). Cf. LSJ, s.v. The two etymologically distinct
roots of the signifiers are connected on the level of the signified in terms of the concept of
purity. Both meanings, that of the unmixed and that of the ritually untouched, play a part in
this case and are retained when used of this claim to originality. Gold is in particular spoken of
as unmixed, unadulterated, noble, and pure: cf. Archil. fr. 91.3 and 93a, 6–7. W. Unmixed wine
(like milk and honey) is unusual and indicates a deviation from the norm: these ingredients are
typical of χοαί; cf. Aesch. *Pers.* 607–622; cf. on this Graf 1980:217: "Strukturalistisch gesehen,
gehört der ungemischte Wein auf die Seite von Milch und Honig: die Mänaden schlagen denn
auch, ausser Milch- und Honigquellen, solche von reinem Wein. . . . Weinlose Libationen—mit
Honig, Milch, Wasser, Melikraton, Öl—und solche mit reinem Wein müssten also zusam-
mengehen, in Opposition zur Spende mit gemischtem Wein und dem Normalopfer, das sie
begleitet, stehen" ["From a structuralist point of view, unmixed wine belongs together with
milk and honey: apart from striking open streams of milk and honey, the maenads also produce
ones of pure wine. . . . Wineless libations—with honey, milk, water, *melikraton*, oil—and those
using unmixed wine thus must belong together, in opposition to libation with mixed wine and
the normal sacrifice that accompanies it"]. Graf emphasizes in particular the symbolic function of pure wine (*ibid.*, 219): "Den Austritt in die Marginalität bezeichnet umgekehrt unter
anderem die Libation mit reinem Wein" ["Libation with pure wine signifies among other things
departure into marginality"]. For wineless libation, see Henrichs 1983 and Henrichs 1984. Wine
was normally drunk mixed with water. Unmixed wine, the sign of the wild and uncivilized,
is only drunk by barbarians, beast-men like centaurs or satyrs, or the Cyclops in the *Odyssey*
(Hom. *Od.* 9.345–974); cf. also the barbarian and bestial in the actors' καυνάκη costume.
    Probably precisely because of the concept of the ἀκήρατον, West treats the song fr. 851b *PMG*
as a "parody" (West 1974:36) or "imitation" (West 1982:147n23) of Eur. *Hipp.* 73–78: σοὶ τόνδε
πλεκτὸν στέφανον ἐξ ἀκηράτου | λειμῶνος, ὦ δέσποινα, κοσμήσας φέρω, | ἔνθ' οὔτε ποιμὴν
ἀξιοῖ φέρβειν βοτὰ | οὔτ' ἦλθέ πω σίδηρος, ἀλλ' ἀκήρατον | μέλισσα λειμῶν' ἠρινὴ διέρχεται
| Αἰδὼς δὲ ποταμίαισι κηπεύει δρόσοις. On ἀκήρατον see the extensive comments of Barrett
1964:171–172 *ad* Eur. *Hipp.* 73–76 and 79–81. Parallels may be found in terms of syntax and partly
in terms of content: σοί in first position, the deictically emphasized object of dedication (τόνδε
στέφανον, τάνδε μοῦσαν), the address in the vocative, the participial style (χέοντες, κοσμήσας),
the performative situation with the verb in the first person, the antithesis οὐ . . . ἀλλά empha-
sizing ritual purity. The decisive difference is that Hippolytos alone speaks, whereas in the
Semos song a group is performing, and Hippolytos offers a garland, while the chorus offers a
hymn; in the utterance in Hippolytos' song there is also of course a "garland" of words alongside the actual object. An important point in common is also its location in a *kômos* (*Hipp.* 55);
the previous strophes stage a *kômos*, where Hippolytos orders his attendants to sing (58–60)

(χοή).[102] Χοαί are poured out completely, are unmixed, in contrast to the mixed wine of the libation used in normal sacrifices, and are intended specifically for the dead as well as for the chthonic deities, which once again symbolizes departure from the everyday order of things and entry into marginality,[103] since the inverted world is also associated with the return of the dead and their terrifying and comic activities.

On the other hand, the ritual meaning, the pure and untouched nature of the offering, is metonymically brought into line with the idea of the unmixed. The ritual of sacrifice blends with the ritual of the choral dance, which excites all the god's senses as well as those of the participants/spectators and which results in the *kharis* of god and human alike. The singers emphasize the newness and authenticity of their song (καινὰν ἀπαρθένευτον, 3) because it is a gift and an offering to the divinity, who is not satisfied with secondhand goods.[104] The composer as *poiêtês* must create the hymn anew on every occa-

---

and as ἔξαρχος then sings the hymn with them (61-72). Cf. Barrett 1964:169 *ad* Eur. *Hipp.* 58-60. Neither Barrett 1964:167-176 *ad* Eur. *Hipp.* 58-87, esp. 170-171 *ad* 73-76, nor Stockert in the latest Teubner edition of the *Hippolytus* (Stuttgart/Leipzig 1994), 10 (in the list of testimonia *ad* 73-87) mentions fr. 851b *PMG*. The commonalities do not appear to be extensive enough to call this an imitation; the parallels depend rather on the fact that both texts express rituality. Hence the emphasis on purity and the stylistic similarity, such as the *Du-Stil* and the participial predication (cf. Norden 1913:143-163, 166-168).

[102] Cf. Dionysius *Eleg.* 3.1 G.-P. ὕμνους οἰνοχοεῖν. For the transferral of the idea of σπένδειν or χέειν to a song, cf. fr. adesp. 941 *PMG* (= carm. pop. 49 D., Terpander fr. 3 B., 4 Loeb, 8 Gostoli): σπένδωμεν ταῖς Μνάμας παισὶν Μούσαις | καὶ τῷ Μουσάρχῳ <τῷ> Λατοῦς υἱεῖ; Pind. *Isthm.* 6, 7-9, esp. line 9: σπένδειν μελιφθόγγοις ἀοιδαῖς; and Pind. *Ol.* 7.1-10, esp. 7-9: καὶ ἐγὼ νέκταρ χυτόν, Μοισᾶν δόσιν, ἀεθλοφόροις | ἀνδράσιν πέμπων, γλυκὺν καρπὸν φρενός, ἱλάσκομαι. The paean, with which the song has sometimes been associated, was closely connected with sacrifice and the symposium. Between the dinner and the actual round of drinking a libation was made to the gods and a paean sung, which served as the opening to the symposium proper. Cf. Käppel 1992:51-54 with test. 73-84.

[103] On libations, see Graf 1980, Burkert 1985:70-73, Jameson/Jordan/Kotansky 1993:70-73. For the distinction between σπονδαί and χοαί, see Rudhardt 1958:240-248 and Casabona 1966:231-297. On the distinction between the more common verb σπένδω and χέω, see Burkert 1985:70 and Jameson/Jordan/Kotansky 1993:71.

[104] Similarly Herter 1947:26: "Zwar haben sich gerade die attischen Komiker etwas darauf zugute getan, wenn sie eine 'neue Idee' vorbringen konnten, aber ihre kultischen Vorläufer empfinden noch ganz unmittelbar, daß der Gottheit etwas Frisches und Unberührtes als Weihegabe gefällt" ["While it was advantageous for Attic comic playwrights if they could present a 'new idea,' their cultic predecessors still have an immediate sense that the god is pleased by an offering that is fresh and untouched"]. Cf. for example the *lex sacra* (text of A and B with translation in Jameson/Jordan/Kotansky 1993:14-17) of Selinous, A 10ff.; the sacrificial context involves various libations of wine (A 10) and a honey mixture (A 13), then a *trapeza* and *klinê* are to be set out for the pure Tritopatores, with a pure covering, olive wreaths, and a honey mixture in *new* vessels (A 15: καιναῖς ποτερίδε[σ]ι). The suggestions here of *theoxenia* and *aparkhê* are noteworthy. Cf. Jameson/Jordan/Kotansky 1993:67-70. New and pure fittings

sion. Within choral culture, self-publicizing occupies a central position as part of the rivalry between poets. The author as *khorêgos*, leader and trainer, is in close contact with the group for a long time. It is therefore only natural that the collective also makes this claim for the poet and speaks with his voice in the same way it does in the *parabasis* of comedy.

Just as the flowers decorating their heads symbolize unwithering vitality, among other things,[105] so too the ritual command for an offering to be presented to a divinity in fresh and untouched form is also reinforced with the above-mentioned adjectives (καινὰν ἀπαρθένευτον, 3).[106] The perfor-

---

and equipment are sometimes strict preconditions for particular rites; cf. Xenoph. fr. 1 G.-P. (offering before symposium) and Jameson/Jordan/Kotansky 1993:35–36 *ad* A 15 with particular reference to conditions in a cult calendar of the fourth century BCE from Kos (Sokolowski 1969 [*LSCG*], Nr. 151 A–C = *SIG*³ 1025–1027).

[105] At the same time the actors are also characterized as "wild men" from the Outside. On dressing as satyrs at the Anthesteria, who represent "wild men" of this type, see Seaford 1984:7n17 and 19 (with reference to the modern Greek Kallikantzaroi as descendants of the satyrs). On the Kallikantzaroi, who still survive in the folk belief of the Peloponnese and the Greek islands, see Lawson 1910:190–255 (on the centaurs) and Ginzburg 1989:186–187, 201–202 (in connection with many other similar groups, e.g. the Eskari, Surovaskari, Coledari, Regös). Cf. the description (Ginzburg 1989:186) of the Kallikantzaroi, who in many ways show points of connection with our actors as well: "Die *Kallikantzaroi* sind scheußliche, schwarze, zottige Wesen, . . . fast immer sind sie männlichen Geschlechts, mit riesigen Genitalien ausgestattet" ["The Kallikantzaroi are repulsive, black, shaggy creatures, . . . they are almost always male, equipped with massive genitalia"]. *Kômos*, beggar ritual, ecstasy, dressing up as animals, vulgar emphasis on the sexual sphere, ridicule, fighting, and the personification of the dead are typical of groups like these, who perform between Christmas and Epiphany (new year's festival!). Leaves and flowers are often ritual indicators of marginality, in particular of youth in the liminal phase of initiation, who embody mythical figures of this type in their groups: see Jeanmaire 1939:174, 177, 179, 181, 189, 221; Brelich 1969 in his excellent introduction (13–112), esp. in the morphology (25–44) of these rites of puberty, 72n60 (leaves), 88n111 (wood spirits). The *kômos*, the procession of drunken players, represents the reactualization of these liminal experiences of puberty initiation rites. In a scholion to Aeschines' speech 1.52 (115 Dilts) we find the following interesting explanation: Κηδωνίδην] οὗτοι παιδερασταί, ἐπωνυμίας ἔχοντες 'ἄγριοι καὶ Τριβαλλοὶ καὶ Κένταυροι.' The figures explained here are thus pederasts (on the connection to pederasty and initiation in the symposium see Bremmer 1990), and in particular they have the bynames "wild ones," "Triballoi" (like the Athenian groups mentioned in Demosth. 54.39), and "centaurs," which also refers to phallic wildness.

[106] Vegetative imagery also lies behind the performative verb ἀγλαΐζομεν, following Hesych. (s.v. ἀγλαΐζει· θάλλει); cf. K.-A. on Eupolis fr. 419. Dionysus was himself described with the name Ἄνθιος (*IG* II/III² 1356.9 and Paus. 1.31.4). Parallel to Thalia (who forms the Kharites along with Aglaia and Euphrosyne) as the name of the personified festival is the verb θάλλειν; cf. Kannicht 1989:31n10. For Dionysus as god of growth, sprouting, and blooming, and for his other cultic epithets corresponding to this idea, see Blech 1982:182–183. The Greeks always connected the Anthesteria via folk etymology with the maturation, or "blossoming," of wine. The Anthesteria have a strong connection with symbolic indications of performance: those who perform the rites are dressed as "wild men," it is a festival of the inverted world, of exception, anarchy, transition, and the new year; masquerade and the dead, the return of the dead as

mative predicate κατάρχομεν is reminiscent of the ἀπαρχή, the first-fruits offering of simple foods in the context of the natural world of the rural population of farmers. Pan, Hermes, the Nymphs, Priapus, Dionysus, and Demeter are the prime recipients of this.[107] The performance and the aesthetic and poetic form of the song culture grounded in the pragmatic are thus viewed as an offering, as a gift for the divinity, who is expected to take pleasure in it.[108] Hymns "begun" (cf. κατάρχομεν τὸν ὕμνον, 5), on the other hand, are sung by performers who have taken up position around an altar where animal sacrifice takes place.[109] In terms of the performative situation of the song the verb natu-

---

ghosts and barbarians, the staging of the origins of civilization, and wine also play a role here. On the Anthesteria in general, see Deubner 1932:93–123, Burkert 1983:213–243, and Auffarth 1991:202–276; on the Anthesteria as the frame of reference of the *Plutus*, see Bierl 1994.

[107] On offerings of first fruits, see Burkert 1985:66–68 and Jameson/Jordan/Kotansky 1993:67–70.

[108] This text thus lends itself extremely well to the approach based on the *Nouvelle Histoire*, which treats poetry as offering; cf. the fundamental study by Svenbro 1984 (who does not mention fr. 851b *PMG*, Dionysius *Eleg.* 3.1 G.-P., and fr. adesp. 941 *PMG* [= Terp. fr. 3 B., 4 Loeb, 8 Gostoli]). Svenbro makes an interesting connection between song (μέλος) and the homonym μέλος, which comes from the same root and means a human or animal limb (221), and analyzes Greek metrics and the bodily nature of its technical terms as a science that bases itself on the model of ritual killing. In a dissertation (1992) supervised by Richard Martin, Sfyroeras attempts to apply this theory to comedy. Cf. esp. 8–13 (unfortunately the examples adduced there, esp. the incorrectly interpreted Herodotean passage [Hdt. 5.67.5], are not very convincing). Nevertheless, Sfyroeras' thesis of a fundamental connection between sacrifice and comedy (see now Sfyroeras 2004) precisely in the light of this ritual song, which shows so many similarities to the *kômos* and ritual poetry, seems well worth considering.

[109] On the practice of performing dithyramb, paean, and hyporcheme in a circle as prelude to a sacrificial rite, see also Furley 1993:35–36. Cf. *ibid.*, 36: "Animal sacrifice survives to this day at some festivals in Greece: hymns are sung while the animal is led round the sacrificial pit." On the presentation of the dithyramb at the *thymelê*, Pratinas fr. 708.1–2 *PMG*: τίς ὁ θόρυβος ὅδε; τί τάδε τὰ χορεύματα; | τίς ὕβρις ἔμολεν ἐπὶ Διονυσιάδα πολυπάταγα θυμέλαν. On the connection between paean and sacrifice, see Käppel 1992:44–47, 49–51, 55–56 (and test. 95), 58–63, 81, 285 and in connection with discussion of the Erythraean paean to Asklepios (Pai. 37) (*ibid.*, 190–192 on the sacred law Pai. 36a) and treatment of the Philodamus paean (Pai. 39), the occasion for which is provided by a *theoxenia* (*ibid.*, 210, 254). The garlands worn by participants at a sacrifice and by symposiasts (Eitrem 1915:64–75, Burkert 1985:56 with 368n5, Jameson/Jordan/Kotansky 1993:68) correspond to those worn by the performers of our song here. On the combination of sacrificial ritual and drama, see Burkert 1966a. The art of drama arose from improvisations at rural goat sacrifices. Intermediary stages remain in the folk custom.

The simplex ἄρχεσθαι and the composite κατάρχειν/ -εσθαι describe both the general beginning of an action and in particular the completion of practices that introduce sacrifices; for κατάρχεσθαι in the meaning "wash hands," "sprinkle barley" (Hom. *Od.* 3.445), "pasture the animal for slaughter," and other preparatory actions before sacrifice, see Dunbar *Birds*, 541–542 *ad* Ar. *Av.* 959. By contrast, ἀπάρχεσθαι is limited to a particular ritual meaning (it is only later attested as synonym for ἄρχεσθαι; LSJ s.v. ἀπάρχομαι). Burkert 1985:56 mentions ἄρχεσθαι, κατάρχεσθαι, and ἀπάρχεσθαι as technical terms for particular rites carried out before sacrifice. The meaning of simply "beginning," "starting out," and the preparatory ceremonies for sacrifice are blended together in the ritual language of the song.

rally means the speech act of beginning; while the comasts produce an utterance about themselves in "we" form, saying that they are beginning a hymn, the presentation is in fact being completed. The choral group thus take over an important convention from song culture as a whole. The proem is where the performers emphasize their intention. This kind of *anabolê* may be improvised in accordance with the rules of oral composition. Various hymns can be introduced using similar set pieces.[110] In the transition to writing, this kind of popular showpiece interwoven with ritual elements may then become fixed as something formulaic, which is transmitted through writing and performed annually.[111] It remains an open question whether the lines were really followed by a hymn or whether this is already achieved through this introduction itself, which then transitions into *tôthasmos*.

[110] The verbs ἄρχειν and κατάρχειν appear with the uncommon accusative construction in the performative context of the introduction; cf. Pind. *Nem.* 3.10–11: ἄρχε . . . | δόκιμον ὕμνον; Alcm. fr. 98 Davies: θοίναις δὲ καὶ ἐν θιάσοισιν | ἀνδρείων παρὰ δαιτυμόνεσσι πρέπει παιᾶνα κατάρχην; and our passage fr. 851b.5 *PMG:* κατάρχομεν τὸν ὕμνον. Cf. also Plat. *Euthyd.* 283b: θαυμαστὸν γάρ τινα, ὦ Κρίτων, ἀνὴρ κατῆρχεν λόγον. For ἄρχεσθαι with the accusative cf. Alcm. fr. 48 Davies: Λατοῖδα, τέο δ᾽ ἀρχ<όμεν>ος χορόν (coni. West); Soph. fr. 737b *PMG* = Käppel 1992:366–367, 366–Pai. 32.2, line 2: σέ[θ]εν ἄρξομαι (coni. Oliver) ὕμ]νον. With this one may also associate ἐξάρχειν, which followed by either accusative or genitive refers to striking up a song, esp. with reference to the choral leader: Hom. *Od.* 4.19: μολπῆς; *Il.* 18.51: γόοιο; with accusative: *Hom. Hymn.* 27.18: χορούς; Archil. fr. 120 W.: διθύραμβον; fr. 121 W.: Λέσβιον παιήονα; for ἐξάρχειν with the accusative, implying a chorus, see Zimmermann 1992:19–23 with further passages 19n3. For the performative future ἀείσομαι (cf. the self-referential ᾠδαῖσιν, fr. 851b.4 *PMG*) cf. Alcm. fr. 28: ἀείσομαι and 29 Davies: ἐγὼν δ᾽ ἀείσομαι. On the topos of the beginning of a song in the Homeric hymns: ἄρχομ᾽ ἀείδειν: *Hom. Hymn.* 2.1, 11.1, 13.1, 16.1, 22.1, 26.1, 28.1; ἀείσομαι: *Hom. Hymn.* 10.1, 15.1, 23.1, 30.1; ἀείδω: *Hom. Hymn.* 12.1, 18.1, 27.1; Μουσάων ἄρχωμαι: *Hom. Hymn.* 25.1; on this introductory formula see Calame 1995a:6–8. For *anabolê* see Comotti 1989 and Zimmermann 1992:22. This has to be understood as originally being an improvised prelude. Zimmermann summarizes Comotti's theory of the content of the *anabolê* as follows (*ibid.*): "Vorstellung des folgenden Chorlieds, Widmung an Dionysos, Kritik anderer Dichter und poetologische Reflexionen dürften der Inhalt solcher ursprünglich zur Kithara, später auch zu Flötenmusik gesungener Proömien gewesen sein, die sich im Verlauf des fünften Jahrhunderts zu regelrechten responsionslosen Bravourarien entwickelt hätten" ["The presentation of the following choral song, dedication to Dionysus, criticism of other poets, and poetological reflections must have been the content of these kinds of *prooimia*, which were originally sung to the accompaniment of the *kithara*, later also to that of the *aulos*, and which during the course of the fifth century would have developed into fixed bravura arias without responsion"]. In this connection Zimmermann 1992:22 refers to the well-known Aristotelian theory of the development of tragedy and comedy (*Poetics* 1449a9–13): γενομένη δ᾽ οὖν ἀπ᾽ ἀρχῆς αὐτοσχεδιαστικῆς—καὶ αὐτὴ καὶ ἡ κωμῳδία, καὶ ἡ μὲν ἀπὸ τῶν ἐξαρχόντων τὸν διθύραμβον, ἡ δὲ ἀπὸ τῶν τὰ φαλλικὰ ἃ ἔτι καὶ νῦν ἐν πολλαῖς τῶν πόλεων διαμένει νομιζόμενα κτλ. Our song could thus relate in self-referential fashion to the prelude of a φαλλικόν. However it is not an ἔξαρχος, rather the entire group, who takes up the introduction.

[111] Zimmermann 1992:22 also makes an interesting reference to a folk song; in fr. 871 *PMG* the women of Elis use the form of a *hymnos klêtikos* to call for the epiphany of Dionysus.

Overlying the dimension of sacrifice and offering, the element of the sexual artfully asserts itself as a further level of meaning. The song is "virginal," untouched, that is, it will bring the god of the phallus particular enjoyment. The performative form ἀγλαΐζομεν implicitly expresses this connection, since Aglaia is viewed as a young maiden on the threshold of womanhood who along with the other Kharites belongs to Aphrodite's retinue and together with Aglauros, associated with her, is often confronted with aggressive, phallic sexuality or threatened with sexual violation.[112] At the same time, the epithet ἀπαρθένευτον can also be interpreted as the negation of the condition of παρθενία, especially in the sense "unfitting for virgins."[113] The "offering" that they bring is "unvirginal" and unseemly for maidens, since the content and the rhythm of the lines correspond to the coarseness and aggression of *iamboi* and the chorus in its function (and dramatic role) is made up of men, preceded in the procession by a mud-covered phallus-bearer. As Phallophoroi they are fitting worshipers of Dionysus Phales, to whom they present their song as a gift. In the performance the words are in a certain sense "deflowered," or offered to the god for his consumption.

In short, then, the following is clear: the ritual *kômos* refers to its own synaesthetic presentation and presents its god with a serenade that is suited to the god in terms of the tropic form "wine, women, and song." The ritual significations are fused with the performative style of speech into a complex speech act. The festive procession (πομπή) with the phallus, the comastic element together with the drinking of wine, its external appearance, its connection with offering and sacrifice, and the element of iambic ridicule reflect on all levels the tensions characteristic of Dionysus that express the marked transi-

---

[112] With their feminizing costumes the presenters through their utterance of ἀγλαΐζομεν themselves become in a sense the Kharites; in other words, they assume in part a feminine role. Girls on the threshold of adulthood are often represented in χοροί. The masculine identity of the actors thereby touches, in terms of content, the border region between man and woman. It is significant that the participle χέοντες does not assume the feminine form relating to the chorus' possible role, but refers to the actual gender of the singers.

[113] Cf. Eur. *Phoen.* 1739: ἀπαρθένευτ' ἀλωμένα and *IA* 993: ἀπαρθένευτα μὲν τάδ'. Navarre 1911:249 thus translates the adjective as "qui n'est pas fait pour des jeunes filles" ["not designed for young girls"]; similarly Horn 1970:68 ("ein Inhalt, der sich nicht für zarte Mädchenohren eignet" ["content not suited for the tender ears of maidens"]); Kugelmeier 1996:154n270 also seems to be of this opinion. The adjective is ambiguous: 1.) It can mean "virginal," i.e. before defloration (as if from παρθενεύω = κορεύω); it is thus treated by the majority of scholars as synonym in asyndeton of καινάν (cf. Soph. fr. 304 Radt). 2.) It may refer to the opposite condition of no longer being a virgin, i.e. "unmaidenly" (cf. schol. Theocr. *Id.* 2.41, 279 Wendel). The above-mentioned meaning "not fitting for a virgin" can be viewed as a subcategory of (2). The metaphor of the song as something mixed or blended is contaminated in the ritual text with the idea of defloration as offering.

tion from the everyday to the sacred and the liminal nature of the comically inverted world. As in comedy, positive worship of the gods is juxtaposed with the radical and carnivalesque elements of comic inversion.

The *Sitz im Leben* of the two songs cannot, unfortunately, be determined with certainty on the basis of the information Athenaeus gives us, since it is only the entertainment value of the amusing performers that interests him in his dinner conversations. Two possibilities present themselves. The ritual complex described is either a preparatory ceremony that precedes the dramatic competition, as in Athens,[114] or a simple performance presented in the theater mainly as a *divertimento*, as became common in the Hellenistic period. Since this is only a brief ritual spectacle there is no integration based on illusion into some form of dramatic plot. The answer to the question of whether in a festive scene of this type we are dealing with proto-theater or ritual has to remain up in the air. Entertainment and the sensory and symbolic experience of transformation are so intertwined that a definitive differentiation of the sort possible in the choral songs of Old Comedy is here impossible.

The *Parabasis* and the Song of the Phallophoroi

As has been emphasized several times, there remains in modern scholarship the assumption that ritual necessarily precedes theater. Relying on the rather vaguely held judgment of Aristotle, who saw the beginnings of comedy in the singers of φαλλικά, scholars have often adduced the song of the Phallophoroi in discussions of the origins of comedy.[115] Faced with the absence of a dramatic plot with fictional roles, they have often connected it with the *parabasis* of Old Comedy, since the latter has long been regarded from the perspective of realistic theater as an unassimilated ritual core because it interrupts the so-called illusion of the dramatic plot.[116] So, for example, the following theory has been

[114] Cf. Cole 1993.

[115] Because the lack of sources the origin can unfortunately probably never be known with certainty.

[116] On the *parabasis* as ritual core and original element: for earlier literature, before the actual influence of the Cambridge ritualists, see Hubbard 1991:16n2; Cornford and Murray as prominent representatives of this direction in scholarship deliver opinions in this vein; Cornford (1961[2]:93) says of the *parabasis* in *The Origin of Attic Comedy*, which appeared in 1914: "With its stiff canonical structure, it has all the air of a piece of ritual procedure awkwardly interrupting the course of the play"; see also Cornford 1961[2]:110. Murray (1933:12) sees it as "a nugget of unassimilated ritual embedded in the structure of the play." This opinion has endured up until comparatively recently; Kranz 1933:25, Herter 1947:31–32, Kranz 1949:1125, Lesky 1971[3]:273 ("Kernstück"), Seaford 1977:85–86, and Reckford 1987:488.

    The origin of comedy has often been connected with the song of the Phallophoroi (the Ithyphalloi, Deikelistai, Autokabdaloi, and *phallika*) but only in a general fashion. Cornford 1961[2]:

proposed: the song of the Phallophoroi could correspond to the ode, and the ridicule connected with the song to the epirrhematic syzygy.[117]

110-111 thinks the development can only have lead to the *parabasis*, because the Phallophoroi did not assume any dramatic role (he does however think the phallic rites were connected with the *kômos, ibid.* 111-114); Herter 1947:16-42 and passim attempts an organic reconstruction using the chorus of the Ithyphalloi in particular; he thinks a plot arose from *parabasis*-like song; Pohlenz 1949 (= Kl. Schr. II 1965:497-510) believes that the song represents only one possible developmental step toward the *parabasis*; cf. also Giangrande 1963, Lesky 1971³:271-273 (relation to carnival and *parabasis*, later mimicry), Reckford 1987:443-498, esp. 487-488 (following Cornford, Semos' song is characterized as a "rudimentary *kômos* from which 'comedy' grew"). Contra, among others, Radermacher *Frösche*, 12, Pickard-Cambridge 1962:133-147, Händel 1963:84, 108, Sifakis 1971:20, 69 and Leonhardt 1991:37-38, who are skeptical about a link between the song of the Phallophoroi and the genesis of comedy or the *parabasis*. For a history of the interpretation of the *parabasis*, see Sifakis 1971:15-20, and now also Imperio 2004:11-14. How a dramatic plot is supposed to have arisen from the undramatic *phallika* has always been viewed as a particularly problematic question. Herter 1938b:1677 replies with the Aristotelian formula that Aristotle does not derive comedy immediately from the φαλλικά themselves, but traces it merely to the ἐξάρχοντες τὰ φαλλικά; he also says the element of improvisation is critical. German scholarship was fond of making a connection between the Phallophoroi and the *parabasis*, which in turn was interpreted as an original song of entry (*parodos*). The main arguments advanced were: a) the term *parabasis* is synonymous with *parodos*; b) anapaests are typical of the marching rhythm of the entry procession; the Phallophoroi also form an entry procession; c) it was the chorus' job to salute the gods immediately after their entry procession (*parabasis* odes). See Sifakis 1971:111-112n21 for literature on the *parabasis-parodos* thesis.

[117] On the comparison between the *parabasis*, especially the epirrhematic syzygy, and the Hellenistic Phallophoroi and Ithyphalloi (hymns and ridicule), see Kolster 1829:51-61, Koester 1835: 16-18 (both derive the *parabasis* directly from phallic songs), Muff 1871:6-7, Herter 1947: Pohlenz 1949:37 (= Kl. Schr. II 1965:503), and Reckford 1987:487-488. The *parabasis* odes as reflexes of cult hymns have been extensively discussed by Fraenkel (1931 and 1962:191-215); he shows that the greeting is directed at all the polis gods, not just Dionysus, as is the case with the Phallophoroi. Kranz thinks (1919:162n4, 163 and 1933:30) that all choruses originally directed their song only to Dionysos Lenaios (on the Phallophoroi, see Kranz 1919:164). Gelzer 1960:210 combines Fraenkel's theory of the dependency of the odes on cult lyric with the German Phallophoroi theory (the epirrhematic syzygy is based on the song of the Phallophoroi, a view held since Kolster 1829:60). Gelzer 1960:210 says: "Das [Phallophoroi-Lied] scheint also eine Art Vorstufe zur Parabase gewesen zu sein, die sich an anderen Orten an bestimmten Festen noch als selbständige Begehung erhalten hatte, in Athen aber in die Komödie eingegangen war. Die Götter werden in der Syzygie unabhängig von der speziellen Funktion des Chors im jeweiligen Stück angerufen, und nur ganz äußerliche Zusätze lassen die Hymnen als vom Chor des jeweiligen Stücks vorgetragen erscheinen" ["The song of the Phallophoroi thus seems to have been a kind of precursor to the *parabasis*, which in other areas was still preserved as an independent celebration at certain festivals, but in Athens became part of comedy. In the syzygy the gods were invoked independently of the chorus' particular function in the given play, and it is only through additions of a completely superficial nature that the hymns appear to be performed by the chorus of that particular play"]. Cf. also Gelzer 1966:69, where the development from indecent φαλλικόν to *parabasis* is described; but it is not quite correct to speak of a "Funktionsänderung zum Rügegedicht" ["change of function to blame poem"], especially since mockery also formed part of the ritual of the Phallophoroi.

Cornford 1961²:95 is skeptical of this; he thinks that the elements of invocation and ridicule were in fact present in the phallic song and in the *parabasis*, but that the structure in

Several misconceptions need to be dealt with here.

1. The interruption of the plot in the Aristophanic *parabasis* is in no way fundamental in nature. Even here elements from the plot are taken up and processed. The lack of dramatic unity and role identity is not confined to this structural element alone, but is part of the open aesthetic and the mode of perception of the genre as a whole.[118]

2. Ritual and theater may certainly be present simultaneously; depending on the interpreter's point of view and on the context, now one, now the other comes to the fore.[119]

Sifakis and Händel reject the connection between the song of the *Phallo-phoroi* and the comic *parabasis* on the not entirely correct basis that we are dealing here exclusively with censure and blame, while in the *parabasis* the "self-presentation of the chorus" is foregrounded.[120] I have attempted to show, however, to what a great extent this fragment of Semos (fr. 851b *PMG*) in fact contains traces of demonstrative self-presentation and self-promotion. On the other hand, blame is also a standard thematic element in the *parabasis*. Both coarse and aggressive ridicule and self-presentation are ritual forms and characteristic of ritual choruses.

the phallic song was different, because invective could be improvised endlessly. He therefore argues against the genesis of the *parabasis* from the phallic song, and sees rather a relationship between the latter and the *exodos*. Cf. also *ibid.* 110–114. The remarks of Pickard-Cambridge 1962, 142–144 are also highly critical.

[118] For the theory of the irrelevant digression, see the earlier bibliography in Hubbard 1991:16n4; cf. further among others Zielinski 1885:184–187, Pickard-Cambridge 1962:199, Kranz 1933:25, Gelzer 1960:208, Händel 1963:85, Sifakis 1971:66, 69, Dover 1972:49, and Heath 1987:18–23, 43–44. Criticism of this position has recently been mounting; cf. Bowie 1982, Harriott 1986:20–36, Reckford 1987, and Hubbard 1991 (Hubbard reads the self-referential remarks of the poet as intertextual commentary and references of the poet to his work). To this debate add now Imperio 2004:13–14.

[119] The characteristic style of speech used between the players and the participants/audience is important here (cf. Athen. 622b: ἐπιστρέφουσιν εἰς τὸ θέατρον with the expression at the beginning of the *parabasis* Ar. *Ach.* 629: οὔπω παρέβη πρὸς τὸ θέατρον, *Equ.* 508: πρὸς τὸ θέατρον παραβῆναι, *Pax* 735: πρὸς τὸ θέατρον παραβὰς ἐν τοῖς ἀναπαίστοις). Cf. early on Schmid 1929:635: "Die Handlung spielt sich zwischen Chor und Publikum ab und entspricht der altattischen Parabase." ["The action is acted out between the chorus and the audience and corresponds to the old Attic *parabasis*."] Cf. also Muff 1871:7 and Kranz 1933:30. The presenters do not play entirely within a dramatic role and within a dramatic plot that the spectators simply witness while submerging themselves therein, but actually enter into direct contact with their surroundings, while oscillating between their real and their fictitious identity. They criticize and ridicule individuals in the surrounding area and they worship the gods of the community in front of and together with the audience.

[120] See Händel 1963:84, 109 and Sifakis 1971:20.

Even if the *parabasis* proper, in contrast to the epirrhematic syzygy, was a late creation of the comic poets,[121] this need not mean at the same time that the entire *parabasis* freed itself of ritual and that only ritual remains are to be found.[122] I come to the following conclusion contrary to the *communis opinio* after thorough investigation and interpretation: the question as to whether the *parabasis* represents a ritual core or a remnant from which comedy developed as a secular, political genre cannot be answered with any certainty. There is much to indicate that the *parabasis*, like many utterances by the comic chorus, in form and content possessed a ritual nature even in the time of Aristophanes. For in Aristophanes too the chorus speaks of its own activity and about its performance, expresses praise, blame, and ridicule, dances (at least in the odes), addresses the community gathered together, and finally, through prayer, hymn, and invocation, brings about contact with the gods of the polis as a whole, among others with Dionysus, the special god of the performative realm. The comic genre is clearly so strongly based on these elements that it can only be purified into a kind of bourgeois comedy by destroying its liveliness and comical nature.

The *parabasis* cannot thus be derived directly from traditional songs of this type, especially since the situation is also complicated by the fact that the fragments transmitted by Semos are perhaps of a later date than Aristophanes and are possibly based on Attic comedy.[123] The relationship is only yielded by the ritual context. Aristophanes reactualizes ritual. He is not an *imitator* or parodist of an age-old tradition, but is within this tradition and, in the pragmatic context of a society whose thinking draws its nourishment entirely from mythical and ritual forms, creates these songs anew and integrates them to a greater or lesser extent into a comic plot that is characterized by a privileging of the paradigmatic, as opposed to syntagmatic, level of action. Both phallic songs are equally performance in the sense of a productive choral culture that relies on traditional models and that is tied to a fixed, pragmatic context, the ritual *Sitz im Leben*. The big difference lies in the fact that these songs are not embedded in a dramatic plot.

---

[121] See Händel 1963:84 and Sifakis 1971:20, 59–70, esp. 68–69.

[122] See Händel 1963:107–109n17 and Sifakis 1971:17–21. Sifakis describes the odes as "a relic of genuine *Kultlyrik*" (*ibid.*, 69).

[123] There is much to suggest this, especially since the examples of the boastful doctor and the Theban mania for strange words in the immediately preceding quotation from Sosibios (Athen. 621d–622a) are drawn from contemporary New Comedy (Alexis fr. 146 K.-A. and Strattis fr. 49 K.-A.). See also the reference to language above, n56. Porson attributed the song of the Phallophoroi to Pratinas (as referred to in Bergk III 1882⁴:657 *ad* carm. pop. 8 B., who does not, however, think the reasoning is sound).

The closeness of the traditional song material to Aristophanes resides, as has been emphasized, not only in the *parabasis*, but in principle in all choral utterances in comedy: for the particular style of the direct address to the audience, the transgression of borders with the polis assembled in the theater, the deficiency of identity in dramatic roles, improvisation, ridicule, and sexual coarseness are all necessary elements for comedy and the laughter essential to it.

The Phallic Procession in a Dramatic Plot
(*Acharnians* 241–279)—the Continued Existence of Rituality

The elements named above are also to be found at the beginning of a comic plot.[124] The parallel between the fragments of Semos (fr. 851a and b *PMG*) and the scene of *phallophoria* at the private celebration of the rural Dionysia in the *parodos* of the *Acharnians* (241–279, in particular with the equally purely iambic Phales song, 263–279), has been observed over and again.[125] As a comic author, Aristophanes naturally sought here too to integrate the φαλλικόν halfway into the dramatic plot, even though, as in several choral songs, the utterance is at the same time a result of the context that determines the plot and also represents independent cult.[126] In particular, for dramaturgical

---

[124] Because of an incorrect interpretation of παραβαίνειν and the entrance-like character of the two phallic songs, it used to be thought that the *parabasis* was originally a song sung while entering.

[125] Consider among others Kolster 1829:52, 59–60, Koester 1835:16–17, Müller II 1857:197–198, van Leeuwen *Ach.*, 50–51 *ad* 261 (also with reference to Sosibios [Athen. 621d] on improvised comic scenes at performances of this kind at the rural Dionysia!), Cornford 1961²:103–109, esp. 103–104, 108, Körte 1921:1218–1219, Herter 1938b:1675ff., Herter 1947:24ff. (who emphasizes the parallels to the song of the Ithyphalloi), Pickard-Cambridge 1962:145–147, Gelzer 1966:69, Horn 1970:63–71, esp. 68, Ghiron-Bistagne 1976:208–213 (who refuses to see any *kômos* either in the Aristophanic song or in that of the Phallophoroi, but sees instead an honorable πομπή), Carrière 1979:19 and 34n14, Zimmermann II 1985:41, Prato 1987:216 with n48 (with special reference to the iambic meter of the Phallophoroi), Cole 1993:26 (only implicitly), Habash 1995:567, Kugelmeier 1996:151–154, and Csapo 1997:284. Cf. now also Olson *Ach.*, 140 *ad* 237–279, 147 *ad* 261, and Pütz 2003:161–163.

[126] Many only see the nondramatic aspect in this song as well; cf. Pickard-Cambridge 1962:146: "In neither is there anything dramatic; the agents represent no one but themselves." Cf. Herter 1938b:1677 and Horn 1970:66–67; likewise Kugelmeier 1996:154 does not recognize an "actual dramatic function" therein. Similarly now Olson *Ach.*, 141 *ad* 241–279: " . . . this scene, which briefly interrupts the forward movement of the action to offer a vision of life in an ideal world of peace . . . " The remarks of Leonhardt 1991:38 in this connection are unclear: "Die berühmte Szene der Acharner des Aristophanes ist in keiner Weise mit der Struktur des Stückes verknüpft, sondern allein von der Handlung her begründet; die Feier der ländlichen Dionysien symbolisiert die Segnungen des Friedens, den der Hauptheld Dikaiopolis mit den Spartanern

reasons Aristophanes has abandoned the choral dimension of the *kômos*, as in the Agathon song in the *Thesmophoriazusae* (101–129), and has turned the song into Dikaiopolis' solo song.

I shall first reproduce the text, continuing to mark performative expressions, and noting correspondences with the Semos fragment:

ΔΙ. εὐφημεῖτε, εὐφημεῖτε.   241
  πρόιθ' εἰς τὸ πρόσθεν ὀλίγον, ἡ κανηφόρος.
  ὁ Ξανθίας τὸν *φαλλὸν ὀρθὸν* στησάτω.
  κατάθου τὸ κανοῦν, ὦ θύγατερ, ἵν' <u>ἀπαρξώμεθα</u>.

ΘΥ. ὦ μῆτερ, ἀνάδος δεῦρο τὴν ἐτνήρυσιν,   245
  ἵν' ἔτνος <u>καταχέω</u> τοὐλατῆρος τουτουί.

ΔΙ. καὶ μὴν καλόν γ' ἔστ'. ὦ Διόνυσε δέσποτα,
  <u>κεχαρισμένως</u> σοι <u>τήνδε τὴν πομπὴν ἐμὲ</u>
  <u>πέμψαντα</u> καὶ <u>θύσαντα</u> μετὰ τῶν οἰκετῶν
  ἀγαγεῖν τυχηρῶς τὰ κατ' ἀγροὺς Διονύσια,   250
  στρατιᾶς ἀπαλλαχθέντα, τὰς <u>σπονδὰς</u> δέ μοι
  καλῶς ξυνενεγκεῖν τὰς τριακοντούτιδας.
  ἄγ', ὦ θύγατερ, ὅπως τὸ κανοῦν καλὴ καλῶς
  οἴσεις βλέπουσα θυμβροφάγον. ὡς μακάριος
  ὅστις σ' ὀπύσει κἀκποήσεται γαλᾶς   255
  σοῦ μηδὲν ἥττους βδεῖν, ἐπειδὰν ὄρθρος ᾖ.
  πρόβαινε, κἂν <u>τὤχλῳ</u> φυλάττεσθαι σφόδρα
  μή τις λαθών σου περιτράγῃ τὰ χρυσία.

---

geschlossen hat. Somit kommt der Parodie des Phallikon kein anderer Stellenwert zu als den zahlreichen Dithyramben-, Tragödien- und Hymnenparodien, die sich in den Komödien allenthalben finden." ["The famous scene from the *Acharnians* of Aristophanes is in no way joined to the structure of the play, but is motivated only in terms of plot; the celebration of the rural Dionysia symbolizes the blessings of the peace that the protagonist Dikaiopolis has concluded with the Spartans. Thus the parody of the *phallikon* possesses no more significance than do the countless parodies of dithyrambs, tragedies, and hymns found everywhere in comedies."] Because it is embedded in the plot of the *Acharnians* the song does not represent a true copy of a *phallophoria*; cf. Herter 1938b:1676. Webster in Pickard-Cambridge 1962:146 refers to the differences between this and Semos' Phallophoroi: a) the latter have a distinctive costume; b) they run toward the spectators and ridicule them; c) the φαλλοφόρος is blackened with soot. Nevertheless, there can be no doubt that the spectacle represents the staging of a cult. According to Gelzer 1992:49 the passage is not a parody at all: "Dieses kompakte Genrebild des ländlichen Dionysosfestes ist gewiss mit der drastischen Verve des damals wohl kaum mehr als 20jährigen Dichters gewürzt; aber es ist als solches kein Witz, sondern die Darstellung eines ländlichen Kultes" ["This compact genre painting of the rural Dionysia is certainly spiced with the graphic verve of the poet, who was probably not much more than twenty at the time; but as such it is not a joke, rather the presentation of a rural cult"].

ὦ Ξανθία, σφῷν δ' ἐστὶν ὀρθὸς ἑκτέος
ὁ φαλλὸς ἐξόπισθε τῆς κανηφόρου·   260
ἐγὼ δ' ἀκολουθῶν ᾄσομαι τὸ φαλλικόν·
σὺ δ', ὦ γύναι, θεῶ μ' ἀπὸ τοῦ τέγους. πρόβα.
   Φαλῆς, ἑταῖρε Βακχίου,
   ξύγκωμε, νυκτοπεριπλάνη-
   τε, μοιχέ, παιδεραστά,   265
   ἕκτῳ σ' ἔτει προσεῖπον εἰς
   τὸν δῆμον ἐλθὼν ἄσμενος,
   σπονδὰς ποησάμενος ἐμαυ-
   τῷ, πραγμάτων τε καὶ μαχῶν
   καὶ Λαμάχων ἀπαλλαγείς.   270
πολλῷ γάρ ἐσθ' ἥδιον, ὦ Φαλῆς Φαλῆς,
κλέπτουσαν εὑρόνθ' ὡρικὴν ὑληφόρον,
τὴν Στρυμοδώρου Θρᾷτταν ἐκ τοῦ φελλέως,
   μέσην λαβόντ', ἄραντα, κατα-
   βαλόντα καταγιγαρτίσαι.   275
   Φαλῆς Φαλῆς,
ἐὰν μεθ' ἡμῶν ξυμπίῃς, ἐκ κραιπάλης
ἕωθεν εἰρήνης ῥοφήσεις τρύβλιον·
ἡ δ' ἀσπὶς ἐν τῷ φεψάλῳ κρεμήσεται.

Dikaiopolis: Silence! Silence! You, basket-carrier, step a little forward! Let Xanthias keep the phallus upright! Put the basket down so we can start.

Daughter: (245) Mother, give me the ladle so I can pour pea soup over this cake here!

Dikaiopolis: That's perfect. – Dionysus, lord, let it be pleasing to you that I send forth this procession and sacrifice with my household! (250) Let me celebrate in good fortune the Dionysia here in the countryside without enemy attack, and bless my libations for a thirty-year peace! Now, daughter, hold that basket up nicely, my pretty, and make sure you put on a face as if you've just eaten bitter herbs! How happy the man (255) who'll take you as his wife and make little weasels with you that fart just as good as you do in the morning! Step forward now, and keep a sharp lookout in the crowd that someone doesn't pinch your jewelry while you're not looking! Xanthias, the phallus has to be kept erect (260) behind the basket-girl! I'll bring up the rear and strike up the phallus song. And you, wife, watch me from the roof! Forward march!

Phales, Bakkhos' friend, fellow comast, nightwanderer, (265) adulterer, pederast, I greet you for the first time in five years, happy now that I've come back to my deme and made my own personal peace-agreement, freed from troubles, wars, and warmongers like Lamakhos. For it's much nicer by far, o Phales, Phales, to snatch Strymodoros' pretty Thracian virgin from the stony ground, grab her by her hips, lift her up, (275) then throw her down and ream her good and proper, o Phales, Phales! If you want to get drunk with us, tomorrow first thing at dawn you'll be hungover and slurping down a bowl of peace, and the shield will be hung up in the chimney.

In this scene Aristophanes draws on the festive life of the polis, embeds the ritual of the *phallophoria* that preceded the actual theatrical performances into the plot, and blends it with the similar rites of the rural Dionysia.[127] The festival of τὰ κατ' ἀγροὺς Διονύσια (250) is mentioned in particular because the πομπή shown on stage also leads the hero from the polis into the countryside, and thus is able to bring the idyllic picture of peace in the countryside into the theater in the city.[128] The thirty-year wine offered by Amphitheos is turned into a correspondingly sacred activity. Σπονδαί in the secondary, metaphorical meaning of peace treaty are transferred by the comic hero into actual

---

[127] According to schol. *Ach.* 202, the rural Dionysia correspond to the Lenaia, the festival of the performance (cf. Pickard-Cambridge 1962:144–145). Actually the Lenaia, celebrated in the month Gamelion, is a quite separate celebration from the rural Dionysia. The latter was celebrated in individual demes already in the month Poseideon. On the inadvertent connection, see Deubner 1932:124. Still, elements of other festivals of Dionysus, such as, for example, mockery delivered by people on carts, were transferred from the Khoes to the Lenaia. Typical of the Lenaia and also of the rural Dionysia were the πομπή, ἀπαρχή, and ἀγών (with presentations of comedies and tragedies). In particular, competitions of κῶμοι are attested for the rural Dionysia, and are of great importance for the origin of comedy. Similar elements (εἰσαγωγή, πομπή, and κῶμος) were also familiar to the audience of the Greater Dionysia. On the individual festivals of Dionysus (Anthesteria, Lenaia, rural and city Dionysia), see Deubner 1932:93–142; on the Lenaia and rural Dionysia, *ibid.*, 123–138. Möllendorff 1995:130–131 in the context of lines 195–202 talks of an interplay of two locations and festival times; still, it is doubtful whether Διονύσια (195) refers to the Lenaia. Throughout the play, rites of Dionysus, in particular the Anthesteria, are reworked in pastiche-like fashion; see Habash 1995 and Fisher 1993.

[128] Cf. the performative announcement in the future *Ach.* 202: ἄξω τὰ κατ' ἀγροὺς εἰσιὼν Διονύσια. The preparatory line 240: θύσων . . . ἐξέρχεται has the hero, who has left in line 202, now return, so that the deme is now to be imagined as the location. For the relation of city and countryside in this passage, see Henrichs 1990:269–270. Cf. also Henderson 1991²:59–60 and Habash 1995:560–567.

libations of wine in honor of the wine-god Dionysus.[129] The completion of this ritual in Dikaiopolis' rural deme of Kholleidai (*Ach.* 406) represents the tangibly expressed realization of the private peace-accord.[130] The reduction of the celebrations to one's own *oikos* and deme reflects the extraordinary nature of the act, which is not based on the inclusion of the whole community. For this reason, the usual collective style of speech is abandoned in favor of a monodic delivery. The offering here is part of the ritual action, but at the same time it is also a metaphor, as in the song of the *Phallophoroi*, for the performance being offered.[131]

Dikaiopolis brings the procession into formation by means of a speech act: his daughter functions as *kanêphoros*, who is responsible for the ἀπαρχή; she is followed by the slave Xanthias as *phallophoros;* Dikaiopolis, following behind as symbol of comic inversion and distortion, fulfills as solo-singer the role of a citizen chorus, while at the same time acting as ἐξάρχων or κορυφαῖος of the mini-procession. After a brief prayer (247ff.), he begins the actual song, all on his own instead of with a chorus, while the role of the crowd participating in the ritual is assumed by his wife on the roof.[132] The ritual of the procession, which is based on the participation of the crowd and on the presence of a comastic choral dance group, which this woman represents, is kept to the bare minimum of performers and participants. From the perspective of the plot we have here imitation and reworking of a familiar ritual, with ritual happening within ritual, theater within theater, but without any real reenactment (μίμησις) as in the other songs.

As in most of the choral utterances in comedy, here too in this pseudo-choral passage there is no commentary or narrative, but only a ritual being

---

[129] For the Eleusinian dimension of Amphitheos as *spondophoros*, see Bowie 1993:21; for the procession *ibid.*, 26–27. On the connection of the Lenaia with Eleusis, see Deubner 1932:125–126. Amphitheos fetches the *spondai* (cf. *Ach.* 131, 178, 186), and Dikaiopolis offers them to the god of the performance as wine (199, 208) and song (263ff.). On the metaphorical usage of *spondai* in the *Acharnians*, see Newiger 1957:104–106.

[130] Similarly Pickard-Cambridge 1962:146.

[131] Cf. above, nn99 and 102 on σπένδω, χέω, and ἀπάρχομαι. In the typical language of ritual, the usual elements are mixed together. Cf. the performative expressions ἀπαρξώμεθα (*Ach.* 244), καταχέω (246), and σπονδὰς (251, 268). In addition, θύσαντα (249) and the accessories for the ἀπαρχή as a whole refer to sacrifice. The scholia to Ar. *Ach.* 242 and 243 seem to relate the text to the *phallophoria* of the Greater Dionysia rather than to the rural Dionysia.

[132] Through the instruction θεῶ μ' ἀπὸ τοῦ τέγους (262), she also becomes the internal female "spectator" in the theatrical spectacle, which is at the same time ritual, being presented on stage. The woman's viewing from the roof is especially connected with the ecstatic ritual of the Adonis procession. See Ar. *Lys.* 389: ὅ τ' Ἀδωνιασμὸς οὗτος οὑπὶ τῶν τεγῶν with Henderson *Lys.*, 119 *ad loc.* See also Baudy 1992:34 with n188. A reason for this may be that the festival of Adonia was thought of as particularly sexual and wild, with the phallus playing a key role; cf. Baudy 1992:38–39, especially the reference to the begetting of illegitimate children at this festival as a motif in comedy.

staged that proceeds as a speech act. Action is completed by utterance. Self-reference also has the function of self-ostentation. In contrast to the songs in Semos, which are given a comprehensive performative context, here the performance of this kind of song is set as a whole into the scene.

It is only in the commands and announcements that come before the song that we get the actual sense of the procession, which would otherwise be lost if only a brief song without these attachments were presented here. It is in the orders of the leader and producer that the formation of the mini-group and its connection with sacrificial ritual is brought about; in the case of the texts in Semos, much of the ritual background has to be surmised because the compiler of the passage did not consider that every detail was worthy of transmission. In this performance it is the other way round: there is no reference to the ὄψις, since this is perfectly plain to the spectator. One cannot, then, entirely exclude the possibility that Dikaiopolis and his assistants wore a particular type of costume or equally that the carrier of the phallus had makeup on his face. The procession derives its particular comic and parodic nature in particular from the sexual remarks directed at the daughter, who leads the parade as bearer of the sacrificial basket. She is a potential victim of the phallus that walks erect behind her. The presence of the girl introduces the suggestion of a sacred marriage into the proceedings.

The iambic vulgarity is in many respects reminiscent of the brief sacrificial procession in the *Thesmophoriazusae* (282-291) that the relative of Euripides stages in order to gain access to the Thesmophorion. There, too, the path to the Other is connected by means of sacrifice and *pompê* with ribald wishes for fertility for the little daughter (cf. *Thesm.* 289-291 with *Ach.* 254-258).[133] In a further command Dikaiopolis positions Xanthias as *phallophoros* behind the virgin. The phallus has to be carried erect behind the maiden. This happens as soon as the procession gets underway. This sexual juxtaposition induces further laughter. Dikaiopolis himself takes up a position at the end of the procession. Using the performative future in the "I" form, Dikaiopolis announces the presentation of his song (ἄσομαι τὸ φαλλικόν, 261) and sends his wife to her post as internal observer. Immediately after the announcement of the performance and the order to proceed (πρόβα, 262),

---

[133] The instruction to her to watch out that nobody snatch and eat her gold jewelry (χρυσία) could also contain a vulgar double entendre, alluding to her endangered virginity. Cf. Hesych., s.v. χρυσίον· τὸ τῶν παιδίων αἰδοῖον. See Henderson 1991²:131 with reference to *Av.* 670 (χρυσόν in the sense of κυσός), who does not however refer to the passage here and its secondary meaning. Cf. Henderson 1991²:144 and 178 on τραγήματα. In contrast to the Thesmophoria (*Thesm.* 293-294), the slave-girl Thratta is not here excluded from the festival; she can be snatched and enjoyed (*Ach.* 271-275).

the procession gets under way to the accompaniment of the song struck up by Dikaiopolis. Actual cult song and improvisation with attacks on individuals are here fused together. The variation between "I" and "we" is striking. The emphatic "I" expresses the isolation of the hero, while the "we" forms and the command for silence and attention in the second-person plural (εὐφημεῖτε, εὐφημεῖτε, 241) involve not only the fellow performers from his household, but also the audience as participants in cult and spectacle.[134] This involvement is also especially brought about by laughter. Dikaiopolis becomes a kind of prayer-leader, and with his refrain-like cry of "O Phales, Phales!" the audience's imagination may be stirred and instead of spectators become in fact fellow players in a communal "we," gradually declaring themselves in agreement with Dikaiopolis' action.

The ritual staged here reflects polis ritual and as with the two songs transmitted in Semos, reworks basic elements—such as the comastic (*Ach.* 264–265, 277–279), the ribald and erotic (254–260, 265, 271–275, 277–278), *aiskhrologia* and personal ridicule of Lamakhos and Strymodoros (270, 273), sacrifice together with pleasure in eating and drinking, the *symposion* (277), and musical performance[135]—into something new. All the rites and pleasures mentioned are fused into the worship of peace (251, 268–270, 278–279) and simultaneously refer to the festival currently taking place.[136] For these are the elements not only of this small φαλλικόν, but also of Old Comedy as a whole. Despite being reduced to a monody, the scene thereby becomes a kind

---

134 On the εὐφημία formula that introduces cultic activity, see Kleinknecht 1937:21n4 with references, 33–34, 38, and 151. Cf. also already *Ach.* 237–238. The address concerns the chorus as well as audience, to which the chorus extends itself. Cf. also the servant's cry before Agathon's performance and Krytilla's before the assembly at the Thesmophoria (Ar. *Thesm.* 39, 295). On the "we" forms: 244, ἀπαρξώμεθα ('let us begin the *aparkhē*'); at the same time it is in turn a reference to the beginning of the performance as offering that the mini-group and the whole community bring to the god. The "we" in the protasis ἐὰν μεθ' ἡμῶν ξυμπίῃς (277) also includes the assembled polis as a collective, especially as Dikaiopolis before this repeatedly emphasizes the fact that he wants to drink alone (199, 251–252, 268–269). The audience thus imperceptibly becomes an accomplice to this peace agreement.

135 Kugelmeier 1996:153 even thinks of "lustige Tanzbewegungen" ["comic dance movements"]. In comedy, a choral dance quite often leads to a solo dance: one has only to think of Philokleon's ecstatic dance at the end of the *Wasps*. In general one may also characterize the body language of the entering comasts as choral kinetics, that is, as dance in the broader sense of the term.

136 Dionysus brings together all these concepts. The idea of worshiping for peace through communal drinking, which symbolizes peace and sacrifice, is likewise quite concrete. On a bone tablet from Olbia (*SEG* 28 [1972]:660, p. 192) there appears next to the name of Dionysus the inscription ΕΙΡΗΝΗ ΠΟΛΕΜΟΣ among other things. This ambivalence is also of great importance for the *Acharnians*. Dionysus is peace, to be sure, but peace cannot be wholly subsumed under Dionysus, because the god also carries within him an element of Ares. For Ares and Dionysus, see Lonnoy 1985 and Bierl 1991:154–157.

of proto-comedy of a sort that could have arisen at the festival of the rural Dionysia.[137]

Redundancy, repetition, simple rhythm, and the blending of the different horizons and ritual aspects characterize this song too as a ritual text.[138] The

[137] Together with the painting of the generic picture one may also think of Dikaiopolis' mimic accompaniment. Even the idea of the rape (cf. now also Olson *Ach.*, 150 *ad* 272–275) of a wood-stealing slave-girl bears a possible similarity to the fruit thieves, who according to Sosibios are simple pranksters (ἐμιμεῖτο γάρ τις ἐν εὐτελεῖ τῇ λέξει κλέπτοντάς τινας ὀπώραν, Athen. 621d). This connection was already thought of by van Leeuwen (*Ach.*, 51 *ad* 272) and more recently also by Habash 1995:566n27. On the mimic and dance-like presentation of meat-stealing, see Pollux 4.105. Aristophanes criticizes this form of cheap farce (cf. *Nub.* 537–560, *Vesp.* 57–63, *Pax* 739–751, *Ran.* 1–18), but himself constantly uses thieving, sex, scatology, and ribald sexual expressions in his comedies in order to raise the laughter essential to comedy from his audience; cf. Halliwell 1991a:290. The proto-comedy of Dikaiopolis would accordingly form a hymn with mimic interludes by the ἐξάρχων, though here he of course performs without a chorus. From this one-man show a scene using actors could have arisen, in which two or three players perform small comic skits of this type, being constantly interrupted by the songs and hymns of a *kômos*-chorus, with a leader who strikes up the song.

Even the sympotic conclusion is combined with allusions to the sexual sphere: Dionysus is summoned to drink with Dikaiopolis; if he does so, he can also slurp a bowl of peace the next morning for his hangover—the notion of cunnilingus also lies behind this. On τρύβλιον cf. Henderson 1991²:143 and 186 with reference to *Pax* 716: ὅσον ῥοφήσει ζωμὸν ἡμερῶν τριῶν (but Olson *Peace*, 214 *ad loc.* now argues against this interpretation). Sommerstein *Acharnians*, 169 *ad* 278 correctly notes that εἰρήνης here comes as a surprise instead of "soup" (ζωμός). For breakfast (cf. ἕωθεν) in this vulgar sense, see Henderson 1991²:186. On the chauvinistic character of the song, see Silk 1980:132–133. The equally strongly performative song of the Frogs (Ar. *Ran.* 209–267) forms a similar *kômos* procession, in which only the transition into another comic world is shown on stage. There, wine-drinking at the Khoes/Khytroi during the Anthesteria is also reworked. The Frogs strike up a song that the hungover crowd sings at the Khytroi (ὁ κραιπαλόκωμος . . . λαῶν ὄχλος, *Ran.* 218–219b with Dover *Frogs*, 223–224 *ad loc.*). The solitary celebration and drinking are generally reminiscent of the eerie ritual of drinking in isolation at the Khoes with which the *Acharnians* ends. Cf. *Ach.* 1068ff. The priest of Dionysus, the representative of the god, really does become his συμπότης (cf. the invitation at 1087). In the end Dikaiopolis becomes the victor in the Khoes competition; as prize he receives a wineskin and enjoys himself with two whores.

[138] Redundancy and repetition are characteristic of the language of cult. The typical doublings are particularly apparent here: εὐφημεῖτε, εὐφημεῖτε (*Ach.* 237, 241) and the refrain-like cultic shout Φαλῆς Φαλῆς (271, 276). On the repeated invocation, cf. Pratinas *TrGF* I 4 F 3.16: θριαμβοδιθύραμβε = fr. 708, 15 *PMG*: θρίαμβε διθύραμβε; Ar. *Ran.* 316–317, 325, 342: Ἴακχ' ὦ Ἴακχε; Ar. *Thesm.* 993b: ὦ Εὔι', Εὔι', εὐοῖ (with Henrichs 1982:230n164). West 1974:23 and Nagy 1979:242–243 point out that the noun ἴαμβος, like διθύραμβος, θρίαμβος, and ἴθυμβος in the cult of Dionysus, refers to a person or type of dance. The Phales shout, which is in *iambic* form, belongs to precisely this style of mocking speech. Repetitions in vocabulary are found in the following passages: σπονδάς—*Ach.* 251, 268; ὀρθός—243, 259; φαλλός—243, 260; στρατιᾶς ἀπαλλαχθέντα, 251—μαχῶν | καὶ Λαμάχων ἀπαλλαγείς, 269–270 (cf. already πολέμου καὶ κακῶν ἀπαλλαγείς, 201); πρόβαινε 257—πρόβα 262. The above-mentioned elements of ritual style do not, however, exclude the possibility that the song was composed following literary standards. For an evaluation, see Silk 1980:131–136, who categorizes this song, despite his tendency generally to relativize the artistic quality of Aristophanic poetry, as "low lyrics *plus*" (133).

monodic form of performance is a striking expression of the lack of pragmatic reality in the imitation of a choral dance song. It is particularly noteworthy that choral self-representation and performative speech acts concerning the performers' own singing and dancing are largely absent in the actual Phales song and are shifted to the speech of preparation. Here there is no chorus that talks with and about itself; rather, Dikaiopolis exercizes an exclusive right to speech in the performative portion as well.[139] The chorus is reserved for the role of the Acharnian charcoal burners, who are opposed to this antisocial behavior by Dikaiopolis and thus attack the individual, after their attention is drawn to him by his sacred activity.

The symbolic meaning of aggressive phallic demonstration and iambic ridicule in the kômos,[140] namely the dissolution of the normal order of things, the separation of the everyday world from the world of the festival, and the marking of the liminal, all serve the plot and the external cultic connection. And even in an instance like this of monodic reworking the ritual choral dimension is apparent. The monodic reactualization of a choral song serves to remind the audience of the actual choral performance of this procession, especially since Aristophanes shapes the scene in such a way that it is played εἰς τὸ θέατρον and that the audience, the whole citizenry, characterized as a great "throng" (ὄχλος; see 257), together with the female spectator in the plot, thereby in fact becomes an active participant in a ritual familiar to it, even though it has been transformed for the comic plot.[141] In the activated imagina-

---

[139] The announcement ἐγὼ δ' ἀκολουθῶν ᾄσομαι τὸ φαλλικόν (261) corresponds to the performative future typical of such songs; cf., for instance, the formula ἀείσομαι in the Homeric hymns above, n110.

[140] Cf. the emphasis on the breaking of sexual norms (pederasty and adultery [265], rape [271–275]) and nocturnal gangs of young men (264–265). The elements are clearly reminiscent of the comastic activity of the Athenian Ithyphalloi and Autolekythoi described in Demosth. 54.14. The comic hero reactualizes practices in ritual action that can be interpreted as the remnants of archaic aristocratic initiation. He thereby undergoes the rejuvenation characteristic of it.

[141] Similarly Möllendorff 1995:131 with n57 and now also Olson Ach., 146 ad 257–258. The expression used by Semos, εἰς τὸ θέατρον λέγοντες (Athen. 622b), is reflected in the expression ἕκτῳ σ' ἔτει προσεῖπον εἰς | τὸν δῆμον ἐλθὼν ἄσμενος (266–267), which has two senses. The surface meaning is that Dikaiopolis, after five years, has at long last returned to his native deme; δῆμος can of course also be understood as the people, assembled in the theater. In the intertwining of places and times, he now performs in the procession in front of the people and in his hymn addresses Dionysos-Phales, who is present in the here and now of the theater. The verb εἰσέρχεσθαι means among other things the entry of chorus or player onto the stage; cf. e.g. Plat. Rep. 580b and Xen. Anab. 6.1.9. The verb is used in the same sense in the opening description of the Ithyphalloi above (Athen. 622b). Dikaiopolis too has entered the orchestra and now addresses the audience. The manner of expression is naturally kept consciously ambivalent; cf. the announcement already in line 202, where εἰσιών refers both to going in behind the stage and to the future entry in lines 237ff. For ὄχλος in the sense of the mass of citizens of the

tion of the audience even this adjusted scene becomes an act of worship and Dionysus takes pleasure in the comedy, even among this kind of this confusion, a ritual within a ritual.[142]

In contrast to the uncontaminated φαλλικά in Semos, then, this song is situated in the context of a plot and in its particular form concentrates distinctive *Leitmotive* in the *Acharnians*. Nevertheless, this text also is clearly located between ritual and theater: for apart from its dramatic function, which until now has been almost entirely overlooked in this scene, the passage also has a particular effect by itself alone as a reenactment of a cultic action.

Within the drama this song as independent episode, which reflects the privileging of paradigmatic over syntagmatic action that is characteristic of comedy, evokes the laughter necessary for its success by concentrating together the elements of ridicule, the sacred, and ribald sexuality.[143] Naturally Dikaiopolis did not really improvise this song; yet around this cultic shout the author composes this simple form with fixed ritual elements corresponding to the improvised models based on orality. At the same time, the song is a staging of an independent ritual, though with features clearly exaggerated for comic purposes. Both in the fragments of Semos and in Aristophanes the phallus song is set in the public space of the theater; in both cases cult becomes spectacle. To draw a precise distinction between art of an entertaining nature and ritual presentation is obviously impossible. Both have in common their char-

---

polis, cf. also Ar. *Ran.* 219b and Demokhares of Athens *FGrHist* 75 F 2 (quoted in Athen. 253c), describing the Ithyphalloi who greeted Demetrios Poliorketes in Athens (. . . ἰθύφαλλοι μετ᾽ ὀρχήσεως καὶ ᾠδῆς ἀπήντων αὐτῷ καὶ ἐφιστάμενοι κατὰ †τοὺς ὄχλους ᾖδον ὀρχούμενοι καὶ ἐπᾴδοντες . . .); for ὄχλος used of a crowd of maenads, cf. Eur. *Ba.* 117 and 1058. On the quasi-choral element in this song, see also Parker 1997:128: "One might speculate that this is a solo, not a choral, hymn-form, but the fact that Dicaeopolis sings it as a solo does not prove that. In his miniature festival, he may be representing a choir, just as his daughter represents a whole troup of basket-carriers and his wife an ὄχλος."

[142] Cf. the adverb κεχαρισμένως (248), which refers to the χάρις of the performance and the pleasure of the god. The song is furthermore a *parodos* within a *parodos*.

[143] According to Warning 1976:283–287, the purposeful plot or *sujet* is, to use terminology derived from a distinction drawn by E. v. Hartmann, an "anderweitige Handlung" ["an additional action/plot (in another time or place)"], on which the paradigmatic comic elements, the "komischen Handlungen" (Hartmann 1887:334) ["comic actions"], "gleichsam parasitär operieren" ["simultaneously operate in parasitic fashion"] (Warning 1976:287). According to Warning (323), the *commedia dell'arte*, with which Aristophanes has much in common in terms of occupying a central position between literature and open ritual form, is an exemplary instance of "wie die schematische anderweitige Handlung als Ermöglichungsstruktur der eigentlich komischen Handlungen fungiert" ["how the schematic other action or plot functions as enabling structure of the actual comic actions"]. Here, as there, we must speak of secondary improvisation.

acteristic theatricality. With the songs of the Ithyphalloi and Phallophoroi the theater, dedicated to the god, serves as a place for carrying out a cultic action. The Greek theater was never understood as a purely profane meeting place for cultural amusement, but as a gathering place for the polis under the auspices of the god and in connection with certain distinct ritual practices.

In Aristophanes, by contrast, the ritual of the everyday world, which serves as a differentiation between what precedes and the actual dramatic *agôn*, is embedded in the spectacle of a comedy. The players here occupy, like the comic chorus, a particular middle position between a role that is connected with the plot and a function as actual performers in a ritual context. It becomes more and more clear in the scholarship on Aristophanes that his plays as a whole are dependent on ritual models, that is to say, on patterns derived from the actual cycle of festivals of the polis. The author integrates these varied ritual subtexts in an intertextual process into a new dramatic text. The scene-like technique of interlacement allows one to see behind the lack of unified plot the independent character of a choral song or cultic performance.

A spectacle of this sort presented before the public is thus both cult and theater. It is difficult in the case of this passage of Aristophanes to determine definitively in terms of *Quellenforschung* what the antecedents and imitators are. As with many choral passages, in particular odes and hymns, one ought not treat even Aristophanes' Phales hymn either as a reflex or as a parody,[144] at least not in the traditional and usual sense of the word, but rather as an authentic product of an artist composing within a living choral culture. In a society that is based on orality and that thinks and acts using fixed forms of myth and ritual, a stable model that is firmly established as a genre is reactualized in a performance for a particular occasion.[145] In the marked form of the

---

[144] Despite "komischer Züge" ["comic traits"] Kleinknecht 1937:53n5, among others, does not see a parody in this "schlicht-volkstümliche Opfergebet und Phallophorenlied" ["simple popular sacrificial prayer and song of Phallophoroi"]; cf. also Prato 1987:216. Similarly, Horn 1970: 57 views the song as "ernstes Gebetspastiche" ["serious prayer pastiche"] based on popular forms. Horn appears to be on the right track, even though he is chiefly thinking (as does previous scholarship) of the problem of written models. The distinction between serious and not serious does not present itself if one uses rituality as a point of departure, since in the religious domain the nonserious, the comic, and the offensive are interwoven with the phallic procession.

[145] The "schwächere Anklänge" ["rather weak reminiscences"]—according to Kugelmeier 1996:154 the command at *Ach.* 253, ἄγ᾽, ὦ θύγατερ an ἀνάγετ᾽, and the content of *Ach.* 257, πρόβαινε, κἄν τῷχλῳ φυλάττεσθαι, are somewhat reminiscent of διὰ μέσου βαδίζειν in lines 1 and 4 of the song of the Ithyphalloi (fr. 851a *PMG*)—are typically motivated by the characteristic performative style of speech. Accordingly, the much more obvious connection between *Ach.* 243, 259 and fr. 851a.3 (ὀρθός; cf. on this Csapo 1997:284) and the relationship of the themes is based on

speech act the spectacle is staged, that is to say, translated into pure action: neither commentary, narration, nor reflection appear.[146] In the case of the phallic songs one can identify the occasion as a festival for Dionysus and the model as a *kômos*. In the texts, accordingly, using a manner peculiar to ritual, the ideas of wine, sacrifice, ribald and aggressive sexuality, and ridicule are fused with the self-referential emphasis of the performative act.[147]

---

the common nature of their occasion and genre. The reference to τήνδε τὴν πομπήν (*Ach.* 248) is comparable to the expression τάνδε μοῦσαν (fr. 851b.1 *PMG*); *deixis* of the here and now is a sign of performance, which refers in self-referential form, using demonstrative pronouns, at one moment to the cultic activity and movement of the procession, at another to the singing. In the same way, the similar syntactic form of *Ach.* 263-270 and fr. 851b with direct address in the vocative, predicate containing a performative verb in the first person, and subsequent elaboration using circumstantial participles, as well as the subsequent γάρ (*Ach.* 271 and fr. 851a.3), belongs to cultic language.

[146] The only thing that is roughly reminiscent of a reflection (*Ach.* 271ff.: πολλῷ γάρ ἐσθ' ἥδιον ...) is actually an order to enact the idea. The construction using a comparative in the neuter singular (generally as a question τί κάλλιον;) with hortatory sense also appears to belong to the language of cult: cf. Eur. *Ba.* 877-881 and 897-901 in the traditional form and Dodds 1960²:186-188 *ad* Eur. *Ba.* 877-881 (contra Blake's conjecture, recently accepted again by Seaford 1996:218-219 *ad* Eur. *Ba.* 877-881). Cf. the *prosodion* Pind. fr. 89a S.-M. and Ar. *Equ.* 1264ff. in connection with the performative activity of the chorus' own singing (τί κάλλιον ... ἀεῖσαι, or ἀείδειν), so that Aristophanes makes an intertextual connection to Pindar; cf. Fraenkel 1962:204-207.

[147] Particularly in the song of the Frogs (Ar. *Ran.* 209-267) and in the procession song of the chorus of initiates as they enter (*Ran.* 316-459), as well as in the *parodos* of Euripides' *Bacchae* (*Ba.* 64-169), the connection of the performative and the cultic (*kômos* and Iakkhos-πομπή) occurs in precisely the same way as in the song of the Phallophoroi (fr. 851b *PMG*); in particular, the short strophes directed at Demeter (*Ran.* 385a-393) and Iakkhos (*Ran.* 398-413) are likewise (following the division made by Radermacher *Frösche* and Coulon) sung in lyric iambics; the purely performative transition to the Iakkhos song with the command to now invoke this god (*Ran.* 394-397) uses the rhythm ia|lec ith||2ia ith (according to the scheme of Dover *Frogs*, 245), which is distantly reminiscent of the Ithyphalloi. For parallels between these passages, see also Silk 1980:145. Radermacher *Frösche*, 190 *ad* 354-371 suggests that an authentic Eleusinian song of initiates functioned as the model for the strophes; Fraenkel 1962:201-202 connects the rhythm with traditional cult songs, while Zimmermann I 1985:130n51 connects that of the Iakkhos invocation particularly with *Ach.* 263-279 and the Phallophoroi.

Summary and Outlook

To talk about ritual requires a great deal of understanding, reflection, and nuanced breadth in order to come even close to doing justice to the complexity of the phenomena involved. Despite the danger of falling prey to simplification after studying the details, I shall nevertheless attempt to summarize my conclusions in brief.

The Aristophanic comic chorus should in large part be understood in the context of ritual utterance and as the expression of a living choral culture that is characteristic of traditional societies based on myth and ritual. I have subjected Aristophanes to an extensive reevaluation. Regardless of all the undeniable contemporary trends pointing to the formation of an autonomous literature and art in the fifth century BCE, the theatrical chorus stands as an immediate ritual presence that also evokes past developments—in short, its own genesis. I have not concerned myself with the investigation of the ritual origins from which comedy might have arisen, but rather with demonstrating in what way these forms are still to be found in Aristophanes. The author's dramatic art is not thereby diminished as literature, but is brought to the fore in all its fundamental Otherness. The criticism voiced in recent times of the apparent lack of literary quality in Aristophanic choral songs is also thereby resolved. The poet ultimately had no desire to create literature of a lofty nature for reading, but instead composed for the performance of a popular genre in accordance with the fixed forms of a song culture that was omnipresent. He integrated this choral tradition into a plot that for its part was based on ritual patterns.

The chorus, or *kômos*, represents the ritual foundation of comedy, around which a comic plot that tends be episodic in nature is entwined. In accordance with the rules of the genre the unity of a so-called illusion is not intended. The chorus represents the element that connects to the real world of the here and now and that has the capacity to remove the distance between itself and the audience.

My investigations proceed from Gregory Nagy's finding that the occasion of a performance originally determines the genre and is identical to it. The festivals of inversion involving dissolution and ridicule, which bring laughter together with the presentation of the lowly and ugly to the center, form the ritual occasion of Old Comedy. Tragedy is performed in the same context, but treats heroic myth, thereby making the supernatural and the tragic fall its theme. Tragedy, in terms of its choral utterances, therefore easily fits into the tradition of high choral lyric, which is characterized by its mythical narrative and didactic content.

Theater appears to have developed in the environment of carnivalesque celebrations out of a comic and grotesque stream that is shared by all its subforms. The tragic art represents a kind of sublimation of this substrate. When the connections to its *Sitz im Leben* threatened to disappear, tragedy was standardized as a serious and lofty genre. We assume that comedy and the satyr play are substantially closer to ritual forms. The comic genre was integrated into the *agôn* only at a much later stage, to reestablish, as it were, the connection with the Dionysiac festival. Popular traditions and customary forms of choral song were preserved for a longer time here. Furthermore, Old Comedy, like the ritual occasion that gives it its context, is based on the conscious regression to the state of man before the advent of civilization—a state from which he is believed to have subsequently emerged; from this contrast with reality arises the laughter that the genre demands.

Nevertheless, Attic comedy and its chorus are not of course identical to ritual in its pure form; rather, Aristophanes in using an intertextual mode of operating also admits the high forms of drama and choral lyric, which in turn have their own ritual *Sitz im Leben* and which because of their mythic narrative underwent a further development into an artistic literary genre. The authoritative nature of the gnomic style is thus influential as a pose, but is constantly undermined in order to provoke the laughter of the audience. Texts that have achieved the status of literature also receive parodic treatment.

Choruses are omnipresent in the culture of the Greek world. One worships the gods in them. In the dance, one learns through one's body the fundamental values and cosmological content of society. In the ritual of movement, myth is translated into action. The education of youth for adulthood represents a central social function of round dancing by age groups. At the same time, the chorus is the place where the critical transition from child to man or woman is experienced in symbolic fashion as social drama. Accordingly, countless reflexes of archaic initiation rituals are found in the ancient chorus. In general most Greek festivals are accompanied by choruses. The critical transitions of the new year's and fertility festivals represent further occasions for *khoreia*. These functions in the real world also cooperate with what happens on stage.

The ritual chorus is marked by a double makeup, by an ambiguity between mimetic role and cultic function that draws on the presence of the actors in the here and now. The boundaries between the fictional represented and the actual representer are consciously fluid and fashioned in such a way that they overlap each other.

The comic chorus and the genre of comedy as a whole are characterized by a transverse openness. The members of the chorus oscillate freely between a plot that is only barely sustained and their cultic task in the actuality of the real world. Through this particular communication situation very close contact with the spectators is achieved, as is also characteristic of ritual. The actors in a certain sense reach out to the bystanders and make them participants. The chorus of Old Comedy always remains in part the social institution "chorus," which correspondingly sings and dances. Integration into the "other," purposeful action never occurs fully. The double communicative capacity of ritual groups is thus also mirrored in the theater. Disambiguity and withdrawal from the actual world in the sense of a closed plot occurs only to a limited extent in Aristophanes. Comedy as a genre obviously needs this transgressive style of discourse in order to move the community to act and laugh together.

Ritual is above all an expressive, symbolic activity that as a synaesthetic event is transmitted between transmitters and recipients using several media. So to what extent, then, is the comic chorus ritual? While the tragic chorus, which remains largely embedded in the plot and which relates mythic events, offers advice and instruction with an authoritative voice, and comments on the events happening on stage, but only performs actions to a relatively small extent, in the comic chorus, by contrast, the narrative content recedes into the background. The chorus is almost completely participant and actor. Gnomic wisdom and commentary are present at most as a reflex to tragedy. Its activity should not, however, be conceived of exclusively in the sense of events on stage, but rather as fundamental performative action, which is central to every chorus: a ritual chorus principally sings and dances. Further, it acts mimetically in dance, while relating its mimetic play to a simple plot. Ritual dances give priority to depicting actions from everyday life. The hunt, sacrifice, military operations, and agricultural practices are the themes favored by this kind of mimesis. It is thus the actions of searching, fleeing, and guarding as well as other minor performances of cult that are at the center.

In particular, the ritual chorus continually presents its activity and its role. The actors describe their exterior and accompany their actions with performative verbs. This self-referentiality represents the transition to the real-world function of the Dionysiac citizen-chorus that worships the divinities of the polis. Thus, on the one hand, it creates the frame for the ritual play. In its self-description it repeatedly draws attention to the fact that it now depicts a bird, for example—it hops, has wings, chirps, whistles, and sings. On the other hand, these self-references fuse with its function in the here and now, in which the chorus sings and dances in honor of the gods.

I have connected these findings with the speech act theory of John L. Austin and John R. Searle, which states that there are utterances whose pronouncement coincides with an action. We have seen that performative references function as a link between the internal and external communication situations of the chorus. Furthermore, I have traced the frequent choral self-references back to the ritual nature of the chorus. In comedy, self-referentiality has not so much to do with an artistic consciousness and reflection about the author's own abilities, but rather stems from a ritual manner of speech. The ritual group requires the illocutionary reinforcement of its current activity. It therefore accompanies the completion of its practices, set aside from the everyday world, with performative verbs. This slightly mimetic activity thus occurs through its utterance. In order that the participant or spectator may follow this behavior, the members of the chorus underscore their actions with the corresponding words of implementation in the here and now. When the chorus sings "I pray," "I sacrifice," "I curse," "I ridicule," etc., it does just that in the moment of utterance. Karl Bühler's concept of *deixis* and Roman Jakobson's linguistic theory of shifters are of great importance in this context. Using the particular speech style of the "I" or "we" and through demonstrative emphasis of place and time, the chorus achieves its characteristic position of mediator between the here and now of the orchestra and the then and there of the fiction of the plot. It functions to a certain extent, then, as a shifter itself between the events imagined on stage and the polis. And it is precisely this that connects it to its ritual models, to which it refers back. Through this exchange of perspectives the chorus becomes a particularly flexible instrument that is opposed, however, to a closed action or plot in the Aristotelian sense.

Speech act theory has shown itself to be particularly useful in the treatment of the chorus. The context can never of course be fully and completely controlled in the pragmatic sense, but it would be a mistake to assume an absolute lack of boundaries in this connection to the real world. As in the case of a ritual dance group, the stage chorus also acts performatively within a relatively limited framework that is predetermined by a concrete situation defined by orality. When the members of the chorus talk of "now" singing and dancing, it may also be assumed that the words are meant sincerely and are translated into action. The spectators become witness to the fact that the speech act is successful.

Through the mimetic dimension the context of meaning on the fictional level becomes more open, and for this reason Austin did not wish to include the theater in his treatment. Yet the occasion as *Sitz im Leben* and its anchoring in the social and cultural fabric act against any expansion of the conceptual horizon *ad infinitum*. Furthermore, the oral medium of the act of communication together with its deictic and performative markings lends it a good deal of presence. That is to say, the free, associative structure of symbolic action is channeled by being embedded in a real-world context.

The symbolic content of the transformation of the chorus through mimetic action and body language—when, for example, it is changed into an animal—can be resolved through the process of signification into a relatively broad spectrum of signifieds. It is thus possible to view such instances of animal procession as groups of primitive monsters or ancestral spirits that are brought back to life and return to the earth for a short time at festivals of inversion in the context of the renewal of fertility and the new year and that celebrate a festive primal state. The *kômos* of comedy can certainly be linked with festivals and interpretive paradigms of this type. Play using the role of an animal reworks in dramatic form the critical transition in status from youth to full citizen, among other things. These rituals experienced on a corporeal level are connected in a very broad sense with tribal initiation. In its comic "leap" into the totally Other and the archaic, comedy falls back on concepts of this type that barely survive and are only reactualized in ritual. But it also reflects contemporary practices in Athenian society that contain traces of these initiatory customs. The chorus is precisely the ritual place *par excellence* where transformative transitions of this type can be experienced in the marked form of movement and body language. In the period of marginality, initiates are imagined as being in a condition of experiencing the complete dissolution of all things that support the established cultural order, until they receive their new role identities as fully adult males or females. During this absolute interim period the young are symbolically stripped of all identity. In the dance of their age group they assume the signification practices of the Other, so that through this contrast they may celebrate in festive fashion and in front of the citizens their entry into their eventual, socially defined gender role, their self.

The *kômos* represents just such a group of youths who fall between all worlds. The wildly celebrating participants drink excessive quantities of wine and behave riotously like people who are free of all norms and values.

They dress up as animals, barbarians, or slaves, assume characteristics of the opposite gender, or even behave as completely grotesque and hybrid beings. They caterwaul, rampage, panhandle, and solicit and ridicule the surrounding crowd. They also do not shrink from the use of violence. The Dionysiac chorus in its real-world function reenacts this uncivilized behavior and stages it in the orchestra.

There are also comastic processions before and after the actual stage performance. The boundaries between the before and after are thus likewise kept open. Here too the actual stage presentation is fused with the ritual framework, with which it is also constantly connected in the case of comedy: for the comic chorus also especially concerns itself with *aiskhrologia*, the ribald mockery of fellow players and fellow citizens.

Using mimesis, the chorus of Old Comedy thus enacts the *kômos* and the marginal condition of the "betwixt and between" in the annually reoccurring restagings. It places itself back in this interim stage immediately before the attainment of maturity and acts out this period of inversion in dance and play. The ephebic members of the chorus temporarily return to the threshold phase of late childhood. They dance like children and their fun and merriment provoke laughter in everybody. They leap and hop about like untamed animals. In its performance the troupe may also assume the role of women, slaves, barbarians, and mythical *daimones*, which over the course of the evolution of comedy then gives rise to a brief and simple plot.

The removal of distinctions from human existence is also translated into movement that resembles military parade and drill. Dances in armor and other exercises that train the body are also supposed to prepare young men for hoplite status. But these potential hoplites swing their weapons and equipment in a different and wild fashion, more like satyrs who swing the *thyrsos*. They transform themselves symbolically into effeminate soldiers and comastic horsemen, before finally being accepted into the society of men as full-fledged members.

Despite the phenomenon of license and the dissolution of all ideological and cosmological norms and values, the order of the polis is nevertheless simultaneously reflected in the performance. Within the cult of the gods who watch over the state and through the staging of their myths, the initiates on the one hand receive the necessary education, while on the other hand the performers strengthen the actual conditions of the here and now. The oscillation back and forth between these positions of reversal and consolidation is extremely complex. The ritual behavior of inversion overlaps with the stabilizing function of the official cult of the gods, who oversee and guarantee life in the community. The energy released in the Dionysiac festival creates *communitas*, which in turn strengthens the cohesion of the performing comasts, the onlookers, and in short the whole city.

Using the example of the *Thesmophoriazusae*, we have seen the interplay of, on the one hand, the unrestrained independence of a group that undertakes the typical ritual actions of the chorus—namely worshiping the gods and dancing—and, on the other hand, its connection to the progress of a simple plot. The embedding is never total: the chorus continually switches into the other communicative perspective of the here and now, giving glimpses of the pragmatic context. Here the parabatic use of language is important, and cannot simply be confined to the *parabasis* itself. The ritual-performative approach I have laid out here ultimately allows us, using the perspective of the chorus, to give a completely new meaning to this comedy, hitherto subjected to a rather stepmotherly neglect by scholars. While in the past scholars, relying on a plot-based mode of interpretation, viewed the song component, relatively detached from the deliberate action of the play, as a step on the path to the ultimate superfluity of the comic chorus, we have now been able to carve out a completely different connection for it to the plot. Because of certain initiation-like elements, the actors in their fictional role and in their cultic function enter into an interaction with the hero, who likewise assumes elements of puberty initiation in his activity. It should here be emphasized once more that the festival of the Thesmophoria, which represents the cultic context for the comedy, is not of course itself an initiation festival at which young maidens are received into adult status: rather, during these autumn days, in accordance with the scheme of ritual inversion, married women temporarily transport themselves back to the highly ambivalent state of their *parthenia* on the threshold of marriage.

In this comedy the chorus creates the fictional context of the celebration of the Thesmophoria, while its songs also implicitly advance the simple plot. The members of the chorus do not of course support the chain of events as carriers of the action, for the chorus does not act as an additional "fellow-player." It only truly interferes in the action once, as a performative searcher in the hunt for male intruders. Otherwise it remains almost entirely in the background. Yet on another marked level, characterized by a multimedia approach, it places a world on stage that accompanies the plot in symbolic fashion and lends it a social and religious depth. The members of the chorus shape the relative in his fictional role in front of an inner audience. At first they construct the relative as enemy; later he is stylized as an initiate in the marginal phase and thus compared to their own role and their reactualized ritual function in their playful dance. By this means, compromise with the men is ultimately able be brought about, so that only then does the sudden happy ending become understandable. In this symbolic performance the hostile intruder becomes a friend and ally. The chorus thus implicitly acts in the orchestra as a secret catalyst for the ritual movement that also imitates the course of the festival of inversion that is the Thesmophoria. After complete reversal and the separation of the sexes, man and wife can once more be united, thus giving rise to prosperity and fertility for the polis. In the hymnic prayer, the gods are drawn into the complex play of oscillating levels of communication. Finally, in the labyrinth of perspectives presented by the ephebic citizen chorus, members of the audience may reflect in humorous fashion on the restrictions of the gender roles constructed by the polis and recall their own initiation.

The observations developed using the *Thesmophoriazusae* as an example can also be transferred to other comedies. To anticipate any misunderstanding: the fact that the comedy I have chosen as my example is set explicitly in a cultic context does not, in general, play a decisive role in my assessment of the comic chorus, for this does not always seem to be the case in the other extant works of Aristophanes. Still, the Eleusinian *mystai* of the *Frogs* represent a further cultic chorus. Furthermore, we have extended to all choral groups the popular rituality of the fictional role that lends individual comedies their names. Finally, to emphasize this point once again: all comic choruses in their pragmatic function outside the plot always represent a ritual association that worships all the gods of the polis within the context of the festival of Dionysus through the use of dance and song.

Up until the *parabasis* the members of the chorus in Old Comedy are, to be sure, often actively involved in the dramatic action as adversaries or helpers of the hero, but here the dramatic perspective is broken time and time again. And here too they complete minor everyday activities in the sense of the speech act. They beat and attack their opponent, they ridicule him, or they enter in the *parodos*: they carry out the action in the sung word. Yet the chorus seldom actually determines action in the way the actors do. It functions rather as a mediator between audience and stage. In what amounts to a synaesthetic spectacle, the singing and dancing actors intensify and lend depth to the action on stage using masks, expensive costumes, striking body language and movements, and performative song accompaniment. Comedy has less to do with the presentation of a complex plot than with a ritual process, a multimedia, aesthetic, and communicative experience that unites spectators, players, and gods. The message is hence to be taken mostly as open and not one-sidedly political. What is important here is the artistic and appellative reenactment of ritual complexes, which in comedy constantly thematize the development from a fundamental crisis and inversion in the world toward healing, fertility, and general well-being. The temporary marginality of the *kômos*, which refers back to critical periods of transition, is reworked in a bewildering, episodic play of laughter. The events typically culminate in a concluding wedding, which puts an end to the breakdown of order. The comastic and joyful celebration at the end of the play transitions into a victory celebration and the exuberant activity of the entire polis before and after the comedy. The presentation on stage ultimately becomes in this sense a ritual within a ritual and the chorus a link that can dynamically decrease, remove, and increase the distance to the *énonciation*, the cultic Dionysiac event in the here and now as well as the audience.

In our discussion of the Ithyphalloi and Phallophoroi we have seen a *kômos* that is not integrated into a purposeful action set "elsewhere." Nevertheless, the performative context, the occasion of the *énonciation*, is transferred to the theater. The two phallic songs cited by Semos as examples of the genre and transmitted by Athenaeus have up until now generally been referred to only in passing and in connection with possible ritual origins of comedy. Since this question is based on modern assumptions and cannot ultimately be resolved, a new approach has been followed in the second chapter. Through an in-depth ritual and performative interpretation of the texts as independent products of a living choral culture, I have been able to show for the first time that the festive hymn to Dionysus, by means of redundancy and fusion, extends the synaesthetic occasion of the choral presentation to the sensual ritual experience of wine-drinking, sexuality, and sacrifice and with allusions to the chorus' own performance merges into a "thick" discourse. The information added by Semos about the songs' embedment in a performative context reveals the connections of ritual, theater, and Hellenistic literature, and the fluid transition between comic theater and the ceremonies surrounding it. Furthermore, the description of the visual, nonverbal semiotic dimension of performance provides evidence of the theme of the reversal of the world, which is characteristic of a *kômos*. In style and diction there are parallels to Aristophanes' choral songs, in particular to the odes of the *parabasis*. It is unlikely that the comic playwright imitated or parodied these popular predramatic forms; rather, as *khorodidaskalos* he composes his songs anew in a productive fashion within a fixed traditional context. Behind this lies a society based on orality that defines itself almost exclusively using myth and ritual.

Of course the thesis advanced here, which is based on the theory of function derived from the study of the sociology of religion—namely that

335

the comic chorus has its foundation in the real world, in the initiation of the youth, and possibly and secondarily also in the fertility cycle and the transition from the old year to the new—implies an alternative hypothesis to the question of origin that conflicts in part with earlier theories about the genesis of the genre. In the view of the ancients, upon which previous scholarship was largely based until quite recently, the origin of comedy is rooted in practices involving blame and begging that were supposed to even out social tensions between city and countryside, rich and poor, powerful and politically underprivileged. All in all, I am convinced that this much-discussed problem cannot be resolved conclusively, and accordingly have pursued other ways of uncovering ritual structures in the extant texts. It should nevertheless be emphasized that even ancient attempts to explain the genre are only hypotheses that were probably extrapolated retrospectively from the surviving comedies. Since the development of Old Comedy under the given conditions of polis democracy did in fact lead to a highly explosive political theater—especially with Aristophanes, whose comedies then gained acceptance in the tradition and were shaped by social antagonisms of this type—is it not then logical that the first literary theoreticians, for whom the dramatic forms used in ritual had already become something foreign, relied on social and political hypotheses in order to be able to explain the contents of Aristophanes' political comedy retroactively in terms of these hypotheses? In the nineteenth and twentieth centuries such ideas of ancient class struggle naturally found favorable reception.

It is not my intention to deny the plausibility of these ancient theories. My suggestion has the advantage, however, of taking into account the Greek chorus' *Sitz im Leben*, something that is today commonly recognized and from which the dramatic chorus among other things apparently evolved. When I associate the comic chorus in this work mainly with initiatory practices, but also with rites connected with fertility and the coming of the new year, which are the three current paradigms in the study of religion, I am also able to subsume the blame practices traditionally advanced by previous theories under these headings. In tribal initiations, but also in the two other categories of festivals, according to Arnold van Gennep's famous tripartite structure, the existing order is repealed in a transitional stage of marginality. The members of the chorus are thus located in an interim phase in an inverted world that is also a fundamental element for comedy as a whole. Choruses in initiation rites do not just work out generational conflicts, but, like the *kômoi*, in their condition of marginality they bring into question all social and cosmological codes. Given this religious and sociological basis, one can thus not only explain the social and political tensions in political comedy between farmers and city dwellers, the poor and the rich, the disadvantaged and the powerful, but also understand practices involving ridicule and, in addition, all the phenomena of the comic and carnivalesque world, such as dressing up as animals, the staging of the Other and the foreign, phallus worship, and transvestism, all of which have their basis in so-called rites of inversion.

In particular, by taking into account conclusions gained from ethnological and anthropological scholarship on ritual, we have also been able in both chapters to trace rituality within the microstructure of the texts. Figures of speech such as metaphor, metonymy, alliteration, anaphora, and rhythmical and metrical structure—commonly described as aesthetic characteristics of poetic style—ultimately have their basis in song culture, out of which literature developed only as a secondary phenomenon. The synaesthetic experience processes various ritual components, unleashing physiological processes within both the actors and the spectators that pave the way for a feeling of unity and group cohesion.

In terms of the scholarship on ritual, the following conclusion emerges: ritual and literature are not complete opposites. In the field of German studies, Wolfgang Braungart, independently of my work, has also made this clear in his 1996 study. Ritual is not simply compulsive and heteronymous, just as literature does not simply mean completely free artistic play. Ritual, like literature, possesses an aesthetic and expressive dimension of theatricality. It, too, works with symbols. Literature and ritual demonstrate common denominators in their formal structure and in their form of public staging.

These inherent connections have long been recognized in the theater of the twentieth century. Modern theatrical forms draw their strength from rituality, especially when one reaches back to modes of drama other than the dominant naturalistic and Aristotelian model. Theater as anti-illusionistic staging and the aesthetic and symbolic performative form make this interdependence clear. This can be seen even more clearly in the case of the conditions of production and reception in antiquity.

The performative approach certainly cannot explain the phenomenon of ritual in its entirety, but it has shown itself to be extremely useful in the context of cultic choruses, which are performed in a form of synaesthetic spectacle in a social space with numerous references to the real world. Chorus, ritual, and theater come together in performativity and in their innate tendency, using several media and levels of expression, to present symbolic connections as spectacle, which in a broad sense connects and transforms both actor and spectator. The comic chorus in this respect, and given its anthropological and social anchoring in real life, acts in a ritual fashion. It not only developed from this stratum, but in all its new formations and contexts remains ritual. Theatricality gives rise to theater: even ancient theater, however, represents only one part of a broader ritual show in honor of Dionysus.

Here a possible misunderstanding clearly needs to be addressed, namely that the broad concept of ritual used in this work renders the latter synonymous with theatrical performance and confuses the distinction between ritualized activity in general and religious activity in particular. We are not concerned here with anchoring the chorus exclusively in festive contexts. Even though the connections to religious festivals are of great importance in the *Thesmophoriazusae* and in the other comedies, it has not been my intention to confine myself to the purely religious. In my investigation, which has a primarily literary orientation, I have traced in an interdisciplinary fashion the attempt to uncover the presence of popular ritual, anti-illusionist, symbolic, and expressive forms of expression in the so-called developed theater of Aristophanes, that is to say the "predramatic" element in drama. The ritual does not of course coincide with the performative, but the latter represents, as has been shown in detail, only one important aspect of explaining the particular transversal openness of the comic chorus that transcends the dramatic theory of the closed plot and illusion based on Aristotle and has its roots in general rituality.

The chorus then is ritual, but not in the sense that modern assumptions about ritual might suggest—namely, that it is something extremely rigid, proceeds in an empty, formulaic fashion, and ultimately exhausts itself in pointless repetition. This description certainly does not apply to the lively and richly expressive theater of Aristophanes. Rather, the chorus and ritual, as with Athenian drama in general, present and process situations of social crisis in a form that is spectacular and in aesthetic terms both directly appealing and powerful. This display functions as communication. In performance, which includes singing, stylized dancing, and mimetic action, the group of performers and the spectators are subjected to a process of transformation that resembles one of van Gennep's *rites de passage*.

In Old Comedy, these rituals anchored in the real world are also connected to the politics of the day. In contrast to the modern world, politics does not represent a diametrically opposed area: instead the whole cosmos of the polis is imbued with rituals. The various discourses of the real world in this genre flow into one another. So, for example, ridicule, a fundamental element of the genre, is transferred to the disparaging of contemporary powerful figures and is turned into a playful and open form of plot. This manner of expression in a carnivalesque context must not, however, be identified in too one-sided a fashion with a definite statement about the politics of the day.

The precise social and cultural backgrounds of this communicative act are ultimately irrevocably lost. Cultural performance in all its dimensions was comprehensible only for the authentic participant. For the modern reader of comedy as literature, this context remains to a large extent buried. Evidence is thus only to be found in traces, because its presence can only be imagined and guessed at through its reception elsewhere and over a distance in time.

Beside all the comic tendencies toward inversion, there are numerous passages in Aristophanes where the members of the chorus strive in cultic worship to draw the gods into the performance unfolding at the moment. Many divinities, who have a function in the actual context surrounding the play while also being involved in the corresponding plot, are often summoned as chorus leaders. In this aspect too, the chorus acts as a shifter between two levels, the human and the divine. The anthropomorphic gods dance and form a chorus, which serves as model for the action proceeding on stage. In their dance, the members of the chorus reenact their divine model and identify themselves to a certain extent with this. Conversely, they also connect their performance in the here and now with the spectators. The chorus with its ritual activity becomes a link between god and human.

Wild, whirling, mimetic, and expressive body movements blend all these modes of perception and ritual concepts into a complex message. Point of departure, center, and periphery, just like the subject, object, and result of the performative act, can no longer be distinguished from each other in this spinning whirlpool. The final verses of William Butler Yeats' *Among Schoolchildren* illuminate these connections:

> O chestnut-tree, great-rooted blossomer,
> Are you the leaf, the blossom, or the bole?
> O body swayed to music, O brightening glance,
> How can we know the dancer from the dance?

The dancer becomes completely absorbed as an entity into his performative activity. Performance and actor are brought into alignment. As it acts, the body becomes an object upon which the music and the rhythm, like some higher power, are inscribed. In the Greek imagination this ecstatic effect is personified in a god of dance, in Dionysus in particular. Dance delights mankind in the same way that play delights children. Joy (χάρις) is inscribed on the body and face, especially in its expression. Dance causes a glowing lustre (ἀγλαΐα) to shine out, shaping bodily attitude in such a way that the dancer as agent can no longer be separated from his activity. When the chorus leader is then finally recognized in the person of a god, ritual unity with the Olympian gods who protect the polis is created in the chorus, and this synaesthetically experienced state of happiness is transferred from the orchestra to the entire body of the polis seated in the circle of the theater of Dionysus.

Bibliography

Editions of Aristophanes

Collected Editions

Biset, O. 1607. *Aristophanis comoediae undecim*. Paris.

Küster (= Kusterus), L. 1710. *Aristophanis comoediae undecim*. Amsterdam.

Brunck, R. F. P. 1783. *Aristophanis comoediae* I–III. Strassburg.

Bothe, F. H. 1845². *Aristophanis comoediae* I–IV. Leipzig.

Bekker, I. 1829. *Aristophanis comoediae* I–V. London.

Meineke, A. 1860. *Aristophanis comoediae* I–II. Leipzig.

Blaydes, F. H. M. 1880–1893. *Aristophanis comoediae* I–XII. Halle.

van Leeuwen, J. 1896–1909. *Aristophanis Acharnenses, Equites, etc.*, I–XI. Leiden.

Rogers, B. B. 1902–1916. *The Acharnians, Knights, etc., of Aristophanes* I–XI. London.

Hall, F. W., and Geldart, W. M. 1906/07². *Aristophanis comoediae* I–II. Oxford.

Coulon, V. 1923–30. *Aristophane* I–V. Paris (all citations are from Coulon's text, unless otherwise indicated; for *Nub., Pax, Av., Lys.,* and *Ran.* the new editions of Dover *Clouds*, Olson *Peace*, Dunbar *Birds*, Henderson *Lys.*, and Dover *Frogs* are used).

Cantarella, R. 1949–1964. *Aristofane, le commedie* I–V. Milan.

Sommerstein, A. H. 1980–2002. *The Comedies of Aristophanes* (thus far vols. I–XII, *Acharnians–Wealth*, and *Indexes*). Warminster.

Individual Comedies

Thesmophoriazusae

Thiersch, B. 1832. *Aristophanis Thesmophoriazusae*. Halberstadt.

Fritzsche, F. V. 1838. *Aristophanis Thesmophoriazusae*. Leipzig.

Enger, R. 1844. *Aristophanis Thesmophoriazusae*. Bonn.

Velsen, A. von. 1883. *Aristophanis Thesmophoriazusae*. Leipzig.

van Leeuwen, J. 1904. *Aristophanis Thesmophoriazusae*. Leiden.

Rogers, B. B. 1904. *The Thesmophoriazusae of Aristophanes*. London.

Gannon, J. F. 1987. *Aristophanes' Thesmophoriazusae* I–II. Bryn Mawr Greek Commentaries. Bryn Mawr.

Bibliography

Sommerstein, A. H. 1994. *Thesmophoriazusae*. Comedies of Aristophanes 8. Warminster.

Prato, C. 2001. *Le donne alle Tesmoforie*. Ed. and trans. D. Del Corno. Milan.

Austin, C., and Olson, S. D. 2004. *Aristophanes. Thesmophoriazusae*. Oxford.

Acharnians

van Leeuwen, J. 1902. *Aristophanis Acharnenses*. Leiden.

Sommerstein, A. H. 1980. *Acharnians*. Comedies of Aristophanes 1. Warminster.

Olson, S. D. 2002. *Aristophanes. Acharnians*. Oxford.

Clouds

Dover, K. J. 1968. *Aristophanes. Clouds*. Oxford.

Wasps

Starkie, W. J. M. 1897. *The Wasps of Aristophanes*. London.

MacDowell, D. M. 1971. *Aristophanes. Wasps*. Oxford.

Sommerstein, A. H. 1983. *Wasps*. Comedies of Aristophanes 4. Warminster.

Peace

Olson, S. D. 1998. *Aristophanes. Peace*. Oxford.

Birds

Rogers, B. B. 1906. *The Birds of Aristophanes*. London.

Dunbar, N. 1995. *Aristophanes. Birds*. Oxford.

Lysistrata

Henderson, J. 1987. *Aristophanes. Lysistrata*. Oxford.

Frogs

Radermacher, L. 1954[2]. *Aristophanes' 'Frösche'* (ed. W. Kraus). Österreichische Akademie der Wissenschaften, philosophisch-historische Klasse, Sitzungsberichte 198.4. Vienna.

Dover, K. J. 1993. *Aristophanes. Frogs*. Oxford.

Scholia

Dübner, F., ed. (1842) 1877. *Scholia Graeca in Aristophanem cum prolegomenis grammaticorum* I–II. Paris.

Rutherford, W. G., ed. 1896. *Scholia Aristophanica*. London.

Koster, W. J. W., et al., eds. 1960–2001. *Scholia in Aristophanem* I.1A–3.2, II.1–4, III.1A–B and 4A–B, and IV.1–3. Groningen (for the scholia to the *Thesmophoriazusae* and *Ecclesiazusae* the edition of Dübner, generally referred to in previous scholarship, must still be consulted).

Works Cited

Adam, J.-M. 1990. "Aspects du récit en anthropologie." In *Le discours anthropologique: Description, narration, savoir* (eds. J.-M. Adam et al.), 251–282. Paris.

Adami, F. 1901. "De poetis scaenicis Graecis hymnorum sacrorum imitatoribus." *Jahrbücher für classische Philologie* supplement 26:213–262.

Adrados, F. R. 1975. *Festival, Comedy, and Tragedy: The Greek Origins of Theatre.* Trans. C. Holme. Leiden.

Agosti, G. 1987/88. "Prometeo incappucciato (Aristoph. *Av.* 1496)." *AION,* filol. 9/10:37–41.

Alexiou, M. 1974. *The Ritual Lament in Greek Tradition.* Cambridge.

Aloni, A. 1998. *Cantare glorie di eroi: Comunicazione e performance poetica nella Grecia arcaica.* Torino.

Anderson, C. A. 1995. *Athena's Epithets: Their Structural Significance in Plays of Aristophanes.* BzA 67. Stuttgart.

Arnoldt, R. 1873. *Die Chorpartien bei Aristophanes: Scenisch erläutert.* Leipzig.

Arnott, P. D. 1989. *Public and Performance in the Greek Theatre.* London.

Arnott, W. G. 1996. *Alexis. The Fragments: A Commentary.* Cambridge.

Aronen, J. 1992. "Notes on Athenian Drama as Ritual Myth-Telling within the Cult of Dionysos." *Arctos: Acta Philologica Fennica* 26:19–37.

Ashmole, B. 1946. "Kalligeneia and Hieros Arotos." *JHS* 66:8–10.

Assmann, J. 1991. "Der zweidimensionale Mensch: Das Fest als Medium des kollektiven Gedächtnisses." In Assmann 1991a:13–33.

——. 1991a. *Das Fest und das Heilige: Religiöse Kontrapunkte zur Alltagswelt.* Studien zum Verstehen fremder Religionen 1. Gütersloh.

——. 1992. *Das kulturelle Gedächtnis: Schrift, Erinnerung und politische Identität in frühen Hochkulturen.* Munich.

Auffarth, C. 1991. *Der drohende Untergang: 'Schöpfung' in Mythos und Ritual im Alten Orient und in Griechenland am Beispiel der Odyssee und des Ezechielbuches.* RGVV 39. Berlin.

——. 1994. "Der Opferstreik: Ein altorientalisches 'Motiv' bei Aristophanes und im homerischen Hymnus." *Grazer Beiträge* 20:59–86.

Ausfeld, C. 1903. "De Graecorum precationibus quaestiones." *Jahrbücher für classische Philologie* supplement 28:505–547.

Austin, C. 1974. "Le rôle de la Coryphée dans les 'Thesmophories.' " *Dioniso* 45:316–325.

——. 1987. "Textual Problems in Ar. *Thesm.*" *Dodone* 16:61–92.

——. 1990. "Observations critiques sur les *Thesmophories* d'Aristophane." *Dodone* 19:9–29.

Austin, J. L. 1975. *How to Do Things with Words* (eds. J. O. Urmson and M. Sbisà). Cambridge, MA.

Bachmann-Medick, D. 1988. "Kulturelle Spielräume: Drama und Theater im Licht ethnologischer Ritualforschung." In *Soziale und theatralische Konventionen als Problem der Dramenübersetzung* (eds. E. Fischer-Lichte et al.), 153–177. Forum modernes Theater 1. Tübingen.

Bacon, H. H. 1994/95. "The Chorus in Greek Life and Drama." *Arion* 3rd ser. 3: 6–24.

Bakhtin, M. M. 1984. *Problems of Dostoevsky's Poetics* (ed. and trans. C. Emerson). Minneapolis.

——. 1984a. *Rabelais and His World*. Trans. H. Iswolsky. Bloomington, IL.

Banova, P. 1994. "Alcibiade in Sofocle e Aristofane (Studio sul secondo stasimo dell'*Edipo Re* e sulle *Tesmoforiazuse*)." *Sileno* 20:145–160.

Baran, H., ed. 1974. *Semiotics and Structuralism: Readings from the Soviet Union*. White Plains, NY.

Barba, E., and Savarese, N. 1991. *A Dictionary of Theatre Anthropology: The Secret Art of the Performer*. Trans. R. Fowler. London.

Barber, E. J. W. 1992. "The Peplos of Athena." In *Goddess and Polis: The Panathenaic Festival in Ancient Athens* (ed. J. Neils), 103–117. Princeton.

Barlow, S. A. 1971. *The Imagery of Euripides: A Study in the Dramatic Use of Pictorial Language*. London.

Barrett, W. S. 1964. *Euripides. Hippolytos*. Oxford.

Barringer, J. M. 1995. *Divine Escorts: Nereids in Archaic and Classical Greek Art*. Ann Arbor.

Barthes, R. 1977. "The Death of the Author." In *Image, Music, Text* (ed. and trans. S. Heath), 142–148. New York.

Barton, A. 1990. *The Names of Comedy*. Toronto.

Batchelder, A. G. 1995. *The Seal of Orestes: Self-Reference and Authority in Sophocles' Electra*. Lanham, MD.

Bateson, G. 1972. *Steps to an Ecology of Mind: Collected Essays in Anthropology, Psychiatry, Evolution, and Epistemology*. San Francisco.

Bateson, M. C. 1974. "Ritualization: A Study in Texture and Texture Change." In *Religious Movements in Contemporary America* (eds. I. I. Zaretsky and M. P. Leone), 150–165. Princeton.

Baudy, D. 1998. *Römische Umgangsriten: Eine ethologische Untersuchung der Funktion von Wiederholung für religiöses Verhalten*. RGVV 43. Berlin.

Baudy, G. J. 1986. *Adonisgärten: Studien zur antiken Samensymbolik*. Beiträge zur Klassischen Philologie 176. Frankfurt.

——. 1992. "Der Heros in der Kiste. Der Erichthoniosmythos als Aition athenischer Erntefeste." *A&A* 38:1–47.

Baur, D. 1997. "Chor und Theater: Zur Rolle des Chores in der griechischen Tragödie unter besonderer Berücksichtigung von Euripides' *Elektra*." *Poetica* 29:26–47.

——. 1999. "Der Chor auf der Bühne des 20. Jahrhunderts: Ein typologischer Überblick." In Riemer and Zimmermann 1999:227–246.

———. 1999a. *Der Chor im Theater des 20. Jahrhunderts: Typologie des theatralen Mittels Chor.* Theatron 30. Tübingen.

Beer, C. 1844. *Ueber die Zahl der Schauspieler bei Aristophanes.* Leipzig.

Bell, C. 1992. *Ritual Theory, Ritual Practice.* Oxford.

———. 1997. *Ritual: Perspectives and Dimensions.* Oxford.

Benveniste, É. 1966. *Problèmes de linguistique générale.* Paris.

Bérard, C. 1974. *Anodoi: Essai sur l'imagerie des passages chthoniens.* Bibliotheca Helvetica Romana 13. Rome.

Bergk, T. 1882⁴. *Poetae Lyrici Graeci.* Leipzig. (= B.)

Bernardini, P. A. 1991. "L'inno agli dei nella lirica corale greca e la sua destinazione sacrale." In Cassio and Cerri 1991:85–94.

Bethe, E. 1907. "Die dorische Knabenliebe: Ihre Ethik und ihre Idee." *RhM* 62:438–475.

Bierl, A. 1986. *Vorkommen und Funktion des Gottes Dionysos bei den griechischen Tragikern außerhalb der 'Bakchen' des Euripides: Eine Stelleninterpretation unter Berücksichtigung der Fragmente.* Unpublished Magisterarbeit. Munich.

———. 1990. "Dionysus, Wine, and Tragic Poetry: A Metatheatrical Reading of P. *Köln* VI 242A = *TrGF* II F 646a." *GRBS* 31:353–391.

———. 1991. *Dionysos und die griechische Tragödie: Politische und 'metatheatralische' Aspekte im Text.* Classica Monacensia 1. Tübingen.

———. 1994. "Karion, die Karer und der *Plutos* des Aristophanes als Inszenierung eines anthesterienartigen Ausnahmefestes." In Bierl and Möllendorff 1994:30–43.

———. 1994a. "Apollo in Greek Tragedy: Orestes and the God of Initiation." In *Apollo: Origins and Influences* (ed. J. Solomon), 81–96 and 149–159. Tucson.

———. 1996. *Die Orestie des Aischylos auf der modernen Bühne: Theoretische Konzeptionen und ihre szenische Realisierung.* Drama: Beiheft 5. Stuttgart.

———. 1999. "Doppeltanz oder doppelte Freude? Gedanken zum umstrittenen διπλῆν (Ar. *Thesm.* 982) aus einer performativen Perspektive." In Riemer and Zimmermann 1999:27–47.

———. 2002. "Religion und Literatur." *Der Neue Pauly: Rezeptions- und Wissenschaftsgeschichte* 15.2 (eds. M. Landfester, H. Cancik, and H. Schneider), 669–677. Stuttgart.

———. 2002a. "Experimentelle Innovation und ihre rituell-pragmatischen Grenzen in der Alten Komödie." *QUCC* n.s. 72.3:7–21.

———. 2004. *L'Orestea di Eschilo sulla scena moderna. Concezioni teoriche e realizzazioni sceniche.* Trans. L. Zenobi. Biblioteca Teatrale–Memorie di Teatro 15. Rome.

———. 2004a. "Alt und Neu bei Aristophanes (unter besonderer Berücksichtigung der *Wolken*)." In *Die Wahrnehmung des Neuen in Antike und Renaissance* (eds. A. von Müller and J. von Ungern-Sternberg), 1–24. Colloquium Rauricum 8. Munich.

Bierl, A. 2006. "Tragödie als Spiel und das Satyrspiel: Die Geburt des griechischen Theaters aus dem Geiste des Chortanzes und seines Gottes Dionysos." In *Kind und Spiel* (eds. J. Sánchez de Murillo and M. Thurner), 111–138. Aufgang: Jahrbuch für Denken, Dichten, Musik 3. Stuttgart.

———. 2007. "Literatur und Religion als Rito- und Mythopoetik: Überblicksartikel zu einem neuen Ansatz in der Klassischen Philologie." In Bierl, Lämmle, and Wesselmann 2007:1–76.

Bierl, A., Lämmle, R., and Wesselmann, K., eds. 2007. *Literatur und Religion: Wege zu einer mythisch-rituellen Poetik bei den Griechen*, I–II. Basiliensia-MythosEikonPoiesis I.1–2. Munich.

Bierl, A., and Möllendorff, P., eds. 1994. *Orchestra: Drama–Mythos–Bühne. Festschrift für Hellmut Flashar anläßlich seines 65. Geburtstages.* Stuttgart.

Binder, G., and Effe, B., eds. 1998. *Das antike Theater: Aspekte seiner Geschichte, Rezeption und Aktualität.* Bochumer Altertumswissenschaftliches Colloquium 33. Trier.

Bing, P. 1988. *The Well-Read Muse: Present and Past in Callimachus and the Hellenistic Poets.* Hypomnemata 90. Göttingen.

Blech, M. 1982. *Studien zum Kranz bei den Griechen.* RGVV 38. Berlin.

Bloch, M. 1974. "Symbols, Song, Dance, and Features of Articulation: Is Religion an Extreme Form of Traditional Authority?" *Archives Européennes de Sociologie* 15:55–81.

Boedeker, D. D. 1974. *Aphrodite's Entry into Greek Epic.* Mnemosyne supplement 31. Leiden.

Bonanno, M. G. 1987. "ΠΑΡΑΤΡΑΓΩΙΔΙΑ in Aristofane." *Dioniso* 57:135–167.

———. 1990. "Metateatro in parodia (sulle 'Tesmoforiazuse' di Aristofane)." In *L'allusione necessaria: Ricerche intertestuali sulla poesia greca e latina* (ed. M. G. Bonanno), 241–276. Filologia e critica 63. Rome.

Bond, G. W. 1981. *Euripides. Heracles.* Oxford.

Bonnette, A. L. 1989. *The Political Wisdom of Women in Aristophanes: A Study of Lysistrata, Ecclesiazusae, and Thesmophoriazusae.* Ph.D. diss. Boston College.

Borgeaud, P. 1988. *The Cult of Pan in Ancient Greece.* Trans. K. Atlass and J. Redfield. Chicago.

Borthwick, E. K. 1967. "Trojan Leap and Pyrrhic Dance in Euripides' *Andromache* 1129–41." *JHS* 87:18–23.

———. 1968. "Notes on the Plutarch *De Musica* and the *Cheiron* of Pherecrates." *Hermes* 96:60–73.

———. 1970. "P. Oxy. 2738: Athena and the Pyrrhic Dance." *Hermes* 98:318–331.

Bourdieu, P. 1977. *Outline of a Theory of Practice.* Trans. R. Nice. Cambridge.

Bowie, A. M. 1982. "The Parabasis in Aristophanes: Prolegomena, *Acharnians*." *CQ* n.s. 32:27–40.

———. 1993. *Aristophanes: Myth, Ritual, and Comedy.* Cambridge.

———. 1993a. "Religion and Politics in Aeschylus' *Oresteia*." *CQ* n.s. 43:10–31.

Bowie, E. 1990. "Marginalia Obsceniora: Some Problems in Aristophanes' *Wasps*." In *'Owls to Athens.' Essays on Classical Subjects Presented to Sir Kenneth Dover* (ed. E. M. Craik), 31–38. Oxford.

Bowra, C. M. 1934. "The Occasion of Alcman's Partheneion." *CQ* 28:35–44.

Braungart, W. 1996. *Ritual und Literatur*. Konzepte der Sprach- und Literaturwissenschaft 53. Tübingen.

Breitholtz, L. 1960. *Die dorische Farce im griechischen Mutterland vor dem 5. Jahrhundert: Hypothese oder Realität?* Studia Graeca et Latina Gothoburgensia 10. Stockholm.

Brelich, A. 1969. *Paides e Parthenoi*, I. Incunabula Graeca 36. Rome.

———. 1975. "Aristofane: Commedia e religione." In *Il mito: Guida storica e critica* (ed. M. Detienne), 103–118. Rome. 3rd ed., 1982.

Bremer, J. M. 1981. "Greek Hymns." In *Faith, Hope, and Worship: Aspects of Religious Mentality in the Ancient World* (ed. H. S. Versnel), 193–215. Studies in Greek and Roman Religion 2. Leiden.

———. 1993. "Aristophanes on His Own Poetry." In Bremer and Handley 1993:125–165.

Bremer, J. M., and Handley, E. W., eds. 1993. *Aristophane*. Entretiens sur l'antiquité classique 38. Vandœuvres-Geneva.

Bremmer, J. 1978. "Heroes, Rituals, and the Trojan War." *Studi Storico-Religiosi* 2:5–38.

———. 1980. "An Enigmatic Indo-European Rite: Paederasty." *Arethusa* 13:279–298.

———. 1990. "Adolescents, *Symposion*, and Pederasty." In Murray 1990a:135–148.

———. 1992. "Dionysos travesti." In Moreau 1992a:189–198.

———. 1994. *Greek Religion*. Greece & Rome: New Surveys in the Classics 24. Oxford.

Brommer, F. 1989. "Antike Tänze." *Archäologischer Anzeiger* 1989:483–494.

Bron, C. 1996. "The Sword Dance for Artemis." *J. Paul Getty Museum Journal* 24:69–83.

———. 1999. "La musique du comos." In *Classical Archaeology Towards the Third Millennium: Reflexions and Perspectives. Proceedings of the XVth International Congress of Classical Archaeology, Amsterdam, July 12–17, 1998* (eds. R. F. Docter and E. M. Moormann), 98–100. Amsterdam.

Broneer, O. 1942. "The Thesmophorion in Athens." *Hesperia* 11:250–274.

Bruit Zaidman, L., and Schmitt Pantel, P. 1992. *Religion in the Ancient Greek City*. Trans. P. Cartledge. Cambridge.

Brulé, P. 1987. *La fille d'Athènes: La religion des filles à Athènes à l'époque classique. Mythes, cultes et société*. Centre de Recherches d'Histoire Ancienne 76. Paris.

Brumfield, A. Chandor. 1981. *The Attic Festivals of Demeter and Their Relation to the Agricultural Year*. Salem.

Bruneau, P. 1970. *Recherches sur les cultes de Délos à l'époque hellénistique et à l'époque impériale*. Paris.

Bubel, F. 1991. *Euripides. Andromeda*. Palingenesia 34. Stuttgart.

Bibliography

Bühler, K. 1934. *Sprachtheorie: Die Darstellungsfunktion der Sprache.* Jena.

Bulloch, A., Gruen, E. S., Long, A. A., and Stewart, A., eds. 1993. *Images and Ideologies: Self-Definition in the Hellenistic World.* Hellenistic Culture and Society 12. Berkeley.

Bundrick, S. D. 2005. *Music and Image in Classical Athens.* Cambridge.

Burkert, W. 1966. "Kekropidensage und Arrhephoria: Vom Initiationsritus zum Panathenäenfest." *Hermes* 94:1–25.

———. 1966a. "Greek Tragedy and Sacrificial Ritual." *GRBS* 7:87–121.

———. 1970. "Buzyge und Palladion: Gewalt und Gericht in altgriechischem Ritual." *Zeitschrift für Religions- und Geistesgeschichte* 22:356–368. Citations refer to Burkert 1990:77–85.

———. 1979. *Structure and History in Greek Mythology and Ritual.* Sather Classical Lectures 47. Berkeley.

———. 1982. "Götterspiel und Götterburleske in altorientalischen und griechischen Mythen." *Eranos-Jahrbuch* 51:335–367.

———. 1983. *Homo Necans: The Anthropology of Ancient Greek Sacrificial Ritual and Myth.* Trans. P. Bing. Berkeley.

———. 1985. *Greek Religion: Archaic and Classical.* Trans. J. Raffan. Cambridge, MA.

———. 1987. "Die antike Stadt als Festgemeinschaft." In *Stadt und Fest: Zu Geschichte und Gegenwart europäischer Festkultur* (eds. P. Hugger, W. Burkert, and E. Lichtenhahn), 25–44. Stuttgart.

———. 1987a. "The Making of Homer in the Sixth Century B.C.: Rhapsodes versus Stesichorus." In *Papers on the Amasis Painter and His World* (eds. M. True, C. Hudson, A. P. A. Belloli, B. Gilman et al.), 43–62. Malibu.

———. 1990. *Wilder Ursprung: Opferritual und Mythos bei den Griechen.* Kleine Kulturwissenschaftliche Bibliothek 22. Berlin.

———. 1992. *The Orientalizing Revolution: Near Eastern Influence on Greek Culture in the Early Archaic Age.* Trans. M. E. Pinder and W. Burkert. Cambridge, MA.

———. 1994. "Griechische Hymnoi." In *Hymnen der Alten Welt im Kulturvergleich* (eds. W. Burkert and F. Stolz), 9–17. Orbis biblicus et orientalis 131. Freiburg.

———. 1996. *Creation of the Sacred: Tracks of Biology in Early Religions.* Cambridge, MA.

Buschor, E. 1923/24. "Das Schirmfest." *JdI* 38/39:128–132.

Butler, J. 1988. "Performative Acts and Gender Constitution: An Essay in Phenomenology and Feminist Theory." *Theatre Journal* 40:519–531.

Calame, C. 1977. *Les chœurs de jeunes filles en Grèce archaïque,* I–II. Filologia e critica 20–21. Rome.

———. 1983. *Alcman.* Rome.

———. 1989. "Démasquer par le masque: Effets énonciatifs dans la comédie ancienne." *Revue de l'Histoire des Religions* 206:357–376.

———. 1990. *Thésée et l'imaginaire athénien: Légende et culte en Grèce antique.* Lausanne.

———. 1992. "Prairies intouchées et jardins d'Aphrodite: Espaces 'initiatiques' en Grèce." In Moreau 1992a:103–118.

——. 1992a. "Narration légendaire et programme poétique dans l'*Hymne à Apollon* de Callimaque." *Études de Lettres* 4:41–65.

——. 1994/95. "From Choral Poetry to Tragic Stasimon: The Enactment of Women's Song." *Arion* 3rd ser. 3:136–154.

——. 1995. *The Craft of Poetic Speech in Ancient Greece.* Trans. J. Orion. Myth and Poetics. Ithaca.

——. 1995a. "Variations énonciatives, relations avec les dieux et fonctions poétiques dans les *Hymnes homériques*." *Museum Helveticum* 52:2–19.

——. 1997. *Choruses of Young Women in Ancient Greece: Their Morphology, Religious Role, and Social Function.* Trans. D. Collins and J. Orion. Greek Studies: Interdisciplinary Approaches. Lanham, MD.

——. 1999. "Performative Aspects of the Choral Voice in Greek Tragedy: Civic Identity in Performance." In Goldhill and Osborne 1999:125–153.

——. 1999a. *The Poetics of Eros in Ancient Greece.* Trans. J. Lloyd. Princeton.

——. 1999b. "Indigenous and Modern Perspectives on Tribal Initiation Rites: Education According to Plato." In *Rites of Passage in Ancient Greece: Literature, Religion, Society* (ed. M. W. Padilla), 278–312. Bucknell Review. Lewisburg, PA.

——. 2004. "Choral Forms in Aristophanic Comedy: Musical Mimesis and Dramatic Performance in Classical Athens." In *Music and the Muses: The Culture of 'Mousikê' in the Classical Athenian City* (eds. P. Murray and P. Wilson), 157–184. Oxford.

——. 2005. "The Tragic Choral Group: Dramatic Roles and Social Functions." In *A Companion to Tragedy* (ed. R. Bushnell), 215–233. Malden, MA.

Calder, W. M., III, ed. 1991. *The Cambridge Ritualists Reconsidered.* Illinois Classical Studies supplement 2. Atlanta.

Campbell, D. A. 1993. *Greek Lyric V.* Loeb Classical Library 144. Cambridge, MA.

Camps-Gaset, M. 1994. *L'année des Grecs: La fête et le mythe.* Centre de Recherches d'Histoire Ancienne 131. Paris.

Carey, C. 1991. "The Victory Ode in Performance: The Case for the Chorus." *CP* 86:192–200.

Carpenter, T. H. 1993. "On the Beardless Dionysus." In Carpenter and Faraone 1993:185–206.

Carpenter, T. H., and Faraone, C. A., eds. 1993. *Masks of Dionysus.* Myth and Poetics. Ithaca.

Carrière, J. C. 1979. *Le carnaval et la politique: Une introduction à la comédie grecque suivie d'un choix de fragments.* Centre de Recherches d'Histoire Ancienne 26. Paris.

Carson, A. 1990. "Putting Her in Her Place: Woman, Dirt, and Desire." In Halperin, Winkler, and Zeitlin 1990:135–169.

Carter, J. B. 1988. "Masks and Poetry in Early Sparta." In Hägg, Marinatos, and Nordquist 1988:89–98.

Cartledge, P. 1981. "The Politics of Spartan Pederasty." *PCPS* n.s. 27:17–36.

Casabona, J. 1966. *Recherches sur le vocabulaire des sacrifices en Grec des origines à la fin de l'époque classique*. Aix-en-Provence.

Casadio, G. 1987. "Antropologia orfico-dionisiaca nel culto di Tebe, Corinto e Sicione." In *Sangue e antropologia biblica nella liturgia. Atti della V Settimana di Studi "Sangue e Antropologia. Riti e culto", Rome, 26 novembre–1 dicembre 1984* (ed. F. Vattioni), 191–260. Rome.

———. 1999. *Il vino dell'anima: Storia del culto di Dioniso a Corinto, Sicione, Trezene*. Biblioteca di Storia delle Religioni 1. Rome.

Caskey, L. D., and Beazley, J. D., eds. 1954. *Attic Vase Paintings in the Museum of Fine Arts, Boston*, II. Oxford.

Cassio, A. C., and Cerri, G., eds. 1991. *L'inno tra rituale e letteratura nel mondo antico. Atti di un colloquio, Napoli 21–24 ottobre 1991*. AION, filol. 13. Rome.

Ceccarelli, P. 1995. "Le dithyrambe et la pyrrhique: À propos de la nouvelle liste de vainqueurs aux Dionysies de Cos (Segre, ED 234)." *ZPE* 108:287–305.

———. 1995a. "Le tissage, la mémoire et la nymphe: Une récente lecture de *l'Odyssée*." *Dialogues d'Histoire Ancienne* 21:181–191.

———. 1998. *La pirrica nell'antichità greco romana: Studi sulla danza armata*. Filologia e critica 83. Rome.

Chapman, G. A. H. 1983. "Some Notes on Dramatic Illusion in Aristophanes." *AJP* 104:1–23.

Chirassi Colombo, I. 1979. "*Paides e Gynaikes*: Note per una tassonomia del comportamento rituale nella cultura attica." *QUCC* n.s. 1:25–58.

Cingano, E. 1986. "Il valore dell'espressione στάσις μελῶν in Aristofane, *Rane*, v. 1281." *QUCC* n.s. 24:139–143.

———. 1993. "Indizi di esecuzione corale in Stesicoro." In Pretagostini 1993:347–361.

Clark, C. A. 1996. "The Gendering of the Body in Alcman's *Partheneion* 1: Narrative, Sex, and Social Order in Archaic Sparta." *Helios* 23.2:143–172.

Clay, D. 1991. "Alcman's *Partheneion*." *QUCC* n.s. 39:47–67.

———. 2004. *Archilochos Heros: The Cult of Poets in the Greek Polis*. Cambridge, MA.

Clinton, K. 1988. "Sacrifice at the Eleusinian Mysteries." In Hägg, Marinatos, and Nordquist 1988:69–80.

———. 1992. *Myth and Cult: The Iconography of the Eleusinian Mysteries*. Acta Instituti Atheniensis Regni Sueciae 8°, 11. Stockholm.

Cole, S. Guettel. 1984. "The Social Function of Rituals of Maturation: The Koureion and the Arkteia." *ZPE* 55:233–244.

———. 1993. "Procession and Celebration at the Dionysia." In *Theater and Society in the Classical World* (ed. R. Scodel), 25–38. Ann Arbor.

Comotti, G. 1989. "L'*anabolé* e il ditirambo." *QUCC* n.s. 31:107–117.

Compton, T. M. 2006. *Victim of the Muses: Poet as Scapegoat, Warrior, and Hero in Greco-Roman and Indo-European Myth and History*. Hellenic Studies 11. Washington, D.C.

Connor, W. R. 1987. "Tribes, Festivals, and Processions: Civic Ceremonial and Political Manipulation in Archaic Greece." *JHS* 107:40–50.

———. 1988. "Seized by the Nymphs: Nympholepsy and Symbolic Expression in Classical Greece." *CA* 7:155–189.

———. 1988a. "Early Greek Land Warfare as Symbolic Expression." *Past & Present* 119:3–29.

———. 1989. "City Dionysia and Athenian Democracy." *Classica et Mediaevalia* 40:7–32.

Contiades-Tsitsoni, E. 1990. *Hymenaios und Epithalamion: Das Hochzeitslied in der frühgriechischen Lyrik*. BzA 16. Stuttgart.

Cornford, F. M. 1961². *The Origin of Attic Comedy* (ed. T. H. Gaster). Garden City, NY. 2nd ed., with introduction by J. Henderson, Ann Arbor 1993.

Cowan, J. K. 1990. *Dance and the Body Politic in Northern Greece*. Princeton.

Craik, E. M. 1987. "'One for the Pot': Aristophanes' *Birds* and the Anthesteria." *Eranos* 85:25–34.

Crusius, O. 1894. *Die delphischen Hymnen: Untersuchungen über Texte und Melodien*. Göttingen.

Csapo, E. 1997. "Riding the Phallus for Dionysus: Iconology, Ritual, and Gender-Role De/Construction." *Phoenix* 51:253–295.

———. 1999/2000. "Later Euripidean Music." *Illinois Classical Studies* 24/25:399–426.

———. 2003. "The Dolphins of Dionysus." In *Poetry, Theory, Praxis: The Social Life of Myth, Word, and Image in Ancient Greece. Essays in Honour of William J. Slater* (eds. E. Csapo and M. C. Miller), 69–98. Oxford.

Csapo, E., and Slater, W. J. 1995. *The Context of Ancient Drama*. Ann Arbor.

Culler, J. 1982. *On Deconstruction: Theory and Criticism after Structuralism*. Ithaca.

Dahl, K. 1976. *Thesmophoria: En græsk kvindefest*. Opuscula Graecolatina 6. Copenhagen.

Dale, A. M. 1969. "Words, Music, and Dance." In *Collected Papers*, 156–169. Cambridge.

D'Alessio, G. B. 1994. "First-Person Problems in Pindar." *BICS* 39:117–139.

———. 2004. "Past Future, and Present Past: Temporal Deixis in Greek Archaic Lyric." *Arethusa* 37:267–294.

Danforth, L. M. 1982. *The Death Rituals of Rural Greece*. Princeton.

Danielewicz, J. 1990. "Deixis in Greek Choral Lyric." *QUCC* n.s. 34:7–17.

d'Aquili, E. G., and Laughlin Jr., C. D. 1979. "The Neurobiology of Myth and Ritual." In d'Aquili, Laughlin, and McManus 1979:152–182 .

d'Aquili, E. G., Laughlin Jr., C. D., and McManus, J., eds. 1979. *The Spectrum of Ritual: A Biogenetic Structural Analysis*. New York.

Davidson, J. F. 1986. "The Circle and the Tragic Chorus." *Greece & Rome* 33:38–46.

De Angeli, S. 1988. "*Mimesis e Techne*." *QUCC* n.s. 28:27–45.

De Falco, V. 1958. "Osservazioni sull'iporchema in Sofocle." In *Studi sul teatro greco* (ed. V. De Falco), 56–88. Naples.

Degani, E. 1987. "Insulto ed escrologia in Aristofane." *Dioniso* 57:31–47.

——. 1988. "Giambo e commedia." In *La polis e il suo teatro* (ed. E. Corsini), II:157–179. Padova.

——. 1993. "Aristofane e la tradizione dell'invettiva personale in Grecia." In Bremer and Handley 1993:1–36.

Delavaud-Roux, M.-H. 1993. *Les danses armées en Grèce antique.* Aix-en-Provence.

——. 1995. "L'énigme des danseurs barbus au parasol et les vases 'des Lénéennes.'" *Révue Archéologique* 1995:227–263.

Derrida, J. 1976. *Of Grammatology.* Trans. G. C. Spivak. Baltimore.

des Bouvrie, S. 1990. *Women in Greek Tragedy: An Anthropological Approach.* Symbolae Osloenses supplement 27. Oslo.

——. 1993. "Creative Euphoria: Dionysos and the Theatre." *Kernos* 6:79–112.

Detienne, M. 1971. "Orphée au miel." *QUCC* 12:7–23.

——. 1979. "Violentes 'eugénies'. En pleines Thesmophories: Des femmes couvertes de sang." In *La cuisine du sacrifice en pays grec* (eds. M. Detienne and J.-P. Vernant), 183–214. Paris.

——. 1988. "Les Danaïdes entre elles ou la violence fondatrice du mariage." *Arethusa* 21:159–175.

Deubner, L. 1932. *Attische Feste.* Berlin.

Diehl, E. 1914. "Hyporchema." *RE* 9:338–343.

——, ed. 1925. *Anthologia Lyrica Graeca* I–II, Leipzig 1925; I, 1–3, curavit R. Beutler, Leipzig 1949–1952[3]; I, 4–II, 5; 6, Leipzig 1935–1940[2]; *Suppl. Addenda et corrigenda fasc. 1–6,* Leipzig 1942[2]. (= D.)

Dillon, M. P. J. 1999. "Post-Nuptial Sacrifices on Kos (Segre, *ED* 178) and Ancient Greek Marriage Rites." *ZPE* 124:63–80.

Di Marco, M. 1981. "Aristoph. Plut. 800: Δεξίνικος." *Bollettino dei Classici* 3rd ser. 2:158–165.

Dobrov, G. W. 2001. *Figures of Play: Greek Drama and Metafictional Poetics.* Oxford.

Dodd, D. B., and Faraone, C. A., eds. 2003. *Initiation in Ancient Greek Rituals and Narratives: New Critical Perspectives.* London.

Dodds, E. R. 1960[2]. *Euripides. Bacchae.* 2nd ed. Oxford.

Donnay, G. 1997. "L'Arrhéphorie: Initiation ou rite civique? Un cas d'école." *Kernos* 10:177–205.

Dorati, M. 1998. "Lisistrata e la tessitura." *QUCC* n.s. 58:41–56.

Dorsch, K.-D. 1983. *Götterhymnen in den Chorliedern der griechischen Tragiker: Form, Inhalt und Funktion.* Ph.D. diss., Westfälische Wilhelms Universität. Münster.

Dover, K. J. 1972. *Aristophanic Comedy.* Berkeley.

——. 1989[2]. *Greek Homosexuality,* Cambridge, MA.

——. 1993. "The Chorus of Initiates in Aristophanes' *Frogs.*" In Bremer and Handley 1993:173–193.

Dowden, K. 1989. *Death and the Maiden: Girls' Initiation Rites in Greek Mythology.* London.

———. 1997. "The Amazons: Development and Functions." *RhM* 140:97–128.

duBois, P. 1982. *Centaurs and Amazons: Women and the Pre-History of the Great Chain of Being.* Ann Arbor.

———. 1988. "Inscription, the Law, and the Comic Body." *Métis* 3:69–84.

Ducrot, O., and Todorov, T. 1972. *Dictionnaire encyclopédique des sciences du langage.* Paris.

Durand, J.-L., and Frontisi-Ducroux, F. 1982. "Idoles, figures, images: Autour de Dionysos." *Révue Archéologique* 1982:81–108.

Easterling, P. E. 1988. "Tragedy and Ritual: 'Cry "Woe, woe," but may the good prevail!'" *Métis* 3:87–109.

———. 1997. "A Show for Dionysus." In *The Cambridge Companion to Greek Tragedy* (ed. P. E. Easterling), 36–53. Cambridge.

Edmunds, L., and Wallace, R. W., eds. 1997. *Poet, Public, and Performance in Ancient Greece.* Baltimore.

Edwards, A. T. 1991. "Aristophanes' Comic Poetics: Τρύξ, Scatology, Σκῶμμα." *TAPA* 121:157–179.

Eitrem, S. 1915. *Opferritus und Voropfer der Griechen und Römer.* Kristiania.

Enger, R. 1846. "Zu Aristophanes Thesmophoriazusen." *RhM* n.F. 4:49–75.

Erken, G. 1997. "Regietheater und griechische Tragödie." In *Tragödie: Idee und Transformation* (ed. H. Flashar), 368–386. Colloquium Rauricum 5. Stuttgart.

Evans-Pritchard, E. E. 1928. "The Dance." *Africa* 1:446–462.

Faraone, C. A. 1985. "Aeschylus' ὕμνος δέσμιος (*Eum.* 306) and Attic Judicial Curse Tablets." *JHS* 105:150–154 .

———. 1993. "Molten Wax, Spilt Wine, and Mutilated Animals: Sympathetic Magic in Near Eastern and Early Greek Oath Ceremonies." *JHS* 113: 60–80.

———. 1995. "The 'Performative Future' in Three Hellenistic Incantations and Theocritus' Second *Idyll.*" *CP* 90:1–15.

———. 1997. "Salvation and Female Heroics in the Parodos of Aristophanes' *Lysistrata.*" *JHS* 117:38–59.

Farnell, L. R. 1907. *The Cults of the Greek States* III. Oxford.

Fauth, W. 1964. "Athena." *Kl. Pauly* 1:681–686.

Fehling, D. 1974. *Ethologische Überlegungen auf dem Gebiet der Altertumskunde.* Munich.

Felson, N., ed. 2004. *The Poetics of Deixis in Alcman, Pindar, and Other Lyric.* Special issue, *Arethusa* 37:253–466. Baltimore.

Ferrari, G. 2002. *Figures of Speech: Men and Maidens in Ancient Greece.* Chicago.

———. 2008. *Alcman and the Cosmos of Sparta.* Chicago.

Ferris, L. 1989. *Acting Women: Images of Women in Theatre.* New York.

Finnegan, R. 1969. "How to Do Things with Words: Performative Utterances among the Limba of Sierra Leone." *Man* 4:537–552.

Firth, J. R. 1957. "Ethnographic Analysis and Language with Reference to Malinowski's Views." In *Man and Culture: An Evaluation of the Work of Bronislaw Malinowski* (ed. R. Firth), 93–118. London.

Fischer-Lichte, E. 1983. *Semiotik des Theaters: Eine Einführung, I: Das System der theatralischen Zeichen.* Tübingen. 1994³.

——. 1998. "Grenzgänge und Tauschhandel: Auf dem Wege zu einer performativen Kultur." In *Theater seit den 60er Jahren: Grenzgänge der Neo-Avantgarde* (eds. E. Fischer-Lichte, F. Kreuder, and I. Pflug), 1–20. Tübingen.

——. 1998a. "Verwandlung als ästhetische Kategorie: Zur Entwicklung einer neuen Ästhetik des Performativen." In *Theater seit den 60er Jahren: Grenzgänge der Neo-Avantgarde* (eds. E. Fischer-Lichte, F. Kreuder, and I. Pflug), 21–91. Tübingen.

——. 1999. "Für eine Ästhetik des Performativen." In *Literaturforschung heute* (eds. E Goebel and W. Klein), 221–228. Berlin.

——. 2004. *Ästhetik des Performativen.* Frankfurt.

Fischer-Lichte, E. and Wulf, C., eds. 2001. *Theorien des Performativen.* Paragrana 10. Berlin.

Fisher, N. R. E. 1992. *Hybris: A Study in the Values of Honour and Shame in Ancient Greece.* Warminster.

——. 1993. "Multiple Personalities and Dionysiac Festivals: Dicaeopolis in Aristophanes' *Acharnians." Greece & Rome* 40:31–47.

Fitton, J. W. 1973. "Greek Dance." *CQ* n.s. 23:254–74.

Flashar, H. 1976. "Die Handlungsstruktur des *König Ödipus." Poetica* 8:355–359.

——. 1977. "König Ödipus: Drama und Theorie." *Gymnasium* 84:120–136.

——. 1979. "Die klassizistische Theorie der Mimesis." In *Le classicisme à Rome aux Iers siècles avant et après J.-C.* (ed. H. Flashar), 79–97. Entretiens sur l'antiquité classique 25. Vandœuvres-Geneva.

——. 1991. *Inszenierung der Antike: Das griechische Drama auf der Bühne der Neuzeit 1585–1990.* Munich.

——. 1994. "Aristoteles, Das Lachen und die Alte Komödie." In *Laughter Down the Centuries, I* (eds. S. Jäkel and A. Timonen), 59–70. Annales Universitatis Turkuensis B 208. Turku.

——. 1996. "Komik und Alte Komödie." *Museum Helveticum* 53:83–90.

Fluck, H. 1931. *Skurrile Riten in griechischen Kulten.* Ph.D. diss., University of Freiburg.

Foley, H. P. 1981. "The Conception of Women in Athenian Drama." In Foley 1981a:127–168.

——, ed. 1981a. *Reflections of Women in Antiquity.* New York.

——. 1982. "The 'Female Intruder' Reconsidered: Women in Aristophanes' *Lysistrat* and *Ecclesiazusae." CP* 77:1–21.

——. 1992. "*Anodos* Dramas: Euripides' *Alcestis* and *Helen.*" In Hexter and Selden 1992:133–160.

———. 2003. "Choral Identity in Greek Tragedy." *CP* 98:1–30.

Foster, M. L., and Brandes, S. H., eds. 1980. *Symbol as Sense: New Approaches to the Analysis of Meaning.* New York.

Foucault, M. 1979. *Discipline and Punish: The Birth of the Prison.* Trans. A. Sheridan. New York.

Fraenkel, E. 1931. "Der Zeushymnus im Agamemnon des Aischylos." *Philologus* 86:1–17.

———. 1962. *Beobachtungen zu Aristophanes.* Rome.

Frank, M. 1984. *Was ist Neostrukturalismus?* Frankfurt.

Fraser, P. M. 1972. *Ptolemaic Alexandria,* I–III. Oxford.

Freidenberg, O. M. 1974. "The Origin of Parody." In Baran 1974:269–283.

Friedrich, R. 1983. "Drama and Ritual." In *Drama and Religion* (ed. J. Redmond), 159–223. Themes in Drama 5. Cambridge.

Frontisi-Ducroux, F., and Lissarrague, F. 1990. "From Ambiguity to Ambivalence: A Dionysiac Excursion through the 'Anakreontic' Vases." In Halperin, Winkler, and Zeitlin 1990:211–256.

Furley, W. D. 1993. "Types of Greek Hymns." *Eos* 81:21–41.

———. 1994. "Apollo Humbled: Phoenix' Koronisma in Its Hellenistic Literary Setting." *Materiali e discussioni per l'analisi dei testi classici* 33: 9–31.

———. 1995. "Praise and Persuasion in Greek Hymns." *JHS* 115:29–46 .

Furley, W. D., and Bremer, J. M. 2001. *Greek Hymns,* I–II. Studien und Texte zu Antike und Christentum 9–10. Tübingen.

Gadamer, H.-G. 1992. "Zur Phänomenologie von Ritual und Sprache." In H.-G. Gadamer, *Gesammelte Werke* VIII: *Ästhetik und Poetik I. Kunst als Aussage,* 400–440. Tübingen.

Gamel, M.-K., ed. 2002. *Performing/Transforming Aristophanes'* Thesmophoriazuae. Special issue, *AJP* 123.3.

Gannon, J. F. 1982. *Thesmophoriazusae restitutae: An Essay in Annotation and Interpretation.* Ph.D. diss., Yale University.

Gardiner, C. P. 1987. *The Sophoclean Chorus: A Study of Character and Function.* Iowa City.

Gardner, D. S. 1983. "Performativity in Ritual: The Mianmin Case." *Man* 18:346–360.

Garvie, A. F. 1965. "A Note on the Deity of Alcman's *Partheneion.*" *CQ* n.s. 15:185–187.

Geertz, C. 1973. *The Interpretation of Cultures: Selected Essays.* New York.

Gellrich, M. 1995. "Interpreting Greek Tragedy: History, Theory, and the New Philoloy." In *History, Tragedy, Theory: Dialogues on Athenian Drama* (ed. B. Goff), 38–58. Austin.

Gelzer, T. 1960. *Der epirrhematische Agon bei Aristophanes: Untersuchungen zur Struktur der attischen Alten Komödie.* Zetemata 20. Munich.

—. 1966. "Dionysisches und Phantastisches in der Komödie des Aristophanes." In *Wandlungen des Paradiesischen und Utopischen: Studien zum Bild eines Ideals*, 39–78. Probleme der Kunstwissenschaft 2. Berlin.

—. 1970. "Aristophanes" (Nachträge). *RE* supplement 12:1392–1569.

—. 1972. "Alte Komödie und hohe Lyrik: Bemerkungen zu den Oden in Pap. Oxy. 2737." *Museum Helveticum* 29:141–152.

—. 1992. "Die Alte Komödie in Athen und die Basler Fastnacht." In *Klassische Antike und neue Wege der Kulturwissenschaften. Symposium Karl Meuli, Basel, 11.-13. September 1991* (ed. F. Graf), 29–61. Basel.

—. 1993. "Feste Strukturen in der Komödie des Aristophanes." In Bremer and Handley 1993:51–90.

Gentili, B. 1952. *La metrica dei Greci*. Messina.

—. 1976. "Il Partenio di Alcmane e l'amore omoerotico femminile nei tiasi spartani." *QUCC* 22:59–67.

—. 1977. *Lo spettacolo nel mondo antico: Teatro ellenistico e teatro romano arcaico.* Rome. 2006².

—. 1984. *Poesia e pubblico nella Grecia antica da Omero al V secolo*. Rome.

—. 1984/85. "Il coro tragico nella teoria degli antichi." *Dioniso* 55:17–35.

—. 1990. "Die pragmatischen Aspekte der archaischen griechischen Dichtung." *A&A* 36:1–17.

—. 1990a. "L' 'io' nella poesia lirica greca." *AION*, filol. 12:9–24.

—. 1991. "*Addendum*. A proposito del Partenio di Alcmane." *QUCC* n.s. 39:69–70.

Gentili, B., and Lomiento, L. 2003. *Metrica e ritmica: Storia delle forme poetiche nella Grecia antica*. Milan.

Gentili, B., and Perusino, F., eds. 1995. *Mousike: Metrica, ritmica e musica greca in memoria di Giovanni Comotti*. Pisa.

—, eds. 2002. *Le orse di Brauron: Un rituale di iniziazione femminile nel santuario di Artemide*. Pisa.

Gerber, D. E. 1994. "Greek Lyric Poetry since 1920, part II: From Alcman to Fragmenta Adespota." *Lustrum* 36:7–188.

Ghiron-Bistagne, P. 1976. *Recherches sur les acteurs dans la Grèce antique*. Paris.

Giangrande, G. 1963. "The Origin of the Attic Comedy." *Eranos* 61:1–24.

Gilula, D. 1996. "A Singularly Gifted Actor (Ar. *Th.* 1056–1096)." *Quaderni di Storia* 44:159–164.

Ginsburg, R. 1989. "Karneval und Fasten: Exzeß und Mangel in der Sprache des Körpers." *Poetica* 21:26–42 .

Ginzburg, C. 1989. *Hexensabbat: Entzifferung einer nächtlichen Geschichte*. Trans. M. Kempter. Berlin. Reprinted Frankfurt a. M. 1993.

Glei, R. 1992. "Aristoteles über Linsenbrei: Intertextualität und Gattungsgenese am Beispiel der antiken Parodie." *Philologus* 136:42–59.

Goffman, E. 1959. *The Presentation of Self in Everyday Life*. New York.

Golder, H. 1996. "Making a Scene: Gesture, Tableau, and the Tragic Chorus." *Arion* 3rd ser. 4:1–19.

Goldhill, S. 1984. *Language, Sexuality, Narrative: The* Oresteia. Cambridge.

——. 1986. *Reading Greek Tragedy.* Cambridge.

——. 1987. "The Great Dionysia and Civic Ideology." *JHS* 107:58–76.

——. 1991. *The Poet's Voice: Essays on Poetics and Greek Literature.* Cambridge.

——. 1996. "Collectivity and Otherness: The Authority of the Tragic Chorus. Response to Gould." In Silk 1996:244–256.

——. 1999. "Programme Notes." In Goldhill and Osborne 1999:1–29.

Goldhill, S., and Osborne, R., eds. 1999. *Performance Culture and Athenian Democracy.* Cambridge .

Gould, J. 1980. "Law, Custom, and Myth: Aspects of the Social Position of Women in Classical Athens." *JHS* 100:38–59.

——. 1996. "Tragedy and Collective Experience." In Silk 1996:217–243.

Gow, A. S. F. 1950/52. *Theocritus,* I–II. Cambridge.

Graf, F. 1980. "Milch, Honig und Wein: Zum Verständnis der Libation im griechischen Ritual." In *Perennitas. Studi in onore di Angelo Brelich,* 209–221. Rome.

——. 1984. "Women, War, and Warlike Divinities." *ZPE* 55:245–254.

——. 1985. *Nordionische Kulte: Religionsgeschichtliche und epigraphische Untersuchungen zu den Kulten von Chios, Erythrai, Klazomenai und Phokaia.* Bibliotheca Helvetica Romana 21. Rome.

——. 1996. *Gottesnähe und Schadenzauber: Die Magie in der griechisch-römischen Antike.* Munich.

——. 1998. "Die kultischen Wurzeln des antiken Schauspiels." In Binder and Effe 1998:11–32.

Grandolini, S. 1991. "Canto processionale e culto nell'antica Grecia." In Cassio and Cerri 1991:125–140.

——. 1995. "Sophocl. *Trach.* 205–24: Peana, ditirambo o iporchema?" *Giornale Italiano di Filologia* 47:249–260.

Greimas, A. J., and Courtés, J. 1979/86. *Sémiotique: Dictionnaire raisonné de la théorie du langage,* I–II. Paris.

Griffith, J. G. 1970. "ΛΗΚΥΘΙΟΝ ΑΠΩΛΕΣΕΝ: A Postscript." *HSCP* 74:43–44.

Griffiths, A. 1972. "Alcman's Partheneion: The Morning after the Night Before." *QUCC* 14:7–30.

Grohs, E. 1993. "Initiation." In *Handbuch religionswissenschaftlicher Grundbegriffe* (eds. H. Cancik, B. Gladigow, and K.-H. Kohl), III.238–249. Stuttgart.

Gruber, W. E. 1983. "Systematized Delirium: The Craft, Form, and Meaning of Aristophanic Comedy." *Helios* 10:97–111.

——. 1986. *Comic Theaters: Studies in Performance and Audience Response.* Athens, GA.

Guépin, J.-P. 1968. *The Tragic Paradox: Myth and Ritual in Greek Tragedy.* Amsterdam.

Habash, M. 1995. "Two Complementary Festivals in Aristophanes' *Acharnians*." *AJP* 116:559–577.

——. 1997. "The Odd Thesmophoria of Aristophanes' *Thesmophoriazusae*." *GRBS* 38:19–40.

Habicht, C. 1970². *Gottmenschentum und griechische Städte*. Zetemata 14. Munich.

——. 1995. *Athen: Die Geschichte der Stadt in hellenistischer Zeit*. Munich.

Hägg, R., Marinatos, N., and Nordquist, G. C., eds. 1988. *Early Greek Cult Practice. Proceedings of the Fifth International Symposium at the Swedish Institute at Athens, 26–29 June 1986*. Acta Instituti Atheniensis Regni Sueciae 4˚, 38. Stockholm.

Haldane, J. A. 1965. "A Scene in the *Thesmophoriazusae* (295–371)." *Philologus* 109:39–46.

Hall, E. M. 1989. "The Archer Scene in Aristophanes' *Thesmophoriazusae*." *Philologus* 133:38–54.

Halliwell, S. 1991. "Comic Satire and Freedom of Speech in Classical Athens." *JHS* 111:48–70.

——. 1991a. "The Uses of Laughter in Greek Culture." *CQ* n.s. 41:279–296.

Halperin, D. M, Winkler, J. J., and Zeitlin, F. I., eds. 1990. *Before Sexuality: The Construction of Erotic Experience in the Ancient Greek World*. Princeton.

Händel, P. 1963. *Formen und Darstellungsweisen in der aristophanischen Komödie*. Heidelberg.

Hanna, J. L. 1979. *To Dance is Human: A Theory of Nonverbal Communication*. Austin.

Hansen, H. 1976. "Aristophanes' *Thesmophoriazusae*: Theme, Structure, and Production." *Philologus* 120:165–185.

Harriott, R. M. 1986. *Aristophanes: Poet and Dramatist*. London.

Harrison, J. E. 1922³. *Prolegomena to the Study of Greek Religion*. Cambridge.

——. 1927². *Themis: A Study of the Social Origins of Greek Religion*. Cambridge.

Hartmann, E. von. 1887. *Philosophie des Schönen: Zweiter systematischer Theil der Aesthetik. Ausgewählte Werke: Wohlfeile Ausgabe*, IV.2. Berlin.

Harvey, A. E. 1955. "The Classification of Greek Lyric Poetry." *CQ* n.s. 5:157–175.

Havelock, E. A. 1963. *Preface to Plato*. Cambridge, MA.

——. 1986. *The Muse Learns to Write: Reflections on Orality and Literacy from Antiquity to the Present*. New Haven.

Headlam, W. 1906. "The Last Scene of the *Eumenides*." *JHS* 26:268–277.

Heath, M. 1987. *Political Comedy in Aristophanes*. Hypomnemata 87. Göttingen.

——. 1988. "Receiving the κῶμος: The Context and Performance of Epinician." *AJP* 109:180–195.

Hedreen, G. 1994. "Silens, Nymphs, and Maenads." *JHS* 114:47–69.

Helbo, A. 1991. "Performance Studies." In Helbo, Johansen, Pavis, and Ubersfeld 1991:1–20.

Helbo, A., Johansen, J. D., Pavis, P., and Ubersfeld, A., eds. 1991. *Approaching Theatre*. Bloomington.

Hempfer, K. W. 1976. *Poststrukturale Texttheorie und narrative Praxis: Tel Quel und die Konstitution eines nouveau nouveau roman*. Romanica Monacensia 11. Munich.

Henderson, J. 1991². *The Maculate Muse: Obscene Language in Attic Comedy*. New York.

———. 1991a. "Women and the Athenian Dramatic Festivals." *TAPA* 121:133–147.

———. 1996. *Three Plays by Aristophanes: Staging Women*. New Classical Canon. New York.

Henkel, J. 1988. "Speech-Act Theory Revisited: Rule, Notions, and Reader-Oriented Criticism." *Poetics* 17:505–530.

Henrichs, A. 1969. "Die Mänaden von Milet." *ZPE* 4:223–241.

———. 1982. "Changing Dionysiac Identities." In *Jewish and Christian Self-Definition, III: Self-Definition in the Graeco-Roman World* (eds. B. F. Meyer and E. P. Sanders), 137–160 and 213–236. London.

———. 1983. "The 'Sobriety' of Oedipus: Sophocles *OC* 100 Misunderstood." *HSCP* 87:87–100.

———. 1984. "The Eumenides and Wineless Libations in the Derveni Papyrus." In *Atti del XVII Congresso Internazionale di Papirologia. Napoli, 19–26 maggio 1983*, II:255–268. Naples.

———. 1990. "Between Country and City: Cultic Dimensions of Dionysus in Athens and Attica." In *Cabinet of the Muses. Essays on Classical and Comparative Literature in Honor of Thomas G. Rosenmeyer* (eds. M. Griffith and D. J. Mastronarde), 257–277. Atlanta.

———. 1991. "Namenlosigkeit und Euphemismus: Zur Ambivalenz der chthonischen Mächte im attischen Drama." In *Fragmenta Dramatica: Beiträge zur Interpretation der griechischen Tragikerfragmente und ihrer Wirkungsgeschichte* (ed. H. Hofmann), 161–201. Göttingen.

———. 1993. "Gods in Action: The Poetics of Divine Performance in the Hymns of Callimachus." In *Callimachus* (eds. M. A. Harder, R. F. Regtuit, and G. C. Wakker), 127–147. Groningen.

———. 1993a. "Response" (to Part Two: "Identity and Crisis in Hellenistic Literature"), in Bulloch, Gruen, Long, and Stewart 1993:171–195.

———. 1994/95. "'Why Should I Dance?': Choral Self-Referentiality in Greek Tragedy." *Arion* 3rd ser. 3:56–111.

———. 1996. "*Warum soll ich denn tanzen?*" *Dionysisches im Chor der griechischen Tragödie*. Lectio Teubneriana 4. Stuttgart.

———. 1996a. "Dancing in Athens, Dancing on Delos: Some Patterns of Choral Projection in Euripides." *Philologus* 140:48–62.

———. 1999. "Demythologizing the Past, Mythicizing the Present: Myth, History and the Supernatural at the Dawn of the Hellenistic Period." In *From Myth to Reason?* (ed. R. Buxton), 223–248. Oxford.

Herington, J. 1985. *Poetry into Drama: Early Tragedy and the Greek Poetic Tradition*. Berkeley.

Herter, H. 1938. "Phales." *RE* 19:1666–1668.

——. 1938a. "Phallen." *RE* 19:1670–1672.

——. 1938b. "Phallophorie." *RE* 19:1673–1681.

——. 1938c. "Phallos." *RE* 19:1681–1748.

——. 1947. *Vom dionysischen Tanz zum komischen Spiel: Die Anfänge der attischen Komödie.* Iserlohn.

Hexter, R., and Selden, D., eds. 1992. *Innovations of Antiquity.* New York.

Hiller, E. 1874. "Über einige Personenbezeichnungen griechischer Dramen." *Hermes* 8:442–456.

Hoffman, R. J. 1989. "Ritual License and the Cult of Dionysus." *Athenaeum* n.s. 67:91–115.

Hofmann, H. 1976. *Mythos und Komödie: Untersuchungen zu den Vögeln des Aristophanes.* Spudasmata 33. Hildesheim.

Høibye, A.-B. 1995. "A Joke with the Inevitable: Men as Women and Women as Men in Aristophanes' Thesmophoriazousai and Ekklesiazousai." In *Greece & Gender* (eds. B. Berggreen and N. Marinatos), 43–54. Papers from the Norwegian Institute at Athens 2. Bergen.

Hölscher, U. 1989². *Die Odyssee: Epos zwischen Märchen und Roman.* Munich.

Hommel, H. 1949. "Tanzen und Spielen." *Gymnasium* 56:201–205.

Horn, W. 1970. *Gebet und Gebetsparodie in den Komödien des Aristophanes.* Erlanger Beiträge zur Sprach- und Kunstwissenschaft 38. Nuremberg.

Hose, M. 1990/91. *Studien zum Chor bei Euripides,* I–II. BzA 10, 20. Stuttgart.

Hubbard, T. K. 1991. *The Mask of Comedy: Aristophanes and the Intertextual Parabasis.* Cornell Studies in Classical Philology 51. Ithaca.

——. 1992. "Tragic Preludes: Aeschylus *Seven Against Thebes* 4–8." *Phoenix* 46:299–308.

Huizinga, J. 1955. *Homo Ludens: A Study of the Play Element in Culture.* New York.

Imperio, O. 2004. *Parabasi di Aristofane: Acarnesi, Cavalieri, Vespe, Uccelli.* Studi e commenti 13. Bari.

Iser, W. 1976. *Der Akt des Lesens: Theorie ästhetischer Wirkung.* Munich. 1994⁴.

——. 1976a. "Das Komische: Ein Kipp-Phänomen." In Preisendanz and Warning 1976:398–402.

Isler-Kerényi, C. 2004. *Civilizing Violence: Satyrs on Sixth-Century Greek Vases.* Orbis Biblicus et Orientalis 208. Fribourg.

Ivanov, V. V. 1974. "The Significance of M. M. Bakhtin's Ideas on Sign, Utterance, and Dialogue for Modern Semiotics (1)." In Baran 1974:310–367.

Jakobson, R. 1960. "(Closing Statement:) Linguistics and Poetics." In *Style in Language* (ed. T. A. Sebeok), 350–377. Cambridge, MA.

——. 1984. "Shifters, Verbal Categories, and the Russian Verb." In R. Jakobson, *Russian and Slavic Grammar: Studies, 1931–1981* (eds. L. R. Waugh and M. Halle), 41–58. Janua Linguarum, Series Maior 106. Berlin.

Jameson, M. H., Jordan, D. R., and Kotansky, R. D. 1993. *A Lex Sacra from Selinous.* Greek, Roman, and Byzantine Monographs 11. Durham.

Jeanmaire, H. 1939. *Couroi et Courètes: Essai sur l'éducation spartiate et sur les rites d'adolescence dans l'antiquité hellénique.* Lille.

Jensen, J. S. 1986. "Ritual between Art and Control." *Temenos* 22:109–128.

Johansen, J. Prytz. 1975. "The Thesmophoria as a Women's Festival." *Temenos* 11:78–87.

Johnson, B. 1980. *The Critical Difference: Essays in the Contemporary Rhetoric of Reading.* Baltimore.

Kachler, K. G. 1974. "Der Tanz im antiken Griechenland." *Antike Welt* 5.3:2–14.

Kaibel, G. 1899. *Comicorum Graecorum Fragmenta* I.1. Poetarum Graecorum Fragmenta 6.1. Berlin.

Kaimio, M. 1970. *The Chorus of Greek Drama within the Light of the Person and Number Used.* Commentationes Humanarum Litterarum 46. Helsinki.

—— et al. 2001. "Metatheatricality in the Greek Satyr-Play." *Arctos* 35:35–78.

Kamerbeek, J. C. 1967. "Notes sur quelques passages des *Thesmophories* d'Aristophane." In *ΚΩΜΩΙΔΟΤΡΑΓΗΜΑΤΑ. Studia Aristophanea Viri Aristophanei W. J. W. Koster in Honorem* (ed. R. E. H. Westendorp Boerma), 74–81. Amsterdam.

Kannicht, R., ed. 1969. *Euripides. Helena* I–II. Heidelberg.

——. 1989. "Thalia: Über den Zusammenhang zwischen Fest und Poesie bei den Griechen." In *Das Fest* (eds. W. Haug and R. Warning), 29–52. Poetik und Hermeneutik 14. Munich.

Käppel, L. 1992. *Paian: Studien zur Geschichte einer Gattung.* UaLG 37. Berlin.

——. 1999. "Die Rolle des Chores in der Orestie des Aischylos: Vom epischen Erzähler über das lyrische Ich zur dramatis persona." In Riemer and Zimmermann 1999:61–88.

Kenner, H. 1970. *Das Phänomen der verkehrten Welt in der griechisch-römischen Antike.* Aus Forschung und Kunst 8. Klagenfurt.

Keyßner, K. 1932. *Gottesvorstellung und Lebensauffassung im griechischen Hymnus.* Würzburger Studien zur Altertumswissenschaft 2. Stuttgart.

Kinzl, K. H. 1980. "Zur Vor- und Frühgeschichte der attischen Tragödie: Einige historische Überlegungen." *Klio* 62:177–190.

Kledt, A. 2004. *Die Entführung Kores: Studien zur athenisch-eleusinischen Demeterreligion.* Palingenesia 84. Stuttgart.

Kleinknecht, H. 1937. *Die Gebetsparodie in der Antike.* Tübinger Beiträge zur Altertumswissenschaft 28. Stuttgart.

——. 1937a. "Zur Parodie des Gottmenschentums bei Aristophanes." *Archiv für Religionswissenschaft* 34:294–313.

Klimek-Winter, R. 1993. *Andromedatragödien: Sophokles, Euripides, Livius Andronikos, Ennius, Accius. Text, Einleitung und Kommentar.* BzA 21. Stuttgart.

Knuf, J., and Schmitz, H. W. 1980. *Ritualisierte Kommunikation und Sozialstruktur.* Forschungsberichte des Instituts für Kommunikationsforschung und Phonetik der Universität Bonn 72. Hamburg.

Koch, K.-D. 1968. *Kritische Idee und Komisches Thema: Untersuchungen zur Dramaturgie und zum Ethos der Aristophanischen Komödie.* Schriften der Wittheit zu Bremen, N.F. 1. Bremen.

Koenen, L. 1969. "Eine Hypothesis zur *Auge* des Euripides und tegeatische Plynterien." *ZPE* 4:7–18.

Koester, H. 1835. "Commentatio de Graecae comoediae parabasi." In *Programm des Stralsunder Gymnasiums* (anläßlich der Examensfeier, 1.–2. Oktober 1835), 1–18. Stralsund.

Koller, H. 1954. *Die Mimesis in der Antike: Nachahmung, Darstellung, Ausdruck.* Dissertationes Bernenses, ser. I, fasc. 5. Bern.

——. 1963. *Musik und Dichtung im alten Griechenland.* Bern.

Kolster, G. H. 1829. *De parabasi, veteris comoediae Atticae parte antiquissima.* Altona.

Köpping, K. P. 1998. "Inszenierung und Transgression in Ritual und Theater: Grenzprobleme der performativen Ethnologie." In *Ethnologie und Inszenierung. Ansätze zur Theaterethnologie* (eds. B. E. Schmidt and M. Münzel), 45–85. Curupira 5. Marburg.

——. 2003. "Ritual and Theatre." In *The Oxford Encyclopedia of Theatre and Performance* (ed. D. Kennedy), 1139–1141. Oxford.

Körte, A. 1921. "Komödie (griechische)." *RE* 11:1207–1275.

Koster, W. J. W., ed. 1975. *Scholia in Aristophanem, pars I, fasc. 1A: Prolegomena de comoedia.* Groningen.

Kotsidu, H. 1991. *Die musischen Agone der Panathenäen in archaischer und klassischer Zeit: Eine historisch-archäologische Untersuchung.* Quellen und Forschungen zur Antiken Welt 8. Munich.

Kranz, W. 1919, "Die Urform der attischen Komödie und Tragödie." *NJbb* 43:145–168.

——. 1933. *Stasimon: Untersuchungen zu Form und Gehalt der griechischen Tragödie.* Berlin.

——. 1949. "Parabasis." *RE* 18:1124–1126.

Kraus, M. 1994. "Erzählzeit und erzählte Zeit im *König Ödipus* des Sophokles." In Bierl and Möllendorff 1994:289–299.

Kron, U. 1992. "Frauenfeste in Demeterheiligtümern: Das Thesmophorion von Bitalemi." *Archäologischer Anzeiger* 1992:611–650.

Krummen, E. 1990. *Pyrsos Hymnon: Festliche Gegenwart und mythisch-rituelle Tradition als Voraussetzung einer Pindarinterpretation (Isthmie 4, Pythie 5, Olympie 1 und 3).* UaLG 35. Berlin.

Kugelmeier, C. 1996. *Reflexe früher und zeitgenössischer Lyrik in der Alten attischen Komödie.* BzA 80. Stuttgart.

Kuhn, T. S. 1968. *The Structure of Scientific Revolutions.* Chicago.

Kuithan, J. W. 1808. *Versuch eines Beweises, dass wir in Pindars Siegeshymnen Urkomödien übrig haben, welche auf Gastmahlen gesungen wurden; und neue Grundideen in der Griechischen Prosodie.* Dortmund.

Kullmann, W. 1993. "Die 'Rolle' des euripideischen Pentheus: Haben die *Bakchen* eine 'metatheatralische' Bedeutung?" In *Philanthropia kai Eusebeia. Festschrift für Albrecht Dihle zum 70. Geburtstag* (eds. G. W. Most, H. Petersmann, and A. M. Ritter), 248–263. Göttingen.

Lada-Richards, I. 1997. "Neoptolemus and the Bow: Ritual *thea* and Theatrical Vision in Sophocles' *Philoctetes*." *JHS* 117:179–183.

——. 1998. "Staging the Ephebeia: Theatrical Role-Playing and Ritual Transition in Sophocles' *Philoctetes*." *Ramus* 27:1–26.

——. 1999. *Initiating Dionysus: Ritual and Theatre in Aristophanes'* Frogs. Oxford.

La Matina, M. 1987. "Donne in Aristofane: Appunti per una semiotica della esclusione." In *Donna e società* (ed. J. Vibaek), 77–89. Quaderni del circolo semiologico Siciliano 26–27. Palermo.

Lamer, H. 1922. "Komos." *RE* 11:1286–1304.

Lanza, D. 1983. "Lo spettacolo." In *Oralità, scrittura, spettacolo* (ed. M. Vegetti), 107–126. Introduzione alle culture antiche I. Turin.

Larson, J. 1995. *Greek Heroine Cults.* Wisconsin Studies in Classics. Madison.

——. 1997. "Handmaidens of Artemis?" *Classical Journal* 92:249–257.

Latacz, J. 1985. "Realität und Imagination: Eine neue Lyrik-Theorie und Sapphos φαίνεταί μοι κῆνος-Lied." *Museum Helveticum* 42:67–94.

——. 1993. *Einführung in die griechische Tragödie.* Göttingen.

Lattke, M. 1991. *Hymnus: Materialien zu einer Geschichte der antiken Hymnologie.* Freiburg.

Laughlin, C. D. 1990 ."Ritual and the Symbolic Function: A Summary of Biogenetic Structural Theory." *Journal of Ritual Studies* 4:15–39.

Lawler, L. B. 1945. "Διπλῆ, διποδία, διποδισμος in the Greek Dance." *TAPA* 76:59–73.

——. 1964. *The Dance in Ancient Greece.* London.

Lawson, J. C. 1910. *Modern Greek Folklore and Ancient Greek Religion.* Cambridge.

Leach, E. 1982. "Introduction." In M. I. Steblin-Kamenskij, *Myth.* Trans. M. P. Coote. 1–20. Ann Arbor.

Lee, K. H. 1997. *Euripides. Ion.* The Plays of Euripides. Warminster.

Lefkowitz, M. R. 1981. *The Lives of the Greek Poets.* London.

——. 1987. "Was Euripides an Atheist?" *Studi Italiani di Filologia Classica* (3 ser.) 5:149–166.

——. 1988. "Who Sang Pindar's Victory Odes?" *AJP* 109:1–11.

——. 1989. "'Impiety' and 'Atheism' in Euripides' Dramas." *CQ* n.s. 39:70–82.

——. 1991. *First-Person Fictions: Pindar's Poetic 'I.'* Oxford.

——. 1995. "The First Person in Pindar Reconsidered–Again." *BICS* 40:139–150.

Lehmann, H.-T. 1991. *Theater und Mythos: Die Konstitution des Subjekts im Diskurs der antiken Tragödie.* Stuttgart. 2001².

———. 1999. *Postdramatisches Theater*. Frankfurt.

Leinieks, V. 1996. *The City of Dionysos: A Study of Euripides' Bakchai*. BzA 88. Stuttgart.

Leitao, D. D. 1995. "The Perils of Leukippos: Initiatory Transvestism and Male Gender Ideology in the Ekdusia at Phaistos." *CA* 14:130–163.

Leonhardt, J. 1991. *Phalloslied und Dithyrambos: Aristoteles über den Ursprung des griechischen Dramas*. Abhandlungen der Heidelberger Akademie der Wissenschaften, philosophisch-historische Klasse 1991.4. Heidelberg.

Lesky, A. 1971³. *Geschichte der griechischen Literatur*. Bern.

———. 1972. *Die tragische Dichtung der Hellenen*. Göttingen.

Levine, D. 1987. "*Lysistrata and Bacchae*: Structure, Genre, and 'Women on Top.'" *Helios* 14:29–38.

Lewis, I. M., ed. 1977. *Symbols and Sentiments: Cross-Cultural Studies in Symbolism*. London.

Lincoln, B. 1979. "The Rape of Persephone: A Greek Scenario of Women's Initiation." *Harvard Theological Review* 72:223–235.

Lohr, G. 1986. *Körpertext: Historische Semiotik der komischen Praxis*. Opladen.

Lonnoy, M.-G. 1985. "Arès et Dionysos dans la tragédie grecque: Le rapprochement des contraires." *REG* 98:65–71.

Lonsdale, S. H. 1993. *Dance and Ritual Play in Greek Religion*. Baltimore.

Loraux, N. 1981. *Les enfants d'Athéna: Idées athéniennes sur la citoyenneté et la division des sexes*. Paris.

———. 1981a. "Le lit, la guerre." *L'Homme* 21:37–67.

Lord, A. B. 1960. *The Singer of Tales*. Harvard Studies in Comparative Literature 24. Cambridge, MA.

MacDowell, D. M. 1989. "Athenian Laws about Choruses." In *Symposion 1982: Vorträge zur griechischen und hellenistischen Rechtsgeschichte. Santander, 1.-4. September 1982* (ed. F. J. Fernández Nieto), 65–77. Akten der Gesellschaft für griechische und hellenistische Rechtsgeschichte 5. Cologne.

———. 1995. *Aristophanes and Athens: An Introduction to the Plays*. Oxford.

MacLachlan, B. 1993. *The Age of Grace: Charis in Early Greek Poetry*. Princeton.

Maehler, H. 1963. *Die Auffassung des Dichterberufs im frühen Griechentum bis zur Zeit Pindars*. Hypomnemata 3. Göttingen.

Malinowski, B. 1935. *Coral Gardens and Their Magic: A Study of the Methods of Tilling the Soil and of Agricultural Rites in the Tobriand Islands, II: The Language of Magic and Gardening*. London.

Marcadé, J. 1969. *Au musée de Délos: Étude sur la sculpture hellénistique en ronde bosse découverte dans l'île*. Paris.

Martin, R. P. 1989. *The Language of Heroes: Speech and Performance in the* Iliad. Myth and Poetics. Ithaca.

Marzullo, B. 1953. "Strepsiade." *Maia* 6:99–124.

Massenzio, M. 1972. "La poesia come fine: La desacralizzazione della tragedia. Considerazioni sulla 'Poetica' di Aristotele." *Religioni e civiltà* 1:285–318.

Mastromarco, G. 1987. "La parabasi aristofanea tra realtà e poesia." *Dioniso* 57:75–93.

Mastronarde, D. J. 1994. *Euripides. Phoenissae.* Cambridge Classical Texts and Commentaries 29. Cambridge.

Mathews, G. 1997. "Aristophanes' 'High' Lyrics Reconsidered." *Maia* 49:1–42.

Mazon, P. 1904. *Essai sur la composition des comédies d'Aristophane.* Paris.

Meier, C. 1980. *Die Entstehung des Politischen bei den Griechen.* Frankfurt.

——. 1985. *Politik und Anmut.* Berlin.

Merkelbach, R. 1972. "Aglauros (Die Religion der Epheben)." *ZPE* 9:277–283.

——. 1988. *Die Hirten des Dionysos: Die Dionysos-Mysterien der römischen Kaiserzeit und der bukolische Roman des Longus.* Stuttgart.

Meuli, K. 1975. *Gesammelte Schriften* (ed. T. Gelzer). Basel.

Miller, M. C. 1992. "The Parasol: An Oriental Status-Symbol in Late Archaic and Classical Athens." *JHS* 112:91–105.

——. 1997. *Athens and Persians in the Fifth Century BC: A Study in Cultural Receptivity.* Cambridge.

——. 1999. "Reexamining Transvestism in Archaic and Classical Athens: The Zewadski Stamnos." *American Journal of Archaeology* 103:223–253.

Mitsdörffer, W. 1954. "Das Mnesilochoslied in Aristophanes' Thesmophoriazusen." *Philologus* 98:59–93.

Möllendorff, P. von. 1995. *Grundlagen einer Ästhetik der Alten Komödie: Untersuchungen zu Aristophanes und Michail Bachtin.* Classica Monacensia 9. Tübingen.

——. 1995a. "Aristophanes und der komische Chor auf der Bühne des 5. Jahrhunderts." In Pöhlmann 1995a:143–154.

Mommsen, A. 1864. *Heortologie: Antiquarische Untersuchungen über die städtischen Feste der Athener.* Leipzig.

Moreau, A. 1992. "Initiation en Grèce antique." *Dialogue d'Histoire Ancienne* 18.1:191–244.

——, ed. 1992a. *L'initiation, I: Les rites d'adolescence et les mystères. Actes du colloque international de Montpellier, 11–14 Avril 1991.* Montpellier.

Moret, J.-M. 1991. "Circé tisseuse sur les vases du Cabirion." *Revue Archéologique* 1991:227–266.

Morgan, K. A. 1993. "Pindar the Professional and the Rhetoric of the κῶμος." *CP* 88:1–15.

Morgan, W., and Brask, P. 1988. "Towards a Conceptual Understanding of the Transformation from Ritual to Theatre." *Anthropologica* 30:175–202.

Morris, I. 1993. "Poetics of Power: The Interpretation of Ritual Action in Archaic Greece." In *Cultural Poetics in Archaic Greece: Cult, Performance, Politics* (eds. C. Dougherty and L. Kurke), 15–45. Cambridge.

Most, G. W. 1985. *The Measures of Praise: Structure and Function in Pindar's Second Pythian and Seventh Nemean Odes.* Hypomnemata 83. Göttingen.

Moulton, C. 1981. *Aristophanic Poetry*. Hypomnemata 68. Göttingen.

Muecke, F. 1982. "A Portrait of the Artist as a Young Woman." *CQ* n.s. 32:41–55.

Muff, C. 1871. "Der Chor in der Attischen Komödie vor Aristophanes." In *Programm der Lateinischen Hauptschule in Halle für das Schuljahr 1870-1871* (ed. F. T. Adler), 1–40. Halle.

———. 1872. *Über den Vortrag der chorischen Partieen bei Aristophanes*. Halle.

Mullen, W. 1982. *Choreia: Pindar and Dance*. Princeton.

Müller, C. W. 1992. "Aristophanes und Horaz: Zu einem Verlaufsschema von Selbstbehauptung und Selbstgewißheit zweier Klassiker." *Hermes* 120:129–141.

Müller, G. 1967. "Chor und Handlung bei den griechischen Tragikern." In *Sophokles* (ed. H. Diller), 212–238. Wege der Forschung 95. Darmstadt.

Müller, K. O. 1857². *Geschichte der griechischen Literatur bis auf das Zeitalter Alexanders*, I–II. Breslau.

Mureddu, P. 1982/83. "Il poeta drammatico da didaskalos a mimetes: Su alcuni aspetti della critica letteraria in Aristofane." *AION*, filol. 4–5:75–98.

———. 1987. "Un caso singolare di 'teatro nel teatro': La scena di Eco nelle *Tesmoforiazuse*." *Annali della Facoltà di Lettere e Filosofia dell'Università di Cagliari* 6 [1985]:15–22.

Murray, G. 1933. *Aristophanes: A Study*. Oxford.

Murray, O. 1990. "The Affair of the Mysteries: Democracy and the Drinking Group." In Murray 1990a:149–161.

———, ed. 1990a. *Sympotica: A Symposium on the* Symposion. Oxford.

Naerebout, F. G. 1997. *Attractive Performances: Ancient Greek Dance. Three Preliminary Studies*. Amsterdam.

Nagy, G. 1979. *The Best of the Achaeans: Concepts of the Hero in Archaic Greek Poetry*. Baltimore.

———. 1990. *Pindar's Homer: The Lyric Possession of an Epic Past*. Baltimore.

———. 1994/95. "Transformations of Choral Lyric Traditions in the Context of Athenian State Theater." *Arion* 3rd ser. 3:41–55.

———. 1994/95a. "Genre and Occasion." *Métis* 9/10:11–25.

———. 1996. *Poetry as Performance: Homer and Beyond*. Cambridge.

Navarre, O. 1911. "Les origines et la structure technique de la comédie ancienne." *Revue des Études Anciennes* 13:245–295.

Neer, R. T. 2002. *Style and Politics in Athenian Vase-Painting: The Craft of Democracy, circa 530-460 B.C.E.* Cambridge.

Neils, J. 1992. "The Panathenaia: An Introduction." In *Goddess and Polis: The Panathenaic Festival in Ancient Athens* (ed. J. Neils), 13–27. Princeton.

Nesselrath, H.-G. 1990. *Die attische Mittlere Komödie: Ihre Stellung in der antiken Literaturkritik und Literaturgeschichte*. UaLG 36. Berlin.

———. 1993. "Parody and Later Greek Comedy." *HSCP* 95:181–195.

Newiger, H.-J. 1957. *Metapher und Allegorie: Studien zu Aristophanes*. Zetemata 16. Munich.

——, ed. 1975. *Aristophanes und die Alte Komödie.* Wege der Forschung 265. Darmstadt.

Nietzsche, F. 1878/79. "Griechische Lyriker: Vorlesungen von Prof. Nietzsche ([WS 1878/79] Nachschrift von unbekannter Hand)." In *Nietzsche Werke: Kritische Gesamtausgabe* II.2 (ed. F. Bornmann), 373–442. Berlin 1993.

Nilsson, M. P. 1967³. *Geschichte der griechischen Religion,* I. Handbuch der Altertumswissenschaft V 2.1. Munich.

Norden, E. 1913. *Agnostos Theos: Untersuchungen zur Formengeschichte religiöser Rede.* Berlin.

——. 1939. *Aus altrömischen Priesterbüchern.* Lund.

Ohmann, R. 1971. "Speech Acts and the Definition of Literature." *Philosophy & Rhetoric* 4.1:1–19.

Olender, M. 1990. "Aspects of Baubo: Ancient Texts and Contexts." In Halperin, Winkler, and Zeitlin 1990:83–113.

Olson, S. D. 1992. "Names and Naming in Aristophanic Comedy." *CQ* n.s. 42:304–319.

Osborne, R. 1993. "Competitive Festivals and the Polis: A Context for Dramatic Festivals at Athens." In *Tragedy, Comedy, and the Polis. Papers from the Greek Drama Conference, Nottingham, 18–20 July 1990* (eds. A. H. Sommerstein et al.), 21–38. Bari.

——. 1993a. "Women and Sacrifice in Classical Greece." *CQ* n.s. 43:392–405.

——. 1994. "Introduction. Ritual, Finance, Politics: An Account of Athenian Democracy." In Osborne and Hornblower 1994:1–21.

Osborne, R., and Hornblower, S., eds. 1994. *Ritual, Finance, Politics: Athenian Democratic Accounts Presented to David Lewis.* Oxford.

Ostwald, M. 1986. *From Popular Sovereignty to the Sovereignty of Law.* Berkeley.

Otto, W. F. 1970⁶. *Die Götter Griechenlands: Das Bild des Göttlichen im Spiegel des griechischen Geistes.* Frankfurt.

Padel, R. 1995. *Whom Gods Destroy: Elements of Greek and Tragic Madness.* Princeton.

Paduano, G. 1982. "Le *Tesmoforiazuse:* Ambiguità del fare teatro." *QUCC* n.s. 11:103–127.

Page, D. L. 1951. *Alcman. The Partheneion.* Oxford.

——. 1962. *Poetae Melici Graeci.* Oxford. (= *PMG*)

Papadopoulou-Belmehdi, I. 1994. *Le chant de Pénélope: Poétique du tissage féminin dans l'Odyssée.* Paris.

Pappas, T. 1987. "Contributo a uno studio antropologico della commedia attica antica: Struttura e funzione degli exodoi nelle commedie di Aristofane." *Dioniso* 57:191–202.

Parke, H. W. 1977. *Festivals of the Athenians.* Aspects of Greek and Roman Life. Ithaca.

Parker, L. P. E. 1997. *The Songs of Aristophanes.* Oxford.

Parker, R. 1996. *Athenian Religion: A History.* Oxford.

Parry, M. 1971. *The Making of Homeric Verse: The Collected Papers of Milman Parry* (ed. A. Parry). Oxford.

Parsons, P. 1993. "Identities in Diversity." In Bulloch, Gruen, Long, and Stewart 1993:152–170.

Paulsen, T. 1989. *Die Rolle des Chors in den späten Sophokles-Tragödien: Untersuchungen zu 'Elektra', Philoktet' und 'Oidipus auf Kolonos.'* Bari.

———. 1998. "Die Funktionen des Chores in der Attischen Tragödie." In Binder and Effe 1998:69–92.

Pavese, C. O. 1968. "Semantematica della poesia corale greca." *Belfagor* 23:389–430.

———. 1979. *La lirica corale greca: Alcmane, Simonide, Pindaro, Bacchilide* I. Rome.

———. 1992. *Il grande Partenio di Alcmane.* Lexis supplement 1. Amsterdam.

Peirce, C. S. 1983. *Phänomen und Logik der Zeichen* (ed. H. Pape). Frankfurt.1993².

Peirce, S. 1993. "Death, Revelry, and *Thysia.*" *CA* 12:219–266.

Pélékidis, C. 1962. *Histoire de l'éphébie attique des origines à 31 avant Jésus-Christ.* Paris.

Peponi, A.-E. 2004. "Initiating the Viewer: Deixis and Visual Perception in Alcman's Lyric Drama." *Arethusa* 37:295–316.

Perlman, P. J. 1995. "*Invocatio* and *Imprecatio*: The Hymn to the Greatest Kouros from Palaikastro and the Oath in Ancient Crete." *JHS* 115:161–167.

Perusino, F., and Colantonio, M., eds. 2007. *Dalla lirica corale alla poesia drammatica: Forme e funzioni del canto corale nella tragedia e nella commedia greca.* Pisa.

Petersmann, H. 1990. "Tithrone als Epiklese der Athene: Ein etymologisch-religionswissenschaftlicher Beitrag zum Wesensverständnis der Göttin." *Historische Namensforschung* 103:38–50.

———. 1991. "Springende und tanzende Götter beim antiken Fest." In Assmann 1991a:69–87.

Petrey, S. 1990. *Speech Acts and Literary Theory.* New York.

Pettersson, M. 1992. *Cults of Apollo at Sparta: The Hyakinthia, the Gymnopaidiai, and the Karneia.* Acta Instituti Atheniensis Regni Sueciae, 8˚, 12. Stockholm.

Pickard-Cambridge, A. W. 1927. *Dithyramb, Tragedy, and Comedy.* Oxford.

———. 1962. *Dithyramb, Tragedy, and Comedy.* 2nd edition rev. T. B. L. Webster. Oxford.

———. 1968. *The Dramatic Festivals of Athens.* 2nd edition rev. J. Gould and D. M. Lewis. Oxford. Reissued with suppl. and corr. 1988.

Poccetti, P. 1991. "Forma e tradizioni dell'inno magico nel mondo classico." In Cassio and Cerri 1991:179–204.

Poe, J. P. 1989. "The Altar in the Fifth-Century Theater." *CA* 8:116–139.

Pohlenz, M. 1949. "Die Entstehung der attischen Komödie." *Nachrichten der Akademie der Wissenschaften in Göttingen*, phil.-hist. Kl., 1949.2:31–44.

Pöhlmann, E. 1981. "Die Proedrie des Dionysos-Theaters im 5. Jahrhundert und das Bühnenspiel der Klassik." *Museum Helveticum* 38:129–146.

———. 1995. "Sucheszenen auf der attischen Bühne des 5. und 4. Jahrhunderts. Zur Bühnentechnik der 'Eumeniden', des 'Aias', der 'Acharner' und des 'Rhesos.' " In Pöhlmann 1995a:117–131.

——, ed. 1995a. *Studien zur Bühnendichtung und zum Theaterbau der Antike.* Studien zur klassischen Philologie 93. Frankfurt.

Poursat, J.-C. 1968. "Les représentations de danse armée dans la céramique attique." *BCH* 92:550–615.

Powell, B. B. 1988. "The Dipylon Oinochoe Inscription and the Spread of Literacy in Eighth-Century Athens." *Kadmos* 27:65–86.

——. 1991. *Homer and the Origin of the Greek Alphabet.* Cambridge.

Powell, J. U., ed. 1925. *Collectanea Alexandrina.* Oxford.

Prato, C. 1987. "I metri lirici di Aristofane." *Dioniso* 57:203–244 .

——. 1993. "Note al testo delle *Tesmoforiazuse.*" In Pretagostini II 1993:695–701.

——. 1995. "La cosiddetta 'versione lirica' dell'*arà* nelle *Tesmoforiazuse* (vv. 352–371)." In Gentili and Perusino 1995:277–285.

——. 1998. "Note esegetico-testuali alle *Tesmoforiazuse* di Aristofane." *Rivista di Cultura Classica e Medioevale* 40:269–273.

——. 1998a. "Note critiche ed esegetiche al testo delle *Tesmoforiazuse.*" *QUCC* n.s. 58:69–74.

Preisendanz, K. 1973/74. *Papyri Graecae Magicae: Die griechischen Zauberpapyri,* I–II. Stuttgart.

Preisendanz, W., and Warning, R., eds. 1976. *Das Komische.* Poetik und Hermeneutik 7. Munich.

Pretagostini, R., ed. 1993. *Tradizione e innovazione nella cultura greca da Omero all'età ellenistica. Scritti in onore di Bruno Gentili,* I–III. Rome.

Price, S. D. 1990. "Anacreontic Vases Reconsidered." *GRBS* 31:133–175.

Prins, Y. 1991. "The Power of the Speech Act: Aeschylus' Furies and Their Binding Song." *Arethusa* 24:177–195.

Pronko, L. C. 1982. "*Kabuki*: Signs, Symbols, and the Hieroglyphic Actor." In *Drama and Symbolism* (ed. J. Redmond), 41–55. Themes in Drama 4. Cambridge.

Prudhommeau, G. 1965. *La danse grecque antique,* I–II. Paris.

Puelma, M. 1977. "Die Selbstbeschreibung des Chores in Alkmans grossem Partheneion-Fragment." *Museum Helveticum* 34:1–55.

Pulleyn, S. 1994. "The Power of Names in Classical Greek Religion." *CQ* n.s. 44:17–25.

Purves, A. 1997. "Empowerment for the Athenian Citizen: Philocleon as Actor and Spectator in Aristophanes' *Wasps.*" In *Griechisch-römische Komödie und Tragödie* II (ed. B. Zimmermann), 5–22. Drama 5. Stuttgart.

Pütz, B. 2003. *The Symposium and Komos in Aristophanes.* Drama: Beiheft 22. Stuttgart.

Race, W. H. 1982. "Aspects of Rhetoric and Form in Greek Hymns." *GRBS* 23:5–14.

Radcliffe-Brown, A. R. 1964. *The Andaman Islanders.* New York.

Radke, G. 2003. *Tragik und Metatragik: Euripides' Bakchen und die moderne Literaturwissenschaft.* Berlin.

Rau, P. 1967. *Paratragodia: Untersuchung einer komischen Form des Aristophanes.* Zetemata 45. Munich.

Rauch, E. 1992. *Sprachrituale in institutionellen und institutionalisierten Text- und Gesprächssorten.* Arbeiten zu Diskurs und Stil 1. Frankfurt.

Reckford, K. J. 1977. "Catharsis and Dream-Interpretation in Aristophanes' *Wasps*." *TAPA* 107:283–312.

——. 1987. *Aristophanes' Old-and-New Comedy* I. Chapel Hill.

Rehm, R. 1988. "The Staging of Suppliant Plays." *GRBS* 29:263–307.

——. 1994. *Marriage to Death: The Conflation of Wedding and Funeral Rituals in Greek Tragedy.* Princeton.

——. 1996. "Performing the Chorus: Choral Action, Interaction, and Absence in Euripides." *Arion* 3rd ser. 4:45–60.

Reich, H. 1903. *Der Mimus: Ein litterar-entwickelungsgeschichtlicher Versuch* I.1. Berlin.

Restani, D. 1995. "I suoni del telaio: Appunti sull'universo sonoro degli antichi Greci." In Gentili and Perusino 1995:93–109.

Revermann, M. 2006. *Comic Business: Theatricality, Dramatic Technique, and Performance Contexts of Aristophanic Comedy.* Oxford.

Richardson, N. J. 1974. *The Homeric Hymn to Demeter.* Oxford.

Richter, W. 1975. "Wendehals." *Kl. Pauly* 5:1366–1367.

Riemer, P., and Zimmermann, B., eds. 1999. *Der Chor im antiken und modernen Drama.* Drama 7. Stuttgart.

Ringer, M. 1998. *Electra and the Empty Urn: Metatheater and Role Playing in Sophocles.* Chapel Hill.

Riu, X. 1999. *Dionysism and Comedy.* Greek Studies: Interdisciplinary Approaches. Lanham, MD.

Robbins, E. 1994. "Alcman's *Partheneion*: Legend and Choral Ceremony." *CQ* n.s. 44:7–16.

Robert, C. 1885. "Athena Skiras und die Skirophorien." *Hermes* 20:349–379.

Robertson, M. 1992. *The Art of Vase-Painting in Classical Athens.* Cambridge.

Robertson, N. 1985. "The Origin of the Panathenaea." *RhM* 128:231–295.

Rode, J. 1971. "Das Chorlied." In *Die Bauformen der griechischen Tragödie* (ed. W. Jens), 85–115. Beihefte zu Poetica 6. Munich.

Rohde, E. 1870. "Unedirte Lucianscholien, die attischen Thesmophorien und Haloen betreffend." *RhM* 25:548–560.

Rolley, C. 1965. "Le sanctuaire des dieux patrôoi et le Thesmophorion de Thasos." *BCH* 89:441–483.

Rose, M. A. 1993. *Parody: Ancient, Modern, and Post-Modern.* Cambridge.

Rosellini, M. 1979. "*Lysistrata*: Une mise en scène de la feminité." In *Aristophane: Les femmes et la cité. Les cahiers de Fontenay 17, Decembre 1979* (eds. D. Auger, M. Rosellini, and S. Saïd), 11–32. Fontenay-aux-Roses.

Rosen, R. M. 1988. *Old Comedy and the Iambographic Tradition.* American Classical Studies 19. Atlanta.

Rösler, W. 1980. *Dichter und Gruppe: Eine Untersuchung zu den Bedingungen und zur historischen Funktion früher griechischer Lyrik am Beispiel Alkaios.* Theorie und Geschichte der Literatur und der Schönen Künste 50. Munich.

———. 1983. "Der Chor als Mitspieler. Beobachtungen zur 'Antigone.'" *A&A* 29:107–124.

———. 1983a. "Über Deixis und einige Aspekte mündlichen und schriftlichen Stils in antiker Lyrik." *WüJbb* n.F. 9:7–28.

———. 1985. "Persona reale o persona poetica? L'interpretazione dell' 'io' nella lirica greca arcaica." *QUCC* n.s. 19:131–144.

———. 1986. "Michail Bachtin und die Karnevalskultur im antiken Griechenland." *QUCC* n.s. 23:25–44.

———. 1993. "Über Aischrologie im archaischen und klassischen Griechenland." In *Karnevaleske Phänomene in antiken und nachantiken Kulturen und Literaturen* (ed. S. Döpp), 75–97. Stätten und Formen der Kommunikation im Altertum I–Bochumer Altertumswissenschaftliches Colloquium 13. Trier.

Rossbach, A., and Westphal, R. 1889³. *Griechische Metrik*, III.2, *Theorie der musischen Künste der Hellenen.* Leipzig.

Rossi, L. E. 1978. "Mimica e danza sulla scena comica greca (A proposito del finale delle *Vespe* e di altri passi aristofanei)." In *Miscellanea di studi in memoria di Marino Barchiesi* II. Special issue, *Rivista di Cultura Classica e Medioevale* 20:1149–1170. Rome.

Rothwell, K. S. 2006. *Nature, Culture, and the Origins of Greek Comedy: A Study of Animal Choruses.* Cambridge.

Rudhardt, J. 1958. *Notions fondamentales de la pensée religieuse et actes constitutifs du culte dans la Grèce classique.* Geneva.

Ruffini, F. 1991. "Theatre Anthropology." In Helbo, Johansen, Pavis, and Ubersfeld 1991:75–91.

Rusten, J. S. 1977. "*Wasps* 1360–1369: Philokleon's ΤΩΘΑΣΜΟΣ." *HSCP* 81:157–161.

Rutherford, I. 1994/95. "Apollo in Ivy: The Tragic Paean." *Arion* 3rd ser. 3:112–135.

Saetta Cottone, R. 2005. *Aristofane e la poetica dell'ingiuria: Per una introduzione alla* λοιδορία *comica.* Aglaia, sez. Greca 6. Rome.

Saïd, S. 1987. "Travestis et travestissements dans les comédies d'Aristophane." In *Anthropologie et théâtre antique* (eds. P. Ghiron-Bistagne and B. Schouler), 217–246. Cahiers du GITA 3. Montpellier.

Schauenburg, K. 1976. "Erotenspiele, 1. Teil." *Antike Welt* 7.3:39–52.

Schechner, R. 1977. *Essays on Performance Theory, 1970–1976.* New York.

———. 1985. *Between Theater and Anthropology.* Philadelphia.

———. 1993. *The Future of Ritual: Writings on Culture and Performance.* London.

Scheid, J., and Svenbro, J. 1996. *The Craft of Zeus: Myths of Weaving and Fabric.* Trans. C. Volk. Cambridge, MA.

Schlegel, A. W. von. 1846. *Vorlesungen über dramatische Kunst und Litteratur*, I, *Sämmtliche Werke*, V (ed. E. Böcking). Leipzig. 3rd ed.

Schlesier, R. 1985. "Der Stachel der Götter: Zum Problem des Wahnsinns in der Euripideischen Tragödie." *Poetica* 17:1–45.

——. 1991. "Prolegomena to Jane Harrsion's Interpretation of Ancient Greek Religion." In Calder 1991:185–226.

Schmid, W. 1929. *Geschichte der griechischen Literatur* I.1. Handbuch der Altertumswissenschaft VII.1. Munich.

——. 1946. *Geschichte der griechischen Literatur* I.4. Handbuch der Altertumswissenschaft VII.1. Munich.

Schmitt, P. 1977. "Athéna Apatouria et la ceinture: Es aspects féminins des Apatouries à Athènes." *Annales (Économie, Sociétés, Civilisations)* 32:1059–1073.

Schmitz, T. A. 1999. "Performing History in the Second Sophistic." In *Geschichtsschreibung und politischer Wandel im 3. Jh. n. Chr. Kolloquium zu Ehren von Karl-Ernst Petzold (Juni 1998) anläßlich seines 80. Geburtstags* (ed. M. Zimmermann), 71–92. Historia Einzelschriften 127. Stuttgart.

Schmitz, W. 2004. *Nachbarschaft und Dorfgemeinschaft im archaischen und klassischen Griechenland*. Klio Beihefte n.F. 7. Berlin.

Schönberger, O. 1980. *Griechische Heischelieder*. Beiträge zur Klassischen Philologie 105. Meisenheim.

Scullion, S. 1998. "Dionysos and Katharsis in *Antigone*." *CA* 17:96–122.

——. 2002. " 'Nothing to Do with Dionysus': Tragedy Misconceived as Ritual." *CQ* 52:102–137.

Seaford, R. 1977. "The 'Hyporchema' of Pratinas." *Maia* 29/30:81–94.

——. 1984. *Euripides. Cyclops*. Oxford.

——. 1987. "The Tragic Wedding." *JHS* 107:106–130.

——. 1988. "The Eleventh Ode of Bacchylides: Hera, Artemis, and the Absence of Dionysos." *JHS* 108:118–136.

——. 1994. *Reciprocity and Ritual: Homer and Tragedy in the Developing City-State*. Oxford.

——. 1996. *Euripides. Bacchae*. Warminster.

——. 2005. "Tragedy and Dionysus." In *A Companion to Tragedy* (ed. R. Bushnell), 25–38. Malden, MA.

Searle, J. R. 1970. *Speech Acts: An Essay in the Philosophy of Language*. Cambridge.

Seeberg, A. 1995. "From Padded Dancers to Comedy." In *Stage Directions. Essays in Ancient Drama in Honour of E. W. Handley* (ed. A. Griffiths), 1–12. BICS supplement 66. London.

Segal, C. 1982. *Dionysiac Poetics and Euripides'* Bacchae. Princeton.

——. 1983. "Sirius and the Pleiades in Alcman's Louvre Partheneion." *Mnemosyne* 36:260–275.

——. 1989. "Song, Ritual, and Commemoration in Early Greek Poetry and Tragedy." *Oral Tradition* 4:330–359.

———. 1992. "Signs, Magic, and Letters in Euripides' *Hippolytus*." In Hexter and Selden 1992:420–456.

———. 1995. "The Gods and the Chorus: Zeus in *Oedipus Tyrannus*." In C. Segal, *Sophocles' Tragic World: Divinity, Nature, Society*, 180–198 and 260–265. Cambridge, MA.

———. 1997. "Chorus and Community in Euripides' *Bacchae*." In Edmunds and Wallace 1997:65–86 and 149–153.

Segre, M. 1993. *Iscrizioni di Cos*, I–II. Rome.

Seidensticker, B. 1972. "Pentheus." *Poetica* 5:35–63.

———. 1979. "Das Satyrspiel." In *Das griechische Drama* (ed. G. A. Seeck), 204–257. Grundriß der Literaturgeschichten nach Gattungen. Darmstadt.

———. 1982. *Palintonos Harmonia: Studien zu komischen Elementen in der griechischen Tragödie*. Hypomnemata 72. Göttingen.

———, ed. 1989. *Satyrspiel*. Wege der Forschung 579. Darmstadt.

———. 1996. "Die griechische Tragödie als literarischer Wettbewerb." *Berlin-Brandenburgische Akademie der Wissenschaften (vormals Preußische Akademie der Wissenschaften), Berichte und Abhandlungen* 2:9–35.

———. 1999. "Philologisch-literarische Einleitung." In *Das griechische Satyrspiel* (eds. R. Krumeich, N. Pechstein, and B. Seidensticker), 1–40. Texte zur Forschung 72. Darmstadt.

Seiterle, G. 1984. "Zum Ursprung der griechischen Maske, der Tragödie und der Satyrn: Bericht über den Rekonstruktionsversuch der vortheatralen Maske." *Antike Kunst* 27:135–143.

———. 1988. "Maske, Ziegenbock und Satyr: Ursprung und Wesen der griechischen Maske." *Antike Welt* 19:2–14.

Sfameni Gasparro, G. 1986. *Misteri e culti mistici di Demetra*. Storia delle Religioni 3. Rome.

Sfyroeras, P. V. 1992. *The Feast of Poetry: Sacrifice, Foundation, and Performance in Aristophanic Comedy*. Ph.D. diss., Princeton.

———. 2004. "From Sacrifice to Feast: A Ritual Pattern in Aristophanic Comedy." In *Law, Rhetoric, and Comedy in Classical Athens. Essays in Honour of Douglas M. MacDowell* (eds. D. L. Cairns and R. A. Knox), 251–268. London.

Shapiro, H. A. 1986. "Dike." *LIMC* III.1:388–391.

Shear, T. L. 1973. "A Votive Relief from the Athenian Agora." *Opuscula Romana* 9:183–191.

———. 1973a. "The Athenian Agora: Excavations of 1971." *Hesperia* 42:121–179.

Sier, K. 1988. *Die lyrischen Partien der Choephoren des Aischylos: Text, Übersetzung, Kommentar*. Palingenesia 23. Stuttgart.

———. 1992. "Die Rolle des Skythen in den *Thesmophoriazusen* des Aristophanes." In *Zum Umgang mit fremden Sprachen in der griechisch-römischen Antike* (eds. C. W. Müller, K. Sier, and J. Werner), 63–83. Palingenesia 36. Stuttgart.

Siewert, P. 1977. "The Ephebic Oath in Fifth-Century Athens." *JHS* 97:102–111.

Sifakis, G. M. 1971. *Parabasis and Animal Choruses: A Contribution to the History of Attic Comedy*. London.

Silk, M. 1980. "Aristophanes as a Lyric Poet." *Yale Classical Studies* 26:99–151.

———, ed. 1996. *Tragedy and the Tragic: Greek Theatre and Beyond*. Oxford.

Simon, E. 1983. *Festivals of Attica: An Archaeological Commentary*. Wisconsin Studies in Classics. Madison.

Slater, N. W. 1993. "From Ancient Performance to New Historicism." In Slater and Zimmermann 1993:1–13.

———. 2002. *Spectator Politics: Metatheatre and Performance in Aristophanes*. Philadelphia.

Slater, N. W., and Zimmermann, B., eds. 1993. *Intertextualität in der griechisch-römischen Komödie*. Drama 2. Stuttgart.

Smith, T. J. 2000. "Dancing Spaces and Dining Places: Archaic Komasts at the Symposion." In *Periplous. Papers on Classical Art and Archaeology Presented to Sir John Boardman* (eds. G. R. Tsetskhladze, A. J. N. W. Prag, and A. M. Snodgrass), 309–319. London.

———. 2003. "Black-Figure Komasts in the 'Age of Red-Figure': Continuity or Change?" In *Griechische Keramik im kulturellen Kontext* (eds. B. Schmaltz and M. Söldner), 102–104. Münster.

Snyder, J. McIntosh. 1974. "Aristophanes' Agathon as Anacreon." *Hermes* 102:244–246.

Sokolowski, F. 1955. *Lois sacrées de l'Asie Mineure*. Paris. (= *LSAM*)

———. 1969. *Lois sacrées des cités grecques*. Paris. (= *LSCG*)

Sommerstein, A. H. 1989. *Aeschylus. Eumenides*. Cambridge Greek and Latin Classics. Cambridge.

———. 1996. "How to Avoid Being a *Komodoumenos*." *CQ* n.s. 46:327–356.

Sourvinou-Inwood, C. 1988. *Studies in Girls' Transitions: Aspects of the Arkteia and Age Representation in Attic Iconography*. Athens.

———. 1994. "Something to Do with Athens: Tragedy and Ritual." In Osborne and Hornblower 1994:269–290.

———. 2003. *Tragedy and Athenian Religion*. Lanham, MD.

———. 2005. "Greek Tragedy and Ritual." In *A Companion to Tragedy* (ed. R. Bushnell), 7–24. Malden, MA.

Spencer, P., ed. 1985. *Society and the Dance: The Social Anthropology of Process and Performance*. Cambridge.

Sperber, D. 1996. "Why Are Perfect Animals, Hybrids, and Monsters Food for Symbolic Thought?" *Method & Theory in the Study of Religion* 8: 143–169.

Staal, F. 1979. "The Meaninglessness of Ritual." *Numen* 26:2–22.

Stark, I. 2004. *Die hämische Muse: Spott als soziale und mentale Kontrolle in der griechischen Komödie*. Zetemata 121. Munich.

States, B. O. 1996. "Performance as Metaphor." *Theatre Journal* 48:1–26.

Stehle, E. 1997. *Performance and Gender in Ancient Greece: Nondramatic Poetry in Its Setting.* Princeton.

———. 2002. "The Body and Its Representation in Aristophanes' *Thesmophoriazousai.*" *AJP* 123.3:369–406.

Steiger, H. 1888. *Der Eigenname in der attischen Komödie.* Ph.D. diss., Erlangen.

Steiner, G. 1988. *Die Antigonen: Geschichte und Gegenwart eines Mythos.* Trans. M. Pfeiffer, Munich.

Steinhart, M. 2004. *Die Kunst der Nachahmung: Darstellung mimetischer Vorführungen in der griechischen Bildkunst archaischer und klassischer Zeit.* Mainz.

Stockert, W., ed. 1994. *Euripides. Hippolytus.* Stuttgart.

Stoessl, F. 1987. *Die Vorgeschichte des griechischen Theaters.* Darmstadt.

Stohn, G. 1993. "Zur Agathonszene in den 'Thesmophoriazusen' des Aristophanes." *Hermes* 121:196–205.

Süß, W. 1954. "Scheinbare und wirkliche Inkongruenzen in den Dramen des Aristophanes." *RhM* n.F. 97:115–159, 229–254, 289–316.

Svenbro, J. 1984. "La découpe du poème: Notes sur les origines sacrificielles de la poétique grecque." *Poétique* 15:215–232.

Szemerényi, O. 1975. "The Origins of Roman Drama and Greek Tragedy." *Hermes* 103:300–332.

Taaffe, L. K. 1993. *Aristophanes and Women.* London.

Tambiah, S. J. 1985. *Culture, Thought, and Social Action: An Anthropological Perspective.* Cambridge, MA.

Taplin, O. 1986. "Fifth-Century Tragedy and Comedy: A *synkrisis.*" *JHS* 106:163–174.

———. 1993. *Comic Angels and Other Approaches to Greek Drama through Vase-Paintings.* Oxford.

———. 1996. "Comedy and the Tragic." In Silk 1996:188–202.

Thiel, R. 1993. *Chor und tragische Handlung im 'Agamemnon' des Aischylos.* BzA 35. Stuttgart.

Thiele, G. 1902. "Die Anfänge der griechischen Komödie." *NJbb* 9:405–426.

Thiercy, P. 1986. *Aristophane: Fiction et dramaturgie.* Paris.

Thompson, H. A. 1936. "Pnyx and Thesmophorion." *Hesperia* 5:151–200.

Thomsen, O. 1973. "Some Notes on the *Thesmophoriazusae* 947–1000." In *Classica et Mediaevalia. Francisco Blatt septuagenario dedicata* (ed. O. S. Due, H. F. Johansen, and B. D. Larsen), 27–46. Classica et Mediaevalia, Diss. 9. Copenhagen.

Thomson, G. 1956. *Aischylos und Athen: Eine Untersuchung der gesellschaftlichen Ursprünge des Dramas.* Trans. H.-G. Heidenreich. Berlin. 1985³.

Thummer, E. 1968/69. *Pindar. Die Isthmischen Gedichte*, I–II. Heidelberg.

Too, Y. L. 1997. "Alcman's *Partheneion*: The Maidens Dance the City." *QUCC* n.s. 56.2:7–29.

Toro, A. de. 1995. "Die Wege des zeitgenössischen Theaters – Zu einem postmodernen Multimedia-Theater oder: das Ende des mimetisch-referentiellen Theaters?" *Forum Modernes Theater* 10:135–183.

Toro, F. de. 1995. *Theatre Semiotics: Text and Staging in Modern Theatre.* Trans. J. Lewis. Rev. and ed. C. Hubbard. Frankfurt.

Totaro, P. 1999. *Le seconde parabasi di Aristofane.* Drama: Beiheft 9. Stuttgart.

Tresp, A. 1914. *Die Fragmente der griechischen Kultschriftsteller.* RGVV 15.1. Giessen.

Treu, M. 1999. *Undici cori comici: Aggressività, derisione e tecniche drammatiche in Aristofane.* Università di Genova, Facoltà di Lettere e Filosofia: Pubblicazioni del Dipartimento di Archeolologia, Filologia Classica e Loro Tradizioni 181. Genova.

Tsakmakis, A. 1997. "Nikandros, Schauspieler des Aristophanes? (Diogenes von Babylon bei Philodemos, περὶ μουσικῆς)." *ZPE* 119:7–12.

Tschiedel, H. J. 1984. "Aristophanes und Euripides: Zu Herkunft und Absicht der Weiberkomödien." *Grazer Beiträge* 11:29–49.

Turner, V. 1967. *The Forest of Symbols: Aspects of Ndembu Ritual.* Ithaca.

——. 1969. "Introduction: Forms of Symbolic Action." In *Forms of Symbolic Action. Proceedings of the 1969 Annual Spring Meeting of the American Ethnological Society* (ed. R. F. Spencer), 3–25. Seattle.

——. 1974. *Dramas, Fields, and Metaphors: Symbolic Action in Human Society.* Ithaca.

——. 1982. *From Ritual to Theatre: The Human Seriousness of Play.* New York.

——. 1984. "Liminality and the Performative Genres." In *Rite, Drama, Festival, Spectacle: Rehearsals toward a Theory of Cultural Performances* (ed. J. MacAloon), 19–41. Philadelphia.

Turner, V., and Turner, E. 1982. "Religious Celebrations." In *Celebration: Studies in Festivity and Ritual* (ed. V. Turner), 201–219. Washington, D.C.

Tzanetou, A. 2002. "Something to Do with Demeter: Ritual and Performance in Aristophanes' *Women at the Thesmophoria.*" *AJP* 123.3:329–367.

Vallois, R. 1922. "L' 'agalma' des Dionysies de Délos." *BCH* 46:94–112.

van Gennep, A. 1909. *Les rites de passage: Étude systematique des rites.* Paris.

Vernant, J.-P. 1990. *Myth and Society in Ancient Greece.* Trans. Janet Lloyd. New York.

Versnel, H. S. 1993. *Inconsistencies in Greek and Roman Religion, II: Transition and Reversal in Myth and Ritual.* Studies in Greek and Roman Religion 6.II. Leiden.

Verweyen, T., and Witting, G. 1982. "Parodie, Palinodie, Kontradiktio, Kontrafaktur – Elementare Adaptionsformen im Rahmen der Intertextualitätsdiskussion." In *Dialogizität* (ed. R. Lachmann), 202–236. Theorie und Geschichte der Literatur und der schönen Künste, Reihe A: Hermeneutik, Semiotik, Rhetorik, Bd. 1. Munich.

Vickers, M. 1989. "Alcibiades on Stage: *Thesmophoriazusae* and *Helen.*" *Historia* 38:41–65.

Vidal-Naquet, P. 1968. "The Black Hunter and the Origin of the Athenian Ephebeia." In *The Black Hunter: Forms of Thought and Forms of Society in the Ancient Greek World.* Trans. A. Szegedy-Maszak. 106–128. Baltimore. 1986.

———. 1986. "The Black Hunter Revisited." *PCPS* n.s. 32 (212):126–144.

Vogt-Spira, G. 1995. "Traditionen improvisierten Theaters bei Plautus: Einige pro-grammatische Überlegungen." In *Griechisch-römische Komödie und Tragödie* (ed. B. Zimmermann), 70–93. Drama 3. Stuttgart.

Wachsmuth, D. 1967. *ΠΟΜΠΙΜΟΣ Ο ΔΑΙΜΩΝ: Untersuchung zu den antiken Sakralhandlungen bei Seereisen.* Ph.D. diss., Freie Universität, Berlin.

Warnecke, B. 1932. "Tanzkunst." *RE* 4 A 2:2233–2247.

Warning, R. 1976. "Elemente einer Pragmasemiotik der Komödie." In Preisendanz and Warning 1976:279–333.

Weaver, B. H. 1996. "A Further Allusion in the *Eumenides* to the Panathenaia." *CQ* n.s. 46:559–561.

Webster, T. B. L. 1970. *The Greek Chorus.* London.

Weege, B. F. 1926. *Der Tanz in der Antike.* Halle.

Wehrli, F. 1945. *Die Schule des Aristoteles: Texte und Kommentar, II: Aristoxenos.* Basel.

Weinreich, O. 1929. *Gebet und Wunder: Zwei Abhandlungen zur Religions- und Literaturgeschichte.* Tübinger Beiträge zur Altertumswissenschaft 5. Stuttgart.

West, M. L. 1965. "The Dictaean Hymn to the Kouros." *JHS* 85:149–159.

———. 1965a. "Alcmanica." *CQ* n.s. 15:188–202.

———. 1974. *Studies in Greek Elegy and Iambus.* UaLG 14. Berlin.

———. 1982. *Greek Metre.* Oxford.

———. 1992. *Ancient Greek Music.* Oxford.

———. 1997. "When Is a Harp a Panpipe? The Meanings of πηκτίς." *CQ* n.s. 47:48–55.

Westphal, R. 1869. *Prolegomena zu Aeschylus Tragödien.* Leipzig.

White, J. W. 1912. *The Verse of Greek Comedy.* London.

Whitman, C. H. 1964. *Aristophanes and the Comic Hero.* Cambridge, MA.

———. 1969. "ΛΗΚΥΘΙΟΝ ΑΠΩΛΕΣΕΝ." *HSCP* 73:109–112.

Wilamowitz, U. von (W.-Moellendorff). 1875. *Analecta Euripidea.* Berlin.

———. 1886. *Isyllos von Epidauros.* Philologische Untersuchungen 9. Berlin.

———. 1893. *Aristoteles und Athen,* I–II. Berlin.

———. 1895². *Euripides. Herakles,* I–III. Berlin.

———. 1921. *Griechische Verskunst.* Berlin.

———. 1924. *Hellenistische Dichtung in der Zeit des Kallimachos,* I–II. Berlin.

———. 1931/32. *Der Glaube der Hellenen,* I–II. Berlin.

Wiles, D. 1997. *Tragedy in Athens: Performance Space and Theatrical Meaning.* Cambridge.

———. 2000. *Greek Theatre Performance: An Introduction.* Cambridge.

Wilkins, J. 1993. *Euripides. Heraclidae.* Oxford.

Wilson, P. 1997. "Leading the Tragic *Khoros*: Tragic Prestige in the Democratic City." In *Greek Tragedy and the Historian* (ed. C. Pelling), 81–108. Oxford.

———. 1999. "The *Aulos* in Athens." In Goldhill and Osborne 1999:58–95.

———. 2000. *The Athenian Institution of the* Khoregia: *The Chorus, the City, and the Stage.* Cambridge.

Wilson, P., and Taplin, O. 1993. "The 'Aetiology' of Tragedy in the *Oresteia*." *PCPS* n.s. 39 (219):169–180.

Winiarczyk, M. 1989. "Bibliographie zum antiken Atheismus." *Elenchos* 10:103–192.

Winkler, J. J. 1985. "The Ephebes' Song: *Tragôidia* and *Polis*." *Representations* 11:26–62.

———. 1990. "The Ephebes' Song: *Tragôidia* and *Polis*." In Winkler and Zeitlin 1990:20–62.

———. 1990a. "Laying Down the Law: The Oversight of Men's Sexual Behavior in Classical Athens." In Halperin, Winkler, and Zeitlin 1990:171–209.

———. 1990b. *The Constraints of Desire: The Anthropology of Sex and Gender in Ancient Greece.* New York.

Winkler, J. J., and Zeitlin, F. I., eds. 1990. *Nothing to Do with Dionysos? Athenian Drama in Its Social Context.* Princeton.

Winnicott, D. W. 1971. *Playing and Reality.* London.

Wirth, U., ed. 2002. *Performanz: Zwischen Sprachphilosophie und Kulturwissenschaften.* Frankfurt.

Wit-Tak, T. M. de. 1968. "The Function of Obscenity in Aristophanes' *Thesmophoriazusae* and *Ecclesiazusae*." *Mnemosyne* 21:357–365.

Wittgenstein, L. 1975. "Bemerkungen über Frazers 'The Golden Bough.'" In *Sprachanalyse und Soziologie: Die sozialwissenschaftliche Relevanz von Wittgensteins Sprachphilosophie* (ed. R. Wiggershaus), 37–57. Frankfurt.

Wolff, C. 1992. "Euripides' *Iphigenia among the Taurians*: Aetiology, Ritual, and Myth." *CA* 11:308–334.

Worman, N. 1997. "The Body as Argument: Helen in Four Greek Texts." *CA* 16:151–203.

Wünsch, R. 1914. "Hymnos." *RE* 9:140–183.

Yatromanolakis, D., and Roilos, P., eds. 2004. *Greek Ritual Poetics.* Washington, D.C.

Zeitlin, F. I. 1981. "Travesties of Gender and Genre in Aristophanes' *Thesmophoriazousae*." In Foley 1981a:169–217.

———. 1982. "Cultic Models of the Female: Rites of Dionysus and Demeter." *Arethusa* 15:129–157.

———. 1990. "Playing the Other: Theater, Theatricality, and the Feminine in Greek Drama." In Winkler and Zeitlin 1990:63–96.

———. 1992. "The Politics of Eros in the Danaid Trilogy of Aeschylus." In Hexter and Selden 1992:203–252.

———. 1999. "Aristophanes: The Performance of Utopia in the *Ecclesiazousae*." In Goldhill and Osborne 1999:167–197.

Zielinski, T. 1885. *Die Gliederung der altattischen Komoedie.* Leipzig.

Zimmermann, B. 1985. *Untersuchungen zur Form und dramatischen Technik der Aristophanischen Komödien,* I–III; I: *Parados und Amoibaion,* 1985² (1984¹); II: *Die anderen lyrischen Partien,* 1985; III: *Metrische Analysen,* 1987. Beiträge zur Klassischen Philologie, 154, 166, 178. Königstein.

———. 1988. "Critica ed imitazione: La nuova musica nelle commedie di Aristofane." In *La musica in Grecia* (eds. B. Gentili and R. Pretagostini), 199–204. Rome.

———. 1992. *Dithyrambos: Geschichte einer Gattung.* Hypomnemata 98. Göttingen.

———. 1993. "Comedy's Criticism of Music." In Slater and Zimmermann 1993:39–50.

———. 1994. "Der Forschungsbericht: Griechische Komödie." *Anzeiger für die Altertumswissenschaft* 47:1–18.

———. 1999. "Chor und Handlung in der griechischen Komödie." In Riemer and Zimmermann 1999:49–59.

Index of Selected Names and Topics

Index of Selected Primary Sources

Index vasorum

Amsterdam 3356: 287n60
Athens, Acropolis 702: 283n47
Athens, Agora P 7242: 133n137
Athens, Kanellopoulos collection
(pyxis cover): 212–213
Athens, National Museum 192
(Dipylon Vase): 68 with n181,
97n23

Berlin, Antikensammlung 1697:
79n210
Bologna 234: 205n354
Boston, Museum of Fine Arts
01.8032: 115n85
20.18: 79n210

Chiusi C 1836: 205n354
Cleveland 26.549: 205n354
Copenhagen, National Museum
13365 (krater by Kleophrades
Painter): 205n354

Dresden 350 (kalyx krater, no
longer extant): 115n85

Erlangen 454 (kylix): 141n146

Florence 3897 (reverse of the
Heydemann Cup): 289n66

London, British Museum
1906.12–15.1 (black-figure vase
from Rhodes): 154n186
E 804: 263n512

Madrid 11009: 205n354
Malibu, J. Paul Getty Museum
86.AE.293 (kylix from Bareiss
collection): 133n137
86.AE.296 (red-figure Sabouroff
cup): 287n60
86.AE.315: 213n380
Munich, Glyptothek 8729 (Exekias
cup): 79

Naples, Museo Nazionale 3240
(Pronomos Vase): 122n110,
189n308, 251n480
New York, Norbert Schimmel
Collection (red-figure psykter
by Oltos): 79n210

Palazzolo Acreide (female comasts
with parasols): 205n354

Made in the USA
Lexington, KY
28 May 2011